W9-BMP-489

W2300

CURRICULUM PLANNING
A Contemporary Approach

SEVENTH EDITION

FORREST W. PARKAY
Washington State University

GLEN HASS
Late, University of Florida

Allyn and Bacon
Boston   London   Toronto   Sydney   Tokyo   Singapore

Senior Series Editor: Virginia Lanigan
Series Editorial Assistant: Bridget Keane
Director of Education Programs: Ellen Mann Dolberg
Marketing Manager: Brad Parkins
Composition and Prepress Buyer: Linda Cox
Manufacturing Buyer: Suzanne Lareau
Cover Administrator: Linda Knowles
Production Editor: Christopher H. Rawlings
Editorial-Production Service: Omegatype Typography, Inc.
Electronic Composition: Omegatype Typography, Inc.

Copyright © 2000, 1993, 1987, 1983, 1980, 1977, 1974 by Allyn & Bacon
A Pearson Education Company
160 Gould Street
Needham Heights, MA 02494

Internet: www.abacon.com

All rights reserved. No part of the material protected by this copyright
notice may be reproduced or utilized in any form or by any means,
electronic or mechanical, including photocopying, recording, or by any
information storage and retrieval system, without written permission from
the copyright owner.

Between the time Website information is gathered and published, some
sites may have closed. Also, the transcription of URLs can result in typo-
graphical errors. The publisher would appreciate notification where these
occur so that they may be corrected in subsequent editions.

Library of Congress Cataloging-in-Publication Data

Curriculum planning : a contemporary approach / [compiled by] Forrest
    W. Parkay, Glen Hass. — 7th ed.
        p.   cm.
    Includes bibliographical references and index.
    ISBN 0-205-30710-8 (alk. paper)
    1. Curriculum planning—United States.   2. Child development—
United States.   3. Learning.   4. Educational psychology.
    I. Parkay, Forrest W.   II. Hass, Glen.
    LB2806.15.C868   2000
    375'.001—dc21   99-17383
                                                      CIP

Printed in the United States of America

10 9 8 7 6 5 4 3   04 03 02 01

Contents

Preface

The seventh edition of *Curriculum Planning: A Contemporary Approach* (formerly *A New Approach*) presents the knowledge, skills, and understandings needed by curriculum planners and teachers at all levels of education, from early childhood through adulthood. This edition of *Curriculum Planning* has been completely revised and updated; fifty-five of the seventy-six articles are new, with most published during the last three years. The book includes a broader spectrum of articles than previous editions—from historical perspectives on curriculum planning, to contemporary analyses of trends and issues, to first-person accounts of curriculum planning and implementation.

Several new features are designed to meet the needs of students with wide-ranging interests, learning styles, and backgrounds. New for each chapter in the seventh edition is a Teachers' Voices—Putting Theory into Practice section that presents a teacher-authored article. In addition, each chapter in Part II includes a Case Study in Curriculum Implementation section that presents a practitioner-authored article that illustrates the complexities of providing leadership for curriculum planning and implementation at the institutional or systemwide level.

To facilitate instruction and to help students study effectively, *Curriculum Planning* includes the following: focus questions at the beginning of each chapter; abstracts and reflection questions for each article; end-of-chapter critical thinking questions, application activities, field experiences, and Internet activities; a total of 645 books and articles to review (75 percent of which are from 1995 or later); and suggested videotapes. In addition, the introductory sections for each chapter have been thoroughly revised and made more reader friendly through a tighter writing style and more extensive use of organizing subheads.

Part I explores the critical elements of curriculum planning: goals and values, the four bases of the curriculum (social forces, human development, learning and learning styles, and the nature of knowledge), and curriculum criteria. Part II emphasizes the application of curriculum planning skills for educational programs for children; early, middle, and late adolescents; and adult and senior learners. At all levels, current trends, innovations, and issues are examined from both theoretical and practical viewpoints.

The key role of educational philosophy in curriculum planning is highlighted in the first chapter. Seminal articles by key figures representing each of the four philosophical orientations that had a major influence on curriculum planning during the twentieth century are presented. These sharply contrasting statements bring contemporary trends and issues into clearer focus, and they highlight how each position will continue to be relevant for curriculum planning during the twenty-first century.

Throughout the book, the interrelationships among past, present, and future perspectives on curriculum planning are stressed. Several articles in this edition address the importance of futures planning. Topics covered include curriculum planning for the future, education and the Information Age, technology and the Internet, cognitive science, the changing workplace, and schools and universities of the future. Other topics that receive increased coverage in this edition are multiple intelligences, learning styles, multicultural education, curriculum standards, and critical perspectives on curriculum planning.

Curriculum Planning is designed for upper-level and graduate students in curriculum and instruction, educational leadership, teacher education, and higher education programs. The key principles and concepts discussed throughout the book apply to educational programs at all levels; and, for each chapter, special attention has been paid to identifying commonalities between curriculum planning at the K–12 and higher education levels.

Acknowledgment is given to the many authors who have contributed to this book. Their willingness to republish their ideas reflects their dedication to the continuous improvement of curriculum as a field of study. I also wish to thank the following reviewers who provided concise, helpful suggestions for this edition: Jan L. Hintz, St. Cloud State University; Dr. Richard Irizarry, University of Texas-Pan American; Dr. Thomas E. Jenkins, University of Maine at Machias.

For her continuing support of the last few editions of *Curriculum Planning* and expert advice during all phases of manuscript preparation, I would like to thank Virginia Lanigan, senior editor at Allyn and Bacon. Additionally, Bridget Keane, editorial assistant at Allyn and Bacon, provided invaluable assistance throughout the revision process. To my wife, Arlene, I give a warm, heartfelt thanks; not only did she provide the constant support that made this edition possible, she cheerfully and competently handled the seemingly endless details related to securing reprint permissions. Lastly, I wish to acknowledge my considerable debt to Glen Hass, who authored the first edition of *Curriculum Planning* and over the years developed a solid conceptual framework for examining the complexities of curriculum planning. He was an impressive curriculum scholar, an inspirational mentor, a valued colleague, and a good friend—it is to his memory that this and future editions of *Curriculum Planning* are dedicated.

F.W.P.

CHAPTER **1**

Goals and Values

FOCUS QUESTIONS

1. What is meant by the term *curriculum?*
2. What is the relationship between curriculum and instruction?
3. What are the bases for curriculum planning?
4. What criteria can be used to plan, develop, and implement curricula?
5. What are four broad, general goals for the curriculum?
6. How do values influence curriculum planning?

The seventh edition of *Curriculum Planning: A Contemporary Approach* contains the knowledge and resources you will need to plan and implement a curriculum. Whether you are a teacher, principal, supervisor, or curriculum coordinator in a K–12 setting; instructor or academic administrator in higher education; or director of an educational program in business or other nonschool setting, you will make a wide array of curriculum-related decisions that will have profound effects on students. To provide all learners—those with diverse cultural backgrounds, needs, abilities, learning styles, and prior educational experiences—with curricular experiences that are meaningful and growth promoting is not an easy task; however, this book is designed to guide you through the complex processes of curriculum planning.

While this book raises many questions about curriculum planning, its purpose is not to settle these questions, but to help you understand the processes involved in planning a curriculum. The book also suggests ways to professionalize decision making in curriculum planning. For example, if excellence in the form of higher standards is currently the public's dominant demand for education (see Daniel Tanner's "Standards, Standards: High and Low" in Chapter 6), then professional educators must raise questions like the following: What is excellence? For what purpose is it sought? How can it be achieved? How can it be measured? Which is more important—the pursuit or the achievement of excellence?

If excellence is to be a major curriculum goal, its attainment will depend substantially on decisions made by curriculum planners and teachers. A goal of *Curriculum Planning: A Contemporary Approach,* then, is to enable you to be professionally accountable when you make those decisions. Such accountability requires that your decisions be informed by an understanding of curriculum goals and values, the bases of the curriculum, and curriculum criteria. In addition, one who is professionally accountable has the ability to use the knowledge, methods, and skills that the profession has developed through past experience, theories, and research. By studying the processes of curriculum planning as perceived by the contributing authors of this book, you will continue to develop your own professional competencies in this area.

To become competent in curriculum planning and decision making, you must understand how society, stages of human development, theories of learning, and the nature of knowledge and cognition influence the curriculum. In addition, you must understand the importance of achieving a balance among these four elements as you plan and implement the curriculum. At the beginning of this complex process, however, you should be able to answer the following question: What is meant by the term *curriculum?*

DEFINITIONS OF *CURRICULUM*

Educational practitioners, theorists, and researchers have used the term *curriculum* in various ways, with no definition universally accepted. Among the definitions currently used are the following:

1. A course of study; derived from the Latin *currere,* meaning to run a course
2. Subject matter; the information or knowledge that students are to learn
3. Planned learning experiences
4. Intended learning outcomes; the *results* of instruction as distinguished from the *means* of instruction
5. All the experiences that students have while at school or in a nonschool educational program
6. The experiences, both planned and unplanned, that enhance (and sometimes impede) the education and growth of students (Parkay & Stanford, 1998, p. 347)

Naturally, no one of these five is the "right" definition. Instead, how we define curriculum reflects our purposes and the educational setting within which we work.

Curriculum and Instruction

When the term *curriculum* is used to refer to planned learning experiences, it is clear that curriculum and instruction are interdependent, not separate and mutually exclusive. Experiences that are planned for learners, of course, include teachers' planning for instruction and the methods they actually use to teach the material. Thus, curriculum and instruction are part of the same process, a process that consists of planning experiences that lead to students' learning and growth.

While there is some warrant for saying that curriculum refers to the *what* of education and instruction the *how*, each has implications for the other. For example, a decision to include certain content in the curriculum means that some methods of instruction will be better suited than others to present that content to learners. Conversely, a given instructional method is more effective for presenting certain types of content than for others. While reading this book, then, you should remember two key points: (1) the terms *curriculum* and *curriculum planning* also refer to the *instruction* and *planning for instruction* which are essential elements of effective educational programs, and (2) effective teachers are those who engage in the full spectrum of curriculum and instruction—from planning the *what* of the curriculum to planning the *how* of instruction.

A Comprehensive Definition of *Curriculum*

None of the preceding views of curriculum are adequate in terms of the needs and trends that will characterize our lives in the twenty-first century. Though mindful of the previous statement that there is no "right" definition of curriculum, we have found the following definition useful: *The curriculum is all of the experiences that individual learners have in a program of education whose purpose is to achieve broad goals and related specific objectives, which is planned in terms of a framework of theory and research or past and present professional practice.*

In this definition, the phrase *program of education* has major significance. It means that the curriculum is a planned program developed by teachers and other professionals. In addition, the phrase means that the planned experiences may occur not only in a school, but in a community agency, a business, or any other setting where a program of education takes place. This definition of *curriculum* also incorporates the following points:

1. The curriculum is preplanned. *Curriculum planning* is the process of gathering, sorting, synthesizing, and selecting relevant information from many sources. This information is then used to design experiences that will enable learners to attain the goals of the curriculum.
2. The planned objectives of a curriculum are developed in light of theories and research on social forces, human development, learning, and knowledge and cognition.
3. Many decisions must be made while planning a curriculum, and these decisions should be made in light of specific, carefully thought out criteria.
4. Planning for instruction is a major part of curriculum planning, since instruction often has a greater influence on learners than the preplanned curriculum, which may be used in part or ignored by the teacher. This is as it should be, since the teacher usually has the greatest knowledge of learners and their needs. Nevertheless, in planning for instruction, the teacher, like the curriculum planner, should

be guided by theories and research on social forces, human development, learning, and knowledge and cognition.

5.   The curriculum that each learner comes to know is the result of experiences had while participating in learning opportunities provided by the teacher. Thus, each student plays an important role in determining the *experienced curriculum*.

BASES OF THE CURRICULUM

The four bases of curriculum planning provide a framework for the organization of much of this book. These bases—*social forces, theories of human development, the nature of learning,* and *the nature of knowledge*—are a major source of guidance for decision making in curriculum planning and planning for instruction. The next four chapters in Part I are devoted to the study of these curriculum bases.

Social Forces

All civilized societies establish schools and programs of education to induct children and youth into the culture and to transmit the society's culture and way of life. At the start of the twenty-first century, K–12 schools, higher education, and educational programs in nonschool settings operate in the midst of an ever-changing array of social forces and trends. Thus, one of the major areas to be considered in curriculum planning must be social forces that include, but are not limited to, the following: (1) social goals, (2) conceptions of culture, (3) the tension between cultural uniformity and diversity, (4) social pressures, (5) social change, and (6) futures planning.

Theories of Human Development

K–12 schools and institutions of higher education emerged in the United States before we knew much about human development and individual differences. However, knowledge of human development and related theories and research expanded significantly during the twentieth century, so that today a vast body of knowledge is available to guide the work of curriculum planners. We understand, for example, that children are not small adults and that human beings are qualitatively different at the various age levels for which we must target curriculum planning and instruction. Therefore, knowledge of human development is an essential basis of the curriculum because it enables curriculum planners to provide for age-related and individual differences among learners.

The Nature of Learning

Knowledge about how human beings learn also increased significantly during the twentieth century. The complexities of learning and individual differences among learners led to the development of several theories of learning that have been tested and refined through carefully controlled research studies. Today's curriculum planners are guided by many of these theories, some of which describe different kinds of learning. Other theories describe the "learning styles" that individuals prefer to use when they process information and seek meaning. Since there are many differences among learners, various learning theories can guide curriculum planners so that they provide for these differences.

The Nature of Knowledge

Today, the nature of knowledge and cognition must be considered one of the essential bases of the curriculum. A key question to be answered anew by all curriculum planners is, of course, What knowledge is of most worth? What to exclude from the curriculum is as difficult to determine as what to include. Other key questions include: How shall knowledge be organized in the curriculum? How does each learner process information? How does he or she seek meaning? Answers to these questions can guide curriculum planners as they develop alternative paths for learning that allow for differences in cognitive style.

Emphasizing Curriculum Bases

What degree of emphasis should be placed on each of the four curriculum bases—social forces, human development, learning, and knowledge—when planning the curriculum? While not easily answered, curriculum planners and teachers should consider this question deliberately and thoughtfully. Therefore, Part I of this book is largely devoted to consideration of this question.

At different intervals throughout the twentieth century, some curriculum planners placed major emphasis on one of the four bases to the exclusion of the others. Often, the emphasis preferred by a curriculum planner reflected that person's philosophical orientation to education or significant historical developments. Prior to the twentieth century, knowledge in the subject matter disciplines and level of schooling provided the primary foci for curriculum planning. After 1900, however, theories and research in the new fields of child development, psychology, anthropology, sociology, and learning gave rise to an emphasis on each of these areas as the basis for curriculum planning and instruction. For curriculum planning in the twenty-first century, however, a multidimensional approach must be used, and all four of the bases considered for their possible contributions toward improving curriculum and instruction.

CURRICULUM CRITERIA

In addition to the four essential bases of the curriculum, other criteria can guide curriculum planners. A *criterion* is a standard on which a decision or judgment can be based; it is a basis for discriminating among elements in a complex field of endeavor. Curriculum criteria, then, are guidelines or standards for addressing the central question in the field of curriculum: What is worth knowing? The articles in Chapter 1 present varying perspectives on the criteria to be followed in answering this question. In "Perspectives on Four Curriculum Traditions," for example, William H. Schubert suggests that four positions characterize the approach curriculum planners use to answer this question: intellectual traditionalist, social behaviorist, experientialist, and critical reconstructionist. And, in "A Morally Defensible Mission for Schools in the 21st Century," Nel Noddings explains why "themes of care," rather than the traditional disciplines, should be the criteria around which the curriculum is organized.

The goals or purposes of a curriculum are among the most significant criteria for guiding the curriculum planning process. Other frequently suggested curriculum criteria are diversity among learners, continuity, balance, flexibility, cooperative planning, international comparisons of achievement, standards developed by professional organizations, student–teacher planning, values to be taught, systematic planning, self-understanding, relevance to learners, and problem solving. The importance of these criteria can be derived from the four essential bases of the curriculum. For instance, an understanding of social forces, human development, learning, and knowledge and cognition will enhance your ability to develop curricula that allow for diversity among learners.

Similarly, an understanding of all four curriculum bases will help you develop a balanced curriculum. Knowledge about human development will enable you to provide for continuity in learning and for the development of self-understanding. Awareness of the nature of knowledge will enable you to plan curricula with learning outcomes that learners find useful and transferable from one situation to another. Lastly, an understanding of social forces will help you provide for relevance and the teaching of values.

The many criteria one can use to make curriculum-related decisions should suggest the need to develop your own set of criteria to guide your planning. These criteria should reflect your thinking as well as the subject area with which you are concerned. The ability to articulate how the four curriculum bases and additional curriculum criteria influence your curriculum planning activities should be one of your goals as you study *Curriculum Planning: A Contemporary Approach.*

CURRICULUM GOALS

While most people would agree that one goal of a curriculum should be to prepare students for the future, there is often little consensus about what knowledge and skills will be required in the future. Debate over this matter is not new, however; for example, Aristotle expressed the dilemma this way: "The existing practice [of curriculum development] is perplexing; no one knows on what principle we should proceed—should the useful in life, or should virtue, or should the higher knowledge, be the aim of our training; all three opinions have been entertained" (1941, p. 1306).

The goals of a curriculum plan provide the first guidelines for determining the learning experiences to be included in the curriculum. Unfortunately, schools commonly lack a comprehensive and reasonably consistent set of goals and related specific objectives on which to base curriculum decisions, and teachers often fail to use these goals to guide their planning for teaching.

Without a set of clearly defined goals in view, teachers and curriculum planners cannot make sound professional judgments. They cannot use their knowledge of the four curriculum bases to make choices of content, materials, or methods that will facilitate students' learning toward intended outcomes. To choose among curriculum alternatives or instructional strategies, educators must know the goals they seek and the curriculum bases on which they will make their choices. Otherwise, their selections will be little more than random, uninformed by today's knowledge of social forces, human development, learning, and knowledge and cognition.

Learners should also be clearly aware of the goals and related specific objectives sought by their teachers and by the curriculum they are experiencing. In fact, the teacher's instructional strategies should "invite" students to share in clarifying and, if appropriate, modifying the objectives. As Glen Hass states in the article, "Who Should Plan the Curriculum?" in Chapter 6, the student is the "major untapped resource in curriculum planning." While the goals the teacher uses to guide his or her planning and those sought by learners need not be identical, they should overlap. The teacher's and learners' goals for a learning experience must be compatible or they are not likely to be achieved. In this chapter's Teachers' Voices section ("The Pot of Goals"), for example, Carol Ann Perks, a teacher of K–5 gifted students, describes how her students set their own goals which, in turn, are related to her aim of teaching children how to plan strategies for attaining goals.

Broad, general goals are needed to determine the related specific objectives of the curriculum. Once developed, these goals and objectives can be used to identify needed courses, activities, and other educational experiences. While there is seldom total agreement about what the goals of a curriculum should be, it is useful to think of curriculum goals as addressing five critical areas: *citizenship, equal educational opportunity, vocation, self-realization,* and *critical thinking.* In addition, curriculum goals can be clustered into two broad areas, each of which should always be considered in curriculum planning: goals that relate to the *society and its values,* and goals that relate to the *individual learner and his or her needs, interests, and abilities.*

VALUES IN CURRICULUM PLANNING

Values enter into every curriculum decision that is made. From planning the curriculum to delivering it in the classroom, there is rarely a moment when teachers are not confronted with situations in which values influence the choices they make. It is their answers (often covert) to questions such as "What is the good person?" "What is the good society?" "What is the good life?" that determine action. While teachers may not consciously pose these philosophical questions, all their curriculum thinking and work are value based.

Four philosophical positions have had a major influence on curriculum planners and teachers during the past sixty years—*perennialism, essentialism, progressivism,* and *reconstructionism.* The struggle for influence among these philosophical positions remains visible today. Because of the significance of values in formulating curriculum goals and developing learning experiences, and in deciding how to evaluate learning, a statement of each philosophical position by an influential historical leader in curriculum planning is included in Chapter 1. Robert F. Hutchins ("The Organization and Subject-Matter of

General Education") represents the perennialists, William C. Bagley ("The Case for Essentialism in Education") the essentialists, William Heard Kilpatrick ("The Case for Progressivism in Education") the progressivists, and Theodore Brameld ("A Cross-Cutting Approach to the Curriculum: The Moving Wheel") the reconstructionists.

That these four positions can lead to heated debate among curriculum planners even today testifies to the continuing relevance of each position. Thus, today's curriculum planners might be well advised to pay more attention to areas of agreement among the positions and less to areas of controversy. Toward this end, John Dewey ("Traditional vs. Progressive Education") cautions curriculum planners against using "either-or" positions to guide their work. His *concept of experience,* for example, includes all the bases of the curriculum—the learner (human development and learning), the society (social forces), and knowledge.

CRITERION QUESTIONS—GOALS AND VALUES

As previously stated, curriculum criteria are guidelines or standards for curriculum decision making. Stating criteria in the form of *criterion questions* is a good way to bring the criteria into clear focus, and we shall use this method in Chapters 1 through 6 of this book. The criterion questions for this chapter on goals and values are as follows:

1. Are the goals of the curriculum clearly stated?
2. To the degree that students' developmental levels will allow, have teachers and students engaged in collaborative planning to define the goals and determine how they will be attained?
3. Do some of the planned goals relate to the society or the community within which the curriculum will be implemented?
4. Do some of the planned goals relate to individual learners and their needs, purposes, interests, and abilities?
5. Are the planned goals used as criteria for selecting and developing learning activities and instructional materials?
6. Are the planned goals used as criteria for assessing students' learning and for further planning of learning subgoals and activities?

The criterion questions bring into clear focus (1) the key role teachers play in curriculum planning and (2) the fact that curriculum planning is not completed until there are engagements with the learners and consideration of the society and community within which the curriculum will be implemented. If most of these criterion questions cannot be answered affirmatively, the goal-setting phase of curriculum planning has probably been inadequate, and steps should be taken to remedy this deficiency.

REFERENCES

Aristotle. *Politics* (Book VIII). In Richard McKoen (Ed.), *The basic works of Aristotle.* New York: Random House, 1941.
Parkay, F. W., & Stanford, B. *Becoming a teacher* (4th ed.). Boston: Allyn and Bacon, 1998.

A Morally Defensible Mission for Schools in the 21st Century

NEL NODDINGS

ABSTRACT: Arguing that the traditional school curriculum is intellectually and morally inadequate for the twenty-first century, Noddings asserts that the goal of education should be the development of students' capacity to find purpose and meaning through their involvement in "centers of care." Thus, education should be organized around "themes of care" rather than the traditional disciplines.

Social changes in the years since World War II have been enormous. We have seen changes in work patterns, in residential stability, in styles of housing, in sexual habits, in dress, in manners, in language, in music, in entertainment, and—perhaps most important of all—in family arrangements. While schools have responded, albeit sluggishly, to technological changes with various additions to the curriculum and narrowly prescribed methods of instruction, they have largely ignored massive social changes. When they *have* responded, they have done so in piecemeal fashion, addressing isolated bits of the problem. Thus, recognizing that some children come to school hungry, schools provide meals for poor children. Alarmed by the increase in teenage pregnancies and sexually transmitted diseases, schools provide sex education. Many more examples could be offered, but no one of these nor any collection of them adequately meets the educational needs of today's students.

What do we want for our children? What do they need from education, and what does our society need? The popular response today is that students need more academic training, that the country needs more people with greater mathematical and scientific competence, that a more adequate academic preparation will save people from poverty, crime, and other evils of current society. Most of these claims are either false or, at best, only partly true. For example, we do *not* need more physicists and mathematicians; many people already highly trained in these fields are unable to find work. The vast majority of adults do *not* use algebra in their work, and forcing all students to study it is a simplistic response to the real issues of equity and mathematical literacy. Just as clearly, more education will not save people from poverty unless a sufficient number of unfortunate people either reject that education or are squeezed out of it. Poverty is a *social* problem. No person who does honest, useful work—regardless of his or her educational attainments—should live in poverty. A society that allows this to happen is not an educational failure; it is a moral failure.

Our society does not need to make its children first in the world in mathematics and science. It needs to care for its children—to reduce violence, to respect honest work of every kind, to reward excellence at every level, to ensure a place for every child and emerging adult in the economic and social world, to produce people who can care competently for their own families and contribute effectively to their communities. In direct opposition to the current emphasis on academic standards, a national curriculum, and national assessment, I have argued that our main educational aim should be to encourage the growth of competent, caring, loving, and lovable people.[1]

At the present time, it is obvious that our main educational purpose is not the moral one of producing caring people but a relentless—and, as it turns out, hapless—drive for academic adequacy.

From *Phi Delta Kappan* 76, no. 5 (January 1995): 365–368. © 1995, Phi Delta Kappa. Used by permission of the author and the publisher.

I am certainly not going to argue for academic *in*adequacy, but I will try to persuade readers that a reordering of priorities is essential. All children must learn to care for other human beings, and all must find an ultimate concern in some center of care: care for self, for intimate others, for associates and acquaintances, for distant others, for animals, for plants and the physical environment, for objects and instruments, and for ideas. Within each of these centers, we can find many themes on which to build courses, topical seminars, projects, reading lists, and dialogue.

Today the curriculum is organized almost entirely around the last center, ideas, but it is so poorly put together that important ideas are often swamped by facts and skills. Even those students who might find a genuine center of care in some arena of ideas—say mathematics or literature—are sorely disappointed. In trying to teach everyone what we once taught only a few, we have wound up teaching everyone inadequately. Further, we have not bothered to ask whether the traditional education so highly treasured was ever the best education for anyone.

I have argued that liberal education (defined as a set of traditional disciplines) is an outmoded and dangerous model of education for today's young. The popular slogan today is "All children can learn!" To insist, however, that all children should get the same dose of academic English, social studies, science, and mathematics invites an important question unaddressed by the sloganeers: Why should children learn what we insist they "can" learn? Is this the material people really need to live intelligently, morally, and happily? Or are arguments for traditional liberal education badly mistaken? Worse, are they perhaps mere political maneuverings?

My argument against liberal education is not a complaint against literature, history, physical science, mathematics, or any other subject. It is an argument, first, against an ideology of control that forces all students to study a particular, narrowly prescribed curriculum devoid of content they might truly care about. Second, it is an argument

in favor of greater respect for a wonderful range of human capacities now largely ignored in schools. Third, it is an argument against the persistent undervaluing of skills, attitudes, and capacities traditionally associated with women. . . .

What do we want for our children? Most of us hope that our children will find someone to love, find useful work they enjoy or at least do not hate, establish a family, and maintain bonds with friends and relatives. These hopes are part of our interest in shaping an acceptable child.[2] What kind of mates, parents, friends, and neighbors will our children be?

I would hope that all our children—both girls and boys—would be prepared to do the work of attentive love. This work must be done in every family situation, whether the family is conventionally or unconventionally, constituted. Both men and women, if they choose to be parents, should participate in the joys and responsibilities of direct parenting, of acting as psychological parents. Too often, women have complained about bearing this responsibility almost entirely. When men volunteer to help with child care or with housework, the very language suggests that the tasks are women's responsibilities. Men "help" in tasks they do not perceive as their own. That has to change.

In education today, there is great concern about women's participation in mathematics and science. Some researchers even refer to something called the "problem of women and mathematics." Women's lack of success or low rate of participation in fields long dominated by men is seen as a problem to be treated by educational means. But researchers do not seem to see a problem in men's low rate of participation in nursing, elementary school teaching, or full-time parenting. Our society values activities traditionally associated with men above those traditionally associated with women.[3]

The new education I envision puts a very high valuation on the traditional occupations of women. Care for children, the aged, and the ill must be shared by all capable adults, not just women, and everyone should understand that these activities bring special rewards as well as burdens. Work with children can be especially rewarding and provides an opportunity to enjoy childhood vicariously. For example, I have often wondered why high school students are not more often invited to revisit the literature of childhood in their high school English classes. A careful study of fairy tales, augmented by essays on their psychology, might be more exciting and more generally useful than, for example, the study of *Hamlet*. When we consider the natural interest we have in ourselves—past, present, and future—it is clear that literature that allows us to look forward and backward is wonderful. Further, the study of fairy tales would provide opportunities for lessons in geography, history, art, and music.

Our children should learn something about life cycles and stages. When I was in high school, my Latin class read Cicero's essay "On Old Age." With all his talk of wisdom—of milk, honey, wine, and cheese; of meditating in the afternoon breeze—I was convinced that old age had its own romance. Looking at the present condition of many elderly people, I see more than enough horror to balance whatever romance there may be. But studies of early childhood, adulthood, and old age (with or without Latin) seem central to education for real life. Further, active association with people of all ages should be encouraged. Again, one can see connections with standard subjects—statistical studies in math; the history and sociology of welfare, medical care, and family life; geographical and cultural differences. We see, also, that the need for such studies has increased as a result of the social changes discussed earlier. Home life does not provide the experience in these areas that it once did.

Relations with intimate others are the beginning and one of the significant ends of moral life. If we regard our relations with intimate others as central in moral life, then we must provide all our children with practice in caring. Children can work together formally and informally on a host of school projects, and, as they get older,

they can help younger children, contribute to the care of buildings and grounds, and eventually—under careful supervision—do volunteer work in the community. Looking at Howard Gardner's multiple intelligences, we see that children can contribute useful service in a wide variety of ways; some have artistic talents, some interpersonal gifts, some athletic or kinesthetic abilities, some spiritual gifts.[4]

A moral policy, a defensible mission, for education recognizes a multiplicity of human capacities and interests. Instead of preparing everyone for college in the name of democracy and equality, schools should instill in students a respect for all forms of honest work done well.[5] Preparation for the world of work, for parenting, and for civic responsibility is essential for all students. All of us must work, but few of us do the sort of work implied by preparation in algebra and geometry. Almost all of us enter into intimate relationships, but schools largely ignore the centrality of such interests in our lives. And although most of us become parents, evidence suggests that we are not very good at parenting—and again the schools largely ignore this huge human task.

When I suggest that a morally defensible mission for education necessarily focuses on matters of human caring, people sometimes agree but fear the loss of an intellectual mission for the schools. There are at least two powerful responses to this fear. First, anyone who supposes that the current drive for uniformity in standards, curriculum, and assessment represents an intellectual agenda needs to reflect on the matter. Indeed, many thoughtful educators insist that such moves are truly anti-intellectual, discouraging critical thinking, creativity, and novelty. Second, and more important from the perspective adopted here, a curriculum centered on themes of care can be as richly intellectual as we and our students want to make it. Those of us advocating genuine reform—indeed, transformation—will surely be accused of anti-intellectualism, just as John Dewey was in the middle of this century. But the accusation is false, and we should have the courage to face it down.

Examples of themes that are especially important to young people are love and friendship. Both can be studied in intellectual depth, but the crucial emphasis should be on the relevance of the subjects to self-understanding and growth. Friends are especially important to teenagers, and they need guidance in making and maintaining friendships.

Aristotle wrote eloquently on friendship, and he assessed it as central in moral life. In the *Nicomachean Ethics,* Aristotle wrote that the main criterion of friendship is that a friend wishes a friend well for his or her own sake. When we befriend others, we want good things for them not because those things may enhance our welfare but because they are good for our friends. Aristotle organized friendships into various categories: those motivated by common business or political purposes, those maintained by common recreational interests, and those created by mutual admiration of the other's virtue. The last was, for Aristotle, the highest form of friendship and, of course, the one most likely to endure.

How do friendships occur? What draws people together? Here students should have opportunities to see how far Aristotle's description will carry them. They should hear about Damon and Pythias, of course. But they should also examine some incongruous friendships: Huck and Jim in Mark Twain's *Adventures of Huckleberry Finn;* Miss Celie and Shug in Alice Walker's *Color Purple;* Lenny and George in John Steinbeck's *Of Mice and Men;* Jane and Maudie in Doris Lessing's *Diaries of Jane Somers.* What do each of these characters give to the friendship? Can friendship be part of a personal quest for fulfillment? When does a personal objective go too far and negate Aristotle's basic criterion?

Another issue to be considered is, When should moral principles outweigh the demands of friendship? The question is often cast this way, even though many of us find the wording misleading. What the questioner wants us to consider is whether we should protect friends who have done something morally wrong. A few years ago,

there was a terrifying local example of this problem when a teenage boy killed a girl and bragged about it to his friends. His friends, in what they interpreted as an act of loyalty, did not even report the murder.

From the perspective of caring, there is no inherent conflict between moral requirements and friendship, because, as Aristotle teaches us, we have a primary obligation to promote our friends' moral growth. But lots of concrete conflicts can arise when we have to consider exactly what to do. Instead of juggling principles as we might when we say, "Friendship is more important than a little theft" or "Murder is more important than friendship," we begin by asking ourselves whether our friends have committed caring acts. If they have not, something has to be done. In the case of something as horrible as murder, the act must be reported. But true friends would also go beyond initial judgment and action to ask how they might follow through with appropriate help for the murderer. When we adopt caring as an ethical approach, our moral work has just begun where other approaches end. Caring requires staying-with, or what Ruddick has called "holding." We do not let our friends fall if we can help it, and if they do, we hold on and pull them back up.

Gender differences in friendship patterns should also be discussed. It may be harder for males to reject relationships in which they are pushed to do socially unacceptable acts, because those acts are often used as tests of manhood. Females, by contrast, find it more difficult to separate themselves from abusive relationships. In both cases, young people have to learn not only to take appropriate responsibility for the moral growth of others but also to insist that others accept responsibility for their own behavior. It is often a fine line, and—since there are no formulas to assist us—we remain vulnerable in all our moral relations.

A transformation of the sort envisioned here requires organizational and structural changes to support the changes in curriculum and instruction. It requires a move away from the ideology of control, from the mistaken notion that iron-handed accountability will ensure the outcomes we identify as desirable. It won't just happen. We should have learned by now that both children and adults can accomplish wonderful things in an atmosphere of love and trust and that they will(if they are healthy) resist—sometimes to their own detriment—in environments of coercion.

Because I would like to present for discussion my basic recommendations for both structural and curricular changes, I will risk setting them forth here in a skeletal form. Of course, I cannot describe and defend the recommendations adequately in so brief a space, but here is a summary.

The traditional organization of schooling is intellectually and morally inadequate for contemporary society. We live in an age troubled by social problems that force us to reconsider what we do in schools. Too many of us think that we can improve education by merely designing a better curriculum, finding and implementing a better form of instruction, or instituting a better form of classroom management. These things won't work.

We need to give up the notion of *a single* ideal of the educated person and replace it with a multiplicity of models designed to accommodate the multiple capacities and interests of students. We need to recognize multiple identities. For example, an 11th-grader may be a black, a woman, a teenager, a Smith, an American, a New Yorker, a Methodist, a person who loves math, and so on. As she exercises these identities, she may use different languages, adopt different postures, and relate differently to those around her. But whoever she is at a given moment, whatever she is engaged in, she needs—as we all do—to be cared for. Her need for care may require formal respect, informal interaction, expert advice, just a flicker of recognition, or sustained affection. To give the care she needs requires a set of capacities in each of us to which schools give too little attention.

I have argued that education should be organized around themes of care rather than around the traditional disciplines. All students should be engaged in a general education that guides them in caring for self, intimate others, global others, plants, animals, the environment, objects and instruments, and ideas. Moral life so defined should be frankly embraced as the main goal of education. Such an aim does not work against intellectual development or academic achievement. Rather, it supplies a firm foundation for both.

How can we begin? Here is what I think we must do:

1. *Be clear and unapologetic about our goal.* The main aim of education should be to produce competent, caring, loving, and lovable people.

2. *Take care of affiliative needs.* We must keep students and teachers together (by mutual consent) for several years, and we must keep students together when possible. We should also strive to keep students in the same building for considerable periods of time and help students to think of the school as theirs. Finally, we must legitimize time spent in building relations of care and trust.

3. *Relax the impulse to control.* We need to give teachers and students more responsibility to exercise judgment. At the same time we must get rid of competitive grading and reduce the amount of testing that we do. Those well-designed tests that remain should be used to assess whether people can competently handle the tasks they want to undertake. We also need to encourage teachers to explore material with students. We don't have to know everything to teach well.

In short, we need to define expertise more broadly and instrumentally. For example, a biology teacher should be able to teach whatever mathematics is involved in biology, while a social studies teacher should be able to teach whatever mathematics is required in that subject. We must encourage self-evaluation and teach students how to do it competently, and we must also involve students in governing their own classrooms and schools. Making such changes means that we accept the challenge to care by teaching well the things that students want to learn.

4. *Get rid of program hierarchies.* This will take time, but we must begin now to provide excellent programs for *all* our children. Programs for the noncollege-bound should be just as rich, desirable, and rigorous as those for the college-bound.

We must abandon uniform requirements for college entrance. What a student wants to do or to study should guide what is required by way of preparation. Here we should not worry greatly about students who "change their minds." Right now we are afraid that, if students prepare for something particular, they may change their minds and all that preparation will be wasted. Thus we busily prepare them uniformly for nothing. We forget that, when people have a goal in mind, they learn well and that, even if they change their minds, they may have acquired the skills and habits of mind they will need for further learning. The one essential point is that we give all students what all students need—genuine opportunities to explore the questions central to human life.

5. *Give at least part of every day to themes of care.* We should discuss existential questions—including spiritual matters—freely. Moreover, we need to help students learn to treat each other ethically by giving them practice in caring. We must help students understand how groups and individuals create rivals and enemies and help them learn how to "be on both sides." We should encourage a way of caring for animals, plants, and the environment that is consistent with caring for humans, and we should also encourage caring for the human-made world. Students need to feel at home in technical, natural, and cultural worlds, and educators must cultivate wonder and appreciation for the human-made world.

6. *Teach students that caring in every domain implies competence.* When we care, we accept the responsibility to work continuously on our competence so that the recipient of our care—person, animal, object, or idea—is enhanced. There is nothing mushy about caring. It is the strong, resilient backbone of human life.

1. Nel Noddings, *The Challenge to Care in Schools* (New York: Teachers College Press, 1992).
2. Sara Ruddick, "Maternal Thinking," *Feminist Studies*, vol. 6, 1980, pp. 342–67.
3. For an extended and powerful argument on this issue, see Jane Roland Martin, *Reclaiming a Conversation* (New Haven, Conn.: Yale University Press, 1985).
4. Howard Gardner, *Frames of Mind* (New York: Basic Books, 1983).
5. John Gardner, *Excellence: Can We Be Equal and Excellent Too?* (New York: Harper, 1961).

Nel Noddings is the Lee Jacks Professor of Child Education at Stanford University.

QUESTIONS FOR REFLECTION

1. Do you agree with Noddings's assertion that the "drive for academic adequacy" characterizes contemporary education? What evidence can you cite to support your position?

2. At the level with which you are most familiar (elementary, middle, secondary, or higher education), what would be the key elements of a curriculum based on Noddings's concept of "themes of care?"

3. Noddings suggests that traditional liberal education may perhaps be "mere political maneuverings." Do you agree or disagree with her position? Why or why not?

4. How can curricula based on "themes of care" be as "richly intellectual" as students and teachers wish them to be?

Perspectives on Four Curriculum Traditions

WILLIAM H. SCHUBERT

ABSTRACT: The history of curriculum planning reveals that various theoretical orientations to curriculum have been proposed. By having hypothetical "speakers" address the central curriculum question, "What is worth knowing?" Schubert suggests that there are four theoretical orientations to curriculum thought—intellectual traditionalist, social behaviorist, experientialist, and critical reconstructionist.

Since the advent of graded textbooks by the mid-1800s, teachers and school administrators have relied on them to such an extent that when many educators and most noneducators hear the term *curriculum,* they think of textbooks. Pioneers in the curriculum field, however (e.g., John Dewey, Franklin Bobbitt, W. W. Charters, Hollis Caswell, Ralph Tyler), argued in the first half of the twentieth century for a much more complex and variegated conceptualization of curriculum. Although these scholars, the array of others who accompanied them, and their more recent descendants have disagreed on many educational issues, they all agreed that curriculum is a great deal more than the textbook.

The most perceptive curriculum scholars throughout history have realized that *curriculum,* at its root, deals with the central question of what is worth knowing; therefore, it deals with what is worth experiencing, doing, and being. Etymologically, *curriculum* is derived from classic meanings associated with the course of a chariot race. Metaphorically, *race course* can be interpreted to mean *journey* or journey of learning, growing, and becoming. As recent interpretation suggests, the verb form of *curriculum* (the noun) is *currere,* and it can be used to focus attention on the act of running the race or experiencing the journey of becoming who we become in life. Thus, the study of curriculum, taken seriously, invokes questions of the good life for individuals and matters of justice in pursuing life together for societies of human beings.

In several of my surveys of curriculum history, I have identified four recurrent positions on curriculum thought, which I have labeled as *intellectual traditionalist, social behaviorist, experientialist,* and *critical reconstructionist.* Although most curriculum scholars, leaders, and teachers are blends of one or more of these orientations, the pure form of each offers its own unique brand of educational possibility that moves far beyond the curriculum as mere textbook. Instead of writing discursively here *about* each, I will ask each *to speak,* as I have done in several publications and as a pedagogical device that I frequently employ through role-playing in courses or in presentations to groups of teachers, administrators, policy makers, and others interested in education. I have asked the *speakers* to share briefly their basic convictions about the major curriculum question(s) noted above and to augment their responses by explaining how curriculum should be restructured beyond the all-too-pervasive reliance on textbooks.

FOUR CURRICULUM TRADITIONS

Intellectual Traditionalist Speaker

[Appearing somewhat formal, self-assured, and willing to deliver the inspirational lecture or to engage in analytic, Socratic dialogue and debate]

The best answers to the basic curriculum question (What is worth knowing?) are found in the

From *Educational Horizons* 74, no. 4 (Summer 1996): 169–176. Used by permission of the author.

great works and in the organized disciplines of knowledge. The great works are the best expressions of human insight, understanding, and wisdom, and the disciplines are the best organizations of knowledge as created by experts in each field. Most certainly, I am an advocate of what is often called "a liberal education" for all. But why? My rationale for advocating study of the great works (in all fields, e.g., arts, sciences, humanities, social sciences) is that they, more than any other source, stimulate human beings to probe deeply into what Mortimer Adler and Robert M. Hutchins have referred to as the *great ideas,* and more recently what Allan Bloom, E. D. Hirsch, Diane Ravitch, Chester Finn, William Bennett, and others have advocated as necessary and neglected knowledge. Adler, for instance, writes of six great ideas: truth, beauty, goodness, liberty, equality, and justice. These ideas transcend matters of culture, race, gender, class, age, ethnicity, location, health or ableness, national origin, and any other aspects of individual and social life that too many consider reasons for gaining separate or individualized treatment.

This focus on individual differences neglects what all human beings have in common—in fact, it omits what makes them essentially human, namely, the great ideas. Every human who has ever lived is concerned about these matters in his or her own life and in the social context of that life. The best expressions of insight into the great ideas is found, not in the intellectual pabulum of textbooks, but in the best expressions that human beings have produced, namely the great works of literature, art, music, philosophy, social and psychological theory, mathematics, history, and the natural sciences.

Whenever possible, the primary sources should be read; however, due to barriers of language, cultural frame of reference, and ability, I admit that secondary sources need to be used. These are adequately found in good translations and in the summaries of essential knowledge available in the disciplines of knowledge.

SOCIAL BEHAVIORIST SPEAKER

[Less formal attire, not quite a lab coat—but in that spirit, oozing with the desire to discover and invent, analytically and scientifically, what works for the needs of today's world; a little rough around the edges]

Basically, I am a grubby empiricist *[with a gleam of eye that shows great respect for scientific investigation, with the "grubby" merely being a way of asking listeners to put more stock in results than in appearances].* I don't ask for too much, only that one have evidence for one's advocacy. The Intellectual Traditionalist seems to think that just because a content area has stood the test of time, so to speak, it is valuable for what students need today.

Textbooks of today carry little more than redigested relics of past textbooks, and the same unquestioned curriculum is passed from generation to generation. These textbooks rarely even get to the level of "great ideas" that the Intellectual Traditionalist promotes. Even those ideas, however, need to be looked at for their relevance to today's students. Taking a cue from one of the greatest Intellectual Traditionalists of all (though I disagree with much that he promotes), I recall that Socrates warned that the unexamined life is not worth living. I want to add that the unexamined curriculum is not worth offering.

To that end I want to tell you a little story from a curriculum classic called *The Saber-Tooth Curriculum,* written by Harold Benjamin in 1939. (By the way, intellectual traditionalists were so powerful in education at the time that Benjamin had to write under a pseudonym, J. Abner Peddiwell.) Being an advocate of economy of time (an earlier version of "time on task"), I am pleased to tell you that the book is short and to the point, even if it is literary and one of the only funny curriculum books in existence!

The story line has a young man who just graduated from college, planning to be a teacher, on a celebratory vacation seated at the longest bar in the world in Tijuana. He sees his old professor from an introduction to education course, strikes up a conversation, and learns that the professor has been on sabbatical studying the educational system of prehistoric peoples.

The conversations are about what he learned. He learned, for example, that prehistoric education classes bore such titles as "Fish Grabbing with the Bare Hands" and "Saber-tooth Tiger Chasing with Fire." The practical value of these courses for prehistoric life is obvious. However, as time went on and as the climate became intensely colder (glaciers arrived), the streams froze up and the saber-tooth tigers migrated to warmer parts of the world. Nevertheless, even then, there were Intellectual Traditionalist educators who argued that the *great ideas* embedded in fish grabbing and tiger chasing would build the mind and must be preserved for all generations. The absurdity of this hardly needs to be noted . . . (or does it, given contemporary intellectual traditionalists?).

With this in mind, I want to say that I am a *behaviorist* in the sense that we need to identify the kinds of behaviors that help students become successful in today's world (as well as the behaviors of teachers that lead to achievement of the desired behaviors in students). I am *social* in the sense that I think that such behaviors should not be taken mindlessly from traditional curriculum values and practices, but rather from systematic investigation of what it takes to be successful in society today.

EXPERIENTIALIST SPEAKER

[Very casual, trying to "tune in" to the audience, obviously desirous of engaging them in an interpersonal fashion, rather than by lecture or by precept]

Sometimes we think of curriculum as a configuration of experiences that leads to the acquisition of skills, bodies of knowledge, and values or beliefs. I am not altogether happy with this three-part separation, and see skill, knowledge, and value as part of a seamless fabric; nevertheless, each of these categories has a heuristic value for my present purposes.

I want you to think of a skill you have that helps you frequently. I want you to think of a body of knowledge that you are glad you have. Similarly, I want you to think of a value or belief that guides your life and helps you deal with difficult circumstances.

Take some time to ponder. *[pause]* Then ask yourself how and where you acquired the skill, or body of knowledge, or guiding value. Tell someone else stories about getting to the place that you now are regarding this skill, knowledge, or value. Try to understand the conditions under which you gained these capacities. If these are powerful learnings, then understanding more about the conditions under which they occurred (in your own life and the lives of others with whom you exchange) will help you to understand powerful learning for your students. Are the conditions of powerful learning in your life, and in the lives of others you know, present in the lives of your students in your school?

What I am trying to convey here is a natural way of learning and teaching, one that we all experience outside of formal learning contexts. Learning, teaching, and curriculum of formal learning contexts, however, are often contrived. My position is that we learn best when learning springs from our genuine interests and concerns.

John Dewey argued this in his many writings. He referred to a progressive curriculum organization centered not in authority outside of the learner, but derived from each learner's experience. He referred to this organization as movement from *the psychological* to *the logical*. By *psychological* he meant concerns and interests of learners and by *logical* he meant the disciplines or funds of knowledge accumulated by the human race. He said that we need to move back and forth on a continuum between the psychological and the logical as we learn and grow.

In other words, Dewey's view is that the usual way of teaching (whether textbook-based, or even as either the Intellectual Traditionalist or the Social Behaviorist recommends) is the antithesis of the natural way of teaching. It is artificial and contrived, and needs to be turned on its head. The *logical* organization of the disciplines of knowledge is fine for encyclopedias and computer banks, but it is not pedagogically sound. The *logical*, however, has the power to inform and illuminate the *psychological*. The reverse is also true.

CRITICAL RECONSTRUCTIONIST SPEAKER

[Starkly serious, upset with injustice and the complicity of the status quo about it; suspicious of conspiracies—intentional and unintentional— restless about the lack of time to right wrongs before injustice reigns supreme]

Although I do agree, in principle, with my Experientialist colleague, I think he is a bit too hopeful—maybe even naive. I am convinced that schools are "sorting machines" for society, as Joel Spring has put it so well. Thus, students are accorded different opportunities to grow and learn, depending on different dimensions of their lives or contexts. I guess that the Social Behaviorist would refer to them as "variables." In any case these dimensions include socioeconomic class, gender, race, ethnicity, health, ableness, appearance, place of living or location, marital status, religion or beliefs, age, nationality, and more.

Much has been written about most of these aspects of life and their impact on providing differential treatment of students, giving them a great disparity of kinds and qualities of educational experiences. For instance, students of a particular race, or ethnicity, or social class background, or status of health, ableness/disableness, and so on may not be given equal access to certain kinds of textbooks, instructional materials, and teaching-learning environments. The variables are often covert sources of tracking students, and it is well-known that students in different tracks are taught in different and unequal ways with materials of unequal quality.

All of this is part of a process that the critical theory literature refers to as *hegemony*. *Hegemony* is the process whereby a society or culture reproduces patterns of inequity. Each institution of a society, school being a prominent one, passes along the hierarchies of the society at large. Students of a given race or social class or gender, for instance, are given messages in schools similar to what they receive from the society at large or from other institutions within the society.

CONCLUSION

The speakers portrayed here represent four quite different curriculum positions. They might be considered akin to archetypes of curriculum that re-emerge in different incarnations and under different labels in each generation all around our globe. Intellectual Traditionalists call for realization of the power of the classics and the great ideas embedded in them (and the accompanying disciplines of knowledge) to overcome the problems of any day. Social Behaviorists, in contrast, call for a new look at what knowledges, skills, and values lead to success in each generation. Experientialists and Critical Reconstructionists decry what they consider to be the authoritarianism of Social Behaviorists and Intellectual Traditionalists, and call for greater grassroots participation. This means that students themselves and the concerns, interests, and injustices they feel deeply must be the starting point for meaningful and worthwhile learning.

What does this all mean? Must the reader (any educator or policymaker, teacher, parent, or student) choose one side or another? In the heat of an earlier battle in the progressive era, John Dewey argued that choosing either progressive or traditional education as superficially practiced was not the main point. In *Experience and Education,* one of Dewey's last books on education, he said prophetically, in the preface, "It is the business of an intelligent theory of education to ascertain the causes for the conflicts that exist and then, instead of taking one side or the other, to indicate a plan of operations proceeding from a level deeper and more inclusive than is represented by the practices and ideas of the contending parties." Dewey's admonition makes it necessary not to become a card-carrying Experientialist, Critical Reconstructionist, Social Behaviorist, or Intellectual Traditionalist, but instead to remember and develop relevant aspects of all of these positions as possibilities for each educational situation encountered.

The fundamental question is not merely whether to have textbooks, but to ask continuously what should be done and why it should be done—with or without textbooks. Each of the curriculum positions offers an avenue to curriculum that transcends most textbooks available, enabling teachers to meet student needs, concerns, and interests more fully. This, however, does not mean that textbooks and other more interactive instructional materials are irrelevant. In fact, rather than rejecting textbooks and related instructional materials, it would be better to ask how instructional media (teacher made, commercially prepared, or student generated) can be created to deeply capture the essence of the Social Behaviorist, Intellectual Traditionalist, Critical Reconstructionist, and Experientialist, alike. Surely, these positions do contradict one another at many points, and practices that bespeak mindless contradiction should be avoided at all costs. However, it is also possible to see each position as complementary to one another, speaking at once to different needs in any complex educational context.

Thus, the great curriculum development task before us is to draw upon all curriculum traditions for the insights and understandings that best fit situations at hand. This means that no text or policy or written curriculum is the final answer. Good answers lie in continuously asking what knowledge and experiences are most worthwhile now, and now, and now . . . throughout the whole panoply of situations that lie ahead. Moreover, such asking must be done by all who are affected by the consequences of that asking, including students who have the greatest vested interest, yet are too often left out of the process of considering matters of purpose that affect them so dearly.

William H. Schubert is Professor of Education and Coordinator of Graduate Curriculum Studies at the University of Illinois at Chicago.

QUESTIONS FOR REFLECTION

1. Is the intellectual traditionalist orientation elitist? How might Schubert's intellectual traditionalist speaker respond to this criticism?
2. The social behaviorist speaker states that "we need to identify the kinds of behaviors that help students become successful in today's world." How would this person determine what will make students "successful"? How would this contrast with the approach used by the other three speakers?
3. If, as the experientialist speaker suggests, the curriculum should be based on students' "genuine interests and concerns," will students acquire the knowledge and skills they will need to function effectively in our society?
4. At this point in your study of curriculum planning, which curriculum orientation is most compatible with your views? Least compatible?

The Organization and Subject-Matter of General Education

ROBERT M. HUTCHINS (1899–1977)

ABSTRACT: *As president of the University of Chicago, Hutchins developed an undergraduate curriculum based on the Great Books. A well-known advocate for using perennialist philosophy to guide curriculum planning, he championed the need to preserve the intellectual traditions of Western culture. This article reflects the key elements of perennialist educational philosophy: education should (1) promote humankind's continuing search for truth, which is universal and timeless; (2) focus on ideas and the cultivation of human rationality and the intellect; and (3) stimulate students to think thoughtfully and critically about significant ideas.*

I assume that we are all agreed on the purpose of general education and that we want to confine our discussion to its organization and subject-matter. I believe that general education should be given as soon as possible, that is, as soon as the student has the tools and the maturity it requires. I think that the program I favor can be experienced with profit by juniors in high school. I therefore propose beginning general education at about the beginning of the junior year in high school. Since I abhor the credit system and wish to mark intellectual progress by examinations taken when the student is ready to take them, I shall have no difficulty in admitting younger students to the program if they are ready for it and excluding juniors if they are not.

The course of study that I shall propose is rigorous and prolonged. I think, however, that the ordinary student can complete it in four years. By the ingenious device I have already suggested I shall be able to graduate some students earlier and some later, depending on the ability and industry that they display.

General education should, then, absorb the attention of students between the ages of fifteen or sixteen and nineteen or twenty. This is the case in every country of the world but this. It is the case in some eight or nine places in the United States.

If general education is to be given between the beginning of the junior year in high school and the end of the sophomore year in college and if a bachelor's degree is to signify the completion of it, the next question is what is the subject-matter that we should expect the student to master in this period to qualify for this degree.

I do not hold that general education should be limited to the classics of Greece and Rome. I do not believe that it is possible or desirable to insist that all students who should have a general education must study Greek and Latin. I do hold that tradition is important in education; that its primary purpose, indeed, is to help the student understand the intellectual tradition in which he lives. I do not see how he can reach this understanding unless he understands the great books of the western world, beginning with Homer and coming down to our own day. If anybody can suggest a better method of accomplishing the purpose, I shall gladly embrace him and it.

Nor do I hold that the spirit, the philosophy, the technology, or the theology of the Middle Ages is important in general education. I have no desire to return to this period any more than I

From an address presented at the annual convention of the National Association of Secondary School Principals at Atlantic City, New Jersey, February 26, 1938. Used by permission of the National Association of Secondary School Principals.

wish to revert to antiquity. Some books written in the Middle Ages seem to me of some consequence to mankind. Most Ph.D.'s have never heard of them. I should like to have all students read some of them. Moreover, medieval scholars did have one insight; they saw that in order to read books you had to know how to do it. They developed the techniques of grammar, rhetoric, and logic as methods of reading, understanding and talking about things intelligently and intelligibly. I think it can not be denied that our students in the highest reaches of the university are woefully deficient in all these abilities today. They cannot read, write, speak, or think. Most of the great books of the western world were written for laymen. Many of them were written for very young laymen. Nothing reveals so clearly the indolence and inertia into which we have fallen as the steady decline in the number of these books read in our schools and colleges and the steady elimination of instruction in the disciplines through which they may be understood. And all this has gone on in the sacred name of liberalizing the curriculum.

The curriculum I favor is not too difficult even for ordinary American students. It is difficult for the professors, but not for the students. And the younger the students are the better they like the books, because they are not old enough to know that the books are too hard for them to read.

Those who think that this is a barren, arid program, remote from real life and devoid of contemporary interest, have either never read the books or do not know how to teach. Or perhaps they have merely forgotten their youth. These books contain what the race regards as the permanent, abiding contributions its intellect and imagination have made. They deal with fundamental questions. It is a mistake to suppose that young people are interested only in football, the dramatic association, and the student newspaper. I think it could be proved that these activities have grown to their present overwhelming importance in proportion as the curriculum has been denatured. Students resort to the extracurriculum because the curriculum is stupid. Young people are interested in fundamental questions. They are interested in great minds and great works of art. They are, of course, interested in the bearing of these works on the problems of the world today. It is, therefore, impossible to keep out of the discussion, even if the teacher were so fossilized as to want to, the consideration of current events. But these events then take on meaning; the points of difference and the points of similarity between then and now can be presented. Think what a mine of references to what is now going on in the world is Plato's "Republic" or Mill's "Essay on Liberty." If I had to prescribe an exclusive diet for young Americans, I should rather have them read books like these than gain their political, economic, and social orientation by listening to the best radio commentators or absorbing the *New York Times.* Fortunately, we do not have to make the choice; they can read the books and listen to the commentators and absorb the *New York Times,* too. I repeat: these important agencies of instruction—the radio and the newspaper—and all other experiences of life, as a matter of fact—take on intelligibility as the student comes to understand the tradition in which he lives. Though we have made great advances in technology, so that the steam turbine of last year may not be of much value in understanding the steam turbine of 1938, we must remember that the fundamental questions today are the same with which the Greeks were concerned; and the reason is that human nature has not changed. The answers that the Greeks gave are still the answers with which we must begin if we hope to give the right answer today.

Do not suppose that in thus including the ancients in my course of study I am excluding the moderns. I do not need to make a case for the moderns. I do apparently need to remind you that the ancients may have some value, too.

Do not suppose, either, that because I have used as examples the great books in literature, philosophy and the social sciences, I am ignoring natural science. The great works in natural science and the great experiments must be a part and an important part of general education.

Another problem that has disturbed those who have discussed this issue is what books I am going to select to cram down the throats of the young. The answer is that if any reasonably intelligent person will conscientiously try to list the one hundred most important books that have ever been written I will accept his list. I feel safe in doing this because (a) the books would all be worth reading, and (b) his list would be almost the same as mine. There is, in fact, startling unanimity about what the good books are. The real question is whether they have any place in education. The suggestion that nobody knows what books to select is put forward as an alibi by those who have never read any that would be on anybody's list.

Only one criticism of this program has been made which has seemed to me on the level. That is that students who can not learn through books will not be able to learn through the course of study that I propose. This, of course, is true. It is what might be called a self-evident proposition. I suggest, however, that we employ this curriculum for students who can be taught to read and that we continue our efforts to discover methods of teaching the rest of the youthful population how to do it. The undisputed fact that some students can not read any books should not prevent us from giving those who can read some the chance to read the best there are.

I could go on here indefinitely discussing the details of this program and the details of the attacks that have been made upon it. But these would be details. The real question is which side are you on? If you believe that the aim of general education is to teach students to make money; if you believe that the educational system should mirror the chaos of the world; if you think that we have nothing to learn from the past; if you think that the way to prepare students for life is to put them through little fake experiences inside or outside the classroom; if you think that education is information; if you believe that the whims of children should determine what they should study—then I am afraid we can never agree. If, however, you believe that education should train students to think so that they may act intelligently when they face new situations; if you regard it as important for them to understand the tradition in which they live; if you feel that the present educational program leaves something to be desired because of its "progressivism," utilitarianism, and diffusion; if you want to open up to the youth of America the treasures of the thought, imagination, and accomplishment of the past—then we can agree, for I shall gladly accept any course of study that will take us even a little way along this road.

Robert M. Hutchins was both President of the University of Chicago and Head of the Center for the Study of Democratic Institutions.

QUESTIONS FOR REFLECTION

1. What is the current "status" of the perennialist orientation to the curriculum? In other words, how widespread is this approach to curriculum planning at the elementary, middle, secondary, and higher education levels?
2. What are the strengths and weaknesses of a perennialist curriculum?
3. Hutchins states that he "wish[es] to mark intellectual progress by examinations." What additional strategies can educators use to assess students' "intellectual progress"?
4. What does Hutchins mean when he says "The curriculum I favor is not too difficult even for ordinary American students. It is difficult for the professors [and teachers], but not for the students."?

The Case for Essentialism in Education
WILLIAM C. BAGLEY (1874–1946)

ABSTRACT: Founder of the Essentialistic Education Society and author of Education and Emergent Man *(1934), Bagley was critical of progressive education, which he believed damaged the intellectual and moral standards of students. This article reflects the essentialist belief that our culture has a core of common knowledge that should be transmitted to students in a systematic, disciplined manner. Though similar to perennialism, essentialism stresses the "essential" knowledge and skills that productive citizens should have, rather than a set of external truths.*

What kind of education do we want for our children? Essentialism and Progressivism are terms currently used to represent two schools of educational theory that have been in conflict over a long period of time—centuries in fact. The conflict may be indicated by pairing such opposites as: effort vs. interest; discipline vs. freedom; race experience vs. individual experience; teacher-initiative vs. learner-initiative; logical organization vs. psychological organization; subjects vs. activities; remote goals vs. immediate goals; and the like.

Thus baldly stated, these pairings of assumed opposites are misleading, for every member of every pair represents a legitimate—indeed a needed—factor in the educative process. The two schools of educational theory differ primarily in the relative emphasis given to each term as compared with its mate, for what both schools attempt is an integration of the dualisms which are brought so sharply into focus when the opposites are set off against one another.

The fundamental dualism suggested by these terms has persisted over the centuries. It appeared in the seventeenth century in a school of educational theory the adherents of which styled themselves the "Progressives." It was explicit in reforms proposed by Rousseau, Pestalozzi, Froebel, and Herbart. It was reflected in the work of Bronson Alcott, Horace Mann, and later of E. A. Sheldon and Francis W. Parker; while the present outstanding leader, John Dewey, first came into prominence during the 1890s in an effort to resolve the dualism in his classic essay, now called "Interest and Effort in Education."

PROBLEMS OF AMERICAN EDUCATION

The upward expansion of mass education first to the secondary and now to the college level, has been an outcome not alone of a pervasive faith in education, but also of economic factors. Power-driven machinery, while reducing occupations on routine levels, opened new opportunities in work for which general and technical training was essential. That young people should seek extended education has been inevitable. In opening high schools and colleges to ever-increasing numbers, it was just as inevitable that scholastic standards should be reduced. Theories that emphasized freedom, immediate needs, personal interest, and which in so doing tended to discredit their opposites—effort, discipline, remote goals—naturally made a powerful appeal. Let us consider, in a few examples, these differences in emphasis.

1. *Effort against Interest*—Progressives have given the primary emphasis to interest, and have maintained that interest in solving a problem or in realizing a purpose generates effort. The Essentialists would recognize clearly enough the

From *Today's Education: Journal of the National Education Association* 30, no. 7 (October 1941): 201–202. Used by permission of the publisher.

motivating force of interest, but would maintain that many interests, and practically all the higher and more nearly permanent interests grow out of efforts to learn that are not at the outset interesting or appealing in themselves. If higher interests can grow out of initial interests that are intrinsically pleasing and attractive, well and good; but if this is not the case, the Essentialists provide a solution for the problem (at least, with some learners) by their recognition of discipline and duty—two concepts which the Progressives are disposed to reject unless discipline is self-discipline and duty self-recognized duty.

2. *Teacher against Learner Initiative*—Progressive theory tends to regard teacher-initiative as at best a necessary evil. The Essentialist holds that adult responsibility for the guidance and direction of the immature is inherent in human nature—that it is, indeed, the real meaning of the prolonged period of necessary dependence upon the part of the human offspring for adult care and support. It is the biological condition of human progress, as John Fiske so clearly pointed out in his essay, "The Meaning of Infancy." The Essentialists would have the teachers responsible for a systematic program of studies and activities to develop the recognized essentials. Informal learning through experiences initiated by the learners is important, and abundant opportunities for such experiences should be provided; but informal learning should be regarded as supplementary rather than central.

3. *Race against Individual Experience*—It is this plastic period of necessary dependence that has furnished the opportunities for inducting each generation into its heritage of culture. The cultures of primitive people are relatively simple and can be transmitted by imitation or by coming-of-age ceremonies. More highly organized systems of education, however, become necessary with the development of more complicated cultures. The need of a firmer control of the young came with this development. Primitive peoples pamper and indulge their offspring. They do not sense a responsibility to provide for their own future, much less for the future of their children. This responsibility, with its correlative duty of

discipline, is distinctly a product of civilization. The Progressives imply that the "child-freedom" they advocate is new, whereas in a real sense it is a return to the conditions of primitive social life.

4. *Subjects against Activities*—The Essentialists have always emphasized the prime significance of race-experience and especially of organized experience or culture—in common parlance, *subject-matter*. They have recognized, of course, the importance of individual or personal experience as an indispensable basis for interpreting organized race-experience, but the former is a means to an end rather than an educational end in itself. The Progressives, on the other hand, have tended to set the "living present" against what they often call the "dead past." There has been an element of value in this position of the Progressives, as in many other of their teachings. Throughout the centuries they have been protestants against formalism, and especially against the verbalism into which bookish instruction is so likely to degenerate. Present day Essentialists clearly recognize these dangers.

5. *Logical against Psychological Organization*—The Essentialists recognize, too, that the organization of experience in the form of subjects involves the use of large-scale concepts and meanings, and that a certain proportion of the members of each generation are unable to master these abstract concepts. For immature learners and for those who never grow up mentally, a relatively simple educational program limited in the earliest years of childhood to the most simple and concrete problems must suffice. This the Essentialists (who do not quarrel with facts) readily admit. The tendency throughout the long history of Progressivism, however, has been to discredit formal, organized, and abstract learnings *in toto*, thus in effect throwing the baby out with the bath, and in effect discouraging even competent learners from attempting studies that are "exact and exacting."

WHAT ABOUT FAILURE?

The Essentialists recognize that failure in school is unpleasant and that repetition of a grade is costly and often not effective. On the other hand, lack of a stimulus that will keep the learner to his task is a serious injustice to him and to the democratic group which has a stake in his education. Too severe a stigma has undoubtedly been placed upon school failure by implying that it is symptomatic of permanent weakness. By no means is this always the case. No less a genius than Pasteur did so poorly in his efforts to enter the Higher Normal School of Paris that he had to go home for further preparation. One of the outstanding scientists of the present century had a hard time in meeting the requirements of the secondary school, failing in elementary work of the field in which he later became world-famous.

WHAT ARE THE ESSENTIALS?

There can be little question as to the essentials. It is no accident that the arts of recording, computing, and measuring have been among the first concerns of organized education. Every civilized society has been founded upon these arts, and when they have been lost, civilization has invariably collapsed. Nor is it accidental that a knowledge of the world that lies beyond one's immediate experience has been among the recognized essentials of universal education, and that at least a speaking acquaintance with man's past and especially with the story of one's country was early provided for in the program of the universal school. Investigation, invention, and creative art have added to our heritage. Health instruction is a basic phase of the work of the lower schools. The elements of natural science have their place. Neither the fine arts nor the industrial arts should be neglected.

ESSENTIALISTS ON DEMOCRACY

The Essentialists are sure that if our democratic society is to meet the conflict with totalitarian states, there must be a discipline that will give strength to the democratic purpose and ideal. If the theory of democracy finds no place for discipline, then before long the theory will have only historical significance. The Essentialists stand for a literate electorate. That such an electorate is indispensable to its survival is demonstrated by the fate that overtook every unschooled democracy founded as a result of the war that was "to make the world safe for democracy." And literacy means the development and expansion of ideas; it means the basis for the collective thought and judgment which are the essence of democratic institutions. These needs are so fundamental that it would be folly to leave them to the whim or caprice of either learner or teacher.

SUMMARY OF THE CASE FOR ESSENTIALISM

To summarize briefly the principal tenets of the present-day Essentialists:

1. Gripping and enduring interests frequently, and in respect of the higher interests almost always, grow out of initial learning efforts that are not intrinsically appealing or attractive. Man is the only animal that can sustain effort in the face of immediate desire. To deny to the young the benefits that may be theirs by the exercise of this unique human prerogative would be a gross injustice.

2. The control, direction, and guidance of the immature by the mature is inherent in the prolonged period of infancy or necessary dependence peculiar to the human species.

3. While the capacity for self-discipline should be the goal, imposed discipline is a necessary means to this end. Among individuals, as among nations, true freedom is always a conquest, never a gift.

4. The freedom of the immature learner to choose what he shall learn is not at all to be compared with his later freedom from want, fraud, fear, superstition, error, and oppression—and the price of this latter freedom is the effortful and systematic mastery of what has been winnowed and refined through the long struggle of mankind upward from the savage—and a mastery that, for most learners, must be under guidance of competent and sympathetic but firm and exacting teachers.

5. Essentialism provides a strong theory of education; its competing school offers a weak theory. If there has been a question in the past as to the kind of educational theory that the few remaining democracies of the world need, there can be no question today.

William C. Bagley was Professor of Education, Teachers College, Columbia University.

QUESTIONS FOR REFLECTION

1. What is the current "status" of the essentialist orientation to the curriculum? How widespread is this approach to curriculum planning at the elementary, middle, secondary, and higher education levels?
2. What are the strengths and weaknesses of an essentialist curriculum?
3. How might Bagley respond to critics who charge that a tradition-bound essentialist curriculum indoctrinates students and makes it more difficult to bring about desired changes in society?
4. Bagley states that "There can be little question as to the essentials. It is no accident that the arts of recording, computing, and measuring have been among the first concerns of organized education." Do you agree with his view? What "basics" might be overlooked in an essentialist curriculum?

The Case for Progressivism in Education
WILLIAM HEARD KILPATRICK (1871–1965)

ABSTRACT: Often called "the father of progressive education," Kilpatrick believed that the curriculum should be based on "actual living." In this article, Kilpatrick sets forth the key tenets of a progressive curriculum: (1) the curriculum, which begins with children's natural interests, gradually prepares them to assume more socially responsible roles; (2) learning is most effective if it addresses students' purposes and concerns; (3) students learn to become worthy members of society by actively participating in socially useful work; (4) the curriculum should teach students to think intelligently and independently; (5) the curriculum should be planned jointly by teachers and students; and (6) students learn best what they practice and live.

The title of this article is the editor's. The writer himself questions whether labels as applied to a living and growing outlook may not do more harm than good. Still, for certain purposes, a name is desirable. In what follows the writer tries to state his own position in a way to seem fair and true to that growing number who approve the same general outlook.

1. The center and nub of what is here advocated is that we start with the child as a growing and developing person and help him live and grow best; live now as a child, live richly, live well; and thus living, to increase his effective participation in surrounding social life so as to grow steadily into an ever more adequate member of the social whole.

From *Today's Education: Journal of the National Education Association* 30, no. 8 (November 1941): 231–232. Used by permission of the publisher.

Among the signs that this desirable living and consequent growth are being achieved, two seem especially significant. One is child happiness—for best work is interested work, and to be zestfully interested and reasonably successful is to be happy. The other, less obvious, but highly desirable is that what is done now shall of itself continually sprout more of life, deeper insights bringing new suggestions with new desires to pursue them.

2. The second main point has to do with learning and how this best goes on so as most surely to come back helpfully into life. For the test of learning is whether it so builds mind and character as to enhance life.

Two types of learning must here be opposed, differing so much in degree as to amount to a difference in kind. In one the learner faces a situation of his own, such that he himself feels inwardly called upon to face it; his own interests are inherently at stake. And his response thereto is also his own; it comes out of his own mind and heart, out of his own very self. He may, to be sure, have had help from teacher or book, but the response when it comes is his.

With the other kind of learning, the situation is set by the school in examination or recitation demands. This accordingly seems to the typical learner as more or less artificial and arbitrary; it does not arise out of his own felt needs. Except for the school demands there would be no situation to him. His response to this hardly felt situation is itself hardly felt, coming mainly out of words and ideas furnished by the textbook or, with older students, by the professor's lectures.

This second, the formal school kind of learning, we all know. Most of us were brought up on it. Except for those more capable in abstract ideas, the learning thus got tends to be wordy and shallow. It does little for mind or heart, and possibly even less for character, for it hardly gets into life.

The first kind has great possibilities. We may call it life's kind. It furnishes the foundation for the type of school herein advocated. Since what is learned is the pupil's own response to a situation felt to be his own, it is at once both heartfelt and mind-created. It is learned as it is lived; in fact, it is learned because it is lived. And the more one's

heart is in what he does, the more important (short of too painful solicitude) it is to him, the more impelling will be the situation he faces; and the stronger accordingly will be his response and in consequence the stronger the learning. Such learning comes from deeper down in the soul and carries with it a wider range of connection both in its backward and in its forward look.

If we take the verb "to live" in a full enough sense, we may then say that, by definition, *learning has taken place when any part or phase of experience, once it has been lived, stays on with one to affect pertinently his further experience.* And we assert that *we learn what we live and in the degree that we live it.*

A further word about the school use of this life-kind of learning may help. Suppose a class is studying Whittier's "Barefoot Boy." I as teacher cannot hand over appreciation to John, nor tell it to him, nor can I compel him to get it. He must in his own mind and heart see something in the poem that calls out in him approval and appreciation. He must first respond that way before he can learn appreciation. Learning here is, in fact, the felt appreciation so staying with John as to get into his mind and character and thence come out appropriately into his subsequent life.

It is the same way with any genuinely moral response attitude. I cannot compel it. John must first feel that way in his own heart and accept it as his way of responding. Such an acceptance on John's part fixes what is thus learned in his character there to stay till the right occasion shall bring it forth again in his life. As it is accepted, so is it learned.

It is the same with ideas. These can be learned only as they are first lived. I cannot simply give John an idea, no matter how skillful I am with words. He may read and I may talk, but he has to respond *out of his own mind* with the appropriate idea as his own personal insight. He has to *see it* himself; something has to *click* inside him; the idea has to come from within, with a certain degree of personal creative insight, as his response to the problematic situation. Otherwise he hasn't it even though he may fool himself and us by using the appropriate words. I as teacher may help John to see better than otherwise he would, and his fellow pupils and I may help him make up his own mind and heart more surely to the good, but he learns only and exactly his own response as he himself accepts this as his way of behaving.

We may sum all this up in the following words: *I learn my responses, only my responses, and all my responses, each as I accept it to act on. I learn each response in the degree that I feel it or count it important, and also in the degree that it interrelates itself with what I already know. All that I thus learn I build at once into character.*

The foregoing discussion makes plain once more how the presence of interest or purpose constitutes a favorable condition for learning. Interest and felt purpose mean that the learner faces a situation in which he is concerned. The purpose as aim guides his thought and effort. Because of his interest and concern he gets more wholeheartedly into action; he puts forth more effort; what he learns has accordingly more importance to him and probably more meaningful connections. From both counts it is better learned.

3. Each learner should grow up to be a worthy member of the social whole. Thus to grow up means to enter more fully and responsibly into the society of which one is a member and in so doing to acquire ever more adequately the culture in terms of which the group lives.

The school exists primarily to foster both these aspects of growing up. The older type school, holding itself relatively secluded within its own four walls, shut its pupils off from significant contact with actual surrounding life and instead had them learn words about life and about the actual culture. The newer school aims explicitly to have its pupils engage actively in life, especially in socially useful work within the community, thus learning to manage life by participation in life, and acquiring the culture in life's varied settings where alone the culture is actually at work.

4. The world in which we live is changing at so rapid a rate that past-founded knowledge no longer suffices. Intelligent thinking and not mere habit must henceforth rule. Youth must learn better to think for themselves. They must understand

the why of our institutions, of our system of legal rights, of moral right and wrong—because only then can they use these essential things adequately or change them intelligently. The newer school thus adds to its learning by living the further fact of pervasive change and undertakes to upbuild its pupils to the kind of thoughtful character and citizenship necessary for adequate living in such a changing social world. The older school cared little either for living or for change. Stressing book study and formal information and minimizing present-day problems, it failed to build the mind or character needed in modern life.

5. The curriculum, where pupil and teacher meet, is of necessity the vital focus of all educational theory.

The older curriculum was made in advance and given to the teacher who in turn assigned it as lessons to the pupils. It was a bookish content divided into separate subjects, in result remote from life. The pupils in their turn "learned" the lessons thus assigned and gave them back to the teacher in recitation or examination, the test being (in the main) whether what was given back was the same as what had been given out. Even the few who "succeeded" on this basis tended to get at best a pedantic learning. The many suffered, being denied the favorable opportunity for living sketched above. The lowest third suffered worst; such a curriculum clearly did not fit them, as becomes now more obvious with each advance of school leaving age.

The newer curriculum here advocated is first of all actual living—all the living of the child for which the school accepts responsibility. As we saw earlier, the child learns what he actually lives and this he builds at once into character. The quality of this living becomes then of supreme importance. The school, as we say, exists precisely to foster good living in the children, the kind of living fit to be built into character. The teacher's work is to help develop and steer this desirable living. This kind of curriculum, being real child living, cannot be made in advance and handed down either to teachers or to pupils. Living at the external command of another ceases by that much to be living for the person himself and so fails to meet desirable learning conditions.

The curriculum here sought is, then, built jointly by pupils and teacher, the teacher remaining in charge, but the pupils doing as much as they can. For these learn by their thinking and their decisions. The teacher helps at each stage to steer the process so as to get as rich living and, in the long run, as all-round living as possible. The richness of living sought includes specifically as much of meaning as the children can, with help from teacher and books, put into their living, meanings as distinctions made, knowledge used, considerations for others sensed, responsibilities accepted. The all-roundedness refers to all sides and aspects of life, immediately practical, social-moral, vocational, esthetic, intellectual. To base a curriculum on a scheme of set subjects is for most children to feed them on husks; the plan here advocated is devised to bring life to our youth and bring it more abundantly.

6. Are we losing anything in this new type school?

a. Do the children learn? Yes. Read the scientific studies (Wrightstone's, for example, and Aikin's report on the Thirty Schools) and see that the evidence is overwhelming. The "tool subjects" are learned at least as well, while the others depending on initiative and creative thinking are learned better. Honesty is much better built.

b. Does the new plan mean pupils will not use books? Exactly no; they do now show far more actual use of books. Textbooks as such will decrease perhaps to nothing, but the use of other books will appreciably increase, as experience already well shows.

c. Will children be "spoiled" by such a regime? Exactly no. For character building, this kind of school far surpasses the old sit-quietly-at-your-desk type of school. Modern psychology is well agreed that one cannot learn what one does not practice or live. The school here advocated offers abundant opportunity to associate on living terms with others and to consider them as persons. The schoolroom of the older school, in the degree that it succeeded with its rules, allowed no communication or other association except through the teacher. Accordingly, except for a kind of negative morality, it gave next to no chance to practice regard for others. The discipline of the school here advocated is positive and inclusive, consciously provided by the school, steered by the teacher, and lived by the pupils. Prejudiced journalists have caricatured the liberty as license; intelligent observation of any reasonably well run school shows exactly the contrary. This discipline is emphatically the constructive kind.

William Heard Kilpatrick was Professor of Education, Teachers College, Columbia University.

QUESTIONS FOR REFLECTION

1. What is the current "status" of the progressive orientation to the curriculum? How widespread is this approach to curriculum planning at the elementary, middle, secondary, and higher education levels?

2. What are the strengths and weaknesses of a progressive curriculum?

3. What does Kilpatrick mean when he says, *"we learn what we live and in the degree that we live it"*? What learning experiences from your own life support Kilpatrick's view?

4. What is Kilpatrick's view of *discipline* as reflected in the following: "The discipline of the school here advocated is positive and inclusive, consciously provided by the school, steered by the teacher, and lived by the pupils"? How does this view differ from that usually associated with the term *discipline*?

A Cross-Cutting Approach to the Curriculum: The Moving Wheel

THEODORE BRAMELD (1904–1987)

ABSTRACT: *Often acknowledged as the founder of reconstructionism, Brameld believed that schools should become the primary agent for planning and directing social change, or "reconstructing" society. Here, he describes a "cross-cutting," integrated approach to the curriculum—an approach that would replace "conventional" subject-matter structures and subdivisions of knowledge. According to the "cross-cutting" approach, the curriculum would be shaped around the critical problems and issues that currently beset humankind. Brameld also explains how the structure of the curriculum can be likened to a wheel, an idea he originally introduced in* Patterns of Educational Philosophy *(1950).*

A number of presuppositions must underlie a cross-cutting approach to the curriculum. Let me merely sketch several of these presuppositions.

1. The prime responsibility of the curriculum on any level, but most focally on the lagging senior high school and undergraduate college levels, is the confrontation of young people with the array of severe, indeed ominous, disturbances that now beset the "naked ape" himself.

2. These disturbances are by no means of exclusive concern to the "social studies." Rather, they pervade every aspect of human life across the planet—whether we are thinking either of the political, economic, esthetic, moral, and religious, or of the so-called "objective" sciences and skills of, say, chemistry, botany, and mathematics. Nothing that man has begun to understand or to utilize can any longer be considered as separable from the crucial roles that he now plays, and the extraordinary obligations that these roles entail.

3. The interpenetrating, interfusing, and evolving character of nature, including human nature, compels us to recognize the universality of the critical period through which we are passing. And education, in turn, is compelled to create new models of the curriculum that express and dramatize this universality.

4. By the same token, the new curriculum models and applications of them in experimental practice repudiate and supersede the entire conventional structure of subjects and subdivisions of knowledge that, for much too long a time, have reflected a grossly outworn, atomistic model of both the universe and man.

5. The legitimate place that special subjects and skills occupy in transformed conceptions of the curriculum undergoes its own metamorphosis. The part no more remains merely a part than does the heart or the hand when it becomes dissevered from the total human body.

6. To follow the same metaphor another step, the human species requires abundant opportunity to reach inward, outward, and upward toward increasing fulfillment of its ever-developing powers both individually and cooperatively. To the degree that men are denied this opportunity, life becomes a failure for them. When education is not completely geared to this same purpose, it too becomes a failure.

7. The necessarily comprehensive presuppositions that we have made above apply, as norms, to any period of culture and history. But they apply with peculiar urgency to our own period. Fearful warnings, often heard, that the birth of the twenty-first century may never be attended

Excerpted from *Phi Delta Kappan* 51, no. 7 (March 1970): 346–348. © 1970, Phi Delta Kappa, Inc. Used by permission of the publisher.

by any historian, because no historian will have survived on our planet thirty years hence, are not warnings that any serious-minded citizen, much less any serious-minded educator, can conscientiously ignore. Unless, of course, he chooses to scoff at such an absurdity.

I am aware that each of these bald statements could be refined and supplemented almost endlessly. Nevertheless, for purposes of discussion, I intend to point directly toward one prospective design for a secondary school curriculum constructed upon the bases that they provide. This is not at all to claim that only one defensible curriculum is possible. It is to claim, however, that models at least comparable to this model should be pulled off the drawing boards and put to the test.

What are the interrelated problems and issues that illustrate the educational agenda inherent in our several presuppositions? I shall state them, again baldly, and without pretense of either order of priority or novelty. They do, however, serve as catalysts for the model to follow.

1. Can the ordinary human being conceivably hope to approach anywhere near optimal fulfillment of his own capacities in the face of accelerating technologized and depersonalized forces?
2. Can the ordinary human being develop a sense of inner personal tranquility and harmony amidst the alienating, divisive, disillusioning experiences by which he is constantly bombarded?
3. Does one (that is, you or I) hold substantial expectations of maintaining any deep sense of relationship with others (that is, with one's mate or family, with one's friends or associates) either amidst chronic instabilities or under the aegis of the folk belief of modern Western culture that self-interest (however "enlightened") still remains the only "realistic" justification for one's daily conduct?
4. Can neighborhoods and other relatively homogeneous communities learn to work together in attacking their own difficulties, in acting concertedly to remove them, and in achieving even a modicum of well-planned, cooperatively organized programs of constructive change?
5. Can racial, ethnic, and other disadvantaged minorities learn to act similarly both among themselves and with other groups of different backgrounds?
6. It is actually plausible to expect that human conflicts—for example between the sexes, the generations, and socioeconomic classes—can be ameliorated by more humane, viable patterns of living and working?
7. Can religious institutions, with all their rigidities of custom and tradition, still find ways to emulate the same general processes suggested above?
8. Can we reasonably aspire to the expectation that nations will find powerful means to conquer and control the ever-advancing threat of human annihilation?
9. Can the fine arts become a vastly wider, richer experience of unique as well as communal creativity for people across the globe, to be shared freely and openly among diverse cultures?
10. Can communication, in every form (such as travel) and through every medium (such as television), occur without restriction or intimidation not only within but between nations?
11. Can the sciences become equally available to all men, devoted to their welfare and advancement (for example, through the sciences of human health or of the control and growth of natural riches), without depletion and decay?
12. Can economic and accompanying political establishments be rebuilt so that people in every part of the earth have access to and become the exclusive directors of (through their chosen representative) physical and human resources?
13. Can a converging awareness and unity of mankind as one species—a species with unique, life-affirming, life-controlling powers—be achieved, and will this awareness and unity

prove translatable into workable guidelines for political, scientific, esthetic, religious direction and renewal?

14. Can education, finally, direct its attention and energy not only toward the past or toward the present of man's experience, but even more persistently and painstakingly toward man's future as well?

That this agenda is far from all-inclusive is surely obvious. Each question could proliferate into dozens of others; indeed, students themselves, stimulated by mankind-oriented teachers, could and should raise innumerable others. All of these questions, moreover, invite explorations into learning not only by means of books and laboratories; above all, they invite firsthand involvement in the experiences of people in nearby or more distant communities who frequently share the same kinds of questions and seek the same kinds of answers.

To approach the problem somewhat more directly, what does all this mean for the organization and operation of the cross-cutting curriculum? It is possible again to summarize only a number of potentialities. According to this normative model:

1. A minimum of one-half of the entire time devoted to the curriculum is spent outside the classroom—in the laboratory of direct participation with people and institutions, and always with the close support of teacher-consultants equipped to deal with whatever situations or issues have been selected for analysis and prognosis.

2. The circumference of this kind of participation is as wide as the earth, extending all the way from the family and neighborhood outward to the region, nation, and eventually to distant nations. Learning therefore occurs *directly* through intra- and international travel (let us not be deluded by financial bugaboos; more than adequate funds are available if we insist upon them enough), and *vicariously* through films, the fine arts, and contact with experts such as anthropologists. There are countless other resources.

3. "Team teaching," so often applied adventitiously these days, is supplanted by flexible partnerships of interdisciplinary study, research, and field involvement.

4. The structure of the curriculum may be symbolized (I have developed this proposal at length elsewhere) in the form of a moving "wheel." The "rim" is the unifying theme of mankind—its predicaments and its aspirations. The "hub" is the central question of any given period of learning (perhaps extending over one week, perhaps a semester), while the "spokes" are the supporting areas of concentrated attention that bear most directly upon each respective question. The "spokes" may thus be termed "courses" in art, science, foreign language, or any other pertinent subject or skills. But these are not to be construed as *mere* courses. At all times they are as supportive of the "hub" as it is of them.

5. To the extent that a particular student discovers whatever special interests and talents he may possess, the individual is given every opportunity to develop fields of concentration in his own "spoke." Never is he encouraged to do so, however, for the sake of completing a "major" or passing "college entrance examinations," or other dubious appendages of conventional school systems.

The normative target of this theme is, I contend, far more "practicable" than are most of those advocated in the name of "practicality." This is so because a cross-cutting curriculum of the kind I urge meets the ever more insistent demands of young people for audacious, unconventional, but directly meaningful experiences in both learning and action.

If it is to succeed, students themselves should, of course, share throughout in the planning and implementation of each year's program. Jointly with their teachers, they should decide what issues are most significant to concentrate upon in a selected period. They should help to pre-plan each successive year. They should take heavy responsibilities for all field involvements both in arranging and in following them through. They should support the deviant student who may not always be interested in "problems" at all, but rather in his own "thing" (music, for example). They should engage in the dialogic process of learning that demonstrates (as Martin Buber has so brilliantly urged) how it is possible to face the profound dilemmas of human existence through the mutualities of shared emotion, reflection, and aggressive action.

I suggest, in short, that the time is long overdue when theories of the integrative curriculum should be revived and reconstructed. The trend among influential curriculum experts who have managed during the post-progressive-education period to reverse those theories should itself now be reversed.

Theodore Brameld was Professor of Education, Boston University.

QUESTIONS FOR REFLECTION

1. What is the current "status" of the reconstructionist orientation to the curriculum? How widespread is this approach to curriculum planning at the elementary, middle, secondary, and higher education levels?
2. What are the strengths and weaknesses of a reconstructionist curriculum?
3. Brameld presents a list of fourteen "interrelated problems and issues" that confronted humankind three decades ago. Which of these problems and issues are still significant today, and should additional ones be added?
4. To what extent do you believe that schools should take an activist position regarding social problems?

Traditional vs. Progressive Education

JOHN DEWEY (1859–1952)

ABSTRACT: The most influential thinker of his time, John Dewey had a profound influence on educational theory and practice, philosophy, psychology, law, and political science. He was an eloquent spokesperson for progressive education; however, his ideas were adopted and often distorted by other educators. He protested these distortions in Experience and Education *(1938), the book from which this article was taken. In what follows, he expresses concern about how some progressive schools of the day were focusing on the learner while giving little or no attention to organized subject matter and the need for adults to provide guidance to learners.*

Mankind likes to think in terms of extreme opposites. It is given to formulating its beliefs in terms of *Either-Ors*, between which it recognizes no intermediate possibilities. When forced to recognize that the extremes cannot be acted upon, it is still inclined to hold that they are all right in theory but that when it comes to practical matters circumstances compel us to compromise. Educational philosophy is no exception. The history of educational theory is marked by opposition between the idea that education is development from within and that it is formation from without;

From John Dewey, *Experience and Education*, pp. 1–10 (New York: The Macmillan Co., 1938), a Kappa Delta Pi Lecture. © Kappa Delta Pi. Used by permission.

that it is based upon natural endowments and that education is a process of overcoming natural inclination and substituting in its place habits acquired under external pressure.

At present, the opposition, so far as practical affairs of the school are concerned, tends to take the form of contrast between traditional and progressive education. If the underlying ideas of the former are formulated broadly, without the qualifications required for accurate statement, they are found to be about as follows: The subject-matter of education consists of bodies of information and of skills that have been worked out in the past; therefore, the chief business of the school is to transmit them to the new generation. In the past, there have also been developed standards and rules of conduct; moral training consists in forming habits of action in conformity with these rules and standards. Finally, the general pattern of school organization (by which I mean the relations of pupils to one another and to the teachers) constitutes the school a kind of institution sharply marked off from other social institutions. Call up in imagination the ordinary schoolroom, its time-schedules, schemes of classification, of examination and promotion, of rules of order, and I think you will grasp what is meant by "pattern of organization." If then you contrast this scene with what goes on in the family for example, you will appreciate what is meant by the school being a kind of institution sharply marked off from any other form of social organization.

The three characteristics just mentioned fix the aims and methods of instruction and discipline. The main purpose or objective is to prepare the young for future responsibilities and for success in life, by means of acquisition of the organized bodies of information and prepared forms of skill which comprehend the material of instruction. Since the subject-matter as well as standards of proper conduct are handed down from the past, the attitude of pupils must, upon the whole, be one of docility, receptivity, and obedience. Books, especially textbooks, are the chief representatives of the lore and wisdom of the past, while teachers

are the organs through which pupils are brought into effective connection with the material. Teachers are the agents through which knowledge and skills are communicated and rules of conduct enforced.

I have not made this brief summary for the purpose of criticizing the underlying philosophy. The rise of what is called new education and progressive schools is of itself a product of discontent with traditional education. In effect it is a criticism of the latter. When the implied criticism is made explicit it reads somewhat as follows: The traditional scheme is, in essence, one of imposition from above and from outside. It imposes adult standards, subject-matter, and methods upon those who are only growing slowly toward maturity. The gap is so great that the required subject-matter, the methods of learning and of behaving are foreign to the existing capacities of the young. They are beyond the reach of the experience the young learners already possess. Consequently, they must be imposed; even though good teachers will use devices of art to cover up the imposition so as to relieve it of obviously brutal features.

But the gulf between the mature or adult products and the experience and abilities of the young is so wide that the very situation forbids much active participation by pupils in the development of what is taught. Theirs is to do—and learn, as it was the part of the six hundred to do and die. Learning here means acquisition of what already is incorporated in books and in the heads of the elders. Moreover, that which is taught is thought of as essentially static. It is taught as a finished product, with little regard either to the ways in which it was originally built up or to changes that will surely occur in the future. It is to a large extent the cultural product of societies that assumed the future would be much like the past, and yet it is used as educational food in a society where change is the rule, not the exception.

If one attempts to formulate the philosophy of education implicit in the practices of the newer education, we may, I think, discover certain common principles amid the variety of progressive schools now existing. To imposition from above is opposed expression and cultivation of individuality; to external discipline is opposed free activity; to learning from texts and teachers, learning through experience; to acquisition of isolated skills and techniques by drill, is opposed acquisition of them as means of attaining ends which make direct vital appeal; to preparation for a more or less remote future is opposed making the most of the opportunities of present life; to static aims and materials is opposed acquaintance with a changing world.

Now, all principles by themselves are abstract. They become concrete only in the consequences which result from their application. Just because the principles set forth are so fundamental and far-reaching, everything depends upon the interpretation given them as they are put into practice in the school and the home. It is at this point that the reference made earlier to *Either-Or* philosophies becomes peculiarly pertinent. The general philosophy of the new education may be sound, and yet the difference in abstract principles will not decide the way in which the moral and intellectual preference involved shall be worked out in practice. There is always the danger in a new movement that in rejecting the aims and methods of that which it would supplant, it may develop its principles negatively rather than positively and constructively. Then it takes its clue in practice from that which is rejected instead of from the constructive development of its own philosophy.

I take it that the fundamental unity of the newer philosophy is found in the idea that there is an intimate and necessary relation between the processes of actual experience and education. If this be true, then a positive and constructive development of its own basic idea depends upon having a correct idea of experience. Take, for example, the question of organized subject-matter—which will be discussed in detail later. The problem for progressive education is: What is the place and meaning of subject-matter and of organization *within* experience? How does

subject-matter function? Is there anything inherent in experience which tends towards progressive organization of its contents? What results follow when the materials of experience are not progressively organized? A philosophy which proceeds on the basis of rejection, of sheer opposition, will neglect these questions. It will tend to suppose that because the old education was based on ready-made organization, therefore it suffices to reject the principle of organization *in toto,* instead of striving to discover what it means and how it is to be attained on the basis of experience. We might go through all the points of difference between the new and the old education and reach similar conclusions. When external control is rejected, the problem becomes that of finding the factors of control that are inherent within experience. When external authority is rejected, it does not follow that all authority should be rejected, but rather that there is need to search for a more effective source of authority. Because the older education imposed the knowledge, methods, and the rules of conduct of the mature person upon the young, it does not follow, except upon the basis of the extreme *Either-Or* philosophy, that the knowledge and skill of the mature person has no directive value for the experience of the immature. On the contrary, basing education upon personal experience may mean more multiplied and more intimate contacts between the mature and the immature than ever existed in the traditional school, and consequently more, rather than less, guidance by others. The problem, then, is how these contacts can be established without violating the principle of learning through personal experience. The solution of this problem requires a well thought-out philosophy of the social factors that operate in the constitution of individual experience.

What is indicated in the foregoing remarks is that the general principles of the new education do not of themselves solve any of the problems of the actual or practical conduct and management of progressive schools. Rather, they set new problems which have to be worked out on the basis of a new philosophy of experience. The problems are not even recognized, to say nothing of being solved, when it is assumed that it suffices to reject the ideas and practices of the old education and then go to the opposite extreme. Yet I am sure that you will appreciate what is meant when I say that many of the newer schools tend to make little or nothing of organized subject-matter of study; to proceed as if any form of direction and guidance by adults were an invasion of individual freedom, and as if the idea that education should be concerned with the present and future meant that acquaintance with the past has little or no role to play in education. Without pressing these defects to the point of exaggeration, they at least illustrate what is meant by a theory and practice of education which proceeds negatively or by reaction against what has been current in education rather than by a positive and constructive development of purposes, methods, and subject-matter on the foundation of a theory of experience and its educational potentialities.

John Dewey was, at various times during his career, Professor of Philosophy, Columbia University; head of the Department of Philosophy and director of the School of Education at the University of Chicago; and Professor of Philosophy at the University of Michigan.

QUESTIONS FOR REFLECTION

1. Using Dewey's concept of *Either-Or* thinking, can you identify other current examples of such thinking in education?
2. A key tenet of progressive education is that there is a close, vital relationship between actual experience and education. What is the nature of this relationship?
3. What does Dewey mean in the following: "When external control is rejected, the problem becomes that of finding the factors of control that are inherent within experience"? In regard to the curricular area with which you are most familiar, what are some examples of how "control" might reside within the experiences students have while they are learning?

Teachers' Voices
Putting Theory into Practice

The Pot of Goals

CAROL ANN PERKS

ABSTRACT: A teacher of K–5 gifted students describes her approach to teaching students how to set goals and plan strategies for attaining those goals in five areas: academics, recreation, personal growth, interpersonal relationships, and careers. Students also learn how to use "benchmark stops" to deal with difficulties that might arise in meeting their goals.

Teachers across the country ask daily: "How do we get the students to stay on task and finish their assignments?" I found an answer in an easy management technique I call the "pot of goals."

Each student needs "A Goals and Strategies Monthly Planner" with the logo *Reach for the Pot of Goals.* The planner is a stapled booklet containing about 25 pages, one for each day of the school month, plus a cover sheet. Along one side (or on top) of each page, there's space to note a goal or goals for that day. There's also space for the children to write in their blocks of time and the activities scheduled for those times; for example, 8:30–9:00 library, 9:00–10:00 Greek myths, and so on. At the bottom of each page, there's room for the children to evaluate their day.

HOW DOES IT WORK?

Each morning, my students record the set routines —such as lunch, PE, art and music. They also put down the time blocks I'll need for mini-lessons, which I write on the chalkboard each day.

The rest of the time left on the planner is theirs to control in quarter-hour, half-hour or hour time blocks. The students are free to plan independent projects and assignments in whatever way they feel most comfortable.

The objective is to teach children how to set goals and plan strategies in the following areas: *Academic, Recreational, Personal Growth, Interpersonal Relationships* and, eventually, *Career.*

BENCHMARK STOPS

Obstacles will almost certainly get in the way of completing strategies and reaching goals, and that's why it's important to use benchmark stops to revisit and revise strategies and goals. Benchmark stops are made in the classroom every half-hour so that peers can check each other's progress. Setting benchmarks helps the children stay on target instead of becoming frustrated when they don't reach their goals.

Sometimes students find their goals unreachable. When than happens, they reconsider and revise their strategies.

One lesson students learn about themselves is how much they can accomplish in a certain period of time. Some students will work on one project for the entire block of time; others will need more diversity with breaks in between. Generally speaking, though, students become more productive when they discover they can control their daily lives and work according to their own clocks, personalities and drives.

Reprinted with permission of the publisher, *Teaching K–8*, Norwalk, CT. From the October 1997 issue of *Teaching K–8*, pp. 48–49.

GOALS AND STRATEGIES

Here are some examples of students' goals and strategies.

One third grader stated his academic goal this way: "I want to make 100 percent on Friday's spelling test of 25 words."

He described his strategy like this: "I'll study six words on Monday, Tuesday and Wednesday and seven on Thursday. I'll break each word into syllables and will look for smaller words or root words to help me remember them. Then I'll ask someone to test me each night, reviewing the previous night's words."

His Monday strategy will be to learn six words. Maybe he'll spend five, 10 or 15 minutes on one word with a block of time to review all words. At benchmark stops, peers will question him. If he's not being successful, they'll figure out what's keeping him from it. They may even rework his strategy.

Recreational Goal

Zachary is a Little League baseball pitcher and dreamed of his team going to the State Playoffs. He wrote, "My goal is to be the best pitcher. My strategy is to practice every day."

"How will you know you're the best pitcher?" I ask. "You can practice every day from now until forever and still not be the best pitcher. You have to be more specific as to how you'll practice every day." He thought about this for a few days and conferred with his coach. A few days later, he said, "Ms. Perks, my coach told me this is my goal: 'My goal is to have a no-hitter game by the end of the month and be Player of the Year! [No doubt the coach was projecting his own goals.] My strategy is to practice throwing strikes every day to get the batter out.' That's specific, isn't it, Ms. Perks?"

By the end of the season, Zack's team made the State Finals and won! Zack was chosen Player of the Year. He reached his goal!

Personal Growth

One morning Kendra whispered her goal in my ear. She wanted to know if she could write, "My goal for today is to be a friend to Shannon, the new girl, because no one wants to. My strategy will be that I will sit next to her and be her peer. My other strategy will be that we will work on a story together and finish it by the end of the day."

By the end of the day a happy little girl, who had set a goal to give friendship to a lonely newcomer, accomplished her mission.

EVALUATION

At the end of each day, the children evaluate themselves at the bottom of the daily planner page. Did they or did they not reach their goal? If not, why not? What can they do tomorrow to make it happen?

If they did achieve their goal, what was the reason for their success? In the beginning, they'll blame anyone and anything for not reaching their goal until they realize that sometimes it's no one's fault, that interruptions during the day will often prevent them from meeting their goals. They must learn to accept this and adjust to it. They may have to carry over the goal, eliminate or revise it.

A PROBLEM SOLVED

Reaching for the Pot of Goals helps students finish their work on time. It becomes a challenge for them to finish the teacher's assignments so they can control their time block.

My students come to school each morning knowing how they want to spend their time blocks, and ready to develop interesting, independent research projects. They become independent, responsible workers able to set goals that will take them into the 21st First Century.

Carol Ann Perks teaches gifted students, K–5, at Comstock Elementary School in Miami, Florida.

QUESTIONS FOR REFLECTION

1. In addition to goal-setting strategies, what values are Perks's students learning?
2. What curriculum criteria are reflected in the learning experiences Perks provides her students?
3. How does the "pot of goals" approach reflect the needs, purposes, interests, and abilities of individual learners in Perks's classroom?

LEARNING ACTIVITIES

Critical Thinking

1. Imagine that Dewey was alive today, teaching in the subject area and at the level with which you are most familiar. Describe the curricular experiences students would have in his classes. Develop similar hypothetical scenarios for the other influential historical curriculum theorists whose work appears in this chapter: Robert M. Hutchins, William C. Bagley, William Heard Kilpatrick, and Theodore Brameld.
2. Think back to the teachers you had during your K–12 and undergraduate years in school. Which ones would you classify as being predominantly perennialist? Essentialist? Progressive? Reconstructionist?
3. How do you imagine teachers at the elementary, middle/junior, senior high, and higher education levels differ in regard to their preferred philosophical orientation to curriculum?
4. Of the four philosophical orientations to curriculum covered in this chapter, which one do you prefer? Least prefer? If you look ahead ten years, do you anticipate any shift in your preference?
5. Study the goals of a curriculum plan of your choice and try to determine whether they are "subject-centered," "society-centered," or "learner-centered." Which do you think they should be? Which of the four philosophical orientations covered in this chapter is closest to each of these three approaches to curriculum goals? Share your findings with other students in your class.
6. There were many important statements about the goals of education during the 1900s, each of which has influenced the processes of curriculum planning. One of the best-known statements of broad goals is known as the "Seven Cardinal Principles of Education," issued in 1918 by the Commission on Reorganization of Secondary Education. The seven goals in *Cardinal Principles of Secondary Education* included the following: health, command of fundamental processes (reading, writing, and computation), worthy home membership, vocation, citizenship, worthy use of leisure time, and ethical character. More recently, the U.S. Department of Education, under the Bush Administration, established six national education

goals (*National Goals for Education,* 1989); and in 1994, President Clinton signed into law the Goals 2000: Educate America Act, which included these six goals plus two additional goals. Goals 2000 called for the attainment of goals in the following eight areas by the year 2000: school readiness; school completion; student achievement and citizenship; mathematics and science; adult literacy and lifelong learning; safe, disciplined, and alcohol- and drug-free schools; teacher education and professional development; and parental participation. Several additional statements of broad goals are included in Books and Articles to Review at the end of this chapter. Find a few of these statements in your library and compare them with the goals and objectives included in the articles in this chapter. How have the goals changed? In what respects have they remained the same?

Application Activities

1.   What specific steps will you take throughout the remainder of your professional career to ensure that your philosophical orientation to curriculum remains dynamic, growing, and open to new perspectives rather than becoming static and limited?
2.   Conduct a survey of current journals in education and try to locate articles that reflect the four philosophical orientations to curriculum that are covered in this chapter: perennialism, essentialism, progressivism, and reconstructionism.
3.   Help your instructor set up a group activity wherein four to six students role-play teachers who are meeting for the purpose of determining broad, general goals for a curriculum. (The students should focus on a level and subject with which they are most familiar.) The rest of the class should observe and take notes on the curricular orientations expressed by the role-players. After the role-play (about 15–20 minutes), the entire class should discuss the curriculum planning process it has just observed.
4.   For a one-month period, keep a tally of all the comments that are made in the mass media regarding what is (or should be) taught in schools, colleges, and universities. Compare your list with those of other students and identify the philosophical orientations to curriculum that are reflected in the comments.

Field Experiences

1.   Visit a school and interview the principal or other member of the administrative team about the broad goals of the school's curriculum. Which of the following educational philosophies are reflected in his or her comments: perennialism, essentialism, progressivism, and reconstructionism? Conduct a similar interview at the higher education level by interviewing one of the following: the director of a university undergraduate honors program, director of general education, dean of instruction, academic dean, or department chair.
2.   Observe the classes of two different teachers at the level with which you are most familiar. Which *one* of the four philosophical orientations to curriculum most characterizes each teacher?

3. Ask your instructor to arrange for a curriculum coordinator from the local school district to visit your class. In addition to finding out about this individual's work, ask him or her to describe the curriculum planning process in the district. On another occasion, ask your instructor to arrange for a similar visit by an individual with responsibility for planning curricula at the higher education level—the director of a university undergraduate honors program, director of general education, dean of instruction, academic dean, or department chair, for example.

Internet Activities

The Internet Activities for each chapter of *Curriculum Planning: A Contemporary Approach* are designed to help you use the Internet to further your study of curriculum planning. As you undertake these online activities, remember that web sites are frequently changed or withdrawn from the Internet. The web site addresses given throughout this book were active at the time of printing. Also, because it is estimated that 10,000 web sites are added each day, you should periodically use key words related to curriculum planning and your favorite search engine to gather the latest information and resources.

1. Visit the following three sites on the Internet and begin a search for materials of interest on philosophical orientations to curriculum: the home page of the American Philosophical Association (APA) (**http://www.oxy.edu/apa/apa.html**), "WWW Philosophy Sites" maintained by the University of Waterloo (**http://watarts.uwaterloo.ca:80/PHIL/cpshelle/sites.html**), and "Philosophy in Cyberspace" (**http://www-personal.monash.edu.au/~dey/phil/**).
2. Visit the Center for Dewey Studies (**http://www.siu.edu/~deweyctr/**) maintained by Southern Illinois University at Carbondale and compile a list of online publications, associations, and reference materials related to the influence of Dewey's work on education.
3. Subscribe to the John Dewey Discussion Group ("open to anyone with an interest in any facet of Dewey's philosophy") on the Internet by writing to **listserv @vm.sc.edu.** Then participate in discussions, seminars, and other online activities of interest.
4. Numerous organizations influence the development of curriculum goals in the United States. Visit the WWW sites of two or more of the following organizations and compare the curriculum goals reflected in their position statements and political activities with regard to education.

Alternative Public Schools Inc. (APS)
American Federation of Teachers (AFT)
National Education Association (NEA)
Goals 2000
Chicago Teachers Union (or other municipal teachers' organization)

National Congress of Parents and Teachers (PTA)
Parents as Teachers (PAT)
Texas State Teachers Association (or other state teachers' organization)

BOOKS AND ARTICLES TO REVIEW

On Curriculum Goals and Objectives

Ayers, William. "Democracy and Urban Schooling for Justice and Care." *Journal for a Just and Caring Education* 2, no. 1 (January 1996): 85–92.

Banks, James A. "Multicultural Education as an Academic Discipline: Goals for the 21st Century." *Multicultural Education* 1, no. 3 (Winter 1993): 8–11, 39.

Beane, James A. *Curriculum Integration: Designing the Core of Democratic Education.* New York: Teachers College Press, 1997.

Beyer, Landon E., ed. *Creating Democratic Classrooms: The Struggle to Integrate Theory and Practice.* New York: Teachers College Press, 1996.

Beyer, Landon E., and Liston, Daniel P. *Curriculum in Conflict: Social Visions, Educational Agenda, and Progressive School Reform.* New York: Teachers College Press, 1996.

Blair, Billie Goode, and Fischer, Cheryl F. *Curriculum: The Strategic Key to Schooling.* Dubuque, IA: Kendall/Hunt, 1995.

Bloom, Benjamin, ed. *Taxonomy of Educational Objectives: The Classification of Educational Goals, Handbook 1: Cognitive Domain.* New York: Davic McKay Co., 1956.

Boyer, Ernest L. "The Commitment to Character: A Basic Priority for Every School." *Update on Law-Related Education* 20, no. 1 (Winter 1996): 4–8.

———. *The Basic School: A Community for Learning.* Princeton, NJ: The Carnegie Foundation for the Advancement of Teaching, 1995.

Brandt, Ronald S., ed. *Content of the Curriculum.* Alexandria, VA: Association for Supervision and Curriculum Development, 1988.

Cheney, Lynne V. *50 Hours: A Core Curriculum for College Students.* Washington, DC: National Endowment for the Humanities, 1989.

Cobb, Nina, ed. *The Future of Education: Perspectives on National Standards in America.* New York: College Entrance Examination Board, 1994.

Commission on the Reorganization of Secondary Education. *Cardinal Principles of Secondary Education.* Washington, DC: U.S. Government Printing Office, 1918.

Costa, Arthur L., and Liebmann, Rosemarie M., eds. *Envisioning Process as Content: Toward a Renaissance Curriculum.* Thousand Oaks, CA: Corwin Press, 1997.

Doll, Ronald C. *Curriculum Improvement: Decision Making and Process,* 9th Ed. Boston: Allyn and Bacon, 1996.

Eisner, Elliot W. *The Educational Imagination: On the Design and Evaluation of School Programs,* 3rd Ed. New York: Macmillan, 1994.

Erickson, H. Lynn. *Concept-Based Curriculum and Instruction: Teaching Beyond the Facts.* Thousand Oaks, CA: Corwin Press, 1998.

Glatthorn, Allan A. *Developing a Quality Curriculum.* Alexandria, VA: Association for Supervision and Curriculum Development, 1994.

———, ed. *Content of the Curriculum.* Alexandria, VA: Association for Supervision and Curriculum Development, 1995.

———. *The Principal As Curriculum Leader: Shaping What Is Taught and Tested.* Thousand Oaks, CA: Corwin Press, 1997.

Goodlad, John. "Agenda for Education in a Democracy." *National Forum* 77, no. 1 (Winter 1997): 15–17.

———. "What Some Schools and Classrooms Teach." *Educational Leadership* 40 (April 1983): 8–19.

Gow, Haven Bradford. "The True Purpose of Education." *Phi Delta Kappan* 70, no. 7 (March 1989): 545–546.

Greene, Maxine. *Releasing the Imagination: Essays on Education, the Arts, and Social Change.* San Francisco: Jossey-Bass Publishers, 1995.

Haworth, Jennifer Grant, and Conrad, Clifton. *Emblems of Quality in Higher Education: Developing and Sustaining High-Quality Programs.* Boston: Allyn and Bacon, 1997.

Heath, Douglas H. *Schools of Hope: Developing Mind and Character in Today's Youth.* San Francisco: Jossey-Bass Publishers, 1994.

Hiebowitsh, Peter S. *Radical Curriculum Theory Reconsidered: A Historical Approach.* New York: Teachers College Press, 1993.

Hirsch, E. D. *The Schools We Need and Why We Don't Have Them.* New York: Doubleday, 1996.

———. *Cultural Literacy: What Every American Needs to Know.* Boston: Houghton Mifflin, 1987.

Hollins, Etta, ed. *Transforming Curriculum for a Culturally Diverse Society.* Mahwah, NJ: Erlbaum, 1996.

Karabenick, Stuart, and Collins-Eaglin, Jan. "Relation of Perceived Instructional Goals and Incentives to

College Students' Use of Learning Strategies." *Journal of Experimental Education* 65, no. 4 (Summer 1997): 331–341.

Kearney, Mary-Louise, and Ronning, Anne Holden, eds. *Women and the University Curriculum: Towards Equality, Democracy, and Peace.* London: J. Kingsley Publishers, 1996.

Kincheloe, Joe L. *Toil and Trouble: Good Work, Smart Workers, and the Integration of Academic and Vocational Education.* New York: P. Lang, 1995.

Krathwol, David, Bloom, Benjamin, and Masia, Bertram. *Taxonomy of Educational Objectives: The Classification of Educational Goals, Handbook II.* New York: David McKay Co., 1956.

Lickona, Thomas. "Eleven Principles of Effective Character Education." *Journal of Moral Education* 25, no. 1 (March 1996): 93–100.

Marsh, Colin, and Willis, George. *Curriculum: Alternative Approaches, Ongoing Issues.* Englewood Cliffs, NJ: Merrill, 1995.

Meier, Deborah. "Supposing That . . . " *Phi Delta Kappan* 78, no. 4 (December 1996): 271–276.

———. "How Our Schools Could Be." *Phi Delta Kappan* 76, no. 5 (January 1995): 369–373.

Morrison, George S. *Contemporary Curriculum K–8.* Boston: Allyn and Bacon, 1993.

National Education Goals Panel. *The National Education Goals Report: Executive Summary: Improving Education through Family-School-Community Partnerships.* Washington, DC: National Education Goals Panel, 1995.

Noddings, Nel. "Teaching Themes of Care." *Phi Delta Kappan* 76, no. 9 (May 1995): 675–679.

Oakes, Jeannie, and Quartz, Karen Hunter, eds. *Creating New Educational Communities.* Chicago: National Society for the Study of Education, The University of Chicago Press, 1995.

Oliva, Peter F. *Developing the Curriculum,* 4th Ed. New York: Longman, 1997.

Ornstein, Allan C., and Hunkins, Francis P. *Curriculum—Foundations, Principles, and Issues,* 3rd Ed. Boston: Allyn and Bacon, 1998.

Pierce, Ronald K. *What Are We Trying to Teach Them Anyway?: A Father's Focus on School Reform.* San Francisco: ICS Press, 1993.

Pinar, William F., et al. *Understanding Curriculum: An Introduction to the Study of Historical and Contemporary Curriculum Discourses.* New York: P. Lang, 1995.

Polite, Vernon C., and Adams, Arlin H. "Critical Thinking and Values Clarification Through So-

cratic Seminars." *Urban Education* 32, no. 2 (May 1997): 256–278.

Richman, Barry M., and Farmer, Richard N. *Leadership, Goals, and Power in Higher Education.* San Francisco: Jossey-Bass Publishers, 1974.

Rusnak, Timothy, ed. *An Integrated Approach to Character Education.* Thousand Oaks, CA: Corwin Press, 1998.

Ryan, Kevin. "Character Education in the United States." *Journal for a Just and Caring Education* 2, no. 1 (January 1996): 75–84.

———. "The Ten Commandments of Character Education." *School Administrator* 52, no. 8 (September 1995): 18–19.

———. "Mining Values in the Curriculum." *Educational Leadership* 51, no. 3 (November 1993): 16–18.

Sarason, Seymour B. *Letters to a Serious Education President.* Newbury Park, CA: Corwin Press, 1993.

Schmitz, Betty. *Core Curriculum and Cultural Pluralism: A Guide for Campus Planners.* Washington, DC: Association of American Colleges, 1992.

Schrag, Francis. *Back to Basics: Fundamental Educational Questions Reexamined.* San Francisco: Jossey-Bass, 1995.

Sowell, Evelyn J. *Curriculum: An Integrative Introduction.* Englewood Cliffs, NJ: Merrill, 1996.

Stark, Joan S. *Designing the Learning Plan: A Review of Research and Theory Related to College Curricula.* Ann Arbor, MI: University of Michigan, 1986.

———. *Shaping the College Curriculum: Academic Plans in Action.* Boston: Allyn and Bacon, 1997.

Tanner, Daniel, and Tanner, Laurel. *Curriculum Development: Theory Into Practice,* 3rd Ed. Englewood Cliffs, NJ: Merrill, 1995.

Thelen, Herbert A. "Authenticity, Legitimacy, and Productivity: A Study of the Tension Among Values Underlying Educational Activity." *Journal of Curriculum Studies* (January–March 1982): 29–41.

U.S. Department of Education. *Achieving the Goals* [reports on progress toward achieving Goals 2000, eight volumes]. Washington, DC: U.S. Department of Education, 1995–1997.

———. *Breaking the Tyranny of Time: Voices from the Goals 2000 Teacher Forum.* Washington, DC: U.S. Department of Education, 1994.

———. *A Bright New Era in Education: Goals 2000, Safer Schools, Family Involvement, Individual Education Accounts, School-to-Work, Improving America's Schools Act.* Washington, DC: U.S. Department of Education, 1994.

Walker, Decker F., and Soltis, Jonas F. *Curriculum and Aims,* 3rd Ed. New York: Teachers College Press, 1997.

———. "Back to the Future: The New Conservatism in Education." *Educational Researcher* 19, no. 3 (April 1990): 35–38.

On Educational Philosophies and Philosophers

Adler, Mortimer J. *Reforming Education: The Opening of the American Mind.* New York: Macmillan, 1990.

Allan, George. *Rethinking College Education.* Lawrence, KN: University Press of Kansas, 1997.

Bagley, William C. *Education and Emergent Man.* New York: Macmillan, 1934.

Brameld, Theodore. *Patterns of Educational Philosophy.* Yonkers-on-Hudson, NY: World Book Co., 1950.

Counts, George S. *Dare the Schools Build a New Social Order?* Carbondale, IL: Southern Illinois University Press, 1978 (originally published in 1932).

Dewey, John. *Democracy and Education.* New York: Macmillan, 1916.

———. "My Pedagogic Creed," pp. 629–638 in Ulich, Robert, ed. *Three Thousand Years of Educational Wisdom: Selections from Great Documents,* 2nd Ed. Cambridge, MA: Harvard University Press, 1954.

———. *The Child and the Curriculum.* Chicago: University of Chicago Press, 1902.

Dougherty, John W. *Four Philosophies that Shape the Middle School.* Bloomington, IN: Phi Delta Kappa Educational Foundations, 1997.

Gadotti, Moacir. *Pedagogy of Praxis: A Dialectical Philosophy of Education.* Albany: State University of New York Press, 1996.

Heslep, Robert D. *Philosophical Thinking in Educational Practice.* Westport, CT: Praeger, 1997.

Hutchins, Robert M. *The Learning Society.* New York: F. A. Praeger Co., 1968.

James, Michael E., ed. *Social Reconstruction Through Education: The Philosophy, History, and Curricula of a Radical Ideal.* Norwood, NJ: Ablex Publishing Corporation, 1995.

Kilpatrick, William H. *Remaking the Curriculum.* New York: Newson and Co., 1936.

Marsh, Colin J. *Key Concepts for Understanding Curriculum.* London: Falmer Press, 1997.

Noddings, Nel. *Philosophy of Education.* Boulder, CO: Westview Press, 1995.

Power, Edward J. *Educational Philosophy: A History From the Ancient World to Modern America.* New York: Garland Publishing, Inc., 1996.

Reagan, Timothy G. *Non-Western Educational Traditions: Alternative Approaches to Educational Thought and Practice.* Mahwah, NJ: Erlbaum Associates, 1996.

Reed, Ronald, and Johnson, Tony W. *Philosophical Documents in Education.* White Plains, NY: Longman Publishers USA, 1996.

Reinsmith, William A. "The True Meaning of Education: A Radical Suggestion." *The Educational Forum* 51, no. 3 (Spring 1987): 249–258.

Schubert, William H. *Curriculum: Perspective, Paradigm, and Possibility.* New York: Macmillan Publishing Co., 1986.

Siegel, Harvey. *Rationality Redeemed?: Further Dialogues on an Educational Ideal.* New York: Routledge, 1997.

Simpson, Douglas, and Jackson, Michael J. B. *Educational Reform: A Deweyan Perspective.* New York: Garland Pub., 1997.

Thelen, Herbert A. *The Classroom Society: The Construction of Educational Experience.* London: Croom Helm, 1981.

———. *Education and the Human Quest.* New York: Harper and Row, 1960.

Videotapes

Ethics in America, Moral Education in Our Schools, and *The Ethics of Teaching* are part of a video series that explores philosophical issues regarding education. (Available from the American Humanistic Association, 7 Harwood Drive, Amherst, NY 14226 (716) 839-5080.)

The Wrong Stuff (58 minutes), a documentary on paradigm shifts in education, includes interviews with Theodore Sizer, Joseph Kellman, and leaders of Chicago's parent Community Council and Indianapolis's Key School Program. (Available from Films for the Humanities & Sciences, PO Box 2055, Princeton, NJ 08543-2053, (800) 257-5126, fax (609) 275-3767.)

Character 101: Reading, Writing, and Respect (21 minutes), a look at the issue of character education in the public schools—who's for it, who's against it, and what some schools are doing about it. (Available from Films for the Humanities & Sciences, PO Box 2055, Princeton, NJ 08543-2053, (800) 257-5126, fax (609) 275-3767.)

CHAPTER 2

Social Forces:
Present and Future

FOCUS QUESTIONS

1. What are ten contemporary social forces that influence the curriculum?
2. What are three developmental tasks that effective curricula help learners accomplish?
3. What are three levels of social forces, and how do they influence the curriculum?
4. Which concepts from the social sciences can help curriculum planners understand the social forces that influence the curriculum?
5. What is the role of futures planning in developing a curriculum that prepares students for an unknown future?

Although education plays an important role in shaping the world of tomorrow, it is also shaped by current and future economic, political, social, demographic, and technological forces. Since education reflects the goals and values of a society and its collective way of life, schools must harmonize with the lives and ideas of people in a particular time and place. Curriculum planners, therefore, must understand how schools and school systems mirror the surrounding societal milieu.

Inasmuch as social environments are dynamic and ever-changing rather than static, descriptions of a society must be refined and modified continually. A critical dimension of curriculum planning and teaching, then, is the continuous reconsideration of present social forces and future trends. Though no one can foretell the future, it has a profound effect on curriculum planning. As Alvin Toffler (1970, p. 363) stated in *Future Shock,* a book that captured the nation's attention three decades ago, "All education springs from some image of the future. If the image of the future held by a society is grossly inaccurate, its educational system will betray its youth." Thus, current social forces and future trends should be examined regularly and an attempt made to understand their meaning and significance for curricula from kindergarten through higher education.

At the beginning of the twenty-first century, we are faced with an array of challenges and opportunities unimagined at the start of the previous century. Though we don't know what the new century holds, we do know that there will be a vital link between education and the quality of that future. Now, more than ever, we are aware of the role education can play in shaping a desired future—virtually every country in the world realizes that education is essential to the individual and collective wellbeing of its citizens in the twenty-first century.

CURRICULUM AND THE CHALLENGE OF THE FUTURE

For curriculum planners, the key question becomes "How do I incorporate an unknown future into my work?" Lined up behind this question, like so many airplanes on a runway, are major trends and issues that will have a profound influence on education at all levels during the twenty-first century: increasing ethnic and cultural diversity; the environment; changing values and morality; the family; the microelectronics revolution; the changing world of work; equal rights; crime and violence; lack of purpose and meaning; and global interdependence. Each of these trends and issues has profound implications for the processes of curriculum planning.

1. *Increasing Ethnic and Cultural Diversity.* Since the end of World War II, the United States has become more ethnically and culturally diverse. The U.S. Bureau of the Census reports that about 820,000 people immigrate into the United States annually, and about one in seven U.S. residents speaks a language other than English at home, most frequently Spanish. The number of students from diverse cultural backgrounds is increasing in most of America's schools, colleges, and universities. It was estimated that by 2000 the majority of students in most urban school districts would be members of those groups traditionally thought of as minorities (National Center for Education Statistics, 1996). Among the districts where non-Hispanic white students number less than 20 percent are Atlanta, Baltimore, Chicago, Detroit, Houston, Los Angeles, Miami, New Orleans, Oakland, Richmond, and San Antonio (National Center for Education Statistics, 1996).

    At one time it was believed that the United States was a "melting pot" in which ethnic cultures would meld into one; however, ethnic and cultural diversity has remained very much a part of our society. A "salad bowl" analogy captures more accurately the cultural pluralism of our society—the distinguishing characteristics of cultures are to be preserved rather than blended into a single culture. The United States has always derived strength from the diversity of its people, and curriculum planners see cultural diversity as an asset to be preserved and valued.

2. *The Environment.* People have become increasingly proficient in their efforts to control and use nature for their safety, comfort, and convenience. Scientific and technological advances and the increased industrialization of the United States led many to believe that people could indeed control and use nature as they pleased. We now realize that such is not the case. Sophisticated computer simu-

lations and ecological experts predict that we are doomed if we don't become careful stewards of the planet. Some people believe that we have already passed the point of no return—that we have so polluted our air and water and plundered our natural resources that it is only a matter of time before we perish, regardless of what corrective measures we now take. The number of species that have become extinct or been placed on the endangered species list during our lifetimes indicates that the worldwide ecosystem is in peril. Clearly, problems such as overpopulation, pollution, depletion of the ozone layer, and the grim possibility of other environmental disasters should be addressed by curricula at all levels.

3. *Changing Values and Morality.* For some time, we have been losing faith in many of our institutions, including government, schools, religion, and the professions. The dizzying pace of events around the globe pushes aside values almost as rapidly as styles come and go in the fashion world. For example, in a short period of time we have undergone a shift in values ranging from frugality to conspicuous consumption to ecologically oriented frugality to renewed conspicuous consumption. There is much unrest in today's middle-aged generation because of its inability to pass its values on to the young. Our fluctuating moral standards contribute to adult and child drug abuse, teen alcoholism, and the divorce rate. Our private lives are played out in a world where much of the landscape seems threatening and constantly changing.

There is an increasing belief on the part of many educators that curricula should include experiences in the process of valuing and values clarification. One approach to teaching values and moral reasoning is known as *character education.* Concern over the moral condition of life in America, as exemplified in the following commentary by Thomas Lickona (1993, p. 6), is leading to a "comeback" of character education in today's curricula:

> Increasing numbers of people across the ideological spectrum believe that our society is in deep trouble. The disheartening signs are everywhere: the breakdown of the family, the deterioration of civility in everyday life, rampant greed at a time when one in five children is poor, an omnipresent sexual culture that fills our television and movie screens with sleaze, beckoning the young toward sexual activity at ever earlier ages, the enormous betrayal of children through sexual abuse; and the 1992 report of the National Research Council that says the United States is now *the* most violent of all industrialized nations.

Other educators, who support their positions with extensive research, assert that the processes of moral judgment can and should be taught at all school levels to help students develop so that they live according to principles of equity, justice, caring, and empathy (see, for example, Lawrence Kohlberg's "The Cognitive-Developmental Approach to Moral Education" in Chapter 3). Many parents and teachers oppose the inclusion of values and morals as part of the curriculum. They believe this is an area of instruction that should be reserved for the home and church or synagogue. However, in this chapter's Teachers' Voices section ("Introducing Censorship: One Teacher's Approach"), Charles M. Ellenbogen explains how he approached classroom discussions of values and morals as they relate to censorship of literature, television, art, and the Internet. At the very least, our various social institutions—the schools, the media, the government, organized religion, the family—must redefine and clarify their responsibilities for instruction in values and morality.

4. *Family*. The family has traditionally been one of the most important institutions in American society. In many cases today, however, the family no longer functions as a closely knit unit. There is great mobility among a large segment of the population—the family is not tied closely to the community, and family members are spread out over a wide geographical area. More and more children are raised without benefit of their natural father's or mother's presence. The roles of father and mother have undergone change.

    There is, however, no evidence of a large-scale rejection of marriage among us—family ties remain a central part of American life. Nevertheless, the stresses that will impact families in the twenty-first century will be extensive, complex, and difficult to manage. The effects of poverty, substance abuse, or violence, for example, can easily cause family units to crumble. As the rate of divorce continues to remain at about 50 percent and as more women enter the workforce, families will feel the strain. The magnitude of this strain is reflected in the fact that the percentage of single-parent families increased from 22 percent in 1985 to 26 percent in 1995 (Annie E. Casey Foundation, 1998).

5. *Microelectronics Revolution*. Learners in the twenty-first century will need to attain extensive skills in computer-based technologies; they will use computers to communicate worldwide and to generate creative solutions to complex problems. To equip students to access vast stores of information available in cyberspace, on CD-ROMs, and in countless data banks, schools, colleges, and universities will need to become more technologically rich and teachers more technologically sophisticated. No longer able to resist the "irresistible force" of Information Age technology (Mehlinger, 1996), they will need to understand that computers are not merely tools—their expanding capabilities and interactivity now provide students with structured learning environments with complex, comprehensive capabilities to access and manipulate information (Morton, 1996).

    Clearly, the Internet, the World Wide Web, and related telecommunications technologies have transformed the world in which we live. This includes the times and places where work is done; the range of products and services available; and how, when, and where we learn. Computers, interactive multimedia, and communication devices that employ the awesome power of tiny silicon microchips are having a profound effect on curriculum and instruction at all levels. For example, in "Future Schools and How to Get There from Here" in this chapter, R. G. Des Dixon states that "The way to make students sophisticated in technology is to make the school a technologically rich environment. . . . Every student must have a notebook computer that is compatible with the school's computer, and every student must make routine use of . . . camcorders, faxes, copiers, phones, and so on."

6. *Changing World of Work*. The microelectronics revolution is radically changing work and the workplace. As Martin Carnoy points out in "The Changing World of Work in the Information Age" in this chapter: "new information technologies facilitate the decentralization of work tasks and their coordination in an interac-

tive network of communication in real time, be it between continents or between floors of the same building." Clearly, we are in the midst of a revolution that will leave virtually no form of work unchanged.

A key aim that should guide curriculum planners from the preschool to the graduate school and beyond is to develop educational experiences that create within students the ability, and the desire, to continue self-directed learning over a lifetime. In a rapidly changing job market, career changes will be the norm, and the ability to continue learning throughout one's career a necessity.

7.   *Equal Rights.* Women and minority groups in America have become more vocal and more active in demanding equal rights. African Americans, Latino and Hispanic Americans, Asian Americans and Pacific Islanders, and Native Americans and Alaskan natives often do not agree among themselves about how to proceed, but they share in a common cause of fighting back against years of inequality, inferior status, marginalization, and often inhumane treatment. In addition, those who know poverty, regardless of ethnicity or race, also struggle for a better life. Lastly, some members of the historically dominant Anglo-European American culture believe that their rights are now being violated in favor of other groups.

Though much has been accomplished to provide equal educational opportunity to all students, regardless of social class, abilities or disabilities, gender, sexual orientation, ethnicity, or race, much remains to be done. The curricular and instructional experiences provided to students are not always appropriate. Many students who have no disabilities now end up in special education classes because of a lack of adequate education options designed to meet the needs of children and youth with diverse learning styles. With the continuing emphasis on higher standards, there is the risk that many low-achieving students will be inappropriately labeled as having a disability.

In spite of a general consensus that schools should promote social change and equal opportunity, some individuals believe that educational practices reproduce the existing social order by providing qualitatively different curricular and instructional experiences to children from different socioeconomic classes. In effect, schools help to maintain the existing stratification in society and the differences between the "haves" and the "have-nots." As Joel Spring (1996, pp. 290–291) asserts: "the affluent members of U.S. society can protect the educational advantages and, consequently, economic advantages, of their children by living in affluent school districts or by using private schools. [T]heir children will attend the elite institutions of higher education, and their privileged educational backgrounds will make it easy for them to follow in the footsteps of their parents' financial success." Similarly, in "Remembering Capital: On the Connections between French Fries and Education" in this chapter, Michael W. Apple maintains that a conservative power bloc in the United States "has integrated education into a wider set of ideological commitments [and] one of its major achievements has been to shift the blame for unemployment and underemployment, for the loss of economic competitiveness, and for the supposed breakdown of 'traditional' values and standards in the family, education, and paid and unpaid workplaces *from* the economic, cultural, and social policies and effects of dominant groups *to* the school and other public agencies."

8. *Crime and Violence.* Ours is a violent, crime-ridden world, as terrorism, street crime, family violence, gang violence, hate crimes, and organized crime attest. Repeated investigations into crime and dishonesty at the highest levels of government, welfare and tax fraud, corruption in business, television and movie violence, and drug abuse have contributed to an alarming erosion of concern for the rights and property of others.

   While the U.S. Department of Justice reported in 1998 that serious violent crime levels and property crime rates had declined during the past few years, other data portrayed a grim picture of crime in America: between 1990 and 1997, the nation's prison population increased by 60 percent; serious violent crime rates for males and females became more equal; about 2 million people were attacked or threatened in the workplace each year; about 1.4 million people were treated in hospital emergency rooms for violence-related injuries; and nearly 11,000 police officers, most of whom are armed, guard the nation's college campuses (U.S. Department of Justice, 1998).

   The impact of crime on education is staggering; more than $600 million is spent annually on school vandalism, a figure the National Parent-Teacher Association pointed out exceeds the amount spent on textbooks for our nation's schools. The National Association of School Security Directors gives the following estimates of school-based crimes committed each year:

   - 12,000 armed robberies
   - 270,000 burglaries
   - 204,000 aggravated assaults
   - 9,000 rapes

   In addition, the U.S. Department of Justice (1996) in its first nationwide survey of gang activity estimated that there are more than 25,000 youth gangs in the United States, with a total of more than 652,000 members. Also, 48 percent of local law enforcement agencies responding to the survey reported that gang problems in their communities were getting worse.

9. *Lack of Purpose and Meaning.* The inability of many individuals to develop and pursue goals they consider worthwhile has led to a lack of purpose and meaning in their lives. Fragmented communities, changes in family structure, the seeming immorality of many leaders, injustice, income disparities, the dizzying pace of technological changes, sharp fluctuations in the global economy, our loss of faith in science and the "experts"—all make it difficult to establish a sense of purpose and meaning. An alarming number of people feel disconnected from the larger society, their families, and themselves. As Paul Bohannan states in "Our Two-Story Culture" in this chapter: "All of us are both running scared and longing for community."

   An increasing number of children and youth live in situations characterized by extreme stress, family violence, grinding poverty, crime, and lack of adult guidance. Searching for purpose and meaning in their lives, they may escape into music, video games, movies, sex, cruising shopping malls, or hanging out with friends on the street. The vulnerability of today's adolescents is vividly portrayed in *Great Transitions: Preparing Adolescents for a New Century,* a report by the Carnegie Council on Adolescent Development: "Altogether, nearly half of American adolescents are at high or moderate risk of seriously damaging their life chances. The damage may be near-term and vivid, or it may be delayed, like a time bomb set in youth" (Carnegie Council on Adolescent Development, 1995). The list of alarming concerns among children and youth is sobering: academic failure, retention, and dropping out; accidents; anorexia; violent behavior; criminal activity; cultism; depression; drug abuse; suicide; teenage pregnancy; and sexually transmitted diseases. In "Full-Service Schools" in this chapter, Joy G. Dryfoos describes how some schools have responded to these concerns by integrating educational, medical, social and/or human services.

10. *Global Interdependence.* The relationships among the nations of the world can have a significant impact on curriculum development at all levels. It is crucial that education help us understand our interconnectedness with all countries and all people and become more sensitive to our own and other's motives and needs. Our future wellbeing depends on being able to participate intelligently and empathetically in the global community. Curricula of the future must emphasize global interdependence, respect for the views and values of others, and an orientation toward international cooperation for resolving global threats to security, health, the environment, and human rights.

Our fate is inextricably bound up with that of the rest of the world. For example, the economic crisis that began in Southeast Asia in 1997 set in motion a ripple effect that was felt in economies around the world. While advances in technology and communications inform us almost instantaneously of such events, the same technology makes those problems our problems. Thus, an important aim of the curriculum at all levels is to cultivate an understanding of the social, psychological, and historical settings that cause others to think and act as they do.

Social Forces and the Individual

The close relationship between the social environment and the development of an appropriate educational program is evident if we consider three developmental tasks that citizens in a democratic society must accomplish. First, some claim that in our society each person's identity is determined largely by his or her occupation. With the exception of the family, the work environment is the setting for most individuals' day-to-day experiences, and friends are often drawn from those with whom one works. Second, a democratic society requires citizens who are prepared to deal with the current issues of government. Finally, each person faces the challenge of achieving self-fulfillment and self-development. Thus, from the individual learner's standpoint, an appropriately developed school program—from preschool through the graduate level—must enhance his or her ability to accomplish developmental tasks in three areas: *vocation, citizenship,* and *self-fulfillment.* In every society the nature of these developmental tasks is different. In industrialized societies such as ours, for example, rapid change is the norm; thus pathways for accomplishing life's developmental tasks are continually changing.

Since social forces are constantly changing, educational programs should change with them. Moreover, few social forces exist independent of each other. They are interrelated, and each individual in the society experiences the influence of most, if not all, of them at the same time. This point is illustrated by the following hypothetical situation.

Liza is an African American who lives in the ghetto of a large city. She is fourteen years old, the oldest of a family of nine children. Her father left the family five years ago because he could not find employment and knew that his children could receive more financial support from the government if he left home. Liza's mother works during the evening, so Liza is expected to care for the apartment and children when she gets home from school. The apartment has only two rooms and is infested with rats. It has poor plumbing and toilet facilities, and the heating system works only occasionally. The children get only one real meal a day and have no money to spend at school. Their clothing is old and worn.

Kevin is a white boy who lives in a middle-class suburb. He is fourteen years old, and has a seventeen-year-old sister. His father is a lawyer who works downtown and commutes daily, often arriving home very late in the evening. Kevin's mother attends many social functions and has a serious drinking problem. His parents often have loud arguments and are openly talking about divorce. Kevin's sister uses cocaine. She often spends the weekend with her boyfriend. Kevin is well fed, lives in an attractive home with a good-sized yard, and is given a generous allowance.

Roy is a white boy who lives near a factory on the outer fringe of the city. He is fourteen years old, and he has one older brother and one older sister. His father is employed at the nearby factory as a blue collar worker. Roy lives in a small but comfortable house. His family does not have many luxuries, but their needs are well satisfied. His parents are deeply religious and take Roy to church with them twice on Sunday and again on Wednesday evening. His father is a veteran and proudly displays several medals. He also belongs to the local VFW. Roy's parents spend much time with their children. He often hears them talk about how radicals and the minority groups are taking over the country.

All three of these young people attend the same school and most of the same classes. Roy walks three blocks to school, but both Liza and Kevin ride the bus. Consider these questions and try to formulate some answers to them in your own mind.

1. How are all three of these young people alike?
2. How are they different?
3. What social forces have played a significant part in their lives?
4. How can the school curriculum plan for meeting the needs of these students, considering the social setting from which they come?
5. How would you, as the teacher of these three students, deal with the similarities and differences they bring from diverse social backgrounds?

It is obvious that each person is unique in the way that social forces have affected his or her life, and the school curriculum is challenged to deal with that individuality. But the curriculum is also asked to meet the needs of the total society. This problem can be seen as you consider the following questions:

1. How actively involved should the school become in dealing with social forces? (Should the faculty lead the students in picket lines?)
2. What percentage of the curriculum should be devoted to learning about and discussing social issues?
3. How should the school respond to parents who feel that the curriculum is either overemphasizing or underemphasizing particular social issues?

Levels of Social Forces

Curriculum planners should consider three levels of social forces that influence the curriculum (see Figure 2.1). First, there is the *national and international level* where concerns such as the preceding ten trends and issues should be identified and utilized in planning.

There is also the level of social forces found in the *local community,* including family structure; class structure; the ethnic, racial, and religious backgrounds of students; and the values of the community in which the curriculum will be implemented. Social forces at the community level significantly affect learners and decidedly influence their perceptions regarding the appropriateness of the curriculum they experience.

Finally, there is the *culture* of the educational setting within which the curriculum is implemented—the social forces that determine the quality of life at the school. The many social forces at this level include the individual learner's social status, the teacher's role in the school, the teacher's role in relation to other professional staff, and the degree of harmony or discord that characterizes school–community relationships. On one level, schools, colleges, and universities are much alike; on another, they are very unique. Each has a distinctive culture—a set of guiding beliefs, assumptions, values, and traditions that distinguish it from other educational settings at the same level. Some may be characterized as communal places where there is a shared sense of purpose and a commitment to providing students with meaningful, carefully thought out curricular experiences. Others lack a unified sense of purpose or direction, and they drift, rudderless from year to year. Still others may be characterized by internal discord, conflict, and devisiveness. Regardless of how they become manifest in a school's culture, social forces at this level are of major significance in curriculum planning and teaching.

FIGURE 2.1
Levels of Social Forces that Influence the Curriculum

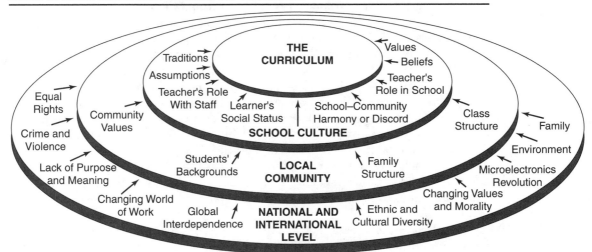

Concepts from the Social Sciences

Several concepts from sociology, anthropology, and social psychology are very useful in defining and describing the social forces to be considered in curriculum planning. Among these concepts are *humanity, culture, enculturation* or *socialization, subculture,* and *cultural pluralism.* This list of relevant concepts could be extended greatly, but these are among the most salient when considering the influence of social forces on contemporary curriculum planning.

The concept of *humanity* can be a significant organizing element in curriculum planning, and it is one that is particularly needed as the nations of the world become more interdependent and together address problems of pollution, energy and food shortages, and terrorism. In addition to trying to understand the social forces that affect society in the United States or Canada, curriculum planners should consider forces that affect humanity as a whole. The issues and information to be considered and the curricular approaches developed should go well beyond national borders. These "cultural universals" would be a major guiding focus in curriculum planning. For example, an increased global perspective on the arts could enlarge students' understanding in many areas of the curriculum.

The concept of culture has been defined in many ways. Simply put, *culture* is the way of life common to a group of people; it represents their way of looking at the world. It also consists of the values, attitudes, and beliefs that influence their behavior. There are hundreds of different cultures, and no one can hope to learn about all of them. In spite of their specific differences, however, all cultures are alike in that they serve important functions within the group. For example, a group's culture may prescribe certain ways of obtaining food, clothing, and shelter. It may also indicate how work is divided up and how relationships among men, women, and children, and between the old and the young, are patterned. Within the United States, we find cultural groups that differ according to language, ethnicity, religion, politics, economics, and region of the country. The regional culture of the South, for example, is quite different from that of New England. North Dakotans are different from Californians, and so on. Socioeconomic factors, such as income and occupation, also contribute to the culture of communities. Recall, for instance, the hypothetical scenario earlier in this chapter—Liza, Kevin, and Roy had very different cultural backgrounds.

From birth to death, each person is immersed in a culture or cultures. Early in life, each person learns the patterns of behavior supported by the culture into which he or she was born. Learning this first culture is called *enculturation* or *socialization.* As our society becomes more complex and places ever-increasing demands and stresses on parents, various agencies assume more responsibility for enculturating and socializing children and youth. Seymour Fersh's "Through the Cultural Looking Glass . . ." in this chapter will help you understand *culture* as a concept that has particular significance for curriculum planners when they analyze the social forces that must be considered for adequate planning. As Fersh asserts: "ignorance of others is not bliss and what you don't know *can* hurt you."

A *subculture* is a division of a cultural group consisting of persons who have certain characteristics in common while they share some of the major characteristics of the larger culture. For example, our society consists of varied subcultures, and many children from these subcultures come to school with life experiences that differ significantly from those of children the schools and teachers are used to encountering. Therefore, curriculum planners and teachers should understand the differences and similarities among the subcultures in a community, as well as those within the national culture. Moreover, as Paul Bohannan points out in "Our Two-Story Culture" in this chapter, our "two levels" of culture must not get too far "out of phase," and we must learn to cherish a "whole spectrum" of subcultures.

An additional critical point is that the individual learner should have positive feelings about his or her culture. This is possible only if curriculum planners and teachers understand that the behaviors, attitudes, and beliefs that children from nonmainstream cultures bring to school are just *different,* not wrong—a point Shirley Brice Heath (1996) brings out in *Ways with Words,* an insightful analysis of how children from two subcultures, "Roadville" and "Trackton," come to school possessing "ways with words" that are incongruent with the "school's ways":

> Roadville and Trackton residents have a variety of literate traditions, and in each community these are interwoven in different ways with oral uses of language, ways of negotiating meaning, deciding on action, and achieving status. . . . Roadville parents believe it their task to praise and practice reading with their young children; Trackton adults believe the young have to learn to be and do, and if reading is necessary for this learning, that will come. . . . In Trackton, the written word is for negotiation and manipulation—both serious and playful. Changing and changeable, words are the tools performers use to create images of themselves and the world they see. For Roadville, the written word limits alternatives of expression; in Trackton, it opens alternatives. Neither community's ways with the written word prepares it for the school's ways (Heath, 1996, pp. 234–235).

Cultural pluralism refers to a comingling of a variety of ethnic and generational lifestyles, each grounded in a complexity of values, linguistic variations, skin hues, and perhaps even cognitive world views. The term *pluralism* implies that, theoretically at least, no one culture takes precedence over any other. Cultural pluralism means that each person, regardless of self- or group-identification, is entitled to the respect, dignity, freedom, and citizen rights promised by law and tradition.

Cultural pluralism requires that curriculum planners and teachers develop learning experiences and environments in which each group's contribution to the richness of the entire society is genuinely validated and reflected to the extent possible in the curriculum. Schools that facilitate understanding of cultural pluralism radiate a tone of inclusiveness in policies, practices, and programs. So significant are the implications of cultural pluralism for contemporary curriculum planning that the concept is discussed in several articles throughout this book; (in this chapter, see Seymour Fersh's "Through the Cultural Looking Glass . . ." and Paul Bohannan's "Our Two-Story Culture;" in Chapter 4, see Cynthia B. Dillard and Dionne A. Blue's "Learning Styles from a Multicultural Perspective: The Case for Culturally Engaged Education;" in Chapter 5, see James A. Banks's "Multicultural Education and Curriculum Transformation;" and in Chapter 10, see Diane Ravitch's "Multiculturalism Yes, Particularism No").

Futures Planning

What curricula will best prepare learners to meet the challenges of the twenty-first century? Of course, no one has *the* answer to this question. Nevertheless, it is important for curriculum planners to think carefully about the future. *Futures planning* is the process of conceptualizing the future as a set of possibilities and then taking steps to create the future we want. As Alvin Toffler (1970, p. 460) pointed out in *Future Shock,* we must choose wisely from among several courses of action: "Every society faces not merely a succession of *probable* futures, but an array of *possible* futures, and a conflict over *preferable* futures. The management of change is the effort to convert certain possibles into probables, in pursuit of agreed-on preferables. Determining the probable calls for a science of futurism. Delineating the possible calls for an art of futurism. Defining the preferable calls for a politics of futurism."

Futures planners project current social forces into the future with the hope of identifying and developing ways to meet the challenges associated with those forces. Unlike past futurists, today's futures planners seldom predict a single future; to use Toffler's term, they develop a set of *possible* futures.

In using the processes of futures planning, curriculum planners and teachers work with students, parents, and other members of the community in identifying and discussing present trends, and forecasting and projecting the effects of one trend compared to another. Alternative scenarios are developed based on efforts to "change" the future, either by taking action or by doing nothing.

For example, the Internet, the World Wide Web, and related telecommunications technologies illustrate how planning for the future in light of present social forces influences the curriculum. For more than thirty years, there have been continued improvements in microelectronics. Computers have moved from the laboratories, universities, and big companies into the mainstream of everyday life. They are at the grocery checkout counter, the neighborhood service station, and in our homes. Each day, millions of people around the world spend countless hours in cyberspace where they visit chat rooms, make business transactions, participate in distance learning programs, and receive instantaneous reports on newsworthy events. In light of the continued dazzling pace of developments in microelectronics, what are the implications for today's curriculum planners? Clearly, a critical form of literacy for the new century is the ability to use computers for learning and solving problems.

The rapid pace of change demands that the curriculum prepare children, youth, and adults for the present as well as the future. Learning to look ahead—to see local, national, and global forces and trends in terms of alternative futures and consequences—must be part of the curriculum. Today, the curriculum should help learners participate in the development of the future through their involvement in meaningful, authentic learning experiences in the present.

CRITERION QUESTIONS—SOCIAL FORCES

What criterion questions may be derived from the social forces discussed in this chapter? Providing for individual differences among learners, the teaching of values, the development of self-understanding, and the development of problem-solving skills are four important curriculum planning criteria that illustrate how social forces influence the curriculum.

First, individual differences among learners are related to family and home background, subculture, and community background. The descriptions of Liza, Kevin, and Roy earlier in this chapter and Fersh's article both illustrate how social forces provide a key to understanding individual differences which should be provided for in the curriculum. In light of individual differences among learners, then, the criterion questions for curriculum planners and teachers are as follows:

1. What social or cultural factors contribute to individual differences among learners?
2. How can the curriculum provide for these differences?

Second, all curricula are implemented within a social climate that teaches values that may or may not be clearly stated, or about which curriculum planners and teachers may be unaware. This "hidden curriculum," as it is commonly termed, also refers to the attitudes and knowledge the culture of a school unintentionally teaches students. The discussion of cultural pluralism earlier in this chapter and Fersh's article, "Through the Cultural Looking Glass . . . ," illustrate the relationship between social forces and the teaching of values. Thus, the criterion questions in regard to teaching values are as follows:

3. What values *are* we teaching?
4. What values do we *wish* to teach?

Third, self-understanding as a curriculum criterion is related to cultural pluralism and to various social forces such as changing values and changes in family life. Effective educational programs help students—regardless of cultural background, family situation, or challenging life circumstances—to understand themselves more fully. Thus, a salient criterion question in regard to facilitating self-understanding is:

5. How can the school program assist learners in achieving their goals of self-understanding and self-realization?

Finally, problem solving as a curriculum criterion asks whether the curriculum and the teaching of that curriculum help learners to clarify problems and develop appropriate problem-solving strategies. Three criterion questions to gauge the effectiveness of a curriculum at promoting problem-solving skills are as follows:

6. Has the curriculum been planned and organized to assist learners in identifying and clarifying personal and social problems?
7. Does the curriculum help learners acquire the problem-solving skills they will need now and in the future?
8. Does the curriculum include the development of skills in futures planning?

REFERENCES

Annie E. Casey Foundation. *Kids Count Data Book 1998.* Baltimore, MD: The Annie E. Casey Foundation, 1998.

Carnegie Council on Adolescent Development. *Great Transitions: Preparing Adolescents for a New Century.* New York: Carnegie Corporation of New York, 1995.

Heath, Shirley Brice. *Ways with Words: Language, Life and Work in Communities and Classrooms.* Cambridge: Cambridge University Press, 1996.

Henry, Eric, et al. *To Be a Teacher: Voices from the Classroom*. Thousand Oaks, CA: Corwin Press, Inc., 1995.

Lickona, Thomas. "The Return of Character Education." *Educational Leadership* 51, no. 3 (November 1993): 6–11.

Mehlinger, Howard D. "School Reform in the Information Age." *Phi Delta Kappan* 77, no. 6 (February 1996): 400–407.

Morton, Chris. "The Modern Land of Laputa: Where Computers Are Used in Education." *Phi Delta Kappan* 77, no. 6 (February 1996): 416–419.

National Center for Education Statistics. *Projection of Education Statistics to 2006*, 25th Ed. Washington, DC: National Center for Education Statistics, 1996.

Spring, Joel. *American Education*, 7th Ed. New York: McGraw-Hill, Inc., 1996.

Toffler, Alvin. *Future Shock*. New York: Random House, 1970.

U.S. Department of Justice. *Sourcebook of Criminal Justice Statistics, 1998*. Washington, DC: U.S. Department of Justice, 1998.

U.S. Department of Justice. *1995 National Youth Gang Survey*. Washington, DC: U.S. Department of Justice, 1995.

Future Schools and How to Get There from Here

R. G. DES DIXON

ABSTRACT: Dixon asserts that current models of schooling fail to reflect the "reality of childhood" and that today's curricula are largely "Victorian." Today's children and youth participate in society in ways that show them to be active, capable, self-directed, assertive, and independent. Teachers, therefore, should take the lead in creating greater public awareness of the contemporary realities of childhood. Schools should be redesigned so that students are empowered to play a key role in shaping their educational experiences.

Our current models of schooling and childhood are of recent origin—only about 600 years old in the 6,000-year history of civilization—and they grew up together influencing each other. Until this century, the model of schooling actually led the model of childhood. Special clothes for children, the separation of children from adults, the ideal of childhood as a form of innocence, punishment used for purification and control, lockstep restrictions on child development—so many characteristics—came to the model of childhood from the model of schooling. Now, in the 1990s, the *reality* of childhood (but not the sentimental model) is changing so fast that it is well in front of the model of schooling.

More than anything else, it was direct access to information that allowed childhood to sprint past schooling and get out in front: first mass-market print, then movies, then radio, then television, now computers. But dozens of other momentous changes speeded the redefinition of childhood in this century: wars, mass migrations, changes in

From *Phi Delta Kappan* 75, no. 5 (January 1994): 360–365. © 1994, Phi Delta Kappa. Used by permission of the author and publisher.

the status of women and minorities, the population explosion, family breakdown, democratization of institutions other than schools, cycles of boom and bust, and so on.

Taken together, a combination of 20th-century circumstances that affect the young constitutes a major—but barely acknowledged—change in society. Neither the media nor our opinion leaders have noticed that children themselves are redefining childhood. The very young consume all types of information via television and computers, while our model of childhood still views them as ignorant and innocent. Teens spend much of their time working for pay, listening to music, and watching television, but the model still pretends that school is their primary activity. They are indispensable to such major industries as fast food, supermarkets, gas stations, retail stores, and hospitals, but the model sees them as outside the labor force. They are looking after themselves and running households for absentee adults, but the model sees them as helpless. They are sexually active, while the sentimental model of childhood says they are nonsexual.

At this moment, millions of high school students are working 55 hours a week or more, when school, home, and paid hours are totaled. But nobody has bothered to create (let alone accept and control) a "total job description" for students that matches the reality of their lives, including school, extracurricular activities, homework, after-hours jobs, household chores, and so on. Children are the most exploited, overworked, and underpaid class in society.

None of the following realities matches the 1940-ish Andy Hardy image of childhood to which society so fervently clings. Children—not old people or women or any racial group—are the poorest members of society. Yet significant numbers of children in their teens attend universities, graduate, and go on to become physicians, engineers, scientists, and mathematicians. Most male and female prostitutes begin working regularly at 16 or younger, and many street-level drug dealers are children. Children are the last visible minority without human rights. For over

a decade boys of 12 to 16 years of age have been fighting in Eritrea, Sudan, Somalia, Israel (in the Intifada), Iraq, Iran, South Africa, Nicaragua, and other countries. Political candidates routinely say that junior high school audiences are among the best informed about issues in federal and state elections.

Our model of childhood dictates that children be passive instead of active, incapable instead of capable, directed instead of self-directed, acquiescent instead of assertive, dependent rather than independent. We have Mickey Moused the lives of children in schools by denying them control, the very thing we should be teaching them so that they can find meaning in life and learn to survive in the real world of childhood. Instead of validating the new self-reliance that is the essence of their reality in the community, schools treat teens as recidivist ring-around-a-rosiers even though, when they're out of school, they may have lovers, drive cars, and work for a living. The young express their frustration by dropping out, smoking, taking drugs, getting pregnant, forming gangs, and committing violent acts.

Our response to their expressed frustration is to set up committees of adults, build more sports facilities to be run by adults, provide more courses to be taught by adults, and improve consultation with parents, who cannot be changed in time to save any current generation of children. Except for a few activists for children's rights, our leading thinkers never set about creating a new model of childhood that matches reality. Instead, we sing praise to the sentimental model of childhood that, as a social convention, parallels 19th-century footbinding in China. Both conventions require a constant restriction, retard growth, subjugate a large minority, deform for life, and are thought by the perpetrators to be beautiful.

As deliberately as the old model disempowers children, the model I propose . . . seeks to empower them. The new model accommodates the new realities of childhood that already exist and simultaneously reclaims for education its historic place as a leader in the development of models of childhood and schooling. For that last reason alone, teachers should be the eager leaders in community discussions that establish new models in the public mind. All the great opportunities for teachers lie in their assuming such leadership. If they fail, corporate giants in telecommunications will assume leadership. The Edison Project of Whittle Communications will then point the way.

Student government has never been taken seriously by school reformers, but it must be central to any new model of schooling. By developing strong and relevant student government, schools will fulfill their long-neglected obligation to teach the democratic process and at the same time will provide sane leadership for society in its inevitable move toward children's rights. The test of student government is this: Is there anything being managed by school or district officials that could be managed by student government? If so, student government is not functioning properly.

In the new model, all school rules issue from and are enforced by student government and its committees. Parents, politicians, administrators, and teachers encourage student governments and student media to deal forthrightly and in-depth with the very matters that are now being censored: sex, politics, social issues, values, trends, children's rights, the redefinition of childhood, and so on. Student governments act as labor unions to promote and protect the interests of students in the part-time job market. If they are thoroughly trained, student governments can be valuable evaluators of all aspects of schooling, including curricula and teachers. In a reconstituted student government, service on the student council is a top-priority learning activity; thus student council meetings must take place during the school day, and office holders must receive academic credit for serving.

In the classroom, my proposed model requires a kind of teacher that has never before existed; I use the name *hi* (plural *hies*)—an abbreviation of human interactor—to convey their new role. And to describe the room in which that role is played, I prefer not to use the term *classroom* (since

classes in the conventional sense are rarely taught there except in the early grades), but to call it instead a *living room*. In the new model, children of all ages, from preschoolers to 18-year-olds, spend about three years in each living room before moving on to the next, so that every child experiences six living rooms before graduation.

Very young children spend most of the day in the living room, but, as students grow older, they make increasing use of other rooms. The living room is home base, and every student keeps returning to it (or checking in by phone or computer when on learning missions outside the school). The hi knows when and why students leave the living room—usually to attend programs in other rooms.

Required programs—those considered essential for enabling students to achieve all forms of literacy, including cultural literacy—are provided in living rooms by hies, but specialized and in-depth courses for college-entry credits are taught elsewhere in the school by teachers called *consultants*. A third category of teachers, called *tutors*, identify and treat specific learning problems. These skill-centered teachers deal with very small groups or with individuals in lab settings, where they do skill-development and remedial work.

Teachers encourage and *train* children to assume all classroom roles, including teaching roles. To this end, obligatory developmental experiences are thoroughly planned, implemented, and evaluated. Remedial programs are provided for those children whose group-process skills are below the levels required for them to participate fully.

In living rooms, groups of students prepare and present most topics in the required curriculum (which I will describe in more detail later). A team made up of the hi, a paid assistant, and three students is in charge of scheduling activities. By age 13 or 14, the three students will be pretty well capable of running the show, with only occasional consultations with the school staff about changes in or additions to the curriculum.

No matter which living room they are in, individual students continue with their own skills programs (in reading, writing, speaking, listening, ciphering, and so on) and with optional programs (electives for credit). The different treatment of the basic required programs in different living rooms is significant only in terms of process, not in terms of sacred content or academic consequence.

Today, the results of standardized testing are widely misused, especially in the U.S. and Britain and especially with regard to the improper comparison of schools. In the Future School, hies routinely administer tests in the usual areas (e.g., reading, writing, listening, ciphering, cultural literacy), but the results are used only as teaching tools. Even more often, individual students test themselves using computerized tests. Content from any source considered essential for the development of any literacy shows up on such tests and so do content and skills considered cumulative and necessary for programs required later in a student's school career. Tutors and consultants also use standardized tests diagnostically. In addition, consultants use examinations they design themselves that are also part of the "standard evaluation criteria and strategies" specified by the government for each subject.

All hies must be outstanding generalists. The best of them blend a number of disciplines in their required programs and special interests. The borders between traditional subjects are already blurring and eventually will disappear. Instead of being sacred packages of content, school programs will become focal points for explorations that include aspects of many traditional disciplines.

In the Future School those in charge of the living rooms, other full-time faculty members, paid assistants, and even students are required to be on the job seven hours a day, five days a week, 220 days a year.

When we do an about-face and expect all children to become self-propelled learners, each will need high self-esteem and an array of skills. These two characteristics are the fuel of self-propulsion. The specific skills essential to self-propulsion that the schools are responsible for developing are the first order of required programs. These include language literacy (reading, writing, and speaking in all their varied forms); listening; numeracy (including addition, subtraction, division, and elements of mathematics that are essential for everyday life); researching; problem solving; organizing; cultural literacy; and computer literacy.

It is the responsibility of the schools to see that all other activities (save only those bearing on health and student government) are held in abeyance each year until such time as an individual student has reached the expected levels of proficiency in each skill essential to self-propulsion. Programs to develop the skills required for self-propulsion (along with all other required programs) must be separate from optional (elective) programs offered for credit. No credit should be given for any required skill development program. In every year of elementary and secondary school, elective programs for credit must be closed to students until they reach the expected level in all required programs.

Another category of required, noncredit programs in which every student must participate every year includes personal fitness (exercise, eating, hygiene, grooming, safety, and drug education), sex education, and student government.

When a student's achievement in these two kinds of required programs has reached the expected level, he or she must also participate every year in a third category of required, noncredit programs, covering such areas of study as international understanding, social service, foreign language, visual and performing arts, children's rights, values (or ethics), current affairs, and media literacy.

A fourth category of required, noncredit programs, equal in status to the third category, are studied at appropriate levels of complexity only at selected ages rather than every year. These include parenting (ages 13 through 18); labor/management relations (ages 6, 11, and 16); law (ages 4, 6, 9, 13, and 16); driving (age 15); science literacy (all ages up to 14); world religions (ages 7, 10, 13, and 16); money and finance (ages 6, 11, and 15); national history (ages 5, 8, 11, and

14); national geography (ages 6, 9, 12, and 15); and job-search and career-planning skills (ages 13, 15, and 17).

Some of the programs in these third and fourth categories will be short units lasting only a few hours, days, or weeks. Others will continue for an entire term or year but will consume only a short time each week. Many programs in all four categories are carried out as living room activities, but others can be assigned to consultants elsewhere in the school.

Students who are achieving at their expected levels in all required programs are allowed to book programs taught by consultants. The electives offered include all the traditional subjects required for college entrance.

As a matter of principle, Future Schools are nongraded and tracked only in the sense that all children have the right and responsibility to choose their living rooms and their electives to suit their individual needs. The current model of schooling is not suited to "schooling" children *out of* lower tracks and *into* higher ones. But it is the model of schooling that is wrong, not the concept of tracking.

The way to make students sophisticated in technology is to make the school a technologically rich environment. That most children are not fully computer literate long before the end of elementary school is a stunning indictment of the present model of schooling and of the people who run it. In a revitalized school system in which self-propelled, active learning is the norm, training for computer literacy must include competency testing on every aspect of using the current generation of computers and specific remedial and developmental training for those whose test results indicate need. Every student must have a notebook computer that is compatible with the school's computer, and every student must make routine use of living room camcorders, faxes, copiers, phones, and so on. If we want controlled evolution from the present publicly operated schools to computerized publicly operated

schools, every nation must create and fund a comprehensive plan that will phase in these changes.

All changes brought by computers have profound implications, but three of them will shake the foundations of schooling more than anything has since Socrates laid those foundations: unleashed creativity, unlimited access to information, and mastery learning. All of these are gigantic square pegs that won't fit the little round hole of traditional schooling.

The purpose of schooling in the twenty-first century is to serve all the needs of children that are not met elsewhere in society. Most lower-, middle-, and upper-class parents, even if they are good people, can't provide optimum learning conditions for infants any more than they can for 8- or 12-year-olds. Schools must welcome everyone, from toddlers up to students in their late teens.

Many aspects of the new model are controversial and are likely to remain so. Consider the following prospects.

- Ultimate allegiance will no longer be to just a single nation-state but rather to the planet and to a planetary moral code that students in compulsory global studies programs must synthesize from all cultures on earth.
- It is possible to teach nearly all young people who pass through schools to read, write, speak, and listen. But profound changes in strategy and priorities will have to be made.
- Teachers of media literacy (along with teachers of English) bear primary responsibility for the well-being of democracy through awakening each generation to assaults on freedom of expression and to the consequent obligations of every citizen to maintain and enhance that pivotal freedom.
- National governments should take a great leap toward the universal health of their citizens by supplying two nutritious meals (and vitamin supplements) daily to all children who wish to partake.
- All school sports teams should be organized, managed, coached, and officiated entirely by

students, with teachers acting only as consultants. Physical education must be compulsory, and programs must guarantee at least 30 minutes per day of sustained, vigorous exercise for every child.

- For both students and teachers, absenteeism more than 2% of the time should be considered unacceptable.
- Instead of compulsory schooling, we must make universal schooling available and guarantee the right to it. Moreover, the right to schooling must carry with it whatever support is needed to make attendance feasible: fees, supplies, food, clothing, housing, emotional nurturance and so on.
- There is no other initiative that any developed country could take to reduce the dropout rate and improve attendance that would be nearly as effective as adding residences to schools.
- Teaching should be like other performing arts: the union should negotiate a minimum rate of pay and leave to individuals the decision of whether to work for scale or negotiate payment above scale. Stars command higher pay.
- Even in the present model of schooling, teaching requires organization. In the schools of tomorrow every teacher will need organi-

zational skills on a par with generals and chief executives.

- Responsibility for the formative evaluation of teachers (and hence the routine supervision that is implicit in formative evaluation) must be taken away from principals and given to counselors, who would be employed by every school board to help teachers plan their professional growth.
- Today's curriculum is largely Victorian, a late 19th-century expression of the Industrial Revolution as applied to the education industry. We have tinkered with it, but we have not changed it. To provide promising alternatives— curriculum ideas that will turn schools around and connect them to the present and future instead of the past—we need permanent international, national, and local curriculum think tanks staffed by visionaries.
- If strong nationhood is the goal (rather than a weaker federation of states), the highest level of government must specify the content of each nation's cultural curriculum, because, without a shared national culture and the shared national values that accompany it, successful nationhood is unlikely.

R. G. Des Dixon is an education analyst and former head of Curriculum and Professional Development for the Ontario Teachers' Federation.

QUESTIONS FOR REFLECTION

1. What evidence can you cite to support Dixon's assertion that "the *reality* of childhood is changing so fast that it is well in front of the model of schooling"?
2. What does Dixon mean when he calls for teachers to become *hies* (human interactors) and students to be educated in "living rooms"?
3. Review the set of recommendations that Dixon presents at the end of his article. What are the strengths and weaknesses of each? What societal barriers might prevent the implementation of each recommendation?

The Changing World of Work in the Information Age

MARTIN CARNOY

ABSTRACT: Most discussions of education and information technology focus on the impact of computers in the classroom and on how students learn. However, the greatest influence of new information technologies on education is related to how they have fundamentally transformed work. Contrary to many projections, Information Age technology will not result in the "end of work" and massive unemployment. To prepare students for tomorrow's work, though, higher levels of education should be expected of all students. Postindustrial countries should move toward universal postsecondary education that enhances students' self-reliance, ability to adjust to rapid change, and mobility.

Most analyses of education and information technology focus on the impact that computers could have on the classroom and on the way children learn. But the much greater effect of new technology on education comes from a different direction. Increased economic competition on a global scale and the massive diffusion of new information and communication technologies are profoundly affecting the nature of work. As they change the nature of work, they put new demands on education, potentially transforming it. Some writers have argued that globalisation and the new technologies portend the 'end of work'.[1] According to these analyses, unless the trend is reversed, education's role would be largely limited to selecting talented individuals for high-paying 'boutique jobs' at the creative end of the global information industry. But notwithstanding real, painful adjustments to a new technological paradigm, the lessons of history, current empirical evidence, employment projections in the OECD countries and economic theory do not support fears of mass unemployment in the long term.[2]

The defining issue of tomorrow's work and education lies elsewhere: although technology does not reduce a nation's jobs, the restructuring of firms and organisations, stimulated by global competition and facilitated by new technology, does indeed fundamentally transform work. It disaggregates labour in the labour process. We are witnessing the reversal of the historical trend of salarisation of work and socialisation of production that was the dominant feature of the industrial era. In its place, new social and economic organisation aims at decentralising management, individualising work and customising markets, thereby fragmenting labour and segmenting societies. At the same time, new information technologies facilitate the decentralisation of work tasks and their coordination in an interactive network of communication in real time, be it between continents or between floors of the same building. The emergence of lean production methods goes hand in hand with widespread business practices of subcontracting, outsourcing, offshoring, consulting and, accordingly, downsizing and customising. Part-time jobs, temporary work, flexible working time and self-employment are on the rise in all countries. The trend points towards a transformation of work arrangements in advanced societies.[3]

The individualisation of work and the disaggregation of labour are processes that affect the entire fabric of our societies. This is because of the centrality of work for social life and because of

From *New Political Economy*, v. 3, no. 1 (March 1998): 123–128. Used by permission of the author and publisher. Copyright 1998, Carfax Publishing Limited, P.O. Box 25, Abingdon, Oxfordshire OX14 3UE, United Kingdom.

the tight connection between work, family, community and the state in our societies. The transformation of the work process shatters the institution of the welfare state, on which the social contract of our societies has been based for the last half-century. How can flexible work and flexible employment possibly coexist with rigid social security entitlements? The individualisation of work and the shrinkage of the public safety net emphasise the main institutions/social forms that help people in the transition periods of their lives—namely families and communities—as they try to adapt to the new requirements of work life. But communities based on shared work practices, such as labour unions and working-class cultures, are gradually fading away. Unions increasingly become micro- and macro-political institutions negotiating the shape of work organisations and family-work relations, rather than salaries and wages per se. Several waves of accelerated urbanisation, suburbanisation and territorial sprawl have undermined the material base of neighbourhood sociability, while new forms of electronic communication are still too limited and too elitist to allow for the widespread emergence of new, virtual communities. As for the traditional family, it has been weakened by the welcome cultural drive for women's equal rights and by the massive incorporation of women into the labour force— all this just when a strong family is most needed during the difficult transition towards new forms of work and personal life.

KNOWLEDGE AND INFORMATION AS THE BASES FOR REINTEGRATING DISAGGREGATED WORKERS

The transformation of work and employment has resulted in a crisis of the relationship between work and society. But it has also created the bases for reintegrating the individual into a highly productive, more egalitarian social structure. These bases are knowledge and information. Knowledge can be defined as the cumulated stock of cognitive skills and information that each individual, family and community (including firms) have that can be applied to work, personal and social situations. Information is the flow of usable knowledge available to individuals, families and communities, including workplaces. The distinguishing feature of work in the information age is the centrality of knowledge, especially 'transportable' general knowledge that is not specific to a single job or firm. The best jobs are those that require a high level of education (high levels of general knowledge) and provide opportunities to accumulate more knowledge. The best firms are those that create the best environment for teaching, learning and interchanging information. It is knowledge and information that creates flexibility in work—the capacity of firms to improve product lines, production processes and marketing strategies, all with the same workforce; and the capacity of workers to learn new processes as they change, to shift jobs several times in the course of a work life, to move geographically and, if necessary, to learn entirely new vocations.

The family and community in the information age should also be organised around the centrality of knowledge and information, both to support new forms of work and to foster human development, which should be the ultimate benefit of human activities. In its most advanced form, the egalitarian family is a supportive environment for interactive teaching and learning, geared to develop adults and children to their highest creative potential. Communities can also be defined in terms of learning networks, including child development centres, educational institutions, municipal organisations providing a range of business services and adult educational networks, and virtual communities connecting individuals through the internet.

More knowledge and information do not, in themselves, create more jobs. Yet a society organised around learning networks provides the basis for much higher productivity, greater equality and the reintegration of individualised citizen-workers. Over the longer run, this will create greater wealth and income, continue to generate higher quality jobs, change the nature of leisure and develop a new set of reintegrative activities that make life more interesting and rewarding.

THE NEW WORKER AND THE INCREASED IMPORTANCE OF FORMAL SCHOOLING

The new information economy places a premium on a worker's ability to move from a job in one firm to another, to learn new jobs in the same firm, to do several different types of tasks in the same day and to adjust quickly to different kinds of employment cultures and different group situations.[4] The firms that reward such flexibility and promote it tend to be more successful than those that do not, creating yet greater demand for workers with these abilities.

Although employers cannot predict which workers will be more flexible, flexibility has consistently been associated with higher levels of general education and general job training. Individual workers with more education are more able to adjust to new situations, learn new tasks and adopt new methods of performing old tasks. At the same time, firms that provide relatively large amounts of general training tied to workers taking on multiple tasks and to wage incentives are more likely to show larger gains in productivity than firms that follow traditional, more inflexible production methods.[5]

This complex interplay between more highly educated workers, prepared to learn more quickly, to take on new tasks and to move from one job to another, and bestpractice firms, promoting increased flexibility through general training, multiple task jobs and employee decision making, is at the core of high productivity work in the information age. Flexible work organisations are necessarily learning organisations and new technologies, including the art of flexible organisation itself, make their maximum contribution to productivity when they are based on learning and teaching as an inherent part of the work place.

HOW EDUCATION WILL NEED TO CHANGE

What goes on in learning organisations suggests that traditional concepts of education will have to change. The workers that do best in flexible, learning organisations are good both at solving problems individually, i.e. the higher order skills normally learned by students going on to post-secondary education; and, as important, at working with others in teams to innovate and motivate—a skill that is hardly touched upon in our present educational system. Such 'cooperative skills' are generally associated with management courses and, indeed, the learning networks require workers to have a 'management mentality', in the sense of 'people skills', including knowing how to motivate individualised fellow workers to commit both to applying their knowledge for maximum efficiency and quality and to learn (and teach others) how to do better. Education for the information age needs to develop workers who have high order problem-solving skills and who can help organise more learning. This suggests profound change in the curriculum of schools and in job training programmes. First, it means that the standard forms of vocational education, organised around specific skills for specific jobs, are almost totally anachronistic, except in the sense that they can be used to teach problem solving and organisational/teaching skills to students who have been alienated from more academic approaches to learning.[6] Second, it suggests that learning in schools should itself be increasingly organised in a cooperative fashion, where students study in groups, present group work and often get evaluated as a group. Third, the curriculum should include the development of networking, motivational and teaching skills so that students develop a clear understanding of human behaviour and the understanding of group processes. In the learning-centred environment of the information age, the process of learning and the motivation to learn should become endogenous to the curriculum itself.

Fourth, general education during youth should be viewed as only the beginning of the learning process. In the not so recent past, young people went to school, got a job and often did that job for much of the rest of their lives. Worker networks were organised to protect the permanence of the worker's job and to build state social welfare programmes around it. In the information age, the worker is no longer defined in terms of a job but in terms of cumulated learning and the capacity to apply that learning to a variety of situations, inside and outside the traditional workplace. These situations include the new egalitarian family and virtual communities. Learning and teaching, therefore, is a continuous process throughout life and should be organised on that basis, with opportunities for workers-citizens-parents to gain knowledge and skills applicable to their varied roles in society at various ages and to exercise them in a variety of ways at the different stages of their lives.

All this does not itself solve the problem of reasonable paying jobs for all those who want them and may even be capable of doing them. More education does not necessarily create new jobs, as shown by the situation in Europe, where average levels of education have been rising rapidly among cohorts of new entrants into the labour force without a secular decline in unemployment rates. In France, for example, in 10 short years (1980–90), the proportion of post-secondary graduates coming out of the educational system climbed from 19 per cent to 31 per cent and the proportion with some post-secondary education from 26 per cent to 44 per cent, while the unemployment rate for young people fell and then rose again to about 25 per cent.[7] Since this trend towards ever higher average levels of education among younger workers is occurring in all OECD countries, one result, if no other measures are taken to incorporate the young into the jobs, could simply be ever higher levels of education among the unemployed.

But keeping young people in school longer has two major advantages: first, it delays them entering the full-time job market; and, second, it provides employers with a much better educated, potentially more flexible, more trainable, more employable and more potentially productive work force. It also develops a work force that is more likely to view further education at older ages as a natural part of their working/learning lives. Combined with best-practice workplaces organised around training and learning, this sets the stage for higher productivity and lower aggregate unemployment rates in the long term.

CONCLUSIONS

Perhaps the most difficult, but necessary, transformation for post-industrial countries to make quickly is to organise schooling around universal post-secondary education that imparts self-reliance, rapid adjustment to change, and mobility. Educational systems in the past have been used not only to impart cognitive skills, but as social selectors, steering children from various socioeconomic backgrounds into 'appropriate' levels of education that then make them eligible for 'appropriate' jobs. This worked reasonably well in a hierarchical industrial system built on career jobs that were mostly semi-skilled and changed little over an individual's work life. The system was stratified but could provide reasonable security and increasing wages, even to those with basic education.[8]

Today, such stratification is much more socially counterproductive than it was in the past, yet societies have not understood the need to overhaul the system that certifies it. Youth with secondary education are increasingly at risk in the labour market, in large part because both the education system and employers regard them as inadequately prepared for higher-skilled, flexible jobs. That has to change and the only way to change it in the current and future environment is to raise expectations and to compress the distribution of education by raising the social minimum. This means not only extending youth education but also focusing more resources on the early childhood development of disadvantaged groups and on the creation of more possibilities for formal schooling in adulthood. Cultural capital, in Bourdieu's and Passeron's terms, must become less of a determining factor in access to knowledge and information.

Higher levels of education in the information age do not just provide more trainable employees for the workplace. One of the most profound transformations of the information age workplace is its increased opportunities for self-employment, especially for people with concrete, high-level service skills. Relatively stable, employed, full-time work has characterised the labour process for only the past 100 years or so. A gradual return to self-employment is a natural outcome of greater work flexibility, the shift to a service economy, the availability of very lowcost information technology and increasing levels of education and knowledge in the labour force. The possibilities for workers to gain skills working as employees also enhances their ability to move out of employment into self-employment.[9]

The difference between the growing self-employment opportunities in the future and those of the past is in their knowledge-intensity. High technology services are organised around information, rather than commodities. Furthermore, information technology makes it possible for small businesses to avail themselves of relatively inexpensive accounting and marketing software, to locate themselves in the home, to be part-time and to be family-centred as part of a mixture of family wage employment activities, self-employment activities and child development activities. Since it is knowledge-intensive, the new self-employment may occupy an increasing proportion of formerly employed workers who have acquired knowledge and skills as employees and then go on to develop their own businesses based on that experience.

Without precluding the positive role of community centres in some cases, the central organising points in our society at the neighbourhood level are rapidly shifting to child development centres and schools (elementary, secondary, community colleges and universities). Because schools' location patterns are pervasive and residence-based and because sociability is made easier

through children's and youth and adult learning connections, schools could become the platforms to deal with a variety of issues in the neighbourhood. They could also be the material support for the formation of networks of solidarity between families of different types, all concerned with the future of their children. Children could be the issue around which family, community and the future worker (the child) could be brought together in a system of interaction that blends instrumental goals (child care, development and education) with expressive, emotional and social interaction. This means transforming the school to make it more open to the community. But it also means—contrary to much of current thinking—providing the public school system with better trained personnel, more resources, better physical facilities and more innovative management.

NOTES

1. See, for example, Jeremy Rifkin, *The End of Work* (Putnam, 1995).
2. Chris Freeman & Luc Soete, *Work for All or Mass Unemployment?* (Pinter, 1994).
3. Bennett Harrison, *Lean and Mean* (Basic Books, 1994); and Martin Carnoy & Manuel Castells, 'Sustainable flexibility', mimeo, Center for Western European Studies, University of California, Berkeley, CA, 1995.
4. Peter Capelli, 'New work systems and skill requirements', paper presented at the Workshop on New Trends in Training Policy, International Labour Organisation, Geneva, October 1993.
5. Theodore Schultz, 'The Value of the Ability to Deal with Disequilibria', *Journal of Economic Literature,* Vol. 13, No. 3 (1975), pp. 827–46; and Clair Brown, Michael Reich, Michael & David Stern, 'Becoming a high performance organization: the role of security, employee involvement and training', mimeo, Center of Labor and Industrial Relations, University of California, Berkeley, CA, 1993.
6. David Stern, M. Raby & C. Dayton, *Career Academies* (Jossey-Bass, 1992).
7. Considering that the unemployment rate for young post-secondary graduates was only 8 percent in the mid 1980s, whereas the average rate for

the young was 25 per cent (INSEE, Donnees Sociales, 1993, p. 146), it can be suggested that the concentration of unemployment among the young was in the groups with secondary schooling or less, just as it was in older groups.

8. Pierre Bourdieu & Jean-Claude Passeron, *Reproduction* (Routledge & Kegan Paul, 1977); and Martin Carnoy & Henry Levin, *Schooling and Work in the Democratic State* (Stanford University Press, 1985). In Europe, the secondary system was organised around vocational education on the premise that young men with mechanical experience and young women with secretarial and other service skills would be assured career jobs.

9. In the USA in the first four months of 1994, new business incorporations hit a record annual rate of 737,000 and the average self-employed worker earned about 40 per cent more per hour than those working for someone else. In addition, capital invested by the self-employed in their own businesses can pay high returns compared with most other investments. See *Business Week,* 17 October 1994.

Martin Carnoy is Professor, School of Education, Stanford University.

QUESTIONS FOR REFLECTION

1. How realistic is the idea of universal postsecondary education?
2. How might the concept of "learning networks" be incorporated into the curricula at the level and in the subject area with which you are most familiar?
3. What does Carnoy mean by the following: "In the learning-centred environment of the information age, the process of learning and the motivation to learn should become endogenous to the curriculum itself"?

Through the Cultural Looking Glass . . .

SEYMOUR FERSH

ABSTRACT: From birth, children are taught to be ethnocentric, to believe that their country—its people, language, and way of life—is not only different from, but superior to other cultures. While this point of view is understandable for an individual within a particular culture, we should become aware of how the culture into which we were born influences what we "see." By understanding how our own cultural context influences our interpretations of behavior and events in other cultural contexts, we can achieve and maintain dual vision in a world that is becoming increasingly pluralistic.

Within the next hour about 7,200 babies will be born. At the moment of birth, the infants will be more like each other than they ever will be again. Their differences will grow because each of them is born into a different family and into a different culture—into a way of living that has developed in a particular place over a long period of time. From birth onward, each child is encouraged to be *ethnocentric*—to believe that his homeland, his people, his language, his everything is not only different but also superior to that of other people. The elders teach that the ways in which we do

From *AAUW Journal* 68, no. 6 (April 1975): 9–12. Used by permission of the author and the publisher.

things are the natural ways, the proper ways, and the moral ways. In other places, they—"barbarians" and "foreigners"—follow a strange way of life. Ours is *the* culture; theirs is *a* culture.

This kind of behavior in favor of one's own culture occurs most frequently when groups of people live in relative isolation from each other.

Survival of the group is believed to depend mainly on each person's acceptance of and loyalty to the group's organizational patterns of life and thought. People from outside the group are unwelcome because their manners and morals, being different, might by example threaten the existing system. These outsiders, in almost all languages, are designated by a word which means "stranger"—one whose beliefs and behavior are, to the insider, strange, eccentric, erratic, odd, queer, quaint, or outlandish.

This hatred of foreigners has a name; it is xenophobia. The anthropologists even have a name for this kind of behavior; it is misoneism, a deep and unreasoned hatred of new ideas. The traditional distrust of foreigners has been intensified by the news media where usually, as Marshall McLuhan observes, "real news is bad news—bad news *about* somebody or bad news *for* somebody." We have been generally conditioned to think of other national groups as either threats or burdens. Terms such as "trouble spots," "powder kegs," and "points of conflict" are often used to describe situations and conditions outside the United States. Such terms carry the feeling that the rest of the world has become a "burdensome" and "troublesome" place which creates a continuous series of problems for us.

Deaths and population decreases among foreigners are often unconsciously welcomed as "good news" because of the feeling that there will be fewer of "them" with whom to compete for worldly resources, which are assumed to be limited. Because each nation tends to exaggerate its own achievements, people everywhere tend not to appreciate how much of their own development—in ideas and in physical survival—has been contributed by "foreigners."

In some ways, however, the ethnocentric view of life is "right"; the pattern of responses that evolved in a particular place may make relatively good sense—for *that* particular people and place.

This generalization was especially true in the past when, according to Professor Elting E. Morison:

> For generations—for centuries—men did their work with the natural resources and energies lying ready at hand—the earth, the beast of burden, the wind and falling water. These materials and sources of power remained on the whole constant and stable; therefore the conditioned reflexes, habits of mind, customary emotional responses—in short, the culture—built up around these agencies remained on the whole relatively constant and stable.

SEPARATE AND RELATED

As human beings become aware of their relatedness, they need not necessarily cease being ethnocentric. When a person begins to identify with a nation, he does not cease being a member of his immediate family; he learns to apportion and extend his loyalties. Ethnocentrism is important and useful because it helps a person to develop a local cultural pattern that is appropriate for specific conditions. It would be unfortunate if the richness of cultural variety were lost to us. In learning about other cultures, the objective is not to discover a "universal culture" suitable for all people, in all places, and for all times. Rather, the objective is to learn the lesson that Aldous Huxley described following his first around-the-world trip in 1926:

> So the journey is over and I am back again, richer by much experience and poorer by many exploded convictions, many perished certainties. For convictions and certainties are too often the concomitants of ignorance. . . . I set out on my travels knowing, or thinking I knew, how men should live, how be governed, how educated, what they should believe. I had my views on every activity of life. Now, on my return, I find myself without any of these pleasing certainties. . . . The better you understand the significance of any question, the more difficult it becomes to answer it. Those who attach a high importance to their own opinion should

stay at home. When one is traveling, convictions are mislaid as easily as spectacles, but unlike spectacles, they are not easily replaced.

A person's awareness of his own ethnocentricity does not mean that he therefore must consider all cultures equally acceptable to him. Awareness can, however, help an observer to realize that what he "sees" is largely already "behind his eyes." Marshall McLuhan says, "Our need today is, culturally, the same as the scientist's who seeks to become aware of the bias of the instruments of research in order to correct that bias." A similar warning comes from Pierre Teilhard de Chardin: "When researchers reach the end of their analysis, they cannot tell with any certainty whether the structure they have made is the essence of the matter they are studying, or the reflection of their own thoughts."

Today, humankind is living in a world where groups are becoming more and more interrelated, less and less isolated. Ignorance of others is *not* bliss and what you don't know *can* hurt you. Moreover, many inventions and styles of life created by individual groups can help others. Each culture does not have to reinvent the wheel or depend exclusively on its own scientists, philosophers, and artists. Learning about other cultures is not something done as a favor to the people who live in them—as an expression of goodwill. Such knowledge can be of immediate and profound benefit and pleasure to the learner.

We should, in the words of James Thurber, "not look back in anger or look forward in fear but look around in awareness." It is too late for us to be unprejudiced, but we can recognize and become alert to our condition. The unprejudiced mind is not without prejudices; it is, says Hans Selye, "a mentality that has control over its numerous prejudices, and is always willing to reconsider them in the face of contrary evidence."

For example, in the United States the currently popular way of dividing the world is in terms of Western and non-Western cultures. In the so-called non-Western parts of the globe are people as different from each other as Chinese, Indians, Nigerians, Egyptians, and Iranians. But

these differences are minimized or, more often, overlooked or ignored. In a similar way, all the peoples who were living in the Americas when Columbus landed were identified by the Europeans as "Indians." The so-called Indians never thought of themselves as one people but considered themselves, more correctly, to be Iroquois, Hopi, Aztecs, Incas, and other tribal groups.

The major purpose, therefore, of learning about other cultures is to discover the ways in which other groups of human beings have organized their lives to answer the perennial questions of survival and fulfillment. Confucius said, "The nature of people is always the same; it is their habits which separate them."

FACTS AND FEELINGS

Each culture has its own kinds of achievements and problems. In comparing his country to the United States, an educated person from India, for example, would not deny that his country is backward with reference to the number of automobiles, amounts of electrical power, and supplies of food and medical services. But he would rightfully resent the conclusion, by inference, that he and his people are less human. Why, for instance, should a photograph of an Indian woman and her children in an American textbook have a caption which reads, "Even in mud huts, Indian parents love their children"? Does love increase with an increase of material goods? A *New York Times* reporter wrote:

> The Easterner seems heartlessly unconcerned about the misery of those to whom he is not related by some tie. But to his family and friends, the Asian commits himself in a way that makes the American appear heartless. The thought of packing one's parents off to some old-age home or retirement colony is shocking to him.

The features and qualities admired in one culture may bring hostility and suspicion in another. What image does the United States present in a world where our people, who number six percent of the population, have half of the material wealth and spend an average of about $90 per person for liquor and tobacco in a year—more than the average *total* income of many of the world's people? How do others see us in a world where most people have too little to eat, while in the United States some of our major health problems come from overeating? It is not really likely that such gaps between the world's rich and poor peoples will be narrowed if conditions continue as they have.

And should the peoples of the so-called "backward" or "undeveloped" countries be impressed with the so-called "developed" countries, which in recent years have spent more money on military matters than on health and education? Their total annual war-related expenditures, if divided among the world's population, would amount to more than $50 for every person. It has been estimated that the elimination of military spending could double the income of the 1.2 billion people who make less than $100 annually. It could also release 25 million soldiers and 75 million workers for constructive work.

It should become clear that choices between cultural patterns need not be rigidly restricted between the "spiritual East" and the "materialistic West." In the United States, many are beginning to learn that people do not live by gross national product alone. Similarly, in countries such as India, there is a growing dissatisfaction with the relatively low material standard of living. As people learn more about cultures other than their own, they begin to apply a variety of measurements in judging their own culture. The result is that waves of "spiritualism" and "materialism" flow around the world, mixing ingredients from one culture into another. It is no longer rare to see an Arab camel driver listening to a transistor radio or to see American students listening to lectures on Hinduism.

But to the overwhelming majority of the world's people, their own culture is still the one against which all others are measured. There is still a strong habit of accepting one's own culture as superior. The need is for alertness to assumptions. What is a person implying when, with apparent goodwill, he says, "Although the people of Asia and Africa are backward, there is no reason for us to feel superior"?

WINDOWS AND MIRRORS

When we become alert to our cultural conditioning, we are ready to continue our study of other peoples. The next concern is one of *cultural contexts*. New information and experiences are likely to be perceived within the framework of one's own cultural background rather than that of the one being studied. Contexts, after all, are invisible. How can the "outsider" possibly hope to create for himself the same cultural contexts which the "insider" carries effortlessly and unconsciously in his head? Here again, the need is for humility and strong motivation.

Until recently, for most people of the world, it really did not matter if understanding stopped at national boundaries, if indeed it stretched that far. Now, however, when international travel is so fast and so frequent, it is hazardous to base our actions solely on our own views. Moreover, ignorance about others perpetuates ignorance about ourselves because it is only through comparisons that we can discover personal differences and similarities. The glass through which we view other cultures serves not only as a window but also as a mirror in which we can see a reflection of our own way of life.

The achievement and maintenance of a dual vision, sometimes called *empathy* (the capacity to imagine what it is like to have the ideas and feelings of another person), is not, however, easily accomplished. Professor Ralph K. White explains that empathy requires us to hold two interpretations of the same facts, the other fellow's interpretation and our own. Because the human mind seeks simplicity and certainty, he feels, it rebels at the complexity and uncertainty of holding two points of view.

For example, most of the reporting in American newspapers about "cow worship" in India has been factually correct but contextually false. Few Americans understand the practical importance of cows in nonindustrial countries such as India. A cow gives milk and provides dung—a dependable source of fuel. The cow also delivers other cows and bulls. And those bulls which are castrated become bullocks (oxen), which are the main work animals in rural India. After they die, the cow, bull, and bullock provide skins for leather. The cow may have become "sacred," as Gandhi suggests, because she has been one of the most useful and docile creatures on earth.

This consideration of the cow's utility within the traditional Indian context is not meant to suggest that the cow will or should continue to be "sacred." In every culture, there are reasons why certain things are done in certain ways. When the reasons are no longer relevant, changes can be introduced without serious damage to the cultural pattern. Many times, however, the relevance of traditional customs is not understood by outsiders. Changes introduced under these conditions are often harmful.

As another example of a point of view based on cultural context, consider that in the United States the automobile holds a special (some would say "sacred") position, even though almost two million Americans have died in motor vehicle crashes—almost twice the number killed in all of our wars. Each year, about 55,000 people in this country die in car accidents—a rate of one every nine minutes. The number seriously injured annually is about five million. The total economic loss is estimated at $50 billion yearly.

If a "non-Western" consultant were to study "the problem of the automobile in the United States" he might start out by considering it basically as a means of transportation. After all, this is how Henry Ford started out when he produced all of his earliest cars in one color and changed models only when there were technological advances. In terms of transportation, the consultant might recommend that we have fewer cars and more express trains and that in fact we should consider "birth control" of cars because they are increasing so rapidly in number. But in making this recommendation, the foreign consultant would reveal that he did not understand the car's place in American culture. The American economy currently depends overwhelmingly on widespread auto transportation, and the car is believed to be an essential part of an American's "pursuit of happiness."

Today, more people throughout the world are trying to understand each other but a willingness is not enough. It takes careful attention and concern. Never before have we had the opportunity to know so much about the world we inhabit—its peoples, its natural resources, its technological potential. But it is also true that the quality of life and respect for the individual worth of each person may be lessening. We need to reaffirm that the proper study of humankind is still humans.

Seymour Fersh is former Professor of Education, College of Education, Fairleigh Dickinson University.

QUESTIONS FOR REFLECTION

1. According to Fersh, in what respects is ethnocentrism "useful"? Do you agree with his argument?
2. In regard to the level and subject area with which you are most familiar, how can the curriculum help students to become more aware of their own ethnocentrism?
3. What contemporary examples can you cite to support Fersh's assertion that "ignorance of others is *not* bliss and what you don't know *can* hurt you"?

Our Two-Story Culture

PAUL BOHANNAN

ABSTRACT: *Our "two-story" culture consists of a large-scale common culture (the "upstairs" of business, politics, and mass communication) and many smaller cultures (the "downstairs" of family and community). Throughout the world, large-scale cultures are interconnected and revolve around power. Small-scale cultures, on the other hand, are not interconnected and are based on intimacy and caring. Both cultures are needed, and each fulfills functions the other can't. Two great challenges confront the world: communication between the two stories and fear among small-scale cultures.*

Only a few years ago it was stylish to say that we could not prepare our children and our students to live in the world because we did not know what their world would be like. Today that world is becoming clear. They will live with—they already live with—a two-story culture. There is a large-scale world, with its common culture. It is primarily economic and political, mediated by dollars and votes, by consumer products and televised national political conventions. There is, at the same time, a small-scale world of family and community, mediated by sympathy and trust in face-to-face relationships. To different degrees, we all live in both.

Both the large-scale and the small-scale world have become complicated; the first by sheer size, the second by sheer variety. All of us must learn to deal with the large-scale culture. We may not seek to participate actively in it, but we cannot ignore it. We must also deal with the fact that most people today—at least those of us who live in an industrialized society—belong to many small intimate groups, and that these are no longer space-bound territorial groups.

We might call ourselves, with our two-story culture, post-peasants. For a long time social scientists have recognized that the essence of the peasant society is that it is divided into two parts; that is, the peasant culture is not capable of survival without joining with other part-cultures

to make up a larger entity. Peasants, although they are self-sufficient in many ways, depend on traders to bring them products (salt, perhaps) that they cannot produce themselves, and on political authorities (earls, perhaps) to protect them.

The large-scale culture—the upstairs culture—revolves around power. There are only a few distinct cultures in the large-scale world: the varieties of democracy, the varieties of communism, and the various socialisms. All the cultures of the large-scale world are interconnected. They are part-cultures in one big world-culture.

The small-scale cultures—downstairs, if you will—are based on intimacy. They are many and varied, and they are *not* interconnected. Or, rather, they are interconnected by individuals who participate in several of them, rather than by institutions in which each individual is a recognizable entity. Some are still tribal; others still peasant. Some are based on religion, some on propinquity. But even more are based on the choice or subscription of individuals and are in that sense "voluntary." The basis for the choice may be rock music, pot, or Masonic ritual. Some small-scale cultures are limited by race or (that most mystical of all concepts) ethnicity.

Small-scale cultures are not usually in touch with one another. Between them are invisible boundaries (or unspoken or disputed boundaries) rather than the overt and known boundaries

From *Saturday Review* 55 (September 2, 1972): 40–41. © 1972, Saturday Review, Inc. Used by permission of the author and the publisher.

established between nations or corporations. Indeed, the only reason that the people of small-scale groups should get to know one another is to reduce fear. But they can go on without one another. They are connected only within the experience of individuals—in the bits of culture that each of us packs within himself.

Obviously, we need both large- and small-scale groups. Consumption aside, the economic and political tasks cannot be done by small-scale groups; welfare aside, providing care and intimacy cannot be done by large-scale groups. The problem is to successfully negotiate the stairs between the two stories.

The two levels of culture with which each of us lives must not get too far out of phase; that is, the stairs between levels must not be allowed to collapse or to be overused. The small-scale cultures, for example, are sometimes dragged into the worldwide framework of large-scale culture. The church in the late fifteenth century had concerned itself with power and hence became a political institution. Nationalism—the practice of building a state on the basis of a nation (a word derived from the Latin word meaning "to be born")—led to a new kind of colonialism and to the widespread problems of minorities because, via the complex idea of "nation," the state could invade ethnic cultures. When power derived from a large-scale culture seeks to destroy or isolate microcultures by controlling entree into the large-scale culture, strife inevitably results.

One of the most common strategies for squeezing people out of the large-scale culture is powerful condemnation of their small-scale cultures. On the other hand, some small-scale cultures are isolated (sometimes voluntarily) in such a way that their members are systematically held back from learning the principles of the large-scale culture.

The most characteristic aspect of what is called the Establishment is that the people in it have no difficulties with the stairs. They can go easily from macroculture to microculture. Their microcultures contain people who run or move easily in the institutions of the large-scale culture. They have a built-in third level that gives easy access to both the others. They often despise people who lack the ability to pass between the two and thus shut themselves off from most microcultures.

We all know that today there are many young people (usually referred to as "middle-class" because of the socioeconomic position of their parents) who can, when they choose, manipulate the large-scale culture very well (but who may consider it immoral to do so) and who feel empty— "alienated"—because they have been " robbed" of the intimacy of a small-scale culture. The countercultures are attempts to create viable and rewarding microcultures, because living only within the large-scale culture is not enough. However, living within the small-scale culture alone is not enough either, as most people in most experimental communities come to realize.

The size of the world population and the excellence of our communications means that we are necessarily living in a world that is truly fraught with danger, danger to our power structures on the one hand, danger to our tribalism on the other. All of us are both running scared and longing for community. So we join the John Birch Society or "the counterculture"–it is the same thing. Yet we are also living in a world potentially fraught with delight. Never have so many people had so wide a choice of cultures open to them.

The goal for America must be to make its two-story culture overt. We must recognize it and learn how to use it toward humane ends. The large-scale culture of America—the culture that accompanies and vivifies our economic and political institutions—must be based on our historically validated doctrines of equality, doctrines that we are still struggling to define. In this context equality means one man, one vote and equal economic opportunity.

At the same time we must cherish a whole spectrum of microcultures. We all know that the melting pot didn't, in fact, melt anything. It was a myth for dealing with the overwhelming migration of "foreigners." The early immigrants to the

New World were not foreigners to anyone except the red Americans. But late in the eighteenth century, when America was becoming an independent state, it also sought to become a nation—a cultural unity based on a common history.

America was probably the first to achieve nation-statehood backward. Whereas Portugal, Britain, France, Spain, and Holland were all nations that founded states, America first made herself a state, and then had to struggle to make herself a nation. Except for the blacks, immigrants before 1776 did indeed merge more or less into "old stock Americans." The first European "foreigners" were the Irish fleeing the famine—the earlier Irish began to call themselves "Scotch-Irish" to keep their "nationality" (a strange new American concept) at the same time they kept their nonforeignness in America.

Equality in small-scale cultures means something very different from what it means in the large-scale culture. Fundamentally, it means a respect for "differentness," without envy and without fear. In these microcultures we can "be ourselves," relax and enjoy with "our own," struggle with the external problems of birth, sex, and death, eat and dance, love and hate, all to the limit of the human capacity for these things.

And what does that mean for people? It means that we have a lot of people who are competent in the large-scale culture and, at the same time, in one or more microcultures. It is happening: One need only look at the variety of people in the televised portion of the Democratic National Convention. There were a lot of two-story people

there, their microcultures showing, working together in the large-scale culture with determination and skill.

But what about a new vision to replace the melting pot? The black revolution has brought black small-scale cultures (the "s" is important) to the attention of everyone, as blacks work to regain rights in the large-scale culture that they almost grasped after the Emancipation Proclamation. And blacks are not the only groups in the public eye. Today we hear of red power, brown power, Greek power, Italian power, Irish power, Polish power, Jewish power, and, feebly but nevertheless audibly, WASP power.

But most microcultures are not, strictly speaking, ethnic. They center upon the hordes of voluntary associations that industrialized people create. This is especially true of Americans, probably as a function of mobility.

There are two great difficulties in the world: communication between the two stories and fear among microcultures. But surely the goals are obvious: civil rights laws based on equality and justice, and sufficient intercultural education so that the differences among microcultures need no longer frighten us. Confusion between the large-scale culture and the microcultures often leads one small group to believe that by putting another group down they thereby control the large-scale culture. They do not reckon that, even if they succeed momentarily, the forces within the total system will destroy them. It is the same kind of futility as the War of the Roses. There can be no victory worth the price.

Paul Bohannan is former Dean, Social Sciences and Communications, University of Southern California.

QUESTIONS FOR REFLECTION

1.   What are the salient characteristics of the small-scale, "downstairs" cultures of which you are a member?
2.   How might Bohannan's concept of the two-story culture be incorporated into the curriculum with which you are most familiar?

3. What are the differences between *equality* in the large-scale culture and in the small-scale cultures?

4. What does Bohannan mean by the following: "The goal for America must be to make its two-story culture overt. We must recognize it and learn how to use it toward humane ends"? To what extent has America achieved this goal?

Remembering Capital: On the Connections between French Fries and Education

MICHAEL W. APPLE

ABSTRACT: Education in the United States is experiencing the effects of a "tense alliance" between neoconservatism and neoliberalism. Neoconservative educational policies and proposals are evidenced by choice plans, the standards movement, increasing attacks on the school curriculum for its failure to promote conservative values, and pressure to make the needs of business and industry the primary goals of education. Neoliberalism, which claims that a democratic society should be founded on a free market perspective, is seen as complementing efforts to implement a neoconservative educational agenda. Thus, schooling should be seen as fundamentally connected to patterns of domination and exploitation in the larger society.

Everyone stared at the department chair in amazement. Jaws simply dropped. Soon the room was filled with a nearly chaotic mixture of sounds of anger and disbelief. It wasn't the first time she had informed us about what was "coming down from on high." Similar things had occurred before. After all, this was just another brick that was being removed. Yet, to each and every one of us in that room it was clear from that moment on that for all of our struggles to protect education from being totally integrated into the rightist project of economic competitiveness and rationalization, we were losing.

It was hard to bring order to the meeting. But, slowly, we got our emotions under control long enough to hear what the State Department of Public Instruction and the Legislature had determined was best for all of the students in Wisconsin—from kindergarten to the university. Starting

the next year, all undergraduate students who wished to become teachers would have to take a course on Education for Employment, in essence a course on the "benefits of the free enterprise system." At the same time, all school curricula at the elementary and secondary levels—from five year olds on up—would have to integrate within their teaching a coherent program of education for employment as well. After all, you can't start too young, can you? Education was simply the supplier of "human capital" for the private sector, after all.

I begin with this story because I think it is often better to start in our guts so to speak, to start with our experiences as teachers and students in this time of conservatism. I begin here as well because, even though the administration in Washington may attempt to rein in some of the excesses of the rightist social agenda—in largely ineffectual

From *The Journal of Curriculum Theorizing* II, no. 1 (1995): 113–128. © 1998, Corporation for Curriculum Research. Used by permission of the author and publisher.

ways—the terms of debate and the existing economic and social conditions have been transformed remarkably in a conservative direction (Apple 1993). We should not be romantic about what will happen at our schools and universities, especially given the fiscal crisis of the state and the acceptance of major aspects of the conservative social and economic agenda within both political parties. The story I told a moment ago can serve as a metaphor for what is happening to so much of educational life at universities and elsewhere.

Let me situate this story within the larger transformations in education and the wider society that the conservative alliance has attempted. Because of space limitations in an article of this size, my discussion here will by necessity be brief. A much more detailed analysis can be found in my newest book, *Cultural Politics and Education* (Apple 1996).

BETWEEN NEO-CONSERVATISM AND NEO-LIBERALISM

Conservatism by its very name announces one interpretation of its agenda. It conserves. Other interpretations are possible of course. One could say, something more wryly, that conservatism believes that nothing should be done for the first time (Honderich 1990, 1). Yet in many ways, in the current situation this is deceptive. For with the Right now in ascendancy in many nations, we are witnessing a much more activist project. Conservative politics now are very much the politics of alteration—not always, but clearly the idea of "Do nothing for the first time" is not a sufficient explanation of what is going on either in education or elsewhere (Honderich 1990, 4).

Conservatism has in fact meant different things at different times and places. At times, it will involve defensive actions; at other times, it will involve taking initiative against the status quo (Honderich 1990, 15). Today, we are witnessing both.

Because of this, it is important that I set out the larger social context in which the current politics

of official knowledge operates. There has been a breakdown in the accord that guided a good deal of educational policy since World War II. Powerful groups within government and the economy, and within "authoritarian populist" social movements, have been able to redefine—often in very retrogressive ways—the terms of debate in education, social welfare, and other areas of the common good. What education is for is being transformed (Apple 1993). No longer is education seen as part of a social alliance which combined many "minority" groups, women, teachers, community activists, progressive legislators and government officials, and others who acted together to propose (limited) social democratic policies for schools (e.g., expanding educational opportunities, limited attempts at equalizing outcomes, developing special programs in bilingual and multicultural education, and so on).[1] A new alliance has been formed, one that has increasing power in educational and social policy. This power bloc combines business with the New Right and with neo-conservative intellectuals. Its interests are less in increasing the life chances of women, people of color, or labor. (These groups are obviously not mutually exclusive.) Rather it aims at providing the educational conditions believed necessary both for increasing international competitiveness, profit, and discipline and for returning us to a romanticized past of the "ideal" home, family, and school (Apple 1993). There is no need to control the White House for this agenda to continue to have a major effect.

The power of this alliance can be seen in a number of educational policies and proposals. These include: 1) programs for "choice" such as voucher plans and tax credits to make schools like the thoroughly idealized free-market economy; 2) the movement at national and state levels throughout the country to "raise standards" and mandate both teacher and student "competencies" and basic curricular goals and knowledge increasingly now through the implementation of statewide and national testing; 3) the increasingly effective attacks on the school curriculum for its anti-family and anti-free enterprise "bias," its secular humanism, its lack of patriotism, and its supposed neglect of the knowledge and values of the "western tradition" and of "real knowledge"; and 4) the growing pressure to make the perceived needs of business and industry into the primary goals of education at all levels (Apple 1988; Apple 1993; Apple 1996). The effects of all this—the culture wars, the immensity of the fiscal crisis in education, the attacks on "political correctness," and so on—are being painfully felt in the university as well.

In essence, the new alliance in favor of the conservative restoration has integrated education into a wider set of ideological commitments. The objectives in education are the same as those which serve as a guide to its economic and social welfare goals. These include the expansion of the "free market," the drastic reduction of government responsibility for social needs (though the Clinton Administration will mediate this in not very extensive—and not very expensive—ways), the reinforcement of intensely competitive structures of mobility, the lowering of people's expectations for economic security, and the popularization of what is clearly a form of Social Darwinist thinking (Bastian, Fruchter, Gittell, Greer, & Haskins 1986).

As I have argued at length elsewhere, the political right in the United States has been very successful in mobilizing support *against* the educational system and its employees, often exporting the crisis in the economy onto the schools. Thus, one of its major achievements has been to shift the blame for unemployment and underemployment, for the loss of economic competitiveness, and for the supposed breakdown of "traditional" values and standards in the family, education, and paid and unpaid workplaces *from* the economic, cultural, and social policies and effects of dominant groups *to* the school and other public agencies. "Public" now is the center of all evil; "private" is the center of all that is good (Apple 1995).

In essence, then, four trends have characterized the conservative restoration both in the United States and Britain—privatization, centralization, vocationalization, and differentiation

(Green 1991, 27). These are actually largely the results of differences within the most powerful wings of this tense alliance—neo-liberalism and neo-conservatism.

Neo-liberalism has a vision of the weak state. A society that lets the "invisible hand" of the free market guide *all* aspects of its forms of social interaction is seen as both efficient and democratic. On the other hand, neo-conservatism is guided by a vision of the strong state in certain areas, especially over the politics of the body and gender and race relations, over standards, values, and conduct, and over what knowledge should be passed on to future generations (Hunter 1988).[2] While these are no more than ideal types, those two positions do not easily sit side by side in the conservative coalition.

Thus the rightist movement is contradictory. Is there not something paradoxical about linking all of the feelings of loss and nostalgia to the unpredictability of the market, "in replacing loss by sheer flux"? (Johnson 1991, 40).

At the elementary and secondary school level, the contradictions between neo-conservative and neo-liberal elements in the rightist coalition are "solved" through a policy of what Roger Dale has called *conservative modernization* (Dale quoted in Edwards, Gewirtz, & Whitty in press, 22). Such a policy is engaged in:

> simultaneously "freeing" individuals for economic purposes while controlling them for social purposes; indeed, in so far as economic "freedom" increases inequalities, it is likely to increase the need for social control. A "small, strong state" limits the range of its activities by transferring to the market, which it defends and legitimizes, as much welfare [and other activities] as possible. In education, the new reliance on competition and choice is not all pervasive; instead, "what is intended is a dual system, polarized between . . . market schools and minimum schools." (Dale quoted in Edwards, Gewirtz, & Whitty in press, 22)

That is, there will be a relatively less regulated and increasingly privatized sector for the children of the better off. For the rest—and the economic status and racial composition in, say, our urban areas of the people who attend these minimum schools will be thoroughly predictable—the schools will be tightly controlled and policed and will continue to be underfunded and unlinked to decent paid employment.

One of the major effects of the combination of marketization and strong state is "to remove educational policies from public debate." That is, the choice is left up to individual parents and "the hidden hand of unintended consequences does the rest." In the process, the very idea of education being part of a *public* political sphere in which its means and ends are publicly debated atrophies (Education Group II 1991, 268).

There are major differences between democratic attempts at enhancing people's rights over the policies and practices of schooling and the neo-liberal emphasis on marketization and privatization. The goal of the former is to *extend politics,* to "revivify democratic practice by devising ways of enhancing public discussion, debate, and negotiation." It is inherently based on a vision of democracy that sees it as an educative practice. The latter, on the other hand, seeks to *contain politics.* It wants to *reduce all politics to economics,* to an ethic of "choice" and "consumption" (Johnson 1991, 68). The world, in essence, becomes a vast supermarket (Apple 1993).

Enlarging the private sector so that buying and selling—in a word competition—is the dominant ethic of society involves a set of closely related propositions. It assumes that more individuals are motivated to work harder under these conditions. After all, we "already know" that public servants are inefficient and slothful while private enterprises are efficient and energetic. It assumes that self-interest and competitiveness are the engines of creativity. More knowledge, more experimentation, is created and used to alter what we have now. In the process, less waste is created. Supply and demand stay in a kind of equilibrium. A more efficient machine is thus created, one which minimizes administrative costs and ultimately distributes resources more widely (Honderich 1990, 104).

This is of course not meant simply to privilege the few. However, it is the equivalent of saying that everyone has the right to climb the north face of the Eiger or scale Mount Everest without exception, providing of course that you are very good at mountain climbing and have the institutional and financial resources to do it (Honderich 1990, 99–100).

Thus, in a conservative society, access to a society's private resources (and, remember, the attempt is to make nearly *all* of society's resources private) is largely dependent on one's ability to pay. And this is dependent on one's being a person of an *entrepreneurial or efficiently acquisitive class type.* On the other hand, society's public resources (that rapidly decreasing segment) are dependent on need (Honderich 1990, 89). In a conservative society, the former is to be maximized, the latter is to be minimized.

However, most forms of conservatism do not merely depend in a large portion of their arguments and policies on a particular view of human nature—a view of human nature as primarily self-interested. They have gone further, they have set out to degrade that human nature, to force all people to conform to what at first could only be pretended to be true. Unfortunately, in no small measure they have succeeded. Perhaps blinded by their own absolutist and reductive vision of what it means to be human, many of our political "leaders" do not seem to be capable of recognizing what they have done. They have set out, aggressively, to drag down the character of a people (Honderich 1991, 81), while at the same time attacking the poor and the disenfranchised for their supposed lack of values and character.

But I digress here and some of my anger begins to show. You will forgive me I trust; but if we cannot allow ourselves to be angry about the lives of our children, what can we be angry about?

Unfortunately, major elements of this restructuring are hardly on the agenda of discussions of some of the groups within the critical and "progressive" communities within education itself, especially by *some* (not all) of those people who have turned uncritically to postmodernism.

LOSING MEMORY

What I shall say here is still rather tentative, but it responds to some of my intuitions that a good deal of the storm and fury over the politics of one form of textual analysis over another or even over whether we should see the world as a text, as discursively constructed, for example, is at least partly beside the point and that "we" may be losing some of the most important insights generated by, say, the neo-marxist tradition in education and elsewhere.

In what I say here, I hope I do not sound like an unreconstructed Stalinist (after all I've spent all too much of my life writing and speaking about the reductive tendencies within the marxist traditions). I simply want us to remember the utterly essential—not essentialist—understandings of the relationships (admittedly very complex) between education and some of the relations of power we need to consider but seem to have forgotten a bit too readily.

The growth of the multiple positions associated with postmodernism and poststructuralism is indicative of the transformation of our discourse and understandings of the relationship between culture and power. The rejection of the comforting illusion that there can (and must) be one grand narrative under which all relations of domination can be subsumed, the focus on the "micro-level" as a site of the political, the illumination of the utter complexity of the power-knowledge nexus, the extension of our political concerns well beyond the "holy trinity" of class, gender, and race, the idea of the decentered subject where identity is both non-fixed and a site of political struggle, the focus on the politics and practices of consumption, not only production—all of this has been important, though not totally unproblematic to say the least (Clarke 1991; Best & Kellner 1991).

With the growth of postmodern and poststructural literature in critical educational and cultural studies, however, we have tended to move too quickly away from traditions that continue to be filled with vitality and provide essential insights into the nature of the curriculum and pedagogy that dominate schools at all levels. Thus, for example, the mere fact that class does not explain all can be used as an excuse to deny its power. This would be a serious error. Class is of course an analytic construct as well as a set of relations that have an existence outside of our minds. Thus, what we mean by it and how it is mobilized as a category needs to be continually deconstructed and rethought. Thus, we must be very careful when and how it is used, with due recognition of the multiple ways in which people are formed. Even given this, however, it would be wrong to assume that, since many people do not identify with or act on what we might expect from theories that link, say, identity and ideology with one's class position, this means that class has gone away (Apple 1992).

The same must be said about the economy. Capitalism may be being transformed, but it still exists as a massive structuring force. Many people may not think and act in ways predicted by class essentializing theories, but this does *not* mean the racial, sexual, and class divisions of paid and unpaid labor have disappeared; nor does it mean that relations of production (both economic *and* cultural, since how we think about these two may be different) can be ignored if we do it in nonessentializing ways (Apple 1992).

I say all this because of very real dangers that now exist in critical educational studies. One is our loss of collective memory. While there is currently great and necessary vitality at the "level" of theory, a considerable portion of critical research has often been faddish. It moves from theory to theory rapidly, often seemingly assuming that the harder something is to understand or the more it rests on European cultural theory (preferably French) the better it is. The rapidity of its movement and its partial capture by an upwardly mobile function of the new middle class within the academy—so intent on mobilizing its cultural resources within the status hierarchies of the university that it has often lost any but the most rhetorical connections with the multiple struggles against domination and subordination at the university and elsewhere—has as one of its effects the denial of gains that have been made in other traditions or restating them in new garb (Apple 1992). Or it may actually move backwards, as in the reappropriation of, say, Foucault into just another (but somewhat more elegant) theorist of social control, a discredited and a-historical concept that denies the power of social movements and historical agents. In our rush toward poststructuralism, we may have forgotten how very powerful the structural dynamics are in which we participate. In the process, we seem to be losing our capacity to be angry.

One of the major issues here is the tendency of all too many critical and oppositional educators to become overly theoretical. Sometimes, in this process, we fail to see things that are actually not that hard to understand. I want to tell a story here that I hope makes my arguments clear. It is a story that perhaps will be all too familiar to those of you who have opposed the North American Free Trade Agreement (NAFTA).

EATING FRENCH FRIES

The sun glared off of the hood of the small car as we made our way along the two lane road. The heat and humidity made me wonder if I'd have any liquid left in my body at the end of the trip and led me to appreciate Wisconsin winters a bit more than one might expect. The idea of winter seemed more than a little remote in this Asian country for which I have a good deal of fondness. But the topic at hand was not the weather; rather, it was the struggles of educators and social activists to build an education that was considerably more democratic than what was in place in that country now. This was a dangerous topic. Discussing it in philosophical and formalistically academic terms was tolerated. Openly calling for it and situating it within a serious analysis of the economic, political, and military power structures that now exerted control over so much of this nation's daily life was another matter.

As we traveled along that rural road in the midst of one of the best conversations I had engaged in about the possibilities of educational transformations and the realities of the oppressive conditions so many people were facing in that land, my gaze somehow was drawn to the side of the road. In one of those nearly accidental happenings that clarify and crystallize what reality is *really* like, my gaze fell upon a seemingly inconsequential object. At regular intervals, there were small signs planted in the dirt a few yards from where the road met the fields. The sign was more than a little familiar. It bore the insignia of one of the most famous fast food restaurants in the United States. We drove for miles past seemingly deserted fields along a flat hot plain, passing sign after sign, each a replica of the previous one, each less than a foot high. These were not billboards. Such things hardly existed in this poor rural region. Rather, they looked exactly–exactly—like the small signs one finds next to farms in the American mid-west that signify the kinds of seed corn that each farmer had planted in her or his fields. This was a good guess it turned out.

I asked the driver—a close friend and former student of mine who had returned to this country to work for the social and educational reforms that were so necessary—what turned out to be a naive but ultimately crucial question in my own education. "Why are those signs for ***** there? Is there a ***** restaurant nearby?" My friend looked at me in amazement. "Michael, don't you know what these signs signify? There's no western restaurant within fifty miles of where we are. These signs represent exactly what is wrong with education in this nation. Listen to this." And I listened.

The story is one that has left an indelible mark on me, for it condenses in one powerful set of historical experiences the connections between our struggles as educators and activists in so many countries and the ways differential power works in ordinary life. I cannot match the tensions and passions in my friend's voice as this story was told; nor can I convey exactly the almost eerie feelings one gets when looking at that vast, sometimes beautiful, sometimes scarred, and increasingly depopulated plain. Yet the story is crucial to hear. Listen to this.

The government of the nation has decided that the importation of foreign capital is critical to its own survival. Bringing in American, German, British, Japanese, and other investors and factories will ostensibly create jobs, will create capital for investment, and will enable the nation to speed into the 21st century. (This is of course elite group talk, but let us assume that all of this is indeed truly believed by dominant groups.) One of the ways the military dominated government has planned to do this is to focus part of its recruitment efforts on agri-business. In pursuit of this aim, it has offered vast tracts of land to international agri-business concerns at very low cost. Of particular importance to the plain we are driving through is the fact that much of this land has been given over to a large American fast food restaurant corporation for the growing of potatoes for the restaurant's french fries, one of the trademarks of its extensive success throughout the world.

The corporation was eager to jump at the opportunity to shift a good deal of its potato production from the U.S. to Asia. Since many of the farm workers in the United States were now unionized and were (correctly) asking for a livable wage, and since the government of that Asian nation officially frowned on unions of any kind, the cost of growing potatoes would be lower. Further, the land on that plain was perfect for the use of newly developed technology to plant and harvest the crop with considerably fewer workers. Machines would replace living human beings. Finally, the government was much less concerned about environmental regulations. All in all, this was a fine bargain for capital.

Of course, *people* lived on some of this land and farmed it for their own food and to sell what might be left over after their own—relatively minimal—needs were met. This deterred neither agri-business nor the government. After all, people

could be moved to make way for "progress." And after all, the villagers along that plain did not actually have deeds to the land. (They had lived there for perhaps hundreds of years, well before the invention of banks, and mortgages, and deeds—no paper, no ownership). It would not be too hard to move the people off of the plain to other areas to "free" it for intensive potato production and to "create jobs" by taking away the livelihood of thousands upon thousands of small scale farmers in the region.

I listened with rapt attention as the rest of the story unfolded and as we passed by the fields with their miniature corporate signs and the abandoned villages. The people whose land had been taken for so little moved, of course. As in so many other similar places throughout what dominant groups call the Third World, they trekked to the city. They took their meager possessions and moved into the ever expanding slums within and surrounding the one place that held out some hope of finding enough paid work (if *everyone*—including children—labored) so that they could survive.

The government and major segments of the business elite officially discouraged this, sometimes by hiring thugs to burn the shanty towns, other times by keeping conditions so horrible that no one would "want" to live there. But still the dispossessed came, by the tens of thousands. Poor people are not irrational, after all. The loss of arable land had to be compensated for somehow and if it took cramming into places that were deadly at times, well what were the other choices? There *were* factories being built in and around the cities which paid incredibly low wages—sometimes less than enough money to buy sufficient food to replace the calories expended by workers in the production process—but at least there might be paid work if one was lucky.

So the giant machines harvested the potatoes and the people poured into the cities and international capital was happy. It's not a nice story, but what does it have to do with *education*? My friend continued my education.

The military dominated government had given all of these large international businesses twenty years of tax breaks to sweeten the conditions for their coming to that country. Thus, there was now very little money to supply the health care facilities, housing, running water, electricity, sewage disposal, and schools for the thousands upon thousands of people who had sought their future in or had literally been driven into the city. The mechanism for not building these necessities was quite clever. Take the lack of any formal educational institutions as a case in point. In order for the government to build schools it had to be shown that there was a "legitimate" need for such expenditure. Statistics had to be produced in a form that was *officially* accepted. This could only be done through the official determination of numbers of registered births. Yet, the very process of official registration made it impossible for thousands of children to be recognized as actually existing.

In order to register for school, a parent had to register the birth of the child at the local hospital or government office—none of which existed in these slum areas. And even if you could somehow find such an office, the government officially discouraged people who had originally come from outside the region of the city from moving there. It often refused to recognize the legitimacy of the move as a way of keeping displaced farmers from coming into the urban areas and thereby increasing the population. Births from people who had no "legitimate" right to be there did not count as births at all. It is a brilliant strategy in which the state creates categories of legitimacy that define social problems in quite interesting ways. (See, e.g., Curtis 1992 and Fraser 1989.) Foucault would have been proud, I am certain.

Thus, there are no schools, no teachers, no hospitals, no infrastructure. The root causes of this situation rest not in the immediate situation. They can only be illuminated if we focus on the chain of capital formation internationally and nationally, on the contradictory needs of the state, on the class relations and the relations between country and city that organize and disorganize that country.

My friend and I had been driving for quite a while now. I had forgotten about the heat. The ending sentence of the story pulled no punches. It was said slowly and quietly, said in a way that made it even more compelling. "Michael, these fields are the reason there's no schools in my city. There's no schools because so many folks like cheap french fries."

I tell this story about the story told to me for a number of reasons. First, it is simply one of the most powerful ways I know of reminding myself and all of us of the utter importance of seeing schooling relationally, of seeing it as connected—fundamentally—to the relations of domination and exploitation of the larger society. Second, and equally as importantly, I tell this story to make a crucial theoretical and political point. Relations of power are indeed complex and we do need to take very seriously the postmodern focus on the local and on the multiplicity of the forms of struggle that need to be engaged in. It is important as well to recognize the changes that are occurring in many societies and to see the complexity of the "power/knowledge" nexus. Yet in our attempts to avoid the dangers that accompanied some aspects of previous "grand narratives," let us *not* act as if capitalism has somehow disappeared. Let us not act as if class relations don't count. Let us not act as if all of the things we learned about how the world might be understood politically have been somehow overthrown because our theories are now more complex.

The denial of basic human rights, the destruction of the environment, the deadly conditions under which people (barely) survive, the lack of a meaningful future for the thousands of children I noted in my story—all of this is not only or even primarily a "text" to be deciphered in our academic volumes as we pursue our postmodern themes. It is a reality that millions of people experience in their very bodies everyday. Educational work that is not connected deeply to a powerful understanding of these realities (and this understanding cannot evacuate a serious analysis of political economy and class relations without losing much of its power) is in danger of losing its soul. The lives of our children demand no less.

NOTES

1. I put the word "minority" in inverted commas here to remind us that the vast majority of the world's population is composed of persons of color. It would be wholly salutary for our ideas about culture and education to remember this fact.
2. Neo-liberalism doesn't ignore the idea of a strong state, but it wants to limit it to specific areas (e.g., defense of markets).

REFERENCES

Apple, Michael W. *Teachers and Texts: A Political Economy of Class and Gender Relations in Education.* New York: Routledge, 1988.

Apple, Michael W. "Education, Culture and Class Power." *Educational Theory* 42 (Spring 1992): 127–145.

Apple, Michael W. *Official Knowledge: Democratic Education in a Conservative Age.* New York: Routledge, 1993.

Apple, Michael W. *Education and Power,* second edition. New York: Routledge, 1995.

Apple, Michael W. *Cultural Politics and Education.* New York: Teachers College Press, 1996.

Bastian, Ann, Fruchter, Norm, Gittell, Marilyn, Greer, Colin & Haskins, Kenneth. *Choosing Equality.* Philadelphia: Temple University Press, 1986.

Best, Steven & Kellner, Douglas. *Postmodern Theory.* London: Macmillan, 1991.

Clarke, John. *New Times and Old Enemies.* London: HarperCollins, 1991.

Curtis, Bruce. *True Government By Choice Men?* Toronto: University of Toronto Press, 1992.

Education Group II, eds. *Education Limited.* London: Unwin Hyman, 1991.

Edwards, Tony, Gewirtz, Sharon, & Whitty, Geoff. "Whose Choice of Schools." *Sociological Perspectives on Contemporary Educational Reforms.* Edited by Madeleine Arnot and Len Barton. London: Triangle Books, in press.

Fraser, Nancy. *Unruly Practices.* Minneapolis: University of Minnesota Press, 1989.

Green, Andy. "The Peculiarities of English Education." *Education Limited.* Edited by Education Group II. London: Unwin Hyman, 1991.

Honderich, Ted. *Conservatism.* Boulder, CO: Westview Press, 1990.

Hunter, Allen. *Children in the Service of Conservatism.* Madison, WI: University of Wisconsin Law School, Institute for Legal Studies, 1988.

Johnson, Richard. "A New Road to Serfdom." *Education Limited.* Edited by Education Group II. London: Unwin Hyman, 1991.

Michael W. Apple is Professor of Curriculum and Instruction and Educational Policy Studies at the University of Wisconsin-Madison.

QUESTIONS FOR REFLECTION

1. What evidence can you cite to illustrate the influence of conservatism on curricula at the K–12 through higher education levels?
2. Do you agree with Apple's assertion that "'Public' now is the center of all evil; 'private' is the center of all that is good"?
3. How might issues of domination and exploitation be incorporated into the curriculum with which you are most familiar?

Full-Service Schools

JOY G. DRYFOOS

ABSTRACT: Full-service schools are designed to provide students and their families with quality educational experiences and support services. At these "one-stop centers," the educational, physical, psychological, and social needs of students and their families are met. Full-service school programs in New York City and Modesto, California, are described. Among the barriers to implementing full-service schools are governance and turf issues, lack of continuity, public controversy, and funding.

In the library of the Salome Urena Middle Academy at Intermediate School 218, three-member teams are hard at work over Spanish lessons. Two members of each group—a student and a parent—are instructing a third member—a police officer from the local precinct. In return for lessons in the language of this Washington Heights neighborhood, the officers—mostly white and non-Hispanic—invite these families to visit the police station and to stay in touch. This mutually beneficial arrangement, which combines educational lessons with parental and community involvement, is the result of a collaboration between a school system and the Children's Aid Society in New York City.

All over the country, school and community people are putting the pieces together to help schools meet the varied needs of today's students and their parents. I call the product of these collaborative efforts "full-service schools," a term first used in Florida's landmark legislation (Department of Health and Rehabilitative Services 1991). The creation of one-stop centers where the educational, physical, psychological, and social requirements of students and their families are addressed in a rational, holistic fashion is attractive to both school people and social service providers. Community agencies can relieve schools of the burden of changing high-risk behaviors and have direct access to the students every day.

What's driving this movement? As anyone who works in a school knows, more and more children are arriving every day not ready to learn. Families who have difficulty clothing, feeding, and housing their children have little time for traditional family nurturing and enrichment. A second factor is the movement toward integrating programs. Everyone is fed up with categorical approaches that don't cure anything. One day it's substance abuse prevention, then teen pregnancy, AIDS, suicide, and, lately, violence. The demands for immunizations, pregnancy tests, mental health counseling, family counseling, and crisis intervention cannot possibly be met by existing school personnel.

CREATING A FULL-SERVICE SCHOOL

. . . Full-service schools aim to provide both quality education and support services. Under the menu for *quality education* are various ingredients that the literature indicates are critical to revitalizing schools (Dryfoos 1994). These items generally fall into the educational domain, and school systems assume fiscal responsibility for providing them.

Under *support services* are examples of health, welfare, recreation, and life-enhancing programs that are in place in various combinations in schools around the country. Most of these programs are operated by community agencies that bring their own funding with them.

From *Educational Leadership* 53, no. 7 (April 1996): 18–23. © 1996, Association for Supervision and Curriculum Development. Used by permission of the author and publisher.

Other services, such as social skills training and life planning, might be provided by either schools or community agencies. The real challenge here is how to create a one-stop unfragmented collaborative institution. The answer is: with great patience and fortitude.

Various models of full-service schools are emerging in communities and schools with the greatest needs and the most disadvantaged populations. In such settings, the principal often acts not only as the leader in the restructuring, but also as the prime facilitator for assuring smooth integration of outside partners into the school environment. Security and maintenance are important issues.

Successful programs also rely on a full-time coordinator or program director, who builds a team of personnel sensitive to issues related to youth development, cultural diversity, and community empowerment. In many locations, bilingual staff are essential. A designated space such as a clinic or a center in a school acts as a focal point for bringing in services from the community. Indeed, the most important outcome of entering into the full-service schools process may be providing a magnet for other resources.

A LOOK AT A FULL-SERVICE SCHOOL

A recent conference on School-Linked Comprehensive Services for Children and Families identified 22 exemplary programs (U.S. Department of Education 1995). Intermediate School 218, mentioned earlier, is one of them. Let's look at some more ways that this New York City school is trying to serve its students and their families.

It's 7 A.M., and Intermediate School 218 is open for breakfast. Before school officially begins, students play sports or attend classes in dance and Latin band. Located in a new building in Washington Heights, the school offers students a choice of five self-contained academies: Business, Community Service, Expressive Arts, Ethics and Law, or Mathematics, Science, and Technology. A store in the school's attractive lobby sells supplies for students.

At the Family Resource Center, parents receive social services, including immigration, employment, and housing consultations. Social workers and mental health counselors are also on hand to serve students and their families. A primary health and dental clinic is on the premises.

After the official school day ends, the building stays open until 10 P.M. for educational enrichment, mentoring, sports, computer lab, music, arts, and entrepreneurial workshops. Teenagers are welcome to use the sports and arts facilities and to take classes along with adults on topics like English, computer work, and parenting skills. The school also stays open weekends and summers, offering the Dominican community many opportunities for cultural enrichment and family participation.

Intermediate School 218 is a true settlement house in a school, made possible through a partnership between the Children's Aid Society and Community School District 6.

MORE EXEMPLARY MODELS

Another promising school-community collaboration can be found in Modesto, California. To better serve students and their families, this school system has formed partnerships with many outside agencies—public mental health, social services, health, probation, police, housing, and drug and alcohol agencies, as well as nonprofit health and service agencies.

The Hanshaw Middle School is open long hours to serve the needs of a deprived, largely Hispanic neighborhood (Modesto City Schools 1995). With support from Healthy Start—California's comprehensive school-linked services program—Hanshaw created a family resource center on the campus. The family center provides a wide range of activities—from aerobics classes to computer workshops. This center also houses an interagency case management team and a primary health care and dental clinic. A mental health clinician, on site every day, provides long-term family therapy and crisis intervention. After-school activities include sports and mentoring, and neighborhood outreach involves parents with school programs.

Another example of educational and support services provided under one roof can be found in the Bedford-Stuyvesant area of Brooklyn. The Decatur-Clearpool School, which opened in 1992, was designed to incorporate the Comer School Development Program (Knowles 1994). To provide varied services to its students and their families, this K–8 school collaborates with Clearpool, Sponsors for Educational Opportunity (both nonprofit organizations), and the Edwin Gould Foundation. An extended day program offers after-school activities for students. The Family Center offers many activities including mentoring, job training, and parent workshops. And, at the school's Health Center, run by the Brooklyn Hospital Center, students and their families receive medical, psychological, and social care.

The most unusual aspect of this school is a 335-acre residential center in the woods, the original Clearpool camp, which has been adapted for day trips and overnight academic retreats for Decatur students and their families. The year-round, two-campus school expects to add an extra 60–75 days to the school year.

BARRIERS TO THE PROCESS

Attempting to provide so many services in one place, not surprisingly, is an immense undertaking. From the experiences of these and other promising models, we can learn about some of the obstacles to success.

- *Governance.* As would be expected, the more complex the model, the more demanding the administrative arrangements. The mounting rhetoric calls for sophisticated collaborative organizations, whereby school systems and community agencies leave behind their parochial loyalties and pitch in to form a new kind of union (Melaville et al. 1993).

In reality, most emerging models are shaped by state and foundation proclivities. A grant goes either to a school system, which then subcontracts for services, or to a community agency (designated as the lead organization), which enters the schools through a memorandum of agreement. In neither case is governance changed.

New Beginnings in San Diego, which has completed its first evaluation, warns that it's "difficult to overestimate the amount of time collaboration takes" (Barfield et al 1994). The New Beginnings collaborative center brings together five major service agencies to run a center in the Hamilton School, staffed with family advocates. Participants there discovered that it was easier to get agencies to make "deals" to sign contracts to relocate workers to schools than to achieve permanent widespread changes in how services are delivered to families in San Diego.

- *Turf.* Related to governance is turf: who owns the school building? When a whole new staff working for an outside agency moves onto school property, many territorial concerns arise. What role does the school nurse play in the school-based clinic? Why not hire more school social workers if family counseling and case management are needed? Issues arise over confidentiality, space, releasing students from classes, and discipline. It takes time and energy and, particularly, skilled principals and program coordinators to work through appropriate policies and practices.

- *Lack of continuity.* To succeed, full-service schools depend on a stable group of people committed to the process. For example, the Decatur-Clearpool School, noted earlier, has operated effectively for several years, but the collaborative is currently facing challenges because of changing leadership. The district has had three superintendents and the school has had three principals in four years. Teacher turnover has been endemic, and each new faculty member must be oriented to the holistic, family-centered approach of the school.

- *Controversy.* Another obstacle to creating full-service schools is communities and/or school boards that resist the idea of using the school building for anything but educational purposes. Experience throughout the country, however, has shown that this resistance has dissipated rapidly with the availability of state and foundation grants. A crucial aspect of launching full-service arrangements is to conduct extensive local needs assessments and planning prior to program development. In general, these early efforts equip parents and school personnel with the necessary data to convince decision makers and educate the media about the importance of integrating services in the school.

- *Funding.* The annual cost for full-service school models ranges from $75,000 for Kentucky's Youth and Family Service Centers to $800,000 for the most comprehensive community-school. School-based clinics cost on the average $150,000 per year, not including large amounts of in-kind and donated goods and services. The annual cost for a school-based clinic user is about $100 per year, while the cost per student in a more complex arrangement is about $1,000.

States are major funders of these initiatives and, even with looming budget cuts, are moving ahead to support more comprehensive school-based programs. Except for a recent initiative in the Bureau of Primary Health Care, no federal grants go directly to communities and schools for integrated services. The full-service school concept has been recognized, however, in new legislative endeavors such as the revisions of Title I, Empowerment Zone grants, and the Crime Bill (but the funding for after-school services did not survive the cuts). Federal regulations could be changed to facilitate the increased use of categorical dollars for integrated services, for example, Drug Free Schools, HIV prevention, special education, and mental health programs.

Many schools are already gaining access to Medicaid funds—for example, the Farrell Area School District near Pittsburgh, Pennsylvania, another comprehensive service provider. This small (1,280 students), extremely disadvantaged district has invited 57 partners to help operate a Family Center and several school-based clinics, which arrange for Medicaid reimbursement.

Two difficulties in using Medicaid money are eligibility determination and reimbursement procedures. The advent of managed care adds to the complexity, with school service providers struggling to establish either fee-for-service or per capita payment contracts with managed care providers. Legislation should guarantee that school-based centers can become "essential community providers" so that enrollees in managed care plans can obtain preventive services, such as mental health and health education, within these plans.

As pointed out by Modesto's superintendent, "the proof of any program funded by grant monies is sustainability after the grant ceases" (Enochs 1995). The Modesto City Schools have demonstrated how programs can be institutionalized. When their large grant from California's Healthy Start (about $400,000 per year over four years) expired, the school system was able to obtain continuing support from county agencies and the local health center while using Community Development Block Grant and Title I funds for core support.

DOES FULL-SERVICE HAVE A FUTURE?

While support for the concept of full-service schools is strong, even the most ardent advocates want assurance that centralizing services in restructured schools will make a difference in the lives of the children and their families. Evaluation results are spotty, not surprising given the early stages of program development and the difficulties inherent in program research. Much of the research has been on autonomous components such as school-based clinics or family resource centers (Dryfoos et al. 1996). Several states—Florida, Kentucky, and California—are beginning to produce reports on the more comprehensive programs that they sponsor (Wagner et al 1994).

In full-service schools with health clinics, clinic users have been shown to have lower substance use, better school attendance, lower dropout rates, and in a few places with targeted reproductive health services, lower birth rates. Students, parents, teachers, and school personnel report a high level of satisfaction with school-based services and particularly appreciate their accessibility, convenience, and confidentiality.

Early reports from the more comprehensive community-schools are encouraging. Attendance and graduation rates are significantly higher than in comparable schools, and reading and math scores have shown some improvement. Students are eager to come to schools that are stimulating, nurturing, and respectful of cultural values. Parents are heavily involved as classroom aides, and advisory board members, in classes and cultural events, and with case managers, and support services. Property destruction and graffiti have diminished, and neighborhood violence rates have definitely decreased.

The full-service school is a home-grown product that can take many shapes: community schools, lighted school-houses called Beacons, school-based clinics, family resource centers. Relatively small investments by state governments and foundations are enabling innovative leaders to better use existing categorical resources to relocate personnel and devise more integrated delivery systems. Research will confirm that combining prevention interventions with school restructuring will create stronger institutions and schools will become neighborhood hubs, places where children's lives are enhanced and families want to go.

We know that the school's role is to educate and the family's responsibility is to raise the children. Many of today's parents need assistance in accomplishing that task. Full-service schools may be the most effective arrangement for achieving school, family, and societal goals.

REFERENCES

Barfield, D., C. Brindis, L. Guthrie, W. McDonald, S. Philliber, and B. Scott. (1994). *The Evaluation of New Beginnings: First Report, February 1994.* San Francisco: Far West Laboratory for Educational Research and Development.

Department of Health and Rehabilitative Services and Department of Education. (1991). *Request for Program Designs for Supplemental School Health Programs, Feb. 1–June 30, 1991.* Tallahassee: State of Florida.

Dryfoos, J. (1994). *Full-Service Schools: A Revolution in Health and Social Services for Children, Youth, and Families.* San Francisco: Jossey-Bass.

Dryfoos, J., C. Brindis, and D. Kaplan. (1996). "Evaluation of School-Based Health Clinics." In *Adolescent Medicine: State of the Art Health Care in Schools,* edited by L. Juszak and M. Fisher. Philadelphia: Hanley and Belfus.

Enochs, J. (August 21, 1995). "Report on Implementation of SB-620 Three-Year Healthy Start Operational Grants to Develop Coordinated School-Based Interagency Services." Memo to Modesto City (California) Schools Board.

Knowles, T. (1994). "The Decatur-Clearpool School: Synthesizing Philosophy and Management." Paper prepared for the annual meeting of the American Educational Research Association meeting in New Orleans.

Melaville, A., M. Blank, and G. Asayesh. (1993). *Together We Can: A Guide for Crafting a Profamily System of Education and Human Services.* Washington, D.C.: U.S. Government Printing Office.

Modesto City Schools. (1995). "Modesto City Schools: 1994–95 Healthy Start Report. Hanshaw Middle School." Modesto, California, City Schools.

U.S. Department of Education. (1995). *School-Linked Comprehensive Services for Children and Families.* Washington, D.C.: Office of Educational Research and Improvement and American Educational Research Association.

Wagner, M., S. Golan, D. Shaver, L. Newman, M. Wechsler, and F. Kelley. (1994). *A Healthy Start for California's Children and Families: Early Findings from a Statewide Evaluation of School-linked Services.* Menlo Park, Calif.: SRI International.

Joy G. Dryfoos is an independent researcher with the Carnegie Corporation.

QUESTIONS FOR REFLECTION

1. To what extent should school curricula address social problems?
2. In your community, what is the level of public support for school-based programs that address social problems?
3. How might an advocate of full-service schools respond to a critic who maintains that the school's role is to educate, and the family's responsibility is to raise the children?

TEACHERS' VOICES
Putting Theory into Practice

Introducing Censorship:
One Teacher's Approach

CHARLES M. ELLENBOGEN

ABSTRACT: A seventh- and eighth-grade teacher describes how he used Inherit the Wind, *a play that deals with the evolution–creationism controversy, to teach about censorship in his language arts and literature class in a community that proclaims itself to be the "buckle of the Bible belt."*

There is a problem inherent in trying to teach a unit on censorship. In order to properly address the issue, the teacher must present the censored objects for debate. In doing so, however, the teacher risks facing consequences from parents and administrators for presenting such materials, I debated the question: how could I have an honest and forthright discussion of censorship without risking censure myself?

My situation was complicated by geography I was teaching junior high Language Arts and Literature at Wharton Arts Magnet Middle School,

in Nashville, Tennessee, the self-proclaimed "buckle of the Bible belt." I had already confronted a parent and the principal over my decision to teach Robert Cormier's *The Chocolate War.* I viewed an independent film called *Damned in the USA* (1994, Valencia, CA: After-Dark), but elected not to show it in class because of its explicit presentation of the controversy surrounding the Robert Mapplethorpe exhibitions. I also decided that my junior high students who, in general, had very strong religious upbringings and convictions would not be able to participate

From *English Journal* 86, no. 2 (February 1997): 65–66. Reprinted with permission. Copyright 1997 by the National Council of Teachers of English.

in an open discussion of the nationwide trend to restrict discussion of homosexual themes in the classroom.

READING *INHERIT THE WIND*

Fortunately, the Tennessee legislature provided a safe, but high-interest gateway to a discussion of censorship. In a situation eerily reminiscent of the Scopes trial of the mid-1920s in nearby Dayton, the legislature began to debate a bill (quickly dubbed "The Monkey Bill") that would enable science teachers to be fired for presenting the theory of evolution as fact.

My next step was easy. I ordered copies of Jerome Lawrence and Robert E. Lee's play, *Inherit the Wind* (1995, New York: Bantam), and we began to discuss the creation of man. I thought I would have to work hard to make Brady's creationist case credible. In our initial conversation, 22 of my 26 students described themselves as creationists, two said that they thought both ideas (creation and evolution) worked together, and two said they believed the theory of evolution. Clearly, it was Drummond and his First Amendment argument that would have to be defended.

CENSORSHIP OF TV, ART, AND THE INTERNET

As we began reading the play out loud in class, I raised other issues of censorship. We discussed the V-chip, and I created a role play based on proposed fictional plots for episodes of "Roseanne" and "NYPD Blue." After a prolonged debate, the students who assumed the roles of the ABC executives decided to air a disclaimer before a "Roseanne" episode that dealt with birth control, but not to move its time slot. They also decided that the standard disclaimer that is run before "NYPD Blue" was sufficient to alert parents about the content (nudity, sexual situations, profanity) in the show.

For our next mini-issue, current events once again provided us with material far superior to anything I could create. In nearby Murfreesboro, a painting of a partially nude woman was removed from City Hall because a female School Board employee who was attending a required meeting there claimed its presence constituted sexual harassment. The artist, in turn, sued, claiming a violation of her First Amendment rights. Since the local newspaper, *The Tennessean*, had run a copy of the painting on the front page (Jennifer Goode, "It's Art vs. Sexual Harassment," *The Tennessean*, March 1, 1996, 1A–2A), I brought it in and gave the students the option of examining it. Most of them did, and they were surprised by its modesty. In class, we enacted the trial, and the painting was returned to City Hall.

We discussed other issues, such as censorship on the Internet and MTV. I invited attorney R. B. Quinn, from Vanderbilt's Freedom Forum First Amendment Center, to speak to the class about the legal issues involved with censorship. But by now, as the class later told me, everyone's position on the issue was becoming familiar. The arguments were becoming stale and repetitive. I was glad I had deliberately saved what I thought of as the best mini-issue for last.

READING RESTRICTED BOOKS

I went to the local library and borrowed copies of many of the books that the Metropolitan-Davidson County School Board had either banned or restricted from the public school and junior high school students in particular. I gave my students copies of the list of restricted books and passed around the copies I had obtained. As with the picture of the partially nude woman, I emphasized to the students that examining the books was entirely at their own discretion.

The conversation was rather subdued because most of the students were eager to inspect Maya Angelou's *I Know Why The Caged Bird Sings* and James Baldwin's *If Beale Street Could Talk*. One student exclaimed in excitement when she discovered that someone who had previously borrowed the library copy of Erich Segal's *Love Story* had crossed out all of the epithets that involved references to God. Many of the students who had been in favor of some limited form of censorship suddenly resented the external authority that was not allowing them the opportunity to discover these books in class or in the school library. (It was interesting to me that when I later offered the students an opportunity to select a novel to read independently, the three titles mentioned above were among the most popular. Ray Bradbury's *Fahrenheit 451* was also a common selection.)

ROLE PLAYING A CENSORSHIP CASE

I followed up this discussion by creating a role play in which a junior high school teacher had his students read Angelou's book even though the school board had restricted it to high schools. I invited two very active parents to join in the role play, including the one who had challenged *The Chocolate War* earlier in the year. After some debate, the students who represented the school's administration decided to transfer the student who objected to the book to another class and to go to court to challenge the legitimacy of the school board's restriction. We concluded this mini-unit by watching the film *The Day They Came To Arrest The Book* (1988, North Hollywood, CA: FilmFair Communications), based on the novel by Nat Hentoff, a fairly balanced story of an attempt to have *The Adventures of Huckleberry Finn* removed from a classroom.

CONCLUSION

As we came to the end of the final arguments in the trial in *Inherit the Wind*, we stopped reading the play, and I asked the students to predict the outcome. Most predicted that Cates (the character based on Scopes) would be found guilty, though they thought that was unjust. Although they still did not agree with the theory of evolution, they thought he ought to have the right to present different ideas. We watched the film, and the students, as usual, were chagrined about all of the departures from the text, and surprised by the court's sentence.

In six short weeks, we covered a lot of ground. The students realized that censorship affects them daily, and is not something to be passively accepted or ignored.

Soon after the Tennessee legislature narrowly defeated the so-called "Monkey Bill" by a narrow margin. But many editorials predicted that we had not heard the end of it (Frank Sutherland, "A Tennessee Journey," editorial, *The Tennessean*, May 26, 1996, 76–77). As long as there are such threats to the presentation of ideas, it is our responsibility as educators to enlist our students as allies in the fight to maintain access to all kinds of ideas in order that they may choose for themselves. Unlike 70 years ago, the newly proposed law would not have forbidden the teaching of evolution, but it would have started us rolling down the slippery and precarious slope that represents academic and intellectual freedom. If we want our students to become good citizens, we cannot impose a certain morality on them; we must allow them the freedom to choose it for themselves.

Charles M. Ellenbogen teaches seventh and eighth grade at Wharton Arts Magnet Middle School in Nashville.

QUESTIONS FOR REFLECTION

1. How should controversial social issues be handled in the curricula with which you are most familiar?

2. What rules of thumb should guide curriculum planners who wish to address controversial social issues in the curriculum? How do these rules of thumb differ for curriculum planners at the elementary, middle and junior high, secondary, and higher education levels?

3. What concerns might some members of the public raise in response to the following statement by Ellenbogen? "If we want our students to become good citizens, we cannot impose a certain morality on them; we must allow them the freedom to choose it for themselves." How should a curriculum planner respond to these concerns?

LEARNING ACTIVITIES

Critical Thinking

1. Have your personal beliefs and attitudes about social forces changed as a result of reading this chapter? If so, how?

2. With respect to a school, college, or university with which you are familiar, describe the social forces that *are* reflected in the curriculum and compare these with the social forces that *should be* reflected in the curriculum. To what extent is there a lack of fit between the two sets of social forces?

3. Paul Gray's article titled "Whose America?" in the July 8, 1991, issue of *Time*, explores the belief of some that "A growing emphasis on the nation's 'multicultural' heritage exalts racial and ethnic pride at the expense of social cohesion." How might a curriculum that emphasizes multicultural diversity also *contribute* to social cohesion?

4. To what extent do you believe that schools in the United States reproduce the existing class and social structure—that curricula tend not to prepare students from the lower socioeconomic classes for upward social mobility?

Application Activities

1. Review the section on futures planning in this chapter and then identify several objectives and some appropriate learning activities for a futures-oriented curriculum at the level of education with which you are most familiar.

2. Herbert A. Thelen has developed a model for teaching called *group investigation*. The model combines the democratic process and the processes of problem solving. (You can read about this model of teaching in Bruce Joyce and Marsha Weil's *Models of Teaching*, fifth edition [Allyn and Bacon, 1996, pp. 73–88]). Describe how you might use this approach to address a social force that influences the curriculum with which you are most familiar.

3. Examine several recent curriculum guides to determine what, if any, provisions have been made to consider changing social forces in the curriculum (e.g.,

changes in values, work, the environment, family). In light of the material presented in this chapter, what changes or additions would you suggest in these curriculum guides?

4.   In this chapter's discussion of concepts from the social sciences, it was pointed out that "the concept of *humanity* can be a significant organizing element in curriculum planning." To gain further understanding of how this concept might be applied to curriculum planning, look at the 503 photographs from 68 countries that Edward Steichen presents in *The Family of Man* (New York: Museum of Modern Art, 1955, 1983). What does one learn about humanity by viewing these photographs, often referred to as the "greatest photographic exhibition of all time"? How might this learning be applied to curriculum planning?

Field Experiences

1.   Visit a local school and then develop a case study of that school's culture. (If your primary interest is at the higher education level, modify this field experience activity as appropriate). Organize your case in terms of the following: (1) *Environment:* Describe the school facility in regard to material and human resources. Describe the climate of the school. To what extent is the surrounding social milieu reflected in the school's curriculum? (2) *Formal practices:* What grades are included at the school? What are the goals of the curriculum? (3) *Traditions:* What events, activities, and rituals are important to students, teachers, administrators, and parents? How do community members describe the school?

2.   Visit a local school and gather information on activities, programs, and services the school has developed to meet the needs of students placed at risk by social problems and their families.

Internet Activities

1.   Visit the Equity Online home page (**http://www.edc.org/CEEC/WEEA/ index.html**), funded by the Women's Educational Equity Act, and compile a list of gender-fair curriculum materials related to the level and subject area with which you are most familiar.

2.   Go to the "Futures-Related Links and World-Wide Resources" home page (**http://www.cl.uh.edu/futureweb/data.html**) and gather resources you could use to incorporate a futures-oriented perspective into your curriculum planning activities.

3.   Explore the U.S. government's Children, Youth and Families Education and Research Network (CYFERNet) at **http://www.cyfernet.mes.umn.edu/** and gather information and resources related to several of the social forces discussed in this chapter.

4.   Conduct an online keyword search for sources of information on one or more of the ten social forces discussed in this chapter. Share your findings with others in your class.

BOOKS AND ARTICLES TO REVIEW

Social Forces and the Curriculum

Anyon, Jean. "Race, Social Class, and Educational Reform in an Inner-City School." *Teachers College Record* 97, no. 1 (Fall 1995): 69–94.

Apple, Michael W. "Justifying the Conservative Restoration: Morals, Genes, and Educational Policy." *Educational Policy* 11, no. 2 (June 1997): 167–182.

———. "Becoming Right: Education and the Formation of Conservative Movements." *Teachers College Record* 97, no. 3 (Spring 1996): 419–445.

———. *Cultural Politics and Education.* New York: Teachers College Press, 1996.

———. "The Politics of Official Knowledge: Does a National Curriculum Make Sense?" *Teachers College Record* 95, no. 2 (Winter 1993): 222–241.

Beyer, Landon E., and Liston, Daniel P. *Curriculum in Conflict: Social Visions, Educational Agendas, and Progressive School Reform.* New York: Teachers College Press, 1996.

Brantlinger, Ellen A. *The Politics of Social Class in Secondary School: Views of Affluent and Impoverished Youth.* New York: Teachers College Press.

Comer, James P., et al. *Rallying the Whole Village: The Comer Process for Reforming Education.* New York: Teachers College Press, 1996.

Elders, Joycelyn. "Violence as a Public Health Issue for Children." *Childhood Education* (Annual Theme Issue 1994): 260–262.

Elkind, David. "The Death of Child Nature: Education in the Postmodern World." *Phi Delta Kappan* 79, no. 3 (November 1997): 241–245.

Hutchinson, David. *Growing Up Green: Education for Ecological Renewal.* New York: Teachers College Press, 1998.

Jenkinson, Edward. "Myths and Misunderstandings Surround the Schoolbook Protest Movement." *Contemporary Education* 66, no. 2 (Winter 1995): 70–73.

Kozol, Jonathan. "Reflections on Resiliency." *Principal* 77, no. 2 (November 1997): 5–7.

———. "Industry's Whims Subjugate Student Needs." *School Administrator* 54, no. 5 (May 1997): 32–34.

Lickona, Thomas. "The Return of Character Education." *Educational Leadership* 51, no. 3 (November 1993): 6–11.

McCarthy, Martha M. "Challenges to the Public School Curriculum: New Targets and Strategies." *Phi Delta Kappan* 75, no. 1 (September 1993): 55–56, 58–60.

Parkay, Forrest W. "The Authoritarian Assault Upon the Public School Curriculum: An Additional 'Indicator of Risk.' " *The High School Journal* 68, no. 3 (February–March 1985): 120–128.

Scheuerer, Daniel T., and Parkay, Forrest W. "The New Christian Right and the Public School Curriculum: A Florida Report." In Smith, Jane Bandy and Coleman, J. Gordon Jr., eds., *School Library Media Annual: 1992,* Volume Ten. Englewood, CO: Libraries Unlimited, 112–118.

Sears, James T., and Carper, James C. *Curriculum, Religion, and Public Education.* New York: Teachers College Press, 1998.

Totten, Samuel, and Pedersen, Jon E. *Social Issues and Service at the Middle Level.* Boston: Allyn and Bacon, 1997.

Walsh, Catherine E. *Education Reform and Social Change: Multicultural Voices, Struggles and Visions.* Mahwah, NJ: Lawrence Erlbaum, 1996.

On Cultural Pluralism

Ball, Howard, Berkowitz, Stephen D., and Mzamane, Mbulelo Vizikhungo, eds. *Multicultural Education in Colleges and Universities: A Transdisciplinary Approach.* Mahwah, NJ: Lawrence Erlbaum, 1998.

Banks, James A. *Teaching Strategies for Ethnic Studies* 6th Ed. Boston: Allyn and Bacon, 1997.

———. *Educating Citizens in a Multicultural Society.* New York: Teachers College Press, 1997.

———, ed. *Multicultural Education, Transformative Knowledge, and Action: Historical and Contemporary Perspectives.* New York: Teachers College Press, 1996.

Banks, James A., and Banks, Cherry A. *Multicultural Education: Issues and Perspectives,* 3rd Ed. Boston: Allyn and Bacon, 1997.

Bennett, Christine. *Comprehensive Multicultural Education: Theory and Practice,* 3rd Ed. Boston: Allyn and Bacon, 1995.

Block, Kathy Collins, and Zinke, JoAnne. *Creating a Culturally Enriched Curriculum for Grades K–6.* Boston: Allyn and Bacon, 1995.

Cohen, Elizabeth, and Lotan, Rachel A. *Working for Equity in Heterogeneous Classrooms.* New York: Teachers College Press, 1997.

Dentler, Robert A., and Hafner, Anne L. *Hosting Newcomers: Structuring Educational Opportunities for Immigrant Children.* New York: Teachers College Press, 1997.

Eldridge, Deborah B. *Teacher Talk: Multicultural Lesson Plans for the Elementary Classroom.* Boston: Allyn and Bacon, 1998.

Friedman, Ellen G., Kolmar, Wendy K., Flint, Charley B., and Rothenberg, Paula. *Creating an Inclusive College Curriculum.* New York: Teachers College Press, 1995.

Hodgkinson, Harold. "Diversity Comes in All Sizes and Shapes." *School Business Affairs* 63, no. 4 (April 1997): 3–7.

———. "Who Will Our Students Be? Demographic Implications for Urban and Metropolitan Universities." *Metropolitan Universities: An International Forum* 7, no. 3 (Winter 1996): 25–39.

Hollins, Etta R., ed. *Transforming Curriculum for a Culturally Diverse Society.* Mahwah, NJ: Lawrence Erlbaum, 1996.

———. *Culture in School Learning: Revealing the Deep Meaning.* Mahwah, NJ: Lawrence Erlbaum, 1996.

Igoa, Cristina. *The Inner World of the Immigrant Child.* Mahwah, NJ: Lawrence Erlbaum, 1995.

Morey, Ann Intili, and Kitano, Margie K. *Multicultural Course Transformation in Higher Education: A Broader Truth.* Boston: Allyn and Bacon, 1997.

Schniedewind, Nancy, and Davidson, Ellen. *Open Minds to Equality: A Sourcebook of Learning Activities to Affirm Diversity and Promote Equality,* 2nd Ed. Boston: Allyn and Bacon, 1998.

On the Family

Dryfoos, Joy G. *Full-Service Schools: A Revolution in Health and Social Services for Children, Youth, and Families.* San Francisco: Jossey-Bass Publishers, 1994.

Elkind, David. "The Young Child in the Postmodern World." *Dimensions of Early Childhood Education* 23, no. 3 (Spring 1995): 6–9, 39.

———. "School and Family in the Postmodern World." *Phi Delta Kappan* 77, no. 1 (September 1995): 8–14.

Fuller, Mary Lou, and Olsen, Glenn. *Home-School Relations: Working Successfully with Parents and Families.* Boston: Allyn and Bacon, 1998.

On Futures Planning and the Information Age

Barker, Joel A. "Preparing for the 21st Century: The EFG Experiment." *Educational Horizons* (Fall 1994): 12–17.

Cetron, Marvin. "Reform and Tomorrow's Schools." *Technos* 6, no. 1 (Spring 1997): 19–22.

———. "What Students Must Know to Succeed in the 21st Century." *Futurist* 30, no. 4 (July/August 1996): S1–S7.

Geisert, Paul G. *Teachers, Computers, and Curriculum: Microcomputers in the Classroom,* 2nd Ed. Boston: Allyn and Bacon, 1995.

Hancock, Vicki. "Creating the Information Age School." *Educational Leadership* 55, no. 3 (November 1997): 60–63.

Knapp, Linda Roehrig, and Glenn, Allen D. *Restructuring Schools with Technology.* Boston: Allyn and Bacon, 1996.

Maddux, Cleborne D., Johnson, D. LaMont, and Willis, Jerry W. *Educational Computing: Learning with Tomorrow's Technologies,* 2nd Ed. Boston: Allyn and Bacon, 1997.

Mehlinger, Howard D. "School Reform in the Information Age." *Phi Delta Kappan* 77, no. 6 (February 1996): 400–407.

Morton, Chris. "The Modern Land of Laputa: Where Computers Are Used in Education." *Phi Delta Kappan* 77, no. 6 (February 1996): 416–419.

Pretzer, William S. "Technology Education and the Search for Truth, Beauty and Love." *Journal of Technology Education* 8, no. 2 (Spring 1997): 5–20.

Postman, Neil. "Making a Living, Making a Life: Technology Reconsidered." *College Board Review* no. 176–77 (1995): 8–13.

———. "Deus Machina." *Technos* 1, no. 4 (Winter 1992): 16–18.

Raizen, Senta A. "Making Way for Technology Education." *Journal of Science Education and Technology* 6, no. 1 (March 1997): 59–70.

Shaw, David E., and the PCAST Panel on Educational Technology. "Report to the President on the Use of Technology to Strengthen K–12 Education in the United States: Findings Related to Research and Evaluation." *Journal of Science Education and Technology* 7, no. 2 (June 1998): 115–126.

Stables, Kay. "Critical Issues to Consider when Introducing Technology Education in the Curriculum of Young Learners." *Journal of Technology Education* 8, no. 2 (Spring 1997): 50–66.

On Sex Roles

Biklen, Sari Knopp. *School Work: Gender and the Cultural Construction of Teaching.* New York: Teachers College Press.

Gaskell, Jane, and Willinsky, John, eds. *Gender In/Forms Curriculum: From Enrichment to Transformation.* New York: Teachers College Press, 1995.

Horgan, Dianne D. *Achieving Gender Equity: Strategies for the Classroom.* Boston: Allyn and Bacon, 1995.

Kleinfeld, Judith S., and Yerian, Suzanne. *Gender Tales: Tensions in the Schools.* Mahwah, NJ: Lawrence Erlbaum, 1995.

McCormick, Theresa Mickey. *Creating the Nonsexist Classroom.* New York: Teachers College Press, 1994.

Pinar, William F., ed. *Queer Theory in Education: Teaching Positions Knowledge of Bodies.* Mahwah, NJ: Lawrence Erlbaum, 1998.

Sadker, Myra, et al. "Gender Equity in the Classroom: The Unfinished Agenda." *College Board Review* no. 170 (1993–94): 14–21.

Sanders, Jo, Koch, Janice, and Urso, Josephine. *Gender Equity Sources and Resources for Education Students.* Mahwah, NJ: Lawrence Erlbaum, 1997.

Schlank, Carol Hilgartner, and Metzger, Barbara. *Together and Equal: Fostering Cooperative Play and Promoting Gender Equity in Early Childhood Programs.* Boston: Allyn and Bacon, 1997.

Videotapes

Bilingual Education (26 minutes) examines the current controversy over bilingual education, and *What Can We Do about Violence,* a four-part series hosted by Bill Moyers, focuses on the growing problem of violence in the United States. (Both available from Films for the Humanities and Sciences, P.O. Box 2053, Princeton, NJ 08543-2053 (800) 257-1526).

Respecting Diversity in the Classroom (60 minutes) illustrates situations involving ethnicity, religion, age, gender, and socioeconomic status; and *School of Many Faces* (18 minutes) is a documentary that examines the history, politics, and conflict surrounding multiculturalism in New York City public schools. (Both available from Insight Media, 2162 Broadway, New York, NY 10024-6642 (212) 721-6316).

Diversity in the Classroom/Multicultural Education presents strategies for presenting the curriculum from different ethnic and cultural points of view. (Available from The Video Journal of Education, 549 West 3560 South, Salt Lake City, UT 84115-4225 (800) 572-1153).

Computer Software

Rossett, Allison, and Hoffman, Bob. "School Technology Planner (STP) Software." An interactive electronic performance support system in CD-ROM format to help educators integrate technology into K–12 schools and classrooms. Boston: Allyn and Bacon, 1998.

CHAPTER 3

Human Development

FOCUS QUESTIONS

1. How do learners differ in their stages of development?
2. What are five aspects of human development that should guide curriculum planners?
3. What is the "problem of the match," and how does it influence curriculum planning?
4. What are the salient characteristics of learners' cognitive, psychosocial, and moral development?

Human development throughout the life span is a significant basis of the curriculum. For decades, the study of child and adolescent development has been regarded as an important part of the knowledge base for K–12 education. Now, with the increasing significance of lifelong learning, curriculum planners must also focus attention on human development during early adulthood, middle age, and later maturity.

The generally accepted stages of human development include infancy, childhood, early adolescence, middle adolescence, late adolescence, and adulthood. The elementary school years correspond roughly to the stage known as childhood. Early, middle, and late adolescence correspond roughly to the middle school, high school, and community college levels of education. And with the current emphasis on lifelong learning, the various stages of adulthood are of considerable importance to curriculum planners at the higher education level.

Knowledge of human development enables curriculum planners to design curricula that are shaped, in part, by the nature and needs of individual learners. Articles that focus on various aspects of human development are included in this chapter. For example, in "Organize Schools around Child Development," James P. Comer discusses how to design school programs around students' developmental needs in several areas; and David A. Hamburg's "Toward a Strategy for Healthy Adolescent Development" examines the biological, physical, behavioral, and social transformations that characterize adolescence. These and other articles in this chapter illustrate the need for curriculum planning to be guided by the five aspects of human development presented in Figure 3.1: the biological basis of individual differences, physical maturation, intellectual development and achievement, emotional growth and development, and cultural and social development.

The concept of stages of human development is a useful tool for understanding the needs of learners at various levels of education, but it cannot define the development of any one learner at a particular age. Each learner is innately unique, and this inborn individuality indicates the importance of providing many alternatives in educational programs. Nevertheless, humans as learners have much in common. In the first article in this chapter, for example, Ashley Montagu ("My Idea of Education") emphasizes the educability of each human being from the perspective of anthropology. Montagu points out that the human person is capable of learning anything, under the appropriate environmental conditions. He states that we need to "grow up into children" and not into adults—that is, we need to preserve some of the traits that children so conspicuously exhibit.

Maturation and change in human development occur over the entire life span, providing one of the bases for curriculum planning at all age levels, including higher

FIGURE 3.1

Five Aspects of Human Development to Guide Curriculum Planning and Planning for Teaching

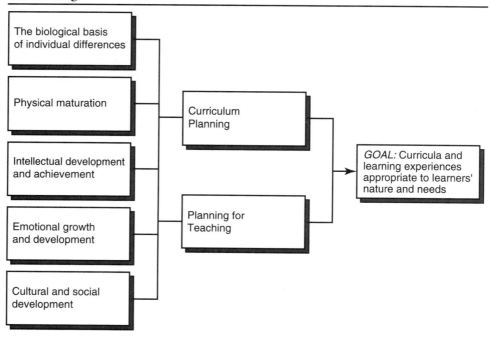

and adult education. Maturation follows different courses of development for different individuals. One of the guidelines for curriculum planning derived from the study of human development, then, is the *problem of the match*. In other words, there must be a match between the learner's developmental stage and the curriculum. For example, in this chapter's Teachers' Voices section, "Walkabout in Sixth Grade," Richard Isenberg describes a curriculum that is congruent with his students' developmental needs in five areas: adventure, creativity, logical inquiry, practical skills, and service.

Research on brain growth periodization has significance for curriculum planning and the problem of the match at various age levels. This research suggests that there are five periods of growth spurt, which alternate with intervals of growth lag, in the development of the human brain from birth to about the age of seventeen. Herman Epstein (1978, 1990), a biologist, reports that growth spurts occur at 3–10 months, 2–4 years, 6–8 years, 10–12 or 13 years, and 14–16 or 17 years. He suggests that "intensive intellectual input should be situated at the spurt ages" (Epstein, 1978, p. 362) and that too much input during the plateau periods may reduce the learner's ability to absorb information at a later, more appropriate age. The challenge for curriculum planners, then, is to make the timing and content of learning experiences fit these known patterns of brain growth.

THEORIES OF HUMAN DEVELOPMENT

Several theorists' and researchers' theories in the area of human development have had a significant influence on curriculum planning. They include Jean Piaget's theory of cognitive development, Erik Erikson's developmental outline for stages of "growth toward a mature personality," and Lawrence Kohlberg's cognitive-developmental view of moral development. These three human development theorists maintain that the developmental stages they describe have a fixed order, and that each person passes through these stages in this order. Sufficient resolution of the challenges and developmental tasks associated with each stage is necessary for the individual to proceed with vigor and confidence to the next stage, and there is a "teachable moment" or opportune time for this development to occur.

Piaget's Model of Cognitive Development

Piaget's theory (as summarized by David Elkind's "Developmentally Appropriate Practice: Philosophical and Practical Implications") maintains that children learn through interacting with their environments, much as scientists do, and that a child's thinking progresses through a sequence of four cognitive stages. At the sensorimotor intelligence stage (birth to 2 years), behavior is largely sensory and motor, and, while cognitive development is occurring, the child does not yet "think" conceptually. At the preoperational thought stage (2–7 years), the development of language occurs, and the child can think of objects and people beyond the immediate environment. At the concrete operations stage (7–11 years), the child explores and masters basic concepts of objects, number, time, space, and causality and can use logical thought to solve problems. Finally, at the formal operations stage (11–15 years), the child can make predictions, think hypothetically, and think abstractly about language.

Erikson's Model of Psychosocial Development

"Erik Erikson's Developmental Stages: A Healthy Personality for Every Child" in this chapter presents Erikson's views on the emotional growth and development of human beings. His model is based on eight stages of growth—from infancy to old age. Each stage is characterized by a psychosocial crisis for the individual's emotional and social growth. These crises are expressed in polar terms; for example, in infancy, the psychosocial crisis is trust versus mistrust. The infant must come to trust the world sufficiently in order to move on to the next stage, autonomy versus share and doubt. Shortly before his death in 1994, Erikson postulated a ninth stage in the human life cycle, *gerotranscendence*, during which some humans confront, and transcend, the reality of their deteriorating bodies and faculties. In the final chapter of an extended version of Erikson's *The Life Cycle Completed*, first published in 1982, his wife and lifelong colleague, Joan M. Erikson, describes the challenges of moving into gerotranscendence:

> Old age in one's eighties and nineties brings with it new demands, reevaluations, and daily difficulties. . . . Even the best cared-for bodies begin to weaken and do not function as they once did. In spite of every effort to maintain strength and control, the body continues to lose its autonomy. Despair, which haunts the eighth stage, is a close companion in the ninth, because it is almost impossible to know what emergencies and losses of physical ability are imminent. As independence and control are challenged, self-esteem and confidence weaken. Hope and trust, which once provided firm support, are no longer the sturdy props of former days. To face down despair with faith and appropriate humility is perhaps the wisest course. (Erikson, 1997, pp. 105–106)

Kohlberg's and Gilligan's Models for Moral Development

Among the many perspectives on the moral development of human beings, Kohlberg's cognitive-developmental approach to moral education, based on Piaget's stages of cognitive development and John Dewey's levels of moral development, has had perhaps the greatest influence on curriculum planning. However, one might ask: Should moral education be an aspect of human development that is considered by curriculum planners and teachers? Perhaps the question is moot, since education is not value-free—it is a moral enterprise whether we wish it to be or not. Students' curricular experiences, including countless hours observing their teachers as moral models, have a profound influence on how they think and behave regarding moral issues.

   In "The Cognitive-Developmental Approach to Moral Education" in this chapter, Kohlberg states that moral principals are ultimately "principles of justice," and that at each stage of moral development the concept of justice is reorganized. However,

Carol Gilligan, at one point a colleague of Kohlberg's, believes that his research depends too heavily on studies of men and that women's moral judgments are more likely to reflect care and concern for others. In "Woman's Place in Man's Life Cycle" in this chapter, Gilligan examines these two perspectives and suggests that the female perspective on morality is based on the understanding of responsibility and relationships, while the male perspective is based on rights and rules.

CRITERION QUESTIONS—HUMAN DEVELOPMENT

Although stages of human development can be identified, no two individuals of the same age are alike in physical, emotional, intellectual, or social development. Knowing how development occurs in each of these areas helps curriculum planners and teachers identify two important curriculum criteria that should be reflected in the curriculum: individual differences and continuity in learning (i.e., the curriculum and teaching begin "where the learner is").

The following are among the criterion questions that can be derived from the theories of human development discussed in this chapter.

1. Does the curriculum reflect the inborn individuality and innate uniqueness of each learner?
2. Does the curriculum provide for developmental differences among the learners being taught?
3. Does the curriculum provide for continuity of learning?
4. Have the significance of developmental tasks, stages of growth toward a mature personality, and the development of morality been considered when planning the curriculum?
5. Does the curriculum attempt to provide for earlier tasks inadequately achieved, and for their maintenance when successfully achieved?
6. Does the curriculum reflect social and cultural changes that have occurred in recent years at each stage of human development?

REFERENCES

Epstein, Herman T. "Stages in Human Mental Growth." *Journal of Educational Psychology* 82, no. 4 (December 1990): 876–880.

———. "Growth Spurts During Brain Development: Implications for Educational Policy and Practice." In Jeanne S. Chall and Allan F. Mirsky, eds., *Education and the Brain, The 77th Yearbook of the National Society for the Study of Education, Part II.* Chicago: University of Chicago Press, 1978.

Erikson, Erik H. *The Life Cycle Competed: Extended Version with New Chapters on the Ninth Stage of Development by Joan M. Erikson.* New York: W. W. Norton & Company, 1997.

My Idea of Education

ASHLEY MONTAGU

ABSTRACT: One of the world's preeminent anthropologists asserts that educability and the need for love distinguishes human beings from other creatures. The implications of childrens' individual rates of development for schools and teachers are discussed.

As an anthropologist who has been studying the six-million-year course of human evolution for nearly sixty years, I have become convinced that the characteristic that distinguishes humans from all other creatures is educability and that the most important of all basic human psychological needs is the need for love. Both of these findings have profound implications for schools and teachers.

The human is capable of learning anything, under the appropriate environmental conditions.

The human brain is an organ for the assimilation of diverse kinds of experiences and for turning accidents into opportunities. It is the most flexible, the most malleable, and the most educable of all the brains in the world.

It is capable of making the most of the improbable. Some people use their brains to arrive at truth and conclusions that others might conceive as utterly impossible. For example, at the very time the flying machine was invented, leading experts of the world said it was a physical impossibility.

We must recognize the educability of the human brain, particularly in dealing with children, who are the most educable of all human beings.

One thing most of us don't understand is the nature of the child and his or her extraordinary educability. Furthermore, we don't understand that we need to grow up into children and not

adults. By this I mean we should preserve some of the traits that the child so conspicuously exhibits.

What are these traits? Besides educability, they are the need to love, sensitivity, the need to think soundly, the need to learn, the need to work, the need to organize, curiosity and wonder, open-mindedness, experimental-mindedness, imagination, creativity, playfulness, sense of humor, joyfulness, laughter, optimism, honesty, trust, compassionate intelligence, and the desire to grow and develop in all these traits.

Frequently, we feel we ought to limit this desire to grow to certain stages that we arbitrarily designate as infancy, childhood, and adolescence or to this one stage or another. Then we treat children of the same chronological age as if they were developmentally of the same age, too.

This is a damaging idea, and it has done an enormous amount of harm to children. Every child has his or her own developmental rate. To treat children, even children the same age, as if they were all equal is to commit a biological and social absurdity. The equal treatment of unequals is the most unequal way of dealing with human beings ever devised. We're all very different, and because we're all very different, we require individual attention. We should not be treated as if we were an agglutinated mass affixed to one another on the basis of our particular age level.

Even though many teachers recognize the great differences among children, they are not in

From *Today's Education,* Journal of the National Education Association, 69, no. 1 (February–March 1980) (General Edition): 48–49. Used by the permission of the author and the publisher.

a position to do anything about them because of the way school systems are organized and the inadequacy of those who are presiding at their top levels. These top level officials are usually unequipped to understand what the child is, what the teacher's needs are, and what education is all about.

What education is all about is being human, in other words, developing those traits that are uniquely human for the benefit of the individual, the family, the community, the society, and the world. Eventually what teachers do in the classroom is going to determine what the world is going to be like; for it is there that children learn all about being human if they have not learned it in the home.

Unfortunately, the probabilities are that children have not learned this in the home, because most parents are not equipped to do the job of parenting. Why? Simply because they have lived in a society that has not recognized the nature of the child, the nature of the human being, and the nature of what the child ought to be.

We now know what human beings ought to be because we understand for the first time in the history of our species that the most important of all human basic psychological needs is the need for love. It stands at the center of all human needs just as our sun stands at the center of our solar system with the planets orbiting around it. So the basic needs, the need for oxygen, food, liquid, rest, for activity, and so on, these revolve around the need for love—the sun of the human being.

It is this need for love that nature designates the mother to satisfy and that we have interfered with for a very long time by having mothers give birth to babies in hospitals, by taking babies away from their mothers in hospitals, by bottlefeeding babies, and by committing many other frightful offenses against babies at the very beginnings of their lives. These are offenses not only against the baby but against the mother and the family. The family should be involved in the ceremony and the celebration of welcoming a new member into the family. It is the family's job to turn this educable creature into the kind of human being that he or she is striving to be from the moment of birth.

Now that's quite a statement for a scientist to make. How do I know what this baby is striving to be? Well, I have discussed this with hundreds of babies. I've observed them, and I've talked with them. So have a good many other people. What they and I have observed is that the baby wants more than anything else to learn to love. Not only to be loved, but to love, because if the baby fails in this, then he or she fails to grow up as a warm, loving human being.

It's as simple as that. Nothing very complicated, but it's taken a long time for us to understand this.

The child who has not been loved is biochemically, physiologically, and psychologically very different from the one who has been loved. The former even grows differently from the latter. What we now know is that the human being is born to live as if to live and love were one.

This is not, of course, new. This is a validation of the Sermon on the Mount. I who am not a Christian and who am not a member of any religious affiliation say this.

The only religion I believe in is goodness and love. This is what we should be teaching in our schools. The greatest gift a teacher has to give a student is his or her love.

A teacher can recognize that the biggest behavior problems in the classroom are the ones who have been failed in their need for love and that what their need is is not to be sent to the principal but to be loved by the teacher. They will try the teacher again and again because they have been failed so many times and they don't trust anyone.

Every time the teacher offers them love, they may not improve their behavior, but if the teacher persists, then the teacher will win the children over. I speak from experience as an old teacher. I know very well how this works, because I've frequently done it myself.

I know this is very difficult in many cases—and it's extremely difficult in certain parts of America where teachers face behavior problems of the worst kind and where violence and vandalism are increasing at an accelerating rate in the schools. Even in those places, however, I think each teacher can make a difference by doing what he or she ought to do: behaving as a warm, loving human being.

How do we become warm, loving human beings? We act *as if* we were warm, loving human beings. If we act as if we were, someday we may find we've become what we've been trying to be, because what we are is not what we say but what we do.

I have been discussing love, but I have not defined it yet for the simple reason that a definition isn't meaningful at the beginning of an inquiry. It can be so only at the end of one.

Love is the ability to communicate by demonstrative acts to others our profound involvement in their welfare. We communicate our deep interest in them because we are aware that to be born human is to be born in danger, and therefore we will never commit the supreme treason against others of not helping them when they are most in need of us. We will minister to their needs and give them all the supports, all the stimulation, all the succor that they need or want.

That's love, and that's what we should be teaching in the schools, and everything else should be secondary to that. Reading, writing, and arithmetic, yes—but not of primary importance, of secondary importance in the development of a warm, loving human being.

This is my idea of education. If we put this idea into action, we stand a chance of solving most of the problems that bedevil the world at the present time, for teachers are the unacknowledged legislators of the world.

Ashley Montagu is an anthropologist. Among the books he has authored are *Growing Young* (1981), *The Human Connection* (1979), *Touching* (2nd Ed., 1978), *Life Before Birth* (2nd Ed., 1978), *The Direction of Human Development* (2nd Ed., 1970), *On Being Human* (2nd Ed., 1966), and *Growing Young* (2nd Ed., 1988).

QUESTIONS FOR REFLECTION

1. What does Montagu mean when he states that "we don't understand that we need to grow up into children and not adults"? Do you agree?

2. To what extent do you agree or disagree with Montagu's statement that "the equal treatment of unequals is the most unequal way of dealing with human beings ever devised"? What implications does his position have for curriculum and teaching?

3. What evidence can you cite to support Montagu's claim that our society "has not recognized the nature of the child, the nature of the human being, and the nature of what the child ought to be"?

4. Do you agree with Montagu when he states that reading, writing, and arithmetic are "of secondary importance in the development of a warm, loving human being"? What would be the key elements of a school curriculum organized around this belief?

Developmentally Appropriate Practice: Philosophical and Practical Implications

DAVID ELKIND

ABSTRACT: Meaningful educational reform will occur only when the reigning psychometric view of educational philosophy is replaced with one that is developmentally appropriate. The developmental and psychometric approaches are contrasted regarding their view of the learner, the learning process, the information to be learned, and educational goals. The implications of a developmental philosophy for teacher training, curriculum, instruction, and assessment are discussed.

The idea of developmentally appropriate educational practice—that the curriculum should be matched to the child's level of mental ability—has been favorably received in education circles.[1] However, this positive reception is quite extraordinary, for developmentally appropriate practice derives from a philosophy of education that is in total opposition to the "psychometric" educational philosophy that now dictates educational practice in the majority of our public schools. Perhaps for this reason developmental appropriateness has been honored more in word than in deed.

In what follows I highlight some of the differences between these two educational philosophies and contrast a few of their practical implications. My purpose in doing so is to argue that true education reform will come about only when we replace the reigning psychometric educational psychology with a developmentally appropriate one.

TWO PHILOSOPHIES

Any philosophy of education must include some conception of the learner, of the learning process, of the information to be acquired, and of the goals or aims of education. The developmental philosophy differs from the psychometric philosophy on all four counts. I should mention that the developmental philosophy that I present here derives from the research and theory of Jean Piaget.[2]

Conception of the Learner

Within a developmental philosophy of education, the learner is viewed as having *developing* mental abilities. All individuals (with the exception of the retarded) are assumed to be able to attain these abilities, though not necessarily at the same age. For example, we expect that all children will attain the concrete operations that Piaget described as emerging at about age 6 or 7. These operations, which function much like the group of arithmetic operations, enable children who have attained them to learn and to apply rules. However, not all children will attain these operations at the same age. Accordingly, a developmental philosophy sees individual differences in ability as differences in *rates* of intellectual growth.

This conception of mental ability contrasts sharply with that of a psychometric philosophy of education. According to the psychometric position, the learner is seen as having *measurable* abilities. This philosophy assumes that any ability that exists must exist in some amount and must, therefore, be quantifiable. For example, intelligence tests—the flagships of the psychometric

From *Phi Delta Kappan* 71, no. 2 (October 1989): 113–117. Used by permission of the author.

philosophy—are designed to assess individual differences in the ability to learn and to adapt to new situations. A psychometric perspective regards individual differences in performance as reflecting differences in *amount* of a given ability.

Both of these opposing conceptions of human ability contain some truth. However, they have far different pedagogical implications.

From a developmental perspective, the important task for educators is *matching curricula* to the level of children's emerging mental abilities: hence the principle of developmental appropriateness. Curriculum materials should be introduced only after a child has attained the level of mental ability needed to master them. This in turn means that curricula must be studied and analyzed to determine the level of mental ability that is required to comprehend them.

From a psychometric point of view, the most important task for educators is *matching children* with others of equal ability. Bright children are assumed to be able to learn more in a given time than less bright children. In practice, this philosophy leads to so-called "ability grouping," which in effect allows bright children to go through the material more quickly than slower children. This psychometric orientation also underlies the provision of special classes for the gifted and for the retarded.

Conception of the Learning Process

Within the developmental philosophy of education, learning is always seen as a *creative* activity. Whenever we learn anything, we engage the world in a way that creates something new, something that reflects both our own mental activity and the material we have dealt with. We never simply copy content; we always stamp it with our unique way of viewing the world. The child from Connecticut who heard the Lord's Prayer as "Our Father, Who art in New Haven, Harold be thy name" is not the exception but the rule. Everything we learn has both a subjective and an objective component.

The conception of learning as a creative or constructive process has a very important practical implication. It means that we cannot talk of learning independently of the content to be learned. The material to be learned will always interact with the learning process in some special way. Long after Piaget discovered the successive stages and organizations of mental operations, he continued to study the ways in which children attained different concepts, such as space, geometry, time, and movement and speed.[3] In so doing he emphasized the fact that merely knowing the stages of mental development does not provide special insight into how children use the operations at any given stage to attain any particular concept. The only way to discover how children go about learning a particular subject is to study children learning.

By contrast, the psychometric philosophy views learning as governed by a set of principles (e.g., intermittent reinforcement) and consisting of the acquisition of a set of skills (e.g., decoding) that are independent of the content to be learned. Early workers in this tradition enunciated such principles as "mass versus distributed" or "whole versus part" learning, which were presumed to operate independently of the content to be learned. Indeed, early studies of memory employed nonsense syllables in order to eliminate the effect of content on the study of memory.

The limitations of this approach were dramatically demonstrated by Jerome Bruner, Jacqueline Goodenough, and George Austin in their seminal work on problem solving.[4] Before the publication of their work, problem solving was spoken of in terms of "trial and error" or "sudden insight" because most of the work had been done with animals. What Bruner and his colleagues demonstrated was that human subjects, when presented with complex problems, employ complex problem-solving activities—in other words, "strategies." Put differently, the content of the problem determines the level of the problem-solving activities that humans employ.

Nonetheless, this insight seems to have been lost. The current interest in teaching young children such things as thinking skills,[5] learning strategies,[6] or computer programming[7] reflects a regression to the idea that thought and content can be treated separately. It is assumed that—once children learn thinking skills or learning strategies or computer programming—these skills will automatically be transferred to different kinds of content. To be sure, transfer of training does occur, but it is far from automatic. Transfer happens when students are active, not passive, learners.[8] But what can we possibly mean by *activity* if not that students are consciously aware of the content they are thinking about or applying strategies to? Mental processes are always content-oriented.

The developmental approach implies that there is little or no automatic transfer from one subject to another, whereas the psychometric approach assumes that the skills and strategies of thinking often transfer spontaneously to new areas.

Conception of Knowledge

From a developmental perspective, knowledge is always a construction, inevitably reflecting the joint contributions of the subject and the object. This is far from a new idea, and it harks back to the Kantian resolution of idealist (all knowledge is a mental construction) and empiricist (all knowledge is a copy of an externally existing world) interpretations of how we come to know the world.[9] Kant argued that the mind provides the "categories" of knowing, while the real world provides the content. Knowledge is thus always a construction of the mind's *interaction* with the world and cannot be reduced to one or the other.

What Piaget added to the Kantian solution— and what makes Piaget a neoKantian—was the demonstration that the categories of knowing (the mental operations of intelligence) are not constant, as Kant had supposed. Rather, the categories change with age. This idea adds a developmental dimension to the Kantian version of the construction of knowledge. As their mental operations develop, children are required to reconstruct the realities they constructed at the previous developmental level. In effect, a child creates and re-creates reality out of his or her experiences with the environment.

The reality of the young child—his or her knowledge of the world—is thus different from the reality of the older child and adult. For example, young children believe that a quantity changes in amount when it changes in appearance—that, say, the amount of liquid in a low, flat container is greater when it is poured into a tall, narrow one. Older children, whose reality is different, can appreciate the fact that a quantity remains the same in amount despite changes in its appearance. In other words, older children recognize that quantity is conserved. From a developmental perspective, the young child's conception of quantity is not "wrong." It is, in fact, as developmentally appropriate as the older child's grasp of conservation.

From the psychometric point of view, knowledge is something that a child acquires and that can be measured independently from the processes of acquisition. This separation is reflected in the distinction between intelligence tests and achievement tests. One consequence of the separation between learning and content is that knowledge is measured against an external standard that is independent of the learner. When compared to such an external standard, a child's responses can be assessed as being either "right" or "wrong."

Certainly, there is a right and a wrong with respect to some types of knowledge. The Bastille was stormed in 1789, not in 1650; two plus two equals four, not five. We have to distinguish here between what I have elsewhere termed *fundamental* knowledge, which we construct on our own, and *derived* knowledge, which is constructed by others and which we must acquire at second hand.[10] The terms *right* and *wrong* are useful only in connection with derived knowledge.

The developmental approach introduces the idea that there can be differences in knowledge without any reference to "right" or "wrong." The idea of difference, rather than of correctness, is important not only with respect to fundamental knowledge, but also with respect to creative thinking. For example, many bright children come up with ideas that are different from those of their peers and teachers. Unfortunately, these ideas are often regarded as wrong rather than as different and original. One bright child, when asked to write something about the color blue, wrote about Picasso's Blue Period and was teased and jeered. A greater appreciation for such differences would make the life of bright children in our schools a lot easier.

Conception of the Aims of Education

The aims of developmental education are straightforward. If the learner is seen as a growing individual with developing abilities, if learning is regarded as a creative activity, and if knowledge is seen as a construction, then the aim of education must surely be to facilitate this development, this creative activity, and this construction of knowledge. Piaget put the aims of education from a developmental perspective this way:

> The principal goal of education is to create men who are capable of doing new things, not simply repeating what other generations have done—men who are creative, inventive, and discoverers. The second goal of education is to form minds which can be critical, can verify, and not accept everything that is offered. The greater danger today is of slogans, collective opinions, ready made trends of thought. We have to be able to resist them individually, to criticize, to distinguish between what is proven and what is not. So we need pupils who are active, who learn early to find out by themselves, partly by their own spontaneous activity and partly through material we set up for them; who learn early to tell what is verifiable and what is simply the first idea to come to them.[11]

The aim of developmental education, then, is to produce thinkers who are creative and critical. This aim will not be achieved, however, by teaching thinking skills to children and adolescents. Rather, the way to pursue this aim is by creating developmentally appropriate learning environments that challenge the child's emerging mental

abilities. Creative thinking and critical thinking are not skills to be taught and learned. They reflect basic orientations toward the self and the world that can be acquired only when children are actively engaged in constructing and reconstructing their physical, social, and moral worlds.

The aim of psychometric education is to produce children who score high on tests of achievement. In other words, the aim of education is to maximize the acquisition of quantifiable knowledge and skills. Perhaps former Secretary of Education William Bennett stated this view of the aims of education as well as anyone:

> We should want every student to know how mountains are made, and that for most reactions there is an equal and opposite reaction. They should know who said "I am the state" and who said "I have a dream." They should know about subjects and predicates, about isosceles triangles and ellipses. They should know where the Amazon flows and what the First Amendment means. They should know about the Donner party and about slavery, and Shylock, Hercules, and Abigail Adams, where Ethiopia is, and why there is a Berlin Wall.[12]

In this statement Bennett echoes a theme that was also sounded in *A Nation at Risk,* which was published three years earlier and decried the poor performance of American students on achievement tests, especially when compared to the performance of children from other nations. Moreover, Bennett's remarks foreshadowed the best-selling critiques of U.S. education by Allan Bloom and E. D. Hirsch, Jr., which charged that American education was failing to provide children with the basic knowledge of western civilization.[13]

Young people should certainly be exposed to Shakespeare, they should know the basics of geography, and they should be familiar with current events. A developmental approach to education does not deny the importance of such knowledge. The difference between the two approaches is a matter of which acquisition comes first. Those who hold a developmental philosophy believe that children who are curious, active learners will acquire much of the knowledge that

Bennett, Bloom, and Hirsch call for—and many other things as well. But, from a developmental perspective, the creation of curious, active learners must *precede* the acquisition of particular information. To put the difference more succinctly, the developmental approach seeks to create students who *want to know,* whereas the psychometric approach seeks to produce students who *know what we want.*

IMPLICATIONS OF A DEVELOPMENTAL PHILOSOPHY

Now that we have looked at these two contrasting educational philosophies, we can review a few of the implications for the practice of education of adopting a developmental perspective. Once again, my interpretation is largely based on the Piagetian idea of the development of intelligence.

Teacher Training

Students of most disciplines must learn the basic material of their discipline. A physics student has to learn about the rules that govern the physical world; a chemistry student must learn how the basic chemical elements interact; a biology student must learn about plants and animals. Education is perhaps the only discipline wherein students do not learn the basic material of the discipline at the outset. Students take courses in curriculum, in methods, in educational philosophy, in assessment, and in classroom management. They take only one (or at most two) courses in educational or developmental psychology.

But the basic material of education is not curriculum. Nor is it assessment or methods. The basic material of education is children and youth. A teacher training program that is truly developmentally appropriate would have its students major in child development. Trained in this way, a teacher would be, first and foremost, a child development specialist. Students with a strong foundation in child development can integrate what they learn about curriculum, assessment,

and management with what they know about how children of various ages think and learn.

From a developmental point of view, the recommendation of the Holmes Group that we do away with the undergraduate major in education and substitute a year or two of graduate training and internship will not produce better teachers. There *is* a need for teacher training at the undergraduate level—not in traditional education courses, but in child development.

Curriculum

From a developmental point of view, there are several principles that should guide the construction of the curriculum. First, a curriculum must be constructed empirically, not a priori. There is no way to figure out how children learn a subject without studying how they actually go about learning it. Thus it is truly a scandal that curriculum publishers not only fail to do research on the materials they produce, but also fail even to field-test them! In no other profession would we allow a product to be placed on the market without extensive field-testing.

In a truly developmental system of education, teachers would have the opportunity to construct and test their own materials. They could see what works and what doesn't, and they could try out different sequences and methods. The way curriculum materials work will always depend on the specific group of children in the classroom in any given year. So a curriculum should never be final; it should always be open, flexible, and innovative. Such a curriculum is exciting for the teacher and for the pupils and makes both learning and curriculum innovation cooperative ventures.

Second, I believe that a curriculum should be localized, particularly for elementary schools. I know that this is contrary to trends in other countries, which have uniform curricula for all children. Japan and France are but two of the countries with such uniform national curricula. England, too, will be initiating a uniform national curriculum in 1990. But such national curricula eliminate the possibility of localizing materials to include particulars from the environment in which children actually live and learn.

Such localized curricula hold a great deal of intrinsic interest for children. For example, in learning math, children living in Hawaii might be asked to match coconuts and palm trees, whereas children living in the Northeast might be asked to match acorns and oaks. Likewise, it would add to children's enjoyment if the stories they read took place in their own community or one similar to it. In social studies, too, children are delighted to find a picture of a building that they have actually been in, rather than one that they have never seen. To be sure, children like stories about places and events that are new to them. Nonetheless, they also enjoy reading stories that relate directly to the world they live in. Children, no less than adults, appreciate *both* fantasy and the realism of local reference.

Finally, we need to study curricula to determine their level of developmental difficulty. Developmental difficulty is quite different from psychometric difficulty. The psychometric difficulty of a curriculum or a test item is determined by the number of children of a particular age who successfully learn the material or who get the item correct. A curriculum or test item is generally assigned to the grade or age level at which 75% of the children can succeed.

Developmental difficulty, by contrast, must be determined by examining the actual "errors" children make in attempting to master a problem or task. For example, when young children who have been taught the short *a* sound are asked to learn the long *a* as well, they have great difficulty. The problem is that they are being asked to grasp the fact that the same letter can have two different sounds. Understanding that the same symbol can stand for two different sounds, however, requires the attainment of the mental abilities that Piaget calls *concrete operations*. A teacher who holds a developmental philosophy would thus avoid teaching phonics until he or she was quite sure that most of the children could handle concrete operations. Because the developmental difficulty of any particular problem or task can be determined only by active investigation, part of

the experimental work of teaching would be to explore the developmental difficulty of the available curriculum materials and to try out new materials that might work differently or better.

Instruction

Developmentally speaking, it is as impossible to separate the learning process from the material to be learned as it is to separate learning from instruction. This is authentic teaching. From this perspective, the teacher is also a learner, and the students are also teachers. The teacher who experiments with the curriculum is learning about the curriculum and about the children he or she teaches. And children who work cooperatively and who experiment with curriculum materials are teaching as well as learning.

One way to highlight the difference between authentic teaching and psychometrically oriented teaching is to look at how each type of instruction handles the asking of questions. In psychometrically oriented teaching, the teacher often asks students questions to which the teacher already knows the answers. The purpose is to determine whether the students have the same information as the teacher. But asking questions to which one already has the answers is not authentic behavior. A much more meaningful approach is to ask children questions to which one doesn't have the answers. Finding the answers can then be a learning experience for teacher and students alike. The authentic teacher asks questions to get information and to gain understanding, not to test what students know or understand. Such questioning reflects the fact that the authentic teacher is first and foremost an enthusiastic learner.

Assessment

Developmental assessment involves documenting the work that a child has done over a given period of time. Usually this is done by having a child keep a portfolio that includes all of his or her writing, drawing, math explorations, and so on. In looking through such a portfolio, we can get a good idea of the quality of work that the child is capable of doing and of his or her progress over the given period.

Psychometric assessment involves measuring a child's achievement by means of commercial or teacher-made tests. A child's progress is evaluated according to his or her performance on such tests. Unlike a portfolio of work, the psychometric approach yields a *grade* that symbolizes both the quantity and the quality of the work that the child has done over a given period of time. Although some testing can be useful, it is currently so overused that many children and parents are more concerned about grades and test scores than about what a child has learned. The documentation of a child's work tends to avoid that danger.

I have tried to demonstrate that, while the idea of developmentally appropriate practice has been well received among educators, it really has little chance of being widely implemented. Without a change in underlying philosophy, changes in educational practice will be superficial at best. No classroom or school can truly be developmentally appropriate if its underlying philosophy is psychometric.

How can we change that underlying educational philosophy? It might seem that what is required is a paradigm shift of the sort described by Thomas Kuhn as characterizing major scientific revolutions.[14] Yet neither the developmental thinking of Freud nor that of Piaget has been sufficient to effect such a shift. This may reflect the fact that educational practice is dictated more by social, political, and economic considerations than it is by science. Unfortunately, a major shift in educational philosophy is more likely to come about as a result of economic necessity than as a result of scientific innovation.

NOTES

1. Sue Bredekamp, *Developmentally Appropriate Practice* (Washington, D.C.: National Association for the Education of Young Children, 1987).

2. Jean Piaget, *The Psychology of Intelligence* (London: Routledge & Kegan Paul, 1950).

3. Jean Piaget and Bärbel Inhelder, *The Child's Conception of Space* (London: Routledge & Kegan Paul, 1956); Jean Piaget, Bärbel Inhelder, and Alina Szeminska, *The Child's Conception of Geometry* (New York: Basic Books, 1960); Jean Piaget, *The Child's Conception of Time* (London: Routledge & Kegan Paul, 1967); and idem, *The Child's Conception of Movement and Speed* (London: Routledge & Kegan Paul, 1970).

4. Jerome S. Bruner, Jacqueline J. Goodenough, and George A. Austin, *A Study in Thinking* (New York: Wiley, 1956).

5. Joan Boykoff Baron and Robert J. Sternberg, *Teaching Thinking Skills: Theory and Practice* (New York: Freeman, 1987).

6. Edwin Weinstein and Richard Edwin Mayer, "The Teaching of Learning Strategies," in Merlin C. Wittrock, ed., *Handbook of Research on Teaching,* 3rd ed. (New York: Macmillan, 1986).

7. Seymour Papert, *Mindstorms* (New York: Basic Books, 1980).

8. David N. Perkins and Gavriel Solomon, "Teaching for Transfer," *Educational Leadership,* vol. 46, 1988, pp. 22–32.

9. Immanuel Kant, *Critique of Pure Reason* (New York: Wiley, 1943).

10. David Elkind, *Miseducation: Preschoolers at Risk* (New York: Knopf, 1987).

11. Quoted in Richard E. Ripple and Verne E. Rockcastle, eds., *Piaget Rediscovered: A Report of the Conference on Cognitive Studies and Curriculum Development* (Ithaca, N.Y.: School of Education, Cornell University, 1964), p. 5.

12. William J. Bennett, *First Lessons: A Report on Elementary Education in America* (Washington, DC: U.S. Department of Education, 1986), p. 3.

13. Allan Bloom, *The Closing of the American Mind* (New York: Simon & Schuster, 1987); and E. D. Hirsch, Jr., *Cultural Literacy: What Every American Needs to Know* (Boston: Houghton Mifflin, 1987).

14. Thomas S. Kuhn, *The Structure of Scientific Revolution,* 2nd ed. (Chicago: University of Chicago Press, 1970).

David Elkind is Professor of Child Development at Tufts University and author of *The Hurried Child* (1981), *All Grown Up and No Place to Go* (1984), and *Miseducation: Preschoolers at Risk* (1987).

QUESTIONS FOR REFLECTION

1. Do you agree with Elkind's statement that "the developmental approach seeks to create students who *want to know,* whereas the psychometric approach seeks to produce students who *know what we want*"? Which approach characterizes the curricula with which you are most familiar?
2. What does Elkind mean when he states that "a curriculum must be constructed empirically, not a priori"?
3. What are several examples of developmentally oriented assessment appropriate for the curriculum with which you are most familiar?

Toward a Strategy for Healthy Adolescent Development

DAVID A. HAMBURG

ABSTRACT: Adolescence is a critical transition period for young people. Contemporary society confronts adolescents with formidable stresses and risks that, for some youth, impair physical and mental health, erode motivation for success in school and workplace, and damage their relationships with others. With support from families, schools, health care professionals, and the community, however, adolescents can grow up to assume the responsibilities of democratic citizenship. For example, schools can promote healthy development by emphasizing a life sciences curriculum, life skills training, and social support.

Adolescence is one of the most complex transitions in the lifespan—a time of metamorphosis from childhood to adulthood. Its beginning is associated with biological, physical, behavioral, and social transformations that roughly correspond with the move from elementary school to middle or junior high school. The events of this crucially formative phase can shape an individual's entire lifespan.

Many adolescents manage to negotiate their way through this critical transition. With caring families, good schools, preventive health care, and supportive community institutions, they grow up healthy and vigorous, reasonably well educated, committed to families and friends, and prepared for the workplace and the responsibilities of democratic citizenship. For many others, however, the obstacles in their path can impair their physical and emotional health, erode their motivation and ability to succeed in school and the workplace, and damage their human relationships.

Adolescents from the ages of 10 to 15 are being confronted with pressures to use legal and illegal drugs and weapons and to engage in premature, unprotected sexual behavior. Many are depressed, and one-third report that they have contemplated suicide. Others lack the compe-

From the *American Journal of Psychiatry* 154, no. 6 (June 1997): 6–12. Used by permission of the author and publisher.

tence to handle interpersonal conflict without re-sorting to violence. By age 17, about one-quarter of all adolescents have engaged in behaviors that are harmful to themselves and others, such as getting pregnant, using drugs, taking part in antisocial activity, and failing in school. Altogether, nearly half of American adolescents are at high or moderate risk of seriously damaging their life chances.

The technological and social changes of recent decades have provided many young people with remarkable material benefits and opportunities but have also brought formidable stresses and risks into the adolescent experience. These changes are most striking in relation to their effect on family configurations: high divorce rates, both parents working full time outside the home, and the growth of single-parent families. Indeed, about half of all young Americans will spend part or all of their childhood and adolescence living with only one parent. These problems are exacerbated by the erosion of neighborhood networks and other traditional social support systems. Children now spend less time in the company of adults than a few decades ago; more of their time is spent either watching television or on the street, generally with peers in age-segregated, largely unsupervised environments.

Such conditions are common among families of all economic strata, social backgrounds, and geographic areas. But these conditions are especially prevalent in neighborhoods of concentrated poverty, where young adolescents so often lack two crucial prerequisites for their healthy growth and development: a close relationship with at least one dependable adult and the perception that meaningful opportunities exist in the adult life course.

What are fundamental requirements for healthy adolescent development? Adolescents must 1) find a valued place in a constructive group; 2) learn how to form close, durable human relationships; 3) feel a sense of worth as individuals; 4) achieve a reliable basis for making informed choices; 5) know how to use the support systems available to them; 6) express constructive curiosity and exploratory behavior; 7) believe in a promising future with real opportunities; 8) find ways of being useful to others; 9) learn to live respectfully with others in circumstances of democratic pluralism; and 10) cultivate the inquiring and problem-solving skills that serve lifelong learning and adaptability.

Early adolescence—the phase during which young people are just beginning to engage in very risky behaviors but before damaging patterns have become firmly established—offers an excellent opportunity for intervention to prevent later casualties and promote successful adult lives. Over a 10-year span in which several major reports were published, the Carnegie Council on Adolescent Development recommended ways in which pivotal institutions can adapt to contemporary circumstances so as to meet the requirements for healthy adolescent development. These institutions are the family, schools, health care systems, community organizations, and the media.

Many current interventions on behalf of young adolescents are targeted to one problem behavior, such as drug abuse or teenage pregnancy. While targeted approaches are useful, they often do not take adequate account of two important findings from research: 1) serious problem behaviors tend to cluster in the same individual and reinforce one another, and 2) such behaviors often have common antecedents in childhood experience.

Therefore, generic approaches that address the fundamental requirements in a comprehensive way—a youth development strategy—are attractive. The pivotal, frontline institutions that have a daily impact on adolescent experience have a special opportunity and obligation to foster healthy lifestyles in childhood and adolescence, while taking into consideration the underlying factors that promote either positive or negative outcomes. For better and worse, these institutions have powerful effects on adolescent development.

DISEASE PREVENTION
IN ADOLESCENCE

Over the past few decades, the burden of adolescent illness has shifted from traditional causes of disease toward the "new morbidities" associated with health-damaging behaviors such as depression, suicide, substance use (alcohol, tobacco, and drugs), sexually transmitted diseases—including HIV and AIDS—and gun-related homicides.

Early adolescence is characterized by exploratory behavior in which the individual seeks adult-like roles and status. This is developmentally appropriate and socially adaptive, even though it involves some high-risk behavior. Yet such behavior can readily become dangerous and inflict damage, such as sexually transmitted diseases, death or trauma from violence, and disabling accidents related to alcohol. In addition, long-term consequences include cancer and cardiovascular disease, which are made more likely by high-calorie, high-fat dietary patterns, inadequate exercise, and heavy smoking. Destructive behaviors may constrict life options. For example, a teenage mother who drops out of junior or senior high school diminishes her prospects for lifetime employment and increases the risk of living in poverty, with the associated risks to her own health and the health of her child.

Early adolescence is a time of opportunity for the formation of healthy practices that have both short-term and long-term effects. Research of recent years has shown how the frontline institutions can provide accurate and personally meaningful information about health risks as well as foster the skills and motivation to avoid these risks and adopt healthy practices.

The health-related perceptions of adolescents can be helpful in motivating them to adopt healthy behavior. Their health concerns vary according to their gender, ethnicity, and socioeconomic status. Still, most are preoccupied with how they look, how they feel about themselves, their relationships to their peers, and educational pressures. Many adolescents are similarly concerned about substance abuse, sexuality, nutrition, and exercise. They tend wishfully to minimize the potentially damaging effects of high-risk behavior, in effect saying, "It can't happen to me." Such views are relevant to the design of social supports to adolescents, including clinical contacts. If health services are not user-friendly, they are not likely to be used by the individuals who need them most. By responding in meaningful ways to the interests, concerns, and perceptions of adolescents, health professionals can be helpful in ways that may have enduring value.

EDUCATION FOR HEALTH
IN EARLY ADOLESCENCE

There is an inextricable link between education and health. Adolescents in poor health have difficulty learning (e.g., substance abuse destroys attention to instruction). Conversely, young people fully engaged in learning tend to form health-promoting habits. Many adolescents arrive at middle school with inadequate skills to cope with their great transition to adulthood. Much of what they need goes beyond the traditional curriculum offered by the public school system.

Middle schools can play a crucial role in fostering health among young adolescents through the curriculum, school policy, and clear examples of health-promoting behavior. A substantial approach to education for health includes 1) teaching adequate nutrition in the classroom and offering a corresponding diet in the cafeteria; 2) smoke-free buildings and programs to help students and staff avoid tobacco; 3) education on the effects of alcohol and illicit drugs on the brain and other organs; 4) opportunities for exercise not just for students in varsity competition but for all in the school community; and 5) emphasis on safety and the prevention of violence, including violence inherently associated with drug dealing and the carrying of weapons.

In 1989, the Carnegie Council on Adolescent Development published an interdisciplinary analysis of middle-grade education entitled *Turning Points*. This task force recommended reforms that were aimed at creating health-promoting, developmentally appropriate middle schools. For example, by organizing smaller units out of large schools, these new units can function on a human scale and provide sustained individual attention to students in a supportive group setting. A mutual aid ethic can be fostered among teachers and students, e.g., through interdisciplinary team teaching, cooperative learning, and academically supervised community service. These units can stimulate thinking skills, especially through a substantial life sciences curriculum, and can offer life skills training, especially in decision making, constructive interpersonal relations, nonviolent problem solving, and the ability to take advantage of opportunities. Since three approaches (life skills curriculum, life skills training, and social supports) offer sufficient potential for healthy development, some further words are in order.

Life sciences curriculum. The life sciences tap into the natural curiosity that surges in early adolescence. Students are intensely interested in the changes taking place in their own bodies. The life sciences clarify growth and development and specifically address adolescent development. The study of human biology includes the scientific study of behavior and illuminates ways in which high-risk behavior, especially in adolescence, bears on health throughout the lifespan.

Life skills training. The vital knowledge obtained from the life sciences curriculum is crucial but needs augmentation to be effective in shaping behavior. Such information becomes more useful when combined with training in interpersonal and decision-making skills. These skills can be useful in a variety of ways, such as helping students to 1) resist pressure from peers or from the media to engage in high-risk behaviors, 2) increase their self-control, 3) acquire ways to reduce stress without engaging in dangerous activity, 4) learn how to make friends and overcome isolation, and 5) learn how to avoid violence. Research shows that such skills can be effectively taught by using systematic instruction and practice through role playing.

Social supports. Research evidence shows that social supports that involve dependable relationships and shared values can provide leverage in the promotion of adolescent health. Schools, community organizations, and health care providers can supplement the family by arranging constructive social support programs.

Taken together, the life sciences curriculum, life skills training, and social supports constitute effective facilitators of healthy adolescent development.

Categorical or targeted approaches are complementary to the generic comprehensive approach of educating youth for lifelong health. Four issues are selected for brief illustration here: responsible sexuality, preparation for parenthood, prevention of youth violence, and prevention of drug abuse. Clearly, other problems also deserve attention and none more so than mental health, particularly depression.

RESPONSIBLE SEXUALITY

Early adolescence is not a time to become seriously engaged in sexual activity, yet adolescents are sorely tempted to do so. They get conflicting messages about desirable body image and appropriate sexual behavior, especially from the media and from peers. They badly need to understand sexuality, including the dynamics of intimate relationships, when to become sexually active, the biological process of conception, and the risks of contracting sexually transmitted diseases, including HIV infection.

Young adolescents get their information about sexuality primarily from peers but also from family, school, television, and movies. Peer information is often inaccurate; for example, the assumption is widespread that "everybody does it." This assumption applies to a variety of risky behaviors such as smoking and alcohol use. Families and schools are in a better position to provide accurate information and health-protective choices. Adolescents who rate communication with their parents as poor are likely to initiate sex, smoking, and drinking earlier than peers who rate communication with their parents as good. However, parents need help in becoming well informed about reproductive health and in overcoming embarrassment about discussing sex with their children.

Adolescents need information about human sexuality and reproduction before they become sexually active. Organized efforts to meet these needs should begin not later than early adolescence in middle schools and in community organizations. Information about preventing the transmission of the AIDS virus is now a crucial although controversial part of health education for young adolescents. Adolescents typically do not know that the incubation period for AIDS can be a decade and that mothers can transmit the virus to their offspring. Interventions should identify the emotionally charged situations that adolescents are likely to encounter and provide life skills training on how to manage or avoid those situations of high risk. Schools, families, and the media, through health-promoting knowledge and skills, can contribute to this effort.

Even so, good information and skills may not be enough; motivation for constructive choices is crucial. Determining how to bring this about remains a formidable task. A recent Institute of Medicine study concluded that fewer than 25 programs to reduce unintended pregnancy have been carefully evaluated; of these programs, about half were found to be effective in the short term. This is one of the many indications that research in this field has not been given adequate priority.

The vast majority of adolescent pregnancies are unintended. Education for health must make it clear that to be sufficiently mature to raise a family, an individual not only must be knowl-

edgeable about reproductive information, birth control, and the prevention of unwanted pregnancies but also must be aware that raising a family brings responsibilities as well as joys and that it takes a lot of learning and coping to become a reliable, competent parent.

PREPARATION FOR PARENTHOOD

Preparing adolescents for the time when they form families of their own is a neglected aspect of healthy development. All too many adolescents become pregnant only to find later that they are poorly prepared for the challenge of raising a child. The fulfillment of each child's potential requires a profound parental investment of time, energy, caregiving, resources, persistence, and resilience in coping with adversity.

The 1994 Carnegie report, *Starting Points: Meeting the Needs of Our Youngest Children,* emphasized the importance of preparing adolescents for responsible parenthood. When people make an informed, thoughtful commitment to have children, they are more likely to be good parents, and their children are more likely to develop in healthy ways. By the same token, when young parents are unprepared for the opportunities and responsibilities of parenthood, the risks to their children are formidable.

Therefore, *Starting Points* recommended a substantial expansion of efforts to educate young people about parenthood. Families are the first source of such education, but schools, places of worship, and community organizations can also be useful. Performing community service in child care centers can provide a valuable learning experience for adolescents about what is required to raise young children. Age-appropriate education about parenthood should begin in late elementary school but no later than early adolescence. It can be a part of either a life sciences curriculum or health education. In either case, it must be substantial and meaningful to adolescents.

PREVENTION OF YOUTH VIOLENCE

Nearly one million adolescents between the ages of 12 and 19 are victims of violent crimes each year. This problem has been accelerating, yet evidence is emerging on ways to prevent adolescent violence. To be effective, prevention requires a comprehensive approach that addresses both individual and social factors. Optimally, this would build on generic approaches that meet essential requirements for healthy adolescent development through developmentally appropriate schools, supportive families, and youth-oriented community organizations. In addition, specific interventions that target youth violence can enhance adolescents' ability to deal with conflict in nonviolent ways. Policy changes, such as implementing stronger measures to restrict the availability of guns, are urgently needed, especially in light of the growing propensity of juveniles to use guns, even semiautomatic weapons.

One promising strategy for preventing youth violence is the teaching of conflict resolution skills as part of health education in elementary and middle schools. Research indicates that conflict resolution programs can reduce violence; best results are achieved if these skills are embedded in long-term, comprehensive programs that address the multiple risk factors that lead to empty, shattered lives, which offer little recourse except violence. Serious, in-depth conflict resolution training over extended periods is increasingly important in a culture that is saturated with media and street violence. Supervised practice of conflict-resolution skills is important. Assertiveness, taught as a social skill, helps young people learn how to resist unwanted pressures and intimidation, resolve conflicts nonviolently, and make sound decisions about the use of weapons.

High-risk youth in impoverished communities urgently need social support networks and life skills training. Both can be provided in schools and school-related health centers as well as in community organizations, including church-related youth activities and sports programs. These programs work best by building enduring relationships with adults as well as with constructive peers. Such an approach offers alternatives to violent groups by providing a sense of belonging, a source of enjoyable activity, a perception of opportunity, a basis for mentoring, and a chance to prepare for social roles that earn respect.

PREVENTION OF DRUG ABUSE

Drugs are cheaper and more plentiful today than they were a decade ago. The United States has the highest addiction rates in its history, and the judicial system is clogged with drug-related cases. Adolescents consider alcohol and other drugs less harmful today than they did a few years ago. For many, the use of drugs, even the sale of drugs, constitutes an attractive path to what they perceive as adult status. Society has been searching desperately for answers. Meanwhile, serious research efforts oriented to prevention have gone through several "generations" of insight, and some promising evidence is at hand.

Community-wide preventive interventions in a few places have substantially diminished the use of "gateway" substances (tobacco, alcohol, and marijuana) in early adolescence, concomitantly enhancing personal and social competence. These efforts have used rigorous research designs on a long-term basis. Several preventive programs for young adolescents have been shown to reduce drug use. The learning of life skills has been effective in the prevention of cigarette smoking and alcohol and marijuana use if applied with sufficient intensity and duration. The systematic, explicit teaching of these skills can contribute to personal competence and provide constructive alternatives to health-damaging behavior.

When booster sessions are provided in high school, the preventive effects of early interventions are sustained through the senior year. The prevention of cigarette smoking is very important, both because of its "gateway" function and the many pathologies throughout the lifespan that flow from this addiction in early adolescence. The well-designed, community-wide interventions are encouraging in this respect. Their success suggests that social norms on cigarette use can be changed by systematic, intensive, and long-term efforts. A striking example is the recent decline in smoking reported by African American adolescents.

Beyond the targeted approach to substance abuse, parents, teachers, and health professionals should understand that adolescent immersion in high-risk behavior is exacerbated by developmental problems such as low self-esteem, poor performance in school, depression, or inability to make deliberate, informed decisions. Using drugs may be a way of feeling mature, courageous, sophisticated, or otherwise grown-up. Disadvantaged youth need to be shown how individuals from comparable backgrounds have done well in the mainstream economy—in contrast to the putatively successful drug dealers who are involved in crime and violence. The fostering of family-augmenting functions by community organizations and health-social services can provide accurate, pertinent information and supportive human relationships that facilitate healthy development even in circumstances of adversity.

STRENGTHENING HEALTH SERVICES FOR ADOLESCENTS

A comprehensive study of adolescent health, conducted by the U.S. Office of Technology Assessment in 1991, pointed to serious barriers to establishing developmentally appropriate health services for adolescents. Current services are particularly lacking in disease prevention and health-promotion services. Recent studies and innovations show what can be done, but there is a long way to go.

One in seven American adolescents has no health insurance coverage; many more have very little. Within the Medicaid population, only one-third of eligible adolescents are currently covered because of funding constraints. Health insurance, even when provided by employers for working families, often excludes their adolescent children.

As managed care spreads rapidly throughout the United States, it is essential to include explicit provisions for coverage of adolescents. This will be especially important to monitor as states increasingly enroll their Medicaid population in managed care plans. Managed care organizations can contract with school-based health centers that serve adolescents. Some community health and school-based adolescent health centers have shown how various barriers can be overcome so that adolescents can get adequate care during these years that are crucially formative for healthy lifestyles.

At present, there is a shortage of experienced and well-trained health providers who can sensitively treat the health problems of adolescents. The conjunction of psychiatry with pediatrics and internal medicine is important in this context.

One promising approach to filling the service gap for adolescents is manifested in school-related health facilities, either at or near the school, and functionally integrated with respect to curriculum and accessibility. Such facilities have demonstrated their ability to deal with acute medical problems, including mental health. They have strong potential for disease prevention and health promotion.

Since students often request help with feelings of depression, loneliness, and anxiety, these centers must provide mental health services. Treatment of depression can represent an important opportunity to prevent further problems, for example, self-medication that leads to substance abuse and addiction.

CONCLUSIONS

The early adolescent years have become the starting point for an upsurge of health-compromising behaviors that have lifelong consequences. Yet early adolescence presents a neglected and overlooked opportunity for health promotion. The interest of adolescents in their own developing bodies can be a potent force for building healthy lifestyles of enduring significance. The best chance to fulfill this promise lies in enhancing understanding of adolescent development among health care professionals, schools, community organizations, families, and media.

A crucial ingredient is the guiding and motivating influence of caring adults. Information and skills are necessary but not sufficient to shape the behavior of adolescents unless they are motivated to put them to use in the service of their own health. This requires the protection and support of families and health professionals who are trained to work effectively with adolescents as distinctive individuals. Health policy makers must find ways to improve adolescents' access to health care through dependable primary care providers and school-linked preventive services, including services for mental health.

A comprehensive health-promotion strategy would optimally involve a community-wide commitment from the full range of institutions with which adolescents are involved. Such a commitment to adolescents is potentially a powerful means of shaping young lives in healthy, constructive patterns of lifelong learning and adaptation. This approach is highly congruent with Mel Sabshin's career-long vision of research, education, and care for healthy development and social responsibility.

David A. Hamburg is President Emeritus of the Carnegie Corporation of New York and former Chair of Psychiatry at Stanford University School of Medicine. In 1996, he received the Presidential Medal of Freedom, the nation's highest civilian honor, and in 1998, he received the Public Welfare Medal from the National Academy of Sciences.

QUESTIONS FOR REFLECTION

1. Reflect on your experiences as an adolescent. In what ways did your school experiences help you to cope with the stresses associated with this transition period?
2. What concerns might some teachers, parents, and community members raise about Hamburg's call for schools to emphasize a life sciences curriculum, life skills training, and social support? How might Hamburg respond to these concerns?
3. What evidence indicates that some adolescents in your local community may not be on the path toward healthy adult development?

Erik Erikson's Developmental Stages:
A Healthy Personality for Every Child

MIDCENTURY WHITE HOUSE CONFERENCE
ON CHILDREN AND YOUTH

ABSTRACT: *This article is based on a paper ("Growth and Crises of the 'Healthy Personality' ") Erik Erikson and his wife, Joan Erikson, presented at the Midcentury White House Conference on Children and Youth in 1950. Erikson's model for the psychosocial development of human beings (see Table 3.1) includes eight stages, from infancy to old age. For each stage a "psychosocial crisis" is central to the individual's emotional and social growth, and this crisis is expressed in polar terms—for example, basic trust versus basic mistrust during the infancy stage. Successful resolution of the crises that come with each life cycle stage increases the individual's overall ego strength, which is characterized by eight "virtues": hope, will, purpose, competence, fidelity, love, care, and wisdom.*

Many attempts have been made to describe the attributes of healthy personality. They have been put succinctly as the ability to love and the ability to work. A recent review of the literature suggests that the individual with a healthy personality is one who actively masters his environment, shows a unity of personality, and is able to perceive the world and himself correctly. Clearly, none of these criteria applies to a child. It seemed to us best, then, to present for the Conference's consideration an outline that has the merit of indicating at one and the same time the main course of personality development and the attributes of a healthy personality.

This developmental outline was worked out by Erik H. Erikson, a psychologist and practicing psychoanalyst who has made anthropological field studies and has had much experience with children. It is an analysis that derives from psychological theory, to which is added knowledge from the fields of child development and cultural anthropology. The whole is infused with the author's insight and personal philosophy.

In each stage of child development, the author says, there is a central problem that has to be solved, temporarily at least, if the child is to proceed with vigor and confidence to the next stage. These problems, these conflicts of feeling and desire, are never solved in entirety. Each shift in experience and environment presents them in a new form. It is held, however, that each type of conflict appears in its purest, most unequivocal form at a particular stage of child development, and that if the problem is well solved at that time the basis for progress to the next stage is well laid.

In a sense personality development follows biological principles. Biologists have found that everything that grows has a groundplan that is laid out at its start. Out of this groundplan the parts arise, each part having its time of special ascendancy. Together these parts form a functioning whole. If a part does not arise at its appointed time, it will never be able to form fully, since the moment for the rapid outgrowth of some other part will have arrived. Moreover, a part that misses its time of ascendancy or is severely damaged during its formative period is apt to doom, in turn, the whole hierarchy of organs. Proper rate and normal sequence is necessary if functional harmony is to be secured.

From a digest of the Fact Finding Report to the Midcentury White House Conference on Children and Youth, 1951, 6–25.

TABLE 3.1
Erikson's Eight Stages of Psychosocial Development

Stages	Approximate Age	Important Event	Description
1. Basic trust versus basic mistrust	Birth to 12–18 months	Feeding	The infant must form a first loving, trusting relationship with the caregiver or develop a sense of mistrust.
2. Autonomy versus shame/doubt	18 months to 3 years	Toilet training	The child's energies are directed toward the development of physical skills, including walking, grasping, controlling the sphincter. The child learns control but may develop shame and doubt if not handled well.
3. Initiative versus guilt	3 to 6 years	Independence	The child continues to become more assertive and to take more initiative but may be too forceful, which can lead to guilt feelings.
4. Industry versus inferiority	6 to 12 years	School	The child must deal with demands to learn new skills or risk a sense of inferiority, failure, and incompetence.
5. Identity versus role confusion	Adolescence	Peer relationships	The teenager must achieve identity in occupation, gender roles, politics, and religion.
6. Intimacy versus isolation	Young adulthood	Love relationships	The young adult must develop intimate relationships or suffer feelings of isolation.
7 Generativity versus stagnation	Middle adulthood	Parenting	Each adult must find some way to satisfy and support the next generation.
8. Ego integrity versus despair	Late adulthood	Reflection on and acceptance of one's life	The culmination is a sense of acceptance of oneself as one is and a sense of fulfillment.

Source: From Lester A. Lefton, *Psychology*, 5th edition. Copyright © 1994 by Allyn and Bacon. Reprinted by permission.

Personality represents the most complicated functioning of the human organism and does not consist of parts in the organic sense. Instead of the development of organs, there is the development of locomotor, sensory, and social capacities and the development of individual modes of dealing with experience. Nevertheless, proper rate and proper sequence are as important here as in physical growth, and functional harmony is achieved only if development proceeds according to the groundplan.

In all this it is encouraging for parents and others who have children in charge to realize that in the sequence of his most personal experiences, just as in the sequence of organ formation, the child can be trusted to follow inner laws of development, and needs from adults chiefly love, encouragement, and guidance.

The operation of biological laws is seen, also, in the fact that there is constant interplay between organism and environment and that problems of personality functioning are never solved once and for all. Each of the components of the healthy personality to be described below is present in some form from the beginning, and the struggle to maintain it continues throughout life.

For example, a baby may show something like "autonomy" or a will of his own in the way he angrily tries to free his head when he is tightly held. Nevertheless, it is not until the second year of life that he begins to experience the whole conflict between being an autonomous creature and a dependent one. It is not until then that he is ready for a decisive encounter with the people around him, and it is not until then that they feel called upon to train him or otherwise curb his free-questing spirit. The struggle goes on for months and finally, under favorable circumstances, some compromise between dependence and independence is reached that gives the child a sense of well-being.

The sense of autonomy thus achieved is not a permanent possession, however. There will be other challenges to that sense and other solutions more in keeping with later stages of development. Nevertheless, once established at two or three years of age, this early sense of autonomy will be a bulwark against later frustrations and will permit the emergence of the next developmental problem at a time that is most favorable for its solution.

So it is with all the personality components to be described. They appear in miniature early in life. The struggle to secure them against tendencies to act otherwise comes to a climax at a time determined by emergence of the necessary physical and mental abilities. There are, throughout life, other challenges and other responses but they are seldom so serious and seldom so decisive as those of the critical years.

In all this, it must be noted in addition, there is not the strict dichotomy that the analysis given below suggests. With each of the personality components to be described, it is not all or nothing: trust *or* mistrust, autonomy *or* doubt, and so on. Instead, each individual has some of each. His health of personality is determined by the preponderance of the favorable over the unfavorable, as well as by what manner of compensations he develops to cope with his disabilities.

THE SENSE OF TRUST

The component of the healthy personality that is the first to develop is the sense of trust. The crucial time for its emergence is the first year of life. As with the other personality components to be described, the sense of trust is not something that develops independent of other manifestations of growth. It is not that the infant learns how to use his body for purposeful movement, learns to recognize people and objects around him, and also develops a sense of trust. Rather the concept "sense of trust" is a shortcut expression intended to convey the characteristic flavor of all the child's satisfying experiences at this early age. Or, to say it another way, this psychological formulation serves to condense, summarize, and synthesize the most important underlying changes that give meaning to the infant's concrete and diversified experience.

Trust can exist only in relation to something. Consequently a sense of trust cannot develop until the infant is old enough to be aware of objects and persons and to have some feeling that he is a separate individual. At about three months of age a baby is likely to smile if somebody comes close and talks to him. This shows that he is aware of the approach of the other person, that pleasurable sensations are aroused. If, however, the person moves too quickly or speaks too sharply the baby may look apprehensive or cry. He will not "trust" the unusual situation but will have a feeling of uneasiness, of mistrust, instead.

Experiences connected with feeding are a prime source for the development of trust. At around four months of age a hungry baby will grow quiet and show signs of pleasure at the sound of an approaching footstep, anticipating (trusting) that he will be held and fed. This repeated experience of being hungry, seeing food, receiving food, and feeling relieved and comforted assures the baby that the world is a dependable place.

Later experiences, starting at around five months of age, add another dimension to the sense of trust. Through endless repetitions of attempts to grasp for and hold objects, the baby is finally successful in controlling and adapting his movements in such a way as to reach his goal. Through these and other feats of muscular coordination the baby is gradually able to trust his own body to do his bidding.

The baby's trust-mistrust problem is symbolized in the game of peek-a-boo. In this game, which babies begin to like at about four months of age, an object disappears and then reappears. There is a slightly tense expression on the baby's face when the object goes away; its reappearance is greeted by wriggles and smiles. Only gradually does the baby learn that things continue to exist even though he does not see them, that there is order and stability in his universe. Peek-a-boo proves the point by playful repetition.

Studies of mentally ill individuals and observations of infants who have been grossly deprived of affection suggest that trust is an early-formed and important element in the healthy personality. Psychiatrists find again and again that the most serious illnesses occur in patients who have been sorely neglected or abused or otherwise deprived of love in infancy. Similarly, it is a common finding of psychological and social investigators that individuals diagnosed as a "psychopathic personality" were so unloved in infancy that they have no reason to trust the human race and, therefore, no sense of responsibility toward their fellow men.

Observations of infants brought up in emotionally unfavorable institutions or removed to hospitals with inadequate facilities for psychological care support these findings. A recent report says: "Infants under six months of age who have been in an institution for some time present a well-defined picture. The outstanding features are listlessness, emaciation and pallor, relative immobility, quietness, unresponsiveness to stimuli like a smile or a coo, indifferent appetite, failure to gain weight property despite ingestion of diets which are entirely adequate, frequent stools, poor sleep, an appearance of unhappiness, proneness to febrile episodes, absence of sucking habits."[1]

Another investigation of children separated from their mothers at six to twelve months and not provided with an adequate substitute comes to much the same conclusion: "The emotional tone is one of apprehension and sadness, there is withdrawal from the environment amounting to rejection of it, there is no attempt to contact a stranger and no brightening if a stranger contacts him. Activities are retarded and the child often sits or lies inert in a dazed stupor. Insomnia is common and lack of appetite universal. Weight is lost, and the child becomes prone to current infections."[2]

Most significant for our present point, these reactions are most likely to occur in children who up to the time of separation at six to nine months of age had a happy relation with their mothers, while those whose relations were unhappy are relatively unaffected. It is at about this age that the struggle between trusting and mistrusting the world comes to a climax, for it is then that the child first perceives clearly that he and his environment are things apart. That at this time formerly happy infants should react so badly to separation suggests, indeed, that they had a faith which now was shattered. Happily, there is usually spectacular change for the better when the maternal presence and love are restored.

It is probably unnecessary to describe the numerous ways in which stimuli from without and from within may cause an infant distress. Birth is believed by some experts to be a painful experience for the baby. Until fairly recently doctors were likely to advise that babies be fed on schedule and that little attention be paid to their cries of hunger at other times. Many infants spent many of the waking hours of the first four months doubled up with colic. All of them had to be bathed and dressed at stated times, whether they liked it or not. Add to these usual discomforts the fact that some infants are handled rather roughly by their parents, that others hear angry words and loud voices, and that a few are really mistreated, and it will not be difficult to understand why some infants may feel the world is a place that cannot be trusted.

In most primitive societies and in some sections of our own society the attention accorded infants is more in line with natural processes. In such societies separation from the mother is less abrupt, in that for some time after birth the baby is kept close to the warmth and comfort of its mother's body and at its least cry the breast is produced. Throughout infancy the baby is surrounded by people who are ready to feed it, fondle it, otherwise comfort it at a moment's notice. Moreover, these ministrations are given spontaneously, wholeheartedly, and without that element of nervous concern that may characterize the efforts of young mothers made self-conscious and insecure by our scientific age.

We must not exaggerate, however. Most infants in our society, too, find smiles and the comfort of mother's soft, warm body accompanying their intake of food, whether from breast or bottle. Coldness, wetness, pain, and boredom—for each misfortune there is prompt and comforting relief. As their own bodies come to be more dependable, there is added to the pleasures of increasing sensory response and motor control the pleasure of the mother's encouragement.

Moreover, babies are rather hardy creatures and are not to be discouraged by inexperienced mother's mistakes. Even a mother cat has to learn, and the kittens endure gracefully her first clumsy efforts to carry them away from danger. Then, too, psychologists tell us that mothers create a sense of trust in their children not by the particular techniques they employ but by the sensitiveness with which they respond to the children's needs and by their over-all attitude.

For most infants, then, a sense of trust is not difficult to come by. It is the most important element in the personality. It emerges at the most vulnerable period of a child's life. Yet it is the least likely to suffer harm, perhaps because both nature and culture work toward making mothers most maternal at that time.

THE SENSE OF AUTONOMY

The sense of trust once firmly established, the struggle for the next component of the healthy personality begins. The child is now twelve to fifteen months old. Much of his energy for the next two years will center around asserting that he is a human being with a mind and will of his own. A list of some of the items discussed by Spock under the heading, "The One Year Old," will serve to remind us of the characteristics of that age and the problems they create for parents. "Feeling his oats." "The passion to explore." "He gets more dependent and more independent at the same time." "Arranging the house for the wandering baby." "Avoiding accidents." "How do you make him leave certain things alone?" "Dropping and throwing things." "Biting humans." "The small child who won't stay in bed at night."

What is at stake throughout the struggle of these years is the child's sense of autonomy, the sense that he is an independent human being and yet one who is able to use the help and guidance of others in important matters. This stage of development becomes decisive for the ratio between love and hate, between cooperation and willfulness, for freedom of self-expression and its renunciation in the make-up of the individual. The favorable outcome is self-control without loss of self-esteem. The unfavorable outcome is doubt and shame.

Before a sense of autonomy can develop, the sense of trust must be reasonably well established and must continue to pervade the child's feeling about himself and his world. Only so dare he respond with confidence to his new-felt desire to assert himself boldly, to appropriate demandingly, and to hurl away without let or hindrance.

As with the previous stage, there is a physiological basis for this characteristic behavior. This is the period of muscle-system maturation and the consequent ability (and doubly felt inability) to coordinate a number of highly conflicting action patterns, such as those of holding on and letting go, walking, talking, and manipulating objects in ever more complicated ways. With these abilities come pressing needs to use them: to handle, to explore, to seize and to drop, to withhold and to expel. And, with all, there is the dominant will, the insistent "Me do" that defies help and yet is so easily frustrated by the inabilities of the hands and feet.

For a child to develop this sense of self-reliance and adequacy that Erikson calls autonomy, it is necessary that he experience over and over again that he is a person who is permitted to make choices. He has to have the right to choose, for example, whether to sit or whether to stand, whether to approach a visitor or to lean against his mother's knee, whether to accept offered food or reject it, whether to use the toilet or to wet his pants. At the same time he must learn some of the boundaries of self-determination. He inevitably finds that there are walls he cannot climb, that there are objects out of reach, that, above all, there are innumerable commands enforced by powerful adults. His experience is much too small to enable him to know what he can and cannot do with respect to the physical environment, and it will take him years to discover the boundaries that mark off what is approved, what is tolerated, and what is forbidden by his elders whom he finds so hard to understand.

As problems of this period, some psychologists have concentrated particularly on bladder and bowel control. Emphasis is put upon the need for care in both timing and mode of training children in the performance of these functions. If parental control is too rigid or if training is started too early, the child is robbed of his opportunity to develop, by his own free choice, gradual control of the contradictory impulses of retention and elimination.

To others who study child development, this matter of toilet training is but a prototype of all the problems of this age-range. The sphincters are only part of the whole muscle system, with its general ambiguity of rigidity and relaxation, of flexion and extension. To hold and to relinquish refer to much more than the bowels. As the child acquires the ability to stand on his two feet and move around, he delineates his world as me and you. He can be astonishingly pliable once he has decided that he wants to do what he is supposed to do, but there is no reliable formula for assuring that he will relinquish when he wants to hold on.

The matter of mutual regulation between parent and child (for fathers have now entered the picture to an extent that was rare in the earlier state) now faces its severest task. The task is indeed one to challenge the most resourceful and the most calm adult. Firmness is necessary, for the child must be protected against the potential anarchy of his as yet untrained sense of discrimination. Yet the adult must back him up in his wish to "stand on his own feet," lest he be overcome by shame that he has exposed himself foolishly and by doubt in his self-worth. Perhaps the most constructive rule a parent can follow is to forbid only what "really matters" and, in such forbidding, to be clear and consistent.

Shame and doubt are emotions that many primitive peoples and some of the less sophisticated individuals in our own society utilize in training children. Shaming exploits the child's sense of being small. Used to excess it misses its objective and may result in open shamelessness, or, at least, in the child's secret determination to do as he pleases when not observed. Such defiance is a normal, even healthy response to demands that a child consider himself, his body, his needs, or his wishes evil and dirty and that he regard those who pass judgment as infallible. Young delinquents may be produced by this means, and others who are oblivious to the opinion of society.

Those who would guide the growing child wisely, then, will avoid shaming him and avoid causing him to doubt that he is a person of worth. They will be firm and tolerant with him so that he can rejoice in being a person of independence and can grant independence to others. As to detailed procedures, it is impossible to prescribe, not only because we do not know and because every situation is different, but also because the kind and degree of autonomy that parents are able to grant their small children depends on feelings about themselves that they derive from society. Just as the child's sense of trust is a reflection of the mother's sturdy and realistic faith, so the child's sense of autonomy is a reflection of the parents' personal dignity. Such appears to be the teaching of the comparative study of cultures.

Personal autonomy, independence of the individual, is an especially outstanding feature of the

American way of life. American parents, accordingly, are in a particularly favorable position to transmit the sense of autonomy to their children. They themselves resent being bossed, being pushed around; they maintain that everybody has the right to express his opinion and to be in control of his affairs. More easily than people who live according to an authoritarian pattern, they can appreciate a little child's vigorous desire to assert his independence and they can give him the leeway he needs in order to grow up into the upstanding, look-you-in-the-eye kind of individual that Americans admire.

It is not only in early childhood, however, that this attitude toward growing children must be maintained. As was said at the outset, these components of the healthy personality cannot be established once and for all. The period of life in which they first come into being is the most crucial, it is true. But threats to their maintenance occur throughout life. Not only parents, then, but everybody who has significant contact with children and young people must respect their desire for self-assertion, help them hold it within bounds, and avoid treating them in ways that arouse shame or doubt.

This attitude toward children, toward all people, must be maintained in institutional arrangements as well. Great differences in educational and economic opportunity and in access to the law, discrimination of all kinds are threats to this ingredient of mental health. So, too, may be the overmechanization of our society, the depersonalization of human relations that is likely to accompany large-scale endeavor of all kinds.

Parents, as well as children, are affected by these matters. In fact, parents' ability to grant children the kind of autonomy Americans think desirable depends in part on the way they are treated as employees and citizens. Throughout, the relation must be such as affirms personal dignity. Much of the shame and doubt aroused in children result from the indignity and uncertainty that are an expression of parents' frustration in love and work. Special attention must be paid to all these matters, then, if we are to avoid destroying the autonomy that Americans have always set store by.

THE SENSE OF INITIATIVE

Having become sure, for the time being, that he is a person in his own right and having enjoyed that feeling for a year or so, the child of four or five wants to find out what kind of person he can be. To be any particular kind of person, he sees clearly, involves being able to do particular kinds of things. So he observes with keen attention what all manner of interesting adults do (his parents, the milkman, the truck driver, and so on), tries to imitate their behavior, and yearns for a share in their activities.

This is the period of enterprise and imagination, an ebullient, creative period when fantasy substitutes for literal execution of desires and the meagerest equipment provides material for high imaginings. It is a period of intrusive, vigorous learning, learning that leads away from the child's own limitations into future possibilities. There is intrusion into other people's bodies by physical attack, into other people's ears and minds by loud and aggressive talking. There is intrusion into space by vigorous locomotion and intrusion into the unknown by consuming curiosity.

By this age, too, conscience has developed. The child is no longer guided only by outsiders; there is installed within him a voice that comments on his deeds, and warns and threatens. Close attention to the remarks of any child of this age will confirm this statement. Less obvious, however, are experts' observations that children now begin to feel guilty for mere thoughts, for deeds that have been imagined but never executed. This, they say, is the explanation for the characteristic nightmares of this age period and for the over-reaction to slight punishment.

The problem to be worked out in this stage of development, accordingly, is how to will without too great a sense of guilt. The fortunate outcome of the struggle is a sense of initiative. Failure to win through to that outcome leaves the personality overburdened, and possibly overrestricted by guilt.

It is easy to see how the child's developing sense of initiative may be discouraged. So many of the projects dreamed up at this age are of a kind which cannot be permitted that the child may come to feel he is faced by a universal "No." In addition he finds that many of the projects are impossible of execution and others, even if not forbidden, fail to win the approval of the adults whom he has come to love. Moreover, since he does not always distinguish clearly between actuality and fantasy, his over-zealous conscience may disapprove of even imaginary deeds.

It is very important, therefore, for healthy personality development that much leeway and encouragement be given to the child's show of enterprise and imagination and that punishment be kept at a minimum. Boys and girls at this stage are extraordinarily appreciative of any convincing promise that someday they will be able to do things as well as, or maybe better than, father and mother. They enjoy competition (especially if they can win) and insistence on goal; they get great pleasure from conquest. They need numerous examples of the kinds of roles adults assume, and they need a chance to try them out in play.

The ability that is in the making is that of selecting social goals and persevering in the attempt to reach them.

If enterprise and imagination are too greatly curbed, if severe rebukes accompany the frequently necessary denial of permission to carry out desires, a personality may result that is overconstricted. Such a personality cannot live up to its inner capacities for imagination, feelings, or performance, though it may overcompensate by immense activity and find relaxation impossible.

Constriction of personality is a self-imposed constriction, an act of the child's over-zealous conscience. "If I may not do this, I will not even think it," says conscience, "for even thinking it is dangerous." Resentment and bitterness and a vindictive attitude toward the world that forces the restriction may accompany this decision, however, and become unconscious but function-

ing parts of the personality. Such, at least, is the warning of psychiatrists who have learned to know the inmost feelings of emotionally handicapped children and adults.

This developmental stage has great assets as well as great dangers. At no time in life is the individual more ready to learn avidly and quickly, to become big in the sense of sharing obligation and performance. If during this preschool period the child can get some sense of the various roles and functions that he can perform as an adult, he will be ready to progress joyfully to the next stage, in which he will find pleasurable accomplishment in activities less fraught with fantasy and fear.

There is a lesson in this for later periods of personality development as well. As has been said before, these conflicts that come to a head at particular periods of a child's life are not settled once and for all. The sense of initiative, then, is one that must be continually fostered, and great care must be taken that youngsters and young people do not have to feel guilty for having dared to dream.

Just as we Americans prize autonomy, so too do we prize initiative; in fact, we regard it as the cornerstone of our economic system. There is much in the present industrial and political mode of life that may discourage initiative, that may make a young person think he had best pull in his horns. What these tendencies are and what they may do to youngsters and to their parents, who too must feel free if they are to cultivate the sense of initiative in their children, is a subject that warrants much serious discussion.

THE SENSE OF ACCOMPLISHMENT

The three stages so far described probably are the most important for personality development. With a sense of trust, a sense of autonomy, and a sense of initiative achieved, progress through the later stages is pretty well assured. Whether this is because children who have a good environment in their early years are likely to continue to be so favored, or whether it is because they have attained such strength of personality that they can successfully handle later difficulties, research has not yet made clear. We do know that nearly all children who get a good start continue to develop very well, and we know that some of those who start off poorly continue to be handicapped. Observations of this sort seem to support psychological theory in the conclusion that personality is pretty well set by about six years of age. Since, however, some children develop into psychologically healthy adults in spite of a bad start, and since some who start well run into difficulties later, it is clear that much research is needed before this conclusion can be accepted as wholly correct.

To return to the developmental analysis, the fourth stage, which begins somewhere around six years of age and extends over five or six years, has as its achievement what Erikson calls the sense of industry. Perhaps "sense of accomplishment" would make the meaning clearer. At any rate, this is the period in which preoccupation with fantasy subsides, and the child wants to be engaged in real tasks that he can carry through to completion. As with other developmental stages, there are foreshadowings of this kind of interest long before six years of age. Moreover, in some societies and in some parts of our own society children are trained very early to perform socially useful tasks. The exact age is not the point at issue. What is to be pointed out is that children, after a period characterized by exuberant imagination, want to settle down to learning exactly how to do things and how to do them well.

In contrast to the preceding stages and to the succeeding ones, this stage does not consist of a swing from a violent inner upheaval to a new mastery. Under reasonably favorable circumstances this is a period of calm, steady growth, especially if the problems of the previous stages have been well worked through. Despite its unspectacular character, this is a very important period, for in it is laid a firm basis for responsible citizenship. It is during this period that children acquire not only knowledge and skills that make for good workmanship but also the ability to cooperate and play fair and otherwise follow the rules of the larger social game.

The chief danger of this period is the presence of conditions that may lead to the development of a sense of inadequacy and inferiority. This may be the outcome if the child has not yet achieved a sense of initiative, or if his experiences at home have not prepared him for entering school happily, or if he finds school a place where his previous accomplishments are disregarded or his latent abilities are not challenged. Even with a good start the child may later lapse into discouragement and lack of interest if at home or school his individual needs are overlooked—if too much is expected of him, or if he is made to feel that achievement is beyond his ability.

It is most important for health of personality, therefore, that schools be conducted well, that methods and courses of instruction be such as will give every child the feeling of successful accomplishment. Autobiographies of juvenile delinquents show time and again a boy who hated school—hated the fact that he was marked out as stupid or awkward, as one who was not as good as the rest. Some such boys find in jobs the sense of accomplishment they miss at school and consequently give up their delinquent ways. Others, however, are handicapped in job finding and keeping by the very fact that in school they did not develop the sense of industry; hence they have work failure added to their other insecurities. Nor is delinquency the only or the most likely outcome of lack of success in school. Many children respond in a quieter way, by passive acceptance of their inferiority. Psychologically they are perhaps even more harmed.

Our Puritan tradition maintains that children will not work except under the spur of competition, so we tend to fear the suggestion that all should succeed. To help children develop a sense of accomplishment does not mean, however, merely giving all of them good marks and passing them on to the next grade. Children need and want real achievement. How to help them secure it, despite differences in native capacity and differences in emotional development, is one of the school's most serious challenges.

School, of course, is not the only place in which children at this stage of development can secure the sense of industry. In work at home there are many opportunities for a child to get a feeling of mastery and worthwhile endeavor. Rural youth groups and their urban counterparts cater to this need, and many recreation programs put as much emphasis on work as on play. School, however, is the legally constituted arrangement for giving instruction to the young, so it is upon teachers that the professional responsibility for helping all children achieve a sense of industry and accomplishment rests.

In addition to aiding personality development in this way, teachers have many opportunities for reconfirming their pupils' sense of trust, autonomy, and initiative or for encouraging its growth in children who have been somewhat hampered by previous life experiences. Teachers cannot work alone, of course, either in aiding a child in the development of new capacities or in strengthening old ones. Jointly with parents and others they can do much, not only for children of already healthy personality but also for many whose development has been handicapped.

THE SENSE OF IDENTITY

With the onset of adolescence another period of personality development begins. As is well known, adolescence is a period of storm and stress for many young people, a period in which previous certainties are questioned and previous continuities no longer relied upon. Physiological changes and rapid physical growth provide the somatic base for the turmoil and indecision. It may be that cultural factors also play a part, for it has been observed that adolescence is less upsetting in some societies than in others.

The central problem of the period is the establishment of a sense of identity. The identity the adolescent seeks to clarify is who he is, what his role in society is to be. Is he a child or is he an adult? Does he have it in him to be someday a husband and father? What is he to be as a worker and an earner of money? Can he feel self-confident in spite of the fact that his race or religion or national background makes him a person some

people look down upon? Over all, will he be a success or a failure? By reason of these questions adolescents are sometimes morbidly preoccupied with how they appear in the eyes of others as compared with their own conception of themselves, and with how they can make the roles and skills learned earlier jibe with what is currently in style.

In primitive societies adolescents are perhaps spared these doubts and indecisions. Through initiation rites, often seemingly cruel in character, young people are tested out (and test themselves out) and are then welcomed into a socially recognized age category in which rights and duties and mode of living are clearly defined. In our society there are few rituals or ceremonies that mark the change in status from childhood to youth. For those who have religious affiliations, confirmation, joining the church, may serve this purpose in part, since the young people are thereby admitted in this one segment of their lives at least, to the company of adults. Such ceremonies serve, in addition, to reaffirm to youth that the universe is trustworthy and stable and that a way of life is clearly laid out.

Graduation ceremonies might play a part in marking a new status were it not that, in present-day America, status is so ill defined. What rules of law and custom exist are too diverse to be of much help. For example, legal regulations governing age of "consent," age at which marriage is permitted, age for leaving school, for driving a car, for joining (or being required to join) the Army or Navy mark no logical progressions in rights and duties. As to custom, there is so much variation in what even families who live next door to each other expect or permit that adolescents, eager to be on their way, are practically forced into standardizing themselves in their search for status. In this they are ably abetted by advertisers and entertainers who seek their patronage, as well as by well-meaning magazine writers who describe in great detail the means by which uniformity can be achieved.

In this urge to find comfort through similarity, adolescents are likely to become stereotyped in behavior and ideals. They tend to form cliques for self-protection and fasten on petty similarities of dress and gesture to assure themselves that they are really somebody. In these cliques they may be intolerant and even cruel toward those they label as different. Unfortunate as such behavior is and not to be condoned, intolerance serves the important purpose of giving the group members at least the negative assurance that there is something they are not.

The danger of this developmental period is self-diffusion. As Biff puts it in *The Death of a Salesman,* "I just can't take hold, Mom, I can't take hold of some kind of a life." A boy or girl can scarcely help feeling somewhat diffuse when the body changes in size and shape so rapidly, when genital maturity floods body and imagination with forbidden desires, when adult life lies ahead with such a diversity of conflicting possibilities and choices.

Whether this feeling of self-diffusion is fairly easily mastered or whether, in extreme, it leads to delinquency, neurosis or outright psychosis, depends to a considerable extent on what has gone before. If the course of personality development has been a healthy one, a feeling of self-esteem has accrued from the numerous experiences of succeeding in a task and sensing its cultural meaning. Along with this, the child has come to the conviction that he is moving toward an understandable future in which he will have a definite role to play. Adolescence may upset this assurance for a time or to a degree but fairly soon a new integration is achieved, and the boy or girl sees again (and with clearer vision) that he belongs and that he is on his way.

The course is not so easy for adolescents who have not had so fortunate a part or for those whose earlier security is broken by a sudden awareness that as members of minority groups their way of life sets them apart. The former, already unsure of themselves, find their earlier doubt and mistrust reactivated by the physiological and social changes that adolescence brings. The latter, once secure, may feel that they must disavow their past and try to develop an "American" personality.

Much has been learned and written about the adolescent problems of the boys and girls whose early personality development has been impaired. How they can be helped, if their disorders are not too severe, is also fairly well known. The full implications of these findings for parents, teachers, and others who would guide youth are still to be worked out but, even so, there is considerable information.

Less well understood are the difficulties and the ways of helping adolescents who grew up in cultures that are not of the usual run. These boys and girls may have been privileged in having had a childhood in which there was little inhibition of sensual pleasures, and in which development proceeded by easy, unselfconscious stages. For them, difficulties arise if their parents lose trust in themselves or if their teachers apply sudden correctives, or if they themselves reject their past and try to act like others. The new role of middle-class adolescent is often too hard to play. Delinquency or bizarre behavior marks the failure.

How to reach these boys and girls, how to help them attain their desire, is a matter not well understood. It is clear, however, that they should not be typed by pat diagnoses and social judgments, for they are ever ready to become the "bums" that they are called. Those who would guide them must understand both the psychology of adolescence and the cultural realities of the day. There is trust to be restored and doubt and guilt and feelings of inferiority to be overcome. The science of how to do this is still pretty much lacking, though here and there teachers, clergymen, probation officers and the like are highly successful in the task.

Hard though it be to achieve, the sense of identity is the individual's only safeguard against the lawlessness of his biological drives and the authority of an over-weening conscience. Loss of identity, loss of the sense that there is some continuity, sameness, and meaning to life, exposes the individual to his childhood conflicts and leads to emotional upsets. This outcome was observed time and again among men hard pressed by the dangers of war. It is clear, then, that if health of personality is to be preserved much attention must be given to assuring that America makes good on its promises to youth.

THE SENSE OF INTIMACY

After the sense of identity, to a greater or lesser extent, is achieved it becomes possible for the next component of the healthy personality to develop. This is the sense of intimacy, intimacy with persons of the same sex or of the opposite sex or with one's self. The youth who is not fairly sure of his identity shies away from interpersonal relations and is afraid of close communion with himself. The surer he becomes of himself, the more he seeks intimacy, in the form of friendship, love and inspiration.

In view of the early age at which boy and girl attachments are encouraged today, it may seem strange to put the critical period for the development of the sense of intimacy late in adolescence. The explanation is that, on the one hand, sexual intimacy is only one part of what is involved, and, on the other, boy-girl attachments of earlier age periods are likely to be of a somewhat different order. Regarding the latter point, it has been observed by those who know young people well that high-school age boys and girls often use each other's company for an endless verbal examination of what the other thinks, feels, and wants to do. In other words, these attachments are one means of defining one's identity.

In contrast to this use of friendship and companionship, boys and girls late in adolescence usually have need for a kind of fusion with the essence of other people and for a communion with their own inner resources. If, by reason of inadequacies in previous personality development, this sense of intimacy cannot be achieved, the youth may retire into psychological isolation and keep his relations with people on a formal stereotyped level that is lacking in spontaneity and warmth or he may keep trying again and again to get close to others, only to meet with repeated failure. Under this compulsion he may even marry, but the role of mate is one he can rarely sustain, for the condition of true two-ness is that each individual must first become himself.

In this area of personality development as in the others, cultural factors play a part in sustaining or in discouraging the individual in his development. American culture is unusually successful in encouraging the development of the feelings of independence, initiative, industry, and identity. It is somewhat less successful in the area of intimacy, for the culture's ideal is the subordination of sexuality and sensuality to a life of work, duty, and worship.

Consequently, American adolescents are likely to be unsupported by their parents and to find little confirmation in story or song for their desire to sense intimately the full flavor of the personality of others. In many of them, then, the sense of intimacy does not develop highly and they have difficulty in finding in close personal relations the outlet for tension that they need.

There is some evidence that a change in conventions and customs in this respect is in the making, however. Too abrupt change in any such cultural matter is not to be urged, but it is to be hoped that gradual, frank discussion can bring about gradual alteration in attitude and overcome the dangers inherent in the traditional rigidity.

THE PARENTAL SENSE

"Parental sense" designates somewhat the same capacity as that implied in the words, creativity or productivity. The individual has normally come to adulthood before this sense can develop fully.

The parental sense is indicated most clearly by interest in producing and caring for children of one's own. It may also be exhibited in relation to other people's children or by a parental kind of responsibility toward the products of creative activity of other sorts. The mere desire for or possession of children does not indicate that this component of the healthy personality has developed. In fact, many parents who bring their children to child guidance clinics are found not to have reached this stage of personality development.

The essential element is the desire to nourish and nurture what has been produced. It is the ability to regard one's children as a trust of the community, rather than as extensions of one's own personality or merely as beings that one happens to live with.

Failure to develop this component of the healthy personality often results in a condition which has not been adequately categorized clinically. Although a true sense of intimacy has not developed, the individual may obsessively seek companionship. There is something of egotism in this as in his other activities, a kind of self-absorption. The individual is inclined to treat himself as a child and to be rivalrous with his children, if he has any. He indulges himself, expects to be indulged, and in general behaves in an infantile or immature manner.

There are both individual and social explanations of the failure to develop an adequate parental sense. Individually, the explanation may be found in the inadequate development of the personality components previously described. In some people this failure goes far back. Because of unfortunate experiences in childhood they did not arrive at a firm sense of trust, autonomy, and the rest. In others it is only inadequacies in later stages, especially in the development of the sense of intimacy, that are at fault.

Socially, as has been suggested throughout this analysis, healthy personality development depends upon the culture's ideals and upon the economic arrangements of the society. In order that most people may develop fully the sense of being a parent, the role of parent, both mother and father, must be a respected one in the society. Giving must rank higher than getting, and loving than being loved. The economy must be such that the future can be depended upon and each person can feel assured that he has a meaningful and respected part to play. Only so can most individuals afford to renounce selfish aims and derive much of their satisfaction from rearing children.

THE SENSE OF INTEGRITY

The final component of the healthy personality is the sense of integrity. In every culture the dominant ideals, honor, courage, faith, purity, grace, fairness, self-discipline, become at this stage the core of the healthy personality's integration. The individual, in Erikson's words, "becomes able to accept his individual life cycle and the people who have become significant to it as meaningful within the segment of history in which he lives."

To continue Erikson's description, "Integrity thus means a new and different love of one's parents, free of the wish that they should have been different, and an acceptance of the fact that one's life is one's own responsibility. It is a sense of comradeship with men and women of distant times and of different pursuits, who have created orders and objects and sayings conveying human dignity and love. Although aware of the relativity of all the various life styles that have given meaning to human striving, the possessor of integrity is ready to defend the dignity of his own life style against all physical and economic threats. For he knows that, for him, all human dignity stands or falls with the one style of integrity of which he partakes."

The adult who lacks integrity in this sense may wish that he could live again. He feels that if at one time he had made a different decision he could have been a different person and his ventures would have been successful. He fears death and cannot accept his one and only life cycle as the ultimate of life. In the extreme, he experiences disgust and despair. Despair expresses the feeling that time is too short to try out new roads to integrity. Disgust is a means of hiding the despair, a chronic, contemptuous displeasure with the way life is run. As with the dangers and the solutions of previous periods, doubt and despair are not difficulties that are overcome once and for all, nor is integrity so achieved. Most people fluctuate between the two extremes. Most, also, at no point, either attain to the heights of unalloyed integrity or fall to the depths of complete disgust and despair.

Even in adulthood a reasonably healthy personality is sometimes secured in spite of previous misfortunes in the developmental sequence. New sources of trust may be found. Fortunate events and circumstances may aid the individual in his struggle to feel autonomous. Imagination and initiative may be spurred by new responsibilities, and feelings of inferiority be overcome by successful achievement. Even late in life an individual may arrive at a true sense of who he is and what he has to do and may be able to win through to a feeling of intimacy with others and to joy in producing and giving.

Evidence of such changes is found in the case records of psychiatrists and social workers. Common sense observation attests that similar changes in health of personality are sometimes accomplished without benefit of any form of psychotherapy. Much remains to be learned about this, however, especially about how life itself may serve as therapeusis.

For the healthy personality development of children and youth it is necessary that a large proportion of adults attain a sense of integrity to a considerable degree. Not only parents but all who deal with children have need of this quality if they are to help children maintain the feeling that the universe is dependable and trustworthy. Integrity is relatively easily attained and sustained when the culture itself gives support, when a meaning to life is clearly spelled out in tradition and ceremony, and roles are clearly defined. Our culture, with its rapidly changing technology and its diversity of value standards, leaves much for the individual to work out for himself. In the American dream, however, and the Judaeo-Christian tradition on which it is based there are values and ideals aplenty. In the interest of the welfare of children and youth, in order that a generation of happy individuals and responsible citizens be reared, it is highly important that these values and ideals be brought into prominence and that the promise of American life be kept.

ENDNOTES

1. Harry Bakwin, "Emotional Deprivation in Infants," *Journal of Pediatrics* (October, 1949): 35, 512–529.
2. John Bowlby, M.D., Summary of Dr. Rene Spitz's observations, unpublished manuscript.

Erik H. Erikson (1902–1994) was a psychoanalyst and Professor of Human Development at Harvard University. *Joan M. Erikson* coauthored many publications with her husband, who prefaced his collected writings from 1930 to 1950 with the following: "The fact is that in this whole collection there does not seem to be one bit of good writing that was not shared by her in thought as well as in formulation."

QUESTIONS FOR REFLECTION

1. If a child has been unsuccessful in his or her first three stages of development, according to Erikson's stages of development theory, what are some of the problems that the child will have that may require the help of his or her elementary teacher?

2. What guidelines for curriculum planning will ensure that the school curriculum provides students with experiences that enhance their feelings of competence during the fourth stage of the life cycle (school age)?

3. According to many leaders in human development, including Erikson, developing a "sense of identity" is the major developmental task of adolescence. Some societies help young people with this task by providing *rites of passage*—rituals and ceremonies that help to establish the individual's identity within the culture. Should schools or other institutions provide more rites of passage for adolescents?

The Cognitive-Developmental Approach to Moral Education

LAWRENCE KOHLBERG (1927–1987)

ABSTRACT: Building on Dewey's and Piaget's ideas about moral development, Kohlberg suggests that the reasoning processes people use to differentiate between right and wrong progress through three levels of development. At the preconventional level, people decide what is right on the basis of personal needs and rules developed by others; at the conventional level, moral decisions reflect a desire for others' approval and a willingness to conform to expectations of family, community, and country; and at the postconventional level, decisions are based on rational, personal choices that can be separated from conventional values.

In this article, I present an overview of the cognitive-developmental approach to moral education and its research foundations, compare it with other approaches, and report the experimental work my colleagues and I are doing to apply the approach.

I. MORAL STAGES

The cognitive-developmental approach was fully stated for the first time by John Dewey. The approach is called *cognitive* because it recognizes that moral education, like intellectual education, has its basis in stimulating the *active thinking* of the child about moral issues and decisions. It is called developmental because it sees the aims of moral education as movement through moral stages. According to Dewey:

> The aim of education is growth or *development,* both intellectual and moral. Ethical and psychological principles can aid the school in the *greatest of all the constructions—the building of a free and powerful character.* Only knowledge of the *order and connection of the stages in psychological development can insure this.* Education is the work of *supplying the conditions* which will enable the psychological functions to mature in the freest and fullest manner.[1]

Dewey postulated three levels of moral development: (1) the *pre-moral* or *preconventional* level "of behavior motivated by biological and social impulses with results for morals," (2) the *conventional* level of behavior "in which the individual accepts with little critical reflection the standards of his group," and (3) the *autonomous* level of behavior in which "conduct is guided by the individual thinking and judging for himself whether a purpose is good, and does not accept the standard of his group without reflection."[2]

Dewey's thinking about moral stages was theoretical. Building upon his prior studies of cognitive stages, Jean Piaget made the first effort to define stages of moral reasoning in children through actual interviews and through observations of children (in games with rules).[3] Using this interview material, Piaget defined the premoral, the conventional, and the autonomous levels as follows: (1) the *premoral stage,* where there was no sense of obligation to rules; (2) the *heteronomous stage,* where the right was literal obedience to rules and an equation of obligation with submission to power and punishment (roughly ages four to eight); and (3) the *autonomous stage,* where the purpose and consequences of following rules are considered and obligation is based on reciprocity and exchange (roughly ages eight to twelve).[4]

From *Phi Delta Kappan* 56, no. 10 (June 1976): 670–677. Used by permission of the author and the publisher.

In 1955 I started to redefine and validate (through longitudinal and cross-cultural study) the Dewey-Piaget levels and stages. The resulting stages are presented in Table 1.

We claim to have validated the stages defined in Table 1. The notion that stages can be *validated* by longitudinal study implies that stages have definite empirical characteristics.[5] The concept of

TABLE 1
Definition of Moral Stages

I. Preconventional level

At this level, the child is responsive to cultural rules and labels of good and bad, right or wrong, but interprets these labels either in terms of the physical or the hedonistic consequences of action (punishment, reward, exchange of favors) or in terms of the physical power of those who enunciate the rules and labels. The level is divided into the following two stages:

Stage 1: *The punishment-and-obedience orientation.* The physical consequences of action determine its goodness or badness, regardless of the human meaning or value of these consequences. Avoidance of punishment and unquestioning deference to power are valued in their own right, not in terms of respect for an underlying moral order supported by punishment and authority (the latter being Stage 4).

Stage 2: *The instrumental-relativist orientation.* Right action consists of that which instrumentally satisfies one's own needs and occasionally the needs of others. Human relations are viewed in terms like those of the marketplace. Elements of fairness, of reciprocity, and of equal sharing are present, but they are always interpreted in a physical, pragmatic way. Reciprocity is a matter of "You scratch my back and I'll scratch yours," not of loyalty, gratitude, or justice.

II. Conventional level

At this level, maintaining the expectations of the individual's family, group, or nation is perceived as valuable in its own right, regardless of immediate and obvious consequences. The attitude is not only one of *conformity* to personal expectations and social order, but of loyalty to it, of actively *maintaining*, supporting, and justifying the order, and of identifying with the persons or group involved in it. At this level, there are the following two stages:

Stage 3: *The interpersonal concordance or "good boy-nice girl" orientation.* Good behavior is that which pleases or helps others and is approved by them. There is much conformity to stereotypical images of what is majority or "natural" behavior. Behavior is frequently judged by intention—"he means well" becomes impor-

tant for the first time. One earns approval by being "nice."

Stage 4: *The "law and order" orientation.* There is orientation toward authority, fixed rules, and the maintenance of the social order. Right behavior consists of doing one's duty, showing respect for authority, and maintaining the given social order for its own sake.

III. Postconventional, autonomous, or principled level

At this level, there is a clear effort to define moral values and principles that have validity and application apart from the authority of the groups or persons holding these principles and apart from the individual's own identification with these groups. This level also has two stages:

Stage 5: *The social-contract, legalistic orientation,* generally with utilitarian overtones. Right action tends to be defined in terms of general individual rights and standards which have been critically examined and agreed upon by the whole society. There is a clear awareness of the relativism of personal values and opinions and a corresponding emphasis upon procedural rules for reaching consensus. Aside from what is constitutionally and democratically agreed upon, the right is a matter of personal "values;" and "opinion." The result is an emphasis upon the "legal point of view," but with an emphasis upon the possibility of changing law in terms of rational considerations of social utility (rather than freezing it in terms of Stage 4 "law and order"). Outside the legal realm, free agreement and contract is the binding element of obligation. This is the "official" morality of the American government and constitution.

Stage 6: *The universal-ethical-principle orientation.* Right is defined by the decision of conscience in accord with self-chosen *ethical principles* appealing to logical comprehensiveness, universality, and consistency. These principles are abstract and ethical (the Golden Rule, the categorical imperative); they are not concrete moral rules like the Ten Commandments. At heart, these are universal principles of *justice*, of the *reciprocity* and *equality* of human *rights*, and of respect for the dignity of human beings as *individual persons* ("From Is to Ought," pp. 164, 165).

From *Journal of Philosophy* 70, no. 18 (October 25, 1973): 631–632. Reprinted by permission.

stages (as used by Piaget and myself) implies the following characteristics:

1. Stages are "structured wholes," or organized systems of thought. Individuals are *consistent* in level of moral judgment.
2. Stages form an *invariant sequence*. Under all conditions except extreme trauma, movement is always forward, never backward. Individuals never skip stages; movement is always to the next stage up.
3. Stages are "hierarchical integrations." Thinking at a higher stage includes or comprehends within it lower-stage thinking. There is a tendency to function at or prefer the highest stage available.

Each of these characteristics has been demonstrated for moral stages. Stages are defined by responses to a set of verbal moral dilemmas classified according to an elaborate scoring scheme. Validating studies include:

1. A twenty-year study of fifty Chicago-area boys, middle- and working-class. Initially interviewed at ages ten to sixteen, they have been reinterviewed at three-year intervals thereafter.
2. A small, six-year longitudinal study of Turkish village and city boys of the same age.
3. A variety of other cross-sectional studies in Canada, Britain, Israel, Taiwan, Yucatan, Honduras, and India.

With regard to the structured whole or consistency criterion, we have found that more than 50 percent of an individual's thinking is always at one stage, with the remainder at the next adjacent stage (which he is leaving or which he is moving into).

With regard to invariant sequence, our longitudinal results have been presented in the *American Journal of Orthopsychiatry* (see endnote 12), and indicate that on every retest individuals were either at the same stage as three years earlier or had moved up. This was true in Turkey as well as in the United States.

With regard to the hierarchical integration criterion, it has been demonstrated that adolescents exposed to written statements at each of the six stages comprehend or correctly put in their own words all statements at or below their own stage but fail to comprehend any statements more than one stage above their own.[6] Some individuals comprehend the next stage above their own; some do not. Adolescents prefer (or rank as best) the highest stage they can comprehend.

To understand moral stages, it is important to clarify their relations to stage of logic or intelligence, on the one hand, and to moral behavior on the other. Maturity of moral judgment is not highly correlated with IQ or verbal intelligence (correlations are only in the 30s, accounting for 10 percent of the variance). Cognitive development, in the stage sense, however, is more important for moral development than such correlations suggest. Piaget has found that after the child learns to speak there are three major stages of reasoning: the intuitive, the concrete operational, and the formal operational. At around age seven, the child enters the stage of concrete logical thought: He can make logical inferences, classify, and handle quantitative relations about concrete things. In adolescence individuals usually enter the stage of formal operations. At this stage they can reason abstractly, i.e., consider all possibilities, form hypotheses, deduce implications from hypotheses, and test them against reality.[7]

Since moral reasoning clearly is reasoning, advanced moral reasoning depends upon advanced logical reasoning; a person's logical stage puts a certain ceiling on the moral stage he can attain. A person whose logical stage is only concrete operational is limited to the preconventional moral stages (Stages 1 and 2). A person whose logical stage is only partially formal operational is limited to the conventional moral stages (Stages 3 and 4). While logical development is necessary for moral development and sets limits to it, most individuals are higher in logical stage than they are in moral stage. As an example, over 50 percent of late adolescents and adults are capable of full formal reasoning, but only 10 percent of these adults (all formal operational) display principled (Stages 5 and 6) moral reasoning.

The moral stages are *structures of moral judgment* or *moral reasoning*. *Structures* of moral judgment must be distinguished from the *content* of moral judgment. As an example, we cite responses to a dilemma used in our various studies to identify moral stage. The dilemma raises the issue of stealing a drug to save a dying woman. The inventor of the drug is selling it for ten times what it costs him to make it. The woman's husband cannot raise the money, and the seller refuses to lower the price or wait for payment. What should the husband do?

The choice endorsed by a subject (steal, don't steal) is called the *content* of his moral judgment in the situation. His reasoning about the choice defines the structure of his moral judgment. This reasoning centers on the following ten universal moral values or issues of concern to persons in these moral dilemmas:

1. Punishment
2. Property
3. Roles and concerns of affection
4. Roles and concerns of authority
5. Law
6. Life
7. Liberty
8. Distributive justice
9. Truth
10. Sex

A moral choice involves choosing between two (or more) of these values as they *conflict* in concrete situations of choice.

The stage or structure of a person's moral judgment defines: (1) *what* he finds valuable in each of these moral issues (life, law), i.e., how he defines the value, and (2) *why* he finds it valuable, i.e., the reasons he gives for valuing it. As an example, at Stage 1 life is valued in terms of the power or possessions of the person involved; at Stage 2, for its usefulness in satisfying the needs of the individual in question or others; at Stage 3,

in terms of the individual's relations with others and their valuation of him; at Stage 4, in terms of social or religious law. Only at Stages 5 and 6 is each life seen as inherently worthwhile, aside from other considerations.

Moral Judgment vs. Moral Action

Having clarified the nature of stages of moral *judgment,* we must consider the relation of moral judgment to moral *action.* If logical reasoning is a necessary but not sufficient condition for mature moral judgment, mature moral judgment is a necessary but not sufficient condition for mature moral action. One cannot follow moral principles if one does not understand (or believe in) moral principles. However, one can reason in terms of principles and not live up to these principles. As an example, Richard Krebs and I found that only 15 percent of students showing some principled thinking cheated as compared to 55 percent of conventional subjects and 70 percent of preconventional subjects.[8] Nevertheless, 15 percent of the principled subjects did cheat, suggesting that factors additional to moral judgment are necessary for principled moral reasoning to be translated into "moral action." Partly, these factors include the situation and its pressures. Partly, what happens depends upon the individual's motives and emotions. Partly, what the individual does depends upon a general sense of will, purpose, or "ego strength." As an example of the role of will or ego strength in moral behavior, we may cite the study by Krebs: Slightly more than half of his conventional subjects cheated. These subjects were also divided by a measure of attention/will. Only 26 percent of the "strong-willed" conventional subjects cheated; however, 74 percent of the "weak-willed" subjects cheated.

If maturity of moral reasoning is only one factor in moral behavior, why does the cognitive-developmental approach to moral education focus so heavily upon moral reasoning? For the following reasons:

1. Moral judgment, while only one factor in moral behavior, is the single most important or influential factor yet discovered in moral behavior.

2. While other factors influence moral behavior, moral judgment is the only distinctively *moral* factor in moral behavior. To illustrate, we noted that the Krebs study indicated that "strong-willed" conventional stage subjects resisted cheating more than "weak-willed" subjects. For those at a preconventional level of moral reasoning, however, "will" had an opposite effect. "Strong-willed" Stages 1 and 2 subjects cheated more, not less, than "weak-willed" subjects, i.e., they had the "courage of their (amoral) convictions" that it was worthwhile to cheat. "Will," then, is an important factor in moral behavior, but it is not distinctively moral; it becomes moral only when informed by mature moral judgment.

3. Moral judgment change is long-range or irreversible; a higher stage is never lost. Moral behavior as such is largely situational and reversible or "losable" in new situations.

II. AIMS OF MORAL AND CIVIC EDUCATION

Moral psychology describes what moral development is, as studied empirically. Moral education must also consider moral philosophy, which strives to tell us what moral development ideally *ought to be*. Psychology finds an invariant sequence of moral stages; moral philosophy must be invoked to answer whether a later stage is a better stage. The "stage" of senescence and death follows the "stage" of adulthood, but that does not mean that senescence and death are better. Our claim that the latest or principled stages of moral reasoning are morally better stages, then, must rest on considerations of moral philosophy.

The tradition of moral philosophy to which we appeal is the liberal or rational tradition, in particular the "formalistic" or "deontological" tradi-tion running from Immanuel Kant to John Rawls.[9] Central to this tradition is the claim that an adequate morality is *principled*, i.e., that it makes judgments in terms of *universal* principles applicable to all mankind. *Principles* are to be distinguished from *rules*. Conventional morality is grounded on rules, primarily "thou shalt nots" such as are represented by the Ten Commandments, prescriptions of kinds of actions. Principles are, rather, universal guides to making a moral decision. An example is Kant's "categorical imperative," formulated in two ways. The first is the maxim of respect for human personality "Act always toward the other as an end, not as a means." The second is the maxim of universalization, "Choose only as you would be willing to have everyone choose in your situation." Principles like that of Kant's state the formal conditions of a moral choice or action. In the dilemma in which a woman is dying because a druggist refuses to release his drug for less than the stated price, the druggist is not acting morally, though he is not violating the ordinary moral rules (he is not actually stealing or murdering). But he is violating principles: He is treating the woman simply as a means to his ends of profit, and he is not choosing as he would wish anyone to choose (if the druggist were in the dying woman's place, he would not want a druggist to choose as he is choosing). Under most circumstances, choice in terms of conventional moral rules and choice in terms of principles coincide. Ordinarily, principles dictate not stealing (avoiding stealing is implied by acting in terms of a regard for others as ends and in terms of what one would want everyone to do). In a situation where stealing is the only means to save a life, however, principles contradict the ordinary rules and would dictate stealing. Unlike rules which are supported by social authority, principles are freely chosen by the individual because of their intrinsic moral validity.[10]

The conception that a moral choice is a choice made in terms of moral principles is related to the claim of liberal moral philosophy that moral principles are ultimately principles of justice. In essence, moral conflicts are conflicts between the claims of persons, and principles for resolving these claims are principles of justice, "for giving each his due." Central to justice are the demands of *liberty, equality,* and *reciprocity.* At every moral stage, there is a concern for justice. The most damning statement a school child can make about a teacher is that "he's not fair." At each higher stage, however, the conception of justice is reorganized. At Stage 1, justice is punishing the bad in terms of "an eye for an eye and a tooth for a tooth." At Stage 2, it is exchanging favors and goods in an equal manner. At Stages 3 and 4, it is treating people as they desire in terms of the conventional rules. At Stage 5, it is recognized that all rules and laws flow from justice, from a social contract between the governors and the governed designed to protect the equal rights of all. At Stage 6, personally chosen moral principles are also principles of justice, the principles any member of a society would choose for that society if he did not know what his position was to be in the society and in which he might be the least advantaged.[11] Principles chosen from this point of view are, first, the maximum liberty compatible with the like liberty of others and, second, no inequalities of goods and respect which are not to the benefit of all, including the least advantaged.

As an example of stage progression in the orientation to justice, we may take judgments about capital punishment.[12] Capital punishment is only firmly rejected at the two principled stages, when the notion of justice as vengeance or retribution is abandoned. At the sixth stage, capital punishment is not condoned even if it may have some useful deterrent effect in promoting law and order. This is because it is not a punishment we would choose for a society if we assumed we had as much chance of being born into the position of a criminal or murderer as being born into the position of a law abider.

Why are decisions based on universal principles of justice better decisions? Because they are decisions on which all moral men could agree. When decisions are based on conventional moral rules, men will disagree, since they adhere to conflicting systems of rules dependent on culture and social position. Throughout history men have killed one another in the name of conflicting moral rules and values, most recently in Vietnam and the Middle East. Truly moral or just resolutions of conflicts require principles which are, or can be, universalizable.

Alternative Approaches

We have given a philosophic rationale for stage advance as the aim of moral education. Given this rationale, the developmental approach to moral education can avoid the problems inherent in the other two major approaches to moral education. The first alternative approach is that of indoctrinative moral education, the preaching and imposition of the rules and values of the teacher and his culture on the child. In America, when this indoctrinative approach has been developed in a systematic manner, it has usually been termed "character education."

Moral values, in the character education approach, are preached or taught in terms of what may be called the "bag of virtues." In the classic studies of character by Hugh Hartshorne and Mark May, the virtues chosen were honesty, services and self-control.[13] It is easy to get superficial consensus on such a bag of virtues—until one examines in detail the list of virtues involved and the details of their definition. Is the Hartshorne and May bag more adequate than the Boy Scout bag (a Scout should be honest, loyal, reverent, clean, brave, etc.)? When one turns to the details of defining each virtue, one finds equal uncertainty or difficulty in reaching consensus. Does honesty mean one should not steal to save a life? Does it mean that a student should not help another student with his homework?

Character education and other forms of indoctrinative moral education have aimed at teaching universal values (it is assumed that honesty or service is a desirable trait for all men in all societies), but the detailed definitions used are relative; they are defined by the opinions of the teacher and the conventional culture and rest on the authority of the teacher for their justification. In this sense character education is close to the unreflective valuings by teachers which constitute the hidden curriculum of the school.[14] Because of the current unpopularity of indoctrinative approaches to moral education, a family of approaches called "values clarification" has become appealing to teachers. Values clarification takes the first step implied by a rational approach to moral education: the eliciting of the child's own judgment or opinion about issues or situations in which values conflict, rather than imposing the teacher's opinion on him. Values clarification, however, does not attempt to go further than eliciting awareness of values; it is assumed that becoming more self-aware about one's values is an end in itself. Fundamentally, the definition of the end of values education as self-awareness derives from a belief in ethical relativity held by many value-clarifiers. As stated by Peter Engel, "One must contrast value clarification and value inculcation. Value clarification implies the principle that in the consideration of values there is no single correct answer." Within these premises of "no correct answer," children are to discuss moral dilemmas in such a way as to, reveal different values and discuss their value differences with each other. The teacher is to stress that "our values are different," not that one value is more adequate than others. If this program is systematically followed, students will themselves become relativists, believing there is no "right" moral answer. For instance, a student caught cheating might argue that he did nothing wrong, since his own hierarchy of values, which may be different from that of the teacher, made it right for him to cheat.

Like values clarification, the cognitive-developmental approach to moral education stresses open or Socratic peer discussion of value dilemmas. Such discussion, however, has an aim: stimulation of movement to the next stage of moral reasoning. Like values clarification, the developmental approach opposes indoctrination. Stimulation of movement to the next stage of reasoning is not indoctrinative, for the following reasons:

1. Change is in the way of reasoning rather than in the particular beliefs involved.
2. Students in a class are at different stages; the aim is to aid movement of each to the next stage, not convergence on a common pattern.
3. The teacher's own opinion is neither stressed nor invoked as authoritative. It enters in only as one of many opinions, hopefully one of those at a next higher stage.
4. The notion that some judgments are more adequate than others is communicated. Fundamentally, however, this means that the student is encouraged to articulate a position which seems most adequate to him and to judge the adequacy of the reasoning of others.

In addition to having more definite aims than values clarification, the moral development approach restricts value education to that which is moral or, more specifically, to justice. This is for two reasons. First, it is not clear that the whole realm of personal, political, and religious values is a realm which is nonrelative, i.e., in which there are universals and a direction of development. Second, it is not clear that the public school has a right or mandate to develop values in general.[15] In our view, value education in the public schools should be restricted to that which the school has the right and mandate to develop: an awareness of justice, or of the rights of others in our Constitutional system. While the Bill of Rights prohibits the teaching of religious beliefs, or of specific value systems, it does not prohibit the teaching of the awareness of rights and principles of justice fundamental to the Constitution itself.

When moral education is recognized as centered in justice and differentiated from value education or affective education, it becomes apparent that moral and civic education are much the same thing. This equation, taken for granted by the classic philosophers of education from Plato and Aristotle to Dewey, is basic to our claim that a concern for moral education is central to the educational objectives of social studies.

The term *civic education* is used to refer to social studies as more than the study of the facts and concepts of social science, history, and civics. It is education for the analytic understanding, value principles, and motivation necessary for a citizen in a democracy if democracy is to be an effective process. It is political education. Civic or political education means the stimulation of development of more advanced patterns of reasoning about political and social decisions and their implementation directly derivative of broader patterns of moral reasoning. Our studies show that reasoning and decision making about political decisions are directly derivative of broader patterns of moral reasoning and decision making. We have interviewed high school and college students about concrete political situations involving laws to govern open housing, civil disobedience for peace in Vietnam, free press rights to publish what might disturb national order, and distribution of income through taxation. We find that reasoning on these political decisions can be classified according to moral stage and that an individual's stage on political dilemmas is at the same level as on nonpolitical moral dilemmas (euthanasia, violating authority to maintain trust in a family, stealing a drug to save one's dying wife). Turning from reasoning to action, similar findings are obtained. In 1963 a study was made of those who sat in at the University of California, Berkeley, administration building and those who did not in the Free Speech Movement crisis. Of those at Stage 6, 80 percent sat in, believing that principles of free speech were being compromised, and that all efforts to compromise and negotiate with the administration had failed. In contrast, only 15 percent of the conventional (Stage 3 or Stage 4) subjects sat in. (Stage 5 subjects were in between.)[16]

From a psychological side, then, political development is part of moral development. The same is true from the philosophic side. In the *Republic*, Plato sees political education as part of a broader education for moral justice and finds a rationale for such education in terms of universal philosophic principles rather than the demands of a particular society. More recently, Dewey claims the same.

In historical perspective, America was the first nation whose government was publicly founded on postconventional principles of justice, rather than upon the authority central to conventional moral reasoning. At the time of our founding, postconventional or principled moral and political reasoning was the possession of the minority, as it still is. Today, as in the time of our founding, the majority of our adults are at the conventional level, particularly the "law and order" (fourth) moral stage. (Every few years the Gallup Poll circulates the Bill of Rights unidentified, and every year it is turned down.) The Founding Fathers intuitively understood this without benefit of our elaborate social science research; they constructed a document designing a government which would maintain principles of justice and the rights of man even though principled men were not the men in power. The machinery included checks and balances, the independent judiciary, and freedom of the press. Most recently, this machinery found its use at Watergate. The tragedy of Richard Nixon, as Harry Truman said long ago, was that he never understood the Constitution (a Stage 5 document), but the Constitution understood Richard Nixon.[17]

Watergate, then, is not some sign of moral decay of the nation, but rather of the fact that understanding and action in support of justice principles are still the possession of a minority of our society. Insofar as there is moral decay, it represents the weakening of conventional morality in the face of social and value conflict today. This can lead the less fortunate adolescent to fixation at the preconventional level, the more fortunate to movement to principles. We find a larger proportion of youths at the principled level today than was the case in their fathers' day, but also a larger proportion at the preconventional level.

Given this state, moral and civic education in the schools becomes a more urgent task. In the high school today, one often hears both preconventional adolescents and those beginning to move beyond convention sounding the same note of disaffection for the school. While our political institutions are in principle Stage 5 (i.e., vehicles for maintaining universal rights through the democratic process), our schools have traditionally been Stage 4 institutions of convention and authority. Today more than ever, democratic schools systematically engaged in civic education are required.

Our approach to moral and civic education relates the study of law and government to the actual creation of a democratic school in which moral dilemmas are discussed and resolved in a manner which will stimulate moral development.

Planned Moral Education

For many years, moral development was held by psychologists to be primarily a result of family upbringing and family conditions. In particular, conditions of affection and authority in the home were believed to be critical, some balance of warmth and firmness being optimal for moral development. This view arises if morality is conceived as an internalization of the arbitrary rules of parents and culture, since such acceptance must be based on affection and respect for parents as authorities rather than on the rational nature of the rules involved.

Studies of family correlates of moral stage development do not support this internalization view of the conditions for moral development. Instead, they suggest that the conditions for moral development in homes and schools are similar and that the conditions are consistent with cognitive-developmental theory. In the cognitive-developmental view, morality is a natural product of a universal human tendency toward empathy or role taking, toward putting oneself in the shoes of other conscious beings. It is also a product of a universal human concern for justice, for reciprocity or equality in the relation of one person to another. As an example, when my son was four, he became a morally principled vegetarian and refused to eat meat, resisting all parental persuasion to increase his protein intake. His reason was, "It's bad to kill animals." His moral commitment

to vegetarianism was not taught or acquired from parental authority; it was the result of the universal tendency of the young self to project its consciousness and values into other living things, other selves. My son's vegetarianism also involved a sense of justice, revealed when I read him a book about Eskimos in which a real hunting expedition was described. His response was to say, "Daddy, there is one kind of meat I would eat—Eskimo meat. It's all right to eat Eskimos because they eat animals." This natural sense of justice or reciprocity was Stage 1—an eye for an eye, a tooth for a tooth. My son's sense of the value of life was also Stage 1 and involved no differentiation between human personality and physical life. His morality, though Stage 1, was, however, natural and internal. Moral development past Stage 1, then, is not an internalization but the reconstruction of role taking and conceptions of justice toward greater adequacy. These reconstructions occur in order to achieve a better match between the child's own moral structures and the structures of the social and moral situations he confronts. We divide these conditions of match into two kinds: those dealing with moral discussions and communication and those dealing with the total moral environment or atmosphere in which the child lives.

In terms of moral discussion, the important conditions appear to be:

1. Exposure to the next higher stage of reasoning
2. Exposure to situations posing problems and contradictions for the child's current moral structure, leading to dissatisfaction with his current level
3. An atmosphere of interchange and dialogue combining the first two conditions, in which conflicting moral views are compared in an open manner.

Studies of families in India and America suggest that morally advanced children have parents at higher stages. Parents expose children to the next higher stage, raising moral issues and engaging in open dialogue or interchange about such issues.[18]

Drawing on this notion of the discussion conditions stimulating advance, Moshe Blatt conducted classroom discussions of conflict-laden hypothetical moral dilemmas with four classes of junior high and high school students for a semester.[19] In each of these classes, students were to be found at three stages. Since the children were not all responding at the same stage, the arguments they used with each other were at different levels. In the course of these discussions among the students, the teacher first supported and clarified those arguments that were one stage above the lowest stage among the children; for example, the teacher supported Stage 3 rather than Stage 2. When it seemed that these arguments were understood by the students, the teacher then challenged that stage, using new situations, and clarified the arguments one stage above the previous one: Stage 4 rather than Stage 3. At the end of the semester, all the students were retested; they showed significant upward change when compared to the controls, and they maintained the change one year later. In the experimental classrooms, from one-fourth to one-half of the students moved up a stage, while there was essentially no change during the course of the experiment in the control group.

Given the Blatt studies showing that moral discussion could raise moral stage, we undertook the next step: to see if teachers could conduct moral discussions in the course of teaching high school social studies with the same results. This step we took in cooperation with Edwin Fenton, who introduced moral dilemmas in his ninth- and eleventh-grade social studies texts. Twenty-four teachers in the Boston and Pittsburgh areas were given some instruction in conducting moral discussions around the dilemmas in the text. About half of the teachers stimulated significant developmental change in their classrooms—upward stage movement of one-quarter to one-half a stage. In control classes using the text but no moral dilemma discussions, the same teachers failed to stimulate any moral change in the students. Moral discussion, then, can be a us-

able and effective part of the curriculum at any grade level. Working with filmstrip dilemmas produced in cooperation with Guidance Association, second-grade teachers conducted moral discussions yielding a similar amount of moral stage movement.

Moral discussion and curriculum, however, constitute only one portion of the conditions stimulating moral growth. When we turn to analyzing the broader life environment, we turn to a consideration of the *moral atmosphere* of the home, the school, and the broader society. The first basic dimension of social atmosphere is the role-taking opportunities it provides, the extent to which it encourages the child to take the point of view of others. Role taking is related to the amount of social interaction and social communication in which the child engages, as well as to his sense of efficacy in influencing attitudes of others. The second dimension of social atmosphere, more strictly moral, is the level of justice of the environment or institution. The justice structure of an institution refers to the perceived rules or principles for distributing rewards, punishments, responsibilities, and privileges among institutional members. This structure may exist or be perceived at any of our moral stages. As an example, a study of a traditional prison revealed that inmates perceived it as Stage 1, regardless of their own level.[20] Obedience to arbitrary command by power figures and punishment for disobedience were seen as the governing justice norms of the prison. A behavior-modification prison using point rewards for conformity was perceived as a Stage 2 system of instrumental exchange. Inmates at Stage 3 or 4 perceived this institution as more fair than the traditional prison, but not as fair in their own terms.

These and other studies suggest that a higher level of institutional justice is a condition for individual development of a higher sense of justice. Working on these premises, Joseph Hickey, Peter Scharf, and I worked with guards and inmates in a women's prison to create a more just community.[21] A social contract was set up in which guards and inmates each had a vote of one and in which rules were made and conflicts resolved through discussions of fairness and a democratic vote in a community meeting. The program has been operating four years and has stimulated moral stage advance in inmates, though it is still too early to draw conclusions as to its overall long-range effectiveness for rehabilitation.

One year ago, Fenton, Ralph Mosher, and I received a grant from the Danforth Foundation (with additional support from the Kennedy Foundation) to make moral education a living matter in two high schools in the Boston area (Cambridge and Brookline) and two in Pittsburgh. The plan had two components. The first was training counselors and social studies and English teachers in conducting moral discussions and making moral discussion an integral part of the curriculum. The second was establishing a just community school within a public high school.

We have stated the theory of the just community high school, postulating that discussing real-life moral situations and actions as issues of fairness and as matters for democratic decision would stimulate advance in both moral reasoning and moral action. A participatory democracy provides more extensive opportunities for role taking and a higher level of perceived institutional justice than does any other social arrangement. Most alternative schools strive to establish a democratic governance, but none we have observed has achieved a vital or viable participatory democracy. Our theory suggested reasons why we might succeed where others failed. First, we felt that democracy had to be a central commitment of a school, rather than a humanitarian frill. Democracy as moral education provides that commitment. Second, democracy in alternative schools often fails because it bores the students. Students prefer to let teachers make decisions about staff, courses, and schedules, rather than to attend lengthy, complicated meetings. Our theory said that the issues a democracy should focus on are issues of morality and fairness. Real issues concerning drugs, stealing, disruptions, and grading are never boring if handled as issues of fairness.

Third, our theory told us that if large democratic community meetings were preceded by small-group moral discussion, higher-stage thinking by students would win out in later decisions, avoiding the disasters of mob rule.[22]

Currently, we can report that the school based on our theory makes democracy work or function where other schools have failed. It is too early to make any claims for its effectiveness in causing moral development, however.

Our Cambridge just community school within the public high school was started after a small summer planning session of volunteer teachers, students, and parents. At the time the school opened in the fall, only a commitment to democracy and a skeleton program of English and social studies had been decided on. The school started with six teachers from the regular school and sixty students, twenty from academic professional homes and twenty from working-class homes. The other twenty were dropouts and trouble-makers or petty delinquents in terms of previous record. The usual mistakes and usual chaos of a beginning alternative school ensued. Within a few weeks, however, a successful democratic community process had been established. Rules were made around pressing issues: disturbances, drugs, hooking. A student discipline committee or jury was formed. The resulting rules and enforcement have been relatively effective and reasonable. We do not see reasonable rules as ends in themselves, however, but as vehicles for moral discussion and an emerging sense of community. This sense of community and a resulting morale are perhaps the most immediate signs of success. This sense of community seems to lead to behavior change of a positive sort. An example is a fifteen-year-old student who started as one of the greatest combinations of humor, aggression, light-fingeredness, and hyperactivity I have ever known. From being the principal disturber of all community meetings, he has become an excellent community meeting participant and occasional chairman. He is still more ready to enforce rules for others than to observe them himself, yet his commitment to the school has led to a steady decrease in exotic behavior. In addition, he has become more involved in classes and projects and has begun to listen and ask questions in order to pursue a line of interest.

We attribute such behavior change not only to peer pressure and moral discussion but to the sense of community which has emerged from the democratic process in which angry conflicts are resolved through fairness and community decision. This sense of community is reflected in statements of the students to us that there are no cliques—that the blacks and the whites, the professors' sons and the project students, are friends. These statements are supported by observation. Such a sense of community is needed where students in a given classroom range in reading level from fifth-grade to college.

Fenton, Mosher, the Cambridge and Brookline teachers, and I are now planning a four-year curriculum in English and social studies centering on moral discussion, on role taking and communication, and on relating the government, laws, and justice system of the school to that of the American society and other world societies. This will integrate an intellectual curriculum for a higher level of understanding of society with the experiential components of school democracy and moral decision.

There is very little new in this—or in anything else we are doing. Dewey wanted democratic experimental schools for moral and intellectual development seventy years ago. Perhaps Dewey's time has come.

ENDNOTES

1. John Dewey, "What Psychology Can do for the Teacher," in Reginald Archambault, ed., *John Dewey on Education: Selected Writings* (New York: Random House, 1964).

2. These levels correspond roughly to our three major levels: the preconventional, the conventional, and the principled. Similar levels were propounded by William McDougall, Leonard Hobhouse, and James Mark Baldwin.

3. Jean Piaget, *The Moral Judgment of the Child*, 2nd ed. (Glencoe, Ill.: Free Press, 1948).

4. Piaget's stages correspond to our first three stages: Stage 0 (premoral), Stage 1 (heteronomous), and Stage 2 (instrumental reciprocity).

5. Lawrence Kohlberg, "Moral Stages and Moralization: The Cognitive-Developmental Approach," in Thomas Lickona, ed., *Man, Morality, and Society* (New York: Holt, Rinehart and Winston, in press).

6. James Rest, Elliott Turiel, and Lawrence Kohlberg, "Relations Between Level of Moral Judgment and Preference and Comprehension of the Moral Judgment of Others," *Journal of Personality,* vol. 37, 1969, pp. 225–52, and James Rest, "Comprehension, Preference, and Spontaneous Usage in Moral Judgment," in Lawrence Kohlberg, ed., *Recent Research in Moral Development* (New York: Holt, Rinehart and Winston, in preparation).

7. Many adolescents and adults only partially attain the stage of formal operations. They do consider all the actual relations of one thing to another at the same time, but they do not consider all possibilities and form abstract hypotheses. A few do not advance this far, remaining "concrete operational."

8. Richard Krebs and Lawrence Kohlberg, "Moral Judgment and Ego Controls as Determinants of Resistance to Cheating," in Lawrence Kohlberg, ed., *Recent Research.*

9. John Rawls, *A Theory of Justice* (Cambridge, Mass.: Harvard University Press, 1971).

10. Not all freely chosen values or rules are principles, however. Hitler chose the "rule," "exterminate the enemies of the Aryan race," but such a rule is not a universalizable principle.

11. Rawls, *A Theory of Justice.*

12. Lawrence Kohlberg and Donald Elfenbein, "Development of Moral Reasoning and Attitudes Toward Capital Punishment," *American Journal of Orthopsychiatry,* Summer, 1975.

13. Hugh Hartshorne and Mark May, *Studies in the Nature of Character: Studies in Deceit,* vol. 1; *Studies in Service and Self-Control,* vol. 2; *Studies in Organization of Character,* vol. 3 (New York: Macmillan, 1928–30).

14. As an example of the "hidden curriculum," we may cite a second-grade classroom. My son came home from this classroom one day saying he did

not want to be "one of the bad boys." Asked "Who are the bad boys?" he replied, "The ones who don't put their books back and get yelled at."

15. Restriction of deliberate value education to the moral may be clarified by our example of the second-grade teacher who made tidying up of books a matter of moral indoctrination. Tidiness is a value, but it is not a moral value. Cheating is a moral issue, intrinsically one of fairness. It involves issues of violation of trust and taking advantage. Failing to tidy the room may under certain conditions be an issue of fairness, when it puts an undue burden on others. If it is handled by the teacher as a matter of cooperation among the group in this sense, it is a legitimate focus of deliberate moral education. If it is not, it simply represents the arbitrary imposition of the teacher's values on the child.

16. The differential action of the principled subjects was determined by two things. First, they were more likely to judge it right to violate authority by sitting in. But second, they were also in general more consistent in engaging in political action according to their judgment. Ninety percent of all Stage 6 subjects thought it right to sit in, and all 90 percent lived up to this belief. Among the Stage 4 subjects, 45 percent thought it right to sit in, but only 33 percent lived up to this belief by acting.

17. No public or private word or deed of Nixon ever rose above Stage 4, the "law and order" stage. His last comments in the White House were of won-derment that the Republican Congress could turn on him after so many Stage 2 exchanges of favors in getting them elected.

18. Bindu Parilch, "A Cross-Cultural Study of Parent-child Moral Judgment," unpublished doctoral dissertation, Harvard University, 1975.

19. Moshe Blatt and Lawrence Kohlberg, "Effects of Classroom Discussions upon Children's Level of Moral Judgment," in Lawrence Kohlberg, ed., *Recent Research*.

20. Lawrence Kohlberg, Peter Scharf, and Joseph Hickey, "The Justice Structure of the Prison: A Theory and an Intervention," *The Prison Journal*, Autumn-Winter, 1972.

21. Lawrence Kohlberg, Kelsey Kauffman, Peter Scharf, and Joseph Hickey, *The Just Community Approach to Corrections: A Manual, Part I* (Cambridge, Mass.: Education Research Foundation, 1973).

22. An example of the need for small-group discussion comes from an alternative school community meeting called because a pair of the students had stolen the school's video-recorder. The resulting majority decision was that the school should buy back the recorder from the culprits through a fence. The teachers could not accept this decision and returned to a more authoritative approach. I believe if the moral reasoning of students urging this solution had been confronted by students at a higher stage, a different decision would have emerged.

Lawrence Kohlberg was Professor of Education and Psychology and Director, Center for Moral Education, Graduate School of Education, Harvard University.

QUESTIONS FOR REFLECTION

1. Are there universal moral values that educators, parents, and community members—regardless of philosophical, political, or religious beliefs—would include in the school curriculum? What are these values?

2. What does Kohlberg mean when he makes a distinction between the *structures* of moral judgment and the *content* of moral judgment? Give an example of a moral dilemma to illustrate this point.

3. What is the relationship between moral *judgment* and moral *action*? What factors determine whether an individual's moral judgment will be translated into moral action?

Woman's Place in Man's Life Cycle

CAROL GILLIGAN

ABSTRACT: Arguing that Kohlberg's model of moral reasoning is based on a male perspective and addresses the rights of the individual, Gilligan suggests that moral reasoning from a female perspective stresses the individual's responsibility to other people. Life-cycle theories, she concludes, should encompass the experiences of both sexes.

. . . Relationships, and particularly issues of dependency, are experienced differently by women and men. For boys and men, separation and individuation are critically tied to gender identity since separation from the mother is essential for the development of masculinity. For girls and women, issues of femininity or feminine identity do not depend on the achievement of separation from the mother or on the progress of individuation. Since masculinity is defined through separation while femininity is defined through attachment, male gender identity is threatened by intimacy while female gender identity is threatened by separation. Thus males tend to have difficulty with relationships, while females tend to have problems with individuation. The quality of embeddedness in social interaction and personal relationships that characterizes women's lives in contrast to men's, however, becomes not only a descriptive difference but also a developmental liability when the milestones of childhood and adolescent development in the psychological literature are markers of increasing separation. Women's failure to separate then becomes by definition a failure to develop.

When one begins with the study of women and derives developmental constructs from their lives, the outline of a moral conception different from that described by Freud, Piaget, or Kohlberg begins to emerge and informs a different description of development. In this conception, the moral problem arises from conflicting responsibilities rather than from competing rights and requires for its resolution a mode of thinking that is contextual and narrative rather than formal and abstract. This conception of morality as concerned with the activity of care centers moral development around the understanding of responsibility and relationships, just as the conception of morality as fairness ties moral development to the understanding of rights and rules.

This different construction of the moral problem by women may be seen as the critical reason for their failure to develop within the constraints of Kohlberg's system. Regarding all constructions of responsibility as evidence of a conventional moral understanding, Kohlberg defines the highest stages of moral development as deriving from a reflective understanding of human rights. That the morality of rights differs from the morality of responsibility in its emphasis on separation rather than connection, in its consideration of the individual rather than the relationship as primary, is illustrated by two responses to interview questions about the nature of morality. The first comes from a twenty-five-year-old man, one of the participants in Kohlberg's study:

[*What does the word morality mean to you?*] Nobody in the world knows the answer. I think it is recognizing the right of the individual, the rights

Reprinted by permission of the publisher from *In a Different Voice: Psychological Theory and Women's Development* by Carol Gilligan, Cambridge, Mass.: Harvard University Press, pp. 8–9, 19–23, copyright © 1982, 1993 by Carol Gilligan.

of other individuals, not interfering with those rights. Act as fairly as you would have them treat you. I think it is basically to preserve the human being's right to existence. I think that is the most important. Secondly, the human being's right to do as he pleases, again without interfering with somebody else's rights.

[*How have your views on morality changed since the last interview?*] I think I am more aware of an individual's rights now. I used to be looking at it strictly from my point of view, just for me. Now I think I am more aware of what the individual has a right to.

Kohlberg (1973) cites this man's response as illustrative of the principled conception of human rights that exemplifies his fifth and sixth stages. Commenting on the response, Kohlberg says: "Moving to a perspective outside of that of his society, he identifies morality with justice (fairness, rights, the Golden Rule), with recognition of the rights of others as these are defined naturally or intrinsically. The human being's right to do as he pleases without interfering with somebody else's rights is a formula defining rights prior to social legislation" (pp. 29–30).

The second response comes from a woman who participated in the rights and responsibilities study. She also was twenty-five and, at the time, a third-year law student:

[*Is there really some correct solution to moral problems, or is everybody's opinion equally right?*] No, I don't think everybody's opinion is equally right. I think that in some situations there may be opinions that are equally valid, and one could conscientiously adopt one of several courses of action. But there are other situations in which I think there are right and wrong answers, that sort of inhere in the nature of existence, of all individuals here who need to live with each other to live. We need to depend on each other, and hopefully it is not only a physical need but a need of fulfillment in ourselves, that a person's life is enriched by cooperating with other people and striving to live in harmony with everybody else, and to that end, there are right and wrong, there are things which promote that end

and that move away from it, and in that way it is possible to choose in certain cases among different courses of action that obviously promote or harm that goal.

[*Is there a time in the past when you would have thought about these things differently?*] Oh, yeah, I think that I went through a time when I thought that things were pretty relative, that I can't tell you what to do and you can't tell me what to do, because you've got your conscience and I've got mine.

[*When was that?*] When I was in high school. I guess that it just sort of dawned on me that my own ideas changed, and because my own judgment changed, I felt I couldn't judge another person's judgment. But now I think even when it is only the person himself who is going to be affected I say it is wrong to the extent it doesn't cohere with what I know about human nature and what I know about you, and just from what I think is true about the operation of the universe, I could say I think you are making a mistake.

[*What led you to change, do you think?*] Just seeing more of life, just recognizing that there are an awful lot of things that are common among people. There are certain things that you come to learn promote a better life and better relationships and more personal fulfillment than other things that in general tend to do the opposite, and the things that promote these things, you would call morally right.

This response also represents a personal reconstruction of morality following a period of questioning and doubt, but the reconstruction of moral understanding is based not on the primacy and universality of individual rights, but rather on what she describes as a "very strong sense of being responsible to the world." Within this construction, the moral dilemma changes from how to exercise one's rights without interfering with the rights of others to how "to lead a moral life which includes obligations to myself and my family and people in general." The problem then becomes one of limiting responsibilities without abandoning moral concern. When asked to describe herself, this woman says that she values "having other people that I am tied to, and also having people that I am responsible to. I have a very strong sense of being responsible to the world, that I can't just live for my enjoyment, but just the fact of being in the world gives me an obligation to do what I can to make the world a better place to live in, no matter how small a scale that may be on." Thus while Kohlberg's subject worries about people interfering with each other's rights, this woman worries about "the possibility of omission, of your not helping others when you could help them."

The issue that this woman raises is addressed by Jane Loevinger's fifth "autonomous" stage of ego development, where autonomy, placed in a context of relationships, is defined as modulating an excessive sense of responsibility through the recognition that other people have responsibility for their own destiny. The autonomous stage in Loevinger's account (1970) witnesses a relinquishing of moral dichotomies and their replacement with "a feeling for the complexity and multifaceted character of real people and real situations" (p. 6). Whereas the rights conception of morality that informs Kohlberg's principled level (stages five and six) is geared to arriving at an objectively fair or just resolution to moral dilemmas upon which all rational persons could agree, the responsibility conception focuses instead on the limitations of any particular resolution and describes the conflicts that remain.

Thus it becomes clear why a morality of rights and noninterference may appear frightening to women in its potential justification of indifference and unconcern. At the same time, it becomes clear why, from a male perspective, a morality of responsibility appears inconclusive and diffuse, given its insistent contextual relativism. Women's moral judgments thus elucidate the pattern observed in the description of the developmental differences between the sexes, but they also provide an alternative conception of maturity by which these differences can be assessed and their implications traced. The psychology of women that has consistently been described as distinctive in its greater orientation toward relationships and interdependence implies a more contextual mode of judgment and a different moral understanding. Given the differences in women's conceptions of self and morality, women bring to the life cycle a different point of view and order human experience in terms of different priorities.

The myth of Demeter and Persephone, which McClelland (1975) cites as exemplifying the feminine attitude toward power, was associated with the Eleusinian Mysteries celebrated in ancient Greece for over two thousand years. As told in the Homeric *Hymn to Demeter,* the story of Persephone indicates the strengths of interdependence, building up resources and giving, that McClelland found in his research on power motivation to characterize the mature feminine style. Although, McClelland says, "it is fashionable to conclude that no one knows what went on in the Mysteries, it is known that they were probably the most important religious ceremonies, even partly on the historical record, which were organized by and for women, especially at the onset before men by means of the cult of Dionysos began to take them over." Thus McClelland regards the myth as "a special presentation of feminine psychology" (p. 96). It is, as well, a life-cycle story par excellence.

Persephone, the daughter of Demeter, while playing in a meadow with her girlfriends, sees a beautiful narcissus which she runs to pick. As she does so, the earth opens and she is snatched away by Hades, who takes her to his underworld kingdom. Demeter, goddess of the earth, so mourns the loss of her daughter that she refuses to allow anything to grow. The crops that sustain life on earth shrivel up, killing men and animals alike, until Zeus takes pity on man's suffering and persuades his brother to return Persephone to her mother. But before she leaves, Persephone eats some pomegranate seeds, which ensures that she will spend part of every year with Hades in the underworld.

The elusive mystery of women's development lies in its recognition of the continuing importance of attachment in the human life cycle. Woman's place in man's life cycle is to protect this recognition while the developmental litany intones the celebration of separation, autonomy, individuation, and natural rights. The myth of Persephone speaks directly to the distortion in this view by reminding us that narcissism leads to death, that the fertility of the earth is in some mysterious way tied to the continuation of the mother-daughter relationship, and that the life cycle itself arises from an alternation between the world of women and that of men. Only when life-cycle theorists divide their attention and begin to live with women as they have lived with men will their vision encompass the experience of both sexes and their theories become correspondingly more fertile.

REFERENCES

Kohlberg, L. (1973). "Continuities and Discontinuities in Childhood and Adult Moral Development Revisited." In *Collected Papers on Moral Development and Moral Education*. Moral Education Research Foundation, Harvard University.

Lovinger, J. and Wessler, R. (1970). *Measuring Ego Development*. San Francisco: Jossey-Bass.

McClelland, D. C. (1975). *Power: The Inner Experience*. New York: Irvington.

Carol Gilligan is Professor in the Human Development and Psychology Program at the Graduate School of Education, Harvard University.

QUESTIONS FOR REFLECTION

1. What does the word *morality* mean to you? With whose view of morality is your answer most congruent—Kohlberg's or Gilligan's?

2. Do you agree with Gilligan's statement that "masculinity is defined through separation while femininity is defined through attachment, [and] male gender identity is threatened by intimacy while female gender identity is threatened by separation"? According to Gilligan, how are these gender differences reflected in moral reasoning?

3. What are the implications for the curriculum of Gilligan's view of male and female moral reasoning?

Organize Schools around Child Development

JAMES P. COMER

ABSTRACT: Drawing from the principles of child development, Comer describes an approach to school re-form (now called the School Development Program) that provides children with the support and role models they need. Through a team approach involving a Governance and Management Team (now called the School Planning and Management Team), a Mental Health Team (now called the Student and Staff Support Team), and the Parents Program (now called the Parent Team), schools are restructured to meet students' developmental needs in the social-interactive, psycho-emotional, moral, linguistic, and intellectual-cognitive areas.

When you don't have a map—or some other way of setting direction—trying to go from New York to Los Angeles by way of Paris is not unreasonable. Americans have been pursuing school improvement in this way—without a conceptual map, without an organizing, direction-giving theme. That's why everything from establishing standards to restructuring to school choice appears to be a reasonable way to improve schools to one group or another.

There is an obvious point of focus for any organizing theme—students—how they grow and learn and, in turn, how policies must be established and resources deployed to promote development and learning. There is abundant evidence that young people learn at an adequate to optimal level when they are able to meet their developmental needs—with support for growth in social-interactive, psycho-emotional, moral, linguistic, and intellectual-cognitive areas. But neither our traditional educational approaches nor our school reform efforts of the past decade has focused adequately on child development.

Many teachers know very little about child development and even less about how to promote it. Until very recently, the pre- and in-service education of teachers largely ignored development; even now, the subject is not taught in a way that prepares teachers to support the development of students in school. Most schools are not organized and managed in a way that facilitates child development. Only recently and grudgingly has it been acknowledged that parents can play a direct role in schooling; and even now, the emphasis is on increasing their power to promote accountability rather than on enabling them to collaborate with the school staff in promoting the development of their children. Most curricula are not informed by an understanding of child development, and education policy often is not made by people with expertise in child development.

Based on our Yale Child Study Center-New Haven School System intervention, I believe school-reform efforts should focus on and be guided by child development principles. The program started in 1968, when a four-person Yale Child Study Center team went into two elementary schools in New Haven that were at the bottom in achievement, attendance, and behavior of the 33 elementary schools in the city. The students were nearly without exception Black, and almost all were from poor families.

In the beginning, our staff had no way to understand the problems of our students that often were manifested in fighting, disrespectful atti-

From *Social Policy* 22, no. 3 (Winter 1992): 28–30. Copyright 1992, Social Policy Corporation. Used by permission of the author and publisher.

tudes towards teachers, an inability to concentrate and take in information when it was important to do so, an inability to be spontaneous and curious when it was important, and to get along well with other students. Staff members often viewed the students as bad or not smart, not interested, and not motivated. Their response—consistent with our cultural norms—was to attempt to punish and control them, and to have low academic expectations for them. And even when staff members wanted to be supportive or better respond to the needs of students, the hierarchical and authoritarian organization and management of the school would not permit it. Teachers were expected to teach and control the children, or refer them to the principal or professional support staff when there was a problem.

In working with the schools, we eventually came to understand the difficult interactions in school to be a result of underdevelopment of children from families under economic and social stress, the punitive and controlling response of teachers that made matters worse, and an organization and management that did not allow the staff to respond in a supportive way. In a chaotic environment, children cannot adequately imitate, identify with, and internalize the attitudes and values of adult caretakers in the way needed to gain the confidence and personal discipline necessary for academic learning.

Our solution was to create a Governance and Management Team representative of all the adult stakeholders in the school—parents, teachers, administrators, and non-professional support staff. The Governance Team enabled parents and staff together to identify problems and opportunities, and to develop strategies and direction for the school, thus gradually decreasing the apathy and chaos, alienation and anger, hopelessness and despair. It was school-based management. But because we were more interested in creating a sense of community in the school, we didn't call it that. Order, control, and accountability eventually increased, largely

due to the work of an effective Governance and Management Team—but even more because the team helped to create a school climate that supported student development and a growth in school effectiveness rather than through a use of rules, regulations, and power.

Our focus on creating a good climate for children led to the creation of a Mental Health Team and a Parents Program. In traditional schools, social workers, psychologists, special education teachers, and other support staff work individually in a way that leads to fragmentation and duplication—expensive and ineffective. By working as a team, our support staff coordinated their efforts, but more importantly, they were able to share systematically their knowledge of child development and relationship skills with other staff and parents. This enabled all the school staff—not just the support staff—to begin to support development rather than simply punish children. The parent program enabled the parents to work with the school staff to create a good social climate in the school.

As we assessed what was going on in our program, we realized that we were giving low-income children the social skills that many middle-class children gained simply by growing up in families engaged in activities utilizing skills that prepared them to meet the expectations of school. We reasoned that our improved social climate in school could accomplish the same thing if we made the effort more systematic. Out of this developed a program called "A Social Skills Curriculum for Inner-City Children."

By 1984, the two project schools we were working with were among the top five in attendance, achievement, and behavior (one of the initial schools was replaced with another with a similar profile in the course of the study). Using the same principles, we are now involved with more than 165 schools in 17 school districts across the country; many are showing improvement, and in several instances there have been dramatic gains—40 to 60 percentile points—measured on nationally standardized achievement tests.

We have seen a large number of school-reform initiatives in this country that have been minimally successful, failed, or are destined to fail because they do not adequately address the developmental issues that should be central to any reform. Many educators have in mind a vaguely industrial model for teaching and learning: students as raw material, staff as assembly-line workers functioning more or less independently of each other. Our work—and that of many others—shows that this system of schooling prevents many capable staff, parents, and students from functioning adequately.

The decision we must now make about how to improve education is similar to the one man-ufacturers were faced with after World War II. American manufacturers chose to stick with the principles advanced by Frederick Taylor tied to mechanistic, assembly-line mass production. Japanese manufacturers were guided by the principles of William Demming, which were people-centered and recognized the interrelatedness of areas of work and the need for continuous quality control, and to change, adapt, and find appropriate ways to do a job rather than be locked into a rigid system. A half-century later, American manufacturing is on the ropes and Japanese manufacturing is thriving. If American education is to thrive, it must be guided by a people-centered—in this case, child-development—approach.

James P. Comer is the Maurice Falk Professor of Child Psychiatry at the Yale University Child Study Center, Associate Dean of the Yale University School of Medicine, and Director of the School Development Program.

QUESTIONS FOR REFLECTION

1. Comer states that "most curricula are not informed by an understanding of child development." What do you think might account for the fact that this important basis of the curriculum is often overlooked?
2. What objections might some teachers, parents, and community members raise about Comer's approach to school reform? As an educational leader, how would you respond to these objections?
3. What evidence can you cite to support Comer's contention that "many educators have in mind a vaguely industrial model for teaching and learning"? How is this model reflected in school curricula?

TEACHERS' VOICES
Putting Theory into Practice

Walkabout in Sixth Grade

RICHARD ISENBERG

ABSTRACT: A sixth-grade teacher describes how he developed a "walkabout program," based on the Australian Aborigine trial of manhood, which provides students with developmental opportunities for self-discovery and challenge. The program is designed around five "challenge areas" of personal development: adventure, creativity, logical inquiry, practical skills, and service.

The term "walkabout"—originating in the Australian Aborigine trial of manhood—is probably more familiar to Americans today than at any time in the past. However, the idea that self-discovery and challenge are important parts of the passage into adulthood is ancient. The beauty of the ancient tradition of the walkabout is that it creates an opportunity for growth as young people move from childhood to adulthood. Those on walkabout are challenged to use all their skills, apply their knowledge to real problems, and see tangible results. The experience also includes time to be introspective and to assimilate what has been learned through the trial itself. When the walkabout is completed, the sojourners return to a new adult life with great pride in their accomplishments. These are worthy goals for any educational setting, but they are especially appropriate for early adolescents.

My first exposure to the idea of walkabout as an educational program was in 1978 when I attended a presentation by the Center for Educational Services and Research in Yorktown Heights, New York. I was intrigued enough to gather the literature that was available at that time. And I was surprised to discover numerous programs evolving throughout the country.

While there was considerable variety, they all shared core principles of walkabout in that they were student-centered, activity-oriented, and focused on authentic life skills. However, I was disappointed to discover that most of them were designed as alternative high school programs for high-risk students. I did not see any reason why the basic principles of walkabout needed to be limited to older students. So, while it took some years to find myself in the right situation to launch a program, in 1986 I began to offer the challenge of walkabout to my sixth-grade students.

Sixth grade seemed like an ideal time to introduce the walkabout concept. Children of 11 or 12 years of age are undergoing rapid physical and emotional change. They are typically given more freedom and independence as well as additional responsibilities at home, in school, and in the community. In my school system in Vermont, students are preparing to make a significant instructional leap from small rural elementary schools into the larger consolidated high school. Most important, many students are eager to become more independent and to expand their opportunities to govern their own learning. Walkabout can channel these natural energies in productive ways.

From *Phi Delta Kappan* 78, no. 7 (March 1997): 513–516. © 1997, Phi Delta Kappa. Used by permission of the author and publisher.

PROGRAM DESIGN

The walkabout program I developed for my sixth-graders was drawn from several models in the literature and adapted for younger students. The basic structure revolves around five areas of personal development:

- *adventure*—a challenge to the student's daring, endurance, and skill in an unfamiliar environment (e.g., rock climbing, backpacking, wilderness fishing, hunting);
- *creativity*—a challenge to explore, cultivate, and express one's own imagination in some aesthetically pleasing form (e.g., oil painting, playing musical instruments, quilting, cartooning);
- *logical inquiry*—a challenge to pursue one's curiosity, to formulate a question of personal importance, and to explore an answer or solution systematically (e.g., police training, llama husbandry, animal anatomy, veterinary medicine);
- *practical skills*—a challenge to explore a utilitarian activity and to acquire the knowledge and skill necessary to work in a given field and to produce something of use (e.g., cooking, sewing, woodworking, house design); and
- *service*—a challenge to identify a need for help and to provide it without expectation of reward (e.g., assisting in a local parent-child center, doing chores for elderly neighbors, assisting at the local humane society).

These categories are somewhat arbitrary, but they are intended to cover a range of potential endeavors that require a variety of skills. Most ideas that students generate can be interpreted or adapted to fit into one of these categories. Since one of the primary goals of walkabout is to encourage students to take responsibility for their own learning, there is a lot of flexibility in how a project is defined, planned, and evaluated. I encourage students to design and carry out a project in each of the areas of personal development.

As they are thinking about an area of challenge to pursue, I ask the students to choose a mentor to help them plan and carry out their project. The mentor will be the student's primary advisor and support. The mentor might be a parent or other interested adult with the special knowledge or skills appropriate for a student's project. The role of the mentor is to provide encouragement, advice, and material support when needed. Mentors are *not* responsible for any part of the process or results. Theirs is strictly a support role.

Experience has shown that students are more enthusiastic when there is a minimum of paperwork required for a project. However, before they begin, I require a simple, one-page planning sheet to be filled out with the help of the student's mentor. To help students organize their thoughts, the planning sheet includes such questions as: What is the goal of your project? How will you know when you have reached your goal? What steps will you have to take to accomplish your goal? What is the estimated time line for your project? I review planning sheets to ensure that students have developed their ideas sufficiently to have a good chance of success and to make certain that they have not taken on anything unreasonable or dangerous.

Students have demonstrated a wide range of interests and considerable creativity in designing their projects. Initially students are particularly interested in *adventure* projects. Rock climbing, living with a family in another state, fishing in remote Canadian lakes, and taking a 50-mile bike trip are examples of adventure projects that students have undertaken. One critical issue is to design a project that is appropriately challenging, given a student's experience. One particularly athletic boy arranged to accompany two expert rock climbers on the ascent of a major rock face in the Adirondack Mountains. Another boy, with little camping experience, planned a short overnight backpacking trip for his family to a shelter on the Long Trail in the Green Mountains. While the climbing was a much more spectacular project, both were appropriate for the experience and ability of the students.

Projects in *creativity* have also been popular. Students have engaged in oil painting, doll house construction, quilting, and dancing, and they have played a variety of musical instruments. One group of four did a joint project by forming a musical combo that performed for commencement.

The distinction between *creativity* and *practical skills* is often unclear and generally unimportant. For example, several students have learned to knit as a project under one or the other category. Typically, practical skills have focused on homemaking or pre-vocational projects. Cooking, sewing, woodworking, and bicycle mechanics are immediately valuable skills, and students are happy to gain experience in them. It is common for students to choose projects that a relative or friend is skilled in and to enlist that person as a mentor.

Logical inquiry projects have been less appealing for most students, perhaps because they are most like other school projects. However, one of the best projects ever done in any category was completed by a student interested in law enforcement. He arranged to attend the actual training sessions conducted by the state police for prospective deputy sheriffs. He received direct instruction from professionals in his field of interest, and he scored higher on the final exam than many of the candidates. My experience has been that students will be more likely to attempt a project if they are encouraged to explore topics of genuine interest and to use direct, experiential learning methods.

Service projects have produced some of the most satisfying and rewarding results. Some have been as simple as helping an elderly neighbor with household chores, participating in a roadside cleanup, or volunteering at the local humane society. One project that was particularly poignant was conducted by two girls who volunteered to help out at the local parent-child center. They helped care for the infants one afternoon a week for several weeks. What they brought back to the class was how demanding child-care responsibilities are and how young many of the mothers and fathers were. It was clear that their own self-perception changed noticeably as a result of their work with children of parents not much older than themselves. When they can contribute in real, tangible ways, students find community service quite appealing.

Students have had the most difficulty in setting a reasonable standard for success. They often have grandiose goals that are only vaguely defined or that they are unlikely to achieve. A student who was interested in hunting as an adventure chose shooting a deer as the criterion for success. Once it was pointed out that many hunters go for years without a kill, the expected outcome was modified to spending two days hunting safely with his father. Students who choose to learn to play musical instruments might conclude their projects with a public performance rather than a subjective assessment of their competence. Such practical skills as knitting, sewing, and woodworking have concluded with a completed product. The key is to have a well-defined, observable outcome as the criterion for success.

I review the steps for pursuing a project and the time line, looking for obvious omissions or unreasonable expectations. However, I still caution students that it may be necessary to modify their plans as the project evolves. Any challenge can present unexpected problems or opportunities that cannot be foreseen in the planning stage. So additional steps must be added or time lines modified as needed. The original planning provides a guide, not a recipe.

Once a project plan is sufficiently developed, students begin their activities independently or in cooperation with their mentors. Since most projects are conducted outside of school, I try to check in with students every couple of weeks to see how things are going. We hold conferences, and we troubleshoot as necessary. Much of the richness of the program lies in this kind of problem solving. Periodically students might be asked to share their work-in-progress with the class. Peers often provide advice and encouragement.

When the goals of a project have been reached, all students are asked to share what they have done with the class and to complete a brief project summary. Again, in an effort to minimize paperwork, the project summary asks only a few simple questions: What happened during the project? What did you learn from the experience? What related areas might you explore someday? The intent of the summary is to serve as a guide for discussion of the project and to give students a record of their work for their formal presentation at the end of the year.

Like other walkabout programs, the formal presentation of a student's accomplishments to peers, family, friends, and other significant people is an important component of my sixth-grade program. In some alternative high school programs, there is a level of accountability implicit in this process since credit or credentials are granted. Because this is not an issue for sixth-graders, we approach it more as a celebration, and it has worked nicely to enhance our traditional sixth-grade commencement.

Before walkabout, our commencements were primarily of interest to adults, and students took little active part. Since the walkabout philosophy requires a formal presentation, we decided to incorporate this into our commencement rather than to create a separate occasion. Now, each student makes a brief speech as part of the commencement program, describing the various projects he or she pursued as part of the walkabout experience. Tangible products are displayed, or students demonstrate the new skills they have acquired. In addition to providing an opportunity for students to present their walkabout accomplishments, this activity has changed the tone of the commencement and made it much more student-centered.

PROGRAM LOGISTICS

Participation in our walkabout program for sixth-graders is optional. The program has no operating budget and takes up little classroom time. True to the spirit of walkabout, most of the impetus and effort come from the students. Thus it is essential to build a climate of enthusiasm, empowerment, and challenge. I rely on students' natural desire for independent learning, testimonials from former students, parents' desire for their children to excel, and my own in-terest in the program to motivate students to take on the extra work and challenges. A letter describing the program is sent home to parents, and an informational meeting is held early in the school year. In class we discuss the walkabout philosophy, the areas of personal development, a brief outline of the steps to follow for a project, sample planning sheets, and projects completed in the past. A chart is displayed on the classroom wall that shows students whose projects are in progress or completed. Individual or group conferences are arranged as needed, and some class time is used to share what students are doing and to solicit comments, questions, and ideas.

Over the past 10 years, about 80% of my students have participated in the program. Most have completed two or three projects. A few complete a project in each of the five challenge areas, and a few choose not to participate at all.

I have found that the most difficult aspect of the program is facilitating students' involvement without directing or rescuing them. I believe that, as soon as the teacher, parent, or mentor becomes more invested in the project than the student, the walkabout idea is dead. It can be very frustrating to encourage without pushing, to guide without directing, and to salvage without rescuing. But the purpose of the program is to give students the opportunity to be responsible for their own learning. While adults do not always find it a comfortable experience to let go, the balance of initiative and effort must be heavily weighted toward students. They must be responsible for the work and worthy of the praise if they are to internalize the habits of educational empowerment.

I cannot emphasize enough the fact that the program's design is only the scaffolding on which students can build their own experiences. The guidelines are intended only to facilitate the process. The program should be undertaken with the expectation and hope that students will stretch the initial boundaries. It is what students bring to, do with, and take from the process that are the essence of walkabout.

Richard Isenberg is a sixth-grade teacher in Cornwall, Vermont.

QUESTIONS FOR REFLECTION

1.   From a human development perspective, why does Isenberg state that "sixth grade seemed like an ideal time to introduce the walkabout concept"?
2.   With reference to the level and the subject area with which you are most familiar, how would you incorporate the walkabout concept in planning learning experiences for students?
3.   Isenberg's walkabout curriculum for sixth-grade students focuses on five "challenge areas." What other "challenge areas" might be appropriate for students at that level?

LEARNING ACTIVITIES

Critical Thinking

1.   With respect to a school, college, or university with which you are familiar, describe the curriculum as it relates to human development. To what extent are the theories of human development presented in this chapter reflected in the curriculum?
2.   In *All Grown Up and No Place to Go: Teenagers in Crisis* (Addison-Wesley, 1998), David Elkind suggests that adolescents behave according to an "imaginary audience" (the belief that others are preoccupied with one's appearance and behavior) and the "personal fable" (the belief that one is immortal and not subject to the limitations that affect other human beings). How might the school curriculum help students to become more realistic in both of these areas?
3.   In *Blackberry Winter: My Earlier Years* (Kodansha, 1995), noted anthropologist Margaret Mead expresses the view that the lack of a close relationship between grandparents and grandchildren in today's society is a serious loss to society and the child. She states that children need to grow up with three generations. Do you agree? Why? Will "adopt a grandparent" programs which many communities have implemented help this developmental need of children?
4.   Studies by the Center on Organization and Restructuring of Schools at the University of Wisconsin-Madison have found that students at "successfully restructured" schools are more likely to conform to their school's expectations if they believe the school "cares" about students. Compare this finding with Ashley Montagu's statement in this chapter that the "greatest gift a teacher has to give a student is his or her love." How can teachers convey this attitude toward their students?
5.   Piaget's theory of cognitive development has been criticized for having only four discrete stages tied to chronological age and for underestimating the cognitive abilities and competence of young children. To what extent do you agree with these criticisms? (For more information see Gelman, R. and Baillargeon, R. (1983). "A Review of Some Piagetian Concepts." In P. Mussen, ed., *Carmichael's*

Manual of Child Psychology, Vol. 3: Cognitive Development (E. Markman and J. Flavel, volume eds.). New York: Wiley, 1983; Woolfolk, A. *Educational Psychology,* 6th Ed. Boston: Allyn and Bacon, 1995, pp. 44–46; and Lourenco, Orlando and Machado, Armando. "In Defense of Piaget's Theory: A Reply to 10 Common Criticisms." *Psychological Review* 103 (January 1996): 143–164.).

6. What are some developmental challenges that today's children and youth must confront that were unknown or little known to their parents or grandparents?

Application Activities

1. Ask your instructor to invite a counselor from the K–12 or higher education levels to your class. Ask this individual to discuss the most frequent developmental needs they encounter among students and to suggest ways that the curriculum can address those needs.

2. The November 1993 issue of *Educational Leadership* is devoted to the theme of character education and includes descriptions of exemplary service learning programs and how they relate to Kohlberg's stages of moral development and Piaget's cognitive stages. Read the articles in this journal and make a list of learning experiences that, with appropriate modification, could be incorporated into the curriculum with which you are most familiar.

Field Experiences

1. Visit a classroom at the level with which you are most familiar. What differences do you note among learners that are related to their stages of development? How might these differences affect their learning?

2. At the level with which you are most familiar, interview a student and, if possible, observe his or her classroom behavior. Then write a brief case study that focuses on common developmental tasks of learners in that age group. As appropriate, make references to the articles on human development included in this chapter.

Internet Activities

1. Go to the home page for James P. Comer's School Development Program (**http://info.med.yale.edu/comer/comer.html**) and gather information on the structure and "operational expectations" of the three "teams" that make up the School Development Program.

2. Visit a few of the following web sites for K–12 students and determine to what extent each site reflects the developmental needs of children and youth:

    The Awesome Lists (**http://www.clark.net/pub/journalism/awesome.html**)
    Berit's Best Sites for Children (**http://db.cochran.com/db_HTML:theopage.db**)
    Canada's SchoolNet (**http://schoolnet2.carleton.ca/**)
    KidLink (**http://www.kidlink.org/**)

Kid's Web (**http://www.npac.syr.edu/textbook/kidsweb/**)
Newton's Apple (**http://ericir.syr.edu/Projects/Newton/**)
Online Educator (**http://www.ole.net/ole/**)
Young Person's Guide to the Internet (**http://www.sos.on.ca/~garym/kids.html**)
Discovery Channel School (**http://school.discovery.com/**)

BOOKS AND ARTICLES TO REVIEW

Allen, Jan. "Promoting Preschoolers' Moral Reasoning." *Early Child Development and Care* 33, no. 1–4 (April 1988): 171–180.

Attanucci, Jane S. "Placing Care in the Human Life Cycle." *Journal for a Just and Caring Education* 2, no. 1 (January 1996): 25–41.

Berk, Laura E. *Child Development,* 4th ed. Boston: Allyn and Bacon, 1997.

———. *Infants, Children, and Adolescents,* 2nd Ed. Boston: Allyn and Bacon, 1996.

———. *Infants and Children: Prenatal through Middle Childhood,* 2nd Ed. Boston: Allyn and Bacon, 1996.

Bickhard, Mark H. "Piaget and Active Cognition." *Human Development* 40, no. 4 (July–August 1997): 238–244.

Blakeney, Ronnie Ann, and Blakeney, Charles David. "A Therapeutic Just Community for Troubled Girls." *Reclaiming Children and Youth: Journal of Emotional and Behavioral Problems* 5, no. 3 (Fall 1996): 163–66, 172.

Boyer, Ernest. "Duty Calls." *Momentum* 27, no. 1 (February–March, 1996): 37–39.

———. "Ready to Learn: A Mandate for the Nation." *Young Children* 48, no. 3 (March 1993): 54–57.

Bradley, Cheryl L. "Generativity-Stagnation: Development of a Status Model." *Developmental Review* 17, no. 3 (September 1997): 262–290.

Burk, Deborah I. "Understanding Friendship and Social Interaction." *Childhood Education* 72, no. 5 (1996): 282–285.

Campbell, Robert L., and Christopher, John Chambers. "Moral Development Theory: A Critique of Its Kantian Presuppositions." *Developmental Review* 16, no. 1 (March 1996): 1–47.

Chaill, Christine, and Silvern, Steven B. "Understanding through Play." *Childhood Education* 72, no. 5 (1996): 274–277.

Chance, Paul. "Speaking of Differences." *Phi Delta Kappan* 78, no. 7 (March 1997): 506–507.

Coyhis, Don. "The Developmental Cycle: Teachings on the Eight Stages of Growth of a Human Being." *Winds of Change* 12, no. 4 (Autumn 1997): 114–119.

Daniels, Judy, et al. "Moral Development and Hawaiian Youths: Does Gender Make a Difference?" *Journal of Counseling & Development* 74, no. 1 (September–October 1995): 90–93.

Daniels, Judy, and D'Andrea, Michael. "Assessing the Moral Development and Self-Esteem of Hawaiian Youth." *Journal of Multicultural Counseling and Development* 23, no. 1 (January 1995): 39–47.

Denton, Johnnie. "Character and Moral Development." *NAMTA Journal* 22, no. 2 (Spring 1997): 111–116.

DeVries, Rheta. "Piaget's Social Theory." *Educational Researcher* 26, no. 2 (March 1997): 4–17.

———, and Zan, Betty S. *Moral Classrooms, Moral Children: Creating A Constructivist Atmosphere in Early Education.* New York: Teachers College Press, 1994.

Edwards, Carolyn Pope. *Promoting Social and Moral Development in Young Children: Creative Approaches for the Classroom.* New York: Teachers College Press, 1986.

Elias, Maurice J., et al. "How To Launch a Social and Emotional Learning Program." *Educational Leadership,* 54, no. 8 (May 1997): 15–19.

Elkind, David. *All Grown Up and No Place to Go: Teenagers in Crisis.* Reading, MA: Addison-Wesley, 1998.

———. *A Sympathetic Understanding of the Child: Birth to Sixteen.* Boston: Allyn and Bacon, 1994.

———. *Ties That Stress: The New Family Imbalance.* Cambridge, MA: Harvard University Press, 1994.

———. "Developmentally Appropriate Education for 4-Year-Olds." *Theory Into Practice* 28, no. 1 (Winter 1989): 47–52.

———. *The Hurried Child: Growing Up Too Fast Too Soon.* Reading, MA: Addison-Wesley, 1988.

Erikson, Erik H. *The Life Cycle Completed: Extended Version with New Chapters on the Ninth Stage of Develop-*

ment by Joan M. Erikson. New York: W. W. Norton & Company, 1997.

Garmon, Lance C., et al. "Gender Differences in Stage and Expression of Moral Judgment." *Merrill-Palmer Quarterly* 42, no. 3 (July 1996): 418–437.

Gellatly, Angus. "Why the Young Child Has Neither a Theory of Mind nor a Theory of Anything Else." *Human Development* 40, no. 1 (January–February 1997): 32–50.

Gilligan, Carol. *In a Different Voice: Psychological Theory and Women's Development.* Cambridge, MA: Harvard University Press, 1993.

———. "Remembering Larry." *Journal of Moral Education* 27, no. 2 (June 1998): 125–140.

Goldberg, Mark F. "Maintaining a Focus on Child Development: An Interview with Dr. James P. Comer." *Phi Delta Kappan* 78, no. 7 (March 1997): 557–559.

Graber, Julia A., Brooks-Gunn, Jeanne, and Petersen, Anne C., eds. *Transitions Through Adolescence: Interpersonal Domains and Context.* Mahwah, NJ: Lawrence Erlbaum, 1996.

Gratz, Rene R., and Boulton, Pamla J. "Erikson and Early Childhood Educators: Looking at Ourselves and Our Profession Developmentally." *Young Children* 51, no. 5 (July 1996): 74–78.

Grossman, Sue. "Passing Vickie's Test: Building Self-Esteem and Trust by Following Through with Rules." *Early Childhood News* 8, no. 5 (September–October 1996): 6–12.

Hansen, David T. "Teaching and the Moral Life of Classrooms." *Journal for a Just and Caring Education* 2, no. 1 (January 1996): 59–74.

Hayes, Richard L. "The Legacy of Lawrence Kohlberg: Implications for Counseling and Human Development. *Journal of Counseling and Development* 72, no. 3 (January 1994): 261–267.

Horst, Elisabeth A. "Reexamining Gender Issues in Erikson's Stages of Identity and Intimacy." *Journal of Counseling & Development* 73, no. 3 (January–February 1995): 271–278.

Hurd, Tracey L., and Brabeck, Mary. "Presentation of Women and Gilligan's Ethic of Care in College Textbooks, 1970–1990: An Examination of Bias." *Teaching of Psychology* 24, no. 3 (1997): 159–167.

Hyson, Marion C. *The Emotional Development of Young Children: Building an Emotion-Centered Curriculum.* New York: Teachers College Press, 1994.

Kagan, Jerome, and Gall, Susan B., eds. *The Gale Encyclopedia of Childhood and Adolescence.* Detroit, MI: Gale Research, 1998.

Kagitcibasi, Cigdem. *Family and Human Development Across Cultures: A View from the Other Side.* Mahwah, NJ: Lawrence Erlbaum, 1996.

Kami, Constance, and Ewing, Janice K. "Basing Teaching on Piaget's Constructivism." *Childhood Education* 72, no. 5 (1996): 260–264.

Kidwell, Jeannie S., et al. "Adolescent Identity Exploration: A Test of Erikson's Theory of Transitional Crisis." *Adolescence* 30, no. 120 (Winter 1995): 785–793.

Killen, Melanie. "Justice and Care: Dichotomies or Coexistence?" *Journal for a Just and Caring Education* 2, no. 1 (January 1996): 42–58.

Kohn, Alfie. "How Not To Teach Values: A Critical Look at Character Education." *Phi Delta Kappan* 78, no. 6 (February 1997): 428–439.

Kohlberg, Lawrence. *The Psychology of Moral Development: The Nature and Validity of Moral Stages.* San Francisco: Harper & Row, 1984.

Koroscik, Judith Smith. "Scholarly Discourse on Art and Human Development." *Human Development* 40, no. 3 (May–June 1997): 181–188.

Kvasz, Ladislav. "Why Don't They Understand Me?" *Science and Education* 6, no. 3 (May 1997): 263–272.

Lamb, Sharon, and Zakhireh, Barry. "Toddlers' Attention to the Distress of Peers in a Day Care Setting." *Early Education and Development* 8, no. 2 (April 1997): 105–118.

Langford, Peter E. "Separating Judicial from Legislative Reasoning in Moral Dilemma Interviews." *Child Development* 68, no. 6 (December 1997): 1105–1116.

Levenson, Michael R., and Crumpler, Cheryl A. "Three Models of Adult Development." *Human Development* 39, no. 3 (May–June 1996): 135–149.

Levinson, Daniel J. *The Seasons of a Woman's Life.* New York: Knopf, 1996.

———. *The Seasons of a Man's Life.* New York: Knopf, 1978.

Lourenco, Orlando. "Reflections on Narrative Approaches to Moral Development." *Human Development* 39, no 2 (March–April 1996): 83–99.

———, and Machado, Armando. "In Defense of Piaget's Theory: A Reply to 10 Common Criticisms." *Psychological Review* 103 (January 1996): 143–164.

Manning, M. Lee. "Erikson's Psychosocial Theories Help Explain Early Adolescence." *NASSP Bulletin* 72, no. 509 (September 1988): 95–100.

Mead, Margaret. *Blackberry Winter: My Earlier Years.* New York: Kodansha America, 1995.

Montangero, Jacques, and Maurice-Naville, Danielle (trans). *Piaget Or the Advance of Knowledge: An Overview and Glossary.* Mahwah, NJ: Lawrence Erlbaum, 1997.

Nabors, Martha L., and Edwards, Linda C. "Creativity and the Child's Social Development." *Dimensions of Early Childhood* 23, no. 1 (Fall 1994): 14–16.

Neysmith-Roy, Joan M., and Kleisinger, Carmel L. "Using Biographies of Adults over 65 Years of Age to Understand Life-Span Developmental Psychology." *Teaching of Psychology* 24, no. 2 (1997): 116–118.

Nisan, Mordecai. "Personal Identity and Education for the Desirable." *Journal of Moral Education* 25, no. 1 (March 1996): 75–83.

O'Neil, John. "Building Schools as Communities: A Conversation with James Comer." *Educational Leadership,* 54, no. 8 (May 1997): 6–10.

Pellegrini, Anthony D. *Observing Children in Their Natural Worlds: A Methodological Primer.* Mahwah, NJ: Lawrence Erlbaum, 1996.

Perry, Constance M. "How Do We Teach What Is Right? Research and Issues in Ethical and Moral Development." *Journal for a Just and Caring Education* 2, no. 4 (October 1996): 400–410.

Peterson, Rosemary, and Felton-Collins, Victoria. *The Piaget Handbook for Teachers and Parents: Children in the Age of Discovery, Preschool-3rd Grade.* New York: Teachers College Press, 1986.

Rodd, Jillian. *Understanding Young Children's Behavior.* New York: Teachers College Press, 1996.

Ryan, Francis J. "Narcissim and the Moral Sense: Moral Education in the Secondary Sociology Classroom." *Social Studies* 88, no. 5 (September–October 1997): 233–237.

Sameroff, Arnold, and McDonough, Susan C. "Educational Implications of Developmental Transitions: Revisiting the 5- to 7-Year Shift." *Phi Delta Kappan* 76, no. 3 (November 1994): 188–193.

Schickedanz, Judith A., Schickedanz, David, Forsyth, Peggy, and Forsyth, G. Alfred. *Understanding Children and Adolescents,* 3rd Ed. Boston: Allyn and Bacon, 1998.

Sheehy, Gail. *New Passages: Mapping Your Life Across Time.* New York: Random House, 1995.

———. *Pathfinders.* New York: Morrow, 1981.

———. *Passages.* New York: E. P. Dutton, Inc. 1976.

Solomon, Gloria B. "Fair Play in the Gymnasium: Improving Social Skills among Elementary School Students." *Journal of Physical Education, Recreation and Dance* 68, no. 5 (May–June 1997): 22–25.

Turner, Pauline H., and Hamner, Tommie J. *Child Development and Early Education: Infancy Through Preschool.* Boston: Allyn and Bacon, 1993.

Wark, Gillian R., and Krebs, Dennis L. "Gender and Dilemma Differences in Real-Life Moral Judgment." *Developmental Psychology* 32, no. 2 (March 1996): 220–230.

Wilson, John. "First Steps in Moral Education." *Journal of Moral Education* 25, no. 1 (March 1996): 85–91.

Wolf, Denise Palmer. "Reimagining Development: Possibilities from the Study of Children's Art." *Human Development* 40, no. 3 (May–June 1997): 189–194.

Videotapes

Erik H. Erikson: A Life's Work, Piaget's Developmental Theory: An Overview, and *Using What We Know: Applying Piaget's Developmental Theory in Primary Classrooms* examine these influential theories of human development. The two videos on Piaget's theory are written and narrated by David Elkind, a former student of Piaget's. (Available from Davidson Films, Inc. 231 E. Street, Davis, CA 95616 (916) 753-9604.)

Supporting Early Adolescents: Grades 5–9 is a 26-minute video that showcases middle school programs that support early adolescents. (Available from Sunburst Communications, Department N S 5 3, 39 Washington Avenue, P.O. Box 40, Pleasantville, NY 10570-9904 (800) 431-1934.)

Theories of Development is a 29-minute video that presents an overview of theories of child development, including Piaget's and Erikson's developmental theories. (Available from Insight Media, 2162 Broadway, P.O. Box 621, New York, NY 10024-0621 (800) 233-9910.)

Learning and Learning Styles

FOCUS QUESTIONS

1. What are the key principles of behavioral learning theories?
2. What role does socialization play in learning?
3. What are the key principles of cognitive learning theories?
4. What is the constructivist view of learning?
5. How do learning styles influence learning?
6. What are multiple intelligences?

The third basis of the curriculum is the nature of learning. An understanding of how human beings learn is obviously of central importance for curriculum planners. Learning theorists and researchers have not arrived at a universally accepted, precise definition of *learning*; however, most agree that learning is a change in an individual's knowledge or behavior that results from experience (Mazur, 1997; Slavin, 1997; Woolfolk, 1998). It is generally acknowledged that there are two families of learning theories—*behavioral* and *cognitive*—and that many subgroups exist within these two families. At the very least, curriculum planners should understand the distinguishing features of each family, because each defines the curriculum differently, and each leads to or supports different instructional strategies. In addition, curricula and teaching practices are usually based on both families of theories to allow for the diverse needs of learners or different types of knowledge to be learned.

BEHAVIORAL LEARNING THEORIES

Behavioral learning theories emphasize observable changes in behavior that result from stimulus-response associations made by the learner. Thinking is part of a stimulus-response (S-R) sequence that begins and ends outside the individual learner, and learning is the product of design rather than accident. Learning is a conditioning process by which a person acquires a new response; and motivation is the urge to act, which results from a stimulus. Behavior is directed by stimuli from the environment, and a person selects one response instead of another because of the particular combination of prior conditioning and physiological drives operating at the moment of action. A person does not have to want to learn something in order to learn it. People can learn anything of which they are capable if they are willing to go through the pattern of activity necessary for conditioning to take place.

A major construct of S-R behavioral learning theories is the *rewarded response.* A response must be rewarded for learning to take place. What counts as a "reward" varies from learner to learner; although the reward must be important to the learner in some way. Rewards are often effective for certain types of learners: slow learners, those less prepared for the learning task, and those in need of step-by-step learning. In "An Analysis of Behavior Modification" in this chapter, Clifford K. Madsen and Charles H. Madsen, Jr., explain how teachers can set up a system of rewards in their classrooms.

John B. Watson (1878–1958) and B. F. Skinner (1904–1990) are the two principal originators of behaviorist approaches to learning. Watson asserted that human behavior was the result of specific stimuli that elicited certain responses. Watson's view of learning was based partially on experiments conducted by Russian psychologist Ivan Pavlov (1849–1936), who noticed that a dog he was working with salivated shortly before he was given food. Pavlov discovered that by ringing a bell when food was given and repeating this several times, the sound of the bell alone (a conditioned stimulus) would make the dog salivate (a conditioned response). Watson believed that all learning conformed to the Pavlovian S-R model, which has become known as *classical* or *type S conditioning.*

Expanding on Watson's basic S-R model, Skinner developed a more comprehensive view of conditioning known as *operant* (or *type R*) *conditioning.* His model was based on the premise that satisfying responses are conditioned, unsatisfying ones are not; as he put it: "the things we call pleasant have an energizing or strengthening effect on our behaviour" (Skinner, 1972, p. 74).

Skinner believed that a "scientific" S-R approach to learning could serve humanitarian aims and help to create a better world. He maintained that notions about human free will based on an eighteenth-century political philosophy should not be allowed to interfere with the application of scientific methods to human affairs. In his novel *Walden Two* (1962), Skinner describes how a utopian society could be created through "behavioral engineering." By focusing on external conditions that shape and maintain human behavior, educators could turn their attention from ill-defined inner qualities and faculties to the observable and manipulable.

Social Learning Theories

While social learning theories reflect many of the principles of behavioral learning theories, they place greater emphasis on the influence of external cues on behavior and on how thinking influences action and vice versa. Social learning theories—which are widely endorsed by sociologists, anthropologists, and social psychologists—maintain that human beings have an unlimited capacity to learn. This capacity, however, *is* limited by social expectations and by constraints on behavior patterns that the immediate social environment considers appropriate. According to this view, the learning process is primarily social, and learning occurs through socialization. Socialization occurs in a variety of social settings, including the family, the peer group, the school, and the job, and it continues throughout life. According to Albert Bandura (1977, p. 12), the originator of social learning theory, "virtually all learning phenomena resulting from direct experience occur on a vicarious basis by observing other people's behavior and its consequences for them." Bandura's view of learning is often referred to as *modeling* or *observational learning*.

COGNITIVE LEARNING THEORIES

Cognitive learning theories focus on the mental processes people use as they acquire new knowledge and skills. Unlike behavioral learning theories which focus on observable behavior, cognitive theories focus on the unobservable processing, storage, and retrieval of information from the brain. According to cognitive learning theories, the individual acts, originates, and thinks, and this is the important source of learning; according to behavioral learning theory, however, the individual learns by reacting to external forces.

Cognitive learning theories emphasize personal meaning, generalizations, principles, advance organizers, discovery learning, coding, and superordinate categories. The next chapter, "The Nature of Knowledge," contains important applications of cognitive learning theory. In "Structures in Learning" in that chapter, Jerome Bruner, a leading cognitive learning theorist, applies generalizations concerning the following to curriculum planning: structure, organization, discovery learning, the "connectedness" of knowledge, meaningfulness, and the "problems approach."

Cognitive Science

By adding to our understanding of how people think and learn, research in the field of cognitive science has contributed to the development of cognitive learning theories. Drawing from research in linguistics, psychology, anthropology, and computer science, cognitive scientists study the mental processes learners use as they acquire new knowledge. Often, cognitive scientists develop computer flow charts to illustrate how learners use their short- and long-term memory to manipulate symbols and process information. In "Cognitive Science and Its Implications for Education" in this chapter, Gary D. Kruse discusses how school programs should be changed to reflect recent findings from cognitive research. And, in "Let's Put Brain Science on the Back Burner," John T. Bruer clarifies the difference between cognitive science and neuroscience (the biological science of the brain) and cautions educators against assuming that developments in neuroscience can serve as a guide for developing curricular and instructional practices.

Gestalt-Field Views of Learning

During the first few decades of the twentieth century, several psychologists in Germany—and later in the United States—began to look at how learners organize information into patterns and wholes. *Gestalt* is a German term meaning "configuration" or "pattern," and Gestalt theorists maintain that "wholeness" is primary; one should start with the total aspects of a learning situation and then move to particulars in light of the whole. Thus, obtaining an "overview" is often an important step in learning, for without it we may be, as the popular saying goes, "unable to see the forest for the trees."

Another major element of the Gestalt view of learning is that the whole is always greater than the sum of its parts. Experiencing a moving symphony is more than hearing individual musical notes; watching a movie is more than looking at the thousands of individual still pictures that make up the movie. The nature of the whole determines the meaning of its parts, and individual perceptions determine meaning.

Constructivist Learning Theories

Since the mid-1980s, several educational researchers have attempted to identify how learners *construct* understanding of new material. Constructivist views of learning, therefore, focus on how learners make sense of new information—how they construct meaning based on what they already know. In part, the roots of constructivism can be traced back to Gestalt views of learning in that learners seek to organize new information into meaningful wholes.

According to constructivism, "*students develop new knowledge through a process of active construction*. They do not merely passively receive or copy input from teachers or textbooks. Instead, they actively mediate it by trying to make sense of it and relate it to what they already know (or think they know) about the topic" (Good and Brophy 1997, p. 398). Constructivist-oriented curricula and instructional strategies focus on students' thinking about the material to be learned and, through carefully thought out prompts and questions, enable students to arrive at a deeper understanding of new material. Among the common elements of constructivist approaches to curriculum and teaching, research has identified the following effective practices:

1. The curriculum is designed to equip students with knowledge, skills, values, and dispositions that they will find useful both inside and outside of school.

2. Instructional goals emphasize developing student expertise within an application context and with emphasis on conceptual understanding of knowledge and self-regulated application of skills.

3. The curriculum balances breadth with depth by addressing limited content but developing this content sufficiently to foster conceptual understanding.

4. The content is organized around a limited set of powerful ideas (basic understandings and principles).

5. The teacher's role is not just to present information but also to scaffold and respond to students' learning efforts.

6. The students' role is not just to absorb or copy input but also to actively make sense and construct meaning.

7. Students' prior knowledge about the topic is elicited and used as a starting place for instruction, which builds on accurate prior knowledge and stimulates conceptual change if necessary (Good and Brophy, 1997, pp. 408–409).

A common element of constructivist approaches to curriculum planning and teaching is known as *scaffolding*—that is, providing learners with greater support during the early phases of learning and then gradually reducing support as their competence and ability to assume responsibility increase. The concept of scaffolding is based on the work of Lev Semenovich Vygotsky (1896–1934), a well-known Russian psychologist. Vygotsky coined the phrase *zone of proximal development* to refer to the point at which the learner needs assistance to continue learning. According to this view, effective instruction neither exceeds the learner's current level of understanding nor underestimates the learner's ability to learn independent of the teacher. The effective teacher varies the amount of help given to learners

> on the basis of their moment-to-moment understanding. If they do not understand an instruction given at one level, then more help is forthcoming. When they do understand, the teacher steps back and gives the child more room for initiative. In this way, the child is never left alone when he [or she] is in difficulty nor is he [or she] "held back" by teaching that is too directive and intrusive. (Wood, 1988, p. 81)

LEARNING STYLES

Much of the recent research on learning focuses on students' learning styles—that is, the approaches to learning that work best for them. Put differently, *learning styles* refers to individual typical ways of processing information and seeking meaning. These differences have also been called *learning modes, learning style preferences* or *cognitive styles*. Implications and applications of learning style research are discussed this chapter's "Matching Learning Styles and Teaching Styles" by Ronald Hyman and Barbara Rosoff. And in this chapter's Teachers' Voices section ("Eric Learns to Read: Learning Styles at Work"), June Hodgin and Caaren Wooliscroft describe how they modified a third-grade inclusion classroom to accommodate students' various learning styles.

Students' preferred learning styles are determined by a combination of hereditary and environmental factors. Some learners rapidly acquire new knowledge that they encounter; others learn best when they are independent and can shape their own learning. Some learn best in formal academic settings, while others learn best in informal, relaxed settings. Some learners require almost total silence, while others learn well in noisy, busy environments. Some learn intuitively, while others learn best in a step-by-step, linear, concrete fashion.

Learning style is an emerging concept, and there is no single "correct" view of learning styles to guide curriculum planners. Cultural differences in learning styles are subtle and difficult to identify. For example, in "Learning Styles from a Multicultural Perspective: The Case for Culturally Engaged Education" in this chapter, Cynthia B. Dillard and Dionne A. Blue point out that no single learning style is preferred by any particular ethnic or cultural group and that learning style diversity within and among cultures is great.

Within the last decade, much research has been conducted on students' preferred learning styles, and scores of conceptual models and accompanying learning-style assessment instruments have been developed. While critics have pointed out flaws in many learning-style schemes and maintain that there is little evidence to support their validity (Snider, 1990, 1992), curriculum planners should be aware of the concept of learning styles and realize that some curricula may be more effective for some students than for others. In addition, though preferences for learning styles can be strong, they can also change as a person matures.

Multiple Intelligences

While many learning theorists believe that intelligence is the general ability to learn—to acquire and use new knowledge—others believe that "the weight of the evidence at the present time is that intelligence is multidimensional, and that the full range of these dimensions is not completely captured by any single general ability" (Sternberg, 1996, p. 11). For example, in response to cognitive theories of learning, which he believed were limited to logical-mathematical or scientific forms of intelligence valued in the West, Howard Gardner proposed in *Frames of Mind: The Theory of Multiple Intelligences* (1983, 1993a, p. 8) that "there is persuasive evidence for the existence of several relatively autonomous human intellectual competencies, [referred to] as 'human intelligences' . . . [The] exact nature and breadth of each has not so far been satisfactorily established, nor has the precise number of intelligences been fixed." Gardner suggested that there were at least seven human intelligences: logical-mathematical, linguistic, musical, spatial, bodily-kinesthetic, intrapersonal, and interpersonal (in the mid-1990s, he identified an eighth intelligence, that of the naturalist).

The concept of multiple intelligences is clearly useful in curriculum planning and teaching. However, in his reflections twelve years after the publication of *Frames of Mind* (Gardner, 1995, p. 206), Gardner asserts that "MI [multiple intelligences] theory is in no way an educational prescription. [E]ducators are in the best position to determine the uses to which MI theory should be put. . . ." And, in "Probing More Deeply into the Theory of Multiple Intelligences" in this chapter, Gardner states that "educators should be cautious about characterizing the intellectual profiles of students."

CRITERION QUESTIONS—LEARNING AND LEARNING STYLES

In light of individual differences among learners, curriculum planners and teachers need many ways to encourage learning. Knowledge and use of theories about learning and learning styles offer important guidelines in providing for individual differences and instructional alternatives. The following are among the criterion questions that can be derived from the theories of learning and learning styles discussed in this chapter.

1. Have both behavioral and cognitive views of learning been considered in planning the curriculum?
2. Has the significance of individual learning styles and how learners construct meaning been considered in planning the curriculum?
3. Does the curriculum include diverse activities for learning?
4. Does the curriculum allow learners to exhibit and develop different forms of intelligence?
5. Is the significance of learning theory concepts such as the following reflected in the curriculum: rewarded response, socialization, modeling, scaffolding, and zones of proximal development?

REFERENCES

Bandura, Albert. *Social Learning Theory.* Englewood Cliffs, NJ: Prentice Hall, 1977.

Gardner, Howard. *Frames of Mind: The Theory of Multiple Intelligences.* New York: Basic Books, 1983. (A tenth-anniversary edition with a new introduction was published in 1993).

———. "Reflections on Multiple Intelligences: Myths and Messages. *Phi Delta Kappan* 77, no. 3 (November 1995): 200–203, 206–209.

Good, Thomas E., and Brophy, Jere E. *Looking in Classrooms,* 6th Ed. New York: Harper-Collins, 1997.

Mazur, J. *Learning and Behavior,* 4th Ed. Englewood Cliffs, NJ: Prentice-Hall, 1997.

Skinner, B. F. "Utopia through the Control of Human Behavior." In John Martin Rich, ed., *Readings in the Philosophy of Education.* Belmont, CA: Wadsworth, 1972.

Slavin, Robert. *Educational Psychology: Theory and Practice,* 5th Ed. Boston: Allyn and Bacon, 1997.

Snider, Vicki E. "Learning Styles and Learning to Read: A Critique." *Remedial and Special Education (RASE)* 13, no. 1 (January–February, 1992): 6–18

———. "What We Know about Learning Styles from Research in Special Education. *Educational Leadership* 48, no. 2 (October, 1990): 53.

Sternberg, Robert J. "Myths, Countermyths, and Truths about Intelligence. *Educational Researcher* 25, no. 2 (March 1996): 11–16.

Wood, David. *How Children Think and Learn.* New York: Basil Blackwell, 1988.

Woolfolk, Anita. *Educational Psychology,* 7th ed. Boston: Allyn and Bacon, 1998.

An Analysis of Behavior Modification

CLIFFORD K. MADSEN
CHARLES H. MADSEN, JR.

ABSTRACT: Learning is seen as a change or modification of behavior that results from the consequences of that behavior. Teachers can enhance students' learning by applying four behavioral principles: (1) pinpoint behaviors to be eliminated or established, (2) record behaviors, (3) choose reinforcers, and (4) evaluate the results.

A teacher stops by a child working on math and checks correct/incorrect responses. This teacher has observed that most students learn more efficiently when they are given academic feedback. She is using a principle of behavior modification to improve academic performance.

The teacher goes back to her desk to correct more academic assignments. A young student comes quickly to her desk and asks a question. She ignores him completely and calmly goes about correcting her papers. He stays about 15 seconds and then goes back to his work. The teacher smiles to herself as she checks a chart designed for this particular child. She has almost extinguished his habit of running to her desk (only once this week; initially he did it 28 times a day and that was *after* she started recording it). The teacher sets her handkerchief on her desk as a reminder to go to this child after he has been in his seat for a few minutes. She hopes that his question was not a really important one, that it can wait two or three minutes.

She goes back to correcting assignments. It is important to her that she finish them by the end of the day. She has discovered that, by randomly picking out a different day of the week for children to take corrected papers home, she can dramatically increase their academic performance. Again, behavior modification.

She takes the time to check on the child who came to her desk—he wanted to know if he could get a book from the library—then returns to her seat. She hears Suzy starting to talk to her neighbor. The teacher immediately gets up, goes to Suzy, and firmly tells her that she should stop visiting until her work is done. The teacher notices that Suzy appears a little sad. She is a sensitive child, and the teacher has long since discovered that a bit of teacher disapproval will halt her inappropriate behavior. Behavior modification.

The teacher remembers that she used to yell nearly all day long (observers actually counted 146 times during one morning session). In those days she used disapproval about 80% of the time in efforts to modify social behavior, generally with little effect. Although she found that this percentage is about average for most teachers, she wanted to be more positive. At first it was difficult not "natural." She had to learn behavioral techniques: the reinforcement of certain academic and social behaviors. Now, when she hears a loud adult voice in an adjoining classroom, she thinks about a discussion of honesty she had with a colleague. Should a teacher be honestly disapproving most of the time because it is a "natural" response? She has learned better.

She stands in front of her class. "Children, I would like you to look at me. Suzy's looking at me. Sam is looking at me. Now David's looking at me. Now everyone is looking at me. That's nice." (Again, behavior modification.) "You may all stop your individual work and visit now until

Article written by Clifford K. Madsen and Charles H. Madsen, Jr., for *Curriculum Planning: A New Approach,* Sixth Edition, 1993. Used by permission of the authors.

it's time for music." (When the youngsters helped make class rules earlier in the year, they expressed a desire for talk time. Establishing rules with student help has *nothing* to do with behavior modification.)

As the students visit, the teacher thinks about the token system the school counselor is trying to establish in some of the rooms. She has read many reports about "token economy" systems and understands that they represent an affective application of behavioral principles, but she does not choose this technique for her class. She has never liked material rewards for learning (except for herself!) and prefers to use social reinforcers instead. Besides, she cannot imagine how her class could be much better than it is. She really likes it. She knows also that the counselor sometimes uses very strong disapproval as well as a special "timeout room" for some children. The effects of these procedures are also well documented and consistent with behavioral approaches, but she prefers not to use them.

WHAT IS BEHAVIOR MODIFICATION? A PROCESS FOR LEARNING

The above paragraphs describe procedures whose efficacy has been documented in behavioral research. In essence, this research shows that behavior is maintained and shaped by its consequences. (Strange, isn't it, that so obvious a truth should be so badly used in practice?) *Behavior* is a common word which is used quite casually in reference to many things. In the literature of behavior modification it refers to *anything* a person *does, says,* or *thinks* that can be observed directly or indirectly. Behavior modification theory deals with techniques of changing behavior as well as specific interaction effects. A "well-behaved student" is, of course, a person who behaves in ways that society (represented in school by the teacher) thinks are appropriate to a given situation.

Some people try to make a case against a behavioral approach by alluding to "attitudes" which are not a part of the process of behavior modification. Actually, these attitudes represent different value systems. *Principles* for teaching (shaping appropriate behaviors) should not be confused with value issues. Many teachers regard the questions of why, what, and who as considerably more important than how. But, after the teacher has decided what is to be learned, why it should be learned, and who is going to learn it, then an effective approach to how it will be taught is vital, or the teacher's efforts as well as the student's might be wasted.

A very simple rationale explains the efficiency of behavioral approaches. *Behavioral change occurs for a reason:* Students work for things that bring them positive feelings, they work for approval from people they admire; students change behaviors to satisfy the desires they have been taught to value; they generally avoid behaviors they associate with unpleasantness; and finally, students develop habitual behaviors when those behaviors are often repeated.

The current emphasis on behavior modification, or reinforcement theory (to use an older term), developed and became popular primarily from the works of B. F. Skinner. Programmed instruction is the best-known result of his initial work. Other teaching systems, treatments of mental illness, and techniques in clinical psychology are based on early experiments by Skinner and his followers. The entire rationale of behavior modification is that most behavior is *learned*. Behavior thus defined includes emotional responses, attitudes, reading, listening, talking, looking into the mirror, liking a person, wanting to talk out a problem, hitting, being frustrated, and so on.

The same principles may be used to teach good social behavior as are used to teach appropriate academic skills (e.g., providing feedback about correct/incorrect responses). If a teacher wishes students to have a real desire to learn something, the teacher may find it necessary to structure the external environment so students will seek structured rewards for their work tasks. After initial manipulation, the rewards for proper behavior will often come from the reinforcement of the particular task itself, i.e., getting the right answer is often all the structure that is needed. Incidentally, this is precisely what most teachers do when they initially make a "game" out of learning. Students become enthusiastic concerning the game per se, not realizing that its purpose is to stimulate effective work. It is curious that some teachers who try desperately to make work fun also say they reject any "manipulation techniques."

BEHAVIOR RESULTS FROM ITS CONSEQUENCES

Behavioral research demonstrates that if work tasks can be 1) geared to the student's own level, 2) presented in logical sequences with 3) appropriate feedback concerning correct/incorrect responses, and 4) rewarded (internal or external) for successively better efforts to reach defined goals, then the student will certainly learn. Exactly the same principles apply to teaching proper social skills.

Critics say, "Yes, but isn't that a cold approach?" Certainly not. While behavior modifications is a branch of applied psychology based on scientific principles verified in the laboratory, it is the nature of the material to be learned that represents important value choices. Actually, because of its consistency and simplicity, behavioral modification effected through contingent reinforcement (approval/disapproval) usually represents a very kind and understandable system to students.

When learning is defined as a change or modification of behavior, then reinforcement principles constitute a method to promote or expedite this learning. In short, behavioral analysis asks, "How should we go about teaching in the best possible manner to ensure correct association?" Or, more specifically, "How should we go about teaching the student to concentrate, to read, to share, to clean his desk, to be honest, to develop his own values and yes, proceed academically?" If a youngster responds favorably to our presentation, we assume that it functions as a reward for the student.

But what if the student does not respond? Then we must restructure the external environment so that the student *does* receive proper motivation.

CHANGING WRONG ASSOCIATIONS

If behavior can be learned, then any behavior can also be unlearned or relearned. Sometimes, in our zeal to get through to our students, we make mistakes. Sometimes we make mistakes regardless of zeal. The efficacy of behavioral techniques with *severe* problem behaviors within mental hospitals and institutions for the retarded and handicapped perhaps should give us the encouragement to move forward. Behavioral techniques have demonstrated that even severely handicapped children can learn much faster and much more than we previously believed possible. And no, one does not need to be a medical or psychological specialist to provide academic and social approval. Teachers have been doing this for centuries.

What are the dynamics of changing social behavior? Since it is impossible for a person to maintain two contradictory responses, the skillful teacher will attempt to elicit responses *incompatible* with deviant behavior and thereby obviate the need for punishment. "Count to 10 before you get angry; think before you begin your work; take three big breaths before you cry." Punishment alone may stop deviant behavior, but it will not necessarily teach correct associations. The child who is hit with a spoon because she cannot use it properly will not necessarily learn proper etiquette. Similarly, the child who is punished for faulty reading will not necessarily learn to read efficiently. The one child might shun the spoon; the other child may stop reading. Setting up incompatible responses is perhaps the most effective behavioral technique of all, because it constitutes a double-edged approach. Not only is the inappropriate behavior eliminated but a correct response replaces it. Thus the child unlearns and relearns at the same time. The procedure eliminates the need for punishment and at the same time teaches correct associations.

WHAT IS A "PAYOFF"? THAT WHICH KEEPS ANY BEHAVIOR ALIVE

One of the discoveries of behavioral science is that it doesn't matter how or where an inappropriate behavior association got started. What does matter is that the behavior is being kept alive by some variety of present "payoff."

The principle can be conceptualized as, "Behavior that goes unrewarded will be extinguished," and, conversely, behavior that does not become extinguished is in some way being rewarded. Although saying so goes against much present-day thinking, looking backward in the history of the student is many times not only unnecessary, it may also be unproductive. This is especially true when unearthing the "reason" for the behavior is used as a substitute for action.

When you want to change a specific behavior, you must first find the payoff and eliminate it. The probability is excellent that this is possible. Some reinforcements, such as those from the student's family or self-concepts concerning thoughts about oneself cannot easily be controlled. But many payoffs are amenable to change.

The teacher must watch the student carefully to find the payoff in each specific case. This is often not easy. Once again, many of us try to simplify our problem by grouping behaviors together or by categorizing students as "types." This is no more successful than other simplistic solutions for inappropriate behavior, such as "These students came from a disadvantaged background and just need experiences," or "This class just needs a teacher with a firm hand." There are too many differences in the behavior of individuals for such thinking to be of any real value.

Individual differences among students can even result in the same behaviors being dependent on different payoffs. For example, Jim, Alex, and Pete are all acting up in class on the same day. They finally become so disruptive that the teacher sends them all to the principal's office. Jim is delighted; his payoff is that he caused the teacher to lose his/her cool. Alex's payoff is that he maintained his reputation among the rest of the class for being a tough guy. Pete doesn't care anything about the teacher or the class; the people he wants to impress are Jim and Alex, and he's happy because their friendship and approval are his payoff. Behaviorally, the teacher's response should have been to ignore them. Consistently ignoring a behavior will go far toward extinguishing it. When the teacher doesn't get angry or disturbed, the problem is forced back where it belongs: on the student, not on the teacher. She/he has not allowed the students to manipulate the situation.

In extinguishing behavior by means of this technique, you must be prepared for the next development, which is that the behavior will initially become worse rather than better! Remember that the student very much desires the payoff, and has learned this particular behavior as the way to achieve it. When the payoff is not forthcoming, the student will redouble his/her efforts to earn it the only way he/she knows. It is not until the student realizes once and for all that the payoff is not going to happen that she/he will stop the behavior. This may happen quickly, and it may happen slowly. Many teachers give up at this stage, saying, "I've tried ignoring, but the student misbehaved even more." Of course.

For this reason, ignoring is not an easy technique. You have to be sure of what you are doing. Sometimes even colleagues or parents won't understand why you're doing it. Explain your reasons and ask for time to achieve results. Stick to your guns. You are extinguishing inappropriate behavior in the student because you care.

WHAT CONSTITUTES REWARD? THAT WHICH THE STUDENT WILL WORK TOWARD

Rewards form pleasant associations and promote the behavior being rewarded. To change a student's inappropriate behavior, often it is enough to track the payoff and eliminate the specific unwanted behavior. It can be even more effective to institute at the same time a reward or system of rewards for desirable behavior, this is a simultaneous attempt to form a new association.

Just as it is necessary to extinguish a behavior, it is necessary to pinpoint the specific behavior to be rewarded. For example, you can't try to reward Lucy for "changing her attitude toward her schoolwork." You must look at the overall picture, assign a hierarchy to Lucy's problems, and decide what behavior you can best work with. First you might decide that Lucy's worst problem is the fact that she does almost anything prior to getting to work, so she gets rushed and never finishes her tasks. The behavior you decide to promote is getting down to work in a reasonable time. You wouldn't at first insist that Lucy start everything immediately, and have her reward contingent on that. You'd allow her five minutes. The five minutes could gradually be cut down until, by buckling quickly down to necessary tasks, Lucy shows that she has learned that it's much better not to procrastinate.

When you have a student with multiple problems, as usually is the case, or when you have many students with problems, your decision about what behaviors to work with first will depend on several factors. You may decide to work with what you judge to be the basic behavior problem. Again, you may choose the problem that is most acute; or you may choose to work on the most accessible problem, considering the time and help you have available.

Extinguishing is best done on an individual basis. A reward system, however, can often be set up for an entire group. This can be helpful if a problem of jealousy develops. This does not happen as often as you might think, once the students recognize that the rewarded student needs help, but the possibility is there.

Any system of rewards, whether individual or group, should be set up so each student knows specifically what she/he must do to earn the reward. What he/she is expected to do should be close enough to the student's present behavior to enable the student to realize that it is within the realm of possibility. The reward should be some-

thing the student desires, the more strongly the desire the better. The reward should be given consistently for each performance of the desired behavior. At first, the reward should be apparent (tangible or verbal), occur immediately, be absolutely certain (no teacher off-task) and should be generous even to the point of being overly so. Do your best to "catch the student being good," even for a moment. It is important to get the student winning as soon as possible.

We suggest that you write the rules in a conspicuous place or have them easily available. Explain the rules every day. If the reward involves a toy, game, or piece of equipment, hold it up or point to it. If it is an activity, explain it. If the reward involves praise, indicate that you will feel good when the student succeeds. If there's a choice of reward, ask each of several students which one they are working for.

Rewards can be anything a student desires. Obviously, the rewards you choose must be within your resources of money, time, and consistent with school policies. A teacher who is setting up a reward system on his/her own probably won't be able to use the more dramatic types of reward. She/he can make use of what is available with imagination and ingenuity.

Traditional teaching takes it for granted that students can be motivated from the beginning by teacher approval. In many cases this is true. However, if approval doesn't work for the problem students, both the ones you notice and those you don't, you must start with the student where she/he is. You motivate him/her by what will work, not by what you think ought to work. Remember it is the student who decides what is important to him/her. When appropriate behavior is followed by teacher approval then the intrinsic rewards of skill achievement and academic achievement will be development and can be combined with approval. Finally, the skillful teacher can structure the classroom environment in such a way that the child can use self-approval as a reward. Motivation by this means is the ultimate purpose of any kind of discipline, but it isn't going to just happen. It is a goal to be worked toward, knowingly and steadily.

CAN BEHAVIOR BE MEASURED? IT CAN EASILY

Teachers are comfortable with spending a good deal of time in devising and employing tests, both formal and informal, for academic skills. To do the same thing for social skills seems a formidable task. Although it takes a little effort, it is not so difficult or time-consuming as it might seem, once the behavior to be tested has been pinpointed. Any specific behavior is observable and occurs during some period of time.

Unlike academic tasks, the behavior modification of social behavior is concerned with measuring the number of times a behavior occurs in a given time period. To do so, you must set up your criteria as to the extent or quality of the behavior to be measured. For example, the length of time disruptive noises go on before they are counted might be set at two seconds. A noisy disturbance may be considered one that causes other student heads to turn; a student's getting out of his/her seat may be counted only when she/he has no legitimate reason.

Even to start the process of behavior modification, the pinpointed behavior must be counted and recorded. Knowing exactly how many times the behavior occurs helps you understand the consequences. It also, of course, tells the teacher when to record again and demonstrates whether the behavior is happening less, more, or continues at the same rate.

The time period to be counted across will have to be estimated at first. If the occurrences happen over quite a long period, the teacher may find it necessary to take samplings and average them. An aide, team member, outside observer, even a student can be of great help, especially to check on the results of interactions between students and teacher. Another observer can also verify your count.

Testing tools consist of pencil, paper, and a watch or clock. Numbers of behaviors can be noted and any comments added. A simple form is adaptable to recording of any behavior.

Videotaping is another method of recording students' behavior. It enables the teacher to observe the results of structuring the classroom environment. It also often happens that teachers can notice behaviors on tape that, in the classroom, they would be too busy to notice. The videotape makes an original record from which the behaviors to be recorded can be counted or rechecked.

Four principles which are important for teachers are as follows:

1. *Pinpoint:* It is necessary to pinpoint explicitly the behavior that is to be eliminated or established. This takes place at many different levels relating to many differentiated academic as well as social behaviors. It leads to a hierarchical arrangement of skills and behaviors based upon expected specific behavioral objectives.
2. *Record:* This is a necessity in behavioral change and actually is what differentiates a behavioral (scientific) approach from other techniques. Specified behaviors must be listed as they occur and thereby provide a precise record from which to proceed. The record must be accurate. If the behavior cannot in some way be measured, then one can never know if it has been established or unlearned. As maladaptive responses are eliminated, more time can then be devoted to teaching other important behaviors and other productive pursuits.
3. *Consequate:* This unique word which you won't find in Webster's means "setting up the external environment contingencies (including one's own personal responses) and proceeding with the teaching programs." Contingencies include approval, withdrawal of approval, disapproval, threat of disapproval and ignoring. Reinforcers may be words (spoken and written), expressions (facial and bodily), closeness (nearness and touching), activities (social and individual), and things (materials, food, playthings, money, etc.). *Choice of reinforcers is an extremely important aspect of behavior modification and is dependent upon the values one holds.* These choices constitute an issue which should receive much discussion, debate, and criticism.
4. *Evaluate:* Evaluation should be continuous, but ultimate effects, which may be different

from immediate effectiveness, must be ascertained. Hence a program must be allowed to operate for some time before final data analysis.

IF AT FIRST YOU DON'T SUCCEED? WELL—YOU KNOW!

Sometimes a teacher who understands behavioral principles and has even successfully applied them will run into trouble. The teacher should first review the way the four steps of behavior modification had been carried out and ask many questions concerning how the principles have been applied. The questions asked could include among others the following:

1. *Pinpoint:* Is the behavior you are trying to extinguish or promote too general? Have you isolated a single behavior sufficiently? Does the behavior you are working with depend on another which you should deal with first? Have you discovered the real payoff? Does the behavior you are building in the student reflect the idea you are trying to get across? What is the response hierarchy of the student?
2. *Record:* Have you chosen the best time period for recording? Does the length indicate the true picture of the frequency of the behavior? If you can't record for the full cycle, have you taken different samplings and averaged them? Have you included all necessary data on your sheet or form? Was your recording technique precise? Did every observer understand and use the criteria correctly? Does your recording need to be modified to take into account differences in duration, intensity or frequency?
3. *Consequate:* Have you made sure that what you think of as a reward really is one for the student? Does disapproval really function as punishment (decrease or suppress behavior)? Does the student understand clearly what she/he has to do to earn the reward? Does the student remember what the reward is? Does the reward need to be changed to add variety? Have you been imaginative in planning rewards? Are you pairing other approval techniques with rewards? Is the contingency applied consistently, appropriately, and timely?
4. *Evaluate:* Have you stayed with your original program long enough to see whether it is actually working or not? Did you remember that behavior you are ignoring will worsen before it disappears, sometimes for a long time? Were the intervals before re-recording long enough? When you became certain one technique wasn't effective, did you go back and try another?

VALUES VERSUS TECHNIQUES

It should be apparent from the frequency discussion that behavior modification represents the use of a series of scientifically verified techniques that may be used to promote more effective learning of both social and academic subject matter. A behavioral approach does not help the teacher decide why, what, and who is going to learn. These issues represent important value choices. However, after questions relating to these values have been answered, behavioral principles may be used to enhance learning of appropriate behavior. Of course, the choice of a particular technique as opposed to other approaches represents a value choice. Also, if a behavioral approach is implemented, then selection of specific behavioral procedures (e.g., approval rather than disapproval), as well as choice of potential reinforcers, represents another value issue.

Opponents of behavior modification would do well to address themselves to the more important issues concerning learning rather than condemn a technique by alluding to many ancillary detriments that they feel might ensue from its application. (Generally, they make these pronouncements in the complete absence of data.)

This point is illustrated in Figure 4.1.

The reader might desire to fill in three or four of the most important values they think should be learned by students (academic, social, or both). For example, reading, writing, consideration for others, honesty, sensitivity, tolerance,

FIGURE 4.1
Values/Techniques Dichotomy Chart

Positive Values

a _____   b _____
c _____   c _____

Behavioral Techniques	**Non-behavioral Techniques**
1. Pinpoint: Observable	1. Non-observable
2. Record: Measurable	2. Non-measurable (Inferential)

Techniques

3. Consequate: Cause and effect relationships	3. Non-determined (random-chance-chaotic)
4. Evaluate: Isolate causes through specific addition and removal of consequences	4. Non-explainable Complex causes Unknown consequences

a _____   b _____
c _____   d _____

Negative Values

self-actualization, etc.—whatever is considered to be positive. It is obvious that behavioral techniques may be used to teach "negative" as well as "positive" values.

The purpose of this exercise is to indicate that behavioral methods, much like any product of man (atomic energy, jet propulsion, governments), may be used either to the benefit or detriment of other human beings. Behavioral techniques are characterized by definitions of behavior that can be observed (pin-pointed) and then measured (recorded and counted). These techniques include the isolation of specific cause and effect methodology for the evaluation of learning. The values that are employed are an entirely different matter. There should be a clear distinction between values and techniques used to implement chosen values.

TEACHING—ART OR SCIENCE?

Through trial and error, it would seem that every teacher who cares can find effective ways to stim-ulate students to realize their full learning potential. With or without a full understanding of behavioral principles, teachers who care will find better methods of behavioral control and character development.

The ability to recognize individual differences and structure the school environment with contingencies relevant to specific situations represents an outstanding accomplishment. Good sense and good taste are important, of course. We know of one seventh-grade teacher who controlled her class by having the problem children participate in a mock wedding ceremony if they were "very, very bad." When the children evidenced proper behavior, they were allowed to "get divorced." This disciplinary procedure was tremendously effective and used behavioral principles. However, the teacher's choice of activity raises serious questions regarding the acquisition of other behaviors and attitudes. Another teacher told of a technique used with 8- and 9-year-old boys: "When one of the boys misbehaves, I make him wear a girl's ribbon in his hair." Does it work? Very well; but again one must question the insensitivity of this teacher to other values. It is ironic that this same person thought it "terrible" to suggest to parents that occasionally they might have a home-based contingency system where proper social behavior at school would eventuate in monetary rewards given at home.

It seems apparent that no teaching technique can be effectively divorced from the person who uses it. This point, however, makes a case for more rigorous screening of prospective teachers, not for the abandonment of effective techniques. It is a curious argument that maintains that effective techniques must be kept from teachers because then teachers may actually teach more efficiently. Because of the effectiveness of behavioral techniques, perhaps the profession may now get down to the truly important issues: What specifically should be learned? Or, more importantly, who will decide what is to be learned, both socially and academically? What values and accompanying behaviors evidencing selected values should be learned? When, where, and by whom?

- Who should be given the responsibility to interact purposefully in the learning process, i.e., to teach?
- Should society require any objective evidence for this learning, i.e., data from observation or other formal means?
- If continued research demonstrates the efficacy of empirical cause and effect relationships (data based on observation), ought derived principles to be systematically implemented within the school?
- If so, then what should be the boundaries concerning choice and application of reinforcers, i.e., approval versus disapproval; punishment versus ignoring; the structuring of incompatible responses; the use of academic subject matter as a reward; social as opposed to material reinforcers. These issues represent the most important value issues within the technique of behavior modification.

Let us not waste time with such irrelevant arguments as "it's unfair." (Of course it's unfair, a teacher must be unfair if it is defined as any individualization or discriminative assessment, e.g., differential grading.)

Then there is the charge: It's totalitarian. Nonsense! Who decides what values/behaviors should be taught to whom has nothing to do with behavior modification. Some schools are run mostly by teachers; others are controlled mostly by students. Another criticism goes something like this: Behavioral techniques teach students to work for rewards. Right! Perhaps after awhile they may even find their subject matter rewarding or even learn to function more efficiently and effectively in a capitalistic social system.

Another criticism: It militates against internal control. Not so; actually, the process of partial reinforcement teaches youngsters to go for longer and longer periods of time without any external rewards. Incidentally, how long do adults maintain appropriate behavior without the occasional reinforcement from a loved one or perhaps a more tangible reward for professional behavior?

Sometimes it is alleged that behavior modification denies human reasoning. If anything it teaches human reasoning—specifying in clear, consistent, and honest ways the cause and effect relationships of life.

Another charge: *It may teach other nonspecified behaviors.* Perhaps. But let's worry about those, if indeed they exist, when there is some evidence for them. And is anyone so naive as to believe that teachers are not already approving or disapproving certain student behaviors with or without a full understanding of behavior modification?

Finally, if we cannot agree on all the issues and values then at least we may begin to take data, i.e., make systematic observations concerning what is presently going on in schools, in order to build a sounder basis for the development of teaching techniques.

It is readily apparent that, regardless of how many "behavioral recipes" are available, the insensitive teacher will still be found wanting. The art of being a good teacher seems directly related to the behaviors of that teacher as a person. Modeling effects of an outstanding individual are still among the most powerful and far-reaching of teacher influences. The truly effective teacher will combine the science of behavior with the art of living to create that exceptionally rare atmosphere: an environment where children not only take excitement from discovery but learn to be nice people.

Clifford K. Madsen is Professor of Music Education at Florida State University, and *Charles H. Madsen, Jr.* is Professor of Psychology at Florida State University.

QUESTIONS FOR REFLECTION

1. Some critics of behavioral approaches to the teaching–learning process are concerned about the ethics of using such methods. What might be some of their concerns?
2. Should students be rewarded for learning?
3. In regard to the curriculum and level with which you are most familiar, what are some examples of how reinforcers could be used to promote students' learning? What are some examples of how reinforcers could be used to reduce or eliminate certain behaviors?

Cognitive Science and Its Implications for Education

GARY D. KRUSE

ABSTRACT: Cognitive science has provided a better understanding of the structure and functions of the human brain—for example, the brain is rarely at rest and constantly searches for meaning. Ten findings from cognitive science that are relevant to the teaching learning process are presented. Schools should incorporate these findings and adopt new views of time, curriculum, learning, and the teacher's role.

A much clearer understanding of the brain's functions and processes has been developed during the last several decades. This growing body of knowledge has far-reaching implications for educational methods and practices. The brain is the result of thousands of years of human evolution. Only recently, largely due to advanced technology, have we begun to unravel the mind's secrets at the molecular, cellular, and functional level.

THE ARCHITECTURE OF THE BRAIN

The basic working units of the brain are 100 billion specialized nerve cells (neurons), each capable of making up to 50,000 connections as meaning is detected. It is this ability to discriminate, register, store, and retrieve meaning that is the essence of all human learning. Neurons communicate or make connections through the use

From *NASSP Bulletin* 82, no. 598 (May 1998): 73–79. Used by permission of the author and publisher.
Copyright 1998, National Association of Secondary School Principals. For more information concerning NASSP services and/or programs, please call (703) 860-0200.

of chemical messengers called neurotransmitters. The process takes the form of electrochemical impulses traveling from one neuron to another by crossing a minute gap called the synapse. This electrochemical "dance" between neurons using chemical messengers is believed to give rise to our power to derive or evoke meaning (Sylwester, 1995).

The earliest structure of the brain, the brain stem, appears to be an extension of our spinal chord. The brain stem contributes to our general alertness and serves as an early warning system to the rest of the brain regarding incoming sensory information. Hence, all learning initially begins at a sensory level of cognitive processing. Meaning and understanding are the result of further cognitive functions within the brain (Ornstein and Thompson, 1984).

Located atop the brain stem lies the limbic system. This system provides the chemicals that influence focus, attention, and concentration. The thalamus, located near the limbic system, is the "gateway valve" for the flow of all information into the brain. The hippocampus, a part of the system, serves as a way station for the temporary storage of information. Short-term memory may reside within this structure.

The largest part of the brain is the cerebrum. It is divided into two hemispheres that are connected by the largest band of neurons found in the brain, the corpus callosum. Its role is to act as a communication "bridge" between hemispheres, which work in concert to make sense out of incoming information. Each hemisphere contributes various forms of thinking to derive meaning.

This lateralization of cognitive processing by hemisphere gives us the ability to think both divergently and convergently. It allows us to approach complexities in life from an intuitive as well as a logical manner. The hemispheres of the cerebrum process information from both a "parts-to-whole" and "whole-to-parts" perspective, allowing us to conceive a holistic as well as a detailed pattern of thought regarding an object, event, or relationship (Ornstein and Thompson, 1984).

Covering the cerebrum is the cortex, which houses two-thirds of all neurons in the brain. It is within this thin layer composed of billions of columns of neurons that genuine learning occurs (Suzuki, 1994).

The cortex is divided into lobes, each lobe carrying out a variety of functions. Researchers have found neurons of similar function grouped together within these lobes. At the rear of the brain lies the visual processing area; within this area are about 100,000 neurons whose purpose is to work to identify facial features such as the height of a hairline or exact distance between the eyes on a facial image (Ackerman, 1994). These "face cells" help us recognize a face as that of a friend or foe, brother or sister.

Temporal lobes contain a number of critical attributes for learning. An area in the left temporal lobe the size of a silver dollar is responsible for receiving all spoken words and forwarding these sounds for further processing to determine semantic meaning. This area discriminates between just 44 "sound bits" that comprise the entire English Language. An area of similar size in the right temporal lobe helps process spatial information for meaning. It is also in the temporal lobes that researchers have found evidence of permanent episodic memory (Ornstein and Thompson, 1984; Damasio and Damasio, 1992).

Frontal lobes of the cortex serve as our center for thought. It is here that such purposeful actions as planning or deciding occur. Neurons found throughout the cortex help to complete the construction of understanding. Alphabet letter symbols, for example, strung together in the temporal lobe to create words are forwarded onto associative fields in the parietal lobes to become sentences, paragraphs and, eventually, a story. These associative fields take in previously processed information and aid in developing conceptual understanding (Damasio and Damasio, 1992).

SOME NOTIONS REGARDING HUMAN LEARNING

Human learning is a direct result of the brain's associative properties and memory systems, the origins of which are currently being investigated by scientists. The ability, however, of one neuron to communicate with another places these associative mechanisms at the heart of all human learning. Though complex, we are moving closer toward the realization that a biological basis exists for learning. The implications of this fact for education are awesome (Kandel and Hawkins, 1992).

Researchers describe the brain as an extremely dynamic organ. It appears that it is rarely at rest and constantly searches for meaning. Moreover, the organ grows as meaning is attached and new synaptic connections are laid down. Hemispheres of the cerebrum provide their owner with a number of different perspectives when interpreting information for meaning. Besides helping to decipher the world outside us, the brain also appears to have the capability to go off on its own to evoke new ideas (Suzuki, 1994).

It is obvious this organ of learning is by no means the passive repository for skills and facts it was once thought to be. Current evidence would suggest the following regarding cognitive processing:

1. The brain is our learning organ.
2. The brain constantly searches for meaning.
3. The brain is a dynamic processor of information.
4. We can enhance or inhibit the operation of the brain.
5. Learning is a "sociocognitive act" tying social interaction, cognitive processing, and language together in an interactive manner.
6. Multi-sensory activities that embed skills and facts into natural experiences appear to enhance the brain's search for meaning.

7. A school day in which "connectiveness" exists between concepts taught enhances the brain's search for meaning.
8. The pace of instruction appears to influence the brain's search for meaning.
9. Information delivered within the student's context, tied to his or her prior understanding, and moving from concrete to abstract levels of processing appears to enhance the brain's search for the meaning.
10. To learn (beyond a perceptual level) requires the student to "act on the learning." To act means involvement.

A MOST IMMODEST PROPOSAL

Educational methods and practices have traditionally treated the brain as a passive repository. Knowledge has been transmitted by subject-area specialists inside a self-contained classroom setting. Current practices promote passive learning through a heavy reliance on students listening, reading, and practicing in isolation. The school day is composed of small increments of time (e.g., 50- to 90-minute periods) in which a subject specialist delivers discrete skills and memorizable facts period by period. In assembly-line fashion, students move from subject to subject, rarely encountering a conceptual tie or relationship (Gardner, 1991; Brooks and Brooks, 1993).

Both traditional instruction and student evaluation have become more a measure of the ability to recognize and recall than a genuine understanding of the concepts. Under the current scheme, curricula are viewed vertically (K–12). No consideration is given to what knowledge and concepts are being taught across the day, week, or semester. No ties or connections exist for the student to attach between subject areas.

This arrangement is built on the false notion that human learning is a linear progression within the mind, a notion that cognitive researchers dispute. They point out that knowledge is constructed by the brain through situational and experiential encounters influenced to a large degree by pace, context, connectiveness, prior understanding, and one's ability or freedom to act on the learning. The traditional vertical view of curriculum has resulted in a system of education driven by a textbook and taught at a rapid pace, causing many students difficulty in cognitively processing information (Brooks and Brooks, 1993).

Many characteristics of our schools disagree with the findings of cognitive research. The isolation as well as fragmentation of knowledge neither complements nor enhances the associative powers of the human mind. The current methods of transmitting knowledge may eliminate the "whole to parts" processing ability of the cerebrum, thereby eliminating the larger picture or understanding for the student. A heavy reliance on the spoken or printed word effectively shuts down other sensory input available to the brain in its search for meaning. At times the message sent to youngsters today is that one's ability to recognize and recall (remember) is of far more value than understanding or applying a concept to life.

Finally, the practice of delivering information out of context, then assuming the student will be able to transfer it to changing life situations, may be totally unrealistic. Information taught out of context is neither meaningful nor relevant to most young people, causing them serious problems in attempting to process it. This common form of instruction could be the major reason we find such inordinate amounts of rote practice occurring in the current school setting.

To move schools toward a greater sensitivity in cognitive processing, we should adopt new views of time, curriculum, learning, and the role of teachers. This will require major shifts on the part of the educational community (Hart, 1983; Kruse and Kruse, 1995).

Our view of time needs to change dramatically. The Carnegie unit equates "seat time" with learning by awarding students credit for successfully completing coursework. For most of the 20th century we have been locked into a view that the

school day should be composed of standard increments of time. Common sense, as well as research, should tell us otherwise. Genuine learning occurs at different rates and to different degrees for each student. The best judges of "how fast" or "how much" are the student and the teacher.

The traditional role of teachers must also change. Teachers should be trained and organized into teams composed of various grade levels or content specialties. The need to create a coherent school day in which the student's mind encounters conceptual ties and connections throughout, necessitates dialogue on a daily basis between subject area specialists. Integration can be two teachers doing something together—however, integration can be a much fuller and richer act, involving an entire team of specialists making conceptual connections as they appear in real life. This type of organization requires a complete change from the traditional "department," which is a working unit originally designed to search for truth, not teach youngsters (Kruse, 1994).

Curriculum should be viewed across the school day. Constant dialogue between team members should occur to make the curriculum coherent. Activities designed by the team embedding essential facts and skills into natural experiences will be a major team responsibility. Finally, the future school day should place utmost value on developing student understanding through honoring student questions, allowing students to work cooperatively, and encouraging student interaction in order to initiate a full array of cognitive functions (Kruse and Zulkoski, 1997).

CONCLUSION

Understanding the ability of the mind to attach novel information to already stored understandings has major implications for current instructional practices, setting, and the manner in which we organize teachers. A greater coherency is needed within the school day to tap into the associative powers of the mind. To accomplish this a new view of time, curriculum, learning, and teacher role will be necessary. Greater authenticity toward knowledge and its delivery is essential to provide relevance and meaning.

To achieve this a much higher degree of collegiality by teachers will be called for in the future, implying a completely different product than has been stamped out over the past century by training institutions. Perhaps the most critical factor being suggested by cognitive research is that of the brain's potential to learn. It appears, barring major insults, this organ's potential to learn is limitless if educational practices and methods "complement, not complicate" its search for meaning.

REFERENCES

Ackerman, S. J. "Face Facts, How Does the Circuitry of Our Brain Allow Us To Recognize Faces?" *Brainwork—The Neuroscience Newsletter,* November/December 1994.

Arwood, E. *Pragmatism, Theory and Application.* London: Aspen, 1983.

Brooks, J. G., and Brooks, M. G. *In Search of Understanding. The Case for Constructivist Classrooms.* Alexandria, Va.: ASCD, 1993.

Caine, R. N., and Caine, G. C. *Making Connections: Teaching and the Human Brain.* Menlo Park, Calif.: Addison Wesley Longman, 1994.

Damasio, A. R., and Damasio, H. "Brain and Language." *Scientific American,* September 1992.

Gardner, H. *The Unschooled Mind. How Children Think and How Schools Should Teach.* New York: Basic Books, 1991.

Goldman-Rakic, P. S. "Working Memory and the Mind." *Scientific American,* September 1992.

Hart, L. *Human Brain and Human Learning.* New York: Longman, 1983.

Kandel, E. R., and Hawkins, R. D. "The Biological Basis of Learning and Individuality." *Scientific American,* September 1992.

Kotulak, R. "Unraveling the Mysteries of the Brain." (A series of articles) *Chicago Tribune,* April 1993.

Kruse, C. A., and Kruse, G. D. "The Master Schedule: Improving the Quality of Education." *NASSP Bulletin,* May 1995.

Kruse, G. D. "Thinking, Learning, and Public Schools: Preparing for Life.' *NASSP Bulletin,* September 1994.

Kruse, G. D., and Zulkoski, M. "The Northwest Experience: A Lesser Road Traveled." *NASSP Bulletin,* December 1997.

LeDoux, J. "Emotion, Memory, and the Brain." *Scientific American,* 1994.

Ornstein, R., and Thompson, R. F. *The Amazing Brain.* Boston, Mass.: Houghton-Mifflin, 1984.

Suzuki, J. *The Brain.* (A five-part television series) Discovery Channel, 1994.

Sylwester, R. *A Celebration of Neurons: An Educators Guide to the Human Brain.* Alexandria, Va.: ASCD, 1995.

Gary D. Kruse is assistant principal of Northwest High School in Grand Island, Nebraska.

QUESTIONS FOR REFLECTION

1. In what ways might a curriculum "enhance or inhibit" the operation of the human brain?
2. Kruse states that "multi-sensory activities that embed skills and facts into natural experiences appear to enhance the brain's search for meaning." What are the implications of this statement for the curriculum with which you are most familiar?
3. In what ways does a curriculum that is "vertically" arranged conflict with findings from cognitive science?
4. To what extent do you believe K–12 schools and higher education will implement the recommendations contained in Kruse's "immodest proposal"?

Let's Put Brain Science on the Back Burner

JOHN T. BRUER

ABSTRACT: Current knowledge of brain development and neural functioning is not adequate to guide educational practice. Three misconceptions about neuroscience and education are discussed, and educators are urged to use cognitive science, rather than brain science, to develop learning environments that exploit the brain's lifelong plasticity.

There has long been a simmering interest in brain research among educators. Recently, however, that interest has gone from simmer to full boil. In the past 18 months, for example, we have seen special issues of *The American School Board Journal* (February 1997), *Educational Leadership* (March 1997), and *The School Administrator* (January 1998). Now the *NASSP Bulletin* addresses the implications of the new brain research for educators.

These issues contain a variety of articles—articles by advocates of brain-based curricula, articles by educational futurists, articles by cognitive (not brain) scientists. In fact, it is rare to find an article written by a neuroscientist in the educational literature. Of these articles, those citing cognitive research on learning, intelligence, memory, and specific subject matter learning provide the most useful advice to educators.

Educators should be aware that cognitive science—the behavioral science of the mind—is not the same as neuroscience—the biological science of the brain. Most cognitive theories are formulated without regard for how the brain might implement or execute mental processes. Nonetheless these cognitive theories are most useful to educators (Bruer, 1993; McGilly, 1994). When "brain-based" curricula do provide sound advice, they might better be called "mind-based," because they often draw from cognitive rather than brain research. Most other claims found in the emerging brain and education literature are

vague, outdated, metaphorical, or based on misconceptions. This article will address some of those misconceptions.

NEUROSCIENCE AND EDUCATION

Despite all the interest and media attention, I do not believe we currently know enough about brain development and neural function to link that understanding, in any meaningful way, to educational practice. Most of the "brain" articles you will read, both in the media and the professional journals, will explicitly state or allude to what I call the "neuroscience and education argument."

The neuroscience and education argument relies on and embellishes three important and reasonably well-established findings from developmental neurobiology. *First,* starting in infancy and continuing into later childhood there is a period of exuberant synapse growth, followed by a period of synaptic "pruning" in the brain. *Second,* there are experience-dependent critical periods in the development of at least some sensory and motor systems. *Third,* in rats, at least, complex or enriched environments cause new synapses to form.

The argument fails to provide guidance to educators because it relies on misconceptions about and overgeneralizations from these three results. I have discussed these misinterpretations elsewhere (Bruer, 1997). Rather than repeat those

From *NASSP Bulletin* 82, no. 598 (May 1998): 9–19. Used by permission of the author and publisher. Copyright 1998, National Association of Secondary School Principals. For more information concerning NASSP services and/or programs, please call (703) 860-0200.

arguments here, I will concentrate on misconceptions about one of the three findings—misconceptions about the significance of synapse formation and loss during childhood—that have crept into the educational literature.

Most neuroscientists agree that the brain is not mature at birth and that significant development events take place post-natally. One such significant developmental event is a postnatal phase of rapid synapse formation. In the mid-1970s, neuroscientists first observed this by counting synapses in samples of brain tissue taken from the visual cortex of cats and monkeys (Cragg, 1975a; Lund, Booth, and Lund, 1977). Since the mid-1970s, research, mostly on rhesus monkeys, has shown that this developmental phase occurs in all areas of the monkey brain that scientists have examined—visual, motor, somatosensory, and frontal cortex—brain areas fundamental for seeing, moving, feeling, and planning/remembering (Rakic, 1994; Rakic, Bourgeois, and Goldman-Rakic, 1994; Goldman-Rakic, Bourgeois, and Rakic, 1997).

In monkeys, rapid synapse formation begins two months before the monkey is born. At birth the number of synapses per unit volume (synaptic density) of tissue in the monkey brain is approximately the same as the synaptic density found in adult monkey brains. This process of rapid synapse formation continues for another two to three months after birth, until synaptic density in the monkey brain far exceeds that found in adult brains.

From age three months to three years, the age of sexual maturity for rhesus monkeys, there is a "high plateau" period for synaptic density. At puberty, a period of rapid synapse elimination begins, during which synaptic densities settle at adult levels by age five years. Thus, in the monkey, synaptic densities (as well as the number of synapses) follow an inverted-U pattern—low at birth, high during adolescence, low thereafter.

Although fewer data are available, it appears that during development the human brain follows the same inverted-U pattern. Since 1979, Peter Huttenlocher at the University of Chicago

has counted synapses in brain tissue taken from 53 human patients at autopsy. The patients' ages at death ranged from pre-term infants to more than 70 years old. Huttenlocher has counted synapses in three brain areas—the visual area, the auditory area, and the frontal area (Huttenlocher, 1979, 1990; Huttenlocher and de Courten, 1987; Huttenlocher and Dabholkar, 1997).

Synapse Formation in Humans

Unlike in the monkey, where rapid synapse formation appears to occur concurrently in all brains, in the human it appears that rapid synapse formation occurs at different times in different brain areas. (Because we do not have comparable data for monkeys and humans, however, this remains an unresolved, contested issue.)

In the human visual cortex, there is a rapid increase in the number of synaptic connections at around 2 months of age, which reaches a peak at 8–10 months. Then there is a steady decline in synaptic density, until it reaches adult levels at around 10 years of age. In the auditory cortex, there is also a rapid rise in the months following birth, with peak density occurring at age 3 months, followed by a plateau period and stabilization at adult levels at puberty. In the human frontal cortex, peak densities occur at around two years of age and remain at these high levels until 8 years of age, when they slowly decline to adult levels at around age 16 (Huttenlocher, 1990).

In humans, there is also indirect evidence for this developmental pattern. Many of the education articles mention brain scanning technologies, such as Positron Emission Tomography (PET), that allow scientists to measure brain activity in normal, living human subjects. PET uses radioactively labeled substances, like oxygen or glucose, that the brain requires for energy. When these substances are administered to a subject, they go via the bloodstream to brain areas requiring energy and there eventually emit positrons. Detectors pick up these emissions, and data on the paths of the emissions allow scientists to construct images of where in the brain the oxygen or glucose is being consumed.

The PET study most often cited in the education literature is a study of 29 epileptic children. (Because PET scans require the injection of a radioactive substance almost no images are available from healthy children [Chugani, Phelps, and Mazziota, 1987].) This study revealed a rapid rise in glucose uptake in children's brains that started at 1 year, peaked at 3 years, and stayed at this level until age 9 or 10, after which levels of glucose uptake receded to adult levels. If one assumes, as the authors of this study do, that the brain's increased energy demands result from the need to fuel and maintain excess synapses, the study provides indirect evidence of the inverted-U developmental pattern.

IMPLICATIONS FOR CHILDREN

Although neuroscientists have documented the time course of this apparent synaptic waxing and waning, they are less sure about what it means for changes in children's behavior, intelligence, and capacity to learn. Generally, they point to correlations between changes in synaptic density or numbers and observed changes in children's behavior documented by developmental and cognitive psychologists. Typically, they all rely on the same small set of examples (Chugani, Phelps, and Mazziota, 1987; Huttenlocher and de Courten, 1987; Goldman-Rakic, Bourgeois, and Rakic, 1997).

At the time rapid synapse formation begins, at around two months of age, human infants start to lose their innate, infantile reflexes. At age three months, when the process is well underway in the visual cortex, infants can reach for an object while visually fixating on it. At four–five months, infants' visual capacities increase. At eight months, when rapid synapse formation begins in the frontal cortex, infants first show the ability to hold information, like the location of hidden objects, in working memory for a short period of time, say several seconds. The time delay over which they can remember this information improves steadily

during the next four months up to more than 10 seconds. These examples are all significant developmental milestones that no doubt depend somehow on brain development. We know these milestones are correlated with changes in synaptic densities and number, but that is all we know.

Educators should note one thing about these examples. They are examples of the emergence or changes in basic sensory, motor, and memory functions. The changes are developmentally significant. These are not abilities and skills children learn in school or pre-school, however. Normal children in almost any environment acquire these capacities at approximately the same age—children in affluent suburbs, children in inner cities, children in rural-pastoral settings throughout the world. It takes severely deprived environments and highly unnatural situations to prevent these skills and abilities from developing, in both children and animals.

No doubt, in some way, the development of these capacities supports future school learning, but currently, we have little idea, certainly no idea based on neuroscientific research, how the emergence of these species-wide capacities relates to later school learning. We do not know much about how these capacities contribute to the acquisition of culturally transmitted knowledge and skills like reading, writing, mathematics, and science.

NEUROSCIENCE AND EDUCATION: MISCONCEPTIONS

This is the neuroscience, most of it more than 20 years old, at the basis of the neuroscience and education argument. Educators interpret these findings to develop what appears to be a commonsense, highly compelling argument. One reason this argument is so beguiling is that it lends itself to a "quantitative" view of brain development, intelligence, and learning. More synapses are better. Saving as many synapses as we can is important. The right experiences at the right times can result in optimal "synaptic conservation" and learning. Beguiling, but misconceived. Here are three of the most common misconceptions.

1. *Enriched early childhood environments causes synapses to multiply rapidly.*

It not unusual to see claims like these: "With proper stimulation brain synapses will form at a rapid pace, reaching adult levels by the age two and far surpassing them in the next several years" (Clinton, 1996, Chapter 4). Or, "Growing evidence indicates that early mental stimulation promotes the growth of synaptic connections between brain cells" (Kotulak, 1996, p. 186).

What little direct evidence we have—all based on studies of monkeys—indicates these claims are inaccurate. Experience, the environment, and sensory stimulation appear to have no impact on the brain's rapid formation of synapses early in life. Evidence comes from both deprivation and stimulation experiments. Rhesus monkeys, whose retinas were removed in utero midway through gestation, had the same synaptic densities in the visual cortex at each stage of development as age-matched normal, sighted monkeys.

Although the visual cortex in the blind animals was smaller than that of the sighted monkeys, total visual deprivation had no impact on the rate of synapse formation (Rakic, 1994; Rakic, Bourgeois, and Goldman-Rakic, 1994; Goldman-Rakic, Bourgeois, and Rakic, 1997).

In the stimulation experiment, monkeys delivered three weeks pre-term received intensive visual stimulation to see if such stimulation would accelerate synapse formation in the visual cortex. Contrary to the experimenters' expectations, the synaptic densities of the pre-term, highly stimulated monkeys were no different than those of the full-term, normally stimulated control monkeys.

The rate of synapse formation and synaptic density seems to be impervious to quantity of stimulation. The rate of synapse formation appears to be linked to the animal's developmental age, the time since it was conceived, and to be under genetic control. It is not linked to birth age and amount of postnatal experience. Some features of brain development, including the rapid burst of synapse formation in infancy and early childhood, rather than being acutely sensitive to deprivation or increased stimulation, are in fact surprisingly resilient to them. Early experience does not cause synapses to form rapidly. Early enriched environments will not put our children on synaptic fast tracks.

2. *More synapses mean more brainpower.*

One often sees claims that neuroscientific evidence indicates that the more synapses you have, the smarter you are. The assumption is that there is a linear relationship between the number of synapses in the brain and brainpower or intelligence (Kotulak, 1996, p. 20; Education Commission of the States, 1997; National Education Association, 1997, p. 9).

The neuroscientific evidence does not support this claim, either. The evidence shows that synaptic numbers and densities follow an inverted-U pattern—low, high, and low—over the life span. However, our behavior, cognitive capacities, and intelligence obviously do not follow an inverted-U pattern over our life span.

Synaptic densities at birth and in early adulthood are approximately the same, yet by any measure adults are more intelligent, have more highly flexible behavior, and learn more readily than infants. Furthermore, early adulthood, the period of rapid synaptic loss, follows the high plateau period of synaptic densities from early childhood to puberty. Young adults do not become less intelligent or less able to learn once they start to lose synapses. Furthermore, learning complex subjects continues throughout life, with no apparent, appreciable change in synaptic numbers.

Studies of brain tissue taken from individuals suffering forms of mental retardation also undermine this claim. Some forms of mental retardation seem to be associated with abnormally low synaptic densities and numbers, but other forms seem to be associated with abnormally high synaptic densities and numbers

(Cragg, 1975b; Huttenlocher and Dabholkar, 1997). Whatever the relationship is between synapses and brain power, it is not a simple, linear, numerical one: " . . . no one believes that there will be a simple and linear relationship between any given dimension of neural development and functional competence" (Goldman-Rakic, 1986, p. 234; Huttenlocher, 1990). It is not true that more synapses mean more brainpower.

3. *The plateau of high synaptic density and high brain metabolism is the optimal period for learning.*

One sees claims that during the plateau period the brain is super-dense and is "a supersponge that is most absorbent from birth to around the age of 12" (Kotulak, 1996, p. 4). "It is a time during which the human computer has so much memory capacity that . . . it can store more information than any army of humans could possibly input" (Clinton, 1996, Chapter 4). This is *the* critical period for learning (Carnegie, 1996, pp. 10–11; Kotulak, 1996; U.S. Department of Education, 1996, p. 22; Shore, 1997).

The idea that periods of high brain growth or activity are optimal periods for learning is an old one. In the 1970s, Herman Epstein argued those periods of high brain growth, as determined by changes in head circumference, might be periods where children are most receptive to learning (1978). To his credit, he put this forward as a hypothesis, not as a fact. There is still not much evidence to support it, but in the brain and education literature, this hypothesis has risen to the status of fact.

The neuroscientific evidence for this claim is extremely weak. The neuroscientists who count synapses in humans and monkeys merely point out that during the plateau period, monkeys and humans develop a variety of skills and behaviors. They develop from infants to adolescents. At adolescence, when rapid synapse loss begins, young primates are essentially like adults in their capacities. They can move, sense, communicate, behave, and procreate like adults.

This is another correlational argument where neuroscientists have observed something about the brain and look to commonsense experience or results from behavioral science in an attempt to explain the possible broader significance of what they have observed. They use what we know about development and behavior to generate hypotheses about the significance of changes observed in the brain. The observed changes in the brain are not being used to explain what we see in child development and classroom behavior. Brain science, at least at the level of studying synapses, is just not that far along yet.

Even, as it appears, that there is this high-plateau period from age 3 to 10, it is still difficult to provide evidence for or against a claim that children learn more during this period than during any other. We have not, and probably have no way, to quantify learning and knowledge. Claims about peak learning periods thus depend more on one's intuitions than on established scientific claims.

When educators say that the first decade of life is a unique time of enormous information acquisition and that the brain is in its most sponge-like phase of learning, they are making an intuitive conjecture, not stating a research result. Needless to say, peoples' intuitions differ. The neuroscientific study that is most often cited to support the claim that age 3–10 is the optimal time for learning is the PET study of brain metabolism. This study showed there was a high plateau period of cerebral metabolism between the ages of 3 and 10. In the educational literature, "high glucose metabolism" becomes "high brain activity," which in turn becomes "high learning potential."

Note, however, that these PET studies did not look at "learning" at all. These studies measured resting brain metabolism—how much energy the brain used when it was doing as little as possible, when the subjects were in a dark room intended to minimize sensory input. We do not know what relationship exists between high resting brain metabolism and learning, any more than we know what relation exists between high synaptic numbers and ability to learn. Any such claims are again conjecture, correlating commonsense behavioral observations with a neuroscientific result in an attempt to understand what the brain is doing.

We can as readily make the opposite conjecture, as one neuroscientist has done. Peter Huttenlocher once speculated that the presence of excess synaptic activity might have negative effects on children's brain function because the large number of unspecified synapses might interfere with efficient information processing in the cortex (Huttenlocher, 1990). This might make it difficult for children to learn.

Although children's brains are metabolically more active than adults, high resting metabolic activity does not necessarily mean high cognitive activity or heightened ability to learn. Childhood is a time of rapid brain growth, as it is a time of rapid physical growth. Growth requires energy. For all we know, and for all that neuroscience can tell us, periods of rapid growth may not be the best time to learn. Little Leaguers should not throw curve balls. It's bad for their growing arms. Maybe they shouldn't learn calculus, either.

WHAT DOES ALL THIS MEAN?

The brain does and should fascinate all of us and we should find advances in neuroscience exciting. As educators, we should also be interested in how basic research might contribute to and improve educational practice. However, we should be wary of claims that neuroscience has much to tell us about educational practice. The neuroscience and education argument attempts to link learning, particularly early childhood learning, with what neuroscience has discovered about neural development and synaptic change.

Neuroscience has discovered a great deal about neurons and synapses, but not nearly enough to guide educational practice in any meaningful way. Currently, it is just too much of a leap from what we know about changes in synapses to what goes on in a classroom. Educators, like all well-informed citizens, should be aware of what basic science can contribute to our self-understanding and professional practice. However, educators should consider carefully what neuroscientists are saying before leaping on the brain and education bandwagon.

Truly new results in neuroscience, rarely mentioned in the brain and education literature, point to the brain's lifelong capacity to reshape itself in response to experience. The challenge for educators is to develop learning environments and practices that can exploit the brain's lifelong plasticity. The challenge is to define the behaviors we want to teach; design learning environments to impart them; and constantly test the educational efficacy of these environments. We will best meet this challenge by careful study of human behavior and behavioral change. How the brain does it will be of less significance. For the present, educators should critically read and evaluate those articles on cognitive science and put brain science on the back burner.

REFERENCES

Bruer, J. T. "Education and the Brain: A Bridge Too Far." *Educational Researcher* 8(1997): 4–16.

———. *Schools for Thought: A Science of Learning in the Classroom.* Cambridge, Mass.: 1993.

Carnegie Corporation of New York. *Years of Promise: A Comprehensive Learning Strategy for America's Children.* New York: Carnegie Corporation, 1996.

Chugani, H. T.; Phelps, M. E.; and Mazziota, J. C. "Positron Emission Tomography Study of Human Brain Function Development." *Annals of Neurology* 22(1987): 487–97.

Clinton, H. *It Takes a Village.* New York: Touchstone, 1996.

Cragg, B. G. "The Density of Synapses and Neurons in Normal, Mentally Defective and Aging Human Brains." *Brain* 98(1975b): 81–90.

———. "The Development of Synapses in the Visual System of the Cat." *Journal of Comparative Neurology* 160(1975a): 147–66.

Education Commission of the States. "1997 Education Agenda/Priorities." September 1997. http://www.ecs.org/ecs/231e.htm.

Epstein, H. T. "Growth Spurts During Brain Development: Implications for Educational Policy and Practice." In *Education and the Brain,* edited by J. S. Chall and A. F. Mirsky, pp. 343–70. Chicago, Ill.: University of Chicago Press, 1978.

Goldman-Rakic, P. S. "Development of Cortical Circuitry and Cognitive Function." *Child Development* 58(1987): 601–22.

———. "Setting the Stage: Neural Development Before Birth." In *The Brain, Cognition, and Education,* edited by S. L. Friedman, K. A. Klivington, and R. W. Peterson. Orlando, Fla.: Academic Press, 1986, pp. 233–58.

Goldman-Rakic, P. S.; Bourgeois, J. P.; and Rakic, P. "Synaptic Substrate of Cognitive Development: Synaptogenesis in the Prefrontal Cortex of the Nonhuman Primate." in *Development of the Prefrontal Cortex: Evolution, Neurobiology, and Behavior,* edited by N. A. Krasnegor, G. R. Lyon, and P. S. Goldman-Rakic, pp. 27–47. Baltimore, Md.: Paul H. Brooks, 1997.

Huttenlocher, P. R. "Morphometric Study of Human Cerebral Cortex Development." *Neuropsychologia* 6(1990): 517–27.

———. "Synaptic Density in Human Frontal Cortex—Developmental Changes of Aging." *Brain Research* 163(1979): 195–205.

Huttenlocher, P. R., and Dabholkar, A. S. "Regional Differences in Synaptogenesis in Human Cerebral Cortex." *The Journal of Comparative Neurology* 387(1997): 167–78.

Huttenlocher, P. R., and de Courten, Ch. "The Development of Synapses in Striate Cortex of Man." *Human Neurobiology* 6(1987): 1–9.

Kotulak, R. *Inside the Brain: Revolutionary Discoveries of How the Mind Works.* Kansas City: Andrews and McNeel, 1996.

Lund, J. S.; Boothe, R. G.; and Lund, R. D. "Development of Neurons in the Visual Cortex (Area 17) of the Monkey (*Macaca Nemestrina*): A Golgi Study From Fetal Day 127 to Postnatal Maturity." *Journal of Comparative Neurology* 176(1977): 149–88.

McGilly, K., ed. *Classroom Lessons: Integrating Cognitive Theory and Classroom Instruction.* Cambridge, Mass.: MIT Press, 1994.

National Education Association. "The Latest on How the Brain Works." *NEA Today,* April 1997.

Rakic, P. "Corticogenesis in Human and Nonhuman Primates." In *The Cognitive Neurosciences,* edited by M. Gazzaniga. Cambridge, Mass.: MIT Press, 1994.

Rakic, P.; Bourgeois, I. P.; and Goldman-Rakic, P. S. "Synaptic Development of the Cerebral Cortex: Implications for Learning, Memory, and Mental Illness." In *Progress in Brain Research,* edited by J. van Pelt, M. A. Corner, H. B. M. Uylings, and F. H. Lopes da Silva. Amsterdam: Elsevier ScienceBV, 1994.

Shore, R. *Rethinking the Brain.* New York: Families and Work Institute, 1997.

U.S. Department of Education. *Building Knowledge for a Nation of Learners: A Framework for Education Research 1997.* Washington, D.C.: U.S. Department of Education, 1996.

John T. Bruer is President, James S. McDonnell Foundation, St. Louis, Missouri.

QUESTIONS FOR REFLECTION

1. Why does Bruer prefer the term *mind-based* curricula than *brain-based* curricula?
2. Bruer discusses several limitations of the "neuroscience and education argument." What might account for the misapplication of neuroscience to the teaching–learning process?
3. In regard to the content area and level with which you are most familiar, what would be the characteristics of a learning environment that exploits the brain's plasticity? In what ways would this environment differ from that which currently exists?

Matching Learning Styles and Teaching Styles

RONALD HYMAN
BARBARA ROSOFF

ABSTRACT: The authors discuss the theoretical and practical limitations of trying to match students' learning styles with teaching styles. Five elements of teaching—teacher, student, subject matter, environment, and time—interact in such a way that students' learning styles are not the main element influencing teacher action. Moreover, students' learning styles are always changing. Teachers should therefore move from a unilateral approach to influencing student actions to a "bilateral" approach based on mutuality and jointness of purpose.

The education literature today often recommends that learning style be matched with teaching style to augment achievement. The paradigm for "learning style based education" (LSBE) is: Examine the student's individual learning style; understand it and classify it according to several large categories; match it with a teaching style of an available teacher or ask that a teacher's teaching style be adjusted to match the student's learning style; and teach teachers to do all this in their preservice and inservice training programs.

Three major issues arising from this paradigm present serious difficulties: The concept of learning style is unclear, even among LSBE advocates; the focus on learning style in determining teaching action is inappropriate theoretically and realistically; and the action strategies and unintended consequences of following this paradigm are undesirable. The following recommendations are not sequential steps but together constitute a reorientation of thinking about matching learning styles and teaching styles.

First, educators who aim to help teachers improve should accept a more inclusive perspective on teaching. Teaching is an act which has three elements—the *teacher,* the *student,* and the *subject matter*—interrelating in an *environment* and in a particular *time* period. Where there is teaching going on, all five elements are present. Thus, it is improper to focus on learning style as the sole

or even main element influencing teacher action. Teachers must always keep in mind the time and place context, the nature of the subject matter under study, and also their own interests, knowledge, skill, and personality because all these are involved.

Second, teachers should realize that the teaching relationship is constantly changing. They ought not to believe that the student's learning style of today is that of next week. All educators, especially LSBE advocates, must be careful not to view scores on learning style preference or description tests as final and unchangeable. Learning style, part of the student element in the teaching relationship, is malleable. The student's learning style is always changing and adapting to the four other elements.

STUDENT ACTIONS

Third, the teacher looking to diagnose learning style should see it as referring to *actions* of the student rather than ability. We also recommend a multidimensional perspective (cognitive, affective, and physiological) on student action. Therefore, teachers should use an informal approach to determining learning style. This approach, which gets information from student feedback and keen observation, will permit teachers to operational-

Excerpted from *Theory Into Practice* 23, no. 1 (Winter 1984): 35–43. © 1984, College of Education, The Ohio State University. Used by permission of the authors and the publisher.

ize a definition of learning style with ease and without waiting for a perfect formal diagnostic instrument.

Fourth, teachers should accept a concept of learning broader than cognitive achievement as determined by a numerical score on a paper-and-pencil test. The task of teachers is complex and diverse. Students learn humanness as they blend the knowledge, the skills, and the values taught by teachers, explicitly or implicitly. What students learn does not remain separated into neat cubby-holes but becomes an integrated whole. Students learn as they experience, reflect individually and with teacher help, and reconstruct experience. Therefore, it is impossible to identify one bit of learning from the other. This broader concept of learning is not compatible with precise measurement. Yet, teachers are in peril if they neglect it.

Fifth, teachers should recognize and attend to the only actions they can control—their own. No one can make students learn and act in specific ways. By attending to their own actions, teachers will come to accept that there are various teaching models or strategies which they can learn and employ in forms adapted to their particular combination of the five teaching elements. Learning, practicing, and utilizing a variety of teaching strategies will give teachers a sense of efficacy in the classroom. Being knowledgeable and skillful regarding their own actions—what they do, control, and are responsible for—is a requisite for teachers to be able to match learning styles with teaching styles. In this regard, we recommend that teachers attend to the literature on teaching and become students of teaching.

BILATERALISM

Sixth, teachers should drop their unilateral approach to influencing student action and accept an approach which rests on mutuality, jointness of purpose, and bilateralism. We oppose the unilateral diagnostic procedure and the resulting unilateral action because they serve only to ac-

complish such negative consequences as lack of trust, low freedom of choice, manipulation, and dependency, while the consequences we want to develop include trust and trustworthiness, high freedom of choice, collaboration, and independence, along with the capacity to make intelligent decisions.

The unilateral LSBE paradigm employs a familiar medical metaphor: Teacher administers the learning style test, diagnoses the test results, prescribes the current teaching style for the "patient," and renders a prognosis for the parents and school officials. A bilateral model leads the teacher to share leadership, encourage students to speak out, and feel successful as a teacher once the students express themselves as individuals. In bilateralism, the students help diagnose their own learning style, help determine the appropriate teaching style, and at times even confront the teacher regarding the teaching situation's five essential elements. The teacher does not act unilaterally, does not define goals unilaterally, and does not impose ideas and values unilaterally.

ILLUSTRATION

We recognize that the six recommendations made here require a different type of preservice and inservice program. For an illustration of change, we refer to what is already in place in one preservice program as one possible implementation step. In the student teaching seminars at the University of Wisconsin, five themes form the essential core of the discussions:

- Helping students to take a critical approach in the examination of educational issues or classroom problems;
- Helping students to see beyond conventional thought about classroom practice;
- Helping students to develop a sense of the history of their particular classroom and to examine the rationales underlying classroom and school regularities;

- Helping students to examine their own assumptions and biases and how these affect their classroom practice; and
- Helping students to examine critically the processes of their own socialization as teachers.

We believe that treatment of these five themes sensitizes the students to the problems of unilateral decision making in our schools, to the issues surrounding currently used paradigms, and to the need for alternative assumptions, strategies, and consequences. Such a seminar can lead to a solution, at least in part, because it guides the students toward a solid examination of the problems that teachers face. We believe it is a step in the right direction.

The issue of matching teaching styles with learning styles is not as simple as some LSBE advocates would have us believe. However, the LSBE advocates are correct in that the learning style issue is important for all teachers concerned with the proper education of their students. The six recommendations made here will, we believe, yield an acceptable way to match learning styles with teaching styles.

Ronald Hyman is Professor, Graduate School of Education, Rutgers University, New Brunswick, New Jersey. *Barbara Rosoff* is a doctoral student at the Graduate School of Education, Rutgers University.

QUESTIONS FOR REFLECTION

1. To what extent do you agree or disagree with Hyman and Rosoff's assertion that "the concept of learning style is unclear"?

2. In regard to the educational setting with which you are most familiar, what steps might you take to use an "informal approach" to determine students' learning styles?

3. Hyman and Rosoff state that "unilateral" approaches to influencing student behavior "serve only to accomplish such negative consequences as lack of trust, low freedom of choice, manipulation, and dependency." Do you agree with their view? What might be said in defense of unilateral approaches?

Learning Styles from a Multicultural Perspective: The Case for Culturally Engaged Education

CYNTHIA B. DILLARD
DIONNE A. BLUE

ABSTRACT: *When developing educational experiences for students from ethnically and culturally diverse backgrounds, teachers should recognize that their personal perspectives influence their curricular decisions. Since no particular learning style is preferred by an ethnic or cultural group, effective teachers use an array of strategies to facilitate students' learning and growth. By using the concept of "culturally engaged education" as a framework for curriculum planning, teachers can create educational experiences that support and develop both their students and themselves.*

The idea of multiculturalism is not new to public education. Although there are still a few public schools in the United States with relatively homogeneous ethnic and linguistic populations, it is difficult to ignore the rapidly changing students in our schools. America is truly a multicultural society.

The number of students from diverse cultural and linguistic backgrounds is increasing. According to estimates in *One Third of a Nation*, a report published in 1988 by the American Council on Education and the Education Commission of the States, at least one-third of Americans will be people of color by the year 2000. Many will come from homes where the primary language is not English. The National Clearinghouse for Bilingual Education (1980) reports that the number of people from non-English-speaking homes and communities is expected to increase from about 33 million in 1987, to nearly 40 million by the year 2000. This increase in multicultural and multilingual populations is creating a new ethos for schooling in our nation.

Providing an appropriate education for students from ethnically and culturally diverse backgrounds is not an easy task. Delpit (1995) reminds us that "it is impossible to create a model for the good teacher without taking issues of culture and community context into account" (p. 37). Unfortunately, some have tended to view these students as inherently deficient—culturally, linguistically, economically, and socially. This deficit perspective has led some teachers to view the education of ethnically diverse students as remedial, rather than developmental or growth-oriented. This view often leads to student alienation. Students may reject the school's culture and codes of power in lieu of patterns that allow for alternative ways of creativity and empowerment, a type of "counter culture" (Delpit, 1995).

Others see ethnically and culturally diverse students as a source of enrichment and embrace diversity as a way to inform their own teaching and enhance all students' learning. They realize the importance of their role in accepting and integrating multicultural perspectives into their teaching.

BEYOND CONTENT: THE ROLE OF TEACHER PERSPECTIVE

Teaching is more than a matter of following a set of strategies. Our choices of subject matter and teaching techniques are grounded in our per-

Article written by Cynthia B. Dillard and Dionne A. Blue for *Curriculum Planning: A Contemporary Approach,* Seventh Edition, 2000. Used by permission of the authors.

sonal perspectives. Shibutani (1955) defines *perspective* as:

> An ordered view of one's world—what is taken for granted about the attributes of various objects, events and human nature. It is an order of things remembered and expected as well as things actually perceived, an organized conception of what is plausible and what is possible; it constitutes the matrix through which one perceives their environment. (p. 564)

Such a perspective guides teachers in making decisions about the curriculum and strategies to be used in the classroom. If we seek to embrace a more culturally diverse perspective related to planning a curriculum, we must also recognize the need to broaden our own perspectives. We must acknowledge, in an explicit manner, the personal perspectives from which we teach and realize, as well as admit to our students, their limited scope (Greene, 1978; Vogeler, 1990). Further, we must acknowledge that in our classrooms there will be a myriad of perspectives held by our students, some of which may be contradictory to the ones we hold. Our own perspective should not become the normative experience by which we judge our students as morally or intellectually correct (Brown, 1988). Instead, our task is one of structuring the curriculum to help our students and ourselves "center" our personal histories and experiences. According to Brown (1988), this is not simply an intellectual process, but rather "about coming to believe in the possibility of a variety of experiences, a variety of ways of understanding the world, a variety of frameworks of operation, without imposing consciously or unconsciously a notion of the norm" (p. 10). What Brown describes has profound implications for curriculum development.

Education, by its very nature, is a social activity. In our classrooms, students observe and experience a wide range of lessons, both intended and unintended. They are involved in relationships of power and authority. They engage in decision making about learning. They see and are involved in a variety of participation structures enacted in classrooms and schools. They are ex-

posed to new and old information and multiple presentations of it. Thus, Harste, Woodward, and Burke (1984) suggest that developing a true multicultural curriculum includes understanding the key role we must play in participating *with* our students in classrooms.

Hence, curriculum development may be seen as a social, collaborative effort involving teachers, students, parents, and others. Further, an understanding of our students' learning styles fosters an awareness of and appreciation for the multitude of experiences represented in our classrooms and our world. It implies that our interpretation of what is important for our students needs to be open for negotiation with our students. Thus, learning styles in an environment that fosters multicultural understandings focuses on the social nature of education, where everyone and everything is a learning possibility. We turn now to an examination of learning styles within the social and cultural environment of the multicultural classroom.

LEARNING STYLES IN A SOCIOCULTURAL CONTEXT

Many attempts have been made to understand learning styles, from the simply definitional, to elaborate categorizations of elements that make up a particular style. However, it is important to remember that no particular learning style is strictly preferred by an ethnic or cultural group. In fact, the diversity within and among cultures is great and depends on such factors as geography, language, and social class. Furthermore, according to Scarcella (1990), the task, subject matter, and curriculum will influence which style of learning students prefer to use in a given situation. Heath (1986), in her research on the sociocultural contexts of language development suggests further that styles of learning can differ dramatically between the home and community and the schools and classroom. Therefore, as Scarcella (1990) suggests, teachers should use a variety of strategies to facilitate learning for students with various learning styles.

Although there are a number of definitions of learning styles, we will use the broad definition advocated by Hunt (1979) in the early learning styles literature: "Learning style describes a student in terms of those educational conditions under which he/she is most likely to learn. Learning style describes *how* a student learns, not what he/she has learned" (p. 27). Hunt's definition implies the need for teachers to consider not only the place where the student's personal culture meets that of the school, but also the nature of the social context of such a meeting. On the one hand, a student's learning style is distinct and personal, inseparable from the lived experiences of that individual. On the other, one's learning style is followed (or not followed) in relation to the larger social contexts of schools. Thus, the concept of *authenticity* is important in building on the learning styles of students in a multicultural setting. For this discussion, *authenticity* refers to *genuinely inviting students to learn in ways that are appropriate and meaningful to them*. Facilitating such authenticity is an important act of personal affirmation for all of our students. Students from historically marginalized backgrounds and linguistic traditions can see that their personal style of learning is as valid as their teacher's and that of other students. Learning that one's way of knowing is valid and important may have profound meaning for students from groups who have been ignored or pushed to the margins of our classrooms (Dillard, 1994). According to Shor and Freire (1987), such knowledge is truly empowering and important for student success. Further, when we provide spaces in the curriculum for a variety of styles to be enacted, we help students understand different approaches to the processes of learning.

NEGOTIATING THE CURRICULUM: CONSIDERATIONS FOR CURRICULUM PLANNERS

From this discussion, it is clear that learning styles must be considered from both a student's individual and personal culture and the sociocultural environment of the school. With so many necessary elements to consider in the development of multicultural curriculum, where does this leave the teacher? How, with such variety both within and across ethnic and cultural groups, can we most appropriately develop a curriculum that responds to and respects such diversity?

Slavin (1987) suggests that the age of negotiation is upon us. In contrast to the teacher-centered instruction often found in our nation's schools, a classroom environment in schools that is founded on collaboration and negotiation can help to provide all learners with access to a meaningful education. The goal of such a multicultural education, according to Bennett (1995), is "to maximize the number of stars that can exist simultaneously in the classroom, to formulate a plan that can work with the most diverse group of students" (p. 163). Such an environment will require alternative ways of thinking about learning and teaching, often simultaneously. It will also require that we "re-think" not only how we facilitate learning for ourselves and our students, but also ways to move the discussion of student learning styles in multicultural classrooms beyond stereotypes and into a more useful conversation about multicultural pedagogy and practice. Banks (1995) also outlines elements of multicultural education that would serve to move that conversation forward. His notion of multicultural education, as "content integration; the knowledge construction process; prejudice reduction; an equity pedagogy; and an empowering school culture and social structure" (p. 4) provides a framework educators can use to create pedagogy which is culturally relevant, that engages each student, and values the various learning styles they bring to the classroom. Understanding learning style patterns that seem to characterize various ethnic groups is not enough. Teachers must also consider ways to restructure the curriculum to truly allow students to learn in different ways, grounded in harmony with their cultural backgrounds. This requires broadening our own perspectives to see learning styles as an extension of who our students are as individuals.

Many scholars advocate an integrated approach for curriculum development that is sensitive to the diverse learning styles of students and applicable to the multicultural and linguistically diverse student populations in our schools. They advocate a curriculum that is a cooperative venture between teachers and students, one that embraces learning styles not so much as ethnic-specific characteristics, but as ways in which all students' culture, language, and ways of being in the classroom are valued. For example, Shor (1986) suggests that the following elements be considered in all curriculum plans if they are to be responsive to multiple learning styles:

1. *Problem solving:* Allowing all students to know that their participation and critical contribution is expected, valued, and needed to solve problems of interest to the learning community.
2. *Critical literacy:* Questioning aspects of literacy, including reading, writing, speaking, listening, and thinking; also extends students' knowledge, and assists them in moving beyond memorization.
3. *Situated pedagogy:* Integrating the experiential with the conceptual, both of which should necessarily be grounded in the life experiences of those in the learning–teaching environment of the classroom.
4. *Cross-cultural communication:* Providing opportunities for students to have long-term and authentic experiences with students and peoples of diverse backgrounds and cultures.
5. *Education as a change agent:* Recognizing that schools are intimately influenced and connected with the broader society.
6. *An integrated interdisciplinary approach:* Seeing the content of schools as related and influential, assisting our students in developing their own understandings and perspectives.
7. *Participatory learning:* Modeling democratic ideals by allowing students to be responsive to and responsible for other persons in the learning environment.

Ladson-Billings's (1994) notion of *culturally relevant pedagogy* provides another model for negotiating multicultural learning styles in curriculum development. Operating along a continuum, Ladson-Billings (1992) operationally describes culturally relevant teaching as an approach that

> serves to empower students to the point where they will be able to examine critically educational content and process and ask what its role is in creating a truly democratic and multicultural society. It uses the students' culture to help them create meaning and understand the world. Thus, not only academic success, but social and cultural success are emphasized. (p. 110)

Thus, culturally relevant teachers make pedagogical moves that envision themselves as part of the communities in which they teach and see their role as giving something back to the community. They believe that success is possible for all students and at least part of that success is helping students make connections between themselves and their communities, as well as their national, ethnic, and global identities. There is a connectedness with all students and encouragement for cooperation and collaboration. Finally, culturally relevant teaching recognizes that knowledge is continuously recreated, reconstructed, and shared. However, culturally relevant teachers take a critical view of knowledge as culturally and socially constructed and demonstrate a passion for teaching critical thinking to their students (Ladson-Billings, 1992, 1994).

A related idea is hooks's (1994) concept of *engaged pedagogy. Engaged pedagogy* is an approach to teaching and learning that acknowledges the politics of both, seeks to engage in reciprocal and authentic ways on more intimate terrain in learning communities, and encourages teachers and students to recognize, discuss, and ultimately act through our politics as dynamic and changing sites of transformation towards freedom. In this way, hooks extends Ladson-Billings' definition by seeing teaching and learning as intimate and reciprocal educative processes.

While Ladson-Billings's culturally relevant pedagogy and hooks's engaged pedagogy provide strong bases for attention to learning styles in a multicultural classroom environment, each construct is limited in its ability to describe a deeply influential, more encompassing way in which students and teachers actually experience the impact of learning styles—as *personal, cultural affirmation and interaction between teachers, students, curriculum, and contexts that attend to and support everyone's educational interests, motivations, and needs as individuals.* Thus, we'd like to introduce another construct, one that might be salient for reconceptualizing learning styles in multicultural education in ways more responsive to the diverse student populations in our nation's schools. This construct is *culturally engaged education* (Dillard & Ransom, 1998). Culturally engaged education seeks the integration, interconnectedness, and extension of teaching and learning relationships for the purposes of the overall support and development of both the teacher and the taught. Thus, pedagogy and curriculum take on an expanded meaning here, beyond simply a set of discreet tasks carried out by teachers, to a confluence of involvement in personal, academic, and intellectual lives, creating relationships that inform and support both teachers and students, as well as a broader agenda of transformation and liberation through education, particularly for people of color.

It is important to note that within this construct, even the terms *teacher* and *student* are problematic, given the hierarchical assumptions embedded within them. While one cannot ignore the relative nature of power held by the teacher, we suggest that culturally engaged education assumes that teachers are also transformed through the act of teaching since they must attempt to be fully present with students as they learn. With this perspective as a more encompassing way to reconceptualize teaching, we close with ten guiding principles for culturally engaged education that meets the diverse styles of learning found in today's multicultural classrooms.

1. Culturally engaged education begins with self-inquiry. Understanding one's self as a culturally constructed being is key, and can be fostered through explorations of one's autobiography, life narratives, and stories as a first step toward understanding one's style of learning (and teaching). It is the basis upon which to build coalitions and connections across cultures.

2. Culturally engaged education must foster and include voices from multiple cultural and ethnic groups and from multiple perspectives. Student and teacher self-knowledge are both valid and relevant versions of "truth."

3. Culturally engaged education is inherently reciprocal, built in relationships based on all parties being both teacher and taught, and contingent upon who has the knowledge and experiences to teach at any given moment.

4. Culturally engaged education sees experiential knowledge as necessary and requires long-term direct experiences with diverse peoples, languages/discourses, and contexts, and cultural and social support for diverse ways of knowing (theory) and ways of being (culture).

5. Culturally engaged education requires acknowledgment of "differences" as real and valuable, not deviant and undesirable.

6. Culturally engaged education requires strong efforts to include all voices in the learning community in issues of curricular, political, and cultural development and in real versus solely symbolic or "token" ways. This includes the voices of children.

7. Culturally engaged education acknowledges the systematic nature of racism, discrimination in all forms, other societal ills, and one's own contributions/complicity in these ills, while also engaging in individual and social action to address and remedy these problems.

8. Culturally engaged education requires ongoing efforts to deconstruct myths and privilege and facilitate access to knowledge and opportunity, particularly in K–12 schools.

9. Culturally engaged education attends to the aesthetic, encourages creativity in knowing and being, and is spiritual, seeking wholeness of individual realities.

10. Culturally engaged education holds humility, passion for education, and caring at the center of all work, seeking the betterment of one's self and humanity as its purpose.

REFERENCES

Banks, J. A. (1995). Multicultural education: Historical development, dimensions and practice. In J. A. Banks & C. A. M. Banks (Eds.), *Handbook of research on multicultural education* (pp. 3–24). New York: Macmillan Publishing.

Bennett, C. I. (1995). *Comprehensive multicultural education: Theory and practice* (4th edition). Boston: Allyn and Bacon.

Brown, E. B. (1988). African-American women's quilting: A framework for conceptualizing and teaching African-American women's history. In M. R. Malson, E. Mudimbe-boyi, J. F. O'Barr & M. Wyer (Eds.), *Black women in America: Social science perspectives.* Chicago: University of Chicago Press.

Commission on Minority Participation in Education and American Life (1988). *One-third of a nation.* Washington, DC: American Council on Education and the Education Commission of the States.

Delpit, L. (1995). *Other people's children: Cultural conflict in the classroom.* New York: The New Press.

Dillard, C. B., & Ransom, R. M. (1998, February). *(Re)defining recruitment and retention: A model of cultural engagement for colleges of education.* Paper presented at the annual meeting of the American Association of Colleges for Teacher Education, New Orleans, LA.

Dillard, C. B. (1994). Beyond supply and demand: Critical pedagogy, ethnicity, and empowerment in recruiting teachers of color. In *Journal of teacher education, 45,* 9–17.

Fine, M. (1989). Silencing and nurturing voice in an improbable context: Urban adolescents in public schools. In H. A. Giroux & P. McLaren (Eds.), *Critical pedagogy, the state and cultural struggle.* New York: SUNY Press.

Greene, M. (1978). Teaching: The question of personal reality. In *Teachers College Record, 80,* 23–35.

Harste, J., Woodward, V., & Burke, C. (1984). Methodological implications. *Language Stories and Literacy Lessons.* Exeter, NH: Heinemann.

Heath, S. B. (1986). Sociocultural contexts of language development. In *Beyond language: Social and cultural factors in schooling language minority students.* Sacramento: California State Department of Education Bilingual Education Office.

Hunt, D. E. (1979). Learning style and student needs: Introduction to conceptual level. In *Student learning styles: Diagnosing and prescribing programs.* Reston, VA: National Association of Secondary School Principals.

hooks, b. (1994). *Teaching to transgress: Education as the practice of freedom.* New York: Routledge.

Ladson-Billings, G. (1994). *The dreamkeepers: Successful teachers of African American children.* San Francisco: Jossey-Bass Publishers.

Ladson-Billings, G. (1992). Culturally relevant teaching: The key to making multicultural education work. In C. Grant (Ed.), *Research and multicultural education: From the margins to the mainstream* (pp. 106–121). London: Falmer Press.

National Clearinghouse for Bilingual Education (1980). *Non-English Language Background Projections by Language Groups, 1976–2000.* Rosslyn, VA: National Clearinghouse for Bilingual Education.

Scarcella, R. (1990). Appealing to a variety of learning styles. In *Teaching language minority students in the multicultural classroom.* Englewood Cliffs, NJ: Prentice-Hall.

Shibutani, T. (1955). Reference group as perspectives. *American Journal of Sociology, LX,* 564.

Shor, I., & Freire, P. (1987). *A pedagogy for liberation.* South Hadley, MA: Bergin and Garvey.

Shor, I. (1986). Equality is excellence: Transforming teacher education and the learning process. *Harvard Education Review, 56.* 406–426.

Slavin, R. (1987). Cooperative learning and the cooperative school. *Educational Leadership, 45,* 7–13.

Vogeler, I. (1990). Cultural diversity: ideology of content. *Issues in Teaching and Learning, 3,* 17–20.

Cynthia B. Dillard is Assistant Dean for Diversity and Outreach, College of Education, and Associate Professor, School of Teaching and Learning, The Ohio State University; and *Dionne A. Blue* is a doctoral candidate and Graduate Associate, School of Teaching and Learning, The Ohio State University.

QUESTIONS FOR REFLECTION

1. What are the "personal perspectives" that influence your curriculum planning activities?
2. What is "culturally engaged education"? In regard to the subject matter and level of schooling with which you are most interested, describe two instances when the concept of "culturally engaged education" might be a useful curriculum criterion.
3. Why do Dillard and Blue suggest that "the terms *teacher* and *student* are problematic, given the hierarchical assumptions embedded within them"?

Probing More Deeply into the Theory of Multiple Intelligences

HOWARD GARDNER

ABSTRACT: The originator of multiple intelligences theory discusses several misconceptions educators have about how to apply the theory to the teaching–learning process. The seven intelligences are based on explicit criteria and "come into being" when they interact with specific real-world content. While educators can assess proficiency at using intelligences for different tasks, they cannot assess intelligences per se.

No one has been more surprised than I by the continuing interest among educators in the theory of multiple intelligences ("MI," as it has become known). Almost 15 years after the manuscript of *Frames of Mind* (1983; 1993a) was completed, I continue on a nearly daily basis to hear about schools that are carrying out experiments in implementing MI. And, on occasion, I encounter a series of thoughtful essays such as the set assembled here.

As a result of the almost constant interaction with the "field," I have come to expect certain understandings and misunderstandings of MI. I began to respond to these interpretations, first through correspondence and then through "replies" to reviews and critiques. In 1995, after 10 years of relative silence, I issued a more formal response, in the form of reflections on seven

"myths about multiple intelligences" (Gardner, 1995). This article gave me an opportunity to address directly some of the most common misconceptions about the theory and, as best I could, to set the record straight.

Since publishing these reflections, I have begun to think about the theory from a different perspective. Like any new formulation, "MI theory" is prone to be apprehended initially in certain ways. Sometimes the initial apprehensions (and misapprehensions) endure; more commonly, they alter over time in various, often in predictable, ways.

It may surprise readers to know that I have observed this process even in myself; I have held some of the common misconceptions about MI theory, even as I have come over time to understand aspects of the theory more deeply. In these

From *NASSP Bulletin* 80, no. 580 (November 1996): 1–7. Used by permission of the author and publisher. Copyright 1996, National Association of Secondary School Principals. For more information concerning NASSP services and/or programs, please call (703) 860-0200.

notes, I identify a series of steps that seem to me to reflect increasingly deep readings of the theory.

Judging the book by its title. Anyone who has published a book of non-fiction will recognize symptoms of the most superficial readings of the book (or, more likely, examination of its cover). Such individuals show no evidence of having even cracked the binding. I have read and heard individuals talk about "multiple intelligence" (sic) as if there were a single intelligence, composed of many parts—in direct contradiction to my claim that there exist a number of relatively autonomous human intellectual capacities. Displaying the ability to read the table of contents but not further, many have written about the "six intelligences," though I have never asserted that there were fewer than seven intelligences. The apparent reason for this misstep: in *Frames of Mind* I devote a single chapter to the two personal intelligences, thus suggesting to the skimmer that I consider these two as if they are one. Finally, I cannot enumerate how often I have been said to posit a "spiritual intelligence" though I have never done so, and have in fact explicitly rejected that possibility both orally and in writings (Gardner, 1995; 1999).

"MI-Lite" based on a skim or a cocktail party conversation. Those who have made at least a half-hearted effort to understand what the author had in mind usually recognize that "multiple intelligence" (sic) is plural, that there are at least seven separate intelligences, and that the only newly accepted intelligence is that of the Naturalist. Of equal importance, they appreciate that my theory constitutes a critique of the hegemony of one or two intelligences—usually the linguistic and logical varieties that are (over-) valued in school. And they infer that I am not fond of tests of the standard psychometric variety. Indeed, such readers are often attracted more by what they think I oppose (IQ tests, the SAT, a one-dimensional approach to students) than by the actual claims of the theory.

Still, these individuals prove most susceptible to the misconceptions to which I earlier referred. It is from them that I am likely to hear that:

1. One ought to have seven tests. (Alas, you can't get from MI to psychometrics-as-usual.)
2. An intelligence is the same as a domain, discipline, or craft. (Actually, any domain can use several intelligences, and any intelligence can be drawn upon in numerous domains.)
3. An intelligence is indistinguishable from a "learning style." (In fact "style" turns out to be a slippery concept, one quite different from an intelligence.)
4. There is an official Gardner or "MI approach" to schools. (There is not such an approach, and I hope there never will be.)

My psychologist colleagues are more likely to succumb to three other myths:

5. MI theory is not based on empirical data. (This nonsensical view could not be held by anyone who has ever spent more than five minutes skimming through the book.)
6. MI theory is incompatible with hereditarian or environmental accounts. (In fact, the theory takes no position on the sources of different intellectual profiles.)
7. Gardner's notion of intelligence is too broad. (Actually, it is the psychometric view that is too narrow, substituting one form of scholasticism for the rich set of capacities that comprise the human mind.)

One further misconception unites many skimmers with those who do not even bother to skim. That is a belief that I favor an un-rigorous curriculum, one that spurns the standard disciplines, hard work, and regular assessment.

Nothing could be further from the truth. I am actually a proponent of teaching the classical disciplines and I attempt to adhere to the highest standards, both for others and for myself. Unlike many readers, I see no incompatibility whatsoever between a belief in MI and pursuit of a rigorous education. Rather, I feel that only if we recognize multiple intelligences can we reach more students, and give those students the opportunity to demonstrate what they have understood.

TOWARD A DEEPER GRASP OF THE THEORY

Those who have studied key writings and have engaged in reflection and dialogue about the theory have come to appreciate a number of important insights. In what follows, I state these insights and suggest their possible educational implications.

The intelligences are based on explicit criteria.

What makes MI theory more than a parade of personal preferences is a set of eight criteria that were laid out explicitly in Chapter 4 of *Frames of Mind*. These range from the existence of populations that feature an unusual amount of a certain intelligence (e.g., prodigies); to localization of an intelligence in particular regions of the brain; to susceptibility to encoding in a symbolic system. Of the many candidate intelligences proposed and reviewed so far (e.g., auditory or visual; humor or cooking; intuitive or moral), only eight have qualified in terms of these criteria. Those who would posit additional intelligences have the obligation to assess candidates on these criteria, and to make available the results of this evaluation (Gardner, 1999).

The intelligences reflect a specific scientific wager. As I envision them, the intelligences have emerged over the millennia as a response to the environments in which humans have lived. They constitute, as it were, a cognitive record of the evolutionary past. If my list of intelligences is close to the mark, it will mean that my colleagues and I have succeeded in figuring out what the brain has evolved to do—to use a current phrase, that we have carved nature at its proper joints.

To be sure, culture has not evolved simply to fit nature, but the kinds of skills that we expect individuals to achieve do reflect the capacities that individuals actually possess. The challenge confronting educators is to figure out how to help individuals employ their distinctive intellectual profiles to help master the tasks and disciplines needed to thrive in the society.

The intelligences respond to specific content in the world.

Scientifically, an intelligence is best thought of as a "biopsychological construct": that is, if we understood much more than we do about the genetic and neural aspects of the human mind, we could delineate the various psychological skills and capacities that humans are capable of exhibiting. Despite the convenient existence of the word, however, it makes little sense to think of intelligences in the abstract. Intelligences only come into being because the world in which we live features various contents—among them, the sounds and syntax of language, the sounds and rhythms of music, the species of nature, the other persons in our environment, and so on.

These facts lead to the most challenging implication of MI theory. If our minds respond to the actual varied contents of the world, then it does not make sense to posit the existence of "all-purpose" faculties. There is, in the last analysis, no *generalized* memory: There is memory for language, memory for music, memory for spatial environments, and so on. Nor, despite current buzzwords, can we speak about critical or creative thinking in an unmodified way. Rather, there is critical thinking using one or more intelligences, and there is creativity in one, or in more than one, domain.

Powerful educational implications lurk here. We must be leery about claiming to enhance general abilities like thinking or problem solving or memory; it is important to examine *which* problem is being solved, *which* kind of information is being memorized. Even more important, the teacher must be wary of claims about transfer. Though transfer of skill is a proper goal for any educator, such transfer cannot be taken for granted—and especially not when such transfer is alleged to occur across intelligences. The cautious educator assumes that particular intelligences can be enhanced, but remains skeptical of the notion that use of one set of intellectual skills will necessarily enhance others.

Despite the seductive terminology, we cannot assess intelligences: We can at most assess proficiency in different tasks.

Given the positing of multiple intelligences, there is an almost inevitable slippage toward the idea that we could assess an individual's intelligences, or profile of intelligences. And even those who recognize the limits (or inappropriateness) of standard measures are still tempted to create some kind of a battery or milieu that "takes the temperature" of different intelligences. I know: I have more than once succumbed to this temptation myself.

But because intelligences are the kinds of constructs that they are, it is simply not possible to assess an individual intelligence or an individual's intelligences with any degree of reliability. All that one can ever assess in psychology is performance on some kind of task. And so, if an individual does well in learning a melody and in recognizing when that melody has been embedded in harmony, we do not have the right to proclaim her "musically intelligent"; the most that we can infer is that the individual has presumptively exhibited musical intelligence on this single measure.

The greater the number of tasks sampled, the more likely it is that a statement about "strength" or "weakness" in an intelligence will acquire some validity, Even here, however, one must be careful. For just because it *appears* that a task was solved by the use of a particular intelligence, we cannot be certain this is so. A person is free to solve a task in whichever manner he likes. Inferences about mind or brain mechanisms can only be made as a result of carefully designed experiments, ones that most educators (and, truth to tell, most researchers) are in no position to conduct.

For informal purposes, it is certainly acceptable to speculate that a person is relying on certain intelligences rather than others, or that she exhibits a strength in one but not another intelligence. Because actual inference about intelligences is problematic, however, educators should be cautious about characterizing the intellectual profiles of students. While seven or eight labels may be preferable to one (smart or stupid), labeling can still be pernicious, and particularly so when there is little empirical warrant for it.

The road between theory and practice runs in two directions.

Many individuals, practitioners as well as researchers, adopt a jaundiced view of the relation between theory and practice. On this "conduit" view, researchers collect data and then develop theories about a topic (say, the nature of human intelligence); the implications of the theories are reasonably straightforward (e.g., let's train all intelligences equally); and practitioners consume the material and attempt to apply the theory as faithfully as possible (Voilà—behold a multiple intelligences classroom!).

This description is wrong in every respect. Within the research world, the relations among theory, data, and inference are complex and ever-changing. Any theoretical statement or conclusion can lead to an indefinite number of possible practical implications. Only actual testing "in the real world" will indicate which, if any, of the implications holds water. And most important, those who theorize about the human world have as much to learn from practitioners as vice versa.

Continuing the confessional mode of this essay, I freely admit that I once held a version of this mental model. While I was not initially bent on applying my theory in practical settings, I assumed that the theory would be revised in the light of further research and nothing else.

Here the events of the past decade have been most auspicious—and most enlightening. My colleagues and I have learned an enormous amount from the various practical projects that have been inspired by MI theory—those that we designed ourselves (Gardner, 1993b) and equally, those generated by ingenious practitioners such as the writers of these essays (cf., Krechevsky, Hoerr, and Gardner, 1995). Readers of this theme section will profit as they ponder Sue Teele's documentation of shifting intellectual enthusiasms over time; Peter Smagorinsky's and Ellen Weber's efforts to engage the passions and imaginations of secondary school students; the pioneering steps taken by Tom Hoerr and his staff to place the personal intelligences at the center of curriculum and assessment; Shirley Jordan's exhortation to broaden our notion of what youngsters can achieve; Richard Colwell and Lyle Davidson's potent arguments for the cultivation of musical intelligence; and Patricia Bolaños' thoughtful reflections on the "mental models" of a staff that is attempting to break open a multiple intelligences pathway. Reminding us that new approaches to intelligence and education are not restricted to the present author, readers may also be instructed by the writings of Robert Sternberg and Joseph Gauld.

Developmental psychology and cognitive psychology confirm an important lesson: It is not possible to short-circuit the learning process. Even those with more than a nodding acquaintance with "MI theory" need to work out their understandings in their own way and at their own pace. And if my own understanding of the theory continues to change, I can hardly expect anyone else to accept any "reading" as conclu-sive—even that of the founding theorist. Still, I hope that these reflections may help to frame readers' encounters with MI theory and efforts to draw on these ideas in ways that are helpful to students.

REFERENCES

Gardner, H. *Frames of Mind: The Theory of Multiple Intelligences.* New York: Basic Books, 1983. (A tenth anniversary edition with a new introduction was published in 1993.)

———. *Multiple Intelligences. The Theory in Practice.* New York: Basic Books, 1993b.

———. "Reflections on Multiple Intelligences: Myths and Messages." *Phi Delta Kappan,* November 1995.

———. "Are There Additional Intelligences?" In *Education, Information, and Transformation: Essays on Learning and Thinking,* edited by J. Kane. Englewood Cliffs, NJ.: Prentice-Hall, 1999.

Krechevsky, M.; Hoerr, T.; and Gardner, H. "Complementary Energies: Implementing MI Theory from the Laboratory and the Field." In *Creating New Educational Communities,* 94th Yearbook of the National Society for the Study of Education (Part 1), edited by J. Oakes and K. H. Quartz. Chicago, Ill.: University of Chicago Press, 1995.

Howard Gardner is professor of education and codirector of Project Zero at the Harvard Graduate School of Education and an adjunct professor of neurology at the Boston University School of Medicine.

QUESTIONS FOR REFLECTION

1. Why does Gardner believe "we must be leery about claiming to enhance general abilities like thinking or problem solving or memory"? What are the implications of this statement for curriculum planners?

2. Why should educators be cautious about characterizing the intellectual profiles of students?

3. What does Gardner mean when he states that "The road between theory and practice runs in two directions"? What professional experiences have you had that confirm Gardner's view?

TEACHERS' VOICES
Putting Theory into Practice

Eric Learns to Read: Learning Styles at Work

JUNE HODGIN
CAAREN WOOLISCROFT

ABSTRACT:　The environment of a third-grade inclusion class was modified to meet the needs of a tactile/kinesthetic learner with an extreme sensitivity to light. As a result, the student's self-esteem, achievement, and participation in classroom activities increased. A learning styles environment can be created by adjusting classroom elements such as noise, light, temperature, design, perception, and intake. Guidelines for introducing students to the concept of learning styles are also presented.

Eric came to our 3rd grade inclusion class from a regular 2nd grade class where he had been referred for an attention deficit screening. His self-esteem was low, and he did not want to participate in classroom activities. We administered the Carbo/Reading Styles Inventory and discovered that Eric was a strong tactile/kinesthetic learner with an extreme sensitivity to light. We decided to allow him to move away from his desk to complete his independent practice.

Each time he went to the same place under a large table at the back of the room. Here he worked in dim lighting and usually swung or tapped his leg or arm. This constant motion had annoyed other students and teachers in the past.

As the year progressed and Eric continued to work in "his spot," we saw a dramatic improvement in his attitude and his academic work. Because he was not always in trouble, other students were more receptive to him. Eric matured academically, and the need for an ADHD evaluation was no longer an issue. In the spring Eric qualified for the gifted program. He had mastered all

objectives on the Texas Assessment of Academic Skills and had received academic recognition for his work.

Eric is not an isolated example. We have seen dramatic changes in many students in our inclusive classroom since we have employed learning styles strategies. In our class of 22 students (10 Hispanic, 12 Anglo), 4 students were identified as learning disabled and qualified for special education and another 3 had attention deficit disorders. The students' IQs ranged from 74 to 126.

From among the many theories about learning styles, we have chosen to base our classroom instruction on the 21 elements of the Dunn and Dunn Learning Styles Model. We believe this classroom design allows for both student preference and student independence. For example, we addressed the following elements in classroom design:

- *Noise*. We have created places where students can listen to classical music while working.

From *Educational Leadership* 54, no. 6 (March 1997): 43–45. © 1997, Association for Supervision and Curriculum Development. Used by permission of the author and publisher.

Other youngsters, who need a quiet area, wear old headphones with the cords cut off.

- *Light.* Because most of our students prefer low light, we asked the custodian to remove half the fluorescent lights in the classroom. Some students work under tables to have even lower lighting levels.
- *Temperature.* We encourage students who prefer a warmer climate to bring a sweater, and those who get hot easily to wear layered clothing that they can remove.
- *Design.* Our classroom has an informal area, as well as a number of learning centers.
- *Sociological stimuli.* We have created areas where students can work alone, in a team with a buddy, or in a group. We seat students who need adult presence close to the front of the room or near the teacher's desk.
- *Perception centers.* Learning centers and daily instruction include activities for the auditory, visual, and tactual/kinesthetic modes. In addition, students can use computers, a language master, and a listening center.
- *Mobility.* We allow our students to move around the room and to use special workplaces of their choice.
- *Intake.* We have built snack times into the classroom schedule. Students are encouraged to bring healthy snacks such as fruit, vegetables, crackers, or cereal.

Although we can measure our success by standardized test scores and other academic indicators, we feel especially successful when we see a frustrated child like Eric begin to relax and enjoy learning.

CREATING A LEARNING STYLES ENVIRONMENT

We teach our students that the freedom to work in their preferred space and style carries certain responsibilities. Our students know we expect them to attend to their lessons and work better than be-

fore, and not to disturb anyone else. They understand that if they abuse a privilege, they will lose it.

As we plan our lessons, we discuss how to group the children for perceptual, sociological, and mobility needs. We use many tactile/kinesthetic materials, a variety of instructional groupings, and other small-group activities. We design our instructional presentations to accommodate the psychological needs of our global students. (Global students must see the whole picture or hear the whole story before learning takes place and before they can see the little pieces that make up the whole.)

INTRODUCING LEARNING STYLES

We introduce learning styles to our students at the beginning of each school year. We expose them to a variety of learning styles elements (for example, working with the lights off, while listening to classical music, or with everyone sitting on the floor) and discuss how the different elements help or hinder learning ability. After reading stories about learning styles and explaining the Learning Styles Model, we hold class discussions.

Then we administer Marie Carbo's Reading Style Inventory (Carbo 1994). After we tabulate the results of the inventory, we give each child a sheet that highlights his or her personal learning styles. We again review the Dunn Learning Styles Model (Dunn 1996). During this discussion, we encourage students to draw pictures or write notes about themselves. We stress that there are no good or bad learning styles. We explain that when students use their preferred learning styles, they will do better work.

After introducing our students to learning styles, we hold a meeting to share each child's Reading Style Inventory with his or her parents. We explain the inventory, show a filmstrip about learning styles, and answer questions. Parents who are unable to attend receive a short letter of explanation with a copy of their child's Reading Style Inventory.

READING STRATEGIES

Although classroom design is important, the methods and the strategies used are the critical factors in teaching children to read. We have found that when we accommodate their reading styles, every child can learn to read. Children with special needs do not always read at grade level, but they can read and participate in classroom activities.

Our goal is to help each student stretch and become the best reader possible. Consider the case of Michael: When Michael came to us from out of state, he was reading on the 1st grade level. Although he qualified for special education services, testing revealed that he was a very capable learner with an above average IQ. He showed large gaps in his reading skills, however. After we introduced Michael to the Carbo Recorded Books system, his reading fluency and comprehension began to increase. Steady improvement continued throughout the year. At the end of the school year, Michael was reading at the 3rd grade level, and he passed the Texas Assessment of Academic Skills. The following year Michael was one of the few children in 4th grade to read all the books on the Texas Bluebonnet list.

We can attribute many successes to our use of the Carbo Recorded Books Method (Carbo 1989) and related strategies. One strategy we have found highly effective is to introduce new information globally. For example, we introduced the book *Shiloh* (Reynolds 1991) by bringing a beagle to school and talking about its characteristics. We also invited a representative from the local animal shelter to visit and talk about abused animals and how to take care of pets. This connected the story to real-life experiences and helped the children focus on the story.

After the global introduction, we initiate activities in which the students can hear, see, and become actively involved in the lesson. Before distributing worksheets, we have students work with tactile/kinesthetic manipulatives or games, or do other group activities. In this way we accommodate all the perceptual strengths so that each student can be successful once the independent practice begins. Our students especially enjoy using tactile/kinesthetic materials such as Electroboards, Flip Chutes, task cards, Pic-a-Holes, and special card and board games related to the learning objectives.

INDICATORS OF SUCCESS

Our students' scores on the Texas Assessment of Academic Skills (TAAS) during the three-year period from 1993 to 1996 demonstrate the effectiveness of reading styles and inclusion practices. During 1993–94, the year before we implemented reading styles and inclusion, only 50 percent of the regular student population passed the test, and none of the special education children passed. We saw dramatic improvements during the next two years as we implemented the reading styles strategies and inclusion practices. All the regular education students passed the test both years, with 25 percent of special education students passing in 1994–95, and 20 percent in 1995–96. In addition, student mastery of all test objectives increased from 11 percent in 1994, to 67 percent in 1995, to 80 percent in 1996.

We saw another indicator of success in the classroom climate. Our students worked together in heterogeneous small and large groups. Because we did not separate students by ability level, our students were not aware of any labels. The self-esteem, motivation, and attitude of all students improved because they did not feel stress, learning was fun and pleasurable, and it was easy to succeed. We had created a real community of learners.

Creating a new classroom environment does not happen quickly. Both Rita Dunn and Marie Carbo stress that it takes three to five years for a teacher to develop a learning styles classroom.

Then, you must update the plan annually to meet the unique needs of each new group of students. But the rewards are great, as each year you tap into your students' strengths and watch them blossom.

REFERENCES

Carbo, M. (1989). *How to Record Books for Maximum Reading Gains.* Syosset, N.Y.: National Reading Styles Institute.

Carbo, M. (1994). *Reading Style Inventory.* Syosset, N.Y.: National Reading Styles Institute.

Dunn, R. (1996). *How to Implement and Supervise a Learning Styles Program.* Alexandria, VA: ASCD.

Reynolds, P. (1991). *Shiloh.* New York: Dell Publishing.

June Hodgin is a consultant for the Special Education Department in Abilene, Texas; and *Caaren N. Wooliscroft* is a third-grade teacher at Alta Vista Elementary School in Abilene.

QUESTIONS FOR REFLECTION

1. How should teachers who wish to create a learning styles environment explain the concept to parents?
2. On what basis might some people criticize the concept of a learning styles environment? How should proponents of a learning styles environment respond?
3. In regard to the educational setting with which you are most familiar (K–12 through higher education), what changes in classroom design elements would accommodate students' diverse learning styles?

LEARNING ACTIVITIES

Critical Thinking

1. In light of constructivist views of learning, how can teachers increase their understanding of students' understanding? How should teachers take into account students' social, cultural, linguistic, and academic backgrounds?
2. What is your preferred learning style? Where, when, and how do you learn best?
3. In regard to multiple intelligences theory, in which intelligences are you most proficient? Least proficient? How do these areas of greatest (and least) proficiency affect your learning?
4. What are the risks of using learning styles and/or multiple intelligences theory to design learning activities for students?

5. Herbert A. Thelen has pointed out that "If we get too comfortable, we stop growing. Students can put pressure on us to work within their comfort zone. Let's be kind about that. Kind enough to help them learn to be uncomfortable" (quoted in *Models of Teaching*, 5th edition [Allyn and Bacon, 1996, p. 385]). What are the implications of Thelen's statement for curriculum planners who develop learning activities to "fit" students' learning styles?

Application Activities

1. Bruce Joyce and Marsha Weil, in their book *Models of Teaching*, 5th edition (Allyn and Bacon, 1996), have included a model for teaching called "Behavior Theory" (pp. 321–329). Read that section in *Models of Teaching* and relate it to Madsen and Madsen's "An Analysis of Behavior Modification" in this chapter. When is it most appropriate for curriculum planners to use behavioral approaches such as these?
2. Examine a recent curriculum guide of interest to you or in your field of study, to identify the learning theory (or theories) that is the basis for the suggested learning activities. What additional learning activities, based on other theories of learning, could be added?
3. In *Practical Intelligence for School* (HarperCollins, 1996), Howard Gardner and a team of researchers have proposed another form of intelligence—*practical intelligence*, "the ability to understand one's environment, and to use this knowledge in figuring out how best to achieve one's goals" (p. ix). They believe that practical intelligence consists of five themes that can be taught: *knowing why, knowing self, knowing differences, knowing process,* and *reworking*. In planning curricula at the level with which you are most interested, how useful is the concept of practical intelligence?
4. At the level and in the content area of greatest interest to you, identify several learning activities that address each of the seven multiple intelligences identified by Gardner.

Field Experiences

1. Interview a teacher at your level of greatest interest, K–12 through higher education, for the purpose of clarifying the learning theory (or theories) that guides the teacher. Formulate your interview questions in light of the material in this chapter.
2. At the level and in the subject area of greatest interest to you, observe a teacher to identify the learning theory (or theories) he or she uses. What differences do you note among the students' responses to their teacher? Is there evidence of different learning styles among the students?

Internet Activities

1. Conduct an Internet and WWW search on one or more of the topics listed below. Gather resources and information relevant to your current, or anticipated, curriculum planning activities.

multiple intelligences	learning styles
learning theories	behavior modification
cognitive science	brain research
constructivism	neuroscience

2. Go to the site for Harvard Project Zero (**http://pzweb.harvard.edu/**) codirected by Howard Gardner. For more than thirty-two years Project Zero has studied how children and adults learn. At this site, gather information relevant to your current, or anticipated, curriculum planning activities.

3. From The Educational Resources Information Center (**http://www.aspensys.com/eric/**), launch a search for resources and information on students' learning at the level and in the subject area of your greatest interest. From this site, you can go to sixteen clearinghouses for information on education from early childhood through higher education and adult education.

BOOKS AND ARTICLES TO REVIEW

On Learning Theories

Anderson, Terry. "What in the World Is Constructivism?" *Learning* 24, no. 5 (March–April 1996): 48–51.

Biggs, Morris L., and Shermis, S. Samuel. *Learning Theories for Teachers,* 5th Ed. New York: HarperCollins, 1992.

Bruner, Jerome. "What We Have Learned about Early Learning." *European Early Childhood Education Research Journal* 4, no 1 (1996): 5–16.

Bruer, John T. "Penicillin for Education: How Cognitive Science Can Contribute to Education." *NASSP Bulletin* 79, no. 571 (May 1995): 68–80.

Byrnes, James. *Cognitive Development and Learning in Instructional Contexts.* Boston: Allyn and Bacon, 1996.

Cameron, D. R. "Self-Directed Learning: Toward a Comprehensive Model." *Adult Education Quarterly* 48, no. 1 (Fall 1997): 18–33.

Carpenter, Thomas P., et al. "Cognitively Guide Instruction: A Knowledge Base for Reform in Primary Mathematics Instruction." *Elementary School Journal* 97, no. 1 (September 1996): 3–20.

Davis, Robert B. "Classrooms and Cognition." *Journal of Education* 178, no. 1 (1996): 3–12.

Dijkstra, Sanne. "The Integration of Instructional Systems Design Models and Constructivist Design Principles." *Instructional Science* 25, no. 1 (January 1997): 1–13.

Duis, Mac. "Using Schema Theory to Teach American History." *Social Education* 60, no. 3 (March 1996): 144–146.

Ebbeck, Marjory. "Children Constructing Their Own Knowledge." *International Journal of Early Years Education* 4, no. 2 (Summer 1996): 5–27.

English, Lyn D., and Sharry, Patrick V. "Analogical Reasoning and the Development of Algebraic Abstraction." *Educational Studies in Mathematics* 30, no. 2 (March 1996): 135–157.

Florence, Namulundah. *bell hooks' Engaged Pedagogy: A Transgressive Education for Critical Consciousness.* Westport, CT: Greenwood Publishing, 1998.

Geisler-Brenstein, E., et al. "An Individual Difference Perspective on Student Diversity." *Higher Education* 31, no. 1 (January 1996): 73–96.

Glatthorn, Allan A. "Constructivism: Implications for Curriculum." *International Journal of Educational Reform* 3, no. 4 (October 1994): 449–455.

Graves, Michael F., and Avery, Patricia G. "Scaffolding Students' Reading of History." *Social Studies* 88, no. 3 (May–June 1997): 134–138.

Grier, Leslie K., and Ratner, Hilary Horn. "Elaboration: The Role of Activity and Conceptual Processing in Children's Memory." *Child Study Journal* 26, no. 3 (1996): 229–252.

Gruender, C. David. "Constructivism and Learning: A Philosophical Appraisal." *Educational Technology* 36, no. 3 (May–June 1996): 21–29.

Guild, Pat Burke. "Where Do the Learning Theories Overlap?" *Educational Leadership* 55, no. 1 (September 1997): 30–31.

Hacker, Douglas J., Dunlosky, John, and Graesser, Arthur C. *Metacognition in Educational Theory and Practice.* Mahwah, NJ: Lawrence Erlbaum, 1998.

Halpern, Diane F. *Critical Thinking Across the Curriculum: A Brief Edition of Thought and Knowledge.* Mahwah, NJ: Lawrence Erlbaum, 1997.

Hargreaves, D. J. "How Undergraduate Students Learn." *European Journal of Engineering Education* 21, no. 4 (December 1996): 425–434.

Hergenhahn, B. R., and Olson, Matthew H. *An Introduction to Theories of Learning,* 5th ed. Upper Saddle River, NJ: Prentice Hall, 1997.

Heuwinkel, Mary K. "New Ways of Learning = New Ways of Teaching." *Childhood Education* 73, no. 1 (Fall 1996): 27–31.

Janssen, P. J. "Studaxology: The Expertise Students Need to Be Effective in Higher Education." *Higher Education* 31, no. 1 (January 1996): 117–141.

Kember, David. "The Intention to Both Memorize and Understand: Another Approach to Learning?" *Higher Education* 31, no. 3 (April 1996): 341–354.

Kruse, Gary. "Thinking, Learning, and Public Schools: Preparing for Life." *NASSP Bulletin* 78, no. 563 (September 1994): 91–96.

Leung, Martin, et al. "Learning from Equations or Words." *Instructional Science* 25, no. 1 (January 1997): 37–70.

Lucking, Robert, and Manning, M. Lee. "Instruction for Low-Achieving Young Adolescents: Addressing the Challenge of a Generation Imperiled." *Preventing School Failure* 40, no. 2 (Winter 1996): 82–87.

Marton, Ference, and Booth, Shirley. *Learning and Awareness.* Mahwah, NJ: Lawrence Erlbaum, 1997.

Matthews, P. S. C. "Problems with Piagetian Constructivism." *Science and Education* 6, no. 1–2 (January 1997): 105–119.

McKinney, C. Warren, and Edginton, William D. "Issues Related to Teaching Generalizations in Elementary Social Studies." *Social Studies* 88, no. 2 (March–April 1997): 78–81.

Mezirow, Jack. "Contemporary Paradigms of Learning." *Adult Education Quarterly* 46, no. 3 (Spring 1996): 158–172.

Murphy, Patricia. "Constructivism and Primary Science." *Primary Science Review* 49 (September–October 1997): 27–29.

Ogborn, Jon. "Constructivist Metaphors of Learning Science." *Science and Education* 6, no. 1–2 (January 1997): 121–133.

Puk, Tom. "The Integration of Extrarational and Rational Learning Processes: Moving Towards the Whole Learner." *Journal of Educational Thought* 30, no. 2 (August 1996): 119–137.

Renzulli, Joseph S. "The Multiple Menu Model: A Successful Marriage for Integrating Content and Process." *NASSP Bulletin* 81, no. 587 (March 1997): 51–58.

Ritchie, Donn, and Karge, Belinda Dunnick. "Making Information Memorable: Enhanced Knowledge Retention and Recall through the Elaboration Process." *Preventing School Failure* 41, no. 28 (Fall 1996): 28–33.

Schunk, Dale H. *Learning Theories: An Educational Perspective,* 2nd ed. Englewood Cliffs, NJ: Merrill, 1996.

Smith, M. Cecil, and Pourchot, Thomas. *Adult Learning and Development: Perspectives from Educational Psychology.* Mahwah, NJ: Lawrence Erlbaum, 1998.

Warrington, Mary Ann. "How Children Think about Division with Fractions." *Mathematics Teaching in the Middle School* 2, no. 6 (May 1997): 390–394.

On the Human Brain and Learning

Anderson, O. Roger. "A Neurocognitive Perspective on Current Learning Theory and Science Instructional Strategies." *Science Education* 81, no. 1 (January 1997): 67–89.

Berger, Eugenia Hepworth, and Pollman, Mary Jo. "Multiple Intelligences: Enabling Diverse Learning." *Early Childhood Education Journal* 23, no. 4 (Summer 1996): 249–253.

Bounds, Christopher, and Harrison, Lyn. "In New South Wales: The Brain-Flex Project." *Educational Leadership* 55, no. 1 (September 1997): 69–70.

Brandt, Ron. "On Using Knowledge about Our Brain: A Conversation with Bob Sylwester." *Educational Leadership* 54, no. 6 (March 1997): 16–19.

Bucko, Richard L. "Brain Basics: Cognitive Psychology and Its Implications for Education." *ERS Spectrum* 15, no. 3 (Summer 1997): 20–25.

Dunn, Rita, et al. "A Meta-analytic Validation of the Dunn and Dunn Model of Learning Style Preferences." *Journal of Educational Research* 88, no. 6 (July–August 1995): 353–362.

Fitzgerald, Ron. "Brain-Compatible Teaching in a Block Schedule." *School Administrator* 53, no. 8 (September 1996): 20–21.

Jones, Rebecca. "Smart Brains." *American School Board Journal* 182, no. 11 (November 1995): 22–26.

King, Jeffrey M. "Brain Function Research: Guideposts for Brain-Compatible Teaching and Learning." *Journal of General Education* 46, no. 4 (1997): 276–288.

Kovalik, Susan, and Olsen, Karen D. "How Emotions Run Us, Our Students, and Our Classrooms." *NASSP Bulletin* 82, no. 598 (May 1998): 29–37.

Languis, Marlin. "Using Knowledge of the Brain in Educational Practice." *NASSP Bulletin* 82, no. 598 (May 1998): 38–47.

Lewis, Ann C. "Learning Our Lessons about Early Learning." *Phi Delta Kappan* 78, no. 8 (April 1997): 591–592.

Nuzzi, Ronald. "A Multiple Intelligence Approach." *Momentum* 28, no. 2 (April–May 1997): 16–19.

Peterson, Rita W. "School Readiness Considered from a Neuro-Cognitive Perspective." *Early Education and Development* 5, no. 2 (April 1994): 120–140.

Poole, Carolyn R. "Maximizing Learning: A Conversation with Renate Nummela Caine." *Educational Leadership* 54, no. 6 (March 1997): 11–15.

Schiller, Pam. "Brain Development Research: Support and Challenges." *Child Care Information Exchange* no. 117 (September–October 1997): 6–10.

Sylwester, Robert. "What the Biology of the Brain Tells Us about Learning." *Educational Leadership* 51, no. 4 (December–January 1993–94): 46–51.

Van Tassell, Gene. "Applied Brain Research." *The Science Teacher* 65, no. 3 (March 1998): 56–59.

On Learning Styles and Forms of Intelligence

Abbott, John. "To Be Intelligent." *Educational Leadership* 54, no. 6 (March 1997): 6–10.

Boulmetis, John, and Sabula, Ann Marie. "Achievement Gains via Instruction That Matches Learning Style Perceptual Preferences." *Journal of Continuing Higher Education* 44, no. 3 (Fall 1996): 15–24.

Burke, Karen G. S. J. "Responding to Participants' Learning Styles During Staff Development." *Clearing House* 70, no. 6 (July–August 1997): 299–301.

Campbell, Linda. "How Teachers Interpret MI Theory." *Educational Leadership* 55, no. 1 (September 1997): 14–19.

Carbo, Marie. "Learning Styles Strategies That Help At-Risk Students Read and Succeed." *Reaching Today's Youth: The Community Circle of Caring Journal* 21, no. 2 (Winter 1997): 37–42.

Checkley, Kathy. "The First Seven . . . and the Eighth: A Conversation with Howard Gardner." *Educational Leadership* 55, no. 1 (September 1997): 8–13.

Clariana, Roy B. "Considering Learning Style in Computer-Assisted Learning." *British Journal of Educational Technology* 28, no. 1 (January 1997): 66–68.

Cohen, Vicki L. "Learning Styles in a Technology-Rich Environment." *Journal of Research on Computing in Education* 29, no. 4 (Summer 1997): 338–50.

Dreher, Sonja. "Learning Styles: Implications for Learning & Teaching." *Rural Educator* 19, no. 2 (Winter 1997): 26–29.

Dunn, Rita, and Griggs, Shirley A. *Multiculturalism and Learning Style: Teaching and Counseling Adolescents.* Westport, CT: Greenwood Publishing, 1998.

Emig, Veronica Borruso. "A Multiple Intelligences Inventory." *Educational Leadership* 55, no. 1 (September 1997): 47–50.

Gardner, Howard. "Multiple Intelligences as a Partner in School Improvement." *Educational Leadership* 55, no. 1 (September 1997): 20–21.

———. "Multiple Intelligences: Myths and Messages." *International Schools Journal* 15, 2 (April 1996): 8–22.

———." 'Multiple Intelligences' as a Catalyst." *English Journal* 84, no. 8 (December 1995): 16–18.

———. "Reflections on Multiple Intelligences: Myths and Messages." *Phi Delta Kappan* 77, no. 3 (November 1995): 200–203, 206–209.

Gregg, Madeleine. "Seven Journeys to Map Symbols: Multiple Intelligences Applied to Map Learning." *Journal of Geography* 96, no. 3 (May–June 1997): 146–152.

Greenhawk, Jan. "Multiple Intelligences Meet Standards." *Educational Leadership* 55, no. 1 (September 1997): 62–64.

Hall, Linda A., and Hyle, Adrienne E. "Learning Styles, Achievement and the Middle Level Student: Useful Facts or Useless Fiction?" *Research in Middle Level Education Quarterly* 19, no. 2 (Winter 1996): 67–88.

Hatch, Thomas. "Getting Specific about Multiple Intelligences." *Educational Leadership* 54, no. 6 (March 1997): 26–29.

———, and Gardner, Howard. "If Binet Had Looked Beyond the Classroom: The Assessment of Multiple Intelligences." *NAMTA Journal* 21, no. 2 (Spring 1996): 5–28.

Hine, Connie. "Developing Multiple Intelligences in Young Learners." *Early Childhood News* 8, no. 6 (November–December 1996): 23–29.

Horton, Connie Burrow, and Oakland, Thomas. "Temperament-Based Learning Styles as Moderators of Academic Achievement." *Adolescence* 32, no. 125 (Spring 1997): 131–141.

Houston, Linda. "Knowing Learning Styles Can Improve Self-Confidence of Developmental Writers." *Teaching English in the Two-Year College* 24, no. 3 (October 1997): 212–215.

Latham, Andrew S. "Responding to Cultural Learning Styles." *Educational Leadership* 54, no. 7 (April 1997): 88–89.

Lazear, David. *Seven Ways of Knowing: Teaching for Multiple Intelligences.* Arlington Heights, IL: IRI/Skylight Training & Publishing, 1991.

Lowenthal, Barbara. "Useful Early Childhood Assessment: Play-Based, Interviews and Multiple Intelligences." *Early Child Development and Care* 129 (February 1997): 43–49.

Matthews, Doris B. "An Investigation of Learning Styles and Perceived Academic Achievement for High School Students." *Clearing House* 69, no. 4 (March–April 1996): 249–254.

McCarthy, Bernice. "A Tale of Four Learners: 4MAT's Learning Styles." *Educational Leadership* 54, no. 6 (March 1997): 46–51.

Merrefield, Gayle Emery. "Three Billy Goats and Gardner." *Educational Leadership* 55, no. 1 (September 1997): 58–61.

Meyer, Maggie. "The GREENing of Learning: Using the Eighth Intelligence." *Educational Leadership* 55, no. 1 (September 1997): 32–34.

Park, Clara C. "Learning Style Preferences of Asian American (Chinese, Filipino, Korean, and Vietnamese) Students in Secondary Schools." *Equity & Excellence in Education* 30, no. 2 (September 1997): 68–77.

———. "Learning Style Preferences of Korean-, Mexican-, Armenian-American, and Anglo Students in Secondary Schools, Research Brief." *NASSP Bulletin* 81, no. 585 (January 1997): 103–111.

Peacock, Thomas D., and Cleary, Linda Miller. "Ways of Learning: Teachers' Perspectives on American Indian Learning Styles." *Tribal College* 8, no. 3 (Winter 1996–97): 36–39.

Reid, Carol, and Romanoff, Brenda. "Using Multiple Intelligences Theory to Identify Gifted Children." *Educational Leadership* 55, no. 1 (September 1997): 71–74.

Reiff, Judith C. "Multiple Intelligences, Culture and Equitable Learning." *Childhood Education* 73, no. 5 (1997): 301–304.

Riding, Richard J., and Read, Geoffrey. "Cognitive Style and Pupil Learning Preferences." *Educational Psychology* 16, no. 1 (March 1996): 81–106.

Silver, Harvey, Strong, Richard, and Perini, Matthew. "Integrating Learning Styles and Multiple Intelligences." *Educational Leadership* 55, no. 1 (September 1997): 22–27.

Sternberg, Robert J. "Myths, Countermyths, and Truths about Intelligence." *Educational Researcher* 25, no. 2 (March 1996): 11–16.

Vialle, Wilma. "In Australia: Multiple Intelligences in Multiple Settings." *Educational Leadership* 55, no. 1 (September 1997): 65–69.

Williams, Wendy, Blythe, Tina, White, Noel, Li, Jin, Sternberg, Robert, and Gardner, Howard. *Practical Intelligence for School.* New York: HarperCollins, 1996.

Videotapes

Learning, a 30-minute video that shows how operant conditioning is used to help children with severe behavioral and learning problems, features an interview with B. F. Skinner. (Available from Insight Media, 121 West 85th Street, New York, NY 10024 (212) 721-6316).

Vygotsky's Developmental Theory: An Introduction is a 28-minute video that illustrates constructivist concepts based on Vygotsky's work. (Available from Davidson Films, Inc. (916) 753-9604).

Memory: Fabric of the Mind is a 28-minute video that visits memory research labs to answer the following: Are different types of memory located in different areas of the brain? Are specific memories stored in separate areas of the brain? Why do we forget? Can memory be improved? (Available from Films for the Humanities and Sciences, P.O. Box 2055, Princeton, NJ 08543-2053, (800) 257-5126, fax (609) 275-3767).

A Conversation with Howard Gardner (30 minutes) and *Multiple Intelligences* (30 minutes) examine the theory of multiple intelligences. (Both available from Agency for Instructional Technology, Box A, Bloomington, IN 47402-0120, (800) 457-4509).

Multiple Intelligences (two videos, 31 minutes and 38 minutes) presents a four-stage model for teaching to multiple intelligences. (Available from Video Journal of Education, 8684 South 1300 East, Salt Lake City, UT 84094 (801) 566-6885).

Learning—A Matter of Style features Rita Dunn, a leader in research on learning styles. (Available from the Association for Supervision and Curriculum Development, 1250 N. Pitt St., Alexandria, VA 22314 (703) 549-9110).

CHAPTER 5

The Nature of Knowledge

FOCUS QUESTIONS

1.   Why is knowledge an important basis for curriculum planning?
2.   What are five ways through which people acquire knowledge?
3.   What is the nature of knowledge according to the *structured disciplines* perspective?
4.   What is the nature of knowledge according to the *personal experience* perspective?
5.   What is the rationale for viewing knowledge as a fusion of the disciplines and personal experience?

Since the 1960s, increasing emphasis has been placed on knowledge as a basis for making curriculum decisions. Prior to that time, human development, learning, and society were seen as the primary bases of curriculum planning. However, in *Experience and Education* (1938, p. 86), John Dewey made the following important distinction regarding knowledge as one of the bases of curriculum planning. He stated that

> finding the material for learning within experience is only the first step. The next step is the progressive development of what is already experienced into a fuller and richer and also more organized form, a form that gradually approximates that in which subject matter is presented to the skilled, mature person.

Curriculum theorists and practitioners of that time were so intent on using human development, learning, or society as the basis for planning that they gave little attention to formal knowledge as a basis for the curriculum. In "Progressive Organization of Subject Matter" in this chapter, Dewey explains how knowledge should be viewed as progressing out of the learner's experiences rather than as something outside of those experiences. Thus, curriculum planning requires consideration of organized bodies of knowledge as well as the nature of the growing child and the nature of our society.

Curriculum planners, of course, have always been concerned with knowledge. Among the questions they must address are the following: What knowledge is true? How does knowing take place? How do we know that we know? How do we decide between opposing views of knowledge (for example, creationist versus evolutionary explanations for life on this planet)? Can knowledge be true at one point in time and then not true at another point? And finally, the perennial curriculum question: What knowledge is of greatest worth?

How curriculum planners answer these questions has extensive implications for their work. They must have an extensive understanding of the nature of knowledge and the processes through which students can most effectively acquire that knowledge. There are five primary ways through which people acquire knowledge.

1. *Knowledge based on authority.* Among the sources of authoritative knowledge in educational settings, K–12 through higher education, are the teacher, the textbook, and experts in the disciplines.
2. *Knowledge based on empiricism (experience).* Much of the knowledge that people hold is based on empirical data—that is, knowledge acquired through the senses. This mode of knowing is exemplified in the experientialist orientation to curriculum that William H. Schubert describes in "Perspectives on Four Curriculum Traditions" (see Chapter 1).
3. *Knowledge based on reason.* People also acquire knowledge as a result of their ability to reason and to use processes of logical analysis. Through curricular experiences that emphasize this mode of knowing, learners solve problems, analyze situations, and prepare arguments. Several articles in the previous chapter on learning and learning styles emphasize this way of knowing.
4. *Knowledge based on divine revelation.* Human history reveals numerous instances where supernatural revelations are reported to be a source of knowledge about the world. Whether it be the many gods of ancient people, the Judeo-Christian god, or the Muslim god, divine revelations have often been a source of knowledge about life.
5. *Knowledge based on intuition.* People can acquire knowledge through intuition—a nondiscursive (beyond reason), instantaneous form of knowing that draws from the imagination. Intuition enables learners to draw from their prior knowledge and experiences and gives them insight into the problem at hand. In this chapter, Maxine Greene's "Art and Imagination: Reclaiming the Sense of Possibility," and Elliot W. Eisner's "Cognition and Representation: A Way to Pursue the American Dream?" explore this mode of knowing.

PERSPECTIVES ON KNOWLEDGE

Scholars have organized portions of knowledge into disciplines. A *discipline* consists of a set of generalizations that explain the relationships among a body of facts and concepts. Also, scholars in each discipline have developed methods of inquiry useful in discovering new knowledge. Each discipline is therefore a human product and is subject to revision if a different organization proves more functional.

Knowledge as Structured Disciplines

Some people think of knowledge as consisting almost exclusively of organized bodies of facts and concepts. They believe that all of the knowledge that has been discovered, learned, or invented has been organized into the most useful structures or disciplines. Further, they often believe that the sole purpose of education is to accept the disciplines of knowledge that have been created in the past and devise ways of helping learners acquire as much of these disciplines of knowledge as they can. William H. Schubert (1986, p. 218) describes this approach in the following:

> . . . each discipline has a deep, inherent structure and that curricular content should be presented in a form that enables students to comprehend this structure. . . .To comprehend the structural framework on which a discipline is built provides efficient access to the wide range of knowledge within that discipline. Bits and pieces of information fit together and make sense when they are viewed through the lenses of, and in relation to, the structure of the discipline. Thus, the intent is to select content that brings the structure into full view and reinforces it.

To follow this approach, curriculum planners and teachers must examine each subject or discipline and determine the sequence, pace, and activities through which the facts, concepts, and generalizations should be presented to learners.

Certain problems have arisen for those who follow this logic exclusively, however. The amount of knowledge available to people grew exponentially during the 1990s, and it will increase even more rapidly during the twenty-first century. It is impossible, and will become even more so, for any one learner to learn all the facts, concepts, generalizations, and methods of inquiry—even in one discipline. Moreover, new knowledge continually makes some previous knowledge in each discipline obsolete. A central question for curriculum planners and teachers, therefore, is what shall be taught from this vast store of available knowledge? And, how shall it be taught to enable learners to use that knowledge to greatest advantage and to be able to accommodate additional, yet-to-be-developed knowledge?

An additional problem with viewing knowledge solely as a set of structured disciplines is the unacknowledged biases and assumptions of those who create "mainstream" academic knowledge. According to the critical reconstructionist perspective on the curriculum (see William H. Schubert's "Perspectives on Four Curriculum Traditions" in Chapter 1), the traditional disciplines can function to maintain the status quo and even reproduce patterns of inequality in society. Similarly, in "Multicultural Education and Curriculum Transformation" in this chapter, James A. Banks explains how the cultural assumptions, frames of reference, and perspectives of mainstream scholars have resulted in the construction of academic knowledge that legitimizes institutional inequality.

Knowledge as Personal Experience

Others view knowledge as a flexible, fluid product of people's experience. People are not merely passive recipients of knowledge; they derive knowledge from their experiences and use that knowledge to pursue their own ends. According to this view, the organization of knowledge by experts in the disciplines is often not useful in life experiences and in new situations or problems. In addition, the definition and structure of a discipline are seen as human inventions which can be revised in light of new knowledge or supplanted by the creation of altogether new disciplines.

Those who believe that knowledge should be more useful point out that the central challenge confronting human beings is to understand themselves and the world around them. As they attempt to do this, people create interpretations of their actions and the environment. These interpretations are unique to each person, and they constitute the knowledge that is "real" and personally meaningful to the individual. Through attempts to understand oneself and the environment, the individual encounters facts and concepts that others have discovered and organized. This knowledge and how it is organized may or may not have meaning for the individual—he or she alone decides. The individual also determines how the newly acquired knowledge will be incorporated into his or her existing framework of knowledge. Thus, the structure of knowledge is personally constructed rather than adopted in toto from the external world. This view of knowledge places a primacy on *personal meaning,* since learners determine what acquired knowledge *means* to them.

Curriculum planners and teachers who hold this second conception of the nature of knowledge approach curriculum development and teaching differently from those who view knowledge as organized bodies of information. The former do not believe that the traditional disciplines should be the primary guide for curriculum planning. Instead, they agree with Dewey that "the starting point for all further learning" must be the learners' experiences, concerns, and needs; and that the teacher's role is to help learners see how they can use knowledge from the disciplines to help them attain their purposes. Similarly, this approach is at the heart of Schubert's experientialist curriculum orientation: "Students must be given opportunity to reconstruct their experience, study its possible meanings, and interpret its significance for their own sense of meaning and direction" (Schubert, 1986, p. 17).

In addition, they believe that if the curriculum is to be related to present social forces, a focus on the separate disciplines will not suffice. Issues and problems related to race relations, the environment, crime and violence, and the impact of technology on our lives can be understood only through interdisciplinary study. Similarly, if the curriculum is to be related to human development theories and research—to the developmental tasks learners face throughout their life spans—an interdisciplinary approach is required. In this chapter, James A. Beane ("Curriculum Integration and the Disciplines of Knowledge") explains how this approach "centers the curriculum on life itself rather than on the mastery of fragmented information within the boundaries of subject areas. It is rooted in a view of learning as the continuous integration of new knowledge and experience so as to deepen and broaden our understanding of ourselves and our world."

Knowledge as a Fusion of the Disciplines *and* Personal Experience

A third position regarding knowledge and how it should be viewed for curriculum planning and teaching emerges if we consider two questions Dewey poses in "Traditional vs. Progressive Education" in Chapter 1: "What is the place and meaning of subject-matter and of organization *within* experience? How does subject-matter function?" Efforts to answer these questions, then, lead us to our third position: structured approaches to the separate disciplines *and* interdisciplinary, problem-based approaches derived from the learner's personal experience provide a balanced view of knowledge and its relationship to the curriculum. Such a position meets Dewey's criteria for "a theory and practice of education which proceeds . . . by a positive and constructive development of purposes, methods, and subject-matter on the foundation of a theory of experience and its educational potentialities."

This position also reminds us that there are different kinds of knowledge and different human purposes for acquiring knowledge. In applying knowledge to his or her purposes—that is, transferring what has been learned—the learner is aided when that knowledge has an orderly structure. If the structure of the disciplines provides insufficient order for this transfer of learning to occur, the learner may need assistance in providing structure to what is to be learned. In this regard, Nita H. Barbour's "Can We Prepackage Thinking?" in this chapter asserts that teachers should model the thinking skills they wish students to acquire rather than "mindlessly following a given set of strategies." Similarly, in "Structures in Learning" in this chapter, Jerome Bruner tells us that knowledge has a structure, an internal connectedness and meaningfulness; and, through "discovery learning," teachers should help learners fit knowledge into that structure. Lastly, in this chapter's Teachers' Voices section ("Redesigning the Model: A Successfully Integrated Approach to Teaching and Learning"), Dennis McFaden, Barbara A. Nelson, and Chip M. Randall describe how they created an interdisciplinary, student-owned curriculum that "blends science and technology with the human experience and need for knowledge, tool use, and skills."

CRITERION QUESTIONS—THE NATURE OF KNOWLEDGE

Curriculum planners and teachers should understand the importance of guiding learners to see how the subject-matter disciplines can be useful in solving personally meaningful problems. They should also understand that, as learners acquire knowledge that is useful, they create a personal structure for that knowledge. To ensure this understanding, the following are among the criterion questions that can be derived from the views of knowledge discussed in this chapter.

1. Does the curriculum assist learners in identifying the key concepts, principles, and structure inherent in the knowledge to be learned?
2. Does the curriculum provide learning opportunities that enable students to acquire knowledge for diverse personally meaningful purposes?

3. Does the curriculum allow students to acquire different types of knowledge in different ways?
4. Does the curriculum allow for a "fusion" of traditional subject-matter disciplines and personal experience?

REFERENCES

Dewey, John. *Experience and Education*. New York: Macmillan, 1938.
Schubert, William H. *Curriculum: Perspective, Paradigm, and Possibility*. New York: Macmillan Publishing Company, 1986.

Structures in Learning

JEROME S. BRUNER

ABSTRACT: *Each discipline of knowledge has a structure, and students should be provided with learning experiences that enable them to "discover" that structure. The aim of learning, therefore, is to acquire the processes of inquiry that characterize the discipline, rather than to merely learn "about" the discipline.*

Every subject has a structure, a rightness, a beauty. It is this structure that provides the underlying simplicity of things, and it is by learning its nature that we come to appreciate the intrinsic meaning of a subject.

Let me illustrate by reference to geography. Children in the fifth grade of a suburban school were about to study the geography of the Central states as part of a social studies unit. Previous units on the Southeastern states, taught by rote, had proved a bore. Could geography be taught as a rational discipline? Determined to find out, the teachers devised a unit in which students would have to figure out not only where things are located, but why they are there. This involves a sense of the structure of geography.

The children were given a map of the Central states in which only rivers, large bodies of water, agricultural products, and natural resources were shown. They were not allowed to consult their books. Their task was to find Chicago, "the largest city in the North Central states."

The argument got under way immediately. One child came up with the idea that Chicago must be on the junction of the three large lakes. No matter that at this point he did not know the names of the lakes—Huron, Superior, and Michigan—his theory was well reasoned. A big city produced a lot of products, and the easiest and most logical way to ship these products is by water.

But a second child rose immediately to the opposition. A big city needed lots of food, and he placed Chicago where there are corn and hogs—right in the middle of Iowa.

A third child saw the issue more broadly—recognizing virtues in both previous arguments. He pointed out that large quantities of food can be grown in river valleys. Whether he had learned this from a previous social studies unit or from

From *Today's Education* 52, no. 3 (March 1963): 26–27. Used by permission of the author and the publisher, the National Education Association.

raising carrot seeds, we shall never know. If you had a river, he reasoned, you had not only food but transportation. He pointed to a spot on the map not far from St. Louis. "There is where Chicago *ought* to be." Would that graduate students would always do so well!

Not all the answers were so closely reasoned, though even the wild ones had about them a sense of the necessity involved in a city's location.

One argued, for example, that all American cities have skyscrapers, which require steel, so he placed Chicago in the middle of the Mesabi Range. At least he was thinking on his own, with a sense of the constraints imposed on the location of cities.

After forty-five minutes, the children were told they could pull down the "real" wall map (the one with names) and see where Chicago really is. After the map was down, each of the contending parties pointed out how close they had come to being right. Chicago had not been located. But the location of cities was no longer a matter of unthinking chance for this group of children.

What had the children learned? A way of thinking about geography, a way of dealing with its raw data. They had learned that there is some relationship between the requirements of living and man's habitat. If that is all they got out of their geography lesson, that is plenty. Did they remember which is Lake Huron? Lake Superior? Lake Michigan? Do you?

Teachers have asked me about "the new curricula" as though they were some special magic potion. They are nothing of the sort. The new curricula, like our little exercise in geography, are based on the fact that knowledge has an internal connectedness, a meaningfulness, and that for facts to be appreciated and understood and remembered, they must be fitted into that internal meaningful context.

The set of prime numbers is not some arbitrary nonsense. What can be said about quantities that cannot be arranged into multiple columns and rows? Discussing that will get you on to the structure of primes and factorability.

It often takes the deepest minds to discern the simplest structure in knowledge. For this reason if for no other, the great scholar and the great scientist and the greatly compassionate person are needed in the building of new curricula.

There is one other point. Our geographical example made much of discovery. What difference does discovery make in the learning of the young? First, let it be clear what the act of discovery entails. It is only rarely on the frontier of knowledge that new facts are "discovered" in the sense of being encountered, as Newton suggested, as "islands of truth in an uncharted sea of ignorance." Discovery, whether by a schoolboy going it on his own or by a scientist, is most often a matter of rearranging or transforming evidence in such a way that one is not enabled to go beyond the evidence to new insights. Discovery involves the finding of the right structure, the meaningfulness.

Consider now what benefits the child might derive from the experience of learning through his own discoveries. These benefits can be discussed in terms of increased intellectual potency, intrinsic rewards, useful learning techniques, and better memory processes.

For the child to develop *intellectual potency*, he must be encouraged to search out and find regularities and relationships in his environment. To do this, he needs to be armed with the expectancy that there is something for him to find and, once aroused by this expectancy, he must devise his own ways of searching and finding.

Emphasis on discovery in learning has the effect upon the learner of leading him to be a constructionist—to organize what he encounters in such a manner that he not only discovers regularity and relatedness, but also avoids the kind of information drift that fails to keep account of how the information will be used.

In speaking of *intrinsic motives* for learning (as opposed to extrinsic motives), it must be recognized that much of the problem in leading a child to effective cognitive activity is to free him from the immediate control of environmental punishments and rewards.

For example, studies show that children who seem to be early over-achievers in school are likely to be seekers after the "right way to do it" and that their capacity for transforming their learning into useful thought structures tends to be less than that of children merely achieving at levels predicted by intelligence tests.

The hypothesis drawn from these studies is that if a child is able to approach learning as a task of discovering something rather than "learning about it" he will tend to find a more personally meaningful reward in his own competency and self-achievement in the subject than he will find in the approval of others.

There are many ways of coming to the *techniques of inquiry,* or the heuristics of discovery. One of them is by careful study of the formalization of these techniques in logic, statistics, mathematics, and the like. If a child is going to pursue inquiry as an eventual way of life, particularly in the sciences, formal study is essential. Yet, whoever has taught kindergarten and the early primary grades (periods of intense inquiry) knows that an understanding of the formal aspect of inquiry is not sufficient or always possible.

Children appear to have a series of attitudes and activities they associate with inquiry. Rather than a formal approach to the relevance of variables in their search, they depend on their sense of what things among an ensemble of things "smell right" as being of the proper order of magnitude or scope of severity.

It is evident then that if children are to learn the working techniques of discovery, they must be afforded the opportunities of problem solving. The more they practice problem solving, the more likely they are to generalize what they learn into a style of inquiry that serves for any kind of task they may encounter. It is doubtful that anyone ever improves in the art and technique of inquiry by any other means than engaging in inquiry, or problem solving.

The first premise in a theory concerning the *improvement of memory processes* is that the principal problem of human memory is not storage, but retrieval. The premise may be inferred from the fact that recognition (i.e., recall with the aid of maximum prompts) is extraordinarily good in human beings—particularly in comparison to spontaneous recall when information must be recalled without external aids or prompts. The key to retrieval is organization.

There are myriad findings to indicate that any organization of information that reduces the collective complexity of material by embedding it into a mental structure the child has constructed will make that material more accessible for retrieval. In sum, the child's very attitudes and activities that characterize "figuring out" or "discovering" things for himself also seem to have the effect of making material easier to remember.

If man's intellectual excellence is the most important among his perfections (as Maimonides, the great Hispanic-Judaic philosopher once said), then it is also the case that the most uniquely personal of all that man knows is that which he discovers for himself. What difference does it make when we encourage discovery in the young? It creates, as Maimonides would put it, a special and unique relation between knowledge possessed and the possessor.

After a career as Professor of Psychology and Director, Center for Cognitive Studies, Harvard University, *Jerome Bruner* was Watts Chair of Experimental Psychology, Oxford University, England, 1972–1979.

QUESTIONS FOR REFLECTION

1. What does Bruner mean when he states that "It often takes the deepest minds to discern the simplest structure in knowledge"? Can you give an example?

2. What is "intellectual potency," and how can it be developed within students?
3. What is "information drift," and what curricular experiences help students avoid it?
4. In recommending the development of "new" curricula, why does Bruner call for the involvement of the "greatly compassionate person" as well as "the great scholar and the great scientist"?

Progressive Organization of Subject Matter

JOHN DEWEY

ABSTRACT: In the following, Dewey explains a key principle of progressive education—the continuity of educative experience. Instead of presenting subject matter that is beyond *the life experiences of learners, the curriculum should begin with material that falls* within *those experiences. Once this connection has been established, the subject can be developed progressively into a fuller, richer, and more organized form; and this new knowledge becomes an "instrumentality" for further learning.*

One consideration stands out clearly when education is conceived in terms of experience. Anything which can be called a study, whether arithmetic, history, geography, or one of the natural sciences, must be derived from materials which at the outset fall within the scope of ordinary life-experience. In this respect the newer education contrasts sharply with procedures which start with facts and truths that are outside the range of the experience of those taught, and which, therefore, have the problem of discovering ways and means of bringing them within experience. Undoubtedly one chief cause for the great success of newer methods in early elementary education has been its observance of the contrary principle.

But finding the material for learning within experience is only the first step. The next step is the progressive development of what is already experienced into a fuller and richer and also more organized form, a form that gradually approximates that in which subject-matter is presented to the skilled, mature person. That this change is possible without departing from the organic connection of education with experience is shown by the fact that this change takes place outside of the school and apart from formal education. The infant, for example, begins with an environment of objects that is very restricted in space and time. That environment steadily expands by the momentum inherent in experience itself without aid from scholastic instruction. As the infant learns to reach, creep, walk, and talk, the intrinsic subject-matter of its experience widens and deepens. It comes into connection with new objects and events which call out new powers, while the exercise of these powers refines and enlarges the content of its experience. Life-space and life-durations are expanded. The environment, the world of experience, constantly grows larger and, so to speak, thicker. The educator who receives the child at the end of this period has to find ways

From John Dewey, *Experience and Education*, pp. 86–93 (New York: The Macmillan Co., 1938), a Kappa Delta Pi Lecture. Kappa Delta Pi. Used by permission.

for doing consciously and deliberately what "nature" accomplishes in the earlier years.

It is hardly necessary to insist upon the first of the two conditions which have been specified. It is a cardinal precept of the newer school of education that the beginning of instruction shall be made with the experience learners already have; that this experience and the capacities that have been developed during its course provide the starting point for all further learning. I am not so sure that the other condition, that of orderly development toward expansion and organization of subject-matter through growth of experience, receives as much attention. Yet the principle of continuity of educative experience requires that equal thought and attention be given to solution of this aspect of the educational problem. Undoubtedly this phase of the problem is more difficult than the other. Those who deal with the preschool child, with the kindergarten child, and with the boy and girl of the early primary years do not have much difficulty in determining the range of past experience or in finding activities that connect in vital ways with it. With older children both factors of the problem offer increased difficulties to the educator. It is harder to find out the background of the experience of individuals and harder to find out just how the subject-matters already contained in that experience shall be directed so as to lead out to larger and better organized fields.

It is a mistake to suppose that the principle of the leading on of experience to something different is adequately satisfied simply by giving pupils some new experiences any more than it is by seeing to it that they have greater skill and ease in dealing with things with which they are already familiar. It is also essential that the new objects and events be related intellectually to those of earlier experiences, and this means that there be some advance made in conscious articulation of facts and ideas. It thus becomes the office of the educator to select those things within the range of existing experience that have the promise and potentiality of presenting new problems which by stimulating new ways of observa-

tion and judgment will expand the area of further experience. He must constantly regard what is already won not as a fixed possession but as an agency and instrumentality for opening new fields which make new demands upon existing powers of observation and of intelligent use of memory. Connectedness in growth must be his constant watchword.

The educator more than the member of any other profession is concerned to have a long look ahead. The physician may feel his job done when he has restored a patient to health. He has undoubtedly the obligation of advising him how to live so as to avoid similar troubles in the future. But, after all, the conduct of his life is his own affair, not the physician's; and what is more important for the present point is that as far as the physician does occupy himself with instruction and advice as to the future of his patient he takes upon himself the function of an educator. The lawyer is occupied with winning a suit for his client or getting the latter out of some complication into which he has got himself. If it goes beyond the case presented to him he too becomes an educator. The educator by the very nature of his work is obliged to see his present work in terms of what it accomplishes, or fails to accomplish, for a future whose objects are linked with those of the present.

Here, again, the problem for the progressive educator is more difficult than for the teacher in the traditional school. The latter had indeed to look ahead. But unless his personality and enthusiasm took him beyond the limits that hedged in the traditional school, he could content himself with thinking of the next examination period or the promotion to the next class. He could envisage the future in terms of factors that lay within the requirements of the school system as that conventionally existed. There is incumbent upon the teacher who links education and actual experience together a more serious and a harder business. He must be aware of the potentialities for leading students into new fields which belong to experiences already had, and must use this knowledge as his criterion for selection and arrangement of the conditions that influence their present experience.

Because the studies of the traditional school consisted of subject-matter that was selected and arranged on the basis of the judgment of adults as to what would be useful for the young sometime in the future, the material to be learned was settled upon outside the present life-experience of the learner. In consequence, it had to do with the past; it was such as had proved useful to men in past ages. By reaction to an opposite extreme, as unfortunate as it was probably natural under the circumstances, the sound idea that education should derive its materials from present experience and should enable the learner to cope with the problems of the present and future has often been converted into the idea that progressive schools can to a very large extent ignore the past.

If the present could be cut off from the past, this conclusion would be sound. But the achievements of the past provide the only means at command for understanding the present. Just as the individual has to draw in memory upon his own past to understand the conditions in which he individually finds himself, so the issues and problems of present *social* life are in such intimate and direct connection with the past that students cannot be prepared to understand either these problems or the best way of dealing with them without delving into their roots in the past. In other words, the sound principle that the objectives of learning are in the future and its immediate materials are in present experience can be carried into effect only in the degree that present experience is stretched, as it were, backward. It can expand into the future only as it is also enlarged to take in the past.

John Dewey was, at various times during his career, Professor of Philosophy, Columbia University; head of the Department of Philosophy and director of the School of Education at the University of Chicago; and Professor of Philosophy at the University of Michigan.

QUESTIONS FOR REFLECTION

1. How does a curriculum that is organized according to Dewey's ideas incorporate the past, present, and future?
2. What criticisms might be made regarding Dewey's position that "the beginning of instruction [should] be made with the experience learners already have"? How would Dewey respond to these criticisms?
3. What techniques can curriculum planners and teachers use to determine the learners' "range of past experiences"?

Curriculum Integration and the Disciplines of Knowledge

JAMES A. BEANE

ABSTRACT: Curriculum integration, appropriately conceived, incorporates the traditional disciplines of knowledge to further the learner's quest to understand self and the world. Thus, curriculum integration facilitates the pursuit of new knowledge and meaning by transcending the disciplines of knowledge rather than abandoning them. However, four factors perpetuate the separate-subjects approach to the curriculum: the institutionalization of subject areas; perceptions of parents and adults; subject-matter professional identities; and conservative political influences.

At a conference on curriculum integration, a speaker who admitted that he had only recently been introduced to the concept said, "From a quick look at various readings, it seems that the disciplines of knowledge are the enemy of curriculum integration." Unwittingly or not, he had gone straight to the heart of perhaps the most contentious issue in current conversations about curriculum integration. Simply put, the issue is this: If we move away from the subject-centered approach to curriculum organization, will the disciplines of knowledge be abandoned or lost in the shuffle?

As an advocate for curriculum integration, I want to set the record straight. In the thoughtful pursuit of authentic curriculum integration, the disciplines of knowledge are not the enemy. Instead they are a useful and necessary ally.

WHAT IS CURRICULUM INTEGRATION?

Curriculum integration is not simply an organizational device requiring cosmetic changes or realignments in lesson plans across various subject areas. Rather, it is a way of thinking about what schools are for, about the sources of curriculum,

and about the uses of knowledge. Curriculum integration begins with the idea that the sources of curriculum ought to be problems, issues, and concerns posed by life itself.[1] I have argued elsewhere that such concerns fall into two spheres: 1) self- or personal concerns and 2) issues and problems posed by the larger world.[2] Taking this one step further, we might say that the central focus of curriculum integration is the search for self- and social meaning.

As teachers facilitate such a search within a framework of curriculum integration, two things happen. First, young people are encouraged to integrate learning experiences into their schemes of meaning so as to broaden and deepen their understanding of themselves and their world. Second, they are engaged in seeking, acquiring, and using knowledge in an organic—not an artificial—way. That is, knowledge is called forth in the context of problems, interests, issues, and concerns at hand. And since life itself does not know the boundaries or compartments of what we call disciplines of knowledge, such a context uses knowledge in ways that are integrated.[3]

Notice that, in order to define curriculum integration, there must be reference to knowledge. How could there not be? If we are to broaden and deepen understandings about ourselves and our

From *Phi Delta Kappan* 76, no. 8 (April 1995): 616–622. © 1995, Phi Delta Kappa. Used by permission of the author and publisher.

world, we must come to know "stuff," and to do that we must be skilled in ways of knowing and understanding. As it turns out, the disciplines of knowledge include much (but not all) of what we know about ourselves and our world and about ways of making and communicating meaning. Thus authentic curriculum integration, involving as it does the search for self- and social meaning, must take the disciplines of knowledge seriously—although, again, more is involved than just the correlation of knowledge from various disciplines.

WHAT IS THE PROBLEM?

Theoretically, defining the relations between curriculum integration and the disciplines of knowledge is easy. But that act does not resolve the tension over how those relations work in the practical context of curriculum integration. Part of the reason is that the problem is not with the disciplines of knowledge themselves but with their representation in the separate-subject approach to the curriculum. Put another way, the issue is not whether the disciplines of knowledge are useful, but how they might appropriately be brought into the lives of young people. And more than that, do they include all that might be of use in the search for self- and social meaning?

A discipline of knowledge is a field of inquiry about some aspect of the world—the physical world, the flow of events over time, numeric structures, and so on. A discipline of knowledge offers a lens through which to view the world—a specialized set of techniques or processes by which to interpret or explain various phenomena. Beyond that, a discipline also provides a sense of community for people with a shared special interest as they seek to stretch the limits of what is already known in that field. Those on the front edges of a discipline know that disciplinary boundaries are fluid and often connect with other disciplines to create interdisciplinary fields and projects.[4]

Though school-based subject areas, like disciplines of knowledge, partition knowledge into differentiated categories, they are not the same thing as disciplines. Some subjects, like history or mathematics, come close, but they are really institutionally based representations of disciplines, since they deal with a limited selection of what is already known within the field. That selection is based on what someone believes ought to be known (or is not worth knowing) about some discipline by people who do not work within it or are unfamiliar with its progress to date. Other subjects, like biology or algebra or home economics, are subsets of disciplines and are limited in even more specialized ways. And still other subjects, like career education or foreign languages, may lay far-reaching claims of connection to some discipline, but their presence in schools really has to do with economic, social, or academic aspirations.

In this sense, a discipline of knowledge and its representative school subject area are not the same things, even though they may be concerned with similar bodies of knowledge. They serve quite different purposes, offer quite different experiences for those who encounter them, and have quite different notions about the fluidity of the boundaries that presumably set one area of inquiry off from others. These differences are substantial enough that the identification of a school subject area as, for example, "history" amounts to an appropriation of the name attached to its corresponding discipline of knowledge. Subject areas are, in the end, a more severe case of "hardening of the categories" than are the disciplines they supposedly represent.

I make this distinction not to demean the work of subject-area teachers or to relegate them to a lower status than disciplinary scholars. Rather, I wish to point out that calling for an end to the separate-subject approach to school curriculum organization is not at all a rejection or abandonment of the disciplines of knowledge. But in saying this, I want to quickly warn that such a claim does not simply open the door to a renewal of "essentialist" conversations about the "structure of disciplines" or their "teachability" that Jerome Bruner and others encouraged in the past[5] and that are now revisited in lists of national and state content standards.

It is worth noting that Bruner himself apparently recognized this risk when, 10 years after the publication of *The Process of Education,* he reconsidered the work's place in education policy. Having just spoken of poverty, racism, injustice, and dispossession, he said this:

> I believe I would be quite satisfied to declare, if not a moratorium, then something of a de-emphasis on matters that have to do with the structure of history, the structure of physics, the nature of mathematical consistency, and deal with curriculum rather in the context of the problems that face us. We might better concern ourselves with how those problems can be solved, not just by practical action, but by putting knowledge, wherever we find it and in whatever form we find it, to work in these massive tasks. We might put vocation and intention back into the process of education, much more firmly than we had it there before.[6]

It is from just this kind of thinking that the case for curriculum integration emerges. Creating a curriculum for and with young people begins with an examination of the problems, issues, and concerns of life as it is being lived in a real world. Organizing themes are drawn from that examination. To work through such themes, to broaden and deepen our understanding of ourselves and our world, and to communicate those meanings, we must necessarily draw on the disciplines of knowledge. Again, therein lies much of what we know about ourselves and our world, ways in which we might explore them further, and possibilities for communicating meanings. Our reach for help in this kind of curriculum is a purposeful and directed activity—we do not simply identify questions and concerns and then sit around and wait for enlightenment to come to us. Instead, we intentionally and contextually "put knowledge to work."

INSIDE THE SUBJECT APPROACH

More and more educators are coming to realize that there is a fundamental tension in schools that current restructuring proposals are simply not addressing, no matter how radical their rhetoric might otherwise be. That tension has to do with the curriculum that mediates the relationships between teachers and young people. After all, teachers and their students do not come together on a random or voluntary social basis—they do not meet casually and decide to "do school." Instead, they are brought together to do something—namely the curriculum—and if that curriculum is fraught with fundamental problems, then the relationships between teachers and students will almost certainly be strained.

Advocates of curriculum integration, myself included, locate a large measure of that tension in the continuing organization of the planned curriculum around separate subject areas. While more complete critiques of the separate-subject approach have been offered elsewhere,[7] I want to touch on the major points of contention in order to clarify the claims made earlier in this article.

First, the separate-subject approach, as a selective representation of disciplines of knowledge, has incorrectly portrayed the latter as "ends" rather than "means" of education.[8] Young people and adults have been led to believe that the purpose of education is to master or "collect"[9] facts, principles, and skills that have been selected for inclusion in one or another subject area instead of learning how those isolated elements might be used to inform larger, real-life purposes.

Second, since the Eight-Year Study of the 1930s, we have been getting signals that the separate-subject approach is an inappropriate route even for those purposes that its advocates claim for themselves.[10] As that study and others after it have indicated, young people tend to do at least as well, and often better, on traditional measures of school achievement when the curriculum moves further in the direction of integration.

Third, the separate subjects and the disciplines of knowledge they are meant to represent are territories carved out by academicians for their own interests and purposes. Imposed on schools, the subject approach thus suggests that the "good life" consists of intellectual activity within narrowly defined areas.[11] The notion that this is the only version of a "good life," or the best one, or even a widely desirable one demeans the lives of others outside the academy who have quite different views and aspirations. It is a remnant of the same "top-down" version of the curriculum that has historically served the people in schools so poorly.

The fact that those academicians who so narrowly define the "good life" happen to be mostly white, upper-middle-class, and male means that the knowledge they prize and select is of a particular kind. Such knowledge, of course, is the cultural capital of that limited group, and thus the cultures of "other" people have been marginalized in the separate-subject approach. This is why the traditional question of the curriculum field, "What knowledge is of most worth?" has been amended to "Whose knowledge is of most worth?" As Michael Apple has pointed out, the fact that subject-centered curricula dominate most schools "is at least partly the result of the place of the school in maximizing the production of high-status knowledge."[12]

Pressing this point a bit further, we can see how such knowledge works in favor of the privileged young people in whose culture it is regularly found while working harshly against those from nonprivileged homes and nondominant cultures. In this way, the separate-subject approach and its selective content plays more than a small role in the "sort and select" system that has been an unbecoming feature of our schools for so long. While curriculum integration by itself cannot resolve this issue, the use of real-life themes demands a wider range of content, while the placement of that content in thematic contexts is likely to make it more accessible for young people.[13]

For most young people, including the privileged, the separate-subject approach offers little more than a disconnected and incoherent assortment of facts and skills. There is no unity, no real sense to it all. It is as if in real life, when faced with problems or puzzling situations, we stopped to ask which part is science, which part mathematics, which part art, and so on.

We are taken aback when young people ask, "Why are we doing this?" And our responses—"Because it will be on the test" or "Because you will need it next year"—are hardly sufficient to answer that question, let alone to justify placing anything in the curriculum.

The deadening effect the separate-subject approach has on the lives of young people cannot be overestimated. In too many places, students are still taught how to diagram complex sentences as if that were the key to the writing process, still made to memorize the names and routes of European explorers, still taught the same arithmetic year after year, page after page, with no particular connection to their lives. I believe such irrelevance has also had a deadening effect on the lives of many teachers. Had they known that this would be their routine for 30 years or more and that high tension would result, many would probably have chosen a different line of work. And who could blame them?

The separate-subject approach is a legacy of Western-style classical humanism, which views the world in divided compartments. This view was shored up in the last century by the theories of faculty psychology and mental discipline that described the mind as a compartmentalized "muscle" whose parts were to be exercised separately by particular disciplines.[14] The reasoning faculty, for example, was supposedly exercised by the "objective logic" of mathematics, and the assumption was that the heightened reasoning abilities could then be applied to any new situations, including social ones.

Though faculty psychology and mental discipline were discredited by the turn of the century, both live on in some interpretations of split-brain and multiple intelligence theories. And suspect as it has now become, classical humanism still looms large in curriculum organization as part of "official knowledge."[15] How can this be so?

The separate-subject approach to the curriculum is protected by four powerful factors. First, any call for rethinking that approach immediately comes up against a network of educational elites whose symbiotic relationships are founded upon it. I refer here to many academicians and teacher educators in universities, state- and district-level subject supervisors, test and text publishers, subject-area associations, and others whose titles and office doors often signify particular subject areas. The struggles to form, institutionalize, and defend the subject areas have not been easy ones, and neither the areas nor the job titles are going to be given up easily, no matter how persuasive the educational arguments to do so.[16]

Second, parents and other adults are reluctant to embrace versions of the curriculum that depart from what they remember from their own schooling. They want assurance that their children will "get what they need." Thus talk about ideas like curriculum integration may feel threatening to them. And their fears are compounded when they hear arguments for national tests and curriculum or are confronted with media critiques of schools, both of which lend support to the separate-subject cause.

Third, inside the schools themselves, teachers and supervisors often build their professional identities along subject-matter lines.[17] They are not just teachers, but "math teachers" or "music teachers" or "language arts teachers." Identities are also tied to status associated with subject areas—"math is more important than physical education" and so on—and that status, in turn, often determines which teachers get preferred schedule slots or their own classrooms. Anyone who has ever worked in a school knows that this is very dangerous territory to invade.

Finally, it is no secret that we are living in a very conservative era in which historically dominant political and economic groups are noisily reclaiming ground and goods they believe have been taken away from them by progressives.[18]

Most of the social road signs advise, "Merge right." In the midst of this conservative restoration comes a call for "curriculum integration"—an approach, as I have defined it, that was historically rooted in the work of the social reconstruction wing of the progressive education movement. Unlike many educators who think that curriculum integration is simply about rearranging lesson plans, conservative critics have figured out that it involves something much larger, and they don't like it.

In constructing a critique of the separate-subject approach, we must remember Dewey's admonition that any nondominant idea about education—in this case curriculum integration—must not be defended solely on the ground of rejection of another idea—here the separate-subject approach.[19] Curriculum integration does not just mean doing the same things differently but doing *something different*. It has its own theories of purpose, knowledge, and learning and is able to stand on those without the necessity of standing on the corpse of the separate-subject approach. However, the subject-centered approach is so rooted in the deep structures and folklore of schooling that its critique is necessary to even raise the possibility of other approaches.[20] It is almost as if it had been conceived supernaturally instead of constructed by real people with particular values and beliefs.[21]

KNOWLEDGE IN AN INTEGRATED CURRICULUM

Having exposed the shortcomings of the separate-subject approach, we may now turn back to the happier relations between curriculum integration and the disciplines of knowledge. How does knowledge look in the context of curriculum integration? What happens to the disciplines of knowledge? How are they used?

In practice, curriculum integration begins with the identification of organizing themes or centers for learning experiences. As previously noted, the themes are drawn from real-life concerns, such as conflict; living in the future; cultures and identities; jobs, money, and careers; or the environment. In some cases the themes are identified by teachers; in the most sophisticated instances, they emerge from collaborative planning with young people.[22] Planning then proceeds directly to creating activities to address the theme and related issues. There is no intermediate step in which attempts are made to identify which subject areas might contribute to the theme.

This is a very important distinction, since curriculum integration, in theory and practice, transcends subject-area and disciplinary identifications; the goal is integrative activities that use knowledge without regard for subject or discipline lines. Pretenders to this approach, such as "multidisciplinary" or "interdisciplinary" arrangements, may not follow a strict subject-centered format, but they nevertheless retain subject-area and disciplinary distinctions around some more or less unifying theme.[23] (This structure is typically demonstrated by the fact that a student's schedule still involves a daily rotation through various subjects, even though the teachers may be attempting to use a common theme.) In curriculum integration, the schedule revolves around projects and activities rather than subjects. The disciplines of knowledge come into play as resources from which to draw within the context of the theme and related issues and activities.

For example, in a unit on "living in the future," young people might survey their peers regarding their visions of the future, tabulate the results, compare them to other forecasts, and prepare research reports. Or they might look at technological, recreational, entertainment, or social trends and develop forecasts or scenarios of probable futures for one or more areas. Or they might study past forecasts made for our own times to see if the predictions actually came true. Or they might develop recommendations for the future of their local communities in areas such as population, health, recreation, transportation, and conservation. Or they might study the effects of aging on facial features to imagine how they might look when they are older.

In a unit on "the environment" they might create simulations of different biomes with real and constructed artifacts and offer guided "tours" of their work. Or they might experiment with the effects of pollutants on plant growth. Or they might set up and manage a recycling program in the classroom or school. Or they might identify the raw products in various clothing items and investigate where they come from, find out who makes them, and analyze the environmental and economic impacts of the entire process. Or they might identify environmental problems in their local community and seek ways to resolve them.

I have used the word "or" between activities, since an integrative unit may involve one or any number of them. The point is this: any careful reading of the activities should reveal that, if they are done thoughtfully, they will draw heavily on a variety of disciplines of knowledge for facts, skills, concepts, and understandings.

For example, in constructing surveys, tabulating data, and preparing reports, one would need to draw heavily from the social sciences, language arts, and mathematics. Suppose that some young people did not know how to compute percentages or make graphs. Obviously the teacher(s) would help them learn how to do these things or, if necessary, find someone else who knew how to do them. In experimenting with the effects of pollutants on plant life, some young people might not know how to carry out controlled tests. In that case, someone would teach them how to do that. Does this mean that schools would intentionally employ teachers who know "stuff" from disciplines of knowledge? Certainly! But in curriculum integration, teachers work first as generalists on integrative themes and secondarily as content specialists.

Note that, in curriculum integration, knowledge from the disciplines is repositioned into the context of the theme, questions, and activities at hand. Even when teaching and learning move into what looks like discipline-based instruction, the theme continues to provide the context and the motivation. It is here that knowledge comes to life, has meaning, and is more likely to be "learned." Particular knowledge is not abstracted or fragmented, as is the case when its identity and purpose are tied only to its place within a discipline or school subject area.

Repositioning knowledge in this way raises two issues that cannot be ignored. First, subject-area sequences that have previously defined the flow of knowledge tend to be rearranged in curriculum integration, since knowledge is called forth when it is pertinent rather than when it is convenient. While this is upsetting to some subject-loyal teachers, we should note the irony that sequences often vary from school to school and from state to state. In other words, sequences are more arbitrary than those who construct and defend them would have us believe.[24] The fact that even some subject-area associations have moved away from traditional notions of sequencing should tell us something. In the end, though, advocates of curriculum integration are more interested in the rhythms and patterns of inquiring young minds than in the scopes and sequences of subject-area specialists. The work done within the context of curriculum integration *is* a curriculum; there is not another "curriculum" waiting in the wings to be taught.

Second, it is entirely possible, even probable, that not all the information and skills now disseminated by separate-subject teaching will come to the surface in the context of curriculum integration. But let's face it: there is a good deal of trivia now being disseminated in schools that would be necessary or meaningful only if and when one actually became a specialist in one or another discipline of knowledge, and even then some of it would probably be superfluous. In some places the separate-subject curriculum looks more like preparation for doing the *New York Times* crossword puzzle than for specializing in a discipline. Besides, the very idea of knowing all that "stuff" is a pipe dream in an era when yesterday's "truths" seem to dissolve in the high tide of today's new knowledge.

Curriculum integration, on the other hand, calls forth those ideas that are most important and powerful in the disciplines of knowledge—the ones that are most significant because they emerge in life itself. And because they are placed in the context of personally and socially significant concerns, they are more likely to have real meaning in the lives of young people, the kind of meaning they do not now have.

As boundaries disappear, curriculum integration is also likely to engage knowledge that ordinarily falls between the cracks of disciplines and subject areas. This is particularly the case as knowledge is applied to problematic situations. For example, in exploring the influences of media, young people might investigate the use of the word "average" in the context of the presumed consumer interests of the "average person." What does "average" mean here? How is "average" arrived at when used in this way? How can mathematics be used to manipulate meanings?

Indeed, this kind of knowledge is being attended to by some scholars who work in disciplines of knowledge (and their work is an important resource for those who advocate curriculum integration). But can the same be said for those who live within the boundaries of school subject areas? And if discipline-based scholars have felt the need to move beyond the boundaries of their home disciplines, why is it that so many people are adamant about leaving those same boundaries intact in schools?

Critics of curriculum integration love to convey their deep concern that it will destroy the integrity of the disciplines of knowledge. I am puzzled by this. What possible integrity could there be for any kind of knowledge apart from how it connects with other forms to help us investigate and understand the problems, concerns, and issues that confront us in the real world? Furthermore, what kind of integrity do the disciplines of knowledge now have in young peoples' minds? Am I missing something? Is "integrity" really a code for "subject boundaries" and "dominant-culture knowledge"?

As a last attempt, some critics suggest that perhaps curriculum integration would be a good idea, but only after a thorough grounding in the separate subjects. If we were talking about house building, the foundation metaphor might work well. However, in the case of learning, it is the "whole" context that gives particular knowledge meaning and accessibility.[25] Besides, if we have to wait for the kind of foundation that such critics mean, we will probably never see any integration.

BEYOND THE DEBATE

Despite the matter-of-fact tone I have used here, it would be a mistake to believe that the understanding and practice of curriculum integration is free of confusion. The very existence of the false dichotomy that I have addressed here between curriculum integration and the disciplines of knowledge is evidence that, as advocates of curriculum integration have criticized the use of a separate-subject approach, they have left the impression that the disciplines of knowledge are to be rejected.

Worse yet, the very meaning of curriculum integration has become so confused that the term is used in association with almost any approach that moves beyond that of strictly separate subjects. For example, "curriculum integration" is often used to describe multidisciplinary arrangements in which themes are found inside the existing subjects (e.g., "colonial living" or "ancient Greece" or "metrics") and the guiding question is, What can each subject contribute to the theme? Subject-loyal teachers typically rebel over the contrived use of their areas in such cases and resent being distracted from their usual focus on content coverage. But that kind of alienation merely signifies that this is an adaptation still closely tied to the separate-subject approach and philosophy. As we have seen, curriculum integration involves a quite different philosophy that goes far beyond these concerns.

The term "integration" has also been used to describe attempts to reassemble fragmented pieces of a discipline of knowledge—such as creating social studies out of history and geography—and to label approaches that emphasize thinking, writing, and valuing across subject areas. One might well argue that the word "integration" is technically acceptable in these instances, but they clearly do not represent what has been meant historically by "curriculum integration."

However, even if the language problem were cleared up, there is still much to learn about curriculum integration as an approach. For example, are some kinds of knowledge more likely than others to emerge in the context of life-centered themes? Are some themes more likely than others to serve well as contexts for integrating wide ranges of knowledge? How big a chunk of life should an integrative theme encompass? How can we be certain that integrated knowledge will not simply accumulate without meaning (as separate-subject knowledge usually does) but will help young people continuously expand meaning?[26]

These kinds of questions are rooted in attempts to understand more fully curriculum integration as well as the place of knowledge within it. Notice that they are not of the sort that asks how curriculum integration might find a peaceful coexistence with current conceptions of a subject-centered curriculum. Again, curriculum integration is not about doing the same things differently but about doing something truly different. For this reason, questions like "How will young people do on our subject-based tests?" or "How does this fit into our current schedule?" are not pertinent (though they are real politically). The structures to which such questions refer grew out of the separate-subject approach to the curriculum. Shifting to a different approach thus calls the structures themselves into question.

Many educators today like to speak of paradigm shifts when describing changes they have made or are trying to make. Such shifts may involve changing the school schedule, more sharply defining outcomes of schooling, or coming up with new methods of assessment. As I understand it, a paradigm shift entails a change in viewpoint so fundamental that much of what is currently taken for granted is called into question or rendered irrelevant or wrong. If we use this definition, it is hard to consider the kinds of changes just mentioned as "paradigm shifts." These, like most of the changes usually associated with "restructuring," ask about "how" we do things and leave alone more fundamental questions about "what" we do and "why."

Curriculum integration centers the curriculum on life itself rather than on the mastery of fragmented information within the boundaries of subject areas. It is rooted in a view of learning as the continuous integration of new knowledge and experience so as to deepen and broaden our understanding of ourselves and our world. Its focus is on life as it is lived now rather than on preparation for some later life or later level of schooling. It serves the young people for whom the curriculum is intended rather than the specialized interests of adults. It concerns the active construction of meanings rather than the passive assimilation of others' meanings.

Described in this way, curriculum integration is more of a real paradigm shift than are the changes usually touted as such. Yet it does not reject outright or abandon all that has been deemed important by other views of schooling. This accommodation is especially apparent with regard to the disciplines of knowledge, which are necessarily drawn on in responsible curriculum integration. This point is not a matter of compromise but of common sense. Advocates of curriculum integration may criticize the separate-subject approach and the purpose of schooling it implies, they may accuse subject-area loyalists of narcissism, and they may decry the deadening effects of the separate-subject curriculum. But they do not intend to walk away from knowledge—and, for that reason, the disciplines of knowledge are clearly not the enemies of curriculum integration.

ENDNOTES

1. L. Thomas Hopkins et al., *Integration: Its Meaning and Application* (New York: Appleton-Century, 1937); Lucille L. Lurry and Elsie J. Alberty, *Developing the High School Core Program* (New York: Macmillan, 1957); Paul L. Dressel, "The Meaning and Significance of Integration," in Nelson B. Henry, ed., *The Integration of Educational Experiences: 57th NSSE Yearbook, Part III* (Chicago: National Society for the Study of Education, University of Chicago Press, 1958); Gertrude

Noar, *The Teacher and Integration* (Washington, D.C.: National Education Association, 1966); James A. Beane, *Affect in the Curriculum: Toward Democracy, Dignity, and Diversity* (New York: Routledge, 1993); and Gordon F. Vars, "Integrated Curriculum in Historical Perspective," *Educational Leadership,* October 1991, pp. 14–15.

2. Beane, op. cit.; and idem, *A Middle School Curriculum: From Rhetoric to Reality,* rev. ed. (Columbus, Ohio: National Middle School Association, 1993).

3. Here and throughout the article, I am using the term "knowledge" generically to include knowing about, knowing how, knowing why, and so on. Thus "knowledge" would include information, skills, concepts, processes, and so on.

4. Julie Thompson Klein, *Interdisciplinarity: History, Theory, and Practice* (Detroit: Wayne State University Press, 1990).

5. Jerome S. Bruner, *The Process of Education* (Cambridge, Mass.: Harvard University Press, 1960); G. W. Ford and Lawrence Pugno, *The Structure of Knowledge and the Curriculum* (Chicago: Rand McNally, 1964); Arthur R. King, Jr., and John A. Brownell, *The Curriculum and the Disciplines of Knowledge* (New York: Wiley, 1966); and Morton Alpern, ed., *The Subject Curriculum: Grades K-12* (Columbus, Ohio: Charles E. Merrill, 1967).

6. Jerome S. Bruner, *"The Process of Education Reconsidered,"* in Robert R. Leeper, ed., *Dare to Care/Dare to Act: Racism and Education* (Washington, D.C.: Association for Supervision and Curriculum Development, 1971), pp. 29–30.

7. Marion Brady, *What's Worth Teaching?* (Albany, N.Y.: State University of New York Press, 1989); Beane, *A Middle School Curriculum;* and R. W. Connell, *Schools and Social Justice* (Philadelphia: Temple University Press, 1993).

8. John Dewey, *The School and Society,* rev. ed. (Chicago: University of Chicago Press, 1915); George Henry, "Foundations of General Education in the High School," in *What Shall the High Schools Teach?: 1956 ASCD Yearbook* (Washington, D.C.: Association for Supervision and Curriculum Development, 1956); and Brady, op. cit.

9. Basil Bernstein, *Class, Codes, and Control, Vol. 3: Towards a Theory of Educational Transmissions,* 2nd ed. (London: Routledge and Kegan Paul, 1975).

10. Wilford Aikin, *The Story of the Eight Year Study* (New York: Harper & Row, 1942).

11. See, for example, Allan Bloom, *The Closing of the American Mind* (New York: Simon & Schuster, 1987); E. D. Hirsch, Jr., *Cultural Literacy* (Boston: Houghton Mifflin, 1987); and Diane Ravitch and Chester E. Finn, Jr., *What Do Our 17-Year-Olds Know?* (New York: Harper & Row, 1987).

12. Michael W. Apple, *Ideology and Curriculum,* 2nd ed. (London: Routledge and Kegan Paul, 1990), p. 38.

13. Ashgar Iran-Nejad, Wilbert J. McKeachie, and David C. Berliner, "The Multisource Nature of Learning: An Introduction," *Review of Educational Research,* Winter 1990, pp. 509–15.

14. Herbert M. Kliebard, "The Decline of Humanistic Studies in the American School Curriculum," in Benjamin Ladner, ed., *The Humanities in Precollegiate Education: 83rd NSSE Yearbook, Part II* (Chicago: National Society for the Study of Education, University of Chicago Press, 1984).

15. Michael W. Apple, *Official Knowledge: Democratic Education in a Conservative Age* (New York: Routledge, 1993).

16. Ivor Goodson, ed., *Social Histories of the Secondary School Curriculum: Subjects for Study* (Philadelphia: Falmer, 1985); Herbert M. Kliebard, *The Struggle for the American Curriculum: 1893–1958* (Boston: Routledge and Kegan Paul, 1986); and Thomas S. Popkewitz, ed., *The Formation of School Subjects: The Struggle for Creating an American Institution* (New York: Falmer, 1987).

17. Bernstein, op. cit.

18. Anne C. Lewis, "The Ghost of November Past," *Phi Delta Kappan,* January 1995, pp. 348–49.

19. John Dewey, *Experience and Education* (New York: Macmillan, 1938).

20. Michael F. D.Young, "An Approach to the Study of Curricula as Socially Organized Knowledge," in idem, ed., *Knowledge and Control* (London: Collier-Macmillan, 1971).

21. Raymond Williams, *The Long Revolution* (London: Chatto and Windus, 1961).

22. Rosalind M. Zapf, *Democratic Processes in the Classroom* (Englewood Cliffs, N.J.: Prentice-Hall, 1959); Noar, op. cit.; James A. Beane, "The Middle School: Natural Home of Integrated Curriculum," *Educational Leadership,* October 1991, pp. 9–13; idem, "Turning the Floor Over: Reflections on *A Middle School Curriculum,*" *Middle School Journal,* January 1992, pp. 34–40; Barbara Brodhagen, Gary Weilbacher, and James A. Beane, "Living in the Future: An Experiment with an Integrative Curriculum," *Dissemination Services on the Middle Grades,* June 1992, pp. 1–7; and Barbara L. Brodhagen, "The Situation Made Us Special," in Michael W. Apple and James A. Beane, eds., *Democratic Schools* (Alexandria, Va.: Association for Supervision and Curriculum Development, 1995).

23. Charity James, *Young Lives at Stake* (New York: Agathon, 1972); Bernstein, op. cit.; and Heidi Hayes Jacobs, ed., *Interdisciplinary Curriculum: Design and Implementation* (Alexandria, Va.: Association for Supervision and Curriculum Development, 1989).

24. It is instructive to note that alphabetical order rather than disciplinary structure created the usual biology-chemistry-physics sequence.

25. Iran-Nejad, McKeachie, and Berliner, op. cit.

26. Arno A. Bellack, "Selection and Organization of Curriculum Content," in *What Shall the High Schools Teach?*

James A. Beane is Professor of Education at the National College of Education, National-Louis University, Evanston, Illinois.

QUESTIONS FOR REFLECTION

1. What is the difference between an *integrated* curriculum and an *interdisciplinary* curriculum?

2. According to Beane, what are some current misconceptions about integrated curricula?

3. What are the differences between a discipline of knowledge—physics, for example—and its corresponding school subject?

Can We Prepackage Thinking?

NITA H. BARBOUR

ABSTRACT: *Materials and programs that have been developed to teach higher-order thinking skills to students are often implemented in a ritualistic, routinized manner that actually curtails thinking. To avoid this, teachers should model the thinking skills they wish students to acquire, and they should emphasize processes rather than outcomes.*

Teaching for thinking has become the new focus in education. Since reports on American education suggest that schools are failing to educate enough students with the ability to do higher order thinking, educators have responded with published programs that suggest specific ways and materials designed to teach thinking skills. Workshops are offered to instruct teachers in the use of these materials and programs.

Certainly, many excellent ideas are available to assist teachers in facilitating development of children's higher order thinking skills. In support of these ideas, educators argue (often for different reasons) about the way thinking should be taught. Some maintain that higher order thinking skills, especially for high-risk students, should not be integrated into the curriculum but instead be taught as a separate training course (Pogrow, 1988). Others who advocate teaching of specific thinking skills argue that these skills should then be applied directly to the school content (Beyer, 1988). Still others insist that learning to think occurs in context, that it is by learning the various disciplines and the structure and problems of these disciplines that children learn to think (Chambers, 1988).

Textbook publishers and curriculum developers have responded to this concept by supplying teachers with prepackaged sets of strategies and tactics as well as step by step procedures for teaching thinking. While they may contain many excellent ideas, often these prepackaged materials lead to ritualistic and routinized practices. When teachers are given, or expect, exact steps on how to conduct lessons for thinking, all too often the results curtail thinking for both children and teachers.

In classrooms where teachers routinely follow given sets of strategies, there is danger that they may not analyze the purpose of the lessons for particular children or think critically about their impact. If teachers want their students to be critical thinkers, Sternberg (1987) points out, then they must practice and model thinking skills themselves instead of mindlessly following a given set of strategies. Unless they do, teachers may fall into the same trap as the teacher in the following episode, who focused more on steps and outcome of the science curriculum guide than on the process.

Children were all given a ball of clay and asked to try to see if they could make it float. When Jamie poked several holes in his ball of clay and dropped it into the water, several children copied his idea—creating a disruption in the classroom. The teacher reprimanded Jamie and the other children, proceeding to tell them how to flatten out the clay "to make it work." The children learned that it was dangerous to venture too much, that eventually the teacher would tell them what they were supposed to discover. With too much routine and direction, the active process of creative and analytical thinking is likely to become stultified for both teachers and children.

From *Childhood Education* 65, no. 2 (Winter 1988), 67–68. Reprinted by permission of the author and the Association for Childhood Education International, 17904 Georgia Avenue, Suite 215, Olney, Maryland. Copyright © by the Association.

Dewey (1910) likens children's thinking to that of a scientist trying to solve problems. Both are experimenters who observe, formulate tentative solutions, try out these solutions, collect more information, summarize what they know and finally draw conclusions. These conclusions may be accurate or inaccurate—and only as children continue to be active observers, to be challenged in their perceptions, to be forced to alter their views will they continue to grow in their thought processes.

What kind of environment nurtures this type of development? Sternberg (1987) suggests that classrooms where critical thinking is developed are places where teachers see themselves and not just children as learners; where discussion is an essential element of the learning process; and where, since children must ultimately teach themselves if they are to find ways to solve problems, teachers are facilitators of children's learning instead of directors.

Bruner (1983) points out that "it is not so much instruction either in language or in thinking that permits the child to develop his powerful combinational skills, but a decent opportunity to play around with language and to play around with his thinking that turns the trick" (p. 66).

In prepackaged lessons on thinking, are children permitted adequate time to play around with their thinking? Do teachers see themselves as learners in the classroom setting? Are children setting up their own problems as they learn content, thus finding ways to solve real-life problems?

In the following scenario the teacher has created an environment where children, while developing skills in one content area (storytelling), practice their reasoning and persuasive skills with each other by solving problems of their own making.

Dan and Zeb are working in the sandbox to build a setting for a cooperative oral story, the day after the 2nd-grade class experimented with siphoning water from one source to another. They have built a sand castle and a "wishing well" at one end of the sandbox and, at the other end,

a "lake." In the process of building, Dan and Zeb have brought plastic tubing from the science area. Zeb places one end of the tube in the "wishing well" and Dan places the other end in the "lake."

Dan: Why don't we make a siphon? [He sucks water into the tube from the "well" and places the tube in the "lake." The water stops flowing.]
Zeb: It isn't working, Dan. [Dan blows into the "wishing well" in an attempt to get the siphon to work.]
Zeb: We don't have to make a siphon. It's a little too equal to the other one [meaning the two water sources are on an equal level.]
Dan: [blows again] No luck. Maybe we shouldn't make one. [The boys drain the water from the "wishing well," but later fill it again as they decide that the tubing will be the water pipes from the well into the castle.]

In the give-and-take of open discussions with each other, these children demonstrate one way of "playing around with [their] thinking." Zeb and Dan have time to explore, to experiment, to discuss the setting and plot of their story. The boys learned about moving water from one area to another in science class, but now they have an opportunity to try the experiment again. Appearing to understand why the experiment doesn't work, Zeb chooses to alter his thinking about how the story should proceed, instead of altering the water level of one of the containers. Observing, collecting data, reformulating their plan of action are all part of Zeb and Dan's experience.

Children's own concepts and ideas are challenged in play situations; at times they are forced to take another's perspective and reformulate their own thinking. If they are not to be dominated by others, then they need to perfect their own reasoning skills so they can persuade peers or teachers of the rightness of their viewpoints. While there are specific activities that may help develop children's analytical or creative thinking in relationship to a particular activity, the habit of questioning and questing develops more slowly and needs constant nurturing. Open-ended child/child and teacher/child discussions, where ideas are generated and challenged, are rich sources of learning potential. Teacher/child discussions are rather common in classrooms, but are they open-ended so that children have time to play around with ideas? How often do teachers plan for a curriculum that permits children the freedom to discuss, agree, argue, inform, regulate and imagine with each other?

RESOURCES

Beyer, B. Y. (1988). *Developing a thinking skills program*. Boston: Allyn & Bacon.

Bruner, J. (1983). Play, thought and language. *Peabody Journal of Education, 60*(3), 60–69.

Chambers, J. H. (1988). Teaching thinking throughout the curriculum—Where else? *Educational Leadership, 45*(7), 4–7.

Costa, A. L. (Ed.) (1987). *Developing minds: A resource book for teaching thinking*. Alexandria, VA: Association for Supervision and Curriculum Development.

de Bono, E. (1983). The Cognitive Research Trust (CoRT) thinking program. In E. Maxwell (Ed.), *Thinking, the expanding frontier*. Hillsdale, NJ: Erlbaum.

Dewey, J. (1910). *How we think*. New York: D.C. Heath.

Gardner, H. (1983). *Frames of mind*. New York: Basic Books.

Nickerson, R. S., Perkins, N., & Smith, E. E. (1985). *The teaching of thinking*. Hillsdale, NJ: Erlbaum.

Pogrow, S. (1988). Teaching thinking to at-risk elementary students. *Educational Leadership, 45*(7), 79–85.

Raths, L. E., Wassermann, S., Jonas, S., & Rothstein, A. (1986). *Teaching for thinking: Theory, strategies, and activities for the classroom*. New York: Teachers College, Columbia University.

Sternberg, R. J. (1987). Teaching critical thinking skills: Eight easy ways to fail before you begin. *Phi Delta Kappan, 68*(6), 456–460.

Nita H. Barbour is the Issues Editor for *Childhood Education,* published by the Association for Childhood Education International.

QUESTIONS FOR REFLECTION

1. In regard to the subject area and the level with which you are most familiar, what curricular approaches are most effective for teaching students the processes of higher-order thinking?

2. Why is it important for learners to "play around" with language and thinking? What distinguishes "playing around" that is beneficial for students from that which is not?

3. What are the benefits of "open-ended" discussions between teacher and students?

Art and Imagination: Reclaiming the Sense of Possibility

MAXINE GREENE

ABSTRACT: In light of the appalling realities of the human condition throughout much of the world and our inability to reduce much of that suffering, current preoccupations with world-class standards and manageable, predictable, and measurable outcomes seem superficial, if not absurd. Through their involvement with the arts, however, the young can "imagine, extend, and renew." By focusing on the arts and imagination, education can facilitate growth, inventiveness, and problem solving and help us all overcome the "tyranny of the technical."

The existential contexts of education reach far beyond what is conceived of in Goals 2000. They have to do with the human condition in these often desolate days, and in some ways they make the notions of world-class achievement, benchmarks, and the rest seem superficial and limited, if not absurd. They extend beyond the appalling actualities of family breakdown, homelessness, violence, and the "savage inequalities" described by Jonathan Kozol, although social injustice has an existential dimension.

Like their elders, children and young persons inhabit a world of fearful moral uncertainty—a world in which it appears that almost nothing can be done to reduce suffering, contain massacres, and protect human rights. The faces of refugee children in search of their mothers, of teenage girls repeatedly raped by soldiers, of rootless people staring at the charred remains of churches and libraries may strike some of us as little more than a "virtual reality." Those who persist in looking feel numbed and, reminded over and over of helplessness, are persuaded to look away.

It has been said that Pablo Picasso's paintings of "weeping women" have become the icons of our time.[1] They have replaced the statues of men on horseback and men in battle; they overshadow the emblems of what once seemed worth fighting for, perhaps dying for. When even the young confront images of loss and death, as most of us are bound to do today, "it is important that everything we love be summed up into something unforgettably beautiful."[2] This suggests one of the roles of the arts. To see sketch after sketch of women holding dead babies, as Picasso has forced us to do, is to become aware of a tragic deficiency in the fabric of life. If we know enough to make those paintings the objects of our experience, to encounter them against the background of our lives, we are likely to strain toward conceptions of a better order of things, in which there will be no more wars that make women weep like that, no more bombs to murder innocent children. We are likely, in rebelling against such horror, to summon up images of smiling mothers and lovely children, metaphors for what *ought* to be.

Clearly, this is not the only role of the arts, although encounters with them frequently do move us to want to restore some kind of order, to repair, and to heal. Participatory involvement with the many forms of art does enable us, at the very least, to *see* more in our experience, to *hear* more on normally unheard frequencies, to *become conscious* of what daily routines, habits, and conventions have obscured.

From *Phi Delta Kappan* 76, no. 5 (January 1995): 378–382. © 1995, Phi Delta Kappa. Used by permission of the author and publisher.

We might think of what Pecola Breedlove in *The Bluest Eye* has made us realize about the meta-narrative implicit in the Dick and Jane basal readers or in the cultural artifact called Shirley Temple, who made so many invisible children yearn desperately to have blue eyes.[3] We might recall the revelations discovered by so many through an involvement with *Schindler's List*. We might try to retrieve the physical consciousness of unutterable grief aroused in us by Martha Graham's dance "Lamentation," with only feet and hands visible outside draped fabric— and agony expressed through stress lines on the cloth. To see more, to hear more. By such experiences we are not only lurched out of the familiar and the taken-for-granted, but we may also discover new avenues for action. We may experience a sudden sense of new possibilities and thus new beginnings.

The prevailing cynicism with regard to values and the feelings of resignation it breeds cannot help but create an atmosphere in the schools that is at odds with the unpredictability associated with the experience of art. The neglect of the arts by those who identified the goals of Goals 2000 was consistent with the focus on the manageable, the predictable, and the measurable. There have been efforts to include the arts in the official statements of goals, but the arguments mustered in their favor are of a piece with the arguments for education geared toward economic competitiveness, technological mastery, and the rest. They have also helped support the dominant arguments for the development of "higher-level skills," academic achievement standards, and preparation for the workplace.

The danger afflicting both teachers and students because of such emphases is, in part, the danger of feeling locked into existing circumstances defined by others. Young people find themselves described as "human resources" rather than as persons who are centers of choice and evaluation. It is suggested that young people are to be molded in the service of technology and the market, no matter who they are. Yet, as many are now realizing, great numbers of our young

people will find themselves unable to locate satisfying jobs, and the very notion of "all the children" and even of human resources carries with it deceptions of all kinds. Perhaps it is no wonder that the dominant mood in many classrooms is one of passive reception.

Umberto Eco, the Italian critic of popular culture, writes about the desperate need to introduce a critical dimension into such reception. Where media and messages are concerned, it is far more important, he says, to focus on the point of reception than on the point of transmission. Finding a threat in "the universal of technological communication" and in situations where "the medium is the message," he calls seriously for a return to individual resistance. "To the anonymous divinity of Technological Communication, our answer could be: 'Not thy, but *our* will be done.' "[4]

The kind of resistance Eco has in mind can best be evoked when imagination is released. But, as we well know, the bombardment of images identified with "Technological Communication" frequently has the effect of freezing imaginative thinking. Instead of freeing audiences to look at things as if they could be otherwise, present-day media impose predigested frameworks on their audiences. Dreams are caught in the meshes of the salable; the alternative to gloom or feelings of pointlessness is consumerist acquisition. For Mary Warnock, imagination is identified with the belief that "there is more in our experience of the world than can possibly meet the unreflecting eye."[5] It tells us that experience always holds more than we can predict. But Warnock knows that acknowledging the existence of undiscovered vistas and perspectives requires reflectiveness. The passive, apathetic person is all too likely to be unresponsive to ideas of the unreal, the as if, the merely possible. He or she becomes the one who bars the arts as frivolous, mere frills, irrelevant to learning in the postindustrial world.

It is my conviction that informed engagements with the several arts would be the most likely way to release the imaginative capacity and give it play. However, this does not happen automatically or "naturally." We have all witnessed the surface contacts with paintings when groups of tourists hasten through museums. Without time spent, without tutoring, and without dialogue regarding the arts, people merely seek the right labels. They look for the artists' names. There are those who watch a ballet for the story, not for the movement or the music; they wait for Giselle to go mad or for the Sleeping Beauty to be awakened or for the white swan to return.

Mere exposure to a work of art is not sufficient to occasion an aesthetic experience. There must be conscious participation in a work, a going out of energy, an ability to notice what is there to be noticed in the play, the poem, the quartet. "Knowing about," even in the most formal academic manner, is entirely different from creating an unreal world imaginatively and entering it perceptually, affectively, and cognitively. To introduce people to such engagement is to strike a delicate balance between helping learners to pay heed—to attend to shapes, patterns, sounds, rhythms, figures of speech, contours, lines, and so on—and freeing them to perceive particular works as meaningful. Indeed, the inability to control what is discovered as meaningful makes many traditional educators uneasy and strikes them as being at odds with conceptions of a norm, even with notions of appropriate "cultural literacy." This uneasiness may well be at the root of certain administrators' current preoccupation with national standards.

However, if we are to provide occasions for significant encounters with works of art, we have to combat standardization and what Hannah Arendt called "thoughtlessness" on the part of all of those involved. What she meant by thoughtlessness was "the heedless recklessness or hopeless confusion or complacent repetition of 'truths' which have become trivial and empty."[6] There is something in that statement that recalls what John Dewey described as a "social pathology"—a condition that still seems to afflict us today. Dewey wrote that it manifests itself "in queru-

lousness, in impotent drifting, in uneasy snatching at distractions, in idealization of the long established, in a facile optimism assumed as a cloak."[7] Concerned about "sloppiness, superficiality, and recourse to sensations as a substitute for ideas," Dewey made the point that "thinking deprived of its normal course takes refuge in academic specialism."[8]

For Arendt, the remedy for this condition is "to think what we are doing." She had in mind developing a self-reflectiveness that originates in situated life, the life of persons open to one another in their distinctive locations and engaging one another in dialogue. Provoked by the spectacle of the Nazi Adolf Eichmann, Arendt warned against "clichés, stock phrases, adherence to conventional, standardized codes of expression and conduct," which have, she said, "the socially recognized function of protecting us against reality, that is, against the claim on our thinking attention that all events and facts make by virtue of their existence."[9] She was not calling for a new intellectualism or for a new concentration on "higher-order skills." She was asking for a way of seeking clarity and authenticity in the face of thoughtlessness, and it seems to me that we might ask much the same thing if we are committed to the release of the imagination and truly wish to open the young to the arts.

Thoughtfulness in this sense is necessary if we are to resist the messages of the media in the fashion Eco suggests, and it is difficult to think of young imaginations being freed without learners finding out how to take a critical and thoughtful approach to the illusory or fabricated "realities" presented to them by the media. To be thoughtful about what we are doing is to be conscious of ourselves struggling to make meanings, to make critical sense of what authoritative others are offering as objectively "real."

I find a metaphor for the reification of experience in the plague as it is confronted in Albert Camus' novel. The pestilence that struck the town of Oran (submerged as it was in habit and "doing business") thrust most of the inhabitants into resignation, isolation, or despair. Gradually revealing itself as inexorable and incurable, the plague froze people in place; it was simply *there*. At first Dr. Rieux fights the plague for the most abstract of reasons: because it is his job. Only later, when the unspeakable tragedies he witnesses make him actually think about what he is doing, does he reconceive his practice and his struggle and talk about not wanting to be complicit with the pestilence. By then he has met Tarrou, who is trying to be a "saint without God" and who has the wit and, yes, the imagination to organize people into sanitary squads to fight the plague and make it the moral concern of all.

Tarrou has the imagination too to find in the plague a metaphor for indifference or distancing or (we might say) thoughtlessness. Everyone carries the microbe, he tells his friend; it is only natural. He means what Hannah Arendt meant—and Dewey and Eco and all the others who resist a lack of concern. He has in mind evasions of complex problems, the embrace of facile formulations of the human predicament, the reliance on conventional solutions—all those factors I would say stand in the way of imaginative thinking and engagement with the arts. "All the rest," says Tarrou, "health, integrity, purity (if you like)—is a product of the human will, of a vigilance that must never falter." He means, of course, that we (and those who are our students) must be given opportunities to choose to be persons of integrity, persons who care.

Tarrou has a deep suspicion of turgid language that obscures the actualities of things, that too often substitutes abstract constructions for concrete particulars. This is one of the modes of the thoughtlessness Arendt was urging us to fight. She, too, wanted to use "plain, clear-cut language." She wanted to urge people, as does Tarrou, to attend to what is around them, "to stop and think." I am trying to affirm that this kind of awareness, this openness to the world, is what allows for the consciousness of alternative possibilities and thus for a willingness to risk encounters with the "weeping women," with Euripides'

Medea, with *Moby Dick*, with Balanchine's (and, yes, the Scripture's) *Prodigal Son*, with Mahler's *Songs of the Earth*.

Another novel that enables its readers to envisage what stands in the way of imagination is Christa Wolf's *Accident: A Day's News*. It moves me to clarify my own response to the technical and the abstract. I turn to it not in order to add to my knowledge or to find some buried truth, but because it makes me see, over the course of time, what I might never have seen in my own lived world.

The power the book holds for me may be because it has to do with the accident at Chernobyl, as experienced by a woman writer, who is also a mother and grandmother. She is preoccupied by her brother's brain surgery, taking place on the same day, and by the consequences of the nuclear accident for her grandchildren and for children around the world. She spends no time wondering about her own response to such a crisis; her preoccupation is with others—those she loves and the unknown ones whom she cannot for a moment forget. It is particularly interesting, within the context of an ethic of care, to contain for a moment within our own experience the thoughts of a frightened young mother, the narrator's daughter, picturing what it means to pour away thousands of liters of milk for fear of poisoning children while "children on the other side of the earth are perishing for lack of those foods."

The narrator wants to change the conversation and asks her daughter to "tell me something else, preferably about the children." Whereupon she hears that "the little one had pranced about the kitchen, a wing nut on his thumb, his hand held high. Me Punch. Me Punch. I was thrilled by the image."[10] Only a moment before, another sequence of pictures had come into her mind and caused her to

admire the way in which everything fits together with a sleepwalker's precision: the desire of most people for a comfortable life, their tendency to believe the speakers on raised platforms and the men in white coats; the addiction to harmony and the fear of contradiction of the many seem to correspond to the arrogance and hunger for power, the dedication to profit, unscrupulous inquisitiveness, and self-infatuation of the few. So what was it that didn't add up in this equation?[11]

This passage seems to me to suggest the kind of questioning and, yes, the kind of picturing that may well be barred by the preoccupation with "world-class achievement" and by the focus on human resources that permeate Goals 2000.

But it does not have to be so. Cognitive adventuring and inquiry are much more likely to be provoked by the narrator's question about "this equation" than by the best of curriculum frameworks or by the most responsible and "authentic" assessment. To set the imagination moving in response to a text such as Wolf's may well be to confront learners with a demand to choose in a fundamental way between a desire for harmony with its easy answers and a commitment to the risky search for alternative possibilities.

Wolf's narrator, almost as if she were one of Picasso's weeping women, looks at the blue sky and, quoting some nameless source, says, "Aghast, the mothers search the sky for the inventions of learned men."[12] Like others to whom I have referred, she begins pondering the language and the difficulty of breaking through such terms as "half-life," "cesium," and "cloud" when "polluted rain" is so much more direct. Once again, the experience of the literary work may help us to feel the need to break through the mystification of technology and the language to which it has given rise.

The narrator feels the need to battle the disengagement that often goes with knowing and speaking. When she ponders the motives of those who thought up the procedures for the "peaceful utilization of nuclear energy," she recalls a youthful protest against a power plant and the rebukes and reprimands directed at the protesters for their skepticism with regard to a scientific utopia.

And then she lists the activities that the men of science and technology presumably do not pursue and would probably consider a waste of time if they were forced to:

> Changing a baby's diapers. Cooking, shopping with a child on one's arm or in the baby carriage. Doing the laundry, hanging it up to dry, taking it down, folding it, ironing it, darning it. Sweeping the floor, mopping it, polishing it, vacuuming it. Dusting. Sewing. Knitting. Crocheting. Embroidering. Doing the dishes. Doing the dishes. Taking care of a sick child. Thinking up stories to tell. Singing songs. And how many of these activities do I myself consider a waste of time?[13]

Reading this passage and posing a new set of questions, we cannot but consider the role of such concrete images in classroom conversation and in our efforts to awaken persons to talk about what ought to be. The narrator believes that the "expanding monstrous technological creation" may be a substitute for life for many people. She is quite aware of the benevolent aspects of technology: her brother, after all, is having advanced neurosurgery (which he does survive). But she is thinking, as we might well do in the schools, about the consequences of technological expansion for the ones we love. Her thinking may remind us of how important it is to keep alive images of "everything we love." I want to believe that by doing so we may be able to create classroom atmospheres that once again encourage individuals to have hope.

This brings me back to my argument for the arts, so unconscionably neglected in the talk swirling around Goals 2000. It is important to make the point that the events that make up aesthetic experiences are events that occur within and by means of the transactions with our environment that situate us in time and space. Some say that participatory encounters with paintings, dances, stories, and the rest enable us to recapture a lost spontaneity. By breaking through the frames of presuppositions and conventions, we may be enabled to reconnect ourselves with the processes of becoming who we are. By reflecting on our life histories, we may be able to gain some perspective on the men in white coats, even on our own desires to withdraw from complexity and to embrace a predictable harmony. By becoming aware of ourselves as questioners, as makers of meaning, as persons engaged in constructing and reconstructing realities with those around us, we may be able to communicate to students the notion that reality depends on perspective, that its construction is never complete, and that there is always more. I am reminded of Paul Cézanne's several renderings of Mont St. Victoire and of his way of suggesting that it must be viewed from several angles if its reality is to be apprehended.

Cézanne made much of the insertion of the body into his landscapes, and that itself may suggest a dimension of experience with which to ground our thinking and the thinking of those we teach. There are some who suggest that, of all the arts, dance confronts most directly the question of what it means to be human. Arnold Berleant writes that

> in establishing a human realm through movement, the dancer, with the participating audience, engages in the basic act out of which arise both all experience and our human constructions of the world. . . . [That basic act] stands as the direct denial of that most pernicious of all dualisms, the division of body and consciousness. In dance, thought is primed at the point of action. This is not the reflection of the contemplative mind but rather intellect poised in the body, not the deliberate consideration of alternative courses but thought in process, intimately responding to and guiding the actively engaged body.[14]

The focus is on process and practice; the skill in the making is embodied in the object made. In addition, dance provides occasions for the emergence of the integrated self. Surely, this ought to be taken into account in our peculiarly technical and academic time.

Some of what Berleant says relates as well to painting, if painting is viewed as an orientation in time and space of the physical body—of both perceiver and creator. If we take a participatory stance, we may enter a landscape or a room or an open street. Different modes of perception are asked of us, of course, by different artists, but that ought to mean a widening of sensitivity with regard to perceived form, color, and space. Jean-Paul Sartre, writing about painting, made a point that is significant for anyone concerned about the role of art and the awakening of imagination:

> The work is never limited to the painted, sculpted or narrated object. Just as one perceives things only against the background of the world, so the objects represented by art appear against the background of the universe. . . . [T]he creative act aims at a total renewal of the world. Each painting, each book, is a recovery of the totality of being. Each of them presents this totality to the freedom of the spectator. For this is quite the final goal of art: to recover this world by giving it to be seen as it is, but as if it had its source in human freedom.[15]

In this passage Sartre suggests the many ways in which classroom encounters with the arts can move the young to imagine, to extend, and to renew. And surely nothing can be more important than finding the source of learning not in extrinsic demands, but in human freedom.

All of this is directly related to developing what is today described as the active learner, here conceived as one awakened to pursue meaning. There are, of course, two contradictory tendencies in education today: one has to do with shaping malleable young people to serve the needs of technology in a postindustrial society; the other has to do with educating young people to grow and to become different, to find their individual voices, and to participate in a community in the making. Encounters with the arts nurture and sometimes provoke the growth of individuals who reach out to one another as they seek clearings in their experience and try to live more ardently in the world. If the significance of the arts for growth, inventiveness, and problem solving is recognized at last, a desperate stasis may be overcome, and people may come to recognize the need for new raids on what T. S. Eliot called the "inarticulate."

I choose to end this extended reflection on art and imagination with some words from "Elegy in Joy," by Muriel Rukeyser:

> Out of our life the living eyes
> See peace in our own image made,
> Able to give only what we can give:
> Bearing two days like midnight. "Live,"
> The moment offers: the night requires
> Promise effort love and praise.
>
> Now there are no maps and no magicians.
> No prophets but the young prophet, the sense
>   of the world.
> The gift of our time, the world to be discovered.
> All the continents giving off their several lights,
> the one sea, and the air. And all things glow.[16]

These words offer life; they offer hope; they offer the prospect of discovery; they offer light. By resisting the tyranny of the technical, we may yet make them our pedagogic creed.

ENDNOTES

1. Judi Freeman. *Picasso and the Weeping Women* (Los Angeles: Los Angeles Museum of Art, 1994).

2. Michel Leiris. "Faire-part," in E. C. Oppler, ed., *Picasso's Guernica* (New York: Norton, 1988), p. 201.

3. Toni Morrison. *The Bluest Eye* (New York: Washington Square Press, 1970), p. 19.

4. Richard Kearney. *The Wake of Imagination* (Minneapolis: University of Minnesota Press, 1988), p. 382.

5. Mary Warnock. *Imagination* (Berkeley: University of California Press, 1978), p. 202.

6. Hannah Arendt. *The Human Condition* (Chicago: University of Chicago Press, 1958), p. 5.

7. John Dewey. *The Public and Its Problems* (Athens, Ohio: Swallow Press, 1954), p. 170.

8. Ibid., p. 168.

9. Hannah Arendt. *Thinking: Vol. II, The Life of the Mind* (New York: Harcourt Brace Jovanovich, 1978), p. 4.

10. Christa Wolf. *Accident: A Day's News* (New York: Farrar, Straus & Giroux, 1989), p. 17.

11. Ibid.

12. Ibid., p. 27.

13. Ibid., p. 31.

14. Arnold Berleant. *Art and Engagement* (Philadelphia: Temple University Press, 1991), p. 167.

15. Jean-Paul Sartre. *Literature and Existentialism* (New York: Citadel Press, 1949), p. 57.

16. Muriel Rukeyser. "Tenth Elegy: An Elegy in Joy." in idem, *Out in Silence: Selected Poems* (Evanston, Ill.: TriQuarterly Books, 1992), p. 104.

Maxine Greene is Professor of Philosophy and Education Emerita at Teachers College, Columbia University, New York.

QUESTIONS FOR REFLECTION

1. What specific evidence suggests that one tendency of education today involves "shaping malleable young people to serve the needs of technology in a postindustrial society"?

2. What is the "mystification" of technology?

3. Do you agree with Greene when she says that "the inability to control what is discovered as meaningful makes many traditional educators uneasy"? What might account for their uneasiness?

4. In regard to the curriculum with which you are most familiar, what role might the arts and imagination play?

Cognition and Representation: A Way to Pursue the American Dream?

ELLIOT W. EISNER

ABSTRACT: "Forms of representation," or symbol systems, play an important part in the development of the mind. However, school curricula do not reflect the full range of ways that humans have thought, felt, and imagined. The "basic skills" represent but a portion of what the mind can do and know. An examination of culture provides the richest repository of what humans are capable of thinking and creating, and the inclusion of these multiple forms of representation in the school curriculum is one way to pursue "the American dream."

In some ways it's an old idea. I'm talking about the idea that the forms we use to represent what we think—literal language, visual images, number, poetry—have an impact on how we think and what we can think about. If different forms of representation performed identical cognitive functions, then there would be no need to dance, compute, or draw. Why would we want to write poetry, history, fiction, drama, or factual accounts of what we have experienced? Yet this apparently obvious idea has not been a prominent consideration in setting curricular agendas in America's schools or in shaping education policy. [This article is] intended to illustrate the ways in which *forms of representation,* or what are sometimes called "symbol systems," function in our mental lives and to explore their contributions to the development of mind.

Among the various aims we consider important in education, two are especially so. We would like our children to be well informed—that is, to understand ideas that are important, useful, beautiful, and powerful. And we also want them to have the appetite and ability to think analytically and critically, to be able to speculate and imagine, to see connections among ideas, and to be able to use what they know to enhance their own lives and to contribute to their culture.

Neither of these two goals is likely to be achieved if schools are inattentive to the variety of ways that humans have represented what they have thought, felt, and imagined. Nor will these goals be achieved if we fail to appreciate culture's role in making these processes of representation possible. After all, human products owe their existence not only to the achievements of individual minds, but to the forms of representation available in the culture—forms that enable us to make our ideas and feelings public. Put another way, we can't have a musical idea without thinking and representing what we have thought musically. We can't have a mathematical idea without mathematics. And neither is possible without a form of representation that affords our ideas the possibility of life. It is the school as a representative of culture that provides access to those forms. It is the school that fosters their skillful use among the young.

Minds, then, in a curious but profound way, are made. Their shape and capacities are influenced by what we are given an opportunity to learn when young. Given this conception of the genesis of mind, the curriculum is a mind-altering device. Decisions that policy makers and educators make about what will be accessible to children help shape the kinds of minds they will come to own. The character of their minds, in turn, will help shape the culture in which we all live.

Brains, in contrast to minds, are biological—they are given by nature. Minds are cultural—

From *Phi Delta Kappan* 78, no. 5 (January 1997): 349–353. © 1997, Phi Delta Kappa. Used by permission of the author and publisher.

they are the result of experience. And the kinds of experience the child secures in school are significantly influenced by the decisions we make about what to teach. As I indicated, as important a consideration as this might be, reflection on the role that forms of representation play in the creation of mind has been all but neglected in framing curricular policy. We need to remedy that.

Ours is a school system that gives pride of place to the skillful use of language and number, the venerable three Rs. No one can cogently argue that the three R's are unimportant. Clearly, competency in their use is of primary importance. But even high levels of skill in their use are not enough to develop the variety of mental capacities that children possess. The three R's tap too little of what the mind can do. Where do we learn what the mind can do? We learn about its potentialities not only from psychologists who study the mind but also by looking at the culture—all cultures—because culture displays the forms humans have used to give expression to what they have imagined, understood, and felt. Each product humans create embodies the forms of thinking that led to its realization, each one of them provides testimony to what humans can achieve, each one represents a silent but eloquent statement concerning the scope and possibilities of the human mind, and each one comes into being through the use of one or more forms of representation.

If culture is, as I have suggested, the most telling repository of human capacity, then I suggest that we inspect the culture to discover what might be called "cognitive artifacts" (the products of thought), that we use these products of thought to understand what we can of the forms of thinking that led to each, and that we try in the process to grasp the kind of meaning that each provides. I am saying that it is the sciences and the arts—the architecture, the music, the mathematics, and the literature found in culture—that give us the clearest sense of what humans are capable of thinking about, the heights their thinking can reach, and the kinds of meaning they are capable of creating. Understanding these achievements

can, and in my view ought to, provide a basis for making decisions about what we teach.

Let's turn now to some of the core ideas [contained in this view]. . . .

First the form of representation we use to represent what we think influences both the processes and products of thinking. Imagine a white horse. Imagine a white horse standing in the corner of a green field and slowly beginning to move. As the horse moves, it gradually turns from white to a brilliant blue. Imagine, as it begins to move from walk to trot, from trot to gallop, large gold wings emerging from its back. Now imagine those wings moving as the blue horse rises slowly into the sky above, getting smaller and smaller and slowly disappearing into a large, soft white cloud.

Now imagine creating a poem that communicates to a reader your experience with that image, or a painting that depicts it, or a literal description that conveys it, or a set of numbers that represents it—a set of numbers? A problem emerges. Poetry, yes; painting, yes; a literal description, yes. But numbers—in this case, numbers won't do.

This example is not an argument against the representational capacities of numbers; it is an effort to demonstrate graphically that you can't represent *everything* with *anything*. What you choose to use to think with affects what you can think about. Furthermore, the ability to represent experience within the limits and possibilities of a form of representation requires that you think *within* the material with which you work. When such thinking is effective, you convert that material into a medium, something that mediates. Mediates what? Mediates your thinking. The choice of a form of representation and the selection of the material to be used both impose constraints and offer possibilities. When the material is employed skillfully, meanings are made that become candidates for interpretation by the "reader."

Reading a form that carries meaning is by no means limited to those who are spectators. Reading the form is required of the maker, of the individual who attempts to use a form of representation to say something. The maker must be able to read the work as it unfolds and, through such a reading, be able to make adjustments. It is in this monitoring process that attention to nuance becomes especially important. Through such attention, when the necessary skills are available, the process is modified to yield a product worth making. In short, the processes of thinking are engaged in the process of making, and the process of making requires the ability to see what is going on in order to make it better. When we modify what we have made as a result of such inspection, we call it "editing." The editing process is employed in all forms of representation.

What is particularly important in this process is that the "standards" the maker uses to make judgments about his or her work are often personal or idiosyncratic—that is, the standards for the work, although influenced by the culture, are often sufficiently open, especially in the arts, to allow the maker to depend on an internal locus of evaluation. Thus thinking is promoted by the character of the task.

Second, different forms of representation develop different cognitive skills. Think about what is required to write a poem or to paint a watercolor or to choreograph a dance. What must someone be able to do? What must a child learn to think about in order to become proficient? First, an idea must be framed that at the very least functions as a launching pad for one's work. Second, the idea itself must be transformed within the terms of the medium. Think again about the horse. To render the experience in dance, what we might call choreographic thinking is required. To render it in paint, another form of thinking is involved. Dance requires movement; painting, the illusion of movement. While both require attention to composition, the terms or conditions of composing in each form are quite different. The choreographer composes through movement framed by a proscenium arch; the artist composes on canvas, a static surface intended to receive a physically static image. The ability to cope successfully with the demands of the former provides no assurance that one will be successful with the demands of the latter. Although both forms of representation are visual, each one is mediated through its own

materials, and each material imposes its own demands. And because the demands of different forms of representation differ, different cognitive skills are developed to cope with them.

Let me offer a specific example of one of those demands in order to better appreciate the forms of cognition it engenders. I turn to watercolor painting. Watercolor painting is an unforgiving process. By this I mean that watercolor requires a directness and confidence in execution that helps one avoid costly mistakes. Unlike oil painting, in which changes can be made by overpainting a section of a canvas, watercolor painting does not accommodate overpainting as a happy solution for correcting unhappy decisions; colors grow muddy, and spontaneity is lost. Thus the person using watercolors must work directly and often quickly. This means becoming sensitive to a wide array of qualities, including the weight of the tip of the brush, for its weight when charged with color tells one about the amount of paint it holds. This is important to know because the amount of paint on the brush's tip will affect the kind of image that will flow from it. But that is not all. The kind of image that flows from the brush is also influenced by the wetness of the paper that receives it. The artist or student has to take that interaction into account as well.

In these assessments of the conditions of one's work, there is no rule to follow and no metric with which to measure weight or to determine wetness. The artist knows through sight and through feel. A unified body and mind must be fully engaged with the material at hand to have a basis for making such judgments.

I have described only a minuscule part of the process of watercolor painting; I have not mentioned any of the formal or expressive considerations that are at the heart of making an art form. These considerations present particularly complex cognitive demands. To regard what is euphemistically called "artwork" as "noncognitive" is to reveal a massive misunderstanding of what such work requires. The task of the teacher is to create the conditions through which the student's thinking about these matters can become more complex, subtler, more effective. In a word, more intelligent.

Third, the selection of a form of representation influences not only what you are able to represent but also what you are able to see. Ernst Gombrich, the noted art historian, has been quoted as saying, "Artists don't paint what they can see; they see what they can paint." Gombrich's point, of course, is that people look for what they know how to find, and what they know how to find is often related to what they know how to do. When what one knows is how to measure, one looks for what one can measure. If the only tool you have is a hammer, you treat almost everything as if it were a nail. Tools are not neutral. Forms of representation are tools, and they are not neutral. If one sees a city in terms of the poetry one wants to write about it, one seeks in one's travels through the city what has poetic potential. If one searches the city for images to record on black-and-white film, one seeks images in light and dark. Put color film in the camera, and another set of criteria emerge for searching the city's landscape. When we emphasize the use of particular forms of representation, we influence what counts as relevant.

Fourth, forms of representation can be combined to enrich the array of resources students can respond to. I alluded earlier to the fact that our schools are deeply immersed in teaching language and number. Working with each one separately, as is often done in school, has the benefit of providing focused attention to a specific task. There is virtue in such focus when trying to learn something complex. At the same time, displays that make available to students ideas couched in visual, verbal, numerical, and auditory forms increase the resources available to the student for making meaning. When resources are rich, the number of avenues for learning expands.

The kind of resource-rich environment I am talking about is much closer to the conditions of life outside of schools than those inside of them. We live our daily lives in an abundant and redundant multimedia environment in which opportunities for iterative forms of learning are common.

This means that if we have difficulty learning something one way, there are often other routes that can be taken. Observing preschoolers explore their surroundings through all their sensory modalities is evidence enough of the variety of ways through which they come to understand the world. Preschool teachers and kindergarten teachers know this, and the environments they create for their students reflect their understanding of the multiple ways through which children learn. These environments also reflect their belief in the importance of providing a wide variety of forms through which their students might represent what they wish to "say."

It is unfortunate that the resource-rich environments that characterize good preschools and kindergartens are typically neutralized as young children move up into the grades. We would do better, I believe, to push the best features of kindergarten upward into the grades than to push the grades into the kindergarten. In many ways the good kindergarten displays features that could serve as a model for the rest of schooling. Kindergarten teachers can create such environments because—at least until recently—kindergarten has not been regarded as "serious" education. As a result, kindergarten teachers are able to utilize the central role sensory experience plays in learning and are free to afford their students many opportunities to find and use forms of representation that stimulate, practice, and develop different cognitive skills.

For older children, imagine programs in science, history, and the arts coming together to provide students with a complete picture of scientific, historical, and artistic content. For example, the early years of the 20th century brought Einstein's special theory of relativity, innovations in visual art and music (Picasso's cubism and Stravinsky's "Firebird"), and Freud's exploration of the unconscious. What would it mean to students to be given the opportunity to explore the relationships between these developments by turning directly to the representational forms in which they were realized—listening to Stravinsky, seeing Picasso's cubism, reading Einstein's comments on his own thought processes and Freud's descriptions of his cases? A curriculum unit designed to introduce students to such material, to ground it in time and in representational form, would multiply the number and types of "cognitive hooks" or forms of scaffolding that students could use to advance their own learning. The enrichment of the environment by the provision of a variety of forms of representation would also increase the array of cognitive abilities that students could develop. The curriculum would become not only a mind-altering device but a mind-expanding one as well.

There is another issue that needs to be recognized. This one pertains to matters of educational equity. The forms of representation that an institution emphasizes influence who succeeds and who does not. At issue is the fit between the aptitudes of the students and the possibilities presented by the forms they are to use. When the primary game in town is the denotative use of language and the calculation of number, those whose aptitudes or whose out-of-school experience utilize such skills are likely to be successful; there is a congruence between what they bring to the school and what the school requires of them. But when the school's curricular agenda is diverse, diverse aptitudes and experience can come into play. Educational equity is provided not merely by opening the doors of the school to the child but by providing opportunities to the child to succeed once he or she arrives. The provision of the resource-rich environment I have described is an extremely important way in which genuine educational equity can be achieved.

This way of thinking about the relationship between the development of cognition and the forms of representation through which it is realized has implications for how we conceive of a successful school. In the conception implicit in what I have said, the mission of the school is decidedly not to bring everyone to the same place but rather to increase the variance in performance among students while escalating the mean for all. The reason I believe that this is an important aim for schools in a democracy is that the cultivation of cognitive diversity is a way of creating citizens who are better able to contribute

uniquely to the commonweal. Look at it this way. If by some magic everyone were transformed into a brilliant violinist, the convocation of all the brilliance among all the violinists on the planet would not make possible the kind of music that equal competencies would achieve if they were distributed among all the instruments. Sometimes you need woodwinds, or percussion, or brass. Schools that cultivate the differences among us while escalating the mean for performance in each of the forms of representation provide for the richness of the full orchestra. We do better as a culture when we are not all violinists—even brilliant ones.

Fifth, each form of representation can be used in different ways, and each way calls on the use of different skills and forms of thinking. We tend to talk about forms of representation as if each of them called on a single set of specific cognitive skills. At a general level they do. Dance, in contrast to computation or the writing of poetry, makes use of the body in motion; thinking must be realized within the capacities of a moving body. But such parameters are general parameters, and within movement itself there are a wide array of options: *how* one chooses to dance, *what* one wishes to express, and the *genre* within which one works also impose requirements that are specific to the particular task to be performed. In the field of painting, the pathos expressed in the drawings of Käthe Kollwitz depend on a marriage between mind, emotion, and body that made the power of her images possible; in a sense, her aesthetic center is located in her guts. Her work is not what one might call cerebral, though surely there are ideas in it. Other artists—for example, the abstractionist Josef Albers—were concerned with color relationships. Albers' paintings deal with what might be called visual vibration. His center is located in a different part of the body from Kollwitz's. And when we look at the work of Salvador Dali, other sources become dominant—these in the meanderings of the unconscious. My point here is that, as Richard Snow points out in his article in this section, many forms of thinking are at play in any single form of representation, even though one may dominate.

What does the foregoing mean for American education? Do the ideas we have examined have any implications for what we do in schools or for the policies we create to guide them? Do they have relevance for how we think about the meaning of education? I think they do, and I believe their implications pertain to matters of *process, content, equity,* and *culture.* I address each briefly here.

By *process* I refer back to where we began, namely with the idea that mind is a cultural achievement, that the form it takes is influenced to a significant degree by the kinds of experience an individual is afforded in the course of a lifetime. In school a major locus of experience for children and adolescents is the curriculum. It performs a major function in shaping those experiences. Decisions regarding which forms of representation will be emphasized, which will be marginalized, and which will be absent constitute decisions about the kinds of processes that will be stimulated, developed, and refined. In short, in schools we influence the forms of cognitive competency that students will develop by providing opportunities for development to occur. In education we are in the construction business.

Process is one side of the coin; *content* is the other. Competency in the use of a form of representation provides access to particular forms of experience and therefore to ways of understanding. In order to be read, a poem, an equation, a painting, a dance, a novel, or a contract each requires a distinctive form of literacy, when literacy means, as I intend it to mean, a way of conveying meaning through and recovering meaning from the form of representation in which it appears. Given this conception of literacy, a conception far broader than its commonly held root "logos" (referring to the word), we ought to be interested in developing multiple forms of literacy. Why? Because each form of literacy has the capacity to provide unique forms of meaning, and it is in the pursuit of meaning that much of the good life is lived. Schools serve children best when their programs do not narrow the kinds of meanings children know how to pursue and capture.

Equity is a third notion that can summarize the contributions that attention to multiple forms of representation can help achieve. As already noted, the equity question is related to aptitude differences among students and to the opportunities they will find in schools to capitalize on their strengths. Equity of opportunity does not reside, as some people seem to believe, in a common program for all. It resides in school programs that make it possible for students to follow their bliss, to pursue their interests, to realize and develop what they are good at. Of course there will need to be limits set with respect to what is possible—a school cannot do everything. Nevertheless, I am talking about ambitions, desiderata, principles. We ought to try to grasp what may be beyond our reach—or what's a heaven for?

Finally, we come to *culture.* What kind of society do we want? What kind of life do we want to be able to lead? What kind of place will America become? The quality of life that America as a culture will make possible will be a function not only of a diversity of traditions and values but also of the varying natures of the contributions that our individual differences allow. In totalitarian societies, Herbert Read reminds us, children are to be shaped by schools to fit an image defined by the state.[1] In democratic societies and in those societies seeking to create a democratic way of life, children are helped to realize their distinctive talents and, through such realization, to be in a position to contribute to the culture as a whole. The presence of multiple forms of representation in the school is one way to try to achieve that democratic ambition.

Ultimately we need to build a culture reflecting the two senses in which the term can be used. One sense of *culture* is biological; the other, anthropological. In the biological sense, a culture is a medium for growing things. In the anthropological sense, a culture is a shared way of life. Our schools should embody both. They should be media for growing things, and what they should grow are minds. They should try to achieve that noble ambition through the shared way of life they make possible, a way of life that recognizes both the differences and the commonalities among us. Understanding the relationship between cognition and representation and its relevance for policy and practice in our schools is one place to begin—and one way to pursue the American dream.[1]

Elliot W. Eisner is Professor of Education and Art at Stanford University.

ENDNOTE

1. Herbert Read, *Education Through Art* (London: Pantheon, 1944).

QUESTIONS FOR REFLECTION

1. What are the implications of Eisner's views for curriculum planning?
2. In what respects is the curriculum a "mind-altering device"?
3. What does Eisner mean when he says that "We would do better . . . to push the best features of kindergarten upward into the grades than to push the grades into the kindergarten"? What are some of the "best features" of kindergartens?
4. What is the relationship between forms of representation and educational equity?

Multicultural Education and Curriculum Transformation

JAMES A. BANKS

ABSTRACT: Mainstream academic knowledge, which represents the established canon in schools, colleges, and universities, reflects cultural assumptions, frames of reference, and perspectives that can legitimize institutionalized inequity. Transformative approaches to academic knowledge, however, recognize that knowledge is related to the cultural experiences of individuals and groups and, by challenging antiegalitarian research, help to maintain democratic values in American society.

The racial crisis in America, the large number of immigrants that are entering the nation each year, the widening gap between the rich and the poor, and the changing characteristics of the nation's student population make it imperative that schools be reformed in ways that will help students and teachers to re-envision, rethink, and reconceptualize America. Fundamental changes in our educational system are essential so that we can, in the words of Rodney King, "all get along." The nation's student population is changing dramatically. By 2020, nearly half (about 48%) of the nation's students will be students of color. Today, about 31% of the youth in the United States under 18 are of color and about one out of every five students is living below the official poverty level (U.S. Bureau of the Census, 1993).

From the *Journal of Negro Education* 64, no. 4 (Fall 1995): 390–399. © 1995, Howard University Press. Used by permission of the author and publisher.

Multicultural education, a school reform movement that arose out of the civil rights movement of the 1960s and 1970s, if implemented in thoughtful, creative, and effective ways, has the potential to transform schools and other educational institutions in ways that will enable them to prepare students to live and function effectively in the coming century (Banks & Banks, 1995a). I will describe the major goals and dimensions of multicultural education, discuss knowledge construction and curriculum transformation, and describe how transformative academic knowledge can be used to re-invent and re-imagine the curriculum in the nation's schools, colleges, and universities.

MULTICULTURAL EDUCATION AND SCHOOL REFORM

There is a great deal of confusion about multicultural education in both the popular mind and among teachers and other educational practitioners. Much of this confusion is created by critics of multicultural education such as Schlesinger (1991), D'Souza (1995), and Sacks and Theil (1995). The critics create confusion by stating and repeating claims about multiculturalism and diversity that are documented with isolated incidents, anecdotes, and examples of poorly conceptualized and implemented educational practices. The research and theory that have been developed by the leading theorists in multicultural education are rarely cited by the field's critics (Sleeter, 1995).

The critics of multicultural education often direct their criticism toward what they call multiculturalism. This term is rarely used by theorists and researchers in multicultural education. Consequently, it is important to distinguish what the critics call multiculturalism from what multicultural education theorists call multicultural education. Multiculturalism is a term often used by the critics of diversity to describe a set of educational practices they oppose. They use this term to describe educational practices they consider antithetical to the Western canon, to the democratic tradition, and to a universalized and free society.

Multiculturalism and multicultural education have different meanings. I have conceptualized multicultural education in a way that consists of three major components: an idea or concept, an educational reform movement, and a process (Banks, 1993a). As an idea or concept, multicultural education maintains that all students should have equal opportunities to learn regardless of the racial, ethnic, social-class, or gender group to which they belong. Additionally, multicultural education describes ways in which some students are denied equal educational opportunities because of their racial, ethnic, social-class, or gender characteristics (Lee & Slaughter-Defoe, 1995; Nieto, 1995). Multicultural education is an educational reform movement that tries to reform schools in ways that will give all students an equal opportunity to learn. It describes teaching strategies that empower all students and give them voice.

Multicultural education is a continuing process. One of its major goals is to create within schools and society the democratic ideals that Myrdal (1944) called "American Creed" values—values such as justice, equality, and freedom. These ideals are stated in the nation's founding documents—in the Declaration of Independence, the Constitution, and the Bill of Rights. They can never be totally achieved, but citizens within a democratic society must constantly work toward attaining them. Yet, when we approach the realization of these ideals for particular groups, other groups become victimized by racism, sexism, and discrimination. Consequently, within a democratic, pluralistic society, multicultural education is a continuing process that never ends.

THE DIMENSIONS OF MULTICULTURAL EDUCATION

To effectively conceptualize and implement multicultural education curricula, programs, and practices, it is necessary not only to define the concept in general terms but to describe it programmatically. To facilitate this process, I have developed a typology called the dimensions of multicultural education (Banks, 1993b, 1995a). This dimensions typology can help practitioners identify and formulate reforms that implement multicultural education in thoughtful, creative, and effective ways. It is also designed to help theorists and researchers delineate the scope of the field and identify related research and theories. The dimensions typology is an ideal-type construct in the Weberian sense. The dimensions are highly interrelated, and the boundaries between and within them overlap. However, they are conceptually distinct.

A description of the conceptual scope of each dimension facilitates conceptual clarity and the development of sound educational practices. As Gay (1995) has pointed out, there is a wide gap between theory, research, and practice in multicultural education. The practices within schools that violate sound principles in multicultural education theory and research are cannon fodder for the field's critics, who often cite questionable practices that masquerade as multicultural education to support the validity of their claims. Although there is a significant gap between theory and practice within all fields in education, the consequences of such a gap are especially serious within new fields that are marginal and trying to obtain legitimacy within schools, colleges, and universities. Thus, the dimensions of multicultural education can serve as benchmark criteria for conceptualizing, developing, and assessing theory, research, and practice.

In my research, I have identified five dimensions of multicultural education (Banks, 1995a). They are: (a) content integration, (b) the knowledge construction process, (c) prejudice reduction, (d) an equity pedagogy, and an (e) empowering school culture and social structure. I will briefly describe each of these dimensions.

Content integration describes the ways in which teachers use examples and content from a variety of cultures and groups to illustrate key concepts, principles, generalizations, and theories in their subject area or discipline. The knowledge construction process consists of the methods, activities, and questions used by teachers to help students understand, investigate, and determine how implicit cultural assumptions, frames of reference, perspectives, and biases within a discipline influence the ways in which knowledge is constructed. When the knowledge construction process is implemented, teachers help students to understand how knowledge is created and how it is influenced by the racial, ethnic, and social-class positions of individuals and groups (Code, 1991; Collins, 1990).

The prejudice reduction dimension of multicultural education relates to the characteristics of students' racial attitudes and strategies that teachers can use to help them develop more democratic values and attitudes. Since the late 1930s, researchers have been studying racial awareness, racial identification, and racial preference in young children (Clark & Clark, 1939; Cross, 1991; Spencer, 1982). This research is too vast and complex to summarize here; however, studies indicate, for example, that both children of color and White children develop a "White bias" by the time they enter kindergarten (Phinney & Rotheram, 1987; Spencer, 1982). This research suggests that teachers in all subject areas need to take action to help students develop more democratic racial attitudes and values. It also suggests that interventions work best when children are young. As children grow older, it becomes increasingly difficult to modify their racial attitudes and beliefs (Banks, 1995b).

An equity pedagogy exists when teachers modify their teaching in ways that will facilitate the academic achievement of students from diverse racial, ethnic, cultural, and gender groups (Banks & Banks, 1995b). A number of researchers such as Au (1980), Boykin (1982), Delpit (1995), Kleinfeld (1975), Ladson–Billings (1995), and Shade and New (1993) have described culturally sensitive (sometimes called culturally congruent) teaching strategies whose purpose is to enhance the academic achievement of students from diverse cultural and ethnic groups and the characteristics of effective teachers of these students. This research indicates that the academic achievement of students of color and low-income students can be increased when teaching strategies and activities build upon the cultural and linguistic strengths of students, and when teachers have cultural competency in the cultures of their students. Kleinfeld, for example, found that teachers who were "warm demanders" were the most effective teachers of Indian and Eskimo youths. Other researchers maintain that teachers also need to have high academic expectations for these students, to explicitly teach them the rules of power governing classroom interactions, and to create equal-status situations in the classroom (Cohen & Lotan, 1995).

An empowering school culture and social structure conceptualizes the school as a complex social system, whereas the other dimensions deal with particular aspects of a school or educational setting. This dimension conceptualizes the school as a social system that is larger than any of its constituent parts such as the curriculum, teaching materials, and teacher attitudes and perceptions. The systemic view of schools requires that in order to effectively reform schools, the entire system must be restructured, not just some of its parts. Although reform may begin with any one of the parts of a system (such as with the curriculum or with staff development), the other parts of the system (such as textbooks and the assessment program) must also be restructured in order to effectively implement school reform related to diversity.

A systemic view of educational reform is especially important when reform is related to issues as complex and emotionally laden as race, class, and gender. Educational practitioners—because of the intractable challenges they face, their scarce resources, and the perceived limited time they have to solve problems due to the high expectations of an impatient public—often want quick fixes to complex educational problems. The search for quick solutions to problems related to race and ethnicity partially explains some of the practices, often called multicultural education, that violate theory and research. These in-

clude marginalizing content about ethnic groups by limiting them to specific days and holidays such as Black History month and Cinco de Mayo. A systemic view of educational reform is essential for the implementation of thoughtful, creative, and meaningful educational reform.

KNOWLEDGE CONSTRUCTION AND CURRICULUM TRANSFORMATION

I will focus on only one of the dimensions of multicultural education: knowledge construction. In my latest book, *Multicultural Education, Transformative Knowledge, and Action* (1996), I describe a typology of knowledge that consists of five types: (a) personal/cultural, (b) popular, (c) mainstream academic, (d) transformative academic, and (e) school knowledge. I will discuss only two of these knowledge types: mainstream academic and transformative academic.

Mainstream Academic Knowledge

Mainstream academic knowledge consists of the concepts, paradigms, theories, and explanations that constitute traditional and established knowledge in the behavioral and social sciences. An important tenet within mainstream academic knowledge is that there is a set of objective truths that can be verified through rigorous and objective research procedures that are uninfluenced by human interests, values, and perspectives. Most of the knowledge that constitutes the established canon in the nation's schools, colleges, and universities is mainstream academic knowledge.

The traditional conceptualization of the settlement of the West is a powerful example of the way in which mainstream academic knowledge has shaped the paradigms, canons, and perspectives that become institutional within the college, university, and school curriculum. In an influential paper presented at a meeting of the American Historical Association in 1893, Frederick Jackson Turner (1894/1989) argued that the frontier, which he regarded as a sparsely populated wilderness and as lacking in civilization, was the main source of American democracy and freedom. Although Turner's thesis is now being criticized by revisionist historians, his paper established a conception of the West that has been highly influential in American scholarship, popular culture, and school books. His ideas, however, are closely related to other European conceptions of the Americas, of "the other" (Todorov, 1982), and of the native peoples who lived in the land that the European conceptualized as "the West." Turner's paradigm, and the interpretations that derive from it, largely ignore the large number of indigenous peoples who were living in the Americas when the Europeans arrived (Thornton [1995] estimates seven million). It also fails to acknowledge the rich cultures and civilizations that existed in the Americas, and the fact that the freedom the Europeans found in the West meant destruction and genocide for the various groups of Native Americans. By the beginning of the 20th century, most American Indian groups had been defeated by U.S. military force (Hyatt & Nettleford, 1995). Their collective will, however, was not broken, as evidenced by the renewed quest for Indian rights that emerged during the civil rights movement of the 1960s and 1970s.

Today, the West paradigm in American history and culture is powerful, cogent, and deeply entrenched in the curriculum of the nation's institutions of learning. As such, it often prevents students at all levels of education from gaining a sophisticated, complex, and compassionate understanding of American history, society, and culture. The West paradigm must therefore be seriously examined and deconstructed in order for students to acquire such an understanding. Students must be taught, for example, that the concept of the West is a Eurocentric idea, and they must be helped to understand how different groups in American society conceptualized and viewed the West differently.

For example, the Mexicans who became a part of the United States after the Treaty of Guadalupe Hidalgo in 1848 did not view or conceptualize the Southwest as the West. Rather, they viewed the territory that Mexico lost to the United States after the war as Mexico's "North." The Indian groups living in the western territories did not view their homelands as the West but as the center of the universe. To the various immigrants to the U.S. from Asia such as those from Japan and China, the land to which they immigrated was "the East" or the "land of the Golden Mountain." By helping students view Eurocentric concepts such as the West, "the Discovery of America," and "the New World" from different perspectives and points of view, we can increase their ability to conceptualize, to determine the implicit perspectives embedded in curriculum materials, and to become more thoughtful and reflective citizens.

Transformative Academic Knowledge

Teachers can help students acquire new perspectives on the development of American history and society by reforming the curriculum with the use of paradigms, perspectives, and points of view from transformative academic knowledge. Transformative academic knowledge consists of the concepts, paradigms, themes, and explanations that challenge mainstream academic knowledge and that expand the historical and literary canon (Banks, 1996). It thus challenges some of the key assumptions that mainstream scholars make about the nature of knowledge as well as some of their major paradigms, findings, theories, and interpretations. While mainstream academic scholars claim that their findings and interpretations are universalistic and unrelated to human interests, transformative scholars view knowledge as related to the cultural experiences of individuals and groups (Collins, 1990). Transformative scholars also believe that a major goal of knowledge is to improve society (Clark, 1965).

TRANSFORMATIVE SCHOLARSHIP AND THE QUEST FOR DEMOCRACY

Within the last two decades, there has been a rich proliferation of transformative scholarship developed by scholars on the margins of society (Banks & Banks, 1995a). This scholarship challenges many of the paradigms, concepts, and interpretations that are institutionalized within the nation's schools, colleges, and universities. Much, but not all, of this scholarship has been developed by scholars of color and feminist scholars. For example, in his book, *Margins and Mainstreams: Asians in American History and Culture*, Gary Okhiro (1994) argues that groups on the margins of society have played significant roles in maintaining democratic values in American society by challenging practices that violated democracy and human rights. Okhiro notes that America's minorities were among the first to challenge institutionalized racist practices such as slavery, the forced removal of American Indians from native lands, segregation, and the internment of Japanese Americans during World War II. By so doing, they helped to keep democracy alive in the United States.

As I point out in my most recent book, transformative scholars and transformative scholarship have long histories in the United States (Banks, 1996). Transformative scholars and their work have helped to maintain democracy in the academic community by challenging racist scholarship and ideologies that provided the ideological and scholarly justification for institutionalized racist practices and policies. This lecture honors Charles H. Thompson, a transformative scholar and educator who was founding editor of the *Journal of Negro Education*. The *Journal* was established to provide a forum for transformative scholars and researchers to publish their findings and interpretations related to the education of Black people throughout the world. Much of their research challenged mainstream research and contributed to the education and liberation of African Americans.

In his editorial comment in the first issue of the *Journal*, entitled "Why a Journal of Negro Education?" Thompson (1932) advocated Black self-determination. He believed that the *Journal* would provide African Americans with a vehicle for assuming a greater role in their own education. As Thompson stated:

. . . leadership in the investigation of the education of Negroes should be assumed to a greater extent by Negro educators . . . [yet there is] no ready and empathetic outlet for the publication of the results of [the Negro's] investigations. . . . Thus, it is believed that the launching of this project will stimulate Negroes to take a greater part in the solutions of the problems that arise in connection with their own education. (p. 2)

Black self-determination is as important today as when Thompson penned these words. The first issue of the *Journal of Negro Education* was published in April 1932. The *Journal* has continued its transformative tradition for 63 years. Other transformative journals founded by African American scholars include the *Journal of Negro History*, founded by Carter G. Woodson in 1916, and *Phylon*, founded by W. E. B. DuBois at Atlanta University in 1940. Prior to the founding of these journals, transformative scholars had few outlets for the publication of their works. The mainstream academic community and its journal editors had little interest in research and work on communities of color prior to the 1960s, especially work that presented positive descriptions of minority communities and that was oppositional to mainstream racist scholarship. When we examine the history of scholarship in the United States, it is striking how both racist scholarship and transformative scholarship have been consistent through time. Near the turn of the century, research and theories that described innate distinctions among racial groups was institutionalized within American social science (Tucker, 1994). A group of transformative scholars including such thinkers as DuBois, Kelly Miller, and Franz Boas seriously challenged these conceptions (Banks, 1996).

The relationship between transformative and mainstream social science is interactive; each influences the other. Over time, transformative knowledge influences mainstream knowledge, and elements of transformative knowledge become incorporated into mainstream knowledge. For example, the conceptions about race that were constructed by transformative scholars near the turn of the century became the accepted concepts and theories in mainstream social science during the 1940s and 1950s. Nevertheless, a group of scholars continued to invent research and construct ideas about the inferiority of particular racial groups.

The history of research about race in America indicates that theories about the racial inferiority of certain groups—and challenges to them from transformative scholars—never disappear (Tucker, 1994). What varies is the extent to which theories of racial inferiority and other theories that support inequality attain public legitimacy and respectability. Since the beginning of the 20th century, every decade has witnessed the development of such theories. The extent to which these theories, and the individuals who purported them, experienced public respectability, awards, and recognitions has varied considerably. The amount of recognition that transformative scholars who challenged these theories have received from the public and academic communities has also varied considerably through time.

Prior to the civil rights movement of the 1960s and 1970s, the White mainstream academic community ignored most of the scholarship created by African American scholars. Most African American scholars had to take jobs in historically Black colleges. Most of these colleges were teaching institutions that had few resources with which to support and encourage research. Professors at these institutions had demanding teaching loads. Nevertheless, important research was done by African American and by a few White transformative scholars prior to the 1960s. Yet, because this research was largely ignored by the mainstream academic community, it had little influence on the knowledge about racial and ethnic groups that became institutionalized within the popular culture and the mainstream academic community. Consequently, it had little influence on the curriculum and the textbooks used in most of the nation's schools, colleges, and universities.

Although it was largely ignored by the mainstream community, a rich body of transformative scholarship was created in the years from the turn of the century to the 1950s. Much of this research was incorporated into popular textbooks that were used in Black schools and colleges. For example, Carter G. Woodson's *The Negro in Our History,* first published in 1930, was published in a 10th edition in 1962. John Hope Franklin's *From Slavery to Freedom,* first published in 1947, is still a popular history textbook in its seventh edition. Scholarly works published during this period included *The Philadelphia Negro* by W. E. B. DuBois (1899/1975), *American Negro Slave Revolts* by Herbert Aptheker (1943), *The Negro in the Civil War* by Benjamin Quarles (1953), *The Free Negro in North Carolina, 1790–1860,* by John Hope Franklin (1943), and Woodson's *The Education of the Negro Prior to 1861* (1919/1968).

THE NEED FOR A TRANSFORMATIVE, LIBERATORY CURRICULUM

Prior to the 1960s, African American scholars and their White colleagues who did research on the African American community remained primarily at the margins of the mainstream academic community. Most of the paradigms and explanations related to racial and ethnic groups that became institutionalized within the mainstream academic community were created by scholars outside these groups. Most of the paradigms, concepts, and theories created by mainstream scholars reinforced the status quo and provided intellectual justifications for institutionalized stereotypes and misconceptions about groups of color. An important example of this kind of scholarship is *American Negro Slavery* by Ulrich B. Phillips, published in 1918. Phillips described slaves as happy, inferior, and as benefiting from Western civilization. His interpretation of slavery became the institutionalized one within American colleges and universities, and he became one of the nation's most respected historians.

Phillips's view of slavery was not seriously challenged within the mainstream scholarly community until historians such as Stanley M. Elkins (1959), Kenneth M. Stampp (1956), John Blassingame (1972), and Eugene D. Genovese (1972) published new interpretations of slavery during the 1950s, 1960s, and 1970s. Transformative scholarship that presented other interpretations of slavery had been published as early as 1943, when Aptheker published *American Negro Slave Revolts*. However, this work was largely ignored and marginalized by the mainstream community partly because it was inconsistent with established views of slaves and slavery.

More recent research on the cognitive and intellectual abilities of African Americans indicates the extent to which antiegalitarian research is still influential in the mainstream academic community. In 1969, for example, the prestigious *Harvard Educational Review* devoted 123 pages of its first issue that year to Arthur Jensen's article on the differential intellectual abilities of Whites and African Americans. Papers by transformative scholars who embraced paradigms different from Jensen's were not published in this influential issue, although comments on the article by other scholars were published in the next issue of the *Review* (Kagan et al., 1969). Even though Jensen's article occupied most of the pages in an issue of a well-known scholarly journal, he experienced much public scorn and rejection when he appeared in public lectures and forums on university campuses.

Published nearly a quarter century after Jensen's article, *The Bell Curve* by Herrnstein and Murray (1994) received an enthusiastic and warm reception in both the academic and public communities. It was widely discussed in the public media and remained on the *New York Times* bestseller list for many weeks. Although it evoked much discussion and controversy (Jacoby & Glauberman, 1995), it attained a high degree of legitimacy within both the academic and public communities.

The publication of *The Bell Curve*, its warm and enthusiastic public reception, and the social and political context out of which it emerged provide an excellent case study for discussion and analysis by students who are studying knowledge construction. They can examine the arguments made by the authors, their major assumptions, and find out how these arguments and assumptions relate to the social and political context. Students can discuss these questions: Why, at this time in our history, was *The Bell Curve* written and published? Why was it so widely disseminated and well-received by the educated public? Who benefits from the arguments in *The Bell Curve*? Who loses? Why do arguments and theories about the genetic inferiority of African Americans keep re-emerging? How do such arguments relate to the social and political climate?

Stephen Jay Gould (1994) responded to the last question in a *New Yorker* article by noting the following:

> *The Bell Curve*, with its claim and supposed documentation that race and class differences are largely caused by genetic factors and are therefore essentially immutable, contains no new arguments and presents no compelling data to support its anachronistic social Darwinism, so I can only conclude that its success in winning attention must reflect the depressing temper of our time—a historical moment of unprecedented ungenerosity, when a mood for slashing social programs can be powerfully abetted by an argument that beneficiaries cannot be helped, owing to inborn cognitive limits expressed as low IQ scores (p. 139)

The publication and public reception of *The Bell Curve* is a cogent example of the extent to which much institutionalized knowledge within our society still supports inequality, dominant group hegemony, and the disempowerment of marginalized groups. *The Bell Curve*, its reception, and its legitimacy also underscore the need to educate students to become critical consumers of knowledge, to become knowledge producers themselves, and to be able to take thoughtful and decisive action that will help to create and maintain a democratic and just society. Works such as *The Bell Curve*, and the public response to them, remind us that democracies are fragile and that the threats to them are serious. Fortunately, the work of transformative scholars indicates that the quest for human freedom is irrepressible.

REFERENCES

Aptheker, H. (1943). *American Negro slave revolts.* New York: International Publishers.

Au, K. H. (1980). Participation structures in a reading lesson with Hawaiian children. *Anthropology and Education Quarterly, 11*(2), 91–115.

Banks, J. A. (1993a). Multicultural education: Characteristics and goals. In J. A. Banks & C. A. M. Banks (Eds.), *Multicultural education: Issues and perspectives* (2nd ed.) (pp. 3–28). Boston: Allyn & Bacon.

Banks, J. A. (1993b). *Multiethnic education: Theory and practice* (3rd ed.). Boston: Allyn & Bacon.

Banks, J. A. (1995a). Multicultural education: Historical development, dimensions, and practice. In J. A. Banks & C. A. M. Banks (Eds.), *Handbook of research on multicultural education* (pp. 3–24). New York: Macmillan.

Banks, J. A. (1995b). Multicultural education: Its effects on students' racial and gender role attitudes. In J. A. Banks & C. A. M. Banks (Eds.). *Handbook of research on multicultural education* (pp. 617–627). New York: Macmillan.

Banks, J. A. (Ed.). (1996). *Multicultural education, transformative knowledge, and action.* New York: Teachers College Press.

Banks, J. A., & Banks, C. A. M. (Eds.). (1995a). *Handbook of research on multicultural education.* New York: Macmillan.

Banks, J. A., & Banks, C. A. M. (1995b). Equity pedagogy: An essential component of multicultural education. *Theory into Practice, 34*(3), 152–168.

Blassingame, J. W. (1972). *The slave community: Plantation life in the antebellum south.* New York: Oxford University Press.

Boykin, A. W. (1982). Task variability and the performance of Black and White school children: Vervistic explorations. *Journal of Black Studies, 12,* 469–485.

Clark, K. B. (1965). *Dark ghetto: Dilemmas of social power.* New York: Harper & Row.

Clark, K. B., & Clark, M. P. (1939). The development of consciousness of self and the emergence of racial identification in Negro preschool children. *Journal of Social Psychology, 10,* 591–599.

Code, L. (1991). *What can she know? Feminist theory and the construction of knowledge.* Ithaca, NY: Cornell University Press.

Cohen, E. G., & Lotan, R. A. (1995). Producing equal-status interactions in the heterogeneous classroom. *American Educational Research Journal, 32*(1), 99–120.

Collins, P. H. (1990). *Black feminist thought: Feminist theory and the construction of knowledge.* New York: Routledge.

Cross, W. E., Jr. (1991). *Shades of Black: Diversity in African American identity.* Philadelphia: Temple University Press.

Delpit, L. (1995). *Other people's children: Cultural conflict in the classroom.* New York: The New Press.

D'Souza, D. (1995). *The end of racism: Principles for a multicultural society.* New York: The Free Press.

DuBois, W. E. B. (1940). Apology. *Phylon, 1*(1), 3–5.

DuBois, W. E. B. (1975). *The Philadelphia Negro: A social study.* Millwood, NY: Kraus–Thomson Organization Limited. (Original work published in 1899)

Elkins, S. M. (1959). *Slavery: A problem in American institutional and intellectual life.* Chicago: The University of Chicago Press.

Franklin, J. H. (1943). *The free Negro in North Carolina, 1790–1860.* New York: Russell & Russell.

Franklin, J. H. (1947). *From slavery to freedom: A history of Negro Americans.* New York: Knopf.

Gay, G. (1995). Curriculum theory and multicultural education. In J. A. Banks & C. A. M. Banks (Eds.), *Handbook of research on multicultural education* (pp. 25–43). New York: Macmillan.

Genovese, E. D. (1972). *Roll, Jordan, roll: The world the slaves made.* New York: Pantheon.

Gould, S. J. (1994, November 28). Curveball. *The New Yorker, 70*(38), 139–149.

Herrnstein, R. J., & Murray, C. (1994). *The bell curve: Intelligence and class structure in American life.* New York: The Free Press.

Hyatt, V. L., & Nettleford, R. (Eds.). (1995). *Race, discourse, and the origin of the Americas: A new world view.* Washington, DC: Smithsonian Institution Press.

Jacoby, R., & Glauberman, N. (Eds.). (1995). *The Bell Curve debate: History, documents, opinions.* New York: Times Books/Random House.

Jensen, A. R. (1969). How much can we boost IQ and scholastic achievement? *Harvard Educational Review, 39*(1), 1–123.

Kagan, J. S., Hunt, J. M., Crow, J. F., Bereiter, C., Elkin, D., & Cronbach, L. (1969). Discussion: How much can we boost IQ and scholastic achievement? *Harvard Educational Review, 39*(2), 274–347,

Kleinfeld, J. (1975). Effective teachers of Eskimo and Indian students. *School Review, 83,* 301–344.

Ladson–Billings, G. (1995). Toward a theory of culturally relevant pedagogy. *American Educational Research Journal, 32*(3), 465–491.

Lee, C., & Slaughter–Defoe, D. T. (1995). Historical and socio-cultural influences on African American education. In J. A. Banks & C. A. M. Banks (Eds.), *Handbook of research on multicultural education* (pp. 348–371). New York: Macmillan.

Nieto, S. (1995). A history of the education of Puerto Rican students in U.S. mainland schools: "Losers," "outsiders," or "leaders"? In J. A. Banks & C. A. M. Banks (Eds.), *Handbook of research on multicultural education* (pp. 388–411). New York: Macmillan.

Myrdal, D. (with R. Sterner & A. Rose). (1944). *An American dilemma: The Negro problem in modern democracy.* New York: Harper.

Okhiro, G. (1994). *Margins and mainstreams: Asians in American history and culture.* Seattle, WA: University of Washington Press.

Phillips, U. B. (1918). *American Negro slavery.* New York: Appleton.

Phinney, J. S., & Rotheram, M. J. (Eds.). (1987). *Children's ethnic socialization: Pluralism and development.* Beverly Hills, CA: Sage Publications.

Quarles, B. (1953). *The Negro in the Civil War.* Boston: Little, Brown.

Sacks, D. O., & Theil, P. A. (1995). *The diversity myth: "Multiculturalism" and the politics of intoler-ance at Stanford.* Oakland, CA: The Independent Institute.

Schlesinger, A., Jr. (1991). *The disuniting of America: Reflections on a multicultural society.* Knoxville, TN: Whittle Direct Books.

Shade, B. A., & New, C. A. (1993). Cultural influences on learning: Teaching implications. In J. A. Banks & C. A. M. Banks (Eds.), *Multicultural education: Issues and perspectives* (2nd ed.) (pp. 317–331). Boston: Allyn & Bacon.

Sleeter, C. A. (1995). An analysis of the critiques of multicultural education. In J. A. Banks & C. A. M. Banks (Eds.), *Handbook of research on multicultural education* (pp. 81–94). New York: Macmillan.

Spencer, M. B. (1982). Personal and group identity of Black children: An alternative synthesis. *Genetic Psychology Monographs, 106,* 59–84.

Stampp, K. M. (1956). *The peculiar institution: Slavery in the ante-bellum south.* New York: Vintage.

Thompson, C. H. (1932). Editorial comment: Why a journal of Negro education? *Journal of Negro Education, 1*(1), 1–4.

Thornton, R. (1995). North American Indians and the demography of contact. In V. L. Hyatt & R. Nettleford (Eds.), *Race, discourse, and the origin of the Americas: A new world view* (pp. 213–230). Washington, DC: Smithsonian Institution Press.

Todorov, T. (1982). *The conquest of America: The question of the other.* New York: HarperCollins.

Tucker, W. H. (1994). *The science and politics of racial research.* Urbana, IL: University of Illinois Press.

James A. Banks is Professor of Education and Director of the Center for Multicultural Education, University of Washington-Seattle.

QUESTIONS FOR REFLECTION

1. What are the salient differences between mainstream academic knowledge and transformative academic knowledge?

2. How are racial, ethnic, and social-class positions of individuals and groups reflected in the knowledge construction process that is most relevant to your area of curricular interest?

3. Regarding the educational setting and level with which you are most familiar, how might the following dimensions of multicultural education be incorporated: content integration, the knowledge construction process, prejudice reduction, an equity pedagogy, and an empowering school culture?

TEACHERS' VOICES
Putting Theory into Practice

Redesigning the Model: A Successfully Integrated Approach to Teaching and Learning

DENNIS M. MCFADEN

BARBARA A. NELSON

CHIP M. RANDALL

ABSTRACT: Three teachers at a science and technology high school describe how they went beyond the "compartmentalization of knowledge" and restructured a ninth-grade curriculum to include a cluster of three core courses in an integrated program. To learn "a new way of doing science," students work with resource managers at a wildlife refuge to gather data on species inhabiting the area. Students also prepare extensive research reports which they present to peers, faculty, and invited guests.

Seven years ago Principal Geoffrey Jones and the department chairpersons of Thomas Jefferson High School for Science and Technology in Alexandria, Va., decided to restructure the ninth grade program by clustering three of its core courses in an integrated program of studies. This was the first step in restructuring a program as a process or way of thinking and acting that blends science and technology with the human experience and need for knowledge, tool use, and skills.

Under the principal's leadership, our management team developed a vision that included a common and directed purpose for the school, empowering faculty members in decision making and application. It was their vision that an interdependent curriculum should foster collaboration as well as independence and lead students to develop their own processes for learning and to

use information as part of a cooperative network. This change created an environment that has led to new teaching strategies, increased learning opportunities for both students and teachers, and a release of the stranglehold that traditional class scheduling had imposed on our programs.

A NEW WAY OF DOING SCIENCE

Our program today has students working as partners with resource managers at the Mason Neck National Wildlife Refuge and at the Mason Neck State Park to gather important data on the species that inhabit the Mason Neck peninsula, a 40-minute drive from school. Students have monitored the daily activity of waterfowl using technology they designed and built in technol-

From *NASSP Bulletin* 80, no. 577 (February 1996): 1–6. Used by permission of the authors and the publisher, the National Association of Secondary School Principals. For more information concerning NASSP services and/or programs, please call (703) 860-0200.

ogy class. They have communicated their results in well-researched and revised technical reports to the refuge and park staff as well as orally in symposium format to peer colleagues, faculty members, and invited guests.

For the students the work is authentic, engaging, and fun. For the teachers it is a new and more effective way of teaching. Working at the refuge and park on real-world problems provides an opportunity for our students to have a field study experience in science and technology, a departure from traditional laboratory-based experiments. Our field projects are designed to be an outreach to our community and a connection with agencies that value our collaboration.

The natural connections that were not immediately obvious to us at the beginning of this restructuring of our curriculum quickly emerged. The real-world connections and experiences at Mason Neck were made possible by the changes in our daily schedule. The Integrated Biology, English, and Technology schedule at Thomas Jefferson clusters three 45-minute class periods, back to back, for each course. We share the same 75 students, divided into classes of 25. Each class rotates through our morning so that each of us sees each class in turn. The linking of these three courses in the daily schedule, fundamental to the success of this program, is a priority of the management team in constructing the master schedule each year. Making this scheduling a priority in developing the master schedule is a necessity in allowing this integration to occur.

An integrated approach has given us the opportunity to create the model for meaningful, contextual learning. In a time of information explosion when even the information may change, the definition of learning and the outcomes we expect from students must reflect our recognition that we are preparing students for a world far different from one in which we currently teach.

Learning is more than a collection and a manipulation of data or facts. Learning that is interactive and enabled by a restructured curriculum is far more powerful than learning content material in courses devoid of context. Learning must be an active process in which students are taught an interdisciplinary algorithm for gathering information, testing ideas, and identifying and solving problems. Learning involves risk taking and a safe arena in which to make mistakes.

Problem solving is what the real world is about. While the validity of specific data or the nature of available tools may change, the problem-solving process will not. The workplace requires people who can integrate skills and information to solve problems: questioning, analyzing, inventing, evaluating, forecasting, making decisions, and communicating. Compartmentalization of courses in a traditional curriculum eliminates this context and opportunity for learning what will be required in the workplace. By eliminating the compartmentalization of knowledge and by making connections, we help our students practice skills that they will use for a lifetime.

THE INTEGRATED PROGRAM

Some courses seem to traditionally connect—social sciences and English, science and math. The clustering of these courses shows students invaluable connections. But, we believe that connections should not be restricted to the links already established in many schools. In fact, the more initially obscure and unconventional the connection, the more creative and innovative the links that the teachers may see between and among courses. While the connections among our courses were not initially obvious, they quickly emerged.

By making integrated project work an important and equal component of our curriculum and restructuring our schedule within a clustered time block, we have fundamentally shifted the paradigm of how we teach and what is taught. It makes us teach what the students need to know when they need to know it, resequencing fundamental concepts to fit the project requirements. It minimizes the content-driven mindset so that needed skills can be taught and reinforced within the context of a legitimate application. These skills can then be transferred from one subject area to another through work on the project itself. This model also allows us to do projects that none of us could do separately or completely without sacrificing the essentials of our individual subject areas.

Critical to the implementation of our integrated program is the realization that we are partners in teaching a single integrated course and are not just trying to combine three separate ones. This does not mean that each of us is expected to be expert in all three disciplines or that the content of the individual courses should be watered down or homogenized.

In fact, we do a better job in teaching the content-specific concepts and skills in our individual courses because we constantly reinforce them, providing a contextual framework. This model requires a transformation in mindset from three separate courses, each vying for its share of time, resources, and importance, to one in which each is integrated naturally into a fabric of instruction and learning that values the contribution each discipline brings to our understanding of the world.

It is the interdisciplinary strand that directs and focuses this integrated approach. In fact, it provides the fundamental framework of how we connect topics, present ideas, and sequence units throughout the school year.

IMPLEMENTING THE PROGRAM

Since we have selected environmental issues as the coordinating strand of our three courses, we plan the field trips and components of the environmental projects at the beginning of the year. To accommodate our integrated strand, each of us has frequently changed the sequence of topics presented in class so that our students will have the background or skill they need at the time they need it. Beginning the school year with technical reading and writing may cause students and their parents to wonder if they are really taking an English course. Some favorite but non-essential topics

may not survive the brutal cost-benefit analysis required to make this kind of program work.

A traditional schedule of separate periods and isolated disciplines that does not link concepts and skills further limits the ability of teachers and students to integrate these problem-solving skills. Time constraints inherent in traditional schedules frustrate teachers, forcing them to follow a line of least resistance in their lesson planning and to limit their creativity.

Integrating and clustering our courses has empowered us to look at new ways of teaching and provided us with the luxury of learning how to manipulate time rather than being manipulated by it. The length of each class period and the pattern in which it is structured has largely determined what we teach, how we teach it, and when it is taught.

Restructuring our daily class schedule has allowed us to create larger blocks of time during the week to accommodate special needs such as field trips, science and technology lab activities, guest speakers, films, or even schedules shortened by inclement weather. By using our collective time we have been able to support these kinds of activities without imposing on other teachers. Even the time used by the rest of the school for passing between classes can be added to the resource pool created by restructuring. We have been able to block time and use it to our advantage, presenting necessary content as well as exploring new ideas. It has meant that we can frequently ignore time as a limiting factor.

One of the requirements for making this model successful is to select appropriate projects. Always, the emphasis is on the process rather than the product. Because it replicates lifelong learning, the problem-solving process is more valuable than simply holding students accountable for factual information. By selecting projects appropriate for ninth graders, we ensure that our students have the opportunity to succeed because the projects are simple and do-able and we have the resources to support them. By carefully selecting projects and working collaboratively, we are able to complete the entire research process from inception to publication.

As part of the process we teach our students how to read and understand technical literature and how to write informationally. They search the literature to establish a hypothesis, design an experiment to test it, run the experiment, collect and analyze data, draw conclusions, and produce a written document that communicates the results of the experiment. Technology, such as simple electronics or prototyping, is introduced as a necessary tool to be used as part of the design to carry out the experimental protocol as well as to measure results. Computer technology enables students to illustrate, spreadsheet, and share their results, using various software applications. Students work interactively and employ the skills learned in each of the content strands to do legitimate research.

In working on a project, we require students to determine what information and resources are needed and how to access them. The integrated projects are long enough to correct mistakes in the original experiment, incorporate revisions to the design and, most important, carry the scientific method completely through all the steps, including publication. By making the commitment to provide the necessary time and resources, we enable students to do what researchers actually do—take risks, learn from their mistakes, and support each other.

Our project model is collegial for both teachers and students. This approach gives us the opportunity to support and learn from each other and serves as a vehicle to model the collaborative team effort we are trying to teach. Students see their teachers collaborating, making decisions, scheduling, and assigning responsibilities as we design and revise *our* project—the course itself. We are modeling the skills we hope to develop in our students.

Students are given the opportunity to design and revise their own projects and to develop important group dynamic skills in working with each other. It allows students and teachers to be-

come partners in a learning process that is authentic and contextual.

Embedded within our project model is the developmental movement throughout the year from a teacher-directed and controlled program to one of increasing student independence in selecting projects, groups, and project designs. By the end of the year, students have more choice, and we teachers function primarily as facilitators and resources for our students. The specific project areas are identified in our meetings with the refuge and park personnel and are developed with student input into specific projects. Past projects have included forest and pond community resource inventories, investigations of deer enclosures, the development of an elementary school curriculum specific to the refuge, and a feasibility study for making the refuge's school group area more accessible to persons with disabilities.

The advantage of this model is not just for the students. The advantages of risk taking, being actively involved in learning, and working and planning with colleagues, all of which we stress as critical with the students, also apply to us. The collegial sharing and support inherent in this model provides a dimension of professional development that is rare in the current educational reality of closed doors and required meetings. This was evident to us even before we recognized the power of students interacting with teachers and among themselves.

As a result of our work together, we have found that skills and information taught in isolation are not as effective or interesting as those taught in the context of student-owned and meaningful community-based projects. Like effective coaches we are able to teach skills, provide practice in these skills, and then allow students to use them in authentic situations.

Teachers must also follow this model: They must stand up to the challenge, learn the process, and develop their model, and then make it happen for the students. Keeping teacher teams together for a significant amount of time gives them time to develop the interactions and trust necessary to take risks and develop innovative curricula.

We are convinced this model is a genuine and powerful form of intercurricular staff development. By establishing an environment that nurtures creativity and flexibility in instruction and curriculum, our principal has empowered us to make decisions about our curriculum that reflect our experience and expertise. We have found this rejuvenating and professionally exciting.

Our administrative staff has given us the resources of restructured class time, equipment, common planning, and autonomy to make this model successful. This integrated model allows the partnership of teachers, students, and administrators to control resources and learning.

Dennis M. McFaden is a science teacher and winner of the 1995 National Science Foundation State Award for Excellence in the Teaching of Secondary Science; *Barbara A. Nelson* is an English teacher; and *Chip M. Randall* is a technology education teacher, all at the Thomas Jefferson High School for Science and Technology in Alexandria, Virginia.

QUESTIONS FOR REFLECTION

1. What is "contextual learning," and how might it be incorporated in the curriculum with which you are most familiar?
2. What is the authors' definition of *learning*?
3. To what extent is the integrated approach to teaching and learning described by the authors applicable to the educational setting with which you are most familiar?

LEARNING ACTIVITIES

Critical Thinking

1. Reflect on your experiences at the elementary, middle/junior, and high school levels. At each level, which view of knowledge seems to have been most salient: knowledge as subject matter or knowledge as personal experience? As you moved from the elementary level through the high school level, was there a shift in the salient view of knowledge that characterized the curriculum?
2. Dewey, in *The Child and the Curriculum* (The University of Chicago Press, 1904, pp. 15–16), says "[One should] get rid of the prejudicial notion that there is some gap in kind (as distinct from degree) between the child's experience and the various forms of subject matter that make up the course of study. From the side of the child, it is a question of seeing how his [or her] experience already contains within itself elements—fact and truths—of just the same sort as those entering into the formulated study. . . ." What does Dewey mean by his statement? Do you agree?
3. At the level of greatest interest to you, to what extent should the curriculum be based on a knowledge-as-subject-matter point of view? A knowledge-as-personal-experience point of view?

4. Reflect on one or two of your most meaningful educational experiences at the K–12 or higher education levels. To what degree were your curricular experiences based on a knowledge-of-subject-matter point of view? A knowledge-as-personal-experience point of view? To what extent were your experiences based on *both* points of view?

Application Activities

1. In the area and at the level with which you are most familiar, examine a set of curriculum materials (a textbook, curriculum guide, etc.) to determine the perception of knowledge upon which the materials are based. In what ways is knowledge seen as a structured discipline? As personal experience?
2. Eisner believes that the curriculum should focus on visual, spatial, auditory, perceptual, and holistic approaches to knowledge, as well as verbal, numerical, logical, and linear approaches. Select a curriculum with which you are familiar and identify which of these approaches it uses. Then identify learning experiences that could be developed to make use of the other approaches.
3. On the basis of Barbour's article in this chapter, "Can We Prepackage Thinking?", design a workshop for teachers at the level and in the subject area with which you are most familiar. The aim of the workshop should be to help teachers design curricula that develop students' analytical and/or creative thinking skills.
4. Obtain a copy of your state's goals for education at the K–12 level and, if available, the postsecondary level. To what extent do these documents reflect a view of knowledge as subject matter? As personal experience?

Field Experiences

1. Visit a curriculum coordinator in a school district in your area and ask him or her to describe the extent to which teachers use integrated curricula in the district. If possible, obtain copies of integrated curriculum materials and share them with your classmates. (If your primary area of interest is at the higher education level, modify the assignment as appropriate. You may, for example, interview a department chair, program director, dean of instruction, director of general education, or an academic dean).
2. Spend a half-day at a school, college, or university observing classes in a subject area of interest. Note the extent to which students' curricular experiences reflect a knowledge-as-subject-matter point of view or a knowledge-as-personal-experience point of view. Share your observations with others in your class.

Internet Activities

1. Go to the WWW site for the national teachers' organization in a subject area of interest, and locate a statement of educational standards for student learning in

that area. To what extent is a subject-matter view of knowledge reflected in the standards? A personal experience view? Internet addresses for several professional teacher organizations are listed in the following:

National Council of Teachers of Mathematics (**www.nctm.org**)
National Council of Teachers of English (**www.ncte.org**)
American Council on the Teaching of Foreign Language
   (**www.Thomson.com.actfl/home.html**)
Music Teachers National Association (**www.mtna.com**)
National Art Education Association (**www.naea-reston.org**)
National Association of Biology Teachers (**www.nabt.org**)
National Business Education Association (**www.nbea.org/nbea.html**)
National Council for the Social Studies (**www.ncss.org**)
Teachers of English to Speakers of Other Languages (**www.tesol.edu**)

2.   Conduct a key-word search in the ERIC (Educational Resources Information Center) database (**http://ericir.syr.edu/**) on integrated and/or interdisciplinary curricula in your area of interest. The ERIC database includes the *Current Index to Journals in Education* (CIJE), which contains more than 800,000 entries from 1983 to the present. In addition, you may want to visit the ERIC Digest Archives (**http://www.ed.gov/databases/ERIC_Digests/index/**) to download overviews on topics of interest.

BOOKS AND ARTICLES TO REVIEW

Altieri, Buy, and Cygnar, Patricia Marvelli. "A New Model for General Education in Associate's Degree Programs: Developing and Teaching a Core Across the Curriculum." *Community College Review* 25, no. 2 (Fall 1997): 3–19.

Banks, Cherry A. McGee, and Banks, James A. "Equity Pedagogy: An Essential Component of Multicultural Education." *Theory Into Practice* 34, no. 3 (Summer 1995): 152–158.

Beane, James A. *Curriculum Integration: Designing the Core of Democratic Education.* New York: Teachers College Press, 1997.

———. "Creating an Integrative Curriculum: Making the Connections." *NASSP Bulletin* 76, no. 547 (November 1992): 46–54.

Blake, Sally. "Integrating Cultural Diversity and Mathematics in the Curriculum." *Dimensions of Early Childhood* 25, no. 2 (Spring 1997): 5–10.

Brady, Marion. "Beyond Interdisciplinary: Preparing Teachers for New Curriculum." *NASSP Bulletin* 80, no. 580 (May 1996): 1–8.

Bruner, Jerome. *Acts of Meaning.* Cambridge, MA: Harvard University Press, 1990.

———. *The Process of Education.* Cambridge, MA: Harvard University Press, 1960.

Clark, John H., and Agne, Russell M. *Interdisciplinary High School Teaching: Strategies for Integrated Learning.* Boston: Allyn and Bacon, 1997.

Davenport, M. Ruth, et al. "A Curriculum of Caring (Integrating Curriculum)." *Reading Teacher* 50, no. 4 (December–January 1996–97): 352–353.

Dewey, John. *Experience and Education.* New York: The Macmillan Co., 1938.

———. *The Sources of a Science of Education.* New York: Horace Liveright, 1929.

Downing, John H., and Lander, Jeffrey E. "Fostering Critical Thinking through Interdisciplinary Cooperation: Integrating Secondary Level Physics into a Weight Training Unit." *NASSP Bulletin* 81, no. 591 (October 1997): 85–94.

Dykman, Ann. "The Great College Divide: Integrating Curriculum at the Postsecondary Level Presents

Unique Challenges." *Techniques: Making Education and Career Connections* 72, no. 2 (February 1997): 36–39.

Eisner, Elliot W. "Commentary: Putting Multiple Intelligences in Context: Some Questions and Observations." *Teachers College Record* 95, no. 4 (Summer 1994): 555–560.

———. *Cognition and Curriculum Reconsidered.* New York: Teachers College Press, 1994.

———. "Forms of Understanding and the Future of Educational Research." *Educational Researcher* 22, no. 7 (October 1993): 5–11.

———. *Cognition and Curriculum: A Basis for Deciding What to Teach.* New York: Longman, Inc. 1982.

———, ed. *Learning and Teaching the Ways of Knowing.* Chicago, IL: National Society for the Study of Education, University of Chicago Press, 1985.

Gehrke, Nathalie J. "Explorations of Teachers' Development of Integrative Curriculums." *Journal of Curriculum and Supervision* 6, no. 2 (Winter 1991): 107–117.

Gordon, Beverly M. "Curriculum, Policy, and African American Cultural Knowledge: Challenges and Possibilities for the Year 2000 and Beyond." *Educational Policy* 11, no. 2 (June 1997): 227–242.

Greene, Maxine. "Metaphors and Multiples: Representation, the Arts, and History." *Phi Delta Kappan* 78, no. 5 (January 1997): 387–394.

———. *Releasing the Imagination: Essays on Education, the Arts, and Social Change.* San Francisco: Jossey-Bass Publishers, 1995.

Halpern, Diane F. *Thought and Knowledge: An Introduction to Critical Thinking,* 3rd Ed. Mahwah, NJ: Lawrence Erlbaum, 1995.

Hicks, Bruno. "Meeting National Science Standards in an Integrative Curriculum: Classroom Examples from a Rural Middle Level Program." *Journal of Research in Rural Education* 13, no. 1 (Spring 1997): 57–63.

Jackson, Philip W. "Thinking about the Arts in Education: A Reformed Perspective." *Teachers College Record* 95, no. 4 (Summer 1994): 542–554.

Janko, Edmund. "Knowing Is Not Thinking." *Phi Delta Kappan* 70, no. 7 (March 1989): 543–544.

Jenkens, John M., and Pelletier, Karen. "Core Knowledge and Cultural Literacy." *International Journal of Educational Reform* 6, no. 4 (October 1997): 476–481.

Katz, Lillian G., and Chard, Sylvia C. "Documentation: The Reggio Emilia Approach." *Principal* 76, no. 5 (May 1997): 16–17.

Korinek, Lori, and Popp, Patricia A. "Collaborative Mainstream Integration of Social Skills with Academic Instruction." *Preventing School Failure* 41, no. 4 (Summer 1997): 148–152.

Marton, Ference, and Booth, Shirley. *Learning and Awareness.* Mahwah, NJ: Lawrence Erlbaum, 1997.

Mauer, Richard E., and Dorner, Anne M. *Designing Interdisciplinary Curriculum in Middle, Junior High, and High Schools.* Boston: Allyn and Bacon, 1994.

Novak, Joseph D. *Learning, Creating, and Using Knowledge: Concept Maps as Facilitative Tools in Schools and Corporations.* Mahwah, NJ: Lawrence Erlbaum, 1998.

Pate, Elizabeth P., Homestead, Elaine R., and McGinnis, Karen L. *Making Integrated Curriculum Work: Teachers, Students, and the Quest for Coherent Curriculum.* New York: Teachers College Press, 1997.

Pinar, William F., and Reynolds, William M., eds. *Understanding Curriculum as Phenomenological and Deconstructed Text.* New York: Teachers College Press, 1992.

Schwab, Joseph J. "The Concept of the Structure of a Discipline." In *Conflicting Conceptions of Curriculum,* Elliot W. Eisner and Elizabeth Vallance, eds. Berkeley, CA: McCutchan Publishing Corp., 1974, 162–175.

Shelly, Richard W., Cannaday, John E., Jr., and Weddle, D. Kenneth. "Product Design Engineering: A Successful Student-Centered Interdisciplinary Elective." *NASSP Bulletin* 81, no. 590 (September 1997): 95–104.

Shutes, Robert, and Peterson, Sandra. "Seven Reasons Why Textbooks Cannot Make a Curriculum." *NASSP Bulletin* 78, no. 565 (November 1994): 11–20.

Stevenson, Chris, and Carr, Judy F., eds. *Integrated Studies in the Middle Grades.* New York: Teachers College Press, 1993.

Tarpy, Maureen E., and Bucholc, Karen. "Making More Sense of America and the World Through Interdisciplinary English." *English Journal* 86, no. 7 (November 1997): 69–74.

Tucker, Brooke, Hafenstein, Norma Lu, Jones, Shannon, Rivian, Bernick, and Haines, Kim. "An Integrated-Thematic Curriculum for Gifted Learners." *Roeper Review* 19, no. 4 (June 1997): 196–199.

Wraga, William G. "Patterns of Interdisciplinary Curriculum Organization and Professional Knowledge of the Curriculum Field." *Journal of Curriculum and Supervision* 12, no. 2 (Winter 1997): 98–117.

Videotapes

Integrating the Curriculum presents steps for developing integrated units that draw from multiple disciplines. (Available from The Video Journal of Education, 549 West 3560 South, Salt Lake City, UT 84115-4225 (800) 572-1153.)

What Should an Educated Person Know? is a 30-minute video featuring Bill Moyers discussing cultural literacy with John Searle. (Available from Films for the Humanities & Sciences, P.O. Box 2055, Princeton, NJ 08543-2053 (800) 257-5126.)

Curriculum Criteria

FOCUS QUESTIONS

1. How should findings from research be used as a curriculum criterion?
2. Why is *student–teacher planning* an important curriculum criterion?
3. What are some possible ways in which the curriculum criterion of *relevance* can be reflected in the curriculum?
4. What are some arguments for and against *higher standards* for the curriculum?
5. Why is an *orientation to the future* an important curriculum criterion?
6. What are some recent trends in using *curriculum design* as a criterion for curriculum planning?

As mentioned in Chapter 1, a *criterion* is a standard on which a decision or judgment can be based. *Curriculum criteria,* then, are guidelines or standards according to which curricular or instructional decisions can be based. The articles in this book present varying perspectives on which criteria should guide curriculum planners and how they should use those criteria.

In many areas of professional practice, findings from research are among the most important criteria for guiding decision making. However, as John Dewey points out in "The Sources of a Science of Education" in this chapter, "No conclusion of scientific research can be converted into an immediate rule of educational art. For there is no educational practice whatever which is not highly complex; that is to say, which does not contain many other conditions and factors than are included in the scientific finding." The significance of any one research study for educational practice, then, can be determined only as the results of that study are balanced with an understanding of the "conditions and factors" that influence the situation. Connections among research results and surrounding environmental influences should be made until they reciprocally confirm and illuminate one another, or until each gives the other added meaning.

When these connecting principles are understood, the practitioner is more likely to take the "best" course of action in response to the educational problem at hand.

To make such informed decisions, Dewey (1904, p. 10) maintains elsewhere that educators should acquire and develop a fundamental mental process the ultimate aim of which is "the intellectual method and material of good workmanship." According to Dewey, this intellectual method is the criterion against which educational decisions—from curriculum planning to selecting instructional strategies—should be made. Dewey also suggests several personal dispositions that characterize those who use the method: intellectual independence (p. 16) and responsibility, initiative, skill in scholarship (p. 21), willingness to be a "thoughtful and alert" student of education (p. 15), and a spirit of inquiry. In addition, Dewey stresses the need to develop the "habit of viewing the entire curriculum as a continuous growth, reflecting the growth of mind itself" (p. 26).

OTHER SIGNIFICANT CURRICULUM CRITERIA

From your reading of Chapters 1–5, you now understand the significance of goals and values and the four bases of curriculum planning—social forces, human development, learning and learning styles, and knowledge—in planning a curriculum. A major aim of this chapter is to emphasize the importance of using not only goals and values and the four bases for curriculum planning, but additional criteria such as student–teacher planning, relevance, standards developed by professional organizations, orientation to the future, and curriculum design.

Student–Teacher Planning

As we pointed out in Chapter 1, learners should be clearly aware of the goals being sought by their teachers and the goals embedded in the curriculum they are experiencing. In addition, though, learners formulate their own curricular goals throughout the process of instruction. While the goals teachers use to guide their planning and those sought by the learners need not be identical, they should overlap. The teacher's and learner's goals for a learning experience must be understood by both the teacher and the learners, and the goals must be compatible or they are not likely to be achieved. An effective way to achieve this congruence is through some form of student–teacher planning. As Glen Hass states in "Who Should Plan the Curriculum?" in this chapter, the student is the "major untapped resource in curriculum planning."

Relevance

In the mid-1960s, there was a strong call at all levels of schooling for curricula that were relevant. During this period, as Forrest W. Parkay points out in "Perspectives on Curriculum Criteria: Past and Present" in this chapter, "many educators, student groups, and political activists charged that school curricula were unresponsive to social issues and significant changes in our culture." At some schools, colleges, and universities, students actually demonstrated against educational programs they believed were not relevant to their needs and concerns. Thus, educators at all levels began to broaden the curriculum, increase the electives students could take, and develop innovative ways of teaching.

For a curriculum to be relevant, its planning should reflect careful consideration of goals and values and all four of the curriculum bases. Moreover, *for whom* and *to what* the curriculum is relevant should be clear. Often, however, relevance in the curriculum reflects only a single criterion. Thus, the curriculum may be almost exclusively relevant to social forces, or relevant to a particular view of human development, or relevant to a multiple intelligences view of knowledge, or relevant to the values preferred by the curriculum planner. Clearly, though, a curriculum must also be relevant to the learner's purposes, needs, and characteristics. For example, if relevance to self-understanding is the criterion being used, one must consider, then, how an understanding of social forces, theories of human development, learning styles, and different types of knowledge might be used to develop a curriculum that promotes the learner's self-understanding.

Higher Standards

A curriculum criterion that gained increasing importance during the last decade of the twentieth century was higher, "world-class" standards. In response to the call for higher standards, schools, colleges, and universities undertook numerous curricular reforms and developed more exacting, authentic methods for measuring educational outcomes. Typically, "higher standards" was interpreted by parents, the public, and lawmakers to mean that teachers should expect more of their students. Toward this end, various macro-level mandates were made: detailed statements of the knowledge and skills students were to acquire under the more rigorous standards; higher test scores to receive passing grades or to be promoted to the next level; and more English, science, and mathematics.

Response to these efforts, however, was mixed. On the one hand, advocates of higher standards agreed with observers such as Diane Ravitch, educational historian and author of *National Standards in American Education: A Citizen's Guide* (1995), who pointed out that:

- Standards can improve achievement by clearly defining what is to be taught and what kind of performance is expected.
- Standards (national, state, and local) are necessary for equality of opportunity.
- National standards provide a valuable coordinating function.
- Standards and assessments provide consumer protection by supplying accurate information to students and parents.
- Standards and assessments serve as an important signaling device to students, parents, teachers, employers, and colleges (Ravitch, 1996, pp. 134–135).

On the other hand, numerous concerns were expressed by opponents of the effort to develop "world-class" standards for America's educational system. The following are among the arguments these critics raised.

- Higher standards further bias educational opportunities in favor of students from advantaged backgrounds, intensify the class-based structure of American society, and increase the disparities between rich and poor schools.
- Raising standards might eventually lead to the development of a national curriculum, thereby increasing the role of federal government in education.
- The push for higher standards is fueled by conservative political groups that wish to undo educational gains made by historically underrepresented groups.
- Preoccupation with raising standards diverts attention from more meaningful educational reform.
- "World-class" standards are often vague and not linked to valid assessments and scoring rubrics.

Perhaps the most controversial standards to come forth during the 1990s were those developed for U.S. and world history by the National Center for History in the Schools. Immediately after the standards were issued in 1994, conservative groups, including the Council for Basic Education, asserted that the standards covered discrimination experienced by minority groups and women, while they omitted certain historical figures and positive features of the westward expansion and other aspects of American life. Some critics even charged that the standards were so "politically correct" that they reflected an anti-Western bias. In response to such widespread criticism, the Center rewrote the standards, this time with input from the Council for Basic Education, thirty-three national education organizations, and more than 1,000 educators. The revised standards were issued in 1996 with endorsements from many groups that were critical of the previous standards.

Two articles in this chapter are representative of the fierce debate over curriculum standards that continues today: Daniel Tanner's "Standards, Standards: High and Low" and Roy Romer's "Today Standards—Tomorrow Success." Tanner asserts that the push for high standards is a "xenophobic reaction to foreign competition for dominance over world industrial markets," while Romer contends that "setting standards, raising expectations, and assessing student progress in a meaningful way will give our students the tools they need to thrive in the twenty-first century."

Orientation to the Future

An orientation to the future is an important curriculum criterion for the twenty-first century. As a criterion, *orientation to the future* is the degree to which a curriculum prepares students to deal with the future—to engage in futures planning, to foresee coming events, and to evaluate medium- and long-range consequences of current trends. The great strains currently placed on our planetary resources and the sometimes bewildering array of social forces influencing our lives (see Chapter 2) require that curricula prepare learners to cope with these challenges in the future. An orientation to the future brings into focus the human character of the problems we face on a local as well as a global basis, and it emphasizes the right of each individual to influence decisions that shape our environment and our lives. In sum, an orientation to the future as a curriculum criterion ensures that the curriculum will be concerned not so much with answers as with strategies, not so much with products as with processes, not so much with things as with persons, and not so much with knowledge as with learners and their welfare now and in the future.

Curriculum Design

The articles on goals and values and the four bases of the curriculum in the first five chapters of this book make it evident that many different designs can be followed in planning a curriculum. These designs are not mutually exclusive; they can be used together or separately to address various types of curricular goals, differences among learners, and different types of knowledge.

While curriculum designs are not intended to provide step-by-step procedures for planning curricula, Ralph Tyler's classic text, *Basic Principles of Curriculum and Instruction,* contained four salient questions, now known as the *Tyler rationale,* that must be considered, in some fashion, at least, when planning a curriculum:

1. What educational purposes should the school seek to attain?
2. What educational experiences can be provided that are likely to attain these purposes?
3. How can these educational experiences be effectively organized?
4. How can we determine whether these purposes are being attained? (Tyler, 1949, p. 1).

The Tyler rationale has been used by many curriculum planners as a set of general guidelines for curriculum planning; however, others have criticized the rationale as being a linear, means–end model that oversimplifies the complexities of curriculum planning. They believe the Tyler rationale advocates a straightforward, step-by-step process that, in reality, is difficult to follow. Nevertheless, as curriculum theorists Francis P. Hunkins and Patricia A. Hammill (1994, p. 7) observe, "Despite all the criticism of Tyler, his thinking is still dominant in schools across the nation."

When first introduced, Tyler's model represented a modern view of curriculum design. Planning the curriculum, according to Tyler, required a mechanical, rational approach that could be followed systematically in any context, with any group of students. Today, however, postmodernist views of the world are leading to curriculum designs that are based on diverse voices, meanings, and points of view. As Hunkins and Hammill (1994, p. 10) point out:

Currently, we are realizing with increasing sophistication that life is organic, not mechanical; the universe is dynamic, not stable; the process of curriculum development is not passive acceptance of steps, but evolves from action within the system in particular contexts; and that goals emerge oftentimes from the very experiences in which people engage.

Similarly, in "Teachers, Public Life, and Curriculum Reform" in this chapter, Henry A. Giroux points out that "the language of curriculum, like other discourses, does not merely reflect a pregiven reality; on the contrary, it selectively offers depictions of the larger world through representations that people struggle over to name what counts as knowledge, what counts as communities of learning, what social relationships matter, and what visions of the future can be represented as legitimate." And, in "Diversity and Inclusion: Toward a Curriculum for Human Beings" in this chapter, Maxine Greene reminds us of the need to include "alternative" perspectives in developing the curriculum. Finally, in this chapter's Teacher's Voices section, Gregory Shafer examines how "romanticism, nostalgia, and the back-to-basics push" have been used to support curricula that are shaped by "a traditional coalition [that] seeks to protect the past and leave it in the hands of a distinct few."

REFERENCES

Dewey, John. "The Relation of Theory to Practice in Education." In *The Relation of Theory to Practice in Education,* the Third Yearbook of the National Society for the Scientific Study of Education, Part 1. Bloomington, IN: Public School Publishing Co., 1904, pp. 9–30.

Hunkins, Francis P., and Hammill, Patricia A. "Beyond Tyler and Taba: Reconceptualizing the Curriculum Process." *Peabody Journal of Education* 69, no. 3 (Spring 1994): 4–18.

Ravitch, Diane. "The Case for National Standards and Assessments." *The Clearing House* 69, no. 3 (January/February 1996): 134–135.

———. *National Standards in American Education: A Citizen's Guide.* Washington, DC: The Brookings Institution, 1995.

Tyler, Ralph W. *Basic Principles of Curriculum and Instruction.* Chicago: The University of Chicago Press, 1949.

The Sources of a Science of Education

JOHN DEWEY (1859–1952)

ABSTRACT: *Dewey suggests that "science" can be seen as a systematic method of inquiry within an area of professional practice. Thus, educational activities such as curriculum planning, instruction, and the organization and administration of schools may be said to be "scientific" if they are done systematically, with particular attention to a rigorous intellectual technique. However, science should not be seen as providing rules that should be applied to the art of education; instead, science enriches professional judgment and provides a wider range of alternatives that can be applied to educational problems.*

EDUCATION AS A SCIENCE

The title may suggest to some minds that it begs a prior question: Is there a science of education? And still more fundamentally, Can there be a science of education? Are the procedures and aims of education such that it is possible to reduce them to anything properly called a science? Similar questions exist in other fields. The issue is not unknown in history; it is raised in medicine and law. As far as education is concerned, I may confess at once that I have put the question in its apparently question-begging form in order to avoid discussion of questions that are important but that are also full of thorns and attended with controversial divisions.

It is enough for our purposes to note that the word "science" has a wide range.

There are those who would restrict the term to mathematics or to disciplines in which exact results can be determined by rigorous methods of demonstration. Such a conception limits even the claims of physics and chemistry to be sciences, for according to it the only scientific portion of these subjects is the strictly mathematical. The position of what are ordinarily termed the biological sciences is even more dubious, while social subjects and psychology would hardly rank as sciences at all, when measured by this definition. Clearly we must take the idea of science with some latitude. We must take it with sufficient looseness to include all the subjects that are usually regarded as sciences. The important thing is to discover those traits in virtue of which various fields are called scientific. When we raise the question in this way, we are led to put emphasis upon methods of dealing with subject-matter rather than to look for uniform objective traits in subject matter. From this point of view, science signifies, I take it, the existence of systematic methods of inquiry, which, when they are brought to bear on a range of facts, enable us to understand them better and to control them more intelligently, less haphazardly and with less routine.

No one would doubt that our practices in hygiene and medicine are less casual, less results of a mixture of guess work and tradition, than they used to be, nor that this difference has been made by development of methods of investigating and testing. There is an intellectual technique by which discovery and organization of material go on cumulatively, and by means of which one inquirer can repeat the researches of another, confirm or discredit them, and add still more to the capital stock of knowledge. Moreover, the methods when they are used tend to perfect themselves, to suggest new problems, new investigations, which refine old procedures and create new and better ones.

From John Dewey, *The Sources of a Science of Education* (New York: Horace Liveright, 1929), pp. 7–22.
© Dewey Center, Southern Illinois University at Carbondale. Used by permission.

The question as to the sources of a science of education is, then, to be taken in this sense. What are the ways by means of which the function of education in all its branches and phases—selection of material for the curriculum, methods of instruction and discipline, organization and administration of schools—can be conducted with systematic increase of intelligent control and understanding? What are the materials upon which we may—and should—draw in order that educational activities may become in a less degree products of routine, tradition, accident, and transitory accidental influences? From what sources shall we draw so that there shall be steady and cumulative growth of intelligent, communicable insight, and power of direction?

Here is the answer to those who decry pedagogical study on the ground that success in teaching and in moral direction of pupils is often not in any direct ratio to knowledge of educational principles. Here is "A" who is much more successful than "B" in teaching, awakening the enthusiasm of his students for learning, inspiring them morally by personal example and contact, and yet relatively ignorant of educational history, psychology, approved methods, etc., which "B" possesses in abundant measure. The facts are admitted. But what is overlooked by the objector is that the successes of such individuals tend to be born and to die with them: beneficial consequences extend only to those pupils who have personal contact with such gifted teachers. No one can measure the waste and loss that have come from the fact that the contributions of such men and women in the past have been thus confined, and the only way by which we can prevent such waste in the future is by methods which enable us to make an analysis of what the gifted teacher does intuitively, so that something accruing from his work can be communicated to others. Even in the things conventionally recognized as sciences, the insights of unusual persons remain important and there is no levelling down to a uniform procedure. But the existence of science gives common efficacy to the experiences of the genius; it makes it possible for the results of

special power to become part of the working equipment of other inquirers, instead of perishing as they arose.

The individual capacities of the Newtons, Boyles, Joules, Darwins, Lyells, Helmholtzes, are not destroyed because of the existence of science; their differences from others and the impossibility of predicting on the basis of past science what discoveries they would make—that is, the impossibility of regulating their activities by antecedent sciences—persist. But science makes it possible for others to benefit systematically by what they achieved.

The existence of scientific method protects us also from a danger that attends the operations of men of unusual power: dangers of slavish imitation, partisanship, and such jealous devotion to them and their work as to get in the way of her progress. Anybody can notice today that the effect of an original and powerful teacher is not all to the good. Those influenced by him often show a one-sided interest; they tend to form schools, and to become impervious to other problems and truths; they incline to swear by the words of their master and to go on repeating his thoughts after him, and often without the spirit and insight that originally made them significant. Observation also shows that these results happen oftenest in those subjects in which scientific method is least developed. Where these methods are of longer standing students adopt methods rather than merely results, and employ them with flexibility rather than in literal reproduction.

This digression seems to be justified not merely because those who object to the idea of a science put personality and its unique gifts in opposition to science, but also because those who recommend science sometimes urge that uniformity of procedure will be its consequence. So it seems worthwhile to dwell on the fact that in the subjects best developed from the scientific point of view, the opposite is the case. Command of scientific methods and systematized subject-matter liberates individuals; it enables them to see new problems, devise new procedures, and, in general, makes for diversification rather than for set uniformity. But at the same time these diversifications have a cumulative effect in an advance shared by all workers in the field.

EDUCATION AS AN ART

This theme is, I think, closely connected with another point which is often urged, namely, that education is an art rather than a science. That, in concrete operation, education is an art, either a mechanical art or a fine art, is unquestionable. If there were an opposition between science and art, I should be compelled to side with those who assert that education is an art. But there is no opposition, although there is a distinction. We must not be misled by words. Engineering is, in actual practice, an art. But it is an art that progressively incorporates more and more of science into itself, more of mathematics, physics, and chemistry. It is the kind of art it is precisely because of a content of scientific subject-matter which guides it as a practical operation. There is room for the original and daring projects of exceptional individuals. But their distinction lies not in the fact that they turn their backs upon science, but in the fact that they make new integrations of scientific material and turn it to new and previously unfamiliar and unforeseen uses. When, in education, the psychologist or observer and experimentalist in any field reduces his findings to a rule which is to be uniformly adopted, then, only, is there a result which is objectionable and destructive of the free play of education as an art.

But this happens not because of scientific method but because of departure from it. It is not the capable engineer who treats scientific findings as imposing upon him a certain course which is to be rigidly adhered to: it is the third- or fourth-rate man who adopts this course. Even more, it is the unskilled day laborer who follows it. For even if the practice adopted is one that follows from science and could not have been discovered or employed except for science, when it is converted into a uniform rule of procedure it becomes an empirical rule-of-thumb procedure—just as a person may use a table of logarithms mechanically without knowing anything about mathematics.

The danger is great in the degree in which the attempt to develop scientific method is recent. Nobody would deny that education is still in a condition of transition from an empirical to a scientific status. In its empirical form the chief factors determining education are tradition, imitative reproduction, response to various external pressures wherein the strongest force wins out, and the gifts, native and acquired, of individual teachers. In this situation there is a strong tendency to identify teaching ability with the use of procedures that yield immediately successful results, success being measured by such things as order in the classroom, correct recitations by pupils in assigned lessons, passing of examinations, promotion of pupils to a higher grade, etc.

For the most part, these are the standards by which a community judges the worth of a teacher. Prospective teachers come to training schools, whether in normals schools or colleges, with such ideas implicit in their minds. They want very largely to find out how to do things with the maximum prospect of success. Put baldly, they want recipes. Now, to such persons science is of value because it puts a stamp of final approval upon this and that specific procedure. It is very easy for science to be regarded as a guarantee that goes with the sale of goods rather than as a light to the eyes and a lamp to the feet. It is prized for its prestige value rather than as an organ of personal illumination and liberation. It is prized because it is thought to give unquestionable authenticity and authority to a specific procedure to be carried out in the school room. So conceived, science is antagonistic to education as an art.

EXPERIENCE AND ABSTRACTION

The history of the more mature sciences shows two characteristics. Their original problems were set by difficulties that offered themselves in the ordinary region of practical affairs. Men obtained fire by rubbing sticks together and noted how things grew warm when they pressed on each other, long before they had any theory of heat. Such everyday experiences in their seeming inconsistency with the phenomena of flame and fire finally led to the conception of heat as a mode of molecular motion. But it led to this conception only when the ordinary phenomena were reflected upon in detachment from the conditions and uses under which they exhibit themselves in practices. There is no science without abstraction, and abstraction means fundamentally that certain occurrences are removed from the dimension of familiar practical experience into that of reflective or theoretical inquiry.

To be able to get away for the time being from entanglement in the urgencies and needs of immediate practical concerns is a condition of the origin of scientific treatment in any field. Preoccupation with attaining some direct end or practical utility, always limits scientific inquiry. For it restricts the field of attention and thought, since we note only those things that are immediately connected with what we want to do or get at the moment. Theory is in the end, as has been well said, the most practical of all things, because this widening of the range of attention beyond nearby purpose and desire eventually results in the creation of wider and farther-reaching purposes and enables us to use a much wider and deeper range of conditions and means than were expressed in the observation of primitive practical purposes. For the time being, however, the formation of theories demands a resolute turning aside from the needs of practical operations previously performed.

This detachment is peculiarly hard to secure in the case of those persons who are concerned with building up the scientific content of educational practices and arts. There is a pressure for immediate results, for demonstration of a quick, short-time span of usefulness in school. There is a tendency to convert the results of statistical inquiries and laboratory experiments into directions and rules for the conduct of school administration and instruction. Results tend to be

directly grabbed, as it were, and put into operation by teachers. Then there is the leisure for that slow and gradual independent growth of theories that is a necessary condition of the formation of a true science. This danger is peculiarly imminent in a science of education because its very recentness and novelty arouse skepticism as to its possibility and its value. The human desire to prove that the scientific mode of attack is really of value brings pressure to convert scientific conclusions into rules and standards of schoolroom practice.

It would perhaps be invidious to select examples too near to current situations. Some illustration, however, is needed to give definiteness to what has been said. I select an instance which is remote in time and crude in itself. An investigator found that girls between the ages of eleven and fourteen mature more rapidly than boys of the same age. From this fact, or presumed fact, he drew the inference that during these years boys and girls should be separated for purposes of instruction. He converted an intellectual finding into an immediate rule of school practice.

That the conversion was rash, few would deny. The reason is obvious. School administration and instruction is a much more complex operation than was the factor contained in the scientific result. The significance of one factor for educational practice can be determined only as it is balanced with many other factors. Taken by itself, this illustration is so crude that to generalize from it might seem to furnish only a caricature. But the principle involved is of universal application. No conclusion of scientific research can be converted into an immediate rule of educational art. For there is no educational practice whatever which is not highly complex; that is to say, which does not contain many other conditions and factors than are included in the scientific finding.

Nevertheless, scientific findings are of practical utility, and the situation is wrongly interpreted when it is used to disparage the value of science in the art of education. What it militates against is the transformation of scientific findings into rules of action. Suppose for the moment that the finding about the different rates of maturing in boys and girls of a certain age is confirmed by continued investigation, and is to be accepted as fact. While it does not translate into a specific rule of fixed procedure, it is of some worth. The teacher who really knows this fact will have his personal attitude changed. He will be on the alert to make certain observations which would otherwise escape him; he will be enabled to interpret some facts which would otherwise be confused and misunderstood. This knowledge and understanding render his practice more intelligent, more flexible, and better adapted to deal effectively with concrete phenomena of practice.

Nor does this tell the whole story. Continued investigation reveals other relevant facts. Each investigation and conclusion is special, but the tendency of an increasing number and variety of specialized results is to create new points of view and a wider field of observation. Various special findings have a cumulative effect; they reinforce and extend one another, and in time lead to the detection of principles that bind together a number of facts that are diverse and even isolated in their *prima facie* occurrence. These connecting principles which link different phenomena together we call laws.

Facts which are so interrelated form a system, a science. The practitioner who knows the system and its laws is evidently in possession of a powerful instrument for observing and interpreting what goes on before him. This intellectual tool affects his attitudes and modes of response in what he does. Because the range of understanding is deepened and widened, he can take into account remote consequences which were originally hidden from view and hence were ignored in his actions. Greater continuity is introduced; he does not isolate situations and deal with them in separation as he was compelled to do when ignorant of connecting principles. At the same time, his practical dealings become more flexible. Seeing more relations he sees more possibilities, more opportunities. He is emancipated from the need of following tradition and special precedents. His ability to judge being enriched, he has a wider range of alternatives to select from in dealing with individual situations.

WHAT SCIENCE MEANS

If we gather up these conclusions in a summary we reach the following results. In the first place, no genuine science is formed by isolated conclusions, no matter how scientifically correct the technique by which these isolated results are reached, and no matter how exact they are. Science does not emerge until these various findings are linked together to form a relatively coherent system—that is, until they reciprocally confirm and illuminate one another, or until each gives the others added meaning. Now this development requires time, and it requires more time in the degree in which the transition from an empirical condition to a scientific one is recent and hence imperfect.

John Dewey was, at various times during his career, Professor of Philosophy, Columbia University; head of the Department of Philosophy and director of the School of Education at the University of Chicago; and Professor of Philosophy at the University of Michigan.

QUESTIONS FOR REFLECTION

1. What does Dewey mean when he says that the effect of an "original and powerful teacher is not all to the good"? What remedy is available to offset the sometimes unfavorable effects of such teachers, according to Dewey? Have you been taught by this type of teacher? If so, how did those experiences influence your learning?

2. Under what circumstances does Dewey consider science to be "antagonistic" to education as an art?
3. When, according to Dewey, is "theory the most practical of all things"? Do you agree with his argument?

Teachers, Public Life, and Curriculum Reform

HENRY A. GIROUX

ABSTRACT: *Discourse related to curriculum and teaching reflects the points of view of those involved and cannot be separated from issues of history, power, and politics. Dominant views of curriculum and teaching claim objectivity, but they fail to link schooling to complex political, economic, and cultural forces; and they see teachers as technicians, bureaucratic agents, and deskilled intellectuals. Thus, a critical theory of curriculum must consider questions of representation, justice, and power. Toward this end, teachers' roles should be restructured so they become critical agents who take risks (or "go for broke") and act as "public intellectuals" who bring issues of equity, community, and social justice to the fore.*

REASSERTING THE PRIMACY OF THE POLITICAL IN CURRICULUM THEORY

The connection between curriculum and teaching is structured by a series of issues that are not always present in the language of the current educational reform movement. This is evident, for instance, in the way mainstream educational reformers often ignore the problematic relationship between curriculum as a socially constructed narrative on the one hand, and the interface of teaching and politics on the other. Mainstream curriculum reformers often view curriculum as an objective text that merely has to be imparted to students.[1]

In opposition to this view, I want to argue that the language used by administrators, teachers, students, and others involved in either constructing, implementing, or receiving the classroom curriculum actively produces particular social identities, "imagined communities," specific competencies, and distinctive ways of life. Moreover, the language of curriculum, like other discourses, does not merely reflect a pregiven reality; on the contrary, it selectively offers depictions of the larger world through representations that people struggle over to name what counts as knowledge, what counts as communities of learning, what social relationships matter, and what visions of the future can be represented as legitimate (Aronowitz & Giroux, 1993).

Of course, if curriculum is seen as a terrain of struggle, one that is shot through with ethical considerations, it becomes reasonable to assume that talk about teaching and curriculum should not be removed from considerations of history, power, and politics. After all, the language of curriculum is both historical and contingent. Theories of curriculum have emerged from past struggles and are

From *Peabody Journal of Education* 69, no. 3 (Spring 1994): 35–47. © 1994, Peabody College of Vanderbilt University. Used by permission of the publisher.

often heavily weighted in favor of those who have power, authority, and institutional legitimation.

Curriculum is also political in that state governments, locally elected schools boards, and powerful business and publishing interests exercise enormous influence over teaching practices and curriculum policies (Apple & Christian-Smith, 1992). Moreover, the culture of the school is often representative of those features of the dominant culture that it affirms, sustains, selects, and legitimates. Thus, the distinction between high and low status academic subjects, the organization of knowledge into disciplines, and the allocation of knowledge and symbolic rewards to different groups indicates how politics work to influence the curriculum.

Within dominant versions of curriculum and teaching, there is little room theoretically to understand the dynamics of power as they work in schools, particularly around the mechanisms of tracking, racial and gender discrimination, testing, and other mechanisms of exclusion (Oaks, 1985). Mainstream educational reformers such as William Bennett, Chester Finn, Jr., and Dianne Ravitch exhibit little understanding of schooling as a site that actively produces different histories, social groups, and student identities under profound conditions of inequality. This is true, in part, because many dominant versions of curriculum and teaching legitimate themselves through unproblematized claims to objectivity and an obsession with empiricist forms of accountability. But, more importantly, many mainstream theorists of curriculum refuse to link schooling to the complex political, economic, and cultural relations that structure it as a borderland of movement and translation rather than a fixed and unitary site.

When inserted into this matrix of power, difference, and social justice, schools cannot be abstracted from the larger society where histories mix, languages and identities intermingle, values clash, and different groups struggle over how they are represented and how they might represent themselves. Questions of representation, justice, and power are central to any critical theory of curriculum. This is especially true in a society in which Afro-Americans, women, and other people of color are vastly underrepresented in both schools and other dominant cultural institutions. Of course, the issue of representation as I am using it here suggests that meaning is always political, actively involved in producing diverse social positions, and inextricably implicated in relations of power.

Educators generally exhibit a deep suspicion of politics, and this is not unwarranted when politics is reduced to a form of dogmatism. And, yet, it is impossible for teachers to become agents in the classroom without a broader understanding of politics and the emancipatory possibilities it provides for thinking about and shaping their own practices. Recognizing the politics of one's location as an educator should not imply that one's pedagogical practice is inflexible, fixed, or intolerant. To insist that teachers recognize the political nature of their own work can be understood as part of a broader critical effort to make them self-reflective of the interests and assumptions that shape their classroom practices. Roger Simon (1992) captures this sentiment by arguing that by inserting the political back into the discourse of teaching educators can "initiate rather than close off the problem of responsibility" (p. 16) for those classroom practices generated by their claim to knowledge and authority.

In what follows, I want to offer an alternative language for defining the purpose and meaning of teacher work. While I have talked about teachers as intellectuals in another context, I want to extend this analysis by analyzing what the implications are for redefining teachers as public intellectuals.[2] In part, I want to explore this position by drawing upon my own training as a teacher and some of the problems I had to face when actually working in the public schools. I will conclude by highlighting some of the defining principles that might structure the content and context of what it means for teachers to assume the role of a public intellectual.

TRADITION AND THE PEDAGOGY OF RISK

Let me begin by saying that we are living through a very dangerous time. . . . We are in a revolutionary situation, no matter how unpopular that word has become in this country. The society in which we live is desperately menaced, not by [the cold war] but from within. So any citizen of this country who figures himself as responsible—and particularly those of you who deal with the minds and hearts of young people—must be prepared to "go for broke." Or to put it another way, you must understand that in the attempt to correct so many generations of bad faith and cruelty, when it is operating not only in the classroom but in society, you will meet the most fantastic, the most brutal, and the most determined resistance. There is no point in pretending that this won't happen. . . . [And yet] the obligation of anyone who thinks of him or herself as responsible is to examine society and try to change it and to fight it—at no matter what risk. This is the only hope society has. This is the only way societies change. (Baldwin, 1988, p. 3)

I read the words of the famed African-American novelist James Baldwin less as a prescription for cynicism and powerlessness than I do as an expression of hope. Baldwin's words are moving because he confers a sense of moral and political responsibility upon teachers by presupposing that they are critical agents who can move between theory and practice in order to take risks, refine their visions, and make a difference for both their students and the world in which they live. In order to take up Baldwin's challenge for teachers to "go for broke," to act in the classroom and the world with courage and dignity, it is important for educators to recognize that the current challenge facing public schools is one of the most serious that any generation of existing and prospective teachers has ever had to face. Politically, the U.S. has lived through 12 years of reforms in which teachers have been invited to deskill themselves, to become technicians, or, in more ideological terms, to accept their role as

"clerks of the empire." We live at a time when state legislators and federal officials are increasingly calling for the testing of teachers and the implementation of standardized curriculum; at the same time, legislators and government officials are ignoring the most important people in the reform effort, the teachers. Within this grim scenario, the voices of teachers have been largely absent from the debate about education. It gets worse.

Economically, the working conditions of teachers, especially those in the urban districts with a low tax base, have badly deteriorated. The story is a familiar one: overcrowded classrooms, inadequate resources, low salaries, and a rise in teacher-directed violence. In part, this is due to the increased financial cutbacks to the public sector by the Federal Government, the tax revolt of the 1970s by the middle-class that put a ceiling on the ability of cities and states to raise revenue for public services, and the refusal by wide segments of the society to believe that public schooling is essential to the health of a democratic society. Compounding these problems is a dominant vision of schooling defined largely through the logic of corporate values and the imperatives of the marketplace. Schools are being treated as if their only purpose were to train future workers, and teachers are being viewed as corporate footsoldiers whose role is to provide students with the skills necessary for the business world. In short, part of the crisis of teaching is the result of a vision of schooling that subordinates issues of equity, community, and social justice to pragmatic considerations that enshrine the marketplace and accountability schemes that standardize the social relations of schooling. The political and ideological climate does not look favorable for teachers at the moment. But it does offer prospective and existing teachers the challenge to engage in dialogue and debate regarding important issues such as the nature and purpose of teacher preparation, the meaning of educational leadership, and the dominant forms of classroom teaching.

I think that if existing and future teachers are willing to "go for broke," to use Baldwin's term, they will need to re-imagine teaching as part of a project of critique and possibility. But there is more at stake here than simply a change in who controls the conditions under which teachers work. This is important, but what is also needed is a new language, a new way of naming, ordering, and representing how power works in schools. It is precisely through a more critical language that teachers might be able to recognize the power of their own agency in order to raise and act upon such questions as: What range of purposes should schools serve? What knowledge is of most worth? What does it mean for teachers and students to know something? In what direction should teachers and students desire? What notions of authority should structure teaching and learning? These questions are important because they force educators to engage in a process of self-critique while simultaneously highlighting the central role that teachers might play in any viable attempt to reform the public schools.

My own journey into teaching was largely shaped by undergraduate education training and my first year of student teaching. While the content and context of these experiences shaped my initial understanding of myself as a teacher, they did not prepare me for the specific tasks and problems of what it meant to address the many problems I had to confront in my first job. In what follows, I want to speak from my own experiences in order to illuminate the shortcomings of the educational theories that both shaped my perceptions of teaching and the classroom practices I was expected to implement.

LEARNING TO BE A TECHNICIAN

During the time that I studied to be a teacher, for the most part I learned how to master classroom methods, read Bloom's taxonomy, and became adept at administering tests, but I was never asked to question how testing might be used as a sorting device to track and marginalize certain groups. Like many prospective teachers of my generation, I was taught how to master a body of knowledge defined within separate academic disciplines, but I never learned to question what the hierarchical organization of knowledge meant and how it conferred authority and power. For example, I was never taught to raise questions about what knowledge was worth knowing and why, why schools legitimated some forms of knowledge and ignored others, why English was more important than art, and why it was considered unworthy to take a course in which one worked with one's hands. I never engaged in a classroom discussion about whose interests were served through the teaching and legitimation of particular forms of school knowledge, or how knowledge served to silence and disempower particular social groups. Moreover, I was not given the opportunity to reflect upon the authoritarian principles that actually structure classroom life and how these could be understood by analyzing social, political, and economic conditions outside of schools. If a student slept in the morning at his or her desk, I was taught to approach the issue as a problem of discipline and management. I was not alerted to recognize the social conditions that may have caused such behavior. That is, to the possibility that the student may have a drug-related problem, be hungry, sick, or simply exhausted because of conditions in his or her home life. I learned quickly to separate out the problems of society from the problems of schooling and hence became illiterate in understanding the complexity of the relationship between schools and the larger social order.

My initial teaching assignment was in a school in which the teacher turnover rate exceeded 85% each year. The first day I walked into that school I was met by some students hanging out in the lobby. They greeted me with stares born of territorial rights and suspicion and one of them jokingly asked me: "Hey man, you're new, what's your name?" I remember thinking they had violated some sort of rule regarding teacher-student relationships by addressing me that way. Questions of identity, culture, and racism had not been factored into my understanding of teaching and schooling at the time. I had no idea that the questions that would be raised for me that year had less to do with the sterile language of methods I had learned as an undergraduate than they did with becoming culturally and politically literate about the context-specific histories and experiences that informed where my students came from and how they viewed themselves and others. I had no idea of how important it was to create a meaningful and safe classroom for them so that I could connect my teaching to their own languages, cultures, and lived experiences. I soon found out that giving students some sense of power and ownership over their own educational experience has more to do with developing a language that was risk taking and self-critical for me and meaningful, practical, and transformative for them. During that first year, I also learned something about the ways in which many school administrators are educated.

LEADERSHIP WITHOUT VISION

During that first year, I rented movies from the American Friends Service Committee, ignored the officially designated curriculum textbooks, and eventually put my own books and magazine articles on reserve in the school library for my students to read. Hoping to give my students some control over the conditions for producing knowledge, I encouraged them to produce their own texts through the use of school video equipment, cameras, and daily journals. Within a very short time, I came into conflict with the school principal. He was a mix between General Patton and the Encino Man. At six foot three, weighing in at 250 pounds, his presence seemed a bit overwhelming and intimidating. The first time he called me into his office, I learned something about how he was educated. He told me that in his mind students should be quiet in classrooms, teachers should stick to giving lectures and writing on the board, and that I was never to ask a student a question that he or she could not answer. He further suggested that rather than developing my own materials in class I should use

the curricula packages made available through the good wishes of local businesses and companies. While clearly being a reflection, if not a parody, of the worst kind of teacher training, he adamantly believed strict management controls, rigid systems of accountability, and lock step discipline were at the heart of educational leadership. Hence, I found myself in a secular version of hell. This was a school in which teaching became reduced to the sterile logic of flow charts. Moreover, it was a school in which power was wielded largely by white, male administrators further reinforcing the isolation and despair of most of the teachers. I engaged in forms of guerrilla warfare with this administration, but in order to survive I had to enlist the help of a few other teachers and some members of the community. At the end of the school year, I was encouraged not to come back. Fortunately, I had another teaching job back east and ended up in a much better school.

In retrospect, the dominant view of educational leadership has had a resurgence during the Reagan and Bush eras. Its overall effect has been to limit teachers' control over the development and planning of curriculum, to reinforce the bureaucratic organization of the school, and to remove teachers from the process of judging and implementing classroom instruction. This is evident in the growing call for national testing, national curriculum standards, and the concerted attack on developing multicultural curricula. The ideology that guides this model and its view of pedagogy is that the behavior of teachers needs to be controlled and made consistent and predictable across different schools and student populations. The effect is not only to remove teachers from the process of deliberation and reflection, but also to routinize the nature of learning and classroom pedagogy. In this approach, it is assumed that all students can learn from the same standardized materials, instructional techniques, and modes of evaluation. The notion that students come from different histories, experiences, and cultures is strategically ignored within this approach. The notion that pedagogy should be attentive to specific contexts is ignored.

TEACHERS AS PUBLIC INTELLECTUALS

I want to challenge these views by arguing that one way to rethink and restructure the nature of teacher work is to view teachers as public intellectuals. The unease expressed about the identity and role of teachers as public intellectuals has a long tradition in the United States and has become the focus of a number of recent debates. On one level, there are conservatives who argue that teachers who address public issues from the perspective of a committed position are simply part of what they call the political correctness movement. In this case, there is a deep suspicion of any attempt to open up the possibility for educators to address pressing social issues and to connect them to their teaching. Moreover, within the broad parameters of this view schools are seen as apolitical institutions whose primary purpose is to both prepare students for the work place and to reproduce the alleged common values that define the "American" way of life.[3] At the same time, many liberals have argued that while teachers should address public issues they should do so from the perspective of a particular teaching methodology. This is evident in Gerald Graff's (1992) call for educators to teach the conflicts. In this view, the struggle over representations replaces how a politics of meaning might help students identify, engage, and transform relations of power that generate the material conditions of racism, sexism, poverty, and other oppressive conditions. Moreover, some radical feminists have argued that the call for teachers to be public intellectuals promotes leadership models that are largely patriarchal and overly rational in the forms of authority they secure. While there may be an element of truth in all of these positions, they all display enormous theoretical shortcomings. Conservatives often refuse to problematize their own version of what is legitimate intellectual knowledge and how it works to secure particular forms of authority by simply labeling as politically correct individuals, groups, or views that challenge the basic tenets of the sta-

tus quo. Liberals, on the other hand, inhabit a terrain that wavers between rejecting a principled standpoint from which to teach and staunchly arguing for a pedagogy that is academically rigorous and fair. Caught between a discourse of fairness and the appeal to provocative teaching methods, liberals have no language for clarifying the moral visions that structure their views of the relationship between knowledge and authority and the practices it promotes. Moreover, they increasingly have come to believe that teaching from a particular standpoint is tantamount to imposing an ideological position upon students. This has led in some cases to a form of McCarthyism in which critical educators are summarily dismissed as being guilty of ideological indoctrination. While the feminist critique is the most interesting, it underplays the possibility for using authority in ways which allow teachers to be more self-critical while simultaneously providing the conditions for students to recognize the possibility for democratic agency in both themselves and others. Operating out of a language of binarisms, some feminist education critics essentialize the positions of their opponents and in doing so present a dehistoricized and reductionistic view of critical pedagogy. Most importantly, all of these positions share in the failure to address the possibility for teachers to become a force for democratization both within and outside of schools.

As public intellectuals, teachers must bring to bear in their classrooms and other pedagogical sites the courage, analytical tools, moral vision, time, and dedication that is necessary to return schools to their primary task: being places of critical education in the service of creating a public sphere of citizens who are able to exercise power over their own lives and especially over the conditions of knowledge acquisition. Central to any such reform effort is the recognition that democracy is not a set of formal rules of participation, but the lived experience of empowerment for the vast majority. Moreover, the call for schools as democratic public spheres should not be limited to the call for equal access to schools, equal opportunity, or other arguments defined in terms of the principles of equality. Equality is a crucial aspect of democratizing schools, but teachers should not limit their demands to the call for equality. Instead, the rallying cry of teachers should be organized around the practice of empowerment for the vast majority of students in this country who need to be educated in the spirit of a critical democracy.[4]

This suggests another dimension in defining the role of public intellectuals. Such intellectuals must combine their role as educators and citizens. This implies they must connect the practice of classroom teaching to the operation of power in the larger society. At the same time, they must be attentive to those broader social forces that influence the workings of schooling and pedagogy. What is at issue here is a commitment on the part of teachers as public intellectuals to extend the principles of social justice to all spheres of economic, political, and cultural life. Within this discourse, the experiences that constitute the production of knowledge, identities, and social values in the schools are inextricably linked to the quality of moral and political life of the wider society. Hence, the reform of schooling must be seen as a part of a wider revitalization of public life.

This should not suggest that as public intellectuals, teachers represent a vanguardist group dedicated to simply reproducing another master narrative. In fact, as public intellectuals it is important for them to link their role as critical agents to their ability to be critical of their own politics while constantly engaging in dialogue with other educators, community people, various cultural workers, and students. As public intellectuals, teachers need to be aware of the limits of their own positions, make their pedagogies context specific, challenge the current organization of knowledge into fixed disciplines, and work in solidarity with others to gain some control over the conditions of their work. At the very least, this suggests that teachers will have to struggle on many different fronts in order to transform the conditions of work and learning that go on in

schools. This means not only working with community people, teachers, students, and parents to open up progressive spaces within classrooms, but also forming alliances with other cultural workers in order to debate and shape educational policy at the local, state, and federal levels of government.

As public intellectuals, teachers need to provide the conditions for students to learn that the relationship between knowledge and power can be emancipatory, that their histories and experiences matter, and that what they say and do can count as part of a wider struggle to change the world around them. More specifically, teachers need to argue for forms of pedagogy that close the gap between the school and the real world. The curriculum needs to be organized around knowledge that relates to the communities, cultures, and traditions that give students a sense of history, identity, and place. This suggests pedagogical approaches that do more than make learning context specific, it also points to the need to expand the range of cultural texts that inform what counts as knowledge. As public intellectuals, teachers need to understand and use those electronically mediated knowledge forms that constitute the terrain of popular culture. This is the world of media texts—videos, films, music, and other mechanisms of popular culture constituted outside of the technology of print and the book. Put another way, the content of the curriculum needs to affirm and critically enrich the meaning, language, and knowledge that students actually use to negotiate and inform their lives.

While it is central for teachers to expand the relevance of the curriculum to include the richness and diversity of the students they actually teach, they also need to correspondingly decenter the curriculum. That is, students should be actively involved with issues of governance, "including setting learning goals, selecting courses, and having their own, autonomous organizations, including a free press" (Aronowitz, in press). Not only does the distribution of power among teachers, students, and administrators provide the conditions for students to become agents in their learning process, it also provides the basis for collective learning, civic action, and ethical responsibility. Moreover, such agency emerges as a lived experience rather than as the mastery of an academic subject.

In addition, as public intellectuals, teachers need to make the issue of cultural difference a defining principal of curriculum development and research. In an age of shifting demographics, large scale immigration, and multiracial communities, teachers must make a firm commitment to cultural difference as central to the relationship of schooling and citizenship (Giroux, 1992). In the first instance, this means dismantling and deconstructing the legacy of nativism and racial chauvinism that has defined the rhetoric of school reform for the last decade. The Reagan and Bush era witnessed a full-fledged attack on the rights of minorities, civil rights legislation, affirmative action, and the legitimation of curriculum reforms pandering to Eurocentric interests. Teachers can affirm their commitment to democratic public life and cultural democracy by struggling in and outside of their classrooms in solidarity with others to reverse these policies in order to make schools more attentive to the cultural resources that students bring to the public schools. At one level, this means working to develop legislation that protects the civil rights of all groups. Equally important is the need for teachers to take the lead in encouraging programs that open school curricula to the narratives of cultural difference, without falling into the trap of merely romanticizing the experience of "Otherness." At stake here is the development of an educational policy that asserts public education as part of a broader ethical and political discourse, one that both challenges and transforms those curricula reforms of the last decade that are profoundly racist in context and content. In part, this suggests changing the terms of the debate regarding the relationship between schooling and national identity, moving away from an assimilationist ethic and the profoundly Eurocentric fantasies of a common culture to one which links national identity to diverse traditions and histories.

In short, as public intellectuals, teachers need to address the imperatives of citizenship. In part, this means addressing how schools can create the conditions for students to be social agents willing to struggle for expanding the critical public cultures that make a democracy viable. Consequently, any notion of pedagogy must be seen as a form of cultural politics, that is, a politic that highlights the role of education, as it takes place in a variety of public sites, to open up rather than close down the possibilities for keeping justice and hope alive at a time of shrinking possibilities.

NOTES

1. This is particularly true with respect to those mainstream reformers arguing for national standards and testing. In this discourse, students are always on the receiving end of the learning experience. It is as if the histories, experiences, and communities that shape their identities and sense of place are irrelevant to what is taught and how it is taught. See, for example, Hirsch (1987); Finn, Jr. and Ravitch (1987); for an alternative to this position, see Apple (1993); Giroux (1988a); Giroux (1993). For an examination of schools that view teachers as more than clerks and technicians, see Wood (1993).
2. I have taken up this issue more extensively in Giroux (1988b), and Aronowitz and Giroux (1993).
3. For a trenchant analysis of the political correctness movement, see Aronowitz (1993), especially Chapter 1; see also Frank (1993).
4. I take this issue up in Giroux (1988b).

REFERENCES

Apple, M. (1993). *Official knowledge*. New York: Routledge.

Apple, M., & Christian-Smith, L. K. (Eds.). (1992). *The politics of the textbook*. New York: Routledge.

Aronowitz, S. (1993). *Roll over Beethoven: The return of cultural strife*. Hanover: Wesleyan University Press.

Aronowitz, S. (in press). A different perspective on educational inequality. *The Review of Education/Pedagogy/Cultural Studies*.

Aronowitz, S., & Giroux, H. A. (1993). *Education still under siege*. Westport, CT: Bergin & Garvey.

Baldwin, J. (1988). A talk to teachers. In Simonson & Waler (Eds.), *Multicultural literacy: Opening the American mind* (pp. 3–12). Saint Paul, MN: Graywolf Press.

Finn, C., Jr., & Ravitch, D. (1987). *What our 17-year olds know*. New York: Harper & Row.

Frank, J. (1993). In the waiting room: Canons, communities, "Political Correctness." In M. Edmunson (Ed.), *Wild Orchids: Messages from American universities* (pp. 127–149). New York: Penguin.

Giroux, H. A. (1988a). *Teachers as intellectuals*. Westport, CT: Bergin & Garvey.

Giroux, H. A. (1988b). *Schooling and the struggle for public life*. Minneapolis: University of Minnesota Press.

Giroux, H. A. (1992). *Border crossings*. New York: Routledge.

Giroux, H. A. (1993). *Living dangerously: The politics of multiculturalism*. New York: Peter Lang.

Graff, G. (1992). Teaching the conflicts. In D. J. Gless & B. H. Smith (Eds.), *The politics of liberal education* (pp. 57–73). Durham: Duke University Press.

Hirsch, E. D. (1987). *Cultural literacy*. Boston: Houghton Mifflin.

Oaks, J. (1985). *Keeping track: How schools structure inequality*. New Haven: Yale University Press.

Simon, R. (1922). *Teaching against the grain*. Westport, CT: Bergin & Garvey.

Wood, G. (1933). *Schools that work*. New York: Penguin Books.

Henry A. Giroux holds the Waterbury Chair Professorship in Secondary Education, Pennsylvania State University, University Park.

QUESTIONS FOR REFLECTION

1.   Why does Giroux advocate "inserting the political back into the discourse of teaching"? Do you agree? What arguments might be raised by critics of Giroux's recommendation?

2.   If teachers were to become "public intellectuals," how would this influence their curriculum planning activities? In other words, what would they do differently?

3.   In regard to the educational setting with which you are most familiar, what would it mean if you were to "go for broke" in the manner that Giroux suggests? What forms of resistance might you encounter? Does Giroux exaggerate when he says that teachers and other responsible citizens who "go for broke" should realize "that in the attempt to correct so many generations of bad faith and cruelty, when it is operating not only in the classroom but in society, [they] will meet the most fantastic, the most brutal, and the most determined resistance"?

4.   Do you agree with Giroux that the dominant view of educational leadership has served to limit teacher involvement in the development and planning of curricula? On the basis of your professional experiences, can you cite evidence that teacher involvement in curriculum planning is increasing?

Diversity and Inclusion: Toward a Curriculum for Human Beings

MAXINE GREENE

ABSTRACT: *The "savage inequalities" in our world marginalize many learners and make it impossible for them to experience curriculum as relevant to improving their lives. A curriculum for human beings, however, would utilize the arts and the imagination to counter patriarchal, rational perceptions of the world and move us toward becoming a truly inclusive society. Such a curriculum would view disciplines of knowledge as provisional, always open to revision; and learners would become engaged* with *objects of study rather than conducting analytic study* on *them. As a result, the curriculum would "provoke persons to reach past themselves and to become."*

This is, in part, an effort to gain perspective on our constructs and our categories, to break through what Dewey once called "the crust of conventionalized and routine consciousness."[1] My reasons for wanting to make this effort have to do with a desire to communicate a sense of how haunted I often feel, how badly I want to break with the taken-for-granted, to see and to say. Like many in our field, I am preoccupied by the "savage inequalities" Jonathan Kozol describes.[2] My interest in coping with diversity and striving toward significant inclusion derives to a large degree from an awareness of the savagery, the brutal marginalizations, the structured sciences, the imposed invisibility so present all around.

Listening to the continuous talk about the AIDS epidemic as an inexorably advancing plague, I have been touched by those who have reminded us of the ways in which marginalization can destroy a community. Excluding and demeaning great numbers of the population, we have not paid heed to what has been happening; we have not responded in time to a catastrophe that now endangers us all, no matter what our class or gender or ethnic origin. How can we not recall the long years in which we were corrupted by our distancing of African Americans in this country, by our institutionalized indifference and neglect?

How can some of us not remember the narratives read by gay and lesbian adolescents in Colorado, confronting not only the law that erodes their civil rights, but constant fears of violence and violation? These are the narratives of young people often deprived of role models, sometimes thrown out of their homes, publicly defined as deviant, feeling wholly alone in the world.

I think of the philosopher's admonition (which most of us would say we believe in absolutely) that all persons should be treated as ends, never as means,[3] and what that obligation entails. I think of what we say to one another about the dignity and integrity of each human being, and about how that relates to our conceptions of democracy. I think of Hillary Rodham Clinton and Marian Wright Edelman emphasizing the importance of children's rights—their rights to good education, corrective health measures, and (yes) to leave neglectful or abusive homes. That reinforces my conviction that the young people in Colorado, like many of those in New York City today, are not only being violated in extremely personal ways. They are being deprived of certain basic rights—in this case, their light to an adequate education, if education is viewed as a consequence of relating to bodies of knowledge in such a fashion that meanings can be made. If the human being is

From *Teachers College Record* 95, no. 2 (Winter 1993): 211–221. © 1993, Teachers College, Columbia University. Used by permission of the author and publisher.

demeaned, if her or his family is delegitimized, crucial rights are being trampled on. This is partly because persons marked as unworthy are unlikely to feel good enough to pose the questions in which learning begins, unlikely to experience whatever curriculum is presented as relevant to their being in the world.

Outrage at this interference with children's becoming and at the violence, the terrorism, the linguistic pornography that often accompany it drives me to try to do something in this domain, at the very least to understand it. We need only think of the pronouncements of the radical Right. We need only summon up the images of the "skinheads." We need only hold in mind the raging against multiculturalism, demonized as communism was not very long ago. Most of us are familiar with the warning that any one of us might well be the next to hear the knocking on our door at night. Recalling what happened in Nazi Germany fifty years ago (when many homosexuals were rounded up along with Jews and Gypsies and sent to concentration camps), I become somewhat obsessive about what diversity ought to signify in a democracy. At once, I keep pondering the meanings of inclusion and wondering how it can occur without the kind of normalization that wipes out differences, forcing them to be repressed, to become matters of shame rather than pride.

In addition to all this, there is my interest in the contemporary modes of thinking described as postmodern: responses to experiences in the shifting, multifaceted world that are more widely shared than ever before. There is the experience of multiplicity itself, what the anthropologist Clifford Geertz calls "the hallmark of modern consciousness.[4] Another scholar speaks of an "irruption of otherness" with which we are still trying to come to terms.[5] Others emphasize the diversity of thought in the realms of scholarship, the radical pluralization of what we think we know in the various disciplines. It becomes, for instance, increasingly indefensible to structure knowledge monologically. We can no longer set aside the ideas of vantage point, dialogue, con-

versation. We cannot forget the "heteroglossia" Mikhail Bakhtin has pointed to: the existence of many voices, some contesting, some cohering, all demanding and deserving attention.[6]

When we relate all this to the acknowledgment of the newcomers in our country, our cities, our classrooms, we come to realize (or ought to come to realize) that there cannot be a single standard of humanness or attainment or propriety when it comes to taking a perspective on the world. There can only be an ongoing, collaborative decoding of many texts. There can only be a conversation drawing in voices kept inaudible over the generations, a dialogue involving more and more living persons. There can only be—there ought to be—a wider and deeper sharing of beliefs, an enhanced capacity to articulate them, to justify them, to persuade others as the heteroglossic conversation moves on, never reaching a final conclusion, always incomplete, but richer and more densely woven, even as it moves through time.

Another notion emerging from contemporary inquiries and talk has to do with the self, the subject, so long thought susceptible to predetermination, to prediction, to framing. There are, at least in recent times, psychologists eager to thrust children's observed behavior into measurable molds. There have been numerous people (mainly white men in power, I must say) hungry to maintain the old hierarchies. Atop those hierarchies, as they saw them, were autonomous, free-wheeling, deep-throated gentlemen (or generals, or corporation managers) who thought themselves entitled to be enthroned. And, of course, there are numerous interdependent, fragile, compassionate, sentimental, dreamy, inefficient people seen to be swarming at the bottom, never meeting world-class standards, never sufficiently efficient, or docile, or controlled.

In both instances, there has been a prevalent conception of the self (grand or humble, master or slave) as predefined, fixed, separate. Today we are far more likely, in the mode of John Dewey and existentialist thinkers, to think of selves as always in the making.[7] We perceive them creating meanings, becoming in an intersubjective world by means of dialogue and narrative. We perceive them telling their stories, shaping their stories, discovering purposes and possibilities for themselves, reaching out to pursue them. We are moved to provoke such beings to keep speaking, to keep articulating, to devise metaphors and images, as they feel their bodies moving, their feet making imprints as they move toward others, as they try to see through others' eyes. Thinking of beings like that, many of those writing today and painting and dancing and composing no longer have single-focused, one-dimensional creatures in mind as models or as audiences. Rather, they think of human beings in terms of open possibility, in terms of freedom and the power to choose. They think of them, as many of us do, as creating themselves in resistance to objectness, in refusal of the abstract formulations presented by the media. They think of them identifying themselves in conscious rebellion against the convergence of masculinity and technology that infuses what may be called the technoculture of our time.

This, of course, arouses me as a feminist, knowing how much there still is to clarify, how much there still is to resist. I am aware (how could I not be?) of the gaps in history and literature where women's lives and ways of knowing are concerned. I know how much had to be hidden and repressed in my life and in lives like mine, if there was to be acceptance by a profession long governed by masculinized and traditional norms. Quite obviously, this intensifies my desire to discover what can be meant by a truly inclusive society and a curriculum for human beings.

There is that; and there is a long commitment to the arts, to aesthetic education, to the life of imagination. It is not because I believe the arts necessarily ennoble or inspire (or can cure toothaches or solve the problems of marginalization). Even the most beautiful Matisse retrospective or the most exquisite American seascape can arouse existential doubts, can remind us of a mystery below the decorative surfaces of things. In all its lulling and thrilling loveliness, the classical ballet is complex enough to arouse an indignation

with regard to women as objects or the chill forms of classical denial. Imagination, for me, cannot be counted on to summon up visions of the romantic, the celestial, the harmonious. It is because I believe that encounters with the arts can awaken us to alternative possibilities of existing, of being human, of relating to others, of *being* other, that I argue for their centrality in curriculum. I believe they can open new perspectives on what is assumed to be "reality," that they can defamiliarize what has become so familiar it has stopped us from asking questions or protesting or taking action to repair. Consider the advancing invisibility of the homeless or how accustomed we have become to burnt-out buildings or to the contrasts between a holiday-decked Fifth Avenue and a desolate "uptown." It may be that some of Beckett's work (*Waiting for Godot,* perhaps, or *Endgame*) might defamiliarize our visions of the lost, the disinherited. It may be that time spent with Edward Hopper's rendering of lonely city streets, of luncheonettes on Sunday mornings, might move us into seeing once again.

In any case, the very conception of disclosure, of perspective, like the possibility that encounters with the arts may overcome what Dewey called the "anaesthetic" in experience[8] and help us break with the mechanical and the routine, feeds my argument for attentiveness to the arts. Equally important is the recognition that they can be opened to consciousness only by intentional imaginative noticing or attending on the part of those who come to them, by a bracketing out of the mundane and the taken-for-granted. I think of novels—Virginia Woolf's and Toni Morrison's and Maxine Hong Kingston's; I think of Jean-Paul Sartre writing of the ways in which the arts appeal to us in our freedom, to our sense that things ought to be, can be otherwise.[9] And I wonder whether the curricula we devise can be of the kind that awaken, awaken sufficiently to move persons to fight the plague. The plague, of course, refers to the metaphor created by Albert Camus, who wrote of it as referring to—not merely a pestilence or the German occupation of Paris—abstract thinking, indifference, depersonalization. Some of you remember how Tarrou in that novel organizes sanitary squads to fight the plague. Some of you recall his saying that, in every predicament, it is necessary to take the victims' side "to reduce the damage done."[10] At the end, Dr. Rieux, who has been the narrator of the story and has tried to bear witness on behalf of those who were stricken, talks of the never-ending fight against terror and its onslaughts and what would have to be done again and again by all who, "while unable to be saints but refusing to bow down to pestilences, strive their utmost to be healers."[11] If pestilence in our time can be identified with exclusion and violation and the marginalization of certain human beings, I would hope to see more and more teachers willing to choose themselves as healers, if not saints.

All this—outrage, an interest in multiplicity and dialogue, feminism, concern for the arts, a hope for healing—leads me to curriculum and the problem of curriculum. Like Elizabeth Minnich, I associate some cultural meaning systems with the curriculum, no matter what the level.[12] She is particularly interested in women's scholarship and the emerging knowledge about women; and she warns against making such scholarship merely additive to what has been recognized as knowledge, or simply mainstreaming it. She says something extremely relevant to the question of diversity with which I am trying to deal when she stresses the need to transform the curriculum rather than merely adding to it. She calls for transformation because the curriculum "remains within a system built on principles of exclusion and characterized by the conceptual errors that those principles necessitate and perpetuate."[13] Among those errors is the one associated with the connection between what has been presented as knowledge and the tendency of the dominant few (those powerful creatures I described) to define themselves not only as the inclusive kind of human but also as the norm and the ideal.

For all the exposure to difference in our world today, for all the increasing interest in multiple realities, for all the questioning with regard to the "canon" or the official tradition of what are con-sidered to be the great works in the history of literature and ideas, we are aware of the persistence of patriarchal thinking where learning and the curriculum are concerned. We have only to read the persisting challenges to multiculturalism viewed as an effort to open the curriculum to works purportedly representing "lesser" cultures and ways of life, civilizations not yet capable of writing *King Lear* or painting the Sistine ceiling. There are still times when the challenge to multiculturalism is linked to attacks on what is called "P.C." (that evil orientation named "political correctness" by those who want things to stay as they have been). There are times when it is linked to the kinds of argument raised by the late Allan Bloom when he lamented the loss of commitment to transcendent values, which he thought ought to ground as well as justify our Western civilization.[14] He blamed the rise of ignorance, banality, vulgarity, and "the closing of the American mind" on rock music, feminism, the protests of the 1960s, and German philosophy, particularly existentialism. We may believe him to be extreme and not really representative of those worried about the disuniting of America[15] or "illiberal education"[16] or a withdrawal of acceptance of official truth in the wake of a reliance on interpretation, even interpretation by the stranger or the least among us. I believe, though, that his book and his argument are paradigm cases that illuminate the ways in which knowledge is and has been constructed and frozen into place.

The categories of sex, gender, race, and class are often thought of in terms of narrative practices today. There are ways of using language that lead to the invention of ethnicities or to the identification of certain kinds of being as undesirable.[17] There are ways of speaking and telling that construct silences, create "others," invent gradations of social difference necessary for the identification of certain kinds of norms. (I have often wondered about the appeal of gradations or hierarchies or "stages" of development in our educational system. We tend so easily to forget that they are human constructions and cannot be found in nature any more than the perfect triangle can be found.)

What good would the patriarchal, rational standard be if it were not defined in opposition to the nonmasculine or the feminine, to the ostensibly irrational, dilatory, serendipitous, illogical, inefficient, playful person who prefers holding hands to staying at the computer, who likes to look at stars for no reason at all, who wonders and wanders beyond technocratic control? There are paradigms throughout our culture that function deliberately to repress, to belittle other ways of being, and sometimes to make those alternative ways appear threatening, requiring censorship or prohibition or even a violent demise. The response to the "Children of the Rainbow" curriculum is a sad example, especially in the way its linking of gay and lesbian families (presented on one page as "real people") to a range of atypical or minority families aroused fear and loathing, and a conscious distortion. Some even said that the very presentation of gay and lesbian families (a way of granting dignity to the children growing up in such families) was a disguised way of teaching sodomy.

Thinking of curriculum, realizing that it always emerges out of an interplay among conceptions of knowledge, conceptions of the human being, and conceptions of the social order, I want to lay stress once more on the way in which universals are structured (like the managerial or the military or the technological norm of what it is to be human), categories are invented, and discourse is manipulated. Just think of the taken-for-granted assumption that heterosexuality is universal, or that the public space is (by definition) a patriarchal space available only to those who live by patriarchal norms. Think again of the dominating visions and prescriptions—if not those of Allan Bloom or the proponents of cultural literacy, the formulations of those who talk in terms of curriculum frameworks for curricula oriented to specified outcomes, outcomes spelled out in terms of competencies and proficiencies demanded by the technological society and by the competitive needs of an economic system evidently in decline.

The preoccupation with standards, with mathematical and scientific superiority, is so great and so convincing that the old categories, the exclusive structures I have been trying to describe, are allowed to stand and to remain unquestioned.

I am not suggesting that we do away with liberal studies or with the disciplines. I am certainly not suggesting that we stop attending to the development of critical and reflective habits of mind. It seems to me, however, that we need to conceive the disciplines provisionally, always open to revision. They provide, after all, perspectives on the lived world; or, as others see them, they offer entry points to the great conversation that has been going on over time. They are, they must be responsive to changing interpretations of what it is to exist in the contemporary world—at the margin, in the center, or in between. Indeed, there has been a growing tendency to look at fields of study or bodies of knowledge contextually. They are cumulative modes of sense-making inevitably influenced by the discontinuous events in history. We need only recall how the work done in women's history has opened new vistas on the landscapes of the past, once wholly demarcated by powerful males. There are the changed ways of seeing identified with what many of us recognize as "women's ways of knowing"—concrete, transactional, narrative in form.[18] There are the approaches to science affected, it is now realized, by gender: engagements *with* the objects of study rather than analytic work *on* them. We are likely to pose questions today that were unlikely before, simply because of the revising that has been going on. Lately, I have been wondering again about American education since the founding of the common school in the early nineteenth century. Such reformers as Horace Mann and Henry Barnard have always dominated the scene presented to us; and suddenly I find myself speculating about the lives of all the single women who taught in the schools. They could not get positions if they were married, you recall; and many were the lonely wards or "spinster" sisters in middle-class families, women and girls who "boarded out" with local families, who may have lived together. We know too little because their voices have been silenced, their faces kept invisible by the way the past has been structured. And, yes, pondering, the insistence on universal heterosexuality, I wonder about the seminarians sent to the frontier towns to distribute tracts; I wonder (recalling the "marriage scene" with Queequeg and Ishmael at the start of *Moby Dick*)[19] about real life on those whaling ships on their two- or three-year journeys around the world. Leslie Fiedler used as a subtitle for a book called *Love and Death in the American Novel*[20] this presumably amusing phrase: "Come back to the raft, Huck honey." He gained a little attention with his suggestions relating to homosexuality, at least in fictional domains; today we might take it more seriously and impart a greater significance than before.

There is some agreement today on the need to reject single dominating visions or interpretations, whether they come from textbook publishers, school superintendents, local religious bodies, teachers, or even students. But we are only beginning to realize the importance of including, whenever possible, alternative visions on what is offered as historical truth or literary renderings or even certain empirical discoveries. We are beginning to learn as well what has to be done to counter the fixed and monological views. At the very least, we have to keep reminding those willing to pay heed that gay people and lesbian people or people from Caribbean islands or women of all races and classes or eastern or mideastern persons have distinctive ways of constituting reality, ways that have—for a decent stretch of time—to be granted integrity. If there is to be a truly humane, plague-free community in this country, it must be one responsive to increasing numbers of life-stories, to more and more "different" voices. Yes, many of the shapes are alike; there are tonalities that resemble one another, that merge. But there are differing nuances, shimmering contours; no one exactly duplicates any other. This is what ought to be attended to, even as we resonate to what is common, what is shared.

Democracy, Dewey wrote, is a community always in the making.[21] If educators hold this in mind, they will remember that democracy is forever incomplete; it is founded in possibility. Even in the small, the local spaces in which teaching is done, educators may begin creating the kinds of situations where, at the very least, students will begin telling the stories of what they are seeking, what they know and might not yet know, exchanging stories with others grounded in other landscapes, at once bringing something into being that is in-between. As they do so, what Hannah Arendt called "webs of relationship" may be woven, webs overlaying the worldly things people normally talk about when they are together. It is when they begin disclosing who they are to one another that worldly things can be overgrown with such a web, "with an entirely different in-between which consists of deeds and words and owes its origin exclusively to people's acting and speaking directly *to* one another."[22] It is at moments like these that persons begin to recognize each other and, in the experience of recognition, feel the need to take responsibility for one another. This means responding to one another as a sister or a brother being in the process of choosing, of becoming what that person (in the midst of others) is not yet.

This brings me back to the ways there are of conceiving learners, those living beings we hope will come to learn by means of what the curriculum presents. Again, it is not a matter of determining the frames into which learners must fit, not a matter of having predefined stages in mind. Rather, it would be a question of releasing potential learners to order their lived experiences in divergent ways, to give them narrative form, to give them voice. Above all, the silencing that takes place in many classrooms must be stopped, as must the blurring over of differences. There is relevance for this in what certain feminist writers have been saying, especially where identity is concerned. Luce Irigaray, for instance, speaks of how important it is to interpret the ways we are determined by and through discourse: as good children, perhaps, or naughty ones, or deviants, or as inverted reproductions of the one who is doing the defining. This can be particularly important for gay and lesbian young people, who may have to be helped to understand the reasons others are defining them as they do, especially when they are too young to see. Irigaray and others today ask girls and women to view themselves as plural, multiple, willing to break with "normal" definitions, sometimes to break up what is generally called the "truth" with laughter.[23] For some it may mean the acknowledgment of desires and fulfillments others deny. For most it should mean a rejection of measuring rods, a refusal to "grade" anyone's story against a standard norm.

Toni Morrison's *The Bluest Eye,* beginning as it does with a treatment of the first paragraph of the "Dick and Jane" basic reader, shows the power of such official stories (or "master narratives") in dominating consciousness. Morrison's Pecola Breedlove is demeaned by the story, since her world ("at the hem of life") is quite the obverse of the one described. She wants desperately to have blue eyes like Shirley Temple, since the culture has imposed on her the idea that only someone blue-eyed partakes in the human reality.[24] We are only now becoming fully aware that it is only when persons are enabled to shape their own experiences in their own fashion, when they become critical of the mystifications that falsify so much, that they become able to name their worlds. At once, they may orient themselves to what they conceive as the good.

I can only say once more that situations have to be deliberately created in order for students to break free in this way. Coming together in their pluralities and their differences, they may finally articulate how they are choosing themselves and what the projects are by means of which they can identify themselves. We all need to recognize each other in our striving, our becoming, our inventing of the possible. And, yes, it is a question of acting in the light of a vision of what might be—a vision that enables people to perceive the voids, take heed of the violations, and move (if they can) to repair. Such a vision, we have found, can be enlarged and enriched by those on the margins, whoever they are. The fine feminist African-American writer bell hooks has written what it is like to be on the margin but at once part of the whole:

> Living as we did—on the edge—we developed a particular way of seeing reality. We looked from the outside in and from the inside out. We focused our attention on the center as well as on the margin. We understood both. This mode of seeing reminded us of the existence of a whole universe, a main body made up of both margin and center. Our survival depended on an ongoing public awareness of the separation between margin and center and an ongoing private acknowledgment that we were a necessary, vital part of the whole. This sense of wholeness, impressed upon our consciousness by the structure of our daily lives, provided us with an oppositional world view—a mode of seeing unknown to most of our oppressors that sustained us, aided us in our struggle to transcend poverty and despair, strengthened our sense of self and solidarity.[25]

I would hope to find that oppositional world view somehow incorporated in or oriented to dimensions of our curriculum. Not only does it offer an alternative perspective. It creates a dissonance, a necessary dissonance between what is taken for granted at the center and what might, what ought to be. It is such dissonance, like the sense of obstacle, that gives rise to the questioning that may move the young to learn to learn. I am reminded by bell hooks of Michel Foucault when he examined the likelihood of a culture without restraints. He said that the point of a system of constraints is whether it leaves individuals the liberty to transform the system. The restrictions that exist, he said, have to be within the reach of those affected by them so they at least have the possibility of altering them.[26] It would appear to me, in an emerging society marked by a rich range of differences, that restrictions do indeed have to be brought within reach so that persons of all sorts can come together to change them. There must be a deepening consciousness of the plague and the need for healing. There must be a confronting of the contradictions, the instances of savagery, the neglect, and the possibility of care. We require curriculum that can help provoke persons to reach past themselves and to become. We want to see them in their multiplicity linking arms, becoming recognized. We want them in their ongoing quests for what it means to be human to be free to move. We want them—and we want to enable them—to exist.

NOTES

1. John Dewey, *The Public and Its Problems* (Athens, Ohio: Swallow Press, 1954), p. 183.

2. Jonathan Kozol, *Savage Inequalities* (New York: Crown Publishers, 1991).

3. Immanuel Kant, *The Doctrine of Virtue* (Part II of *The Metaphysic of Morals*) (New York: Harper Torchbooks, 1964), pp. 42ff.

4. Clifford Geertz, *Local Knowledge* (New York: Basic Books, 1983), p.161.

5. James Clifford, *The Predicament of Culture: Twentieth-Century Ethnography, Literature, and Art* (Cambridge: Harvard University Press, 1988), p. 17.

6. Mikhail M. Bakhtin, *The Dialogic Imagination* (Austin: The University of Texas Press, 1981), pp. 288–93.

7. See John Dewey, *Democracy and Education* (New York: The Macmillan Co., 1916), p. 408; and Jean-Paul Sartre, *Search for a Method* (New York: Alfred A. Knopf, 1963), p. 91.

8. John Dewey, *Art as Experience* (New York: Minton, Balch, & Co., 1934), pp. 53–54.

9. Jean-Paul Sartre, *Literature and Existentialism* (New York: Citadel Press, 1963), pp. 62–63.

10. Albert Camus, *The Plague* (New York: Alfred A. Knopf, 1948), p. 230.

11. Ibid., p. 278.

12. Elizabeth Kamarck Minnich, *Transforming Knowledge* (Philadelphia: Temple University Press, 1990), pp. 11–13.

13. Ibid., pp. 31–32.

14. Allan Bloom, *The Closing of the American Mind* (New York: Simon & Schuster, 1987).

15. See Arthur M. Schlesinger, Jr., *The Disuniting of America: Reflections on a Multicultural Society* (New York: W. W. Norton, 1992).

16. Dinesh D'Souza, *Illiberal Education: The Politics of Race and Sex on Campus* (New York: Free Press, 1991).

17. See, for example, Jacques Derrida, *Of Grammatology* (Baltimore: The Johns Hopkins University Press, 1976). Note, especially, Part II, "Nature, Culture, and Writing," pp. 95–192.

18. Mary Belenky et al., *Woman's Ways of Knowing* (New York: Basic Books, 1986).

19. Herman Melville, *Moby Dick* (Berkeley: University of California Press, 1981), pp. 27, 28.

20. Leslie A. Fiedler, *Love and Death in the American Novel* (New York: Criterion Books, 1960).

21. Dewey, *The Public and Its Problems,* pp. 148ff.

22. Hannah Arendt, *The Human Condition* (Chicago: University of Chicago Press, 1958), p. 182.

23. Luce Irigaray, *Towards a Culture of Difference* (New York: Routledge, 1991).

24. Toni Morrison, *The Bluest Eye* (New York: Washington Square Press, 1972).

25. Bell Hooks, *Yearning: Race, Gender, and Cultural Politics* (Boston: South End Press, 1990), p. 149.

26. Michel Foucault, *Power/Knowledge* (New York: Pantheon Books, 1977). See, especially, "Two Lectures," pp. 78–108.

Maxine Greene is Professor of Philosophy and Education Emerita at Teachers College, Columbia University, New York.

QUESTIONS FOR REFLECTION

1. What are the key elements of a "curriculum for human beings"?
2. What is the function of the arts in the curriculum Greene envisions?
3. What examples can you cite of "the persistence of patriarchal thinking where learning and the curriculum are concerned"?

Who Should Plan the Curriculum?

GLEN HASS (1915–1997)

ABSTRACT: Several groups have important roles to play in curriculum planning. Scholars from the disciplines can provide input on what should be taught and how to implement the curriculum. Parents and other citizens in our pluralistic society can help to formulate goals and values to be included in the curriculum. Students, since they are well positioned to identify advantages and disadvantages of the current curriculum, can participate in seven aspects of curriculum planning, from determining what shall be studied to identifying methods for evaluating success in learning. Lastly, educators can play a key role by creating structures that facilitate the processes of collaborative curriculum planning.

In these times of complex, often insoluble problems and rapid change, it is urgent that professionals in curriculum planning take a new look at the question, "Who Should Plan the Curriculum?" It is apparent that the curriculum planning and teaching that is needed involves many factors that go beyond the scope of any single discipline or profession. In addition, change is now so rapid in our society and world, that today's curriculum is unsuited for tomorrow's world and is as outmoded as the Model T for the world of twenty years from tomorrow—the world whose leaders are now in the classrooms.

THE CURRICULUM WE NEED

Today's curriculum planners should study conditions and trends in contemporary society and probable conditions and requirements for democratic living . . . at the beginning of the twenty-first century. Education for the future is almost useless unless it prepares learners to meet problems that are new and that neither they nor anyone else has ever encountered before. All professionals in education need an image of tomorrow as curricula are planned. All too often we now see a "good curriculum" as the present one with its problems removed.

In facing toward the future we must find ways to teach innovation, problem solving, a love of learning; students must acquire the tools of analysis, expression, and understanding. We will surely find that learners of all ages must be prepared for work that does not yet exist. We will see that we all will have numerous increasingly complex tasks as buyers, voters, parents, legislators, and cooperative planners.

All interested citizens, parents, learners, and scholars from many of the disciplines should be encouraged to work with teachers, principals, curriculum leaders, state department of education and federal education agency personnel in the planning. This involvement in planning by all interested parties should begin in the local school and school district, but it should also occur regularly on a state, national and international basis. A democratic society cannot permit uniformity and centralization. The undefined, but onrushing future requires many different autonomous, alternative efforts to cope with its challenges and problems.

In the past many curriculum writers have stated that laypersons and scholars should be encouraged to work with professional educators in planning the curriculum. They have also frequently stated that collaborative models for planning are needed. They have, however, often

Revised, 1979 by Glen Hass. Portions drawn from *Educational Leadership* 19, no. 1 (October 1961): 2–4, 39. Used by permission of the author and the publisher.

given inadequate attention to the particular role of each type of planner in the planning process. Lacking adequate role definition we have often, as educators, overemphasized our mission to instruct the public, and have been undersensitive to, or intolerant of, suggestion and dissent. Let us try to define the particular role of each group in curriculum planning.

ROLE OF SCHOLARS

What is the role in curriculum planning of scholars from disciplines other than education? There are at least two ways in which they can help. They can often give crucial advice regarding *what* should be taught; and they can often suggest *means of implementing* curriculum decisions.

For instance, in the 1960s, scholars in biology, mathematics, and physics worked with teachers and other curriculum workers in determining what should be taught. These planners found that the textbooks in use contained almost none of the modern concepts, although greater change in knowledge had occurred in the past fifty years than in the preceding 500. They also learned that greater emphasis was needed on unifying concepts so that the total number of basic ideas to be learned might be reduced. Now the collaboration of scholars is needed to identify the concepts which are most relevant to alternative futures so that they may become the focus of the curriculum.

Sociologists can give particular assistance in determining the means by which goals of education may be achieved and in identifying the essential values and behavior patterns which must be learned as society changes. Of equal importance is the fact that sociologists, as future planners, can aid the educator in understanding some of the characteristics of the society in which his or her students will live in the future. Together they can devise a better educational program to prepare for it.

Anthropologists can shed light on the reasons for the direction of the development of various aspects of the culture. They can help the school to plan to counterbalance pressures for confor-

mity and to attach greater emphasis to creativity and critical judgment. They can help in planning to develop in each student an understanding of his or her powers and limitations for creating and modifying society. Anthropologists can also help in developing curriculum plans for the future.

Scholars from many disciplines can aid in curriculum planning by identifying the central concepts and rules for discovering the nature of the discipline. In the terms in which they are now represented, many of the disciplines are increasingly unteachable. We need a philosophical synthesis, appropriate to our world, the future, and to the learners, that can be taught—and only the scholars working alongside educators can achieve this synthesis.

ROLE OF PARENTS AND OTHER CITIZENS

In the long run, we can only build the curriculum and use the teaching methods which the active public will accept. We must work with the public and have orderly patterns for its participation. People need to be involved in the process of planning the curriculum in order to change their beliefs, attitudes, and behavior regarding it.

A fundamental question is, whose values are to be represented in the curricula for the learners of a particular community? Curriculum planners must recognize that a monolithic curriculum is not acceptable to parents and other citizens in a pluralistic society. Curriculum leaders and teachers should work with parents and other active citizens in setting the yearly educational goals for a particular classroom, school, or district. Within the larger framework of the school system, local communities, teachers, and principals should define *together* what each school community sees as the most important focus for the coming year. Public education transmits values and beliefs as well as knowledge. Since values and beliefs are very much family and community matters, parents and other citizens must be involved in curriculum planning.

From 1960 to the present, the prevailing practice in many school districts has been to curtail opportunities for citizen participation, and, increasingly, to try to confine curriculum decision-making to the professional educators. In the late 1960s this led to the press for community control through decentralization of large, urban school districts—a prime example of our failure to involve citizens in curriculum planning. Such involvement would have helped teachers and other curriculum planners to be sensitive to the realities of life in the school community.

Many parents are concerned today about whether their children seem to be learning the "basics" needed for survival in our society. Some parents are concerned as to whether the content and operation of the school and its curriculum give students pride in their own race and ethnic background. All parents often wonder whether teachers genuinely accept and share their concern about the learning of their children. Without cooperative planning each group often sees the other as insensitive, as having unreasonable expectations, and as making unrealistic demands.

It is a matter of crucial importance that many school systems invent and use structural devices to bring about a sharing of thinking about the curriculum by the lay citizens of the community and professional staff members.

Staff members must learn to work with citizens; citizens must take part but not take over. This should begin at the level of the parents planning with the teacher about their concerns for their children and should move from there to the citizens advisory council and the systemwide curriculum committee. The profession, in each community, and the teacher, in each classroom, is responsible for establishing these channels.

ficiencies of the present curriculum. Their ideas and reactions are of very great importance. Research has shown many times that learning is significantly improved when students share in planning and evaluating the curriculum.

In the process of instruction, learners should share in setting goals and objectives. In a particular learning experience the initial objectives should be those that the student sees, at that time, as interesting and meaningful. While the objectives the teacher uses to guide his or her planning and those sought by learners need not be identical, there should be much overlapping. The teachers and learner's goals for a learning experience certainly must be understood by both, and they must be compatible or they are not likely to be achieved.

Too little use is made of teacher-student planning. The understanding and skills of planning are among the most important outcomes of education. Perhaps more teachers would plan with their students if they realized that student-teacher planning has at least seven aspects, and that they might begin to plan with students about any one of them:

1. What is to be studied?
2. Why are we having this learning activity?
3. How shall we go about it?
4. Where might we do what needs to be done?
5. When shall we do it?
6. Who will do each part of the job?
7. How can we evaluate our success in learning?

While student participation in the choice of topics may be possible only in certain subjects, there is no reason why extensive use of the other aspects of teacher-student planning should not be used in all subjects.

ROLE OF STUDENTS

The student is the major untapped resource in curriculum planning. Students are in the best position to explain many of the advantages and de-

ROLE OF EDUCATORS

The role of professional educators is one that will grow and develop as they work with the scholars, parents, other citizens, and students.

It is the job of the teacher, principal, and curriculum consultant to provide structure for planning with others, to inform, to offer recommendations, to bring together contributions from many sources, and to work out a recommended plan of action. In the analysis of the curriculum that is planned, professional educators must be certain that it takes account of the nature of the learner, of the society of which he or she is a part, and of the future. This part of the educator's role is not new, but it has increasing importance as he plans with others who are not so likely to give adequate attention to the various bases for curriculum decisions.

The professional curriculum planner should be alert to the necessity for relating schools to the surrounding political, economic, and social forces so that the means and goals of the curriculum harmonize with the lives of learners in particular circumstances.

Frequently, educators need to take a stand for what they believe, sharing what they know and feel. The public relies on the vision and courage of educators to present recommendations for curriculum improvement. Such recommendations should be related to a sense of purpose, the ability to think and analyze, and a proper respect for the requirements of human response. The educator, in recommending, must carefully avoid the appearance that the curriculum is solely the professional's business. Experience over time in working together helps to solve this problem.

A most important part of the teacher's role is to communicate to students his or her own valuing of learning. Teachers often motivate learners by their own motivations. Learners learn to like to learn from teachers who exhibit the intellectual accomplishment of regularly acquiring and acting on new knowledge.

Finally, professional educators must evaluate and interrelate the contributions from other planners and evolve a curriculum plan which they implement in their own classrooms or which they submit for the approval of the curriculum council or committee.

MOVING AHEAD

If it is recognized that all public policy in education is the product of professional-lay interaction, then one of the main roadblocks to progress can be removed. Increasing the communication between scholars in various disciplines and professional educators would be a valuable step forward. A next step is to make greater use of that largely untapped resource—student contributions to curriculum planning. In each community, professional educators should move to establish the structural devices needed so that scholars, citizens, students, and professional educators may share in planning the curriculum needed. Because of the importance of education, each should be enabled to make his or her particular contribution to curriculum planning.

Who should plan the curriculum? Everyone interested in the future; everyone concerned for the quality of education being experienced by the leaders of the future who are now in our classrooms.

Glen Hass was Professor of Education, Emeritus, University of Florida, Gainesville, and twice National President of the John Dewey Society.

QUESTIONS FOR REFLECTION

1.   Do you agree that "The student is the major untapped resource in curriculum planning?" Why or why not?

2. In regard to the level and curricular area with which you are most interested, what "structures" could you create to increase the involvement of the following groups in planning the curriculum: students, parents, and community members, and other educators?
3. What guidelines should educators follow in facilitating collaborative curriculum planning?

Perspectives on Curriculum Criteria: Past and Present

FORREST W. PARKAY

ABSTRACT: Three interrelated and continually changing criteria have influenced school curricula during our nation's history: vocation, citizenship, and self-fulfillment. These criteria, in turn, have been influenced by historical forces. Religion and the need to educate for citizenship in a democracy have played important roles in the development of curricula. Recent systematic efforts to establish curriculum reforms have focused on curriculum standards, core curricula, and education for equity and excellence.

The content of the curricula in America's schools has changed frequently since the colonial period. These modifications came about as the goals of the schools were debated, additional needs of society became evident, and the characteristics of student populations shifted. The following list is a sampling of goals the schools have set for themselves at different times in our history.

- Prepare students to carry out religious and family responsibilities
- Provide employers with a source of literate workers
- Desegregate society
- Reduce crime, poverty, and injustice
- Help our country maintain its competitive edge in the world economy

- Provide the scientists needed to keep our country strong
- Educate students for intelligent participation in a democracy

Three interrelated and continually changing criteria have influenced school curricula during our nation's history: vocation, citizenship, and self-fulfillment. These criteria, in turn, have been influenced by historical forces. The timeline presented in Figure 6.1 indicates the approximate periods during which these three criteria exerted their strongest influence on the curriculum. (Each criterion, of course, continues to be used as a guideline for curriculum planning). In addition, the timeline shows several of the major shifts in what was actually taught.

Excerpted from "Developing and Implementing the Curriculum," a chapter written by Forrest W. Parkay for *Becoming a Teacher,* fourth edition (by Forrest W. Parkay and Beverly Stanford), Boston: Allyn and Bacon, 1998, pp. 344–377. Used by permission of the author and publisher.

FIGURE 6.1
A Chronology of Major Emphases in the School Curriculum

1620	1620	Emphasis on basic skills needed to learn religious cate- chisms and read prayers.
		Curriculum also includes surveying, navigation, and bookkeeping. Education primarily for the elite.
1640	1636	Latin grammar (college-prep) schools established and, like Harvard and Yale Colleges, emphasize Latin, Greek, theology, and philosophy for those preparing to enter law or religion.
	1647	Massachusetts Law of 1647 mandates a reading and writing teacher for towns of 50 or more families; a Latin teacher for towns of 100 or more. Females taught basics to enable them to carry out religious and family responsibilities.
1660		
1680		
Religious Emphasis		
1700	1700	Public schools teach reading, writing, and basic mathe- matics (counting, adding, and subtracting) to prepare students for jobs and apprenticeships.
1720		
1740		
	Early 1750s	Academies teach secondary students a practical curricu- lum (drawing, surveying, navigation, merchant's ac- counting, etc.) to become tradespeople and workers.
1760		
Political Emphasis on Citizenship	1780	
1800		
1820		
	1821	First public high school teaches basic skills and history, geography, health, and physical training.
Vocational Emphasis	1840	
1860	1860	First English-speaking kindergarten emphasizes growth, activity, play, songs, and physical training.
	1874	Free public schooling now includes high schools that place strong emphasis on vocational education and reading, writing, and mathematics.
1880		

FIGURE 6.1
(continued)

Education for Masses	1893	Committee of Ten asserts that high schools are for college-bound and curriculum should emphasize mental disciplines in humanities, language, and science.
1900	1918	Commission on Reorganization of Secondary Education focuses on individual differences. Curriculum to stress Seven Cardinal Principles.

Time Period	Year	Event
	1920	
The Excellence Movement	1940	1930s — 1940s — Progressive education movement stresses curriculum based on student's needs and interests. Home economics, health, family living, citizenship, and wood shop added to the curriculum.
	1957	Russia's Sputnik sparks emphasis on science, mathematics, and languages.
1960	1960s	Calls for relevancy result in expanded course offerings and electives.
	Mid-1970s	Back-to-basics movement emphasizes reading, writing, mathematics, and oral communication.
1980		
	1983	*Nation at Risk* report calls for "five new basics"— English, mathematics, science, social studies, and computer science.
	1985	Rigorous core curricula advocated at all levels in an effort to increase standards and to ensure quality.
	1989	The Carnegie Council on Adolescent Development report, *Turning Points,* recommends the creation of learning communities and a core academic program for middle-level students.
1990	1990	President Bush unveils national educational goals in six areas: readiness for school; high school completion; student achievement and citizenship; science and mathematics; adult literacy and lifelong learning; and safe, disciplined, and drug-free schools.
	1992	President Clinton proposes a program of national service for America's youth.
	Mid-1990s	National standards committees meet in the subject areas. Renewed emphasis on developing curricula for schooling in an increasingly diverse society.
2000		

CHURCH, NATION, AND SCHOOL

From 1620 to 1760, the primary aim of the curriculum was to train students in religious beliefs and practices. It was only later that a distinction was made between civil and religious life. Basic skills were taught for the purpose of learning religious catechisms and reading prayers. In addition to taking courses with religious content, students also studied such practical subjects as surveying, navigation, bookkeeping, architecture, and agriculture.

From 1770 to 1860 the development of citizenship provided the curriculum's major focus. The U.S. had just won its independence from England, and many policymakers believed that literacy was essential to the preservation of freedom. Accordingly, students were taught history, geography, health, and physical training, as well as the basic skills of reading, writing, and computation. In 1821, the nation's first public high school was opened in Boston, and two years later the first private normal school for teachers opened in Concord, Vermont. The first English-speaking kindergarten, taught by Elizabeth Peabody, opened in Boston in 1860.

By the beginning of the Civil War, the basic skills of reading, writing, and mathematics were well established in the curriculum. Various types of schools had been incorporated into state systems, and in 1852 the first compulsory school attendance law was passed in Massachusetts. Parents in every section of the country wanted more and better opportunities for their children. Through a curriculum that stressed individual virtue, literacy, hard work, and moral development, reformers wished to improve social conditions and to provide more opportunities for the poor.

The development of citizenship continues to influence school life and school curricula. All students, for example, are required to study United States history and the United States Constitution at some time during their school career. Presidents' birthdays and national holidays are built into the school year calendar. Issues concerning civil liberties and the expression of patriotism often become educational issues, as in controversies during the last decades over treatment of the American flag and the recitation of the Pledge of Allegiance in schools.

CHILDREN AND SCHOOL

Vocational goals for the curriculum were most prominent from 1860 to 1920. The turn of the century brought with it many changes that profoundly influenced the curriculum. The dawning of the machine age altered the nature of industry, transportation, and communication. The growth of cities and the influx of millions of immigrants resulted in new functions for all social institutions, and home life was forever changed. As a result, curricula came to be based on vocationally oriented social and individual need rather than on subject matter divisions. Subjects were judged by the criterion of social utility rather than by their ability to develop the intellect.

During this period, several national committees met for the purpose of deciding what should be taught in elementary and secondary schools. Initially, these committees espoused goals formed by educators at the college and private secondary school levels—that is, uniform curricula with standardized methods of instruction. Gradually, though, these appointed groups began to recommend curricula that were more flexible and based on the needs of children. This shift is seen clearly in the recommendations made by three of the more influential committees during this period: the Committee of Ten, the Committee of Fifteen, and the Commission on Reorganization of Secondary Education.

The Committee of Ten

During 1892–93, the directors of the National Education Association appropriated $2,500 for a

Committee of Ten to hold nine conferences that focused on the following subjects in the high school curriculum: (1) Latin; (2) Greek; (3) English; (4) other modern languages; (5) mathematics; (6) physics, astronomy, and chemistry; (7) natural history (biology, botany, and zoology), (8) history, civil government, and political science; and (9) geography (physical geography, geology, and meteorology). The group's members decided that the primary function of high schools was to take intellectually elite students and prepare them for life. Their recommendations stressed mental discipline in the humanities, languages, and science.

The Committee of Fifteen

The report of the Committee of Ten sparked such discussion that in 1893 the National Education Association appointed the Committee of Fifteen to examine the elementary curriculum. In keeping with the view that high schools were college preparatory institutions, the committee's report, published in 1895, called for the introduction of Latin, the modern, languages, and algebra into the elementary curriculum. In addition, the curriculum was to be organized around five basic subjects: grammar, literature, arithmetic, geography, and history.

The Reorganization of Secondary Education

In 1913 the National Education Association appointed the Commission on the Reorganization of Secondary Education. The commission's report, *Cardinal Principles of Secondary Education,* was released in 1918 and called for a high school curriculum designed to accommodate individual differences in scholastic ability. Seven educational goals were to provide the focus for schooling at all levels: health, command of fundamental processes (reading, writing, and computation), worthy home membership, vocation, citizenship, worthy use of leisure time, and ethical character.

STANDARDS AND THE SCHOOLS

From 1920 to the present, schools have become increasingly accountable for providing all students with curricular experiences based on high standards. The following comments made by U.S. Education Secretary Richard Riley at a Washington, D.C., junior high school in 1993, for example, reflect the nation's concern about current standards in schools (1993/1994, 3):

> We are not doing any children any favors by praising them for their skill on the basketball court but continuing the conspiracy of low expectations. Excellence and equality are not incompatible. We've just never tried hard enough to achieve them for all of our children.
>
> Ultimately, if we want our children to get smart and come into their own as full citizens of this great democracy, we need to raise the bar and help our children jump a little higher academically

To meet these demands for higher standards, schools have undertaken numerous curricular reforms over the years and used more sophisticated methods for measuring the educational outcomes of these reforms.

The Push for Mass Education

Since 1920, schools have been expected to provide educational opportunities for all Americans. During this period, curricula have been developed to meet the needs and differences of many diverse student groups: disabled, bilingual, gifted, delinquent, and learning-disabled students, for example. Moreover, these curricula have been used not only in public and private schools but also in alternative schools: night schools, schools without walls, summer schools, vocational schools, continuation schools, schools-within-schools, magnet schools, and so on. In 1973 there were more than 600 alternative public schools. A survey done in 1981 found that the number of public alternative schools had mushroomed to over 10,000, with an estimated three million children enrolled (Raywid 1981, 551–554)!

The Progressive Curriculum

The concern in this country for educating all our youth has drawn much of its initial energy from the progressive education movement. During the 1920s, the Progressive Education Association reacted against the earlier emphasis on the mental disciplines and called for elementary schools to develop curricula based on the needs and interests of all students. Throughout the 1930s, progressive ideas were promoted on the secondary level as well.

Though there was no single set of beliefs that united all Progressives, there was general agreement that students should be involved in activities that parallel those found in society. Furthermore, those activities should engage students' natural interests and contribute to their self-fulfillment. With these guidelines in mind, the progressive education movement expanded the curriculum to include such topics as home economics, health, family living, citizenship, and wood shop. The spirit of the progressive education movement is expressed well in a statement made in 1926 by the Director of the School of Organic Education in Fairhope, Alabama (Johnson 1926, 350–351):

> We believe that education is life, growth; that the ends are immediate; that the end and the process are one. We believe that all children should have the fullest opportunity for self-expression, for joy, for delight, for intellectual stimulus through sub-

ject matter, but we do not believe that children should be made self-conscious or externalized by making subject matter an end. Our constant thought is not what do the children learn or do, but what are the "learning" and the "doing" doing to them. . . .

> We believe that society owes all children guidance, control, instruction, association, and inspiration—right conditions of growth—throughout the growing years until physical growth is completed. No child may know failure—all must succeed. Not "what do you know" but "what do you need," should be asked, and the nature of childhood indicates the answer.

The Eight-Year Study.   One of the most ambitious projects of the progressive education movement was the Eight-Year Study, which ran from 1932 to 1940. During this period, thirty public and private high schools were given the opportunity to restructure their educational programs according to progressive tenets and without regard for college and university entrance requirements. Over 300 colleges and universities then agreed to accept the graduates of these schools. The aim of the study, according to its director, was "to develop students who regard education as an enduring quest for meanings rather than credit accumulation" (Aiken 1942, 23). The curricula developed by these schools emphasized problem solving, creativity, self-directed study, and more extensive counseling and guidance for students.

Ralph Tyler evaluated the Eight-Year Study by matching nearly 1,500 graduates of the experimental schools who went on to college with an equal number of college freshmen who graduated from other high schools. He found that students in the experimental group received higher grades in every subject area except foreign languages and had slightly higher overall grade point averages. Even more significant, perhaps, was the finding that the experimental group had higher performance in such areas as problem solving, inventiveness, curiosity, and motivation to achieve. Unfortunately, the Eight-Year Study failed to have any lasting impact on American education—possibly because World War II overshadowed the study's results.

The Push for Excellence

Concern with excellence in our schools ran high during the decade that spanned the late 1950s to the late 1960s. The Soviet Union's launching of the satellite Sputnik in 1957 marked the beginning of a great concern in this country over the content of the schools' curricula. Admiral Hyman G. Rickover was a leading proponent of an academically rigorous curriculum and urged the public to see that our strength as a nation was virtually linked to the quality of our educational system. He wrote in his 1959 book *Education and Freedom* (188):

> The past months have been a period of rude awakening for us. Our eyes and ears have been assaulted by the most distressing sort of news about Russia's giant strides in technology, based on the extraordinary success she has had in transforming her educational system. All but in ruins twenty-five years ago, it is today an efficient machine for producing highly competent scientists and engineers—many more than we can hope to train through our own educational system which we have so long regarded with pride and affection.
>
> We are slowly thinking our way through a thicket of bitter disappointment and humiliating truth to the realization that America's predominant educational philosophy is as hopelessly outdated today as the horse and buggy. Nothing short of a complete reorganization of American education, preceded by a revolutionary reversal of educational aims, can equip us for winning the educational race with the Russians.

Fueled by arguments like Rickover's, many curriculum reform movements were begun in the 1950s and 1960s. The federal government became involved and poured great sums of money into developing curricula in mathematics, the sciences, modern languages, and, to a lesser extent, English and history. Once again, the focus of the curriculum was on the mental disciplines and the social and psychological needs of children were secondary. Testing and ability grouping procedures were expanded in an effort to identify and to motivate academically able students.

The Inquiry-Based Curriculum

The prevailing view of what should be taught in the schools during this period was influenced significantly by Jerome Bruner's short book, *The Process of Education.* A report on a conference of scientists, scholars, and educators at Woods Hole, Massachusetts, in 1959, Bruner's book synthesized current ideas about intelligence and about how to motivate students to learn. Bruner believed that students should learn the "methods of inquiry" common to the academic disciplines. For example, in an inquiry-based curriculum, instead of learning isolated facts about chemistry, students would learn the principles of inquiry common to the discipline of chemistry. In short, students would learn to think like chemists; they would be able to use principles from chemistry to solve problems independently.

Bruner's ideas were used as a rationale for making the curriculum more rigorous at all levels. As he pointed out in an often-quoted statement in *The Process of Education,* "Any subject can be taught effectively in some intellectually honest form to any child at any stage of development' (1960, 33). Bruner advocated a spiral curriculum wherein children would encounter the disciplines at ever-increasing levels of complexity as they progressed through school. Thus, elementary students could be taught physics in a manner that would pave the way for their learning more complex principles of physics in high school.

The Relevancy-Based Curriculum

The push for a rigorous academic core curriculum was offset in the mid-1960s by a call for a relevancy-based curriculum. Many educators, student groups, and political activists charged that school curricula were unresponsive to social issues and significant changes in our culture. At some schools, largely high schools, students actually demonstrated against educational programs they felt were not relevant to their needs and concerns. In response to this pressure, educators began to add more courses to the curriculum, increase the number of elective and remedial courses offered, and experiment with new ways of teaching. This concern with relevancy continued until the back-to-basics movement began in the mid-1970s.

The Core Curriculum

In the early 1980s, the public was reminded anew that our country's well-being depended on its system of education, and once again our schools were found lacking in excellence. Several national reports claimed that curriculum standards had eroded. The 1983 report by the National Commission on Excellence in Education asserted, for example, that secondary school curricula had become "homogenized, diluted, and diffused." And even Admiral Rickover, in his characteristically terse, hard-hitting manner, pointed out in 1983 that school curricula had become less rigorous (Rickover 1983):

> Student performance is lower than in 1957 at the time of Sputnik, when many so-called reforms were initiated. Some curricula involve expensive gimmicks, trivial courses and quick fixes of dubious value. Teachers are often poorly trained and misused on nonacademic tasks. Many students have settled for easy, so-called relevant and entertaining courses. They and their parents are deceived by grade inflation. And the lack of national standards of performance blinds everyone to how poor our education system is.

The push for excellence in the high school curriculum received a boost at the end of 1987 when U.S. Secretary of Education William J. Bennett proposed an academically rigorous core curriculum for all high school students. In a U.S. Department of Education booklet entitled *James Madison High School: A Curriculum for American Students,* Bennett described what such a curriculum might look like for an imaginary high school. His course of study called for four years of English consisting of four year-long literature courses; three years each of science, mathematics, and social studies; two years of foreign language; two years of physical education; and one semester each of art and music history. Twenty-five percent of his program would be available for students to use for electives.

Outcome-Based Education

A recent approach to reforming the curriculum to ensure that all students learn and perform at higher levels is known as performance-based or outcome-based education. The performance-based approach focuses on assessing students' mastery of a set of rigorous learning goals or outcomes. By the early 1990s, Kentucky, Oregon, Connecticut, and Washington were among the states that had begun to develop statewide performance-based curriculum goals. Washington, for example, passed the Performance-Based Education Act of 1993 calling for the implementation of a performance-based education system by 2000–2001. The system, which will include mandatory assessments of students' performance at the elementary, middle, and high school levels, is based on the following four goals, each of which includes several outcomes and essential learning requirements:

Goal 1: Communicate effectively and responsibly in a variety of ways and settings

Goal 2: Know and apply the core concepts and principles of mathematics; social, physical, and life sciences; arts; humanities; and healthful living

Goal 3: Think critically and creatively, and integrate experience and knowledge to form reasoned judgments and solve problems

Goal 4: Function as caring and responsible individuals and contributing members of families, work groups, and communities

As the preceding historical review of curriculum criteria has shown, the content of the curriculum does not remain static. It is continuously refined, added to or subtracted from, based upon the prevailing needs of society, our views of children and how they learn, and our conceptions of the larger purposes of education. Nevertheless, the curriculum must, somehow, reflect the beliefs, values, and needs of widely different groups: liberals and conservatives, rich and poor, gifted and remedial, college-bound and work-bound, and immigrants and native-born.

REFERENCES

Aiken, Wilford Merton. *The Story of the Eight-Year Study.* New York: Harper and Row, 1942.

Bruner, Jerome S. *The Process of Education.* New York: Random House, 1960.

Johnson, M. "The Educational Principles of the School of Organic Education, Fairhope, Alabama." In Whipple, G. M., ed., *The Twenty-sixth Yearbook of the National Society for the Study of Education.* Bloomington, IL: Public School Publishing Company, 1926.

Raywid, Mary Anne. "The First Decade of Public School Alternatives." *Phi Delta Kappan* (April 1981), 551–554.

Rickover, Hyman G. "Educating for Excellence." *Houston Chronicle.* (February 3, 1983).

———. *Education and Freedom.* New York: E. P. Dutton, 1959.

Riley, Richard. Quoted in *Goals 2000 Educate America Community Update.* Washington, DC: U.S. Department of Education, 1993/1994.

Forrest W. Parkay is Professor of Educational Leadership, Washington State University, Pullman.

QUESTIONS FOR REFLECTION

1. At the level and in the curricular area with which you are most familiar, how are these criteria reflected in the curriculum: vocation, citizenship, and self-fulfillment?

2. Examine the timeline presented in Figure 6.1. What do you think will be the major emphases on the curriculum during the next 10 years? The next 20 years?

3. What are some examples of the current impact of religion and nationalism on the curriculum?

Today Standards—Tomorrow Success

ROY ROMER

ABSTRACT: *If students are to become members of the worldwide community, they must possess globally competitive skills, according to the governor of Colorado, a leading advocate of higher standards. The author and the Colorado General Assembly passed legislation that identified "model" content standards in mathematics, science, geography, history, reading, and writing at three grade levels: K–4, 5–8, and 9–12. Four years later, assessment data show higher achievement levels and narrowing gaps among ethnic and socioeconomic groups. Effective standards-based education requires (1) a re-examination of what is or should be taught, (2) professional development for teachers, (3) up-to-date instructional materials and resources, and (4) ongoing assessments of students' learning.*

Preliminary results in Colorado imply that uniform standards not only raise student achievement, but also close gaps between various ethnic and socioeconomic groups. Setting standards, raising expectations, and assessing student progress in a meaningful way gives students the tools they need to thrive in the 21st century and the tools parents and teachers need to help them.

One of my highest priorities as governor of Colorado for the last 10 years has been to better prepare our children for the future. I am constantly looking for guidance in shaping public policy decisions to create a better tomorrow. I have learned many lessons that have shaped our work, both in Colorado and nationally, through governors and business leaders involved in ACHIEVE, an effort by America's governors and major corporate leaders. This organization assists governors and business leaders in their efforts to raise student achievement to world-class levels through the development and implementation of high academic standards, assessments, and accountability systems, and the effective use of technology.

I am more convinced than ever that how we educate, train, and develop the potential of our children will do more to determine their future than anything else we do; we cannot afford to jeopardize that future.

DEFINING COMMUNITY

There was a time, not so long ago, when a child's community was defined by his or her family and neighbors. The neighborhood schoolhouse helped to pass on its community's values and the knowledge that children needed to succeed. Today, television, movies, and the World Wide Web are transforming our definition of community. More and more, our children's lives are shaped as much by people and events all over the world as by those in their neighborhood. Our sense of community is no longer limited to our family and neighbors.

Membership in the worldwide community has important implications for local education. It has opened up horizons that once were limited by geography or resources. Our children's education is no longer restricted to what their particular school has to offer. Students can interact with teachers and students hundreds of miles away as part of a distance education program, or log on to the Internet to find information and resources unmatched by any school library. These are obvious benefits to the global community.

Membership in the worldwide community also puts pressure on local education. With increased exposure to more information from more sources, we must redouble our efforts to ensure

From *NASSP Bulletin* 81, no. 590 (September 1997): 7–11. Used by permission of the publisher. For more information concerning NASSP services and/or programs, please call (703)860-0200.

our children possess the knowledge and skills they need to succeed. Our notion of what children need to know and be able to do expands in a global community. They need to know more about this world and how to function in it.

COMPONENTS OF STANDARDS-BASED EDUCATION

I am convinced our children must receive standards-based education to succeed. Let me define what standards-based education means. Content standards are a compilation of specific statements of what students should know or be able to do. They do not represent the totality of what students should learn at school. They are not curriculum. When standards are well-conceptualized and written, they can focus the education system on common, explicit goals; ensure that rigorous academic content is taught by all teachers in all classrooms; and raise expectations for all students.

In 1993, the Colorado General Assembly worked with me to pass a comprehensive reform strategy to improve students' academic performance. As part of House Bill 93–1313, each school and community in the state is working together to reach an explicit and common understanding about what students should learn in core subject areas. State "model" content standards have been adopted by the Colorado State Board of Education in six subject areas: mathematics, science, geography, history, reading, and writing. We have written model standards in each of these subject areas for three groupings of grades—Kindergarten through grade 4, grades 5–8, and grades 9–12.

Some examples of Colorado "model" standards are helpful in understanding. In reading, for grades 5–8, "model" standards include:

- Writing stories, letters, and reports with greater detail and supporting material
- Choosing vocabulary and figures of speech that communicate clearly

- Drafting, revising, editing, and proofreading for a legible final copy
- Applying skills in analysis, synthesis, evaluation, and explanation to writing and speaking
- Incorporating source materials into speaking and writing
- Writing and speaking in the content areas using the technical vocabulary of the subject accurately
- Recognizing stylistic elements such as voice, tone, and style

All 176 Colorado school districts have adopted their own standards, which must meet or exceed state model content standards. Locally elected school boards make decisions regarding local curriculum, teaching materials, and instructional approaches to ensure that students meet content standards.

Our approach also aims to provide educators, parents, students, and others with specific information about how well students are doing at meeting these standards. To gather this information, the legislation created two different levels of testing, state and local. State assessments will be used to monitor state trends, verify district results, and give Coloradans an overall view of how well students are performing. District testing will be used to measure individual student progress and the effectiveness of school programs and instructional strategies. The new state testing system will not replace traditional college entrance examinations such as the ACT or SAT, nor will it be used to determine graduation eligibility. Local districts will continue to determine graduation requirements.

STANDARDS-BASED EDUCATION AS A STATE-LEVEL REFORM TOOL

For most of us, standards are already a familiar part of life. Before acquiring a driver's license, applicants must demonstrate the knowledge and skills necessary to drive a car. Employees must live up to the standards set by their employers. Yet, in many circles, the introduction of standards into public education is not a simple matter. In Colorado, we introduced standards-based education to make sure our children were being adequately prepared for the challenging demands of tomorrow. The general agreement was that holding students to higher expectations would get better results.

Before I went to the National Education Summit in New York last spring, I talked to a group of teachers across the state. I asked them for their views; I wanted to get the real scoop. One of them told me that the Colorado standards and assessment changes have made her completely redefine the way she approaches school. She said, "I used to have the concept that in fourth grade math, I had to do 176 particular things during the school year. So I laid them out, I just checked them off. I went through this laundry list. I felt if I got them done, I was a good teacher. Standards have set me back on my heels. The point wasn't to get 176 little ideas in the head of a kid. Focusing on the bigger picture of understanding certain materials and standards made me reorganize my whole approach to the fourth grade year. I need to say if this is what we are really trying to do, let's get at it. We're trying to teach a child to think, trying to use this language of math and problem solving in communicating."

This teacher's revelations made me realize a number of issues related to the implementation of standards-based education that I need to consider as a state policymaker. First, standards-based education will push many educators, either individually or collectively in a school, as well as their local communities to re-examine what should be or is being taught in the classroom. This re-examination is important, especially if it results in a closer alignment between local standards and classroom curriculum. As I noted above, we must make sure our children have the opportunity to learn the knowledge and skills they will need to succeed.

Second, many teachers need help in figuring out how to revise their classroom curriculum and instruction to help students meet local standards. As we learned in the recent release of the TIMSS (U.S. Department of Education, 1996), 95 percent of the sampled U.S. teachers re-

ported they were aware of the National Council of Teachers of Mathematics curriculum and evaluation standards (often used as a model for states or local districts). Nevertheless, observations conducted as part of TIMSS revealed that classroom instruction was not always matched to these standards. Teachers need access to professional development to help them reshape classroom curriculum and instruction to be consistent with whatever standards are in place in their particular districts.

Third, we must figure out ways to make sure the necessary materials and resources are available in all classrooms. Too many of the textbooks used in U.S. classrooms are outdated, and cover content frequently unrelated to the recently established standards. Students in classrooms without Internet connections and other technology are clearly at a disadvantage.

Finally, standards, without some means for assessing their attainment, is a fairly weak policy tool for reform. We must measure students' progress in meeting these standards. We must help parents monitor the progress of their children, and we must help citizens monitor the progress of their schools. That's why in Colorado we gather data not only on how the individual child is doing, but also aggregate data so we can judge the performance of an individual school or district. Until we have in place a system that provides ongoing, up-to-date information about each child's progress, we cannot be sure we are doing all we can to help our children reach their potential.

We've made great progress in Colorado with standards and assessments. Preliminary results from these school districts imply that uniform standards not only raise student achievement, but also close gaps between various ethnic and socioeconomic groups. I am convinced that setting standards, raising expectations, and assessing student progress in a meaningful way will give our students the tools they need to thrive in the 21st century and the tools parents and teachers need to help them. I'm excited about the possibilities these policies hold. I know they will make a difference.

REFERENCES

U.S. Department of Education. *Pursuing Excellence: A Study of U.S. Eighth Grade Mathematics and Science*

Teaching, Learning, Curriculum, and Achievement in International Context. National Center for Educational Statistics 97–198. Washington, D.C.: U.S. Government Printing Office, 1996.

Roy Romer is governor of Colorado, chair of the National Education Goals Panel, and co-vice chairman of ACHIEVE, an effort by America's governors and major corporate leaders to reform education by using standards and assessments.

QUESTIONS FOR REFLECTION

1. According to the point of view developed in Henry A. Giroux's "Teachers, Public Life, and Curriculum Reform" in this chapter, what concerns might teachers as "public intellectuals" raise in response to Romer's recommendations?
2. Romer and Maxine Greene ("Diversity and Inclusion: Toward a Curriculum for Human Beings") stress the importance of *community* in the educational enterprise. What are the similarities and differences between their views of community?
3. Romer discusses four "issues" related to the implementation of standards-based education. What additional issues could be raised?

Standards, Standards: High and Low

DANIEL TANNER

ABSTRACT: *A noted curriculum theorist and historian traces the origins of the current standards movement and suggests that a "xenophobic national policy" aimed at restoring the nation's dominance over a global economy has led to the development of inappropriate "benchmarks" for learning. Lacking continuity and interconnectedness, the benchmarks are problematic for teachers and curricularists who wish to develop articulated curricula. Moreover, the benchmarks' emphasis on what students should know does not allow for interesting, provocative, and useful questions such as* Why? How come? How to? So what? *and* What if? *Also, many standards reflect fallacious dualistic thinking, fail to indicate the means by which teachers and students are to reach the standards, are arbitrary and inappropriate for targeted grade levels, and neglect the central curriculum question "What knowledge is of most worth?"*

To the layperson the concept of *standards* connotes levels of excellence as determined through authoritative and objective scientific measures. The mere mention of the term *education standards* to a layperson, or its use in a news caption or in a television interview with a politician, typically conveys the message that the topic is on the measurement or advocacy of academic excellence to which students are to be held. However, the very formulation, selection, interpretation, and modes of implementation and evaluation of *standards* are essentially value-based and quite arbitrary.

From *Educational Horizons* 73, no. 3 (Spring 1997): 115–120. © 1997, Pi Lambda Theta. Used by permission of the author and publisher.

MISEDUCATIVE EFFECTS

The movement for *standards* is not without political valuation and opportunism. In fact the contemporary movement has stemmed largely from political sources and interests. From the 1970s through the 1980s many of the states were using various forms of statewide competency tests as a gatekeeping mechanism for grade promotion or high school graduation. Commonly, the test results were being used to measure the adequacy of the quality of "delivery" of education by schools and school districts for purposes of "accountability" and school "reform."

Some of the miseducative effects of such tests have begun to emerge, such as the adverse impact of the tests for blacks and Hispanics, along with the unanticipated effects of the high school graduation sanction for increasing dropouts, thereby exerting deleterious economic effects on the student and society.[1]

There was a time when teaching-the-test was widely regarded as miseducative and even as a kind of fraudulent practice, such as in the case of the early adventures with performance contracting,[2] but today it is widely practiced and even sanctioned under the practice of "curriculum alignment."[3] The high-stakes consequences of test results for students and the schools, coupled with state-mandated graduation requirements, have impacted the curriculum significantly by giving priority to the academic subjects that connect with the tests, as against electives and other studies that serve comprehensive curricular functions of exploratory education, enrichment education, and career education.[4] Paradoxically, as Jaeger points out, "the higher the stakes associated with competency tests, the lower is their utility as valid barometers of students' knowledge and skills," and "in their quest for control of public education through testing, state legislatures might well have adopted a strategy that undermines the very reforms they seek to achieve."[5]

I am ashamed to say that my own state of New Jersey administers a statewide Early-Warning Test for eighth-graders in March of every year. Taking its name from the era of global nuclear missile threat, the Early Warning Test carries the implicit message to eighth-graders that their entire educational worth is being evaluated and their entire future is threatened by a low score. The tests are used by the state and the media for school and district comparisons and, as expected, the inner-city districts, the children in poverty, and the new immigrant children pay the penalty on the test results. The schools commonly teach-the-tests at the expense of productive engagement in the adventures of learning.

THE XENOPHOBIA SYNDROME

The current standards movement directly stems from the xenophobic national policy reports on education calling for the restoration of the nation's dominance over global economic markets by establishing of world-class standards for academic achievement and as measured by "new" standardized tests.[6] The political push for national standards has changed the purpose and function of the National Assessment of Educational Progress (NAEP) from its original design as a census-gathering instrument based on national sampling of test findings (to protect against invidious state-by-state comparisons). Presently it is being transformed into a national program of education accountability through state-by-state assessments, with Educational Testing Service as the primary contractor.[7] Ironically, as originally conceived and developed, the NAEP tests were not to be geared to the school curriculum in any direct way, but rather to assess learning outcomes as related to practical life for enlightened citizenry.[8]

THE BEST-LAID PLANS GO AWRY

Within two years following the issuance of *A Nation at Risk,* the American Association for the

Advancement of Science (AAAS) initiated Project 2061—a long-term program for the improvement of science, mathematics, and technology education. Named for the year when Halley's comet will pass again through our solar system, the rationale for Project 2061 rejected the notion that more and more subject matter should be required, but opted for a comprehensive, interdisciplinary approach. The curriculum was to be reconstructed "to reduce the sheer amount of material covered; to weaken or eliminate rigid subject-matter boundaries; to pay more attention to the connections among science, mathematics, and technology; to present the scientific endeavor as a social enterprise that strongly influences—and is influenced by—human thought and action."[9]

The basic approach was to build upon the curiosity of the learner. Instead of emphasizing answers to be learned, it was contended that the teaching-learning process should start with questions about interesting phenomena, and students should become actively engaged in investigation and knowledge application. The rationale taken for Project 2061 was in sharp contrast to the puristic and abstract approach embraced by the national discipline-centered projects of the Cold War and space-race era that produced the so-called "new mathematics" and "new science"—a federally financed curriculum-reform movement that eventually collapsed for failure to consider the nature of the learner, failure to deliver the promised results, and failure to connect with societal problems and needs.[10]

Unfortunately, "literacy" was selected as the conceptual goal for Project 2061 rather than general education—unfortunate because of the great proliferation of separate literacies denoting separate subject fields and reflecting the curriculum fragmentation resulting from each special-interest group's seeking to promote its own literacy in the school curriculum. It should be mentioned that general education is not to be confused with the general track of the secondary school or the practice of student tracking. Traditional European societies provided for literacy education or basic education for the masses and liberal education for the privileged. General education, as an American invention, was conceived to provide for all a common universe of discourse, understanding, and competence necessary for an enlightened citizenry in a free society.[11]

For the initial phase of Project 2061, various panels were convened to establish the interdisciplinary rationale for the knowledge and skills needed to understand the social dimensions of the sciences, mathematics, and technology. However, warning signs appeared in the Social and Behavioral Sciences Panel's report, which opted for a disciplinary bias for the separate social sciences and a focus on abstract concepts rather than life problems and knowledge applications for democratic citizenship.[12]

Inexplicably, the Social and Behavioral Sciences Panel for Project 2061 embraced the discipline-centered rationale, contrary to the interdisciplinary rationale that was supposed to undergird Project 2061. This contradictory orientation was reflected without challenge in *Benchmarks for Science Literacy,* issued by AAAS in 1993—a 400-plus-page compendium of "benchmarks" or statements of what students "should know and be able to do" by the time they reach certain grade levels.[13] The interdisciplinary rationale for *Benchmarks* is clearly explicated in the prefatory statement of the report.

> The common core of learning in science, mathematics, and technology should center on science literacy, not on an understanding of each of the separate disciplines. Moreover, the core studies should include connections among science, mathematics, and technology and between those areas and the arts and humanities and the vocational subjects.[14]

However, this is once again contradicted in the prefatory statement for the social sciences section of *Benchmarks,* which opens with the declaration: "Social science is a collection of disciplines, each of which examines human behavior from a different perspective and has its own particular techniques, modes of expression, and history."[15] The prefatory statement goes on to disclaim the citizenship function of education—the very key to the idea and practice of general education and the core curriculum.

"STUDENTS SHOULD KNOW THAT . . ."

The claim that *Benchmarks* identifies what students should "be able to do by the time they reach certain grade levels" is most intriguing. However, the *Benchmarks* compendium is focused almost entirely on factual statements and generalizations denoting what students should know by the end of certain grade levels. The lists are very short, generally consisting of from three to ten benchmarks for each topic by grade levels. Examples of the benchmarks are presented in Figure 6.2. As shown, each benchmark is couched in the phrase "students should know that"; in turn, this is followed by a factual statement or generalization.

It is notable that the lists of benchmarks under each topic for the various grade levels lack continuity and relationship. This is a critical problem for the teacher or the curricularist who is trying to use the benchmarks for an articulated science curriculum for general education. Moreover, . . . the emphasis for each benchmark is on "students should know that." But in scientific thinking, the focus should be on the following simple questions as guides for inquiry:

- Why? (causation)
- How come? (explanation)
- How to? (application)
- So what? (significance, consequences)
- What if? (hypothesis-making and prediction for testing)

These kinds of questions are far more interesting, provocative, and useful for students than

questions directed at "what students should know." Further, they are *generative* questions—questions that generate ideas and lead to further inquiry in spiraling-up fashion, as contrasted to end-point questions that require mere recall.

DUALISTIC THINKING

Figure 6.2 presents some examples of benchmarks for the study of human society, focusing on "trade-offs"—a key concept in the social sciences. This concept is so widely accepted in the social sciences that it has become a veritable doctrine. Like the algebraic equation or the balance sheet, any taking of a quantity from one side must be accounted for on the other side. But life is not an algebraic equation. Nor is life a balance sheet. The notion of necessary trade-offs in human dealings suffers from dualistic thinking, such as in the aphorism "You can't have your cake and eat it too." But if one can't eat the cake (or loaf of bread), it has no nutritional value. The point is that in the real world the situation is not necessarily dualistic—or a matter of give and take and recompense. In fact the various sides may indeed be complementary. For example, in American democracy individual rights need not be in conflict with the social good, but serve to protect the social good. Complementarity is not compromise, but actually creates new and stronger relationships and structures.

Perhaps the most pernicious and fallacious dualism that has plagued traditional societies is that of quantity versus quality in terms of educational opportunity. Traditionalists have held that "more means worse" with regard to the extension of educational opportunity to the masses. But the American experience has demonstrated that the upward extension of educational opportunity produces the greatest educational yield for society, creates a more productive and enlightened citizenry, and opens to the individual the greatest life chances.[16] American democracy is built upon the belief in human possibilities, not limitations.

FIGURE 6.2
Examples of Benchmarks for Social Science Literacy

Social Trade-Offs

By the end of the 8th grade, students should know that

- There are trade-offs that each person must consider in making choices—about personal popularity, health, family relations, and education, for example—that often have lifelong consequences.

- One common aspect of all social trade-offs pits personal benefit and the rights of the individual, on one side, against the social good and rights of society, on the other.

By the end of the 12th grade, students should know that

- In deciding among alternatives, a major question is who will receive the benefits and who (not necessarily the same people) will bear the costs.

Source: American Association for the Advancement of Science, *Benchmarks for Science Literacy*, Project 2061 (New York: Oxford University Press, 1993), 166.

ENDS SEVERED FROM MEANS

Since the initiation of Project 2061 by the American Association for the Advancement of Science in 1985, various professional associations representing the different subject fields also responded to *A Nation at Risk* (1983) by fashioning standards and benchmarks for various grade levels. Again, much lip service was given to an interdisciplinary rationale and framework. However, for the most part, each association developed and issued "standards" for "content knowledge" for its own field or for a separate subject field.[17]

Virtually all the various associations claim that they developed their standards for content knowledge to be articulated with the emphasis on the enhancement of thinking.[18] Although the standards formulated for each subject field are generally focused on learning outcomes for the development of higher-order thinking, they fall short on several counts. As mentioned, the proposed standards are devoid of the means for teachers and students to develop the capabilities reflected in the standards. The standards are ends, severed from the means and severed from the curriculum. We shall return to this problem later.

INAPPROPRIATENESS OF MANY STANDARDS

Other difficulties with the lists of standards are encountered when considering their appropriateness for the designated grade levels; the unevenness in the number of standards identified for the various grade groupings; the lack of continuity and relationship within the grade-level designations; and the need to build the standards through an articulated spiral curriculum attuned to the developmental levels of the learners. For example, one is impelled to wonder whether K–2 youngsters in mathematics can be expected to "effectively use a variety of strategies in the problem-solving process" and "make organized lists or tables of information necessary for solving a problem."[19]

Similarly, one is impelled to question whether the K–2 child should be expected to meet this standard: "Understands changes in community life over time (e.g., changes in goods and services, changes in architecture and landscape, changes in jobs, schooling, transportation, communication, religion, recreation)."[20] Or, for that matter, this standard for grades 5–6: "Understands how economic and political, and environmental factors influenced the civilizations of Mesopotamia, Egypt, and the Indus Valley (e.g., the impact of trade networks connecting various regions of Southwest Asia or Mesopotamian civilization, the importance of commercial, cultural, and political connections between Egypt and peoples of Nubia along the upper Nile; how geography and climate affected trade in the Nile Valley)."[21]

Many of the standards appear to be arbitrarily conceived and inappropriately placed by grade level. It is exceedingly doubtful to my mind whether the authors of the following standard in language arts can actually be met by the very authors of the standard, let alone by children in grades 3–5:

> Demonstrates competence in narrative writing (e.g., engages the reader by establishing a context, creating a point of view, and otherwise developing reader interest; establishes a situation, plot, point of view, setting, and conflict; creates an organizing structure that balances and unifies all narrative aspects of the story; includes sensory details, and concrete language to develop plot and character; uses a range of appropriate strategies such as dialogue and tension or suspense).[22]

These quite typical standards lead one to wonder whether the authors, critics, and policymakers are demanding much more of children and adolescents than they could ever demand of themselves. This may best be illustrated once again by the following standard formulated at the English Coalition Conference and issued by the National Council of Teachers of English and the Modern Language Association, to be attained by fourth-graders in the year 2000: Fourth-graders "will write and speak eloquently about observations and experiments."[23]

Now I doubt very much whether many scientists are able to "write and speak eloquently" about their observations and experiments, let alone fourth-graders. In fact I doubt whether there are many social scientists, linguists, philosophers, and even professional writers who "write and speak eloquently" about their observations. Held to such standards, the fourth-graders might well expect a life sentence in the fourth grade.

Alfred North Whitehead may well have been right when he commented early in this century that it is primarily the schools and not the students who should be held to standards.[24]

"WHAT KNOWLEDGE IS OF MOST WORTH?"

Strange it is indeed that contemporary education reformers are beginning at the end by formulating standards to be attained without asking the curriculum question of questions: "What knowledge is of most worth?"[25]—to which might be added, "for the development of an enlightened, productive, and responsible citizen in a free society?" This in turn would require the development of the many emergent pathways and means (curriculum) to develop the outcomes.

In effect, the formulations of standards without the means serves to perpetuate a dualism between ends and means that is counterproductive for education. To conceive of knowledge as merely results as measured by "standards" neglects the processes or means through which the learner is to become increasingly knowledge/able (the capability of putting knowledge into use). For the process or means is the truly significant aspect of giving meaning to experience and to the outcomes of the educative journey. As Dewey pointed out, when one is shooting at a target, "not the target but *hitting* the target is the end in view."[26] The standards makers have given teachers and learners the targets without the resources and means for hitting the targets.

Then there remains the nagging question: Even if the child should be capable of meeting certain standards of "content knowledge" such as "the impact of trade networks on Mesopotamia," should the child be required to study for this end, or should the child be learning something that relates integrally with his or her life and growth and the life of society? "Life is the great thing after all; the life of the child at its time and in its measure no less than the life of the adult," observed Dewey at the opening of the twentieth century.[27] A century later, despite all the advances in understanding the developmental stages of the learner, Dewey's findings for the learner, the curriculum, and society remain largely an unlearned lesson.

To set "world-class standards" for school children and youth in xenophobic reaction to foreign competition for dominance over world industrial markets is to surrender the cause of education. If our society is to be true to itself, the nation's strength will not derive from turning our schools to serve narrow nationalistic interests. Schools must be dedicated to the release of students' fullest possible potentials for growth in personal and social insight for democratic social responsibility.

NOTES

1. R. M. Jaeger, "Competency Testing," in *Encyclopedia of Educational Research*, 6th ed., ed. M. C. Alkin (New York: Macmillan Publishing Company, 1992), 228.
2. D. Tanner, "Performance Contracting: Contrivance of the Industrial-Governmental-Educational Complex," *Intellect* (March 1973):63,64.
3. D. Tanner and L. Tanner, *Curriculum Development: Theory into Practice*, 3rd ed. (Englewood Cliffs, N.J.: Prentice-Hall, Inc., 1995), 262, 269, 293, 606.
4. D. Tanner, "The Structure and Function of the American Secondary School: A National Survey," in *Annual Review of Research for School Leaders*, ed. P. H. Hlebowitsh and W. G. Wraga, (New York: Scholastic, Inc., 1996), 105–106.
5. R. M. Jaeger, "Competency Testing," 230.
6. National Commission on Excellence in Education, *A Nation at Risk: The Imperative for Educational Reform* (Washington, D.C.: U.S. Department of Education, 1983), 27, 28, and *America 2000: An Education Strategy Sourcebook* (Washington, D.C.: U.S. Department of Education, 1991), 5.
7. J. Epstein, "The National Assessment of Educational Progress and Educational Policy Making," in *Annual Review of Research*, ed. Hlebowitsh and Wraga, 26–40.
8. R. W. Tyler, "A Program of National Assessment," in *National Assessment Pro and Con* (Washington, D.C.: American Association of School Administrators, 1966), 11–18.
9. American Association for the Advancement of Science, *Science for All Americans*, Project 2061 (Washington, D.C.: AAAS, 1989), 5.
10. D. Tanner and L. Tanner, *Curriculum Development*, 428–453.
11. Harvard Committee Report, *General Education in a Free Society* (Cambridge, Mass.: Harvard University Press, 1945).
12. American Association for the Advancement of Science, *Social and Behavioral Sciences*, Project 2061 (Washington, D.C.: AAAS, 1989), 26–29.
13. American Association for the Advancement of Science, *Benchmarks for Science Literacy*, Project 2061 (New York: Oxford University Press, 1993), XI.
14. Ibid., 152.
15. Ibid.
16. T. Husen, "Does Broader Educational Opportunity Mean Lower Standards?" *International Review of Education* (Fall 1971): 77, 79, 88.
17. J. S. Kendall and R. J. Marzano, *Content Knowledge: A Compendium of Standards for K–12 Education* (Aurora, Colo.: Mid-Continent Regional Educational Laboratory, 1996).
18. Ibid., 14.
19. Ibid., 44.
20. Ibid., 124.

21. Ibid., 196.
22. Ibid., 295.
23. Council for Basic Education, "Standards: A Vision for Learning," *Perspective* 4, Table insert, n.p.
24. A. N. Whitehead, *The Aims of Education and Other Essays* (New York: Macmillan Publishing Company, 1929), 21.
25. H. Spencer, "What Knowledge Is of Most Worth?" Chapter 1 in *Education* (New York: Appleton, 1860), 21–97.
26. J. Dewey, *Democracy and Education* (New York: Macmillan Publishing Company, 1917), 123.
27. J. Dewey, *The School and Society* (Chicago: University of Chicago Press, 1990), 60 (originally published in 1900).

Daniel Tanner is Professor, Department of Educational Theory, Policy, and Administration, Graduate School of Education, Rutgers University, New Brunswick, New Jersey.

QUESTIONS FOR REFLECTION

1. What can be done to reduce the "high-stakes consequences" of test results for students and their schools?
2. According to Tanner, why are school-by-school comparisons of test results "miseducative"?
3. What does Tanner mean when he says that "The standards are ends, severed from the means and severed from the curriculum"?

TEACHERS' VOICES
Putting Theory into Practice

Nostalgia and Back to Basics

GREGORY SHAFER

ABSTRACT: *A high school English teacher examines how a sense of nostalgia and a desire to "get back to basics" can result in a curriculum that is "inimical to sound educational practice." For example, in spite of overwhelming evidence of its ineffectiveness, the teaching of grammar persists. Similarly, historical events can be distorted to retain a "pristine" view of the past, or attempts to broaden the voices included in the American literary canon can be resisted. While such efforts may reflect a natural desire to salvage a bit of the past while dealing with the unpredictability of the present, educators have a responsibility to portray the past accurately and truthfully.*

In the United States, people love a good romance, especially when it involves their history and a chance to reminisce about supposed victories and elusive accomplishments. As a teacher for the past two decades, I have noticed this curious case of selective memory seeping into the dialogue about education and the call to "get back to basics." Perhaps it began in the Reagan era or perhaps we have always had a reverence for the past. Whatever the reason, the back-to-basics movement and the regressive practices that accompany it too often lead to curriculum changes that satisfy this penchant for nostalgia.

We all probably have a slightly different perception of what it means to get back to basics. As an English teacher, I have seen the movement usher in some very odd ideas about how language is taught. Often, when such practices are unraveled and their weaknesses exposed, they are quickly returned to the shelf and happily forgotten. For an alarming number, however, the life span is longer and more inimical to sound educational practice.

Consider, for a moment, the example of grammar and the incredible staying power this relic has enjoyed. In language arts classes all across our nation, hapless students are diagramming sentences and labeling parts of speech in the same fashion their great-grandparents did. Despite volumes of studies on its inability to improve writing or knowledge of language, the study of syntax—of nouns, adverbial conjunctions, and other labels—lingers on.

Such a phenomenon becomes especially glaring when one considers the size of the opposition to the practice. Many leading scholars deride its practice and lampoon its results. Connie Weaver, a leading author on grammar instruction, reminds us that even history militates against the teaching of grammar as a way to enhance composition skills. Weaver contends that the historical reason for including grammar had more to do with mental discipline than any connection to writing (1996).

Since the twentieth century, however, grammar has been taught less for the mental discipline

From *NASSP Bulletin* 81, no. 590 (September 1997): 117–119. Used by permission of the publisher. For more information concerning NASSP services and/or programs, please call (703)860-0200.

it was supposed to foster and more for its supposed ability to improve writing. With this claim came a flurry of studies on the efficacy of grammar as a way to facilitate better compositions. Here, too, grammar struck out. George Hillocks summarized the results by concluding:

> In short, the findings of research on the composing process give us no reason to expect the study of grammar or mechanics to have any substantial effect on the writing process or on writing ability as reflected in the quality of written products. These findings have been consistent for many years (p. 227).

With such conclusions, it would seem impossible for such a practice to survive. And yet, its prominence in public and private schools—its secure, time-honored place—only highlights the power of romanticism, nostalgia, and the back-to-basics push. Like phonics and the rote memorization of facts, grammar's place is sacred—its role far transcending its status among students. Indeed, for many community members and politicians, the demise of grammar is a symptom of a general fall from standards, a betrayal of cultural mythology.

Today, most classrooms devote a few perfunctory weeks to nouns, verbs, adverbs, and adjectives—to parsing sentences and reviewing the quickly forgotten parts of speech—despite the incredible linguistic knowledge students already have when they enter school.

The romance and nostalgia that is inherent in the back-to-basics movement is not limited to the language arts. While Johnny labors through a meaningless labyrinth of conjunctions, pronouns, and gerunds, his sister is being subjected to a romantic distortion of history in her class down the hall. The back-to-basics movement and its devotion to golden oldies is truly interdisciplinary when it comes to whom we honor and our very traditional vision of the past.

Perhaps there is no better example of this than the story of Helen Keller, who learned to speak and graduated from college despite being both deaf and blind. History tells us that Helen Keller overcome incredibly daunting odds; she is an inspiration of hope, a font of optimism. However, U.S. romanticism, with its loyalty to ideals like capitalism and the "American way," stops there, failing to tell students the whole story. The fact is, writes James Loewen in *Lies My Teacher Told Me,* "Helen Keller was a radical socialist. She joined the Socialist Party of Massachusetts in 1909 and later sang the praises of the new Communist nation after the Russian Revolution" (p. 20). Because Keller was an outspoken critic of sweatshops, crowded slums, and the uneven distribution of wealth in America, our system has conveniently and discreetly omitted those facts with which it is uncomfortable. As with the grammar movement in English, the back-to-basics agenda aspires to protect the past and leave its memory pristine. Sordid details are swept up and quickly expunged, leaving us half-informed and blissfully ignorant.

Of course, secrets that reveal the darker side of history and human nature are often difficult to cover, especially in a nation that seeks information voraciously. For the back-to-basics team, the response to such lurid details is to accuse the speaker of being "politically correct." Today, in campuses across the nation, students are witness to an ongoing, often vitriolic debate about the protection of the canon of American literature—one that is predominantly white, male, and of European descent. While many professors call for a more inclusive, representative sample of voices—including people of color and of different genres—a traditional coalition seeks to protect the past and leave it in the hands of a distinct few.

The list is endless and forever provocative. Thomas Jefferson, who may enjoy a deification unlike any other hero, is too often insulated from legitimate criticisms of racism and hypocrisy. Half the history textbooks reviewed by James Loewen failed to even mention that Jefferson owned slaves. Textbooks as a whole tend to stress Jefferson's written opposition to slavery—his words rather than his deeds. As with grammar, literature, and the Helen Keller story, an invisible agenda seems at work, one that leaves us feeling good if not a little empty.

Many theories have been advanced as to the source of this disquieting movement. Some claim it is conservative in nature, and there clearly is evidence that a vocal coalition is promoting this quixotic movement. However, it is more plausible, I believe, to see the back-to-basics agenda as a natural reaction from people of all political and cultural persuasions—people who want to salvage a bit of their past, to honor and protect history at a time when the present seems more and more unpredictable. Whatever the cause or reason, back-to-basics promises to be a regressive component in America as long as schools allow myths and clichés to flourish over truth and hard

facts. As educators, it is our responsibility to separate appearance from reality and acknowledge our past with all its dubious heroes and time-honored practices.

REFERENCES

Hillocks, George. *Research on Written Composition.* Urbana, Ill.: E.R.I.C. Clearinghouse on Reading and Composition Skills and the National Conference on Research in English. Distributed by the National Council of Teachers of English, 1986.

Loewen, James. *Lies My Teacher Told Me.* New York: Touchstone, 1995.

Weaver, Connie. *Teaching Grammar in Context.* Portsmouth, N.H.: Boynton/Cook Heinemann, 1996.

Gregory Shafer teaches English at Charlotte High School in Battle Creek, Michigan.

QUESTIONS FOR REFLECTION

1. At the level and in the subject area with which you are most familiar, can you cite examples of curriculum practices that satisfy a "penchant for nostalgia"?
2. Why do you suppose the teaching of grammar endures in spite of voluminous evidence that it does not enhance composition skills?
3. What does the phrase *back to basics* mean to you? Based on your experiences, what are the origins of the back-to-basics movement?

LEARNING ACTIVITIES

Critical Thinking

1. Do you think teachers at the elementary, middle-junior, senior high, and post-secondary levels differ in regard to the curriculum design they prefer to follow? What differences might one expect to find among teachers at different levels?
2. Most educators consider *collaborative planning* to be an important curriculum criterion. Whom do you believe should be involved in planning a curriculum? What role(s) do you suggest for each planner?
3. In addition to the curriculum criteria discussed in this chapter—student–teacher planning, relevance, higher standards, and curriculum design—and the four

curriculum bases discussed in the previous chapters, what criteria are important for you to follow in planning educational programs for students?

4.   At the level and in the content area of greatest interest to you, what curriculum topics do today's students find most relevant? How do these topics compare with topics viewed as relevant when you were a student?

Application Activities

1.   If possible, obtain a set of state-wide educational standards for your state and critique them according to the points made in Tanner's "Standards, Standards: High and Low."

2.   Examine a recent curriculum guide, of interest to you or in your field of study, to identify the criteria used in developing the guide. Does the curriculum adequately address the criteria? What additional criteria might improve the curriculum?

3.   Review the work of various curriculum committees (e.g., the Committee of Ten, 1892–93) and major curriculum reform efforts (e.g., The Eight-Year Study, 1932–40) that are summarized in Parkay's "Perspectives on Curriculum Criteria: Past and Present." Which bases and curriculum criteria were predominant at these points during our nation's history?

Field Experiences

1.   Develop a rank-ordered list of four or five curriculum criteria that you believe are most important for developing curricula at your level of interest. Then, conduct an informal survey of students at that level to find out how they rank the items. In addition, ask them if there are other criteria they believe should be on the list. Compare your findings with your classmates'.

2.   Using the rank-ordered list of curriculum criteria described in #1 above, survey several teachers to find out how they rank the items. Also, ask them if they use other criteria in planning their curriculum. If you completed #1 above, compare the responses of students and teachers.

Internet Activities

1.   Go to the home page of the Putnam Valley, New York, School District, rated by *Classroom Connect* magazine as the "best Web site" in February 1996, where you will find extensive information on the standards movement at the state and national levels. From this point, conduct a search of national standards in content areas of interest. Share your findings with other members of your class.

2.   Find the national curriculum standards for your subject area(s) online and compare them with the curriculum standards for your state. For example, you might download the National Council for Teachers of Mathematics (NCTM) standards

(**http://www.nctm.org**) and then compare them with the mathematics standards (termed "Essential Academic Learning Requirements") developed by Washington State's Commission on Student Learning (**http://csl.wednet.edu**). What similarities and differences do you note?

BOOKS AND ARTICLES TO REVIEW

On Curriculum Standards

Allen, Dwight W., and Brinton, Robert C. "Improving Our Unacknowledged National Curriculum." *The Clearing House* 69, no. 3 (January/February 1996): 140–143.

Anderson, Erma. "Meeting the Challenges of the National Science Education Standards." *NASSP Bulletin* 80, no. 577 (February 1996): 24–26.

Aronowitz, Stanley. "National Standards Would Not Change Our Cultural Capital." *The Clearing House* 69, no. 3 (January/February 1996): 144–147.

Berube, Maurice R. "The Politics of National Standards." *The Clearing House* 69, no. 3 (January/February 1996): 151–153.

Cross, Christopher T., and Joftus, Scott. "Are Academic Standards a Threat or an Opportunity?" *NASSP Bulletin* 81, no. 590 (September 1997): 12–20.

Eisner, Elliot W. "Do American Schools Need Standards?" *The School Administrator* 51, no. 5 (May 1994): 8–11, 13, 15.

———. "Invitational Conference on the Hidden Consequences of a National Curriculum." *Educational Researcher* 22, no. 7 (October 1993): 38–39.

Gittell, Marilyn. "National Standards Threaten Local Vitality." *The Clearing House* 69, no. 3 (January/February 1996): 148–150.

Greene, Maxine. "The Arts and National Standards." *The Educational Forum* 58, no. 4 (Summer 1994): 391–400.

Hass, Jim. "Standards, Assessments, and Students: Encouraging Both Equity and Excellence." *NASSP Bulletin* 79, no. 573 (October 1995): 95–101.

Ladson-Billings, Gloria. "Watching a Naked Emperor: A Critique of National Standards Efforts." *The Educational Forum* 58, no. 4 (Summer 1994): 401–408.

LeMahieu, Paul G., and Foss, Helen K. "Standards at the Base of School Reform: What Are the Implications for Policy and Practice?" *The School Administrator* 51, no. 5 (May 1994): 16–22.

Marzano, Robert J., and Kendall, John S. "National and State Standards: The Problems and the Promise." *NASSP Bulletin* 81, no. 590 (September 1997): 26–41.

Monson, Robert J., and Monson, Michele Pahl. "Professional Development for Implementing Standards: Experimentation, Dilemma Management, and Dialogue." *NASSP Bulletin* 81, no. 590 (September 1997): 65–73.

Myers, Miles. "Standards in the English Language Arts: Meeting the Challenge." *NASSP Bulletin* 81, no. 590 (September 1997): 42–47.

Popham, W. James. "The Standards Movement and the Emperor's New Clothes." *NASSP Bulletin* 81, no. 590 (September 1997): 21–25.

Ravitch, Diane. "The Case for National Standards and Assessments." *The Clearing House* 69, no. 3 (January/February 1996): 134–135.

———. "50 States, 50 Standards? The Continuing Need for National Voluntary Standards in Education." *Brookings Review* 14, no. 3 (Summer 1996): 6–9.

———. *National Standards in American Education: A Citizen's Guide.* Washington, DC: The Brookings Institution, 1995.

Sutton, John T., and Krueger, Alice B. "Do We Need New National Standards in Mathematics and Science?" *NASSP Bulletin* 81, no. 590 (September 1997): 48–55.

Zemelman, Steven, Daniels, Harvey, and Hyde, Arthur. *Best Practice: New Standards for Teaching and Learning in America's Schools,* 2nd Ed. Westport, CT: Heinemann, 1998.

On Curriculum Design

Apple, Michael. "Is There a Curriculum Voice to Reclaim?" *Phi Delta Kappan* 71, no. 7 (March 1990): 526–530.

———. "Restoring the Voice of Curriculum Specialists." *Educational Digest* 56, no. 2 (October 1990): 48–52.

Ayers, William. "The Shifting Ground of Curriculum Thought and Everyday Practice." *Theory into Practice* 31, no. 3 (Summer 1992): 259–263.

Beauchamp, George A. *Curriculum Theory,* 4th Ed. Itasca, IL: Peacock Publishing Co., 1981.

Connelly, E. Michael, and Clandimin, D. Jean. *Teachers as Curriculum Planners: Narratives of Experience.* New York: Teachers College Press, 1988.

Cuban, Larry. "The Lure of Curricular Reform and Its Pitiful History." *Phi Delta Kappan* 75, no. 2 (October 1993): 181–185.

Giroux, Henry A. "Teachers, Public Life, and Curriculum Reform." *Peabody Journal of Education* 69, no. 3 (Spring 1994): 35–47.

Hunkins, Francis P., and Hammill, Patricia. "Beyond Tyler and Taba: Reconceptualizing the Curriculum Process." *Peabody Journal of Education* 69, no. 3 (Spring 1994): 4–18.

Klein, M. Frances. "The Toll for Curriculum Reform." *Peabody Journal of Education* 69, no. 3 (Spring 1994): 19–34.

———. "A Perspective on the Gap between Curriculum Theory and Practice." *Theory into Practice* 31, no. 3 (Summer 1992): 191–197.

Ornstein, Allan C. "Curriculum Trends Revisited." *Peabody Journal of Education* 69, no. 4 (Summer 1994): 4–20.

———. "The Textbook-Driven Curriculum." *Peabody Journal of Education* 69, no. 3 (Spring 1994): 70–85.

Schubert, William H. *Curriculum: Perspective, Paradigm, and Possibility.* New York: Macmillan Co., 1986.

Tanner, Daniel. *Curriculum Development: Theory into Practice,* 3rd Ed. Englewood Cliffs, NJ: 1995.

Tyler, Ralph W. *Basic Principles of Curriculum and Instruction.* Chicago: The University of Chicago Press, 1949.

On Curriculum Evaluation Criteria

Banks, James A. "Transforming the Mainstream Curriculum." *Educational Leadership* 51, no. 8 (May 1994): 4–8.

Eisner, Elliot W. "Who Decides What Schools Teach?" *Phi Delta Kappan* 71, no. 7 (March 1990): 523–526.

Goldberg, Mark F. "Doing What Works: An Interview with E. D. Hirsch, Jr." *Phi Delta Kappan* 79, no. 1 (September 1997): 83–85.

Greene, Maxine. "Diversity and Inclusion: Toward a Curriculum for Human Beings." *Teachers College Record* 95, no. 2 (Winter 1993): 211–221.

Jackson, Philip W. "Thinking about the Arts in Education: A Reformed Perspective." *Teachers College Record* 95, no. 4 (Summer 1994): 542–554.

Paris, Cynthia L. *Teacher Agency and Curriculum Making in Classrooms.* New York: Teachers College Press, 1993.

Schubert, William H. "Toward Lives Worth Sharing: A Basis for Integrating Curriculum." *Educational Horizons* 73, no. 1 (Fall 1994): 25–30.

Tyler, Ralph W. "Equity as a Priority for Education in a Democratic Society." *Equity & Excellence in Education* 74, no. 1 (April 1996): 9–10.

Videotapes

An Introduction to Outcome-Based Education features teachers who have implemented outcome-based curricula in the classroom. (Available from The Video Journal of Education, 549 West 3560 South, Salt Lake City, Utah 84115-4225 (800) 572-1153).

A Quest for Education (60 minutes) and *The Education Race* (60 minutes) examine why U.S. students consistently rank below their counterparts in Japan in achievement in mathematics, science, and other subjects. (Both available from PBS Video, 1320 Braddock Place, Alexandria, VA 22314-1698 (800) 344-3337).

Teach Me! a Chicago Emmy Award winner, Outstanding Achievement for a Documentary of Current Significance, is based on *Best Practice: New Standards for Teaching and Learning in America's Schools* by Steven Zemelman, Harvey Daniels, and Arthur Hyde, (Heinemann, 1998). Available from Heinemann, 88 Post Road West, P.O. Box 5007, Westport, CT 06881, (800) 793-2154).

CHAPTER **7**

Education for Children

FOCUS QUESTIONS

1. Why should curriculum planners be familiar with educational programs at levels other than the one at which they work?
2. How can preschool and elementary-level education contribute to the long-range growth and development of students?
3. In light of the four curriculum bases and other relevant curriculum criteria, what are several goals for childhood educational programs?

In keeping with the definition of *curriculum* presented in Chapter 1, the chapters in Part II of this book focus on *programs of education* that occur not only in schools, but in community agencies, businesses, or other settings where education is provided. The chapters are organized, however, according to the institutional, grade-level structure of education in the United States. For the purposes of this chapter, *education for children* refers to early childhood programs (sometimes called *nursery* or *preprimary* programs) for children between the ages of three and five, and elementary-level programs for children between the ages of six and eleven or twelve. Chapter 8, "Education for Transescents and Early Adolescents," discusses junior high and middle-level education programs; Chapter 9, "Education for Middle Adolescents," discusses secondary-level programs; and Chapter 10, "Education for Late Adolescents and Adults," discusses postsecondary programs.

To help you understand some of the "real world" challenges associated with curriculum planning at each level, the chapters in Part II of this book, like those in Part I, include a Teachers' Voices section that presents first-person, classroom-based accounts of teachers' experiences with curriculum planning. In addition, each chapter includes a Case Study in Curriculum Implementation that is designed to illustrate some of the complexities of providing leadership for curriculum implementation at the institutional or system-wide level.

Curriculum planners and teachers should be acquainted with educational programs at all levels, regardless of the level at which they work. For instance, you should know about goals and trends in childhood education even if your primary interest is at another level. Familiarity with your students' prior educational experiences, or those they will have in the future, will better equip you to meet their needs in the present. Knowledge of educational programs at other levels will also enable you to address important curriculum criteria such as continuity in learning, balance in the curriculum, and provision for individual differences.

ELEMENTARY-LEVEL PROGRAMS

Graded elementary schools as we know them today were established in the nineteenth century when educators had little knowledge of the nature and extent of individual differences or of the stages of human development. Prior to the nineteenth century, elementary-level education was primarily for boys from the middle and upper classes; however, boys from the lower classes and girls were often taught basic literacy skills so they could read the Bible and recite religious catechisms.

Elementary schools were developed in conformity with the then prevalent ideas of child development and education. For the most part, it was believed that individual differences in education were undesirable and that the government had an obligation to educate citizens in the new republic. Horace Mann (1796–1859), Massachusetts senator and the first secretary of a state board of education, championed the *common school movement* which led to the free-public, locally controlled elementary schools of today. Mann was a passionate advocate of a system of universal free schools for all children—as he wrote in one of his *Annual Reports on Education:*

> It [a system of free common schools] knows no distinction of rich and poor, of bond and free, or between those, who, in the imperfect light of this world, are seeking, through different avenues, to reach the gate of heaven. Without money and without price, it throws open its doors, and spreads the table of its bounty, for all the children of the State. (Mann, 1968, 754)

Today's elementary school typically consists of self-contained classrooms in which one teacher teaches all or nearly all subjects to a group of about twenty-five children. The curriculum is often integrated, with one activity and subject area flowing into another. Teacher and students usually spend most of the day in the same classroom, with students often going to other rooms for instruction in art, music, and physical education. Individual students may also attend special classes for remedial or enriched instruction, speech therapy, choir, and band.

Some elementary schools are organized around team teaching arrangements, in which two teachers are responsible for two groups of students. One teacher might present lessons in mathematics, science, and health, while another teaches reading, language arts, and history. A variation on this arrangement is for teacher responsibilities to be made according to students' ability levels. For example, one teacher might teach reading to lower-ability students and all remaining subjects to middle- and higher-ability students; while the other teaches reading to middle- and higher-ability students and all remaining subjects to lower-ability students.

The Importance of Elementary-Level Programs

"The early years are transcendentally the most important, and if this nation wishes ultimately to achieve excellence, we will give greater priority and attention to the early years and start affirming elementary teachers instead of college professors as the centerpiece of learning." This statement by the late Ernest L. Boyer, President of the Carnegie Foundation for the Advancement of Teaching, reminds us that the experiences children have in elementary school provide the foundation upon which their education through adulthood is built. Clearly, the elementary school has an intense influence on children; the year the child spends in the first grade is one-sixth of his or her entire life to that point. Therefore, the lack of adequate provision for individual differences in the elementary-level curriculum can result in intense feelings of failure and rejection for some children. Failure to acquire sufficient knowledge and skills at the elementary level can exact a high price at other levels where the resulting deficiencies are very difficult to overcome.

Social changes are placing enormous new pressures on the elementary school. All of the social forces discussed in Chapter 2 are having a major impact on education for children. A major challenge for elementary schools in the twenty-first century is to establish meaningful contact with children from diverse backgrounds. The scope of this challenge is captured well in the following excerpt from Ernest Boyer's last book, *The Basic School: A Community for Learning:*

> Last fall, more than three million kindergarten children enrolled in over fifty thousand public and private schools from Bangor, Maine, to the islands of Hawaii. Most of these young students arrived at school anxious, but also eager. Some were cheerful, others troubled. Some skipped and ran, others could not walk. This new generation of students came from countless neighborhoods, from a great diversity of cultures, speaking more languages than most of us could name. And the challenge we now face is to ensure that every child will become a confident, resourceful learner. (Boyer, 1995, 3)

Provision for individual differences, and flexibility and continuity in learning are thus curriculum criteria of major significance.

EARLY CHILDHOOD PROGRAMS

During the last few decades, early childhood programs have received increasing attention and support, and the thrust toward education at this level will continue to be a significant educational trend into the twenty-first century. United States Census

Bureau data, for example, revealed that 65 percent of all five-year-olds attended kindergarten in 1965; by 1980, this figure had risen to almost 96 percent; and in 1999, virtually all five-year-olds attended (National Center for Education Statistics, 1999a). The preprimary enrollment rates for three- and four-year-olds have also continued to rise steadily. In 1991, 31 percent of three-year-olds and 52 percent of four-year-olds were enrolled in preprimary educational programs, including Head Start, nursery school, and prekindergarten; by 1996, these percentages had risen to 37 percent and 90 percent, respectively (National Center for Education Statistics, 1999a). In 1982, about 3.2 million children attended kindergarten; by 2007, it is estimated that almost 4 million children will attend (National Center for Education Statistics, 1999b).

Educational programs for preschool-age children are provided by public and private schools, churches, and for-profit and not-for-profit day care centers; in addition, a growing number of preschool educational programs are being offered to employees in business and industry. Early childhood education may be a half-day nursery school program organized around play and socialization, or it may be a full-day academic program that focuses on teaching reading and math readiness skills to children. Several articles in this chapter focus on the content and organization of early childhood education programs. In "Early Childhood Education: What Should We Expect?" David Elkind suggests that preschool curricula should not focus on school readiness. And, in "Weaving the Web," Suzanne Lowell Krogh explains how an early childhood curriculum can be developed along the lines of a theme or web rather than according to subject areas. Lastly, in "The Reggio Emilia Approach," Lilian G. Katz and Sylvia C. Chard explain how teachers can add a new dimension to early childhood education by carefully observing and recording, or "documenting," children's learning and progress in a wide variety of media.

Unfortunately, there is no institutionalized system of early childhood education that guarantees preschool experiences for all children, and resources to support preschool education programs have been inconsistent. Chapter 1 Programs such as Head Start, Follow Through, and Success for All have continually been in jeopardy of being phased out and have never served all eligible students. It has been estimated that Head Start and similar programs serve fewer than half of the nation's three- and four-year-olds living in poverty (Elam, Rose, and Gallup, 1992). While some research studies concluded that the benefits of Head Start tend to disappear as children move through elementary school, others concluded that the program was effective and provided a $3 return for every dollar invested (Elam, Rose, and Gallup, 1993, 143).

Throughout the country, the number of prekindergarten and full-day kindergarten programs is increasing, mainly as a result of studies confirming the value of early childhood education, especially for "disadvantaged" children (Karweit, 1993, 1987; McKey, et al., 1985; Nieman & Gastright, 1981). A few states—Pennsylvania, Alabama, and Virginia—have modified their certification policies to include a birth through third-grade certificate, and some states are seeking to create formal public school programs for four-year-olds.

The growth of early childhood education is also due to theories of human development and learning that emphasize the need for early stimulation and encouragement of curiosity in infants and young children if their intellectual potential is to be developed. Since research indicates that much of a child's intellectual development has taken place by the age of six (Woolfolk, 1998; Slavin, 1997), instruction at the preschool level helps to increase a child's interest in learning at a critical period in his or her development. Two of the most successful early childhood education programs are the federally funded Head Start program and Follow Through.

Head Start

Since 1965, Head Start has served almost 16 million three- to five-year-old children from low-income families. Head Start services, many of which are delivered by parents and volunteers, focus on education, socioemotional development, physical and mental health, and nutrition. In 1996, $3.5 billion was allocated to Head Start, and almost 751,000 children were enrolled in 37,000 Head Start Classrooms (Administration for Children and Families, 1998).

The educational component of Head Start provides children with curricular experiences designed to foster their intellectual, social, and emotional growth. In addition, Head Start curricula reflect the community being served, its ethnic and cultural characteristics. Research on the effectiveness of Head Start indicates that participating children show immediate gains in cognitive test scores, socioemotional test scores, and health status (McKey, et al., 1985; Love, Meckstroth, and Sprachman, 1997). Over time, however, cognitive and socioemotional gains dissolve, and former Head Start students tend not to score above nonparticipants. Nevertheless, some studies have shown that former Head Start students are more likely to be promoted to the next grade level and less likely to be assigned to special education classes than their peers (McKey, et al., 1985).

A unique feature of Head Start is the staff development and training provided by the program. Head Start operates the Child Development Associate (CDA) program that gives professional and nonprofessional employees an opportunity to pursue academic degrees or certification in early childhood education. Currently, almost 80,000 persons hold a CDA credential (Administration for Children and Families, 1998).

Follow Through

The purpose of Follow Through is to sustain and augment, in kindergarten and the primary grades, the gains children from low-income families make in Head Start and similar preschool programs. Follow Through meets the educational, physical, and psychological needs of children, including supplementary or specialized instruction in regular classrooms. The program's impact was greatest in the 1970s when hundreds of thousands of children were served and the annual budget was more than $55 million; by 1998, funding had fallen to less than $10 million per year. The Follow Through program is a good example of how the curriculum criterion of individual differences can be used to develop appropriate learning experiences for students. By developing a variety of innovative educational programs for children and then evaluating those approaches over time, Follow Through has produced knowledge about programs that best facilitate the growth and development of children (Wang and Ramp, 1987; Wang and Walberg, 1988).

In the past, parents and guardians may have felt that they were to bring their children to the elementary school door and then leave. But evidence from programs such as Head Start and Follow Through indicate that parents can play an important role in the early mental development of their children. As a result, parents should have a more active role in developing and delivering programs of education for young children. One novel way to induct parents and their children into the life of the school was suggested by John I. Goodlad (1984) in *A Place Called School,* one of the more influential educational reform reports to be released in the early 1980s. Goodlad proposed that children enter school during the month of their fourth birthday. The proposed practice would make possible a warm welcome for each child since school could begin with a birthday party. The child would then participate in subsequent birthday parties for children who followed. Needless to say, the challenge of socializing twenty or more beginning students each fall would be greatly minimized, and schooling could take on a highly individualized character. Teachers could become acquainted with just a few new children and their families each month at the time of admission, and the children would enter a stable classroom environment.

GOALS FOR CHILDHOOD EDUCATION

What should be the goals of educational programs for children? Many goals might be suggested—some derived, of course, from the four curriculum bases: social forces, theories of human development, the nature of learning, and the nature of knowledge. A list of goals would surely include many of the following:

1. Helping learners develop a sense of trust, autonomy, and initiative
2. Introducing structure and organization without curbing self-expression and creativity (In "Playing Is My Job" in this chapter, Elizabeth Jones reminds us that children's play is an important form of self-expression and creativity as well as "a crucial precursor to the convergent, right-answer thinking required in school.")
3. Developing social skills through large group, small group, and individualized activities
4. Providing adequate and appropriate physical and health education
5. Teaching the fundamental skills of communication and computation
6. Establishing a desire to learn and an appreciation for education by providing experiences that enhance interest and curiosity
7. Developing interests in many subject areas through exposure to diverse fields of knowledge
8. Developing feelings of self-worth and security by providing opportunities for each child to build on his or her successes
9. Providing many opportunities for children to experience the satisfaction of achievement
10. Developing appreciation for the worth and differences of others (This chapter's Case Study in Curriculum Implementation article, "Preparing Children for a

Global Society: Integrating Foreign Languages into the Elementary School Curriculum" by Gisela Ernst-Slavit, Kerri J. Wenger, and Lana Krumweide, describes how one elementary school provides foreign language instruction to children in grades 1–5.)

11. Developing the processes of conceptualizing, problem solving, self-direction, and creating

12. Developing a concern for the environment, the local and global communities, the future, and the welfare of others

13. Helping learners to examine and develop moral values (In "What's Ahead in Elementary Education" in this chapter, Gerald W. Bracey points out that many people do *not* want the elementary curriculum to address values.)

What additions or changes would you propose for this list of goals? Review William H. Schubert's "Perspectives on Four Curriculum Traditions" in Chapter 1; what goals would an intellectual traditionalist suggest for childhood education programs? Similarly, what goals would a social behaviorist, experientialist, and critical reconstructionist suggest?

REFERENCES

Administration for Children and Families. *Fact Sheet.* Washington, DC: The Administration for Children and Families, 1998.

Boyer, Ernest L. *The Basic School: A Community for Learning.* Princeton, NJ: The Carnegie Foundation for the Advancement of Teaching, 1995.

Elam, Stanley M., Rose, Lowell C., and Gallup, Alex M. "The 25th Annual Phi Delta Kappa Gallup Poll of the Public's Attitudes Toward the Public Schools." *Phi Delta Kappan* (1993, September).

———. "The 24th Annual Phi Delta Kappa Gallup Poll of the Public's Attitudes Toward the Public Schools." *Phi Delta Kappan* (1992, September).

Goodlad, John I. *A Place Called School.* New York: Highstown, NJ: McGraw-Hill, 1984.

Karweit, Nancy. "Effective Preschool and Kindergarten Programs for Students at Risk." In Bernard Spodek, ed., *Handbook of Research on the Education of Young Children.* New York: Macmillan, 1993, pp. 385–411.

———. "Full Day or Half Day Kindergarten: Does It Matter? (Report No. 11). Baltimore, MD: The Johns Hopkins University, Center for Research on Elementary and Middle Schools, 1987.

Love, John M., Mechstroth, Alicia, and Sprachman, Susan. *Measuring the Quality of Program Environments in Head Start and Other Early Childhood Programs: A Review and Recommendations for Future Research: Working Paper Series.* Washington, DC: National Center for Education Statistics, 1997.

Mann, Horace. *Annual Reports on Education.* In Mary Mann, ed., *The Life and Works of Horace Mann,* vol. 3. Boston: Horace B. Fuller, 1968.

McKey, Ruth Hubbell, et al. *The Impact of Head Start on Children, Families, and Communities. Final Report of the Head Start Evaluation, Synthesis and Utilization Project, Executive Summary* ERIC Documents No. ED 263 984, 1985.

National Center for Education Statistics. *The Condition of Education 1999.* Washington, DC: National Center for Education Statistics, 1999a.

———. *Projection of Education Statistics to 2007.* Washington, DC: National Center for Education Statistics, 1999b.

Nieman, R., and Gastright, Joseph F. "The Long-term Effects of Title I Preschool and All-day Kindergarten," *Phi Delta Kappan* 63 (1981, November): 184–185.

Slavin, Robert E. *Educational Psychology: Theory and Practice,* 5th Ed. Boston: Allyn and Bacon, 1997.

Wang, Margaret C., and Ramp, Eugene A. *The National Follow Through Program: Design, Implementation, and Effects.* Philadelphia, PA, 1987.

Wang, Margaret C., and Walberg, Herbert J. *The National Follow Through Program: Lessons from Two Decades of Research Practice in School Improvement.* ERIC Document No. ED 336 191, 1988.

Woolfolk, Anita E. *Educational Psychology,* 7th Ed. Boston: Allyn and Bacon, 1998.

Weaving the Web

SUZANNE LOWELL KROGH

ABSTRACT: *An integrated early childhood curriculum can be compared to a spider's web with intricate interrelationships among its elements. The subject areas may be likened to the "radials" of a web, with each subject offering the "strength" that is necessary to weave a whole web. As children learn, they naturally integrate subjects into a complex whole, in effect creating the "orb lines" that go from one radial to the next. Philosophically and practically, curriculum webs are effective because they provide curriculum coverage, recognize how children naturally learn, build on children's interests, develop skills in meaningful context, allow flexibility, and serve as a planning device.*

In his book *Charlotte's Web,* E. B. White spun a tale of fantasy that pits a spider-heroine against a family of farmers who plan to "murder" and eat her friend, a young pig. Throughout this enchanting fantasy are woven elements of reality. In describing Charlotte's masterful spelling of words across her web, as no other spider before her had done, White chose to explain in detail the making of a real spider's web. He explained that to the unpracticed eye the completed web would appear to be a single entity of patterned thread, but that a more careful observer could see that the basis for the web was an intricate interrelationship between very distinct components. Each

of these components had its separate and indispensable purpose.

We can view the early childhood curriculum in much the same way. When children learn in a way that is most natural to themselves, they unconsciously integrate subject areas into a complex whole based on their current interests. Teachers who consciously adapt this method of learning to the classroom see the curriculum as a fully spun web that incorporates a number of components at one time. However, they also know that it is important to take a careful look at each of these components individually to be sure it is sufficiently represented. Without the radials to connect them,

From *The Integrated Early Childhood Curriculum* (New York: McGraw-Hill, 1990), 77–83. Used by permission of the publisher.

the orb lines in Charlotte's web would surely have collapsed. Without each subject area in the curriculum, the totality would lack strength. Before focusing on the positive ways in which a curriculum web can be woven, let us take a look at how these webs are weakened if the "radials," or subject areas, are deleted from the whole "web."

THE SUBJECT AREAS, OR RADIALS

We will consider each subject area in turn, surmising what might happen if it were to be deleted from the curriculum. As you will see, each area offers its own special strength which, when woven into the whole, provides children with a fully and richly rewarding school experience.

1. *Language:* The need to communicate is basic to human beings. Children need many language experiences in school, if they are to learn to communicate with others effectively. Fewer experiences will lead to less effective communication. In addition, children need to understand why we write, read, and talk. Without experiences that give purpose to the learning of letters, words, and sounds, children will fail to understand why they need to learn reading and writing skills. What could be an exciting experience in learning to read and write may become a tedious chore devoid of meaning.

2. *Reading:* This subject might have been included under "Language." Yet, its importance is so critical that it has been given its own listing. Literacy is the foundation of any civilized society. Without success in reading, children are deprived of their rightful membership in the advanced cultures of today. This is not to say that preschool children need to be drilled in reading or even prereading exercises. They do need activities and experiences that show them the importance, excitement, and possibilities offered by the reading they will do one day. In the primary grades, it is amazingly possible to provide the class with reading books, reading

groups, and reading assignments and still have little real reading. Real, meaningful, enjoyable reading is what children crave and need.

3. *Mathematics:* Particularly in the earliest years it is tempting to save mathematics for later, for "real" school. This point of view argues for a dull, drill approach to learning mathematics and divorces the subject from real life. Yet, mathematics is all around us, in everyday experiences, waiting to be discovered and explored. Without the introduction of math in the early years, children miss out on learning this important point, and this subject, too, becomes another exercise in tedium.

4. *Science:* Teachers often feel weak in the sciences and so neglect their teaching in the early childhood classroom. To do so perpetuates this weakness in school learning to future generations. This weakness has already been observed across the grades and throughout the entire country. Worse, the deletion of science from the curriculum over recent years is beginning to have a profound effect on an entire society's ability to keep up with the rest of the world in the development of technology. If children have little or no experience with the sciences in the early years, they may never develop an interest in them, or worse yet, they may develop an antipathy or fear toward them.

5. *Social studies:* This is a subject that is often left at the wayside when the day becomes too filled with demands. Yet, learning to participate in their society is one of the most important reasons for children to be educated. Simply passing down the culture from one generation to the next can be done without a study of the social sciences; for children to understand their culture, however, and to learn to make decisions about its future, social studies must be part of the curriculum.

6. *Art:* When the curriculum becomes crowded, this is one of the first subjects to go. Yet when we look back through the history of the ages, the art produced by any society or culture is one of the most salient and telling things

about it. The art we and our children produce will be one of the most important legacies we leave for the generations to come. Speaking for the present, art adds richness and beauty to life. It provides children with skills in observation, hand-eye coordination, and methods of communication. Without art the curriculum becomes drier, duller, more tedious.

7. *Movement and drama:* Young children learn, not just with their eyes and ears, but with their entire bodies. To deprive them of movement experiences is to deprive them of a primary method of gaining knowledge. In the primary grades, organized sports are just beginning to be of interest. Throughout all the early years, less organized experiences are crucial to physical, emotional, and intellectual growth. Expressing themselves dramatically is an outgrowth, in part, of children's physical expression. Sometimes when children cannot verbalize what they are thinking and feeling, they can act it out. Without drama, a primary means of communication is eliminated from children's repertoires.

8. *Music:* Like art, music adds richness to children's lives. And like art it frequently disappears from the curriculum. When children are occupied in unsupervised play, they can be observed quite naturally and unconsciously singing, humming, and chanting their way through various activities and experiences. To eliminate music from the curriculum is to eliminate a primary means of children's communication and enjoyment.

It should be apparent that every curricular subject is important to the development of the children we teach. At the same time, children do not naturally learn through isolating specific subjects. These have been determined by adult definition. Children's natural learning is more likely to take place across a theme of interest: building a fort, exploring a sandbox, interacting with the first snow of winter. Teachers can create a good deal of their curriculum by building webs made up of these themes of interest. Done with knowl-

edge and care, a web can be created that incorporates most, or even all, of the required and desired curriculum. In the earliest years, these webs may be built as loosely structured themes. In the primary grades, the requirements and expectations for learning may argue for more structured units. In either case, children's natural inclinations for learning are catered to and exploited in the most positive sense of the word.

WHY CURRICULUM WEBS

We have already hinted at some of the advantages of planning a curriculum through the use of webs. A more in-depth discussion will point up their overall value.

Curriculum Coverage One concern many teachers have is that if they teach along the line of themes, or webs, some curricular areas will be overemphasized or undertaught. On the contrary, planning with a web provides an overview of the entire curriculum and gives the teacher a basis for decision making of this sort.

Natural Learning Children do not naturally learn by focusing first on history, then on science, then on math, and so on. These divisions have been created by adults who may (or may not) learn more efficiently that way themselves. Young children are interested in making sense of the world around them, and they are hungry to learn ever more about what they see, hear, and feel. Breaking their learning down into categories by subject area is less natural, more forced, and therefore less interesting and exciting than is working with thematic webs.

Building on Children's Interests This advantage to integrating subject matter is an extension of natural learning. Choosing subjects interesting to children means children will be much more involved in the learning process and more enthusiastic about being in school. When learning is simply done by isolated subject matter, it is difficult to heed children's interests as planning is done; through integrated webbing, it is the most natural thing to do.

Skills in Meaningful Context   When learning is done along the line of themes interesting to children, skills need not be neglected. They can have just as much attention paid them as in more subject-oriented learning. They simply need to become part of the planning web. Done within the context of thematic learning, the skills become much more meaningful to children. A spelling word that needs to be right because it is part of an invitation to a holiday party has more meaning than a spelling word that is memorized because it is on this week's list.

Flexibility   Teaching along the line of themes or units takes away the need to be on page 83 by Thanksgiving. It may be more important to read page 155 first and page 72 next month if the current theme calls for that. Further, it is possible to emphasize some curricular areas now and save others for later. . . . If the teacher keeps the overall needs of the year in mind, children can cover just as much of the curriculum as is expected (and more), without ever feeling the pressures of getting to page 83 on time.

A Planning Device   Once a teacher has determined that a teaching project or unit will be integrated across the curriculum, the actual making of a web provides a way of organizing that has specific advantages. A web is less structured and more tentative than an outline, while it still provides a focused means of organization. Further, if the web is regarded as a work in progress, rather than as a finished product, it can be added to or subtracted from at any given time.

Some teachers may find that after creating the web, an outline format is a good finished product. This can be done as a chronology, providing a schedule of activities in their proper sequence. Or it can be done by listing the subject areas. Or, the teacher may find that the web provides enough structure.

The advantages of viewing the school curriculum as a web of learning range from the philosophical (webbed learning as natural learning) to the practical (using webs as a planning device). Despite the many sound arguments in favor of integrated teaching and learning, of a curriculum that on paper looks like an illustration for an article about spiders, it doesn't always come naturally at first. However, the advantages of a webbed curriculum are extensive, and the first hurdles of planning and teaching can be overcome.

BIBLIOGRAPHY

White, E. B. *Charlotte's Web*. New York: Harper & Row, 1952.

Suzanne Lowell Krogh is Professor, Elementary Education, Woodring College of Education, Western Washington University, Bellingham, Washington.

QUESTIONS FOR REFLECTION

1.   In the subject area and at the level of greatest interest to you, how might you use the curriculum web concept?
2.   What are the characteristics of children's "natural learning"?
3.   What are the philosophical and practical advantages of a webbed curriculum?
4.   What problems might arise when trying to develop an early childhood curriculum along the lines of a theme or web rather than according to the subject areas? How might these problems be solved?

The Reggio Emilia Approach

LILIAN G. KATZ
SYLVIA C. CHARD

ABSTRACT: Schools in the Italian city of Reggio Emilia have made documentation of children's classroom experiences a central feature of early childhood education. The Reggio Emilia Approach involves displaying students' work throughout the school and carefully documenting their progress through such means as teachers' comments; observations; photographs; and transcriptions of children's discussions, comments, and explanations. The approach enhances students' learning, takes their ideas and work seriously, allows for continuous planning and evaluation, encourages parent participation, extends teachers' understanding of how children learn, and makes learning visible.

The municipal preprimary schools in the northern Italian city of Reggio Emilia have been attracting worldwide attention for more than a decade (see "Lessons from Reggio Emilia," *Principal,* May 1994). While interest in what is now called the Reggio Emilia Approach is focused on many of its impressive features (Gandini 1993; Katz and Cesarone 1994), perhaps its unique contribution to early childhood education is the documentation of children's experience as a standard classroom practice.

Documentation, in the forms of observation of children and extensive record-keeping, has long been encouraged and practiced in many early childhood programs. However, documentation in Reggio Emilia focuses more intensively on children's experience, memories, thoughts, and ideas during the course of their work. It emphasizes the importance of displaying children's work with great care and attention, both to content and aesthetic qualities.

In Reggio Emilia schools, documentation typically includes samples of a child's work at several different stages of completion; photographs showing work in progress; comments written by the teacher or other adults working with the children; transcriptions of children's discussions, comments, and explanations of intentions about the activity; and comments made by parents. Observations, transcriptions of tape recordings, and photographs of children discussing their work also may be included. Examples of children's work and written reflections on the processes in which they engaged are displayed in classrooms or hallways. The documents reveal how the children planned, carried out, and completed the displayed work.

We believe this type of documentation of children's work and ideas contributes to the quality of an early childhood program in at least six ways.

1. ENHANCED LEARNING

Documentation can contribute to the range and depth of children's learning from their projects and other work. As Malaguzzi (1993) points out, it is through documentation that children "become even more curious, interested, and confident as they contemplate the meaning of what they have achieved." The process of preparing and displaying documentaries of children's efforts and

From *Principal* 76, no. 5 (May 1997): 16–17. © 1997, National Association of Elementary School Principals. Used by permission of the author and publisher.

experiences provides a kind of debriefing or revisiting, during which new understandings can be clarified and strengthened.

Observation of children in Reggio Emilia preprimary classes indicate that they also learn from and are stimulated by each other's displayed work. A display documenting the work of a child or group often encourages other children to become involved in a new topic or to adopt a new representational technique. For example, Susan and Leroy conducted a survey on which grocery stores their classmates' families patronized. When Susan wanted to make a graph of her data, she asked Jeff about a graph he had displayed to demonstrate his earlier survey about the kinds of cereal their classmates ate for breakfast.

2. TAKING CHILDREN'S IDEAS AND WORK SERIOUSLY

Careful and attractive documentary displays can convey to children that their ideas, intentions, and efforts are taken seriously, and that the displays are not intended simply for decoration. For example, an important element in the project approach is preparing documents for display so that classmates working on different aspects of a topic can learn from each other's findings. Taking children's work seriously in this way encourages in them the disposition to approach their work responsibly, with energy and commitment, and to take satisfaction in the processes and results.

3. CONTINUOUS PLANNING AND EVALUATION

One of the most salient features of project work is continuous planning based on progressive evaluations. As children undertake complex tasks—individually or in small groups—over a period of several days or weeks, teachers examine the work each day and discuss with the children their ideas and new options for the following days. Planning decisions can be based on whatever the children have found interesting, puzzling, or challenging.

In one early childhood center where teachers meet to review children's work weekly—and often daily—they plan activities for the following week collaboratively, based in part on their review. Activities are never planned too far in advance, so that new strands of work can emerge and be documented. After the children have left for the day, teachers can reflect on and discuss the work in progress, and consider possible new directions the work might take. They also become more aware of each child's participation and development, which helps teachers maximize children's opportunities to represent their ideas in interesting and satisfying ways.

When teachers and children plan together, with openness to each other's ideas, the resulting activity is likely to be undertaken with greater interest and skill than if the child had planned alone. The documentation provides a kind of ongoing planning and evaluation by the adults working with the children.

4. PARENT PARTICIPATION

Documentation makes it possible for parents to become intimately aware of their children's experience in the school. As Malaguzzi (1993) points out, documentation "introduces parents to a quality of knowing that tangibly changes their expectations. They . . . take a new and more inquisitive approach toward the whole school experience. . . ."

Parents' comments on children's work contribute to the value of documentation. As they learn about the work in which their children are engaged, parents may be able to contribute ideas for field experiences, especially when they can offer help in gaining access to a field site or relevant expert. One parent brought in a turkey from her uncle's farm after she learned that the teacher was trying to help children visualize what a live turkey looks like.

The opportunity to examine a project's documentation can also help parents think of ways they might contribute time and energy to their child's classroom, such as listening to children's intentions, helping them find the materials they need, making suggestions, helping children write their ideas, offering assistance in finding and reading books, and measuring or counting things in the context of a project.

5. TEACHER RESEARCH AND AWARENESS

Documentation is an important kind of teacher research, sharpening and focusing teachers' attention on children's plans and learning, and on their own role in children's experiences. As teachers examine children's work and prepare to document it, their understanding of children's development and their insight into children's learning is deepened in ways not likely to occur from simply inspecting test results.

Documentation provides a basis for modifying and adjusting teaching strategies, and a source of ideas for new strategies, while deepening teachers' awareness of each child's progress. On the basis of rich data made available through documentation, teachers are able to make informed decisions about appropriate ways to support each child's development and learning.

The final product of a child's work rarely allows one to appreciate the false starts and persistent efforts entailed. By examining the documented steps that children take during their investigations, teachers and parents can appreciate the uniqueness of each child's construction of experience, and the ways that group efforts contribute to learning.

6. MAKING LEARNING VISIBLE

Of particular relevance to American educators, documentation provides information about children's learning and progress that cannot be demonstrated by the formal standardized tests and checklists we commonly employ. While U.S. teachers often gain important information and insight from their firsthand observations of children, documentation of the children's work in a wide variety of media provides compelling public evidence of the intellectual powers of young children that is not available in any other way.

REFERENCES

Gandini, L. "Educational and Caring Spaces." In *The Hundred Languages of Children: The Reggio Emilia Approach to Early Childhood Education* by Edwards, C.; Gandini, L.; and Forman, G. Norwood, N.J.: Ablex, 1993.

Katz, L. G. *Talks with Teachers of Young Children: A Collection*. Norwood, N.J.: Ablex, 1995. ED 380 232.

Katz, L. G.; Chard, S. C. *Engaging Children's Minds: The Project Approach*. Norwood, N.J.: Ablex, 1989.

Katz, L. G.; Cesarone, B. (eds.). *Reflections on the Reggio Emilia Approach*. Urbana, Ill.: ERIC Clearinghouse on Elementary and Early Childhood Education, 1994. ED 375 986.

Malaguzzi, L. "History, Ideas, and Basic Philosophy." In *The Hundred Languages of Children: The Reggio Emilia Approach to Early Childhood Education* (op. cit.).

Lilian G. Katz is professor of early childhood education at the University of Illinois at Urbana-Champaign and director of the ERIC Clearinghouse on Elementary and Early Childhood Education; *Sylvia C. Chard* is associate professor of early childhood education at the University of Alberta, Canada.

QUESTIONS FOR REFLECTION

1. In the subject area and at the level of greatest interest to you, would careful documentation of students' work à la the Reggio Emilia Approach enhance their learning? How might you implement such an approach?
2. The Reggio Emilia Approach has attracted worldwide attention. What do you think accounts for the effectiveness of the program?
3. In addition to creating documentary displays of students' work, how can teachers indicate that they "take students' ideas and work seriously"?

Playing Is My Job

ELIZABETH JONES

ABSTRACT: The trend to use direct teaching, worksheets, and drill in many kindergartens and some preschools may undermine children's competence and self-esteem. According to Erik Erikson and Jean Piaget's developmental theories, becoming a "master player" is a critical learning task for young children. Through play, children begin to shape their identities, acquire language and social skills, and explore the world around them. A "play curriculum" is therefore a developmentally appropriate learning environment for three- to five-year-olds.

During the past few decades, increased awareness of the importance of the preschool years has led to greater public interest and investment in early childhood education. In many programs, however, the developmental theory base for appropriate practice in the education of young children (Bredekamp 1987; Elkind 1986; Kamii 1985) has been neglected in favor of the behaviorist theory that characterizes common practice in elementary education.

A "push-down" of direct teaching, worksheets, and drill is found in many kindergartens and even in preschools. Such programs, designed to give children a head start in school, fail to take into account the active-learning mode in which young children are most competent. Thus, for some children, early schooling may undermine rather than contribute to their competence and self-esteem.

The developmental stage theories of Erik Erikson (1950) and Jean Piaget (Labinowicz 1980), which are basic to early childhood education, emphasize the different tasks to be accomplished at each stage. Infancy and toddlerhood offer the opportunity to learn first to trust and then to separate from one's primary caregiver, and to gain sensory-motor knowledge through active exploration of one's own physical self and the physical world.

Three- to five-year-olds who have mastered these tasks move on to the exercise of initiative, making choices and learning to sustain their play,

From *Principal* 76, no. 5 (May 1997): 18–19. © 1997, National Association of Elementary School Principals. Used by permission of the author and publisher.

relationships, and oral language—their modes for developing knowledge about the world. Children in the primary grades are moving into the next stage, in which they practice tasks to meet others' standards, and develop greater understanding of the logical relationship among the concrete objects in their world.

While the stages overlap, mastery of tasks at each stage is the most important preparation for the next stage, rather than practicing the next stage's tasks.

MASTERING PLAY

To become a master player is the height of achievement for children ages three to five. Master players are skilled at representing their experiences symbolically in self-initiated improvisational drama. Sometimes alone, sometimes in collaboration with others, they play out their fantasies and feelings about the events of their daily lives. Through their pretend play, young children consolidate their understanding of the world, their language, and their social skills. The skillful teacher of young children is one who makes such play possible and helps children to keep getting better at it.

Children at play are constructing their individual identities as well as their knowledge of the world. The child is saying, in effect, "This is who I am. This is what I want to do. This is what I need to do it with. I need to keep playing until I'm done."

Play, for young children, is active; the child does what he or she is thinking about, using body language as well as words. Younger children (ages 2 to 5) need props because they are the actors; older children (ages 4 to 8) increasingly create dramas in miniature by manipulating puppets, blocks, cars, and small animal and people figures.

Children's play is open-ended and builds skills in divergent thinking, a crucial precursor to the convergent, right-answer thinking required in school. The child who has learned, through play,

that he or she is a person-who-knows is then ready to adapt to the knowledge of others-who-know, including teachers.

Becoming a master player is an intermediate stage in the development of representation, a complex sequence that culminates in the child becoming a writer and reader. All human beings, beginning in early childhood, not only have experiences, they *represent* them for purposes of personal reflection and interpersonal communication. Like the life cycle stages, these stages overlap, with the later stages becoming more abstract (see Table 7.1).

Children invent writing in a process very similar to their invention of talking if they receive comparable response from adults (Ferreiro and Teberosky 1982; Harste *et al.* 1984; Bissex 1980). Talking begins with babbling; writing begins with scribbling. Just as early talkers move from spontaneous babble to conscious imitation of sounds made by mature talkers, so early writers move from spontaneous scribbling to conscious imitation of the print in their environment. The errors made in each case are not random; they reflect the child's systems of knowledge at that point in his or her development.

APPROPRIATE LEARNING ENVIRONMENTS

A developmentally appropriate classroom for three- to five-year-olds has a play curriculum. Children choose their activities during extended time periods, act physically on available materials, and talk to each other. The environment is rich in props for dramatic play, tools for image-making, and print. Teachers spend only brief periods talking to the whole group; while children are playing, teachers circulate, respond, mediate, enrich, observe, and plan (Jones and Reynolds 1992).

Children are ready for the challenges of the primary grades not when they have memorized colors, shapes, and numbers, but when they have

TABLE 7.1
The Development of Representation

Body language is the first mode of representation used by infants. As the child reaches for an object, the adult interprets the gesture as communication and responds accordingly.

Talk, which follows not long after, develops in the same way, as the adult interprets random babbling as communicative language, causing the child to babble with increased selectivity.

Play likewise begins as exploration of the physical world. The toddler puts things in and dumps them out, picks up, stacks, and knocks things over. A cup may elicit the beginning of make-believe as the child pretends to drink from it or give a drink to a stuffed toy. But as the child continues to master play, a real cup is unnecessary; a block or imaginary cup is sufficient to sustain play.

Image-making marks a stage in which children first explore and then make representations using markers, crayons, paint, clay, blocks or wood scraps. Scribbles are given names and move toward increasingly recognizable approximations of what they are meant to represent.

Writing evolves when children as young as three identify some of their scribbles as words while playing at drawing signs, making lists, or writing letters.

Reading begins not with decoding, but with the sequence, learned by watching adult readers, of picking up a book, turning it right side up, opening it, turning the pages one by one, and saying remembered words if the book is a familiar one.

mastered play and the dynamics of being a member of a group. A developmentally appropriate classroom for six- to eight-year-olds continues to build on all the skills of representation that children have been practicing since infancy.

Integrated curriculum in the primary grades (Katz and Chard 1989) encourages children to reflect on their meaningful experiences through many different modes of representation. For example, children in a coastal town, who have many reasons to be interested in fish, will gain both in basic skills and general information if they visit a fish market, talk with a visiting fisherman, feed goldfish, build a fishing boat with large blocks, play at working on the boat, read fish stories, sing chanties, and draw, paint, and write their own related experiences.

School should be a place that provides children tools and time to reflect on personal experiences, to understand them, and to communicate about them (Ashton-Warner 1963; Johnson 1987). Children are highly motivated to talk, play, draw, and write about the important people, places, and events in their lives outside school (Graves 1983; Dyson 1989).

From a developmental perspective, children learn to write by writing and to read by reading. "Readiness" activities which break down global tasks into incremental practice are likely to be both irrelevant and confusing to children. Development, both physical and intellectual, proceeds from whole to part, not from part to whole. A babbling infant acquires the inflections of the family's language before breaking them down into words; a three-year-old plays competently at the drama of reading a book long before becoming interested in the words.

Children should come to school with a repertoire of play skills that represent their understanding of the world as they have so far encountered it. A developmentally appropriate school acknowledges and expands that repertoire while extending children's skills in creating representations of their experience.

REFERENCES

Ashton-Warner, Sylvia. *Teacher.* New York: Simon and Schuster, 1986.

Bissex, Glenda. *GYNS at Work: A Child Learns to Read and Write.* Cambridge, Mass.: Harvard University Press, 1980.

Bredekamp, Sue. *Developmentally Appropriate Practice in Early Childhood Programs Serving Children from Birth through Age 8.* Washington, D.C.: National Association for the Education of Young Children, 1987.

Dyson, Anne Haas. *Multiple Worlds of Child Writers.* New York: Teachers College, 1989.

Elkind, David. "Formal Education and Early Childhood Education: An Essential Difference." *Phi Delta Kappan* 67:9 (May 1986): 631–636.

Erikson, Erik. *Childhood and Society.* New York: Norton, 1950.

Ferreiro, Emilia; and Teberosky, Ana. *Literacy before Schooling.* Exeter, N.H.: Heinemann, 1982.

Graves, Donald. *Writing: Teachers and Children at Work.* Exeter, N.H.: Heinemann, 1983.

Harste, Jerome; Woodward, Virginia; and Burke, Carolyn. *Language Stories and Literature Lessons.* Exeter, N.H.: Heinemann, 1984.

Johnson, Katie. *Doing Words.* Boston: Houghton Mifflin, 1987.

Jones, Elizabeth; and Reynolds, Gretchen. *The Play's the Thing: The Teacher's Role in Children's Play.* New York: Teachers College, 1992.

Kamii, Constance. "Leading Primary Education toward Excellence: Beyond Worksheets and Drill." *Young Children* 40:6 (September 1985): 3–9.

Katz, Lilian G.; and Chard, Sylvia C. *Engaging Children's Minds: The Project Approach.* Norwood, N.J.: Ablex, 1989.

Labinowicz, Ed. *The Piaget Primer.* Menlo Park, Cal.: Addison-Wesley, 1980.

Elizabeth Jones is a member of the early childhood education faculty at Pacific Oaks College and Children's School, Pasadena, California.

QUESTIONS FOR REFLECTION

1. How should teachers of three- to five-year-olds respond to parents who do not believe that "Children are ready for the challenges of the primary grades not when they have memorized colors, shapes, and numbers, but when they have mastered play and the dynamics of being a member of a group"?

2. In what ways might the concept of *play* be used to enhance curricula at the K–12 and postsecondary levels?

3. Explain the following statement: "Development, both physical and intellectual, proceeds from whole to part, not from part to whole." Does this perspective apply to development after the early childhood years?

What's Ahead in Elementary Education?

GERALD W. BRACEY

ABSTRACT: While secondary education has undergone many changes, elementary education has shown remarkable continuity over the years. Although a vigorous national dialogue on the need for national standards, the role of technology in education, interdisciplinary instruction, and charter schools continues, these trends will take years to affect teaching and learning in elementary schools. For example, the potential of technology in education is largely untapped due to software that simply "automate[s] the past" and the lack of infrastructure in the schools. In sum, a significant reason for the slow pace of change in the elementary curriculum is parents' nostalgia and "amnesia" regarding schools of a bygone era.

In ["Change and Continuity in Elementary Education," *Principal*, January 1996] I noted the remarkable continuity of elementary education over the years, in contrast to the many changes undergone by secondary education. I closed with a vision of America's elementary schools "oozing into the future." Let's be more specific.

STANDARDS

The governors and business leaders who attended the "Education Summit" at Palisades, New York, in March 1996 talked about higher standards, but none of the participants expressed a need for national standards. This dismayed former Assistant Secretary of Education Diane Ravitch, who declared, "Apparently, the United States should have 50 state standards or even 16,000 local standards. But not national standards. The governors, Democratic and Republican, said it; the President said it. And they are all wrong."

Although Ravitch and President Albert Shanker of the American Federation of Teachers continue to beat the drums for national standards, it's impossible at this time to predict the future of the standards movement, and its impact on 21st century elementary curricula. However, the National Governors Association and business executives are working together to create an organization that would serve as a clearinghouse for standards issues.

TECHNOLOGY

Certainly the next century will see an enormous increase in the use of technology at all grade levels. At present, though, the potential of technology remains largely untapped. Part of the reason can be seen by examining available educational software, most of which breaks no new ground but simply attempts, in the words of one critic, to "automate the past." The bells and whistles are all there—dynamite graphics, cute interactivity, and even jangling music—but much of it was created by "techies" who haven't a clue about how kids learn. While some software suppliers bring in educators to help develop or critique their products, many do not.

A hopeful trend is an effort currently being undertaken by moviemaker George Lucas, whose *Star Wars* films feature some of the most spectacular images ever seen on the silver screen. The latest project of his Lucas Educational Foundation is to produce images of another kind that should help schools make better and wiser use of technology. It is a documentary film that shows what technology can do, to be accompanied by a source book that the Lucas Foundation's Patricia

From *Principal* 76, no. 1 (September 1996): 6–10. © 1996, National Association of Elementary School Principals. Used by permission of the author and publisher.

Burness describes as the "*Whole Earth Catalog* for technology."

Another reason why technology's potential is not being realized lies in the lack of suitable infrastructure. Most schools don't have anything close to the wiring required to handle the new and sophisticated information technologies. A 1994 report found that most schools had woefully inadequate wiring, including a number of situations where circuit breakers tripped if more than four computers were used at once.

When Sun Microsystems sponsored Netday '96, using volunteers to wire 1,000 California schools, the company was flooded with inquiries from 15 nations and 41 states. As a result, plans are under way to make Netday a national event.

If a combination of Netdays and Lucas images help move elementary school technology into the next century—and adequate resources are provided for necessary staff development—fabulous things are possible: Instead of reading about Apollo 13 or watching the movie, students can experience the virtual reality of space travel. Instead of reading about weather cycles, they can download weather maps from satellites. Instead of studying marine life in the Florida Keys, they can electronically accompany a scientist on an exotic field trip. At a more mundane level, e-mail could provide a strong communication link connecting children, teachers, and parents.

An inexpensive video camera will permit students in different countries to see each other as they communicate through the Internet, which literally connects the user to the world. President Clinton has promised to give every school access to the Internet by 2000. Already the Internet is slowly changing from a largely text-oriented medium to one making increasing use of multimedia.

INTERDISCIPLINARY INSTRUCTION

Something likely to change elementary education even more quickly than technology is interdisciplinary instruction—a term that defies precise

definition but that I choose to call any instruction that integrates material from more than one discipline in a given project.

There are several forces pushing interdisciplinary instruction into the elementary classroom. One is the standards movement. For the elementary school teacher, incorporating standards from various curriculum areas into meaningful daily instruction can be a daunting task. But interdisciplinary instruction offers the appealing prospect of including two or more sets of standards in a given set of activities.

In addition to interdisciplinary instruction, there has been a recent resurgence of interest in interdisciplinary *learning* in an attempt to make the elementary curriculum more relevant to real life. Students, perhaps out of habit, tend to separate subjects that were learned separately, not recognizing their interconnections. But this separation does not exist in the world outside the classroom, where they must be prepared to interrelate what they have learned.

Interdisciplinary learning already has a strong foothold at the secondary school level, and it may be only a matter of time before elementary schools begin to emulate interdisciplinary programs like Chemcom, a chemistry project in which students investigate a fish kill to determine how it happened, how it might have been prevented, and how it can be cleaned up. To find answers, the students must relate facts and principles of biology, ecology, and chemistry.

CHARTER SCHOOLS

In their old movies, Judy Garland and Mickey Rooney would solve problems by shouting, "Let's put on a show!" If they were around today to confront the problems of elementary education, the cry would be, "Let's start a charter school!"

Charter schools are popping up all over the country, but it is too early to tell if they will be a long-lasting reform or just another disappointing educational fad. At the moment, the movement is being backed by enthusiasts representing diverse ideologies. Those on the left see charter schools as an outgrowth of the 1970s alternative schools movement. Those on the right are using charter schools as a stalking horse for a market-driven school system and further deregulation of education.

There are no specific characteristics that define charter schools, many of which represent the vision of one person or a small group. Typically they are small, can hire and fire teachers, have governing boards made up of parents, teachers, and administrators, and are exempt from some district rules and regulations (though not those imposed by state and federal agencies). Many are required to show improvement by their students.

Because they are small and independent, charter schools can act quickly, avoiding the sometimes cumbersome and slow processes of a central office. But also because they are small and independent, they often lack specialized knowledge, and their lack of expertise in business and finance has already caused a number of them to fail.

In addition, lack of assessment expertise may make them vulnerable when it comes time to demonstrate the accountability specified by most charter school legislation. Some years ago, researchers concluded that different curricula give rise to different patterns of achievement. Measuring the success of any new curriculum depends, in part, on whether the pattern of achievement sought by testing matches the pattern of achievement sought by the curriculum. Without some expertise in linking curriculum to assessment, the assessments may mislead. Nor are the states prepared to render assistance. According to a recent report, no state has a plan for evaluating its charter schools.

BARRIERS TO CHANGE

One often hears the words "values" and "character" in connection with elementary education these days, in part reflecting the rise of juvenile crime. But studies by the Public Agenda Foundation indicate that what the public prefers is a curriculum emphasizing the basic three R's, and that values and character belong at home (which is all well and good when there *is* a home, with parents in it.) While it's dangerous to generalize about the impact of increasingly conservative school boards and parent groups on the elementary curriculum, it will obviously become more difficult in many districts to introduce material that does not narrowly attend to cognitive outcomes.

Public Agenda found that people want their kids to learn the same things they did. They are afraid that if children learn different things or in different ways, their chances in later life will somehow be limited. These attitudes are motivated less by politics and religion than by a tendency to glorify schools of bygone years.

The late Secretary of Education Terrel Bell typified this kind of wistful thinking when he wrote, "How do we get back to a time when we were a nation of learners?" In penning these words, Bell displayed two qualities often seen when people reflect on earlier times: nostalgia and amnesia. In fact, we have *never* been a nation of learners, and we are probably closer to deserving that title today than at any time in the past.

It is this false nostalgia that makes many parents suspicious of change, especially in the elementary grades where the foundation for later learning is laid down. This suspicion is compounded when people misinterpret such changes as whole language and invented spelling.

"Not with my kid, you don't," they say, and it is this sort of attitude that will inhibit any major changes in the elementary curriculum in the near future. Continuity rather than change remains the dominant mode as our elementary schools "ooze into the future."

Gerald W. Bracey is an education consultant and writer in Alexandria, Virginia, and executive director of the Alliance for Curriculum Reform.

QUESTIONS FOR REFLECTION

1.   What evidence can you cite to support Bracey's claim that "continuity rather than change remains the dominant mode as our elementary schools 'ooze into the future' "? Evidence to refute his claim?
2.   What are the differences between *interdisciplinary instruction* and *interdisciplinary learning*?
3.   Do you agree or disagree with Bracey's statement that "we have *never* been a nation of learners, and we are probably closer to deserving that title today than at any time in the past"? Explain your answer.

Early Childhood Education: What Should We Expect?

DAVID ELKIND

ABSTRACT: *The benefits of early education for children depend upon program quality and the number of socioeconomic risk factors (low maternal education, poverty, mother's minority-language status, etc.) the children possess. Researchers cite gains in literacy and numeracy skills as the most important program benefits, while kindergarten teachers believe social and emotional skills are most important. In light of these variables, it is not possible to make generalizations about the benefits of early programs. Moreover, early childhood should be seen as a unique stage of life, a time for liberation and exploration rather than intervention and remediation.*

What have young children to gain from participating in early education programs? Although a number of investigations have been conducted in recent years (*e.g.,* Haskins 1989, McKey *et al.* 1985, Schweinhart and Weikert 1980), a 1995 study of young children, conducted by West and Hausken for the U.S. Department of Education, is unique in two respects.

First, it explores the extent to which one or more socioeconomic risk factors (low maternal education, poverty, mother's minority-language status, unmarried mother, and single parenthood) impairs the effectiveness of a child's early education experience. Second, it compares what

are perceived as critical readiness skills with the traits that kindergarten teachers believe are essential for success in their classrooms.

West and Hausken surveyed a representative sample of 4,423 children, aged 3 to 5, who had not yet attended kindergarten. They measured six different areas of development: emerging literacy and numeracy, small motor development, gross motor function, general health, social and emotional development, and speech development. The researchers found that young children who attended a center-based preschool program attained significantly more preliteracy skills (*e.g.,* recognized all or most letters) and numeracy

From *Principal* 75, no. 5 (May 1996): 11–13. © 1996, National Association of Elementary School Principals. Used by permission of the author and publisher.

skills (*e.g.*, counted to 20) than did comparable children who did not attend such programs. Preschool attendance was not associated with higher performance in any of the other five health/behavioral parameters.

However, the study found that gains in preliteracy and numeracy skills were reduced when risk factors were included. The higher the number of risk factors impacting on the child, the lower the number of skills. This finding adds yet another to the many qualifications that must preface any statement heralding the benefits of early childhood education.

One such qualification, which the study did not evaluate, is the *character* of the early childhood education program. The effectiveness of each such program varies with the teachers' training, child-to-teacher ratio, availability of educational materials, and adequacy of the physical facilities. With all of these variables, it is not possible to make any generalizations about the benefits of early education programs. This is a very important point that is rarely acknowledged or acted upon.

A PERSISTENT MISCONCEPTION

Educators often assume that young children who have participated in a preschool program are ready for academic instruction when they enter kindergarten or first grade. Since about 85 percent of today's young children have been in some type of out-of-home setting before entering school, administrators expect that most of them will already know their numbers and letters, and they structure kindergarten and first-grade classes accordingly.

As a result, it is the at-risk children least likely to benefit from a preschool program, according to the West and Hausken study (1995), who are often held back or placed in transition classes—reinforcing their already poor self-images and solidifying their already negative attitudes towards school and learning.

Educators are not entirely to blame for misconceptions regarding the benefits of early education programs. The introduction of Head Start and other early intervention programs in the 1960s was accompanied by a barrage of claims that such programs would raise the IQs and academic achievement levels of disadvantaged children. Although these promises were never fulfilled, the perception that early intervention is beneficial for all children, under all circumstances, persists.

REVISITING AN OLD PERSPECTIVE

It seems to me that we need to look at early childhood education from a different perspective—the one held by those who first proposed the idea of educating young children outside the home. Frederick Froebel (1893) created the first kindergarten and introduced the idea that play was the young child's natural mode of learning and self-expression.

For her part, Maria Montessori (1964) fervently believed that even three- and four-year-old children could profit from an educational program outside the home. She described these children as being in a "sensitive period" for development of their sensory and motor abilities, for which she prescribed a wide array of manipulative tasks.

Unfortunately, the social and political upheavals of the 1960s have distorted Froebel's and Montessori's conceptions of early childhood education. Today their views are being placed further at risk by the growing use of technology. Computers, unlike teaching machines and other educational fads, are here to stay. But young children's facility with computers should not be misread. They may be able to "point and click" without really understanding all they are doing. We need to remember that computers deal with symbols, and young children need hands-on experience before symbols have meaning for them. Without seeing "red" or tasting "sweet," a child can have no understanding of what these words symbolize.

We need to move away from the idea that the first years of life are a time for intervention and school readiness. Early childhood is a stage of life that should be considered on its own terms, not as preparation for later stages. If we think of early childhood in this way, we will create kindergarten and first-grade environments that are flexible, activity-oriented, and filled with plants and animals. Such environments liberate young children's abilities and provide them opportunities to experience the special pleasures—as well as the awful fears—that are unique to this stage of life.

RESEARCHERS VS. TEACHERS

Another important feature of the West and Hausken study (1995) was the contrast between the conceptions of school readiness held by educational researchers and classroom teachers. While the study identifies emerging literacy and numeracy skills as the most important tools for children entering kindergarten, its authors acknowledge that kindergarten teachers do not agree with this assessment.

In fact, a survey of kindergarten teachers (Heaviside and Harris 1993) reveals that only a small minority of them believe that knowledge of primary colors and shapes, and the ability to count and recognize letters, are essential for success in kindergarten. Instead, they tend to emphasize the importance of health and of such skills as the ability to communicate needs and thoughts; to participate without disrupting the classroom; and to follow instructions.

It seems to me that educational administrators often place too much importance on the theories of researchers and too little on the experiential wisdom of teachers. For more than a quarter of a century, researchers have been touting the academic benefits of early childhood education, while teachers have consistently argued for the importance of social and emotional skills. Yet the findings of longitudinal studies indicate that the long-term benefits of participating in a quality early childhood program, such as lower delinquency and dropout rates, are more social than academic (Schweinhart and Weikart 1980).

A LIBERATING ENTERPRISE

Teachers who work with young children every day understand that early childhood is a period of rapid intellectual growth, much as adolescence is a time of rapid physical growth. During both periods, differences in individual growth rates are pronounced. Just as some adolescents may attain their full height at 13 while others are still growing at 14 and 15, some young children acquire the mental abilities that Jean Piaget (1950) called "concrete operations" (for example, understanding that the same letter can have two sounds) at age 4, others at age 6, and still others at age 7. The different rates at which they acquire these abilities are relatively independent of IQ.

Because young children's rates of intellectual attainment are so variable, it makes little sense to have uniform, standardized kindergarten and first-grade curricula. Even children with similar intellectual potential may be at very different intellectual levels, and this diversity is only enhanced by participation in early childhood programs.

We can address this diversity best if we regard early education as a liberating, rather than a remedial, enterprise, and organize our kindergarten and first-grade classrooms accordingly. Early education programs that accommodate this diversity will provide a suitable environment for the young child's abilities, needs, and interests.

In the end, a setting in which children can fully experience all the vicissitudes of their early childhood years is the very best preparation for a successful transition to the later stages of the human life cycle.

REFERENCES

Froebel, F. *The Education of Man*. New York: Appleton, 1893.

Haskins, I. "Beyond Metaphor: The Efficacy of Early Childhood Education." *American Psychologist* 44:2 (February 1989): 274–282.

Heaviside, S.; Farris, E. *Public School Kindergarten Teachers' Views on Children's Readiness for School*. Washington, D.C.: U.S. Department of Education, National Center for Education Statistics, 1993.

McKey, R.; Condelli, L.; Ganson, H.; Barrett, J.; McConkey, C.; Plantz, M. *The Impact of Head Start on Children, Families and Communities*. DHHS Publication No. OHDS 85-31193. Washington, D.C.: U.S. Department of Health and Human Services, 1985.

Montessori, M. *The Montessori Method*. New York: Shocken, 1964.

Piaget, J. *The Psychology of Intelligence*. London: Routledge & Kegan Paul, 1950.

Schweinhart, L.; Weikart, D. *Young Children Grow Up: The Effects of the Perry Preschool Project on Youths Through Age 15*. Ypsilanti, Mich.: High Scope Press, 1980.

West, J.; Hausken, E. G. *Approaching Kindergarten: A Look at Preschool in the United States*. Washington, D.C.: U.S. Department of Education, National Center for Education Statistics, 1955.

David Elkind is Professor of Child Development at Tufts University and the author of *The Hurried Child* (1981), *All Grown Up and No Place to Go* (1984), and *Miseducation: Preschoolers at Risk* (1987).

QUESTIONS FOR REFLECTION

1. Why does Elkind believe that the educational views of Froebel and Montessori are being placed "at risk" by the growing use of technology? Do you agree?

2. What reasons can you cite to support the view that "early childhood is a stage of life that should be considered on its own terms, not as preparation for later stages"?

3. According to Elkind's views, what curriculum criteria would be helpful in developing an "ideal" kindergarten or first-grade program?

Case Study in Curriculum Implementation

Preparing Children for a Global Society: Integrating Foreign Languages into the Elementary School Curriculum

GISELA ERNST-SLAVIT

KERRI J. WENGER

LANA KRUMWEIDE

ABSTRACT: Although our educational system has not changed much from the early twentieth century, the linguistic and cultural backgrounds of students have changed dramatically. To meet the challenge of preparing students for a global, diverse world, a K–5 school in Washington state collaborated with a local university to create a program that integrates instruction in K–5 Spanish with the content areas. The program, named Compañeros (partners), gives university students enrolled in a bilingual/English as a Second Language (ESL) program opportunities to teach weekly Spanish lessons at the school. Compañeros teachers use visuals, games, music, and manipulatives to present lessons organized around Gardner's multiple intelligences theory.

INTRODUCTION

Two elementary teachers are talking in the faculty lounge.

"Today, one of my kids found archaeology articles for a class project on the Internet written in Spanish," said Monica Jones. "As students talked about it, my student from Laos was amazed that none of her classmates could read a language other than English!"

"I have a student who writes in Spanish and English to her e-mail pal at Washington State University," said the other. "I wish we could offer a second language to all our kids. But how would we fit it in?"

We face a new millennium in education, with concomitant changes in the students we teach

and the materials we use to teach them. The increase in the linguistic and cultural diversity in our schools, the changes in the domestic and world economy, and a burgeoning dependency on technology are perhaps the three most important factors affecting educational efforts.

According to data from the 1990 census, of the 42,791,000 public and nonpublic students enrolled during the 1991–92 school year, approximately 6 percent were language minority students, that is, students in the process of learning English as a Second Language (ESL). More specifically, 2,430,712 ESL students were enrolled in elementary or secondary schools during this period. As Valdés (1998) points out, this situation is by no means uncommon. While many nations adopt one official language, "few are ei-

Article written by Gisela Ernst-Slavit, Kerri J. Wenger, and Lana Krumweide for *Curriculum Planning: A Contemporary Approach,* Seventh Edition, 2000. Used by permission of the authors.

ther mono-lingual or mono-ethnic" with respect to citizens and students in school (p. 12).

The linguistic and cultural makeup of the children in our classrooms has changed significantly. However, the characteristics of the teaching force, the basic curriculum, and most teaching methodologies used today still reflect an educational system based on America's early twentieth century industrial society. Stated differently, our country's demographics reflect the planet's global diversity, but our schools are not equipped to take advantage of such linguistic and cultural diversity. Students who wish to study languages other than English are traditionally forced to wait until secondary school to begin such study.

Meanwhile, the global economy is changing in ways that have sharply increased the demand for an educated workforce well versed in many modes of communication. Heath (1993) indicates that the United States is facing an economic-educational crisis at all levels of business and education. She explains that the role played by schools as a main source of economic vitality has changed; now schools seem to be out of step with the times. To reverse this current trend, changes in the public educational system will have to include the ability to perceive our economic vitality in terms of a multilingual, multicultural, integrated world economy.

We are currently in the midst of a technological and information revolution, spawned by new information technologies, networks and combinations of computer databases, telephones, and satellite and cable transmission systems. Computer literacy has become a fundamental skill, and knowing how to retrieve information, as opposed to having access to it, has become the mark of an educated person (Ornstein, 1993). But computers, like people, do not exist in a vacuum; as more schools around the world are wired, children whose language and cultural backgrounds are increasingly divergent will travel the "information superhighway." Within this context, then, foreign language teachers are working to design curricula for children who will interact with peers whose languages and cultures are different from their own, using a range of technological resources to access information in ways heretofore unimagined.

The good news is that changes are happening—although sometimes too slowly. As we understand more about optimum conditions for second language learning, foreign language teachers have advocated a move away from the teaching of foreign languages at the high school level by stressing grammar and vocabulary lists. Rather, the emphasis is now on beginning language instruction at the elementary level, using a variety of communicative and engaging activities. Today, teachers are being prepared to integrate foreign language education with the content areas (Ernst & Richard, 1994; Ernst-Slavit, Wenger, & Statzner, 1998). Integrated language and content instruction allows language students to develop fuller proficiency in a second language while reinforcing ongoing content area instruction. These changes are clearly evident as we eavesdrop on three elementary classrooms:

Vignette 1

Amy Muller, a student teacher at Washington State University, kneels before her class of twenty-five squirming six- and seven-year-olds after reading a story about *la familia* (the family). Referring to colorful pictures of family members labeled in Spanish, she asks her students—in Spanish—to tell her how many *hermanas y hermanos* (sisters and brothers) they have.

"Jason, *cuántos hermanos y hermanas tienes?*" Muller asks.

"*Dos hermanas*" he says, pointing to the "sisters" pictures.

"Ginger?"

"*Un hermano, dos hermanas.*"

"Bruno?"

"*No, nada,*" Bruno shakes his head.

To a visitor, all twenty-five students appear quite versed in Spanish. Yet these students have had only four months of Spanish instruction.

Vignette 2

Fifth graders are engaged in a treasure hunt on the World Wide Web as they look for the current exchange rate between the United States and twenty nations in which Spanish is the official language. In his efforts to find information, we observe Max reading words aloud from *El Comercio,* a Peruvian newspaper; Patricia, skimming through several screens—in Spanish—of news reports from Spain; Jofen browsing through a list of bilingual sites about Panama and the Panama Canal; and Misha using a search engine to locate exchange rates for different currencies within the World Bank site.

Vignette 3

In a second grade classroom, Yi-Wen approaches her regular teacher.

"Mrs. Bental, we learned the Spanish names for different dinosaurs in our Spanish class last week. Could we add those words to our 'Dinosaur Dig' lists for this week?"

"Yeah, we could write the words down in English on one side like we always do, and the *Español* words over here," another student chimes in.

"And then Maestra Anita[1] can help us write the rest of our science stories in *Español* words next week!"

Mrs. Bental, though she speaks no Spanish, readily agrees. "Maestra Anita and I will get together and work on them when you're finished, okay?"

These vignettes—all of which involve real students and teachers observed at Franklin Elementary School—illustrate the curricular changes occurring in foreign language education. In these classrooms, children no longer learn *about* a new language and how it works by practicing isolated grammar skill sequences; they are now learning a language by using it for real communicative pur-

poses. How was this curriculum developed and implemented? Using Franklin Elementary School as an example, we discuss the process and the partners involved in this curriculum development effort and suggest a model for a school's efforts to provide students with foreign language instruction at all grade levels.

FRANKLIN ELEMENTARY SCHOOL

"Preparing students for their world" is the motto for Franklin Elementary School in Pullman, Washington. The great diversity of cultural and linguistic backgrounds which characterize people in this state is evident at Franklin, where approximately 30 percent of students come to school speaking languages other than English, and anywhere from two to ten different languages may be represented in a given classroom.

Located in a small, state-of-the-art new building in a university community surrounded by rolling wheat and lentil fields, Franklin's staff attempts to address the needs of this rapidly changing student population. In 1994, the school staff and site council developed a Student Learning Improvement Plan, which was shaped by the following overarching goals:

"To create a multicultural, global community where:

- all members interact in ways which recognize both their individual strengths and their interdependence;
- a systematic plan for curriculum and instruction meets the diverse academic and social needs of all members; and
- all members are encouraged to take risks, think creatively, and grow intellectually and socially."

To reach these objectives, Franklin faculty and its partner, Washington State University's Bilingual/ESL Education Program, developed a K–5 Spanish Foreign Language in the Elementary School (FLES) program named *Compañeros* (partners). Through this partnership, WSU graduate and undergraduate students in the Bilingual/ESL education program use their recently acquired knowledge about pedagogy, languages, and cultures in real classrooms with real children when they teach weekly Spanish classes at Franklin Elementary School (Ernst & Richard, 1994).

THE *COMPAÑEROS* SPANISH PROGRAM

After considerable study and dialogue involving teachers, the district ESL coordinator, principal, parents, and university language specialists, Franklin's site council voted in 1994 to provide modest funding for a one-year pilot program in Spanish for all children in kindergarten through grade five. The establishment of a FLES program would offer Franklin Elementary School a rich opportunity for innovative curriculum development and afford regular grade-level teachers time for faculty collaboration and planning.

Since then, Spanish instruction has been offered to all children in the school. Although the time allocation and scheduling have changed somewhat over the years, all children in grades 1–5 are exposed to the language and cultures of over twenty Spanish-speaking nations for an average of sixty minutes a week; kindergartners receive thirty minutes weekly. In the initial phases of the program, classes were staffed by pairs of preservice teachers enrolled in a second language methods class at Washington State University. Although education majors are still actively involved in the program, the school hired a part-time FLES teacher to coordinate the program in 1997.[2]

The K–5 curriculum for *Compañeros,* described as a FLES content-related program, exposes young children to Spanish native speech and to several of the historical and folk traditions of twenty Spanish-speaking countries. The organizing model for this program is depicted in Figure 7.1. As the arrows between the three circles indicate, each dimension—the K–5 curriculum, *Standards for Foreign Language Learning: Preparing for the 21st Century* (1996), and Howard

FIGURE 7.1
Compañeros **K–5 Spanish Curriculum**

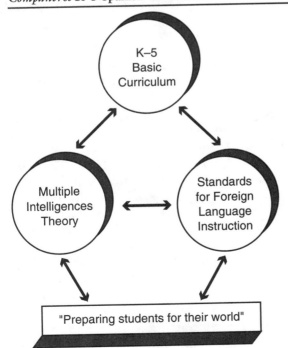

Gardner's Multiple Intelligences Theory (1983, 1989)—informs the other two. Each dimension is explained below.

1. THE K–5 CURRICULUM: INTEGRATING LANGUAGE AND CONTENT

During the last decade, the integration of language and content instruction has been advocated by many (e.g., Curtain & Pesola, 1994; Dulay, Burt, & Krashen, 1982; Mohan, 1986; Omaggio, 1993). That is, second-language teachers use instructional materials, learning tasks, and classroom techniques from academic content areas as the vehicle for developing language, content, cognitive, and study skills. In the *Compañeros* program, Spanish instruction is interwoven as much as possible with the children's basic grade-level curriculum. This means that FLES teachers need to have a thorough knowledge of the scope and sequence of the school curriculum to build upon children's experiences across the curriculum and, whenever appropriate, to integrate skills and activities across diverse subject areas.

Early in the year, regular grade-level teachers provide outlines to Spanish teachers of the main themes which shape the curriculum for that year. With this information in hand, Spanish instructors attempt to connect Spanish instruction with the topic of the week or month. For example, every February, second graders become archaeologists and historians for three weeks as they participate in dinosaur digs, read about prehistoric times, produce colorful timelines, and manipulate plaster molds of dinosaur bones. Accordingly, during Spanish instruction, it is not unusual to observe these second graders grappling with the Spanish past tense as they talk about "dinosaurios," "tiranosaurios," and "brontosaurios." This articulation between the content areas and the Spanish curriculum facilitates learning a second language while at the same time offering students opportunities to reinforce their recently acquired knowledge in the academic subjects. The following list includes the main curriculum themes introduced in the early grades in both Spanish instruction and in the primary curriculum, which are reinforced and extended during ensuing years:

1. Home and the classroom
2. Pollution and the environment
3. Customs and celebrations
4. Calendar and time
5. Animals
6. Grammatical constructs
7. Foods
8. Courtesy expressions (school and home)
9. The body/self-concept
10. Classifications

It is important to remember that in a 60-minute FLES lesson it is not realistic to assume that all foreign language instruction is going to be based on all concepts taken from that week's grade-level curriculum. While foreign language teachers base their units on the overarching themes presented above, many specific content-area objectives (for example, written comparisons of different holiday celebrations, which require high language fluency) are not included in FLES lessons, due to students' developing language abilities.

2. STANDARDS FOR FOREIGN LANGUAGE LEARNING: THE FIVE C'S

The content of the *Compañeros* curriculum weaves grade level content area objectives with the *Standards for Foreign Language Learning: Preparing for the 21st Century* (1996). These national standards, guided by the assumption that all students should develop and maintain proficiency in English and at least one other language, are designed around the five C's of foreign language education—communication, cultures, connections, comparisons, and communities. Brief explanations of each of these goals in foreign language instruction in relation to the *Compañeros* program appear below.

Communication: To communicate in languages other than English. *Compañeros'* goal is

FIGURE 7.2
Unit: La Casa (The House), Grade 2

Unit Goals and Objectives				
Connections	*Communication*	*Culture*	*Comparisons*	*Communities*
• Identifies materials needed to build different types of homes. • Demonstrates understanding of chart making and chart reading.	• Comprehends at least 12 words related to: — house — household items — furnishings • Responds accurately to questions: "Camina hacia el/la" "¿Qué es esto?" "¿Es la sala?" • Comprehends TPR commands: "Camina hacia el/la . . ." "Toca la/el"	• Demonstrates understanding of different types of homes in at least one Spanish-speaking country. • Demonstrates understanding of different types of ancient homes in one Spanish-speaking country (e.g., Mayan, Incan, Spanish). • Knows one Spanish song, "La Casa."	• Recognizes differences and similarities among different types of homes (e.g., igloos, cabins, mobile homes, teepees, trailers). • Identifies similarities and differences among students' houses.	• Shows evidence of understanding the situation of homeless people.

to facilitate genuine interaction with others whether they are on another continent, across town, or within the neighborhood.

Cultures: To gain knowledge and understanding of other cultures. This FLES program exposes students to the historical and folk traditions in more than twenty Spanish-speaking countries.

Connections: To connect with other disciplines and acquire information. The *Compañeros* program is built around the belief that learning other languages will aid young learners as they make connections with other disciplines and learn to recognize and value a diversity of viewpoints.

Comparisons: To develop insight into the nature of language and culture. An important goal of a language program is to help students develop an awareness of the similarities and differences between different cultures and languages.

Communities: To participate in multilingual communities at home and around the world. *Compañeros* seeks to help students find opportunities to use Spanish beyond the classroom and school settings.

Although clear and ambitious goals are the first step in designing an elementary FLES program, developing curriculum and planning for

each day's instruction are pivotal to the success of the program. Figure 7.2 presents an example of a unit on *La Casa* (The House) designed around the five C's. Although this particular unit for grade two is traditionally taught in three lessons of thirty minutes each, it is not difficult to see how it can be adapted for other grade levels and timeframes.

3. MULTIPLE INTELLIGENCES THEORY

Compañeros utilizes a multiplicity of second-language methodologies and teaching strategies such as visuals, games, music, and manipulatives. In addition, lessons are organized around Gardner's Multiple Intelligences theory (Gardner, 1983; Gardner & Hatch, 1989). Gardner proposes the existence of a number of relatively autonomous capacities to solve problems or to fashion products that are valued in one or more settings. These different ways of knowing and understanding the world include: 1) verbal/linguistic —the ability to use words and language; 2) logical/mathematical—the capacity for inductive and deductive thinking/reasoning, the use of numbers, and the recognition of abstract patterns; 3) visual/spatial—the ability to visualize objects and spatial dimensions; 4) bodily/kinesthetic—the ability to control bodily motion; 5) musical—the ability to recognize tonal patterns, sounds, and rhythm and beats; 6) interpersonal—the ability to communicate with others and establish meaningful relationships; and 7) intrapersonal—the ability to engage in self-reflection and analysis.

To refer to our earlier example as depicted in Figure 7.3, the unit of *La Casa* includes a diversity of activities such as drawing an imaginary house in a selected Spanish-speaking country (visual/spatial); imagining who the occupants are and what their lifestyles are (intrapersonal); surveying class members and graphing results about types of homes and furnishings (logical-mathematical); commands such as *"Camina hacia la/el..."* (Walk to the ...), *"Abre la/el..."* (Open the ...) (bodily/kinesthetic); singing a song about the house (musical); learning new vocabulary about the house and home furnishings (linguistic); and practicing in pairs questions *"¿Dónde está la/el...?"* (Where is the ...) and *"¿Quién está en la/el...?"* (Who is in the ...) (interpersonal). In

FIGURE 7.3
Unit: La Casa (The House), Grade 2

Activities and Strategies

Anticipated Learning Outcomes: Students will be able to . . .

- comprehend basic vocabulary related to the house
- react to TPR commands
- identify similarities and differences among students' houses
- recognize differences and similarities among different types of houses (e.g., igloo, teepee, mobile home, trailer, apartment, condo, house boat)
- recognize certain types of houses common to particular areas in one South American country (i.e., Peru)
- learn a Spanish song: "El Patio de Mi Casa"
- show evidence of awareness of and compassion for the homeless

Linguistic

1. Talk about how we all live in different houses.
2. Read or tell a story about houses (e.g., *La Casa donde vivo* by Isadore Seltzer).
7. Learn new vocabulary through visual aids and repetition.

Intrapersonal

3. Imagine a house in a selected Spanish-speaking country. Who might live in that house? What do they do? What does the house look like? Discuss questions about the poor and homeless.

Visual-Spatial

4. Draw an imaginary house in selected Spanish-speaking country.
6. View slides of houses in selected Spanish-speaking country.

Musical

5. Sing a song in Spanish about the casa (from CD of Spanish songs).

Interpersonal

10. In pairs practice questions "¿Qué es esto?" (What is this?) "¿Es la sala?" (Is this the living room?).

Logical-Mathematical

9. Survey class and graph results about types of homes and furnishings.

Bodily-Kinesthetic

8. React to TPR Commands: "Camina hacia el/la . . ." (Walk to the . . .) "Toca la/el . . ." (Touch the . . .).

Assessment: Students will be assessed through their participation and performance in all activities (e.g., observe students' use of new vocabulary by showing pictures and asking students "¿Qué es esto?" "¿Es la sala?" and observe students' actions following TPR commands). During seat work, teacher will walk around and ask questions to individual students. Grade ditto activity (day 3).

this way, students who may not learn best via traditional methods of foreign language teaching (which emphasize only discrete listening and repetition skills) are engaged and challenged as they use many modes of learning to practice thinking and communicating in a second language.

SUMMARY

The three dimensions of the *Compañeros* Spanish program—the children's basic grade-level curriculum, new standards for foreign language education, and Gardner's multiple intelligences theory—can provide a framework for curriculum developers who wish to "fit" quality second language instruction into the crowded school day. Implicit in this approach is the notion that the success of such a curriculum lies in the willingness of all partners to constantly adapt and re-articulate program goals to meet student needs, and to communicate effectively with each other. Sometimes it is not easy! Both grade-level teachers and FLES teachers must be highly committed and flexible, as together they attempt to coordinate and reinforce thematic content-area instruction in English and in the weekly Spanish lesson.

In the final analysis, perhaps the words of Franklin students best demonstrate the worth of foreign language study at an early age. "I love Spanish time," says one third-grader. "I like the songs and our Spanish cartoon . . . but most of all I like to learn it because now I can talk to *all* my friends."

NOTES

1. The term *Maestra* means *female teacher*. *Maestra* is also the "official" title for Spanish teachers in the *Compañeros* program.
2. As a result of the successful implementation of the *Compañeros* program at Franklin Elementary School, the Pullman School District allocated funds in 1997 to the community's other two elementary schools to begin FLES programs modeled after *Compañeros*.

REFERENCES

American Council on the Teaching of Foreign Languages. (1996). *Standards for Foreign Language Learning: Preparing for the 21st Century*. Yonkers, NY: ACTFL.

Curtain, H. A., & Pesola, C. A. (1994). *Languages and Children: Making the Match*. Reading, MA: Longman Publishing Company.

Dulay, H., Burt, M., & Krashen, S. (1982). *Language two*. New York: Oxford University Press.

Ernst, G., & Richard, K. (1994). Teacher preparation: Using videotapes in a teaching practicum. *FLES News, 8:* 2, pp. 1, 5–6.

Ernst-Slavit, G., & Pierce, A. O. (1998). Introducing foreign languages in elementary school. *Principal*, January, pp. 31–33.

Ernst-Slavit, G., Wenger, K., & Statzner, E. (1998). "*Compañeros*": A teacher preparation partnership model for teaching FLES. *Hispania, 81*, pp. 379–391.

Gardner, H. (1983). *Frames of Mind*. New York: Basic Books.

Gardner, H., & Hatch, T. (1989). Multiple intelligences go to school. *Educational Researcher, 18:* 8, pp. 4–10.

Heath, I. A. (1993). Foreign language immersion programs: Reforms that consider a global perspective for a changing world economy. *The Journal for the Education of Language Minority Students*. Vol. 12, Summer.

Mohan, B. (1986). *Language and Content*. Reading, MA: Addison-Wesley.

Omaggio, H. A. (1993). *Teaching Language in Context*. Boston, MA: Heinle and Heinle Publishers.

Ornstein, A. C. (1993). Emerging curriculum trends: An agenda for the future. In: G. Hass & F. Parkay (Eds.), *Curriculum Planning: A New Approach* (6th edition), pp. 57–65.

Pierce, A., Richard, K. J., & Ernst, G. (1995). *Compañeros*: A school-university partnership for teaching foreign languages. *Curriculum in Context 22*, 4: 25–27.

Valdés, G. (1998). The world outside and inside schools: Language and immigrant children. *Educational Researcher 27* (6), pp. 4–18.

Gisela Ernst-Slavit is Associate Professor, Department of Teaching and Learning, Washington State University-Vancouver; Kerri J. Wenger is Assistant Professor, Elementary Education, Eastern Oregon University, La Grande, Oregon; and Lana Krumweide is a bilingual elementary teacher in the Pasco School District, Pasco, Washington.

QUESTIONS FOR REFLECTION

1. How does the *Compañeros* approach to early instruction in foreign languages differ from traditional approaches?
2. How are the five C's of foreign language instruction—communication, cultures, connections, comparisons, and communities—reflected in the *Compañeros* program? Can you suggest any additional guiding assumptions for foreign language learning?
3. What evidence do the authors present to document the success of *Compañeros*? What factors contribute to the success of a school–university partnership such as *Compañeros*?

Teachers' Voices
Putting Theory into Practice

"We Are Friends When We Have Memories Together"

MERLE WEISS SCHARMANN

ABSTRACT: *Inspired by her kindergartners' end-of-year recollections of the experiences they had and the connections they felt with one another, a teacher realizes the importance of encouraging children to reflect on their learning and growth. An opportunity to interact with teachers from the Reggio Emilia early childhood programs in Italy further confirms the importance of giving students the opportunity to revisit prior learning. The author explains how creating a "Memory Wall" for each school year enhances students' learning, reinforces the school's spiral curriculum, and contributes to her understanding of how children learn.*

As you walk through the halls and classrooms of Greeley School, you may see this memory statement in various forms and places. This beautiful refrain is usually accompanied by pieces of collaborative work generated by our children. These works cause one to pause—amazed by the power, elaborate use of material, and obvious level of knowledge expressed. How do these pieces come to be? What is the process that children go through that generates these wonderful expressions?

RELIVING THEIR CLASS EXPERIENCES

One spring I was listening to my senior kindergartners reflect on their year. It was a joyful mo-

From *Young Children* 53, no. 3 (March 1998): 27–29. Used by permission of the author.

ment for us all, as they relived experience after experience from our rich kindergarten curriculum. "Remember when the butterfly came out of its chrysalis and needed time to dry? I was sitting right next to John!" was one child's recollection. "I remember the log at the forest. Together Mary Claire and I pushed that log hard to see all those insects," said another. This conversation went on and on. I immediately noticed the clarity and depth of the children's memories, but it was the joy and sense of connection they obviously felt to one another that stayed in my mind.

Later that same spring I had the opportunity to visit one of my children's homes. His mother led me to a back room. When I entered this room, my breath was taken away. All around me were projects and artifacts that reflected every topic we had explored in class. The experiences of the classroom were being relived and enjoyed at home.

In our classrooms much care is given to the selection of topics for study. We begin by inviting the children to explore a topic of their own interest or an aspect of the curriculum that is particularly engaging. The learning environment becomes a rich creation and reflection of the children's experiences.

At the end of each study, we clear the environment so we can prepare for the next topic. As I remove each artifact, I feel a great sense of loss. And if I feel this way, could the children be feeling the same sense of loss? How could I expect them to see the connections that each study has to the next if all physical evidence of these experiences is removed?

During that same year several of my colleagues began to share experiences from their study of the Reggio Emilia early childhood programs in Italy. That summer several of the Reggio educators came to share their knowledge with Winnetka, Illinois, teachers. Learning about the philosophy and approach of the Reggio program was exciting, but it was the discussion of giving children the opportunity and time to revisit prior learning that caught my attention. I wondered what activity or project would invite children to revisit, remember, and reflect on a very rich curriculum? And then in the final meeting we were shown slides of several of the schools in Reggio. Over the portal of one of the schools hung these words: "We are friends when we have memories together." I knew then how I wanted to explore with my class.

ENCOURAGING CHILDREN'S CONTINUED REFLECTION

At Greeley we continually look for ways to encourage children to be reflective about their own learning and growth. For the young child this is a very difficult task. After watching the children carefully, I began a Memory Wall project. This experience was designed to make concrete the value of remembering and sharing our discoveries and revisiting prior knowledge. This was to be reflective of both the curriculum in place and curriculum that would emerge out of the children's interests.

At the end of each study we discuss what we would like to remember relative to that study and how we can express that knowledge. As each collaborative piece is completed, we mount it on the wall. Subsequent pieces follow after each study.

During the creation of the first Memory Wall, the kindergartners chose a mural format, using very simple materials. In a discussion with those same children later as second graders, they remembered the exact point at which they felt the limitation of using only markers and paint. "We were finishing the Gray Squirrel memory and we had trouble. The marker couldn't show his fur and the nature around him."

On the next memory piece, the children began to ask for more extensive materials with which to express themselves. On the fourth memory piece, the children discovered for themselves the value of collaboration. Up to that point each child had an individual job to do on the piece being created. The consensus, to blend their ideas, is reflected in each subsequent mural. "Remember the fight about making the big Great Plains?" recalled one of the second graders. The children's growth and learning was reflected not only on the emerging memory wall but also, with time, within the child's own mind.

SAVING AND CARRYING ON WORKS

The value of recording and selecting work to be saved and carried on became apparent to the children at the end of the year. When I took my class on to first grade, moving into another classroom, we were confronted with the problem of taking our huge Memory Wall with us. As one girl said, "We must take our memories with us—we need them to know." After many discussions, we decided to reduce the murals in size, make a big book, and take our memories with us to first grade.

All during their first-grade year the children would revisit this book for many reasons—always adding to our sense of community and joy. By the end of the year the children had created another wall of memories that included the printed word and more extensive use of materials, reflecting their growth and development. As the school year drew to a close, the children asked for this wall to be left intact for them to visit as second-graders. Many times during the day I would hear soft voices of children, who lingered in the hallway, remembering the experiences recalled by a certain piece.

SEEING HOW LEARNING IS ENHANCED

The experience of the Memory Wall offered another window into assessing and understanding the children. As children go back and explore previous studies, their use of drawing and materials encourages them to form questions and to refine previous understandings. This enhances and reinforces our spiraling curriculum. One can see children beginning to formulate hypotheses about their studies with the use of materials. If we look at memory as an aptitude for learning, we notice those children who are more concrete using the wall to remind them of an experience. Still others, at a more abstract level, use the wall to build new ideas and make comparisons.

The benefits of this experience are many, but the fact that learning is enhanced when it is memorable becomes abundantly clear. The glorious aspect of the experience is watching how the emotion attached to the experience creates true learning—not mere rote learning.

The classrooms at Greeley are busy places, alive with interesting experiences for all of our children. The excitement and joy one feels during holidays is evident in our schoolhouse all the year round. Why? Because you never know when you're going to make a memory.

Merle Weiss Scharmann teaches junior and senior kindergarten at the Greeley School in Winnetka, Illinois, and serves as chair of her district's kindergarten grade level.

QUESTIONS FOR REFLECTION

1. Does the concept of a "Memory Wall" have application, in some form, to the subject area and level of greatest interest to you? Explain your answer.
2. In the subject area and at the level of greatest interest to you, how might teachers enhance students' learning by making greater use of the "projects and artifacts" that students produce?

3. What are the implications of the following statement for curriculum planners: "learning is enhanced when it is memorable"? Is memorableness a valid curriculum criterion?

LEARNING ACTIVITIES

Critical Thinking

1. In what ways does the Reggio Emilia Approach reflect John Dewey's educational philosophy? (See the following articles by Dewey: "Traditional vs. Progressive Education," Chapter 1; "Progressive Organization of Subject Matter," Chapter 5; and "The Sources of a Science of Education," Chapter 6.

2. Review "Erik Erikson's Developmental Stages" in Chapter 3. What problems might a young child have in elementary school if he or she failed to resolve sufficiently the psychosocial crises of Erikson's first three stages of development?

3. What are the characteristics of learning experiences in the elementary curriculum that help children master the challenges that come with each stage of their development as human beings?

4. What are some of the challenges that children face today that were unknown or little known to their parents or grandparents? To what extent can (or should) these challenges be addressed in childhood education?

5. Reflect on your experiences as an elementary student. What curricular experiences enhanced your growth and development? Impeded your growth and development? What implications do your reflections have for your curriculum planning activities, regardless of the level of education which interests you most?

Application Activities

1. Invite a group of elementary-level teachers to your class and ask them to describe the steps they take in planning curricula for their students. What do they see as the most important curriculum criteria to use in planning?

2. Obtain a statement of philosophy (or mission statement) from a nearby elementary school. Analyze the statement in regard to the thirteen goals for childhood education presented in this chapter. How many of the goals are reflected in the statement?

3. Conduct a comparative survey, at ten-year intervals, of an education journal that addresses childhood education. Have there been any significant changes over the years in regard to curriculum-related issues and trends discussed in the journal? Among the journals to consider are *Child Development, Child Study Journal, Childhood Education, Children Today, Early Childhood Research Quarterly,*

Elementary School Journal, Exceptional Children, Gifted Child Quarterly, Gifted Child Today, International Journal of Early Childhood, Journal of Early Intervention, Journal of Research in Childhood Education, New Directions for Child Development, Teaching Exceptional Children, and *Young Children.*

Field Experiences

1. Interview a school psychologist, mental health worker, child protective services (CPS) worker, or similar individual to find out about the sources, signs, and treatment of psychosocial problems that can interfere with children's learning. Ask him or her to suggest ways that teachers can help students overcome these problems.
2. Visit a nearby elementary school and obtain permission to interview a few students about their curricular experiences. Take field notes based on these interviews. The following questions might serve as a guide for beginning your interviews: Do the students like school? What about it do they like and dislike? What are their favorite subjects? What about those subjects do they like? Then, analyze your field notes; what themes or concerns emerge that would be useful to curriculum planners at this level?
3. Visit an agency in your community that offers services to children and their families. Ask a staff member to explain the services that are offered. Report your findings to the rest of your class.

Internet Activities

1. Go to the home page for the National Clearinghouse for Bilingual Education (NCBE) at **http://www.ncbe.gwu.edu** and gather information and resources on effective elementary-level programs for limited English proficiency (LEP) students. Also visit NCBE's page titled "School Reform and Student Diversity: Case Studies of Exemplary Practices for LEP Students"; from this location, "visit" several exemplary elementary schools and gather additional information and resources.
2. Go to the George Lucas Educational Foundation (referenced in Gerald W. Bracey's "What's Ahead in Elementary Education?" in this chapter) at **http://glef.cog/** and gather curriculum resources and ideas relevant to your subject area and level of interest. For example, you may wish to examine the *Learn & Live* kit which contains a documentary film, hosted by Robin Williams, and a resource book that showcases innovative K–12 schools.
3. Go to one or more of the following professional organization web sites dedicated to the education of young children and gather information, fact sheets, research results, resources, and publications of interest.

   Association for Childhood Education International (ACEI)
       http://www.udel.edu/bateman/acei/

Early Childhood Care and Development (ECCD)
 http://ecdgroup.harvard.net/
National Association for the Education of Young Children (NAEYC)
 http://www.naeyc.org/default.htm
Professional Association for Childhood Education (PACE)
 http://www.careguide.net/careguide.cgi/pace/about.htm

BOOKS AND ARTICLES TO REVIEW

Research and Theory in Education for Children

Alter, Gloria. "Transforming Elementary Social Studies: The Emergence of a Curriculum Focused on Diverse, Caring Communities." *Theory and Research in Social Education* 23, no. 4 (Fall 1995): 355–374.

Bracey, Gerald W. "Change and Continuity in Elementary Education." *Principal* 75, no. 3 (January 1996): 17, 19–21.

Cadwell, Louise Boyd. *Bringing Reggio Emilia Home.* New York: Teachers College Press, 1997.

Chenfeld, Mimi B. *Creative Experiences for Young Children.* New York: Harcourt Brace & Company, 1994.

Colker, Laura J., et al. "Curriculum for Infants and Toddlers: Who Needs It?" *Child Care Information Exchange* no. 112 (November–December 1996): 74–78.

Elkind, David. "The Death of Child Nature: Education in the Postmodern World." *Phi Delta Kappan* 79, no. 3 (November 1997): 241–245.

———. "Young Children and Technology: A Cautionary Note." *Young Children* 51, no. 6 (September 1996): 22–23.

———. "The Young Child in the Postmodern World." *Dimensions of Early Childhood* 23, no. 3 (Spring 1995): 6–9, 39.

———. "Early Childhood Education and the Postmodern World." *Principal* 73, no. 5 (May 1994): 6–7.

———. "Whatever Happened to Childhood?" *Momentum* 24, no. 2 (April–May 1993): 18–19.

———, ed. *Perspectives on Early Childhood Education: Growing with Young Children Toward the 21st Century.* Washington, DC: NEA Professional Library, 1991.

———. *The Hurried Child: Growing Up Too Fast Too Soon.* Reading, MA: Addison-Wesley, 1989.

———. *Miseducation: Preschoolers at Risk.* New York: Knopf, 1987.

Faulkner, Dorothy. "Workshop Four: Encouraging Social Collaboration through Play 'The Flourishing Child.'" *International Journal of Early Years Education* 4, no. 2 (Summer 1996): 81–89.

Fortson, Laura Rogers, and Reiff, Judith C. *Early Childhood Curriculum: Open Structures for Integrative Learning.* Boston: Allyn and Bacon, 1994.

Glassner, Sid S. "I'm Going to Sit Right Down and Write Myself Some Standards." *Teaching and Learning Literature with Children and Young Adults* 6, no. 5 (May–June 1997): 81–83.

Hamman, Vincent E. "Children's Literature in Social Studies. Is It Used?" *Rural Educator* 17, no. 1 (Fall 1995): 3–4.

Haugland, Susan W., and Wright, June L. *Young Children and Technology: A World of Discovery.* Boston: Allyn and Bacon, 1997.

Hendrick, Joanne. *The Whole Child: Developmental Education for the Early Years,* 6th Ed. Englewood, Cliffs, NJ: Merrill, 1996.

Jalongo, Mary Renck. "On Behalf of Children: 'Why Cute is Still a Four-Letter Word.'" *Early Childhood Education Journal* 24, no. 2 (Winter 1996): 67–70.

Jalongo, Mary Renck, and Stamp, Laurie Nicholson. *The Arts in Children's Lives: Aesthetic Education in Early Childhood.* Boston: Allyn and Bacon, 1997.

James, Allison, Jenks, Chris, and Prout, Alan. *Theorizing Childhood.* New York: Teachers College Press, 1998.

Kagan, Sharon L. "Early Care and Education: Beyond the Fishbowl." *Phi Delta Kappan* 76, no. 3 (November 1994): 184–187.

Katz, Lilian G. "Affirming Children's Minds." *Montessori Life* 10, no. 1 (Winter 1998): 33–36.

———. *What Should Be Learned in Kindergarten?* Washington, DC: ERIC, 1993.

———. *Early Childhood Education: What Research Tells Us.* Bloomington, IN: Phi Delta Kappa Educational Foundation, 1988.

Kobak, Dorothy. "Raising the Caring Quality (CQ) in Education: A Moral Imperative." *Childhood Education* 74, no. 2 (Winter 1997–98): 97–98.

Miller, Linda. "A Vision for the Early Years Curriculum in the United Kingdom." *International Journal of Early Childhood* 29, no. 1 (1997): 34–41.

Montagu, Ashley, et al. "Beginnings Workshop: Meeting Children's Needs." *Child Care Information Exchange,* no. 106 (November–December 1995): 41–64.

Petersen, Evelyn A. *A Practical Guide to Early Childhood Planning, Methods and Materials: The What, Why and How of Lesson Plans.* Boston: Allyn and Bacon, 1996.

Platten, Linda. "Talking Geography: An Investigation into Young Children's Understanding of Geographical Terms: Part 2." *International Journal of Early Years Education* 3, no. 3 (Autumn 1995): 69–84.

Riley, Tracy L., and Karnes, Frances A. "Tracking Interest Rates: Curriculum Interests of Elementary Intellectually Gifted Students." *Gifted Child Today Magazine* 19, no. 1 (January–February 1996): 36–37.

Safford, Philip L., ed. *Early Childhood Special Education.* New York: Teachers College Press, 1994.

Saracho, Olivia, and Spodek, Bernard, eds. *Multiple Perspectives on Play in Early Childhood Education.* Albany: State University of New York Press, 1998.

Schickedanz, Judith A., et al. *Curriculum in Early Childhood: A Resource Guide for Preschool and Kindergarten Teachers.* Boston: Allyn and Bacon, 1997.

Schubert, William H. "The Plight of Children Is Our Plight: Thoughts Based on John Dewey and Charles Dickens." *Educational Horizons* (Winter 1998): 69–72.

Seefeldt, Carol, ed. *The Early Childhood Curriculum: A Review of Current Research,* 2nd Ed. New York: Teachers College Press, 1992.

Sefer, Jasmina. "The Effects of Play Oriented Curriculum on Creativity in Elementary School Children." *Gifted Education International* 11, no. 1 (1995): 4–7.

Sharpe, Tom, et al. "The Effects of a Sportsmanship Curriculum Intervention on Generalized Positive Social Behavior of Urban Elementary School Students." *Journal of Applied Behavior Analysis* 28, no. 4 (Winter 1995): 401–416.

Siraj-Blatchford, Iram. "Workshop One: Values, Culture, and Identity in Early Childhood Education." *International Journal of Early Years Education* 4, no. 2 (Summer 1996): 63–69.

Smith, Anne B. "The Early Childhood Curriculum from a Sociocultural Perspective." *Early Child Development and Care* 115 (January 1996): 51–64.

———. "Quality Programs That Care and Educate." *Childhood Education* 72, no. 6 (1996): 330–336.

Spodek, Bernard, ed. *Handbook of Research on the Education of Young Children.* New York: Macmillan, 1993.

———. *Educationally Appropriate Kindergarten Practices.* Washington, DC: NEA Professional Library, 1991.

Spodek, Bernard, and Saracho, Olivia N., eds. *Issues in Early Childhood Educational Assessment and Evaluation.* New York: Teachers College Press, 1997.

———. "Culture and the Early Childhood Curriculum." *Early Child Development and Care* 123 (September 1996): 1–13.

———. *Dealing with Individual Differences in the Early Childhood Classroom.* White Plains, NY: Longman, 1994.

———. *Right From the Start: Teaching Children Ages Three through Eight.* Boston: Allyn and Bacon, 1994.

———, eds. *Language and Literacy in Early Childhood Education.* New York: Teachers College Press, 1993.

———, eds. *Issues in Early Childhood Curriculum.* New York: Teachers College Press, 1991.

———, and Davis, Michael D. *Foundations of Early Childhood Education: Teaching Three-, Four-, and Five-Year-Old Children.* Englewood Cliffs, NJ: Prentice Hall, 1991.

Sunal, Cynthia Szymanski, et al. "Introducing the Use of Communication Technology into an Elementary School Social Studies Curriculum." *International Journal of Social Education* 10, no. 2 (Fall–Winter 1995–1996): 106–123.

Tinworth, Sue. "Whose Good Idea Was It? Child Initiated Curriculum." *Australian Journal of Early Childhood* 22, no. 3 (September 1997): 24–29.

Turner, Joy. "How Do You Teach Reading?" *Montessori Life* 7, no. 3 (Summer 1995): 25–29.

Wade, Rahima. "Civic Ideal into Practice: Democracy in the Elementary School." *Social Studies and the Young Learner* 8, no. 1 (September–October 1995): 16–18.

Theory into Practice: Strategies for Elementary Education Programs

Bracken, Khlare R. "Integrating Classical Music into the Elementary Social Studies Curriculum." *Social Studies Journal* 26 (Spring 1997): 36–42.

Eade, Joanna. "Using a Core Text with Bilingual Children." *English in Education* 31, no. 3 (Autumn 1997): 32–39.

Ernst-Slavit, Gisela, and Pierce, Ardith O. "Introducing Foreign Languages in Elementary School." *Principal* 77, no. 3 (January 1998): 31–33.

Haynes, Richard M., and Chalker, Donald M. "The Making of a World-Class Elementary School." *Principal* 77, no. 3 (January 1998): 5–6, 8–9.

Kassell, Cathy Page. "Music in the Classroom." *Primary Voices K–6* 5, no. 2 (April 1997): 26–31.

Lewis, Catherine C. "My Job Is to Create Happy Memories." *Principal* 76, no. 1 (September 1996): 21–22, 24.

Peters, Tim, et al. "A Thematic Approach: Theory and Practice at the Aleknagik School." *Phi Delta Kappan* 76, no. 8 (April 1995): 633–636.

Placek, Judith H., and O'Sullivan, Mary. "The Many Faces of Integrated Physical Education." *Journal of Physical Education, Recreation and Dance* 68, no. 1 (January 1997): 20–24.

Slattery, Patrick. "Curriculum Is the Key to Total Education." *Momentum* 26, no. 3 (August–September 1995): 31–33.

Smith-Gratto, Karen, and Blackburn, Marcy A. "The Computer as a Scientific Tool: Integrating Spreadsheets into the Elementary Science Curriculum." *Computers in the Schools* 13, no. 1–2 (1997): 125–131.

Stewart, Loraine Moses. "Developing Basic Mathematics Skills through the Use of African-American Children's Literature." *Reading Horizons* 37, no. 4 (1997): 315–320.

Towers, G. Charles, and Towers, James M. "An Elementary School Principal's Experience With Implementing an Outcome-Based Curriculum." *Contemporary Education* 68, no. 1 (Fall 1996): 67–72.

Vail, Kathleen. "Core Comes to Crooksville." *American School Board Journal* 184, no. 3 (March 1997): 14–18.

Theory into Practice: Strategies for Early Childhood Education Programs

Dahl, Keith. "Why Cooking in the Classroom?" *Young Children* 53, no. 1 (January 1998): 81–83.

Davies, Margaret M. "Outdoors: An Important Context for Young Children's Development." *Early Child Development and Care* 115 (January 1996): 37–49.

Fischer, Bobbi. "Moving Beyond 'Letter of the Week.'" *Teaching PreK–8* 26, no. 4 (January 1996): 74–76.

Harding, Nadine. "Family Journals: The Bridge from School to Home and Back Again." *Young Children* 51, no. 2 (January 1996): 27–30.

Jungers, Sue. "Teaching Young Children about Nutrition." *Principal* 75, no. 5 (May 1996): 26–27.

May, Helen, and Carr, Margaret. "Making a Difference for the Under Fives? The Early Implementation of Te Whaariki: The New Zealand National Early Childhood Curriculum." *International Journal of Early Years Education* 5, no. 3 (October 1997): 225–236.

McClurg, Lois Gail. "Building an Ethical Community in the Classroom: Community Meeting." *Young Children* 53, no. 2 (January 1998): 30–35.

Patton, Mary Martin, and Kokoski, Teresa M. "How Good Is Your Early Childhood Science, Mathematics, and Technology Program? Strategies for Extending Your Curriculum." *Young Children* 51, no. 5 (July 1996): 38–44.

Sheerer, Marilyn A., et al. "Off with a Theme: Emergent Curriculum in Action." *Early Childhood Education Journal* 24, no. 2 (Winter 1996): 99–102.

Spring, Barbara. "Physics Is Fun, Physics Is Important, and Physics Belongs in the Early Childhood Curriculum." *Young Children* 51, no. 5 (July 1996): 29–33.

Stone, Sandra J. "Teaching Strategies: Integrating Play into the Curriculum." *Childhood Education* 72, no. 2 (Winter 1995–1996): 104–107.

Williams, Karen Cachevki. " 'What Do You Wonder?' Involving Children in Curriculum Planning." *Young Children* 52, no. 6 (September 1997): 78–81.

Videotapes

The Whole Child: A Caregiver's Guide to the First Five Years, a set of six videos that first appeared on PBS in 1997, addresses children's physical, emotional, and cognitive development; and features Head Start classrooms, a private urban infant center and preschool, a suburban preschool, and two university child care centers. *A Class Divided* is a classic, award-winning program that shows how racial stereotypes affect young children. (Both available from PBS Video, 1320 Braddock Place, Alexandria, VA 22314-1698 (800) 344-3337).

Socrates for Six-Year-Olds is a 30-minute video featuring Matthew Lipman, who shows how children can benefit from philosophical inquiry. *Evaluating Preschool Education* examines the effectiveness of preschool programs. *Daycare Grows Up* focuses on new societal attitudes about child care; features corporations that are incorporating daycare into the workplace. (All available from Films for the Humanities & Sciences, P.O. Box 2055, Princeton, NJ 08543-2053, (800) 257-5126, fax (609) 275-3767).

Becoming Bilingual, Part I, focuses on the education of elementary-level ESL students; Part II focuses on the high school level. (Available from Extension Media Center, University of California, 2176 Shattuck Avenue, Berkeley, CA 94704 (415) 642-0460).

Education for Transescents and Early Adolescents

FOCUS QUESTIONS

1. What important developmental tasks characterize transescence and early adolescence?
2. How do transescents and early adolescents differ in their physical, social, psychological, and cognitive maturation?
3. What factors can threaten the healthy development of transescents and early adolescents?
4. What are some appropriate curricular goals for transescents and early adolescents?
5. How do educational programs organized around middle school concepts address the unique needs of transescents and early adolescents?

Simply defined, a *transescent* is a person passing from childhood to early adolescence. In our society, transesence and early adolescence is a period from about age ten to age fifteen. Young people at this age must cope with a wide range of life stresses because they mature physically more quickly than they mature cognitively or socially. For example, the average age of menarche has dropped from sixteen years of age 150 years ago to twelve and one-half today; similarly, boys reach reproductive maturity at an earlier age. As a result, young people often do not have the social and emotional maturity to handle the freedoms and stressors that characterize our modern society. "Many life-threatening behaviors, such as drug and alcohol abuse and early sexual experiences, begin in early adolescence," Peggy A. Grant points out in "Middle School Students and Service Learning: Developing Empowered, Informed Citizens," in this chapter. The vulnerability of today's adolescents is portrayed graphically in *Great Transitions: Preparing Adolescents for a New Century*, a report by the Carnegie Council on Adolescent Development (1995) which built on an earlier Council report, *Turning Points: Preparing American Youth for the 21st Century* (1989): "Altogether, nearly half of American adolescents are at high or moderate risk of seriously damaging their life chances. The damage may be near-term and vivid, or it may be delayed, like a time bomb set in youth."

MAJOR TRANSITIONS AND CRITICAL TURNING POINTS

Individual differences among students are greater during transesence and early adolescence than at other stages of life. There is a four-year range within each sex group from the time that the first significant fraction of the group attains puberty to the time that the last member of that sex reaches it. Generally, by the time they are twenty, both boys and girls have reached full physical growth and biological maturity. But social, psychological, and cognitive maturation are usually not in step with physical maturation. Many pressures in modern society tend to force the social, psychological, and cognitive changes of this period on the young person ahead of the biological.

As with any age group, it is important to consider the four bases of curriculum—social forces, human development, learning, and knowledge—when planning curricula for transescents and early adolescents. Toward this end, it may be helpful to review the perspectives on human development covered in Chapter 3, particularly Erik Erikson's theory as discussed in "A Healthy Personality for Every Child," David A. Hamburg's "Toward a Strategy for Healthy Adolescent Development," and James P. Comer's "Organize Schools around Child Development." These articles identify cultural, psychological, cognitive, and social factors that influence students' learning during this period.

Transescence and early adolescence are characterized by rapid physical growth, which is frequently uneven, with some parts of the body growing faster than others. As these physical developments occur, self-concepts must often be adjusted. Both boys and girls may go through periods where they are clumsy and awkward, only to become graceful and athletic as they become older. Since rapid growth requires a great deal of physical energy, children need plenty of food and sleep to maintain good health during this period. On many occasions, though, they may have excess energy that needs to be discharged through vigorous physical activity.

The physical changes that take place during this period are not the only changes that are occurring. In regard to Erik Erikson's eight-stage model for the human life cycle, identity versus identity confusion is the salient psychosocial crisis for early adolescents. During this time, early adolescents use new, more complex thinking abilities and begin to shape a sense of personal identity. Identity confusion can result, however, when the early adolescent is confronted with the variety of roles available to him or her.

Erikson's theory suggests that when early adolescents identify with a peer group, with their school, or with a cause beyond themselves, their sense of *fidelity*—the "virtue" of this stage—can be the "cornerstone of identity." During this stage, early adolescents are loyal and committed—in fortunate instances, they are motivated by growth-enhancing goals, aspirations, and dreams; in unfortunate instances, by people, causes, and life styles that alarm parents, teachers, and other adults in their lives. An example of how curricular experiences can help early adolescents "sort out [their] place in the world" and identify with a worthwhile cause is found in this chapter's Teachers' Voices article, "The Educational Benefits to Middle School Students Participating in a Student/Scientist Project." The teacher-author, Mary Fougere, describes how participation in the "Forest Watch Program" helps her students "gain some control and hope over their future."

The transescent child who has looked to his or her family for care, affection, and guidance must begin to find independence in order to fulfill the developmental tasks of this period and to prepare for adulthood. They must learn to make decisions on their own and to accept the consequences of those decisions. Parents and teachers can facilitate the growth of early adolescents by praising their accomplishments and not over-dwelling on shortcomings, encouraging independence with appropriate limitations, and giving affection without expecting too much in return. The "practical counseling skills" that teachers at this level should possess are discussed in Judith A. Brough's "The Teacher as Counselor: Some Practical Considerations" in this chapter.

Great Transitions, an excerpt of which appears in this chapter, reminds us that, indeed, education can be a "turning point" in the lives of early adolescents: "early adolescence is the phase when young people begin to adopt behavior patterns in education . . . that can have lifelong consequences. At the same time, it is an age when, much like younger children, individuals still need special nurturing and adult guidance. For these reasons, early adolescence offers a unique window of opportunity to shape enduring patterns of healthy behavior" (Carnegie Council on Adolescent Development, 1995, p. 1) The same point, perhaps more compelling because it is in the language of her peers, is made elsewhere in *Turning Points* by sixteen-year-old Sarah:

> I think that being a kid is the most important stage of your life. It's a time when you start to develop a personality. It's when you start to learn about who you are, and what you want to do with yourself. And it's a time when you develop trust. It's a time when you learn how to be a person in society. Unfortunately a lot of kids don't have that. If you don't grow up learning how to be a productive person, then you're going to have a problem once you grow up. (Carnegie Council on Adolescent Development, 1995, p. 2)

CURRICULAR GOALS FOR TRANSESCENTS AND EARLY ADOLESCENTS

Turning Points asserts that there is a "volatile mismatch . . . between the organization and curriculum of middle grade schools and the intellectual and emotional needs of young adolescents" (Carnegie Council on Adolescent Development, 1989, p. 2). Similarly, Tariq T. Akmal, in "Teach Middle School and All This, Too? Teachers' Concerns about Standards-Based Curricula" in this chapter, points out that "middle schools must develop curricula that are built around concepts that are important in the lives of early adolescents."

What, then, should be the goals of educational programs for transescents and early adolescents? Many goals might be suggested; some derived from social forces, some from theories of human development and learning, and some from theories of knowledge. The list would surely include helping learners to:

1. Build self-esteem and a strong sense of identity, competence, and responsibility
2. Understand and adjust to the physical changes they are experiencing
3. Deal with wider social experiences and new social arrangements
4. Explore different areas of knowledge and skill to help determine potential interests
5. Make the transition between childhood education and education for middle adolescents, and prepare for the eventual transition to senior high school
6. Deal with value questions that arise because of their developing cognitive abilities, their growing need for independence, and rapid changes in society
7. Cope with social pressures from some of their peers to engage in risk-taking behaviors
8. Develop concern for the environment, the local and global communities, and the welfare of others

DEVELOPMENT OF THE MIDDLE SCHOOL

A major issue for transescents and early adolescents is whether their education is best provided in a junior high school, a middle school, or some other form of school organization. During the 1950s and 1960s, dissatisfaction with junior high schools became evident as many people pointed out that junior high schools were "scaled-down" versions of high schools, complete with departmentalization, extensive athletic programs, and age-inappropriate social activities. Junior high schools, it was felt, were not providing students with a satisfactory transition into the high school, nor were they meeting the unique needs of early adolescents.

During the early 1960s, an organizational framework for a "school in the middle" was introduced. The new middle school arrangement called for moving the ninth grade into the high school, placing grades 5–8 in the middle school, and developing curricula to meet the needs of ten- to fourteen-year-olds. By 1970, almost 2,500 middle schools had been created, and by 1990 this number had increased to almost 15,000 (George, 1993).

At first, middle schools were quite different from junior high schools—often, middle schools had more interdisciplinary, exploratory curricula; team teaching; teacher/advisor programs; flexible scheduling; smaller athletic programs; and less ability grouping. Today, the distinctions between junior high schools and middle schools have become somewhat blurred, and many innovative practices initially developed to meet the needs of students in middle schools have been incorporated in junior high schools as well. However, as James A. Beane points out in "The Search for a Middle School Curriculum" in this chapter, "we often find the most promising and exciting reforms at the middle level. School climate is more positive, adults are more sensitive to the experience of puberty, and educators are willing to try team arrangements, new schedules, advisory programs, and a range of other organizational patterns."

Evidence to support the effectiveness of middle school concepts—whether they were part of middle-level or junior-high programs—accumulated as the middle school movement expanded during the 1970s and 1980s. The August 1985 issue of *Middle School Journal* presented the results of a major study of "schools in the middle" (grades 5–9), which found that most of the "effective schools" in the study were organized in 6-7-8 or 5-6-7-8 grade patterns. Moreover, principals of these schools were knowledgeable about middle-level programs and research, and they evidenced familiarity with block scheduling, interdisciplinary teaming, cocurricula programs, learning styles, teacher/advisor programs, and developmental age grouping.

As we enter the twenty-first century, the well-documented effectiveness of educational programs organized around middle school concepts is having a positive influence on schooling at other levels. For example, in this chapter's Case Study in Curriculum Implementation article, "Revitalizing the Middle School: The Guilford County Process," Jerry Weast and his colleagues point out that the county's revitalization effort at the middle level will be extended to the high school level, and they conclude by asking "what more positive evidence could there be?"

REFERENCES

Carnegie Council on Adolescent Development. *Great Transitions: Preparing Adolescents for a New Century,* abridged version. New York: Carnegie Council on Adolescent Development, Carnegie Corporation of New York, 1995.

Carnegie Council on Adolescent Development. *Turning Points: Preparing American Youth for the 21st Century.* Carnegie Council on Adolescent Development, Carnegie Corporation of New York, 1989.

George, Paul. "The Middle School Movement: A State-of-the-Art Report and a Glimpse Into the Future." In Hass, Glen, and Parkay, Forrest W., eds., *Curriculum Planning: A New Approach,* 6th Ed. Boston: Allyn and Bacon, 1993, pp. 446–455.

Educating Young Adolescents for a Changing World

CARNEGIE COUNCIL ON ADOLESCENT DEVELOPMENT

ABSTRACT: This excerpt from the Carnegie Council on Adolescent Development's report, Great Transitions: Preparing Adolescents for a New Century, *stresses the importance of education for early adolescents in a complex, changing world. Eight principles for developing new middle-level education programs based on research and the experiences of educators, policy makers, and advocates for children and youth are described. A program to improve curricula, instruction, and assessment at middle schools in fifteen states resulted in achievement gains for students, increased self-esteem, and reduced feelings of alienation, fearfulness, and depression.*

If it were possible to reach any consensus about high-priority solutions to our society's problems, a good education throughout the first two decades of life would be a prime candidate. Every modern nation must develop the talents of its entire population if it is to be economically vigorous and socially cohesive. A well-educated young adult is rarely found in our nation's prisons. In the past two decades, however, the achievement levels of American adolescents have virtually stagnated. The performance of our students is too low to support adequate living standards in a high-technology, information-based, transnational economy.

A persistent misconception among many educators is that young adolescents generally are incapable of critical or higher-order reasoning. Many school systems do a disservice to middle grade students by not offering challenging instruction. Education to capture the young person's emergent sense of self and the world, and to foster inquiring, analytical habits of mind, is not only feasible but constitutes essential preparation for life.

FACILITATING THE TRANSITION TO THE MIDDLE GRADES

In the move from elementary school, where a student has spent most of the day in one classroom with the same teacher and classmates, to the larger, more impersonal environment of middle school or junior high school farther from home, an adolescent's capacities to cope are often severely tested. Such an abrupt transition coincides with the profound physical, cognitive, and emotional changes of puberty, a juxtaposition that for some students can result in a loss of self-esteem and declining academic achievement.

Middle grade education was largely ignored in the education reforms of the 1980s. With the publication in 1989 of the Carnegie Council's report, *Turning Points: Preparing Youth for the 21st Century,* however, the nascent movement to reorganize middle schools to make them more developmentally appropriate for young adolescents was powerfully reinforced.

Middle grade education, said the report, should be more intellectually challenging, in line

From Executive Summary of *Great Transitions: Preparing Adolescents for a New Century,* Carnegie Council on Adolescent Development, Carnegie Corporation of New York, 1995. Used by permission of the publisher.

with young adolescents' new appreciation for the complexity of knowledge and ideas, and supportive of their desire for individual attention. Schools should have curricula that provide the information, skills, and motivation for adolescents to learn about themselves and their widening world. They should promote a mutual aid ethic among teachers and students, manifest in team teaching and cooperative learning. They should integrate students of varying ability levels in a single classroom, and they should provide opportunities for academically supervised community service.

EIGHT PRINCIPLES FOR TRANSFORMING THE EDUCATION OF YOUNG ADOLESCENTS

At the heart of *Turning Points* is a set of eight principles for transforming the education of young adolescents. These rest on a foundation of knowledge from current research and from the experience of leading educators, policymakers, and advocates for children and youth.

Create Communities for Learning

Large schools should be brought to human scale through the creation of smaller units, or schools-within-schools, where stable relationships between teachers and students and among students can be cultivated and smaller class sizes can ensure that each student is well known and respected.

Teach a Core of Common Knowledge

In many middle grade schools, the curriculum is so fragmented by subject matter that students have few opportunities to make connections among ideas in the different academic disciplines. A primary task for middle grade educators, especially as part of teaching teams, is to identify the most im-

portant principles and concepts within each discipline and concentrate their efforts on integrating the main ideas to create a meaningful interdisciplinary curriculum. The current emphasis on memorization of a large quantity of information must yield to an emphasis on depth and quality of understanding of the major concepts in each subject area as well as the connections between them.

Provide an Opportunity for All Students to Succeed

Numerous studies of cooperative learning approaches, in which students of varying ability learn together, have demonstrated their efficacy for everyone. Cooperative learning helps high achievers to deepen their understanding of the material by explaining it to lower achievers, who in turn benefit by receiving extra help as needed from their peers. Students master course material faster, retain the knowledge longer, and develop critical reasoning powers more rapidly than they would working alone. Cooperative refining also enables young people to get to know classmates from backgrounds different from their own, which sets the stage for them to learn the requirements for living together in a pluralistic society.

Prepare Teachers for the Middle Grades

At the present time, there are only a few graduate education programs that prepare middle grade teachers, as opposed to elementary or secondary school teachers. Yet the early adolescent transition is a distinct phase requiring special understanding of the conjunction of changes that a young person is undergoing and that have a bearing on learning. To orient teachers effectively for the middle grades, professional education programs must incorporate courses in adolescent development, team teaching, and the design and assessment of demanding interdisciplinary curricula. They must also offer special training to work with students and families of different economic, ethnic, and religious backgrounds.

Improve Academic Performance through Better Health and Fitness

Middle grade schools often do not have the support of health and social service agencies to address young adolescents' physical and mental health needs. Developmentally appropriate adolescent health facilities, in or near schools, are urgently needed for middle and high school students, especially in areas where there is a high proportion of uninsured families. Such school-related health centers should be linked to health education programs and a science curriculum that helps students understand the biological changes they are experiencing and the impact of various health-damaging as well as health-promoting practices.

Reengage Families in the Education of Adolescents

As discussed in the previous chapter, schools must involve parents of young adolescents in all aspects of their education. As it is, they are often considered as part of the problem of educating adolescents rather than as a potentially important educational resource.

Strengthen Teachers and Principals

States and school districts should give teachers and principals the authority to transform middle grade schools. They and other members of the school staff know more about how to do their jobs than those far removed from the classroom. Teachers, especially, need control over the way they meet curricular goals. The creation of governance committees composed of teachers, ad-

ministrators, health professionals, support staff, parents, and representatives from community organizations is one way to make schools more effective.

Connect Schools with Communities

In the 1980s, social service professionals and community organization leaders began moving their youth services into the schools, where the young people are. The result is a major innovation called "full-service schools." Led by individual states, full-service schools offer a variety of social and health services to young people and their families, paid for and rendered by outside agencies. As an example of a school-community partnership, these interventions are showing that they not only can help to reduce high-risk behavior in adolescents, but they enhance the environment for learning.

THE MIDDLE GRADE SCHOOL STATE POLICY INITIATIVE

Turning Points' comprehensive framework became the basis of a Carnegie Corporation effort to stimulate widespread middle grade reform beginning in 1990. Called the Middle Grade School State Policy Initiative (MGSSPI), it is a program of grants to fifteen states (usually the state department of education) whose schools are adopting promising practices in line with *Turning Points'* principles. Included are schools using approaches that are effective with young adolescents from disadvantaged communities, who make up a growing proportion of the nation's public school enrollments.

To improve curricula, instruction, and assessment under MGSSPI, the states have developed week-long summer institutes on interdisciplinary instruction, portfolio-based assessment, on-site professional development seminars facilitated by university faculty, formal networks to exchange information and resources between schools, systems for deploying expert consultants, and many other forms of assistance. At the local level, MGSSPI has stimulated improvements in curricula, instruction, and assessment in more than one hundred middle schools, some of which have worked to integrate education and health services for young adolescents and anchored health education firmly in the middle grade curriculum.

A group of Illinois middle grade schools, first as part of a federally supported effort called Project Initiative Middle Level, and now as part of the MGSSPI, has been implementing *Turning Points'* recommendations. Results thus far from an evaluation of the Illinois project show that, in forty-two schools participating at least one year, students are showing significant improvements in their reading, mathematics, and language achievement. They have higher self-esteem and are less likely to feel alienated, fearful, or depressed in school than they otherwise would, as a result of the implementation of reforms.

These promising findings demonstrate that, although most schools do not now meet the needs of young adolescents, the potential is there and can be readily tapped. With the support of schools redesigned expressly to prepare youth for the future, all adolescents will have a better chance at educational and personal success.

The *Carnegie Council on Adolescent Development* was established in 1985 by the Carnegie Corporation of New York to generate public and private interest in measures that prevent problems during adolescence and promote healthy adolescent development. *Great Transitions* was the Council's concluding report.

QUESTIONS FOR REFLECTION

1. Review the eight principles for transforming the education of young adolescents. What can curriculum planners, teachers, parents, and community leaders do to implement these principles? To what extent do you believe these principles will characterize educational programs for early adolescents during the first decade of the twenty-first century?

2. The Carnegie report states that "In the past two decades . . . the achievement levels of American adolescents have virtually stagnated. The performance of our students is too low to support adequate living standards in a high-technology, information-based, transnational economy." How might the following authors whom you read in the preceding chapters react to this point of view: Nel Noddings, Michael W. Apple, Ashley Montague, Maxine Greene, Elliot W. Eisner, and Henry A. Giroux?

3. Imagine that you are a member of a middle-level teaching team that is following the Carnegie Council's recommendation "to identify the most important principles and concepts within each discipline." How would you proceed?

The Search for a Middle School Curriculum

JAMES A. BEANE

ABSTRACT: Rather than imitating high school programs, middle-level educators are developing curricula that are connected, coherent, meaningful, and relevant. Three case studies illustrate innovative approaches to integrating the curriculum. Middle school curriculum reform should adhere to five guidelines: (1) there is no "recipe or packaged program" to follow; (2) time and resources should be provided for teachers interested in curriculum reform, and reluctant teachers should not be "forced" to participate; (3) subject area lines, which are often related to teachers' (and supervisors') self-concept and self-esteem, should not be "tampered with"; (4) integrated and integrative curricula are more than methods—they are a way of thinking about curriculum and education; and (5) the ideas that guide curriculum reform should be "brought to life" in various ways.

Remember for a moment that first day of junior high school. It doesn't matter whether it involves a trip to a new school building or a move to grade seven in a K–8 or K–12 building. It was still the "junior high school."

Recall the feeling that things were about to change in our school lives, the teachers exhorting us that this was no longer elementary school ("the fun and games are over"), the baffling new locker combinations, and, of course, the confusing schedule of classes and the fear of getting lost and being late.

Think about that schedule of classes. It meant all kinds of things: expectations of several different teachers, the rule of the clock in defined time slots, and the daunting pile of books and notebooks for each one.

Behind all of this, though, was a new way of looking at learning and knowledge. Now our work would be divided into a number of areas called subjects, each with its own separate language, facts, ideas, assignments, tests, and teacher. The boundaries were drawn, the lines were cast. Throughout the day we would move from one subject to another, each one neatly de-fined and separated, concentrating our minds on the particular subject at that given moment. And when the bell rang, we would turn our attention to another subject, another teacher.

This seemed to make sense. After all, we were in junior high school. How else would the curriculum be than a junior version of the high school model? Being in junior high school made us sound big and sophisticated. We were only one step removed from the one step from college where the curriculum was organized this way. We were getting ready! Besides, this is how it was for our parents and, no doubt, how it would be for our children. And so it has been.

SKEWED PICTURE

For a growing number of middle school educators today, many of whom carry much the same memory, something is wrong with that picture and they have a metaphor to help us understand.

Imagine for a moment we were given a random handful of jigsaw puzzle pieces and told to put them together. No doubt most of us would

Reprinted with permission from the March 1993 issue of *The School Administrator* magazine. Copyright 1993, American Association of School Administrators.

ask questions like, "Where is the picture? When we put a jigsaw puzzle together we usually have a picture in front of us." "Are there enough pieces, too few, too many?" "Do these pieces make a picture?"

By asking these questions we demonstrate our understanding that the pieces have no real meaning apart from the picture and that it is the picture that sustains and motivates us as we put the puzzle together.

This jigsaw puzzle metaphor helps us to see what was, and is, wrong with that indelible image of the junior high school. Those separate subjects, with their isolated bits of information and skill, were little more than disconnected and fragmented puzzle pieces. We "learned" them because the teacher said they were important, mostly because they would appear on the next test. But their real purpose was unclear. Nothing brought them together so that they had meaning. There was no picture!

Middle-level educators and many others recognize the middle school movement has made dramatic progress over the past 30 years. Charles Silberman, writing in *Crisis in the Classroom* some two decades ago, characterized this level as the "cesspool" of education in the United States.

Yet in a great many school districts today we often find the most promising and exciting reforms at the middle level. School climate is more positive, adults are more sensitive to the experience of puberty, and educators are willing to try team arrangements, new schedules, advisory programs, and a range of other organizational patterns.

REDESIGNING CURRICULA

During the past few years a new kind of conversation has been heating up among middle-level educators about what the middle school curriculum should be. This is not as simple as saying what ought to be taught in one subject or another, but rather considering what ought to be the broad underlying conception of the curriculum as a whole.

This new focus involves asking questions like: What learning experiences should we offer to early adolescents? How might these learning experiences differ from those offered to children and adolescents? How should the curriculum be organized? How can external knowledge and skill be brought to early adolescents in a meaningful way? What is the middle school curriculum for? And who is it for?

A central part of this conversation has focused on the problem illustrated by our memories of junior high school and the jigsaw metaphor. How can we create a curriculum that is connected and coherent, that has meaning and relevance, that has a picture to guide it? A few schools may tell us how some middle-level educators are attempting to answer this question.

In one middle school, outside of Boston, a team of teachers decided to organize a unit on ancient Greece. They began by asking what each subject area might contribute to that theme. Near the end of the unit, students entered a classroom that had been transformed to the inside of an Egyptian tomb.

With the help of art and industrial arts teachers, they built a substructure complete with alcoves, hieroglyphics, sarcophagi, and Canopic jars. The math teacher helped with necessary measurements and taught them about number systems and currency in ancient Greece. The science teacher introduced information about health, superstitions, mummies, technical aspects of tomb construction, and environmental problems.

Also, the social studies teacher has taught about history and government of the period, and about education. The home economics teacher has brought information about family structures, work, and nutrition. Language arts, music, and physical education also contributed, relating their areas to life in ancient Greece.

These teachers and their students have developed a "multi-disciplinary" unit. The various subject areas have retained their identity but are correlated around the theme of ancient Greece. In this way, a "picture" guides the unit, tying together what otherwise would be abstract and disconnected information from each subject.

Along the way, students have developed and applied a number of skills like measuring, researching, constructing, writing, and so on. The theme or picture might have been colonial living, the environment, metrics, or the local community. The point is that subject areas begin to relate to one another rather than being isolated.

INTEGRATED UNITS

At another middle school in Bedford, N.H., eighth-grade students spend four days camping on nearby Mt. Cardigan. Their days are filled with activities like constructing a camp, collecting data on forestation, studying streams, observing weather, keeping journals, preparing meals, exploring trails, and reflecting on how they have lived as a group.

What began some years ago as a multi-disciplinary unit, correlating pieces from various subject areas, has now become a curriculum in and of itself. Teachers and students recognize they are learning and applying content and skills from many subjects but as they plan and carry out each activity they do not stop to ask what each subject can contribute. Rather, they see that each activity simultaneously calls forth content and skills from several subjects. They cannot be separated out because to do so would detract from the power of the activity.

These teachers and students are engaged in an "integrated" unit. Once the central theme and related activities are identified, an array of pertinent knowledge and skill is called forth naturally without attempting to retain the boundaries of the subject areas from which they are drawn. These boundaries are maintained by scholars for their specialized studies, but are unproductive in creating a curriculum that is life-like and appropriate for early adolescents.

As in the multi-disciplinary example, the theme itself can be drawn from many sources, but the point here is that knowledge and skill are integrated in the context of the theme rather than treated as separate subjects. The day itself is organized around the integrated activities rather than a string of subject areas.

INTEGRATIVE APPROACH

A variation on the integrated curriculum is encountered in a middle school in Madison, Wis. Here teachers guide students as they identify questions and concerns about themselves and their world. Students then cluster their questions into themes and, with help from the teachers, plan activities they might do to address each theme and the questions and concerns related to it.

For example, in a unit on "the future," students may investigate their own expected lifespans through family health histories, make recommendations for various aspects of their own community, investigate the accuracy of past predictions for contemporary times, suggest new technologies that might be invented, survey others for future forecasts, and explore the impact of population trends. In addition to helping plan the theme and activities, students are finding resources and evaluating their own work as well as the unit as a whole.

These teachers and students are carrying out an "integrative" curriculum. Like the "integrated" version, knowledge and skill are unified in the context of the theme and activities. Here, though, the teachers have extended the jigsaw puzzle metaphor by asking, "Whose picture is it?" They would argue that when we purchase a puzzle, we do so after sorting through the pile looking for a picture that we like, one whose significance will sustain us as we put it together.

In planning with students, they are attempting to find out what "fuzzy" pictures are compelling for their students so that the curriculum will have both meaning and significance.

When asked what students learn in the integrative curriculum, the teachers list a wide range of content and skills that virtually all states and districts call for, but they put particular emphasis on those that have so often been elusive: problem-solving, critical thinking, application, question posing, valuing, and so on.

They also are quick to point out their work does not involve simply asking young people what they are interested in or what they want to study. Rather, it is a carefully constructed way of helping them expand their understanding of themselves and their world under the guidance of teachers who are also concerned about helping them to be knowledgeable and skilled.

DIFFERING VERSIONS

These cases are examples of the three major types of curriculum organizational reform that are surfacing in middle schools around the country. They share a sense that we must move beyond the fragmented separate subject approach and search instead for themes around which the curriculum might be organized.

In doing so, the teachers are prepared to give up the systematized, subject-by-subject scope and sequence that may appear coherent on paper but is unproductive in organizing meaningful and successful learning for young people.

Substantial differences exist among the three versions themselves. The multi-disciplinary approach, the most widespread of the three, represents a major breakthrough for strict subject loyalists. Yet while a central theme exists for correlating subject areas, their place and space in the curriculum is maintained.

Moreover, unlike the example cited above, areas like art, music, home economics, and so on are still left off "interdisciplinary" teams and out on the edges of the curriculum. And with variations in teacher commitment and time allotment, one can never be sure exactly how much correlation is really occurring. In cases where a multi-disciplinary approach is used, we should celebrate the breakthrough but wonder if that is nearly as far as we ought to go.

The integrated approach brings us much closer to the kind of curriculum reform we ought to be after, especially when the theme presents a real-life problem or puzzling situation. After all, in real life, when we are confronted by a significant issue, we do not stop to ask which part is mathematics, which part home economics, which part language arts, and so on.

Furthermore, most educators (and others) have long recognized that content and skills are best learned in a functional context where their meaning and application are immediate and visible. These reasons make the integrated approach so powerful as a curriculum possibility.

The integrative approach proceeds from this same reasoning but offers the additional advantage of building upon the questions and concerns young people have about themselves and their world. It more clearly promotes elusive skills like problem posing and solving, critical thinking, and meaningful application.

Beyond this, it introduces the concept of democratic planning and respects the dignity of young people by taking their concerns seriously, ideas that are much more likely to enhance self-esteem than the separate time-slot, packaged programs so widely used.

SUPPORTING REFORM

Obviously, much more could be said about the prospects for these versions of middle school curriculum reform: the role of teachers, the place of assessment, their relation to state and impending national curriculum forms, and so on. However, in the space remaining I want to say something about the role of administrative and supervisory persons in relation to middle school curriculum reform.

First, there is no recipe or packaged program for the curriculum work we need to do. Implementation questions are premature until we know exactly what we are trying to accomplish. The first priority is to support conversations about the middle school curriculum question: What and who is the curriculum for? What learning experiences should we offer to early adolescents?

Think of this work as following a parallel structure in which we first carefully consider what we want and how the curriculum might generally look before asking how those ideas might be brought to life in practice. As we now know from quantum physics, parallel lines do meet and, in curriculum work, when they do, we will learn a great deal to support continuing conversations about theory and practice and create stories to explain what we are doing.

Incidentally, it might make sense to invite some elementary and high school teachers, as well as parents, to be part of the dialogue. Do not assume parents are against curriculum reform; after all, not all of them had exactly wonderful experiences in school.

Second, and along those same lines, seek out interested persons for the dialogue and for initial attempts at implementation. Many teachers have had experience with serious curriculum reform, sometimes behind closed classroom doors. Just as many, if not more, have reached a point where they want to talk.

On the other hand, it makes little sense to force reluctant teachers into the initial undertaking, especially with the idea of trying to change a whole building or district. I believe it is fair to expect curriculum change along the lines I have described. But if we wait for those who are reluctant, we will all go to our graves waiting for something to happen. Find those who are interested in doing something and move ahead with them. Be sure to provide support in terms of time and resources for those who want to do so.

Third, remember that tampering with subject area lines means entering into the self-concept and self-esteem of teachers and subject supervisors. Many see themselves not simply as teachers (or supervisors) but as "language arts teachers," "science teachers," "math teachers," (and supervisors).

Furthermore, certain subjects have higher status than others, and status influences schedules, room assignments, and other institutional perks. Deep loyalties to these things are not given up easily. People need time to think about what all this means.

Fourth, understand that the curriculum versions I have described, particularly the integrated and integrative ones, are not simply methods— they are a way of thinking about curriculum and education. It is hard to pull them off if one has only the words and not the music. For this reason, workshops may help but nothing is likely to succeed more than chances to try these ideas out in real classrooms in partnership with colleagues who have already done so.

In other words, staff development should center on real action in classrooms. It also makes sense that administrative and supervisory persons should find time to observe these classrooms firsthand so their contributions to curriculum dialogue are based upon experience with new ideas.

Fifth, following the idea of a parallel structure, the curriculum guidelines or ideas in our conversations may well be brought to life in various ways. Many possibilities exist for creating themes and planning with students. Whatever is done ought to bring to life those ideas that we want to promote.

GUIDING PURPOSE

I have left the idea of a curriculum conversation fairly open, but I believe we might begin by reminding ourselves that the middle school is for early adolescents. Adult needs are important and so are state and district mandates, parental expectations, and other pressures on the curriculum.

But the central purpose of the curriculum ought to be to help early adolescents move toward broader and deeper understanding of themselves and their world. This concept ostensibly guides the middle school movement and should surface most visibly in our curriculum practice. If the growing curriculum conversation is any indication, we are finally on our way to making that rhetoric a reality.

James A. Beane is Professor, National College of Education, National-Louis University, Beloit, Wisconsin.

QUESTIONS FOR REFLECTION

1. What is the "picture" that guides your curriculum planning efforts?
2. What "fuzzy" pictures are compelling for students at the level with which you are most interested?
3. To what degree do subject area lines contribute to your self-concept and self-esteem as an educator?

Middle School Students and Service Learning: Developing Empowered, Informed Citizens

PEGGY A. GRANT

ABSTRACT: Service learning provides students with opportunities to serve their communities while engaging in reflection on the meaning of those experiences. Several examples illustrate how service learning helps middle school students—who are at a critical point in their personal, moral, social, and cognitive development—create a sense of who they are and what they can contribute to the world around them. Successful service learning activities require organization, careful planning, and commitment.

Students are growing vegetables for a homeless shelter in a school garden using recycled water. They have created a computer database on the nutritional content and growth cycles of different plants, solicited donations of materials, and even written a grant to the National Gardening Association for equipment (Hayes, 1997, p. 12).

Seventh graders are reading to preschool children. They have selected and critiqued appropriate children's books and developed oral reading skills. "We liked the look on [the children's] faces when we read them stories and gave them cookies and stuff," they explain (Simon, Parks, & Beckerman, 1996, p. 175).

These teenagers were participating in service learning projects, an educational idea whose pur-

pose is to reconnect young people to their communities while providing real-life contexts for academic learning. This article will discuss the following aspects of service learning: 1) its definition and purpose, 2) how it meets the goals for school reform and content area standards, 3) the ways in which it fits the particular needs of middle school students, and 4) guidelines for incorporating service learning into the middle school classroom.

WHAT IS SERVICE LEARNING?

The twenty-first century is one fraught with dangers and with opportunities, especially for teachers

Article written by Peggy A. Grant for *Curriculum Planning: A Contemporary Approach,* Seventh Edition, 2000. Used by permission of the author.

and the young people they serve. Although many teenagers seem to be experiencing, as the former Executive Director of the National Association of Secondary School Principals claims, ". . . disinterest in classwork, a tragic 'drift' and lack of motivation" (Eberly, 1989, p. 53), many are idealists, eager to make a positive difference in their world. Service learning, while not a panacea for what ails us in these postmodern times, does offer exciting possibilities for rejuvenation among teachers and pupils alike.

Teachers who practice service learning create activities in which their students apply the knowledge and skills of their academic classes to improve the communities in which they live, both locally and globally. These activities fall generally into one of the following categories: 1) cross-age tutoring or teaching, such as reading to kindergarten children or helping new immigrants learn English, 2) creation of a product within the classroom to be donated to an outside agency, institution, or other classroom, such as translating government pamphlets about recycling for non-English speaking citizens or performing skits about peer pressure for elementary age students, 3) taking on an issue and attacking it from several fronts, such as working for flood relief or supporting drunk driving legislation, or 4) going into the community to perform service, such as working in a soup kitchen or creating an inner-city flower garden. These areas overlap to a great degree, as authentic learning experiences do, but all of them serve to use skills from the classroom, whether it is the learning of a foreign language to knowledge about reading strategies, to help others that need the service.

THE ROLE OF SERVICE LEARNING IN SCHOOL REFORM

Several of the reform movements of the eighties included involving students in service within their communities in their recommendations. Ernest Boyer, John Goodlad, and the Carnegie Foundation all suggested community service as

an important part of the traditional school program. More recently, goal number 3 of the National Education Goals: Building a Nation of Learners, includes the following objectives:

- All students will be involved in activities that promote and demonstrate good citizenship, good health, community service, and personal responsibility.
- The percentage of all students who demonstrate the ability to reason, solve problems, apply knowledge, and write and communicate effectively will increase substantially (National Education Goals Panel, 1998).

Service learning is also compatible with the standards currently being written and implemented in the content areas, such as science, mathematics, social studies, and the language arts. The standards in science demand a "classroom that is inquiry-oriented, activity-based, and engaging. The role of the teacher changes from that of disseminator of information to one of a mentor-scholar as children present ideas, challenge ideas, and reconceptualize these ideas" (Shymansky, Jorgensen, & Marberry, 1997). The K–12 standards for the teaching of mathematics also require a pedagogy radically different from that currently practiced in many of today's schools, one that is compatible with the goals and practice of service learning. "These goals imply that students should be exposed to numerous and varied interrelated experiences that encourage them to value the mathematical enterprise" (National Council of Teachers of Mathematics, 1989). Real-life connections between science and mathematics, such as those made by students who created a garden to raise vegetables for the homeless using recycled water, embody what is described in the standards for conceptual learning (Hayes, 1997).

The most natural content link for service learning is the social studies. According to Hatcher (1997), "[S]ervice learning is distinguished from other types of experiential education by its commitment to and its potential to clarify values related to social responsibility and civic literacy." Benjamin Barber (1992), a leading proponent of community service, writes, "Civic empowerment and the exercise of liberty are simply too important to be treated as extracurricular electives" (p. 25).

The content of the social studies is also being conceived in a new light, beyond just learning important names and dates in order to be familiar with our nation's history and culture. According to the National Council for the Social Studies, teaching and learning are powerful when they are active, when they "emphasize authentic activities that call for real-life applications using the skills and content of the field" (NCSS, 1994).

An excellent example of how service learning can provide authentic application of classroom subjects and foster civic action is the unit "Trails to Colorado: Past and Present" designed by teachers in the SSEC service learning project. In this unit, students studied "the impact of human settlement and economic development on the environment." They held community information sessions about "environmental problems related to economic development" and educated the local businesses about environmentally responsible endeavors (Schukar, 1997, p. 181).

A complex, student-driven activity such as this one gives young people an opportunity to combine the knowledge from their math and science classes with what they were learning in social studies about world problems to create something original and useful. Working together, they practiced problem-solving and developed interpersonal skills, all the while using the communication skills from their language arts classes. What they produced became an ongoing, self-sustaining project that improved the quality of life in their neighborhood.

With the inclusion of students with disabilities into regular classrooms, instructors must also think about how educational programs such as service learning will affect these students who have special needs and must be dealt with on an individual basis. Fortunately, there is also support within the special education community for service activities. Special educators recommend an "integrated, activity-based learning model" in which the "learning must take place in a community context" where students work cooperatively with others (Edgar & Polloway, 1994). Contact with community agencies gives students with special needs exposure to a variety of vocational opportunities, and working collaboratively with their peers can provide them with modeling of the social and academic skills they will need for success both in and out of school.

A reporter was interviewing a group of eighth graders who were building bat houses in a local park. To his question, "Why bat houses?" a student replied, "We have reclaimed this park for the people of our community who want to enjoy the surroundings." Unfortunately, the environment was also enjoyable to unpleasant insects, especially mosquitoes. Another student explained, "In class we learned that bats consume thousands of insects each day." Thus, middle school students used their science knowledge, their communication and interpersonal skills to solve a problem in their local neighborhood. This environmental lesson, learned in a social context, in the real world of mud and grass and bugs could be the beginning of an environmental awareness that will grow as these children mature into informed adult citizens.

Clearly there is broad support for service learning as an instructional activity. Activity-based, experiential learning is in alignment with the standards of the subject area organization and is appropriate for those students with special needs. It also addresses those skills important in business and personal relationships, working with others, taking on different points of view, in addition to strategic planning and evaluation.

WHY SERVICE LEARNING WORKS IN THE MIDDLE SCHOOL

Service learning is an instructional strategy that is especially appropriate for middle school students who are at a crucial point in their personal, moral, social, and cognitive development. Exposure to diverse work environments, numerous adult role models, and real-life problem solving can provide students in the middle-school years with more options for their future. Many of the most important skills required in service learning projects, although necessary for academic, emotional, and social growth, are not addressed specifically in the academic curriculum. Schine (1997) describes these areas of emphasis:

> Among these [skills] are the need to acquire and test new skills, develop a range of relationships with both peers and adults, be permitted to make real decisions within appropriate and clearly understood limits, have the opportunity to speak and be heard, and discover that young people can make a difference. (p. 171)

When preteenagers enter the middle school years they begin to acquire the ability to think abstractly, to engage in "reflection, introspection, comparisons with others and a sensitivity to the opinions of other people" (Irwin, 1996). They begin a search for identity, especially in relationship to career choices, sexuality, and a view of life (Marcia, 1987). Young people moving from concrete thinking to more formal reasoning are at an ideal place to begin looking at themselves and the world around them in a new light.

Self-esteem is an important issue for middle school students, especially for young women. Kohn (1994) observes that, "When members of a class meet to make decisions and solve problems, they get the self-esteem building message that their voices count, they experience a sense of belonging to a community, and they hone their ability to reason and analyze" (p. 279). This assertion is supported by the experiences of middle school students working with young children. The teacher reports that "helpers become more mature, responsible and self-assured as a result of their service" and "can see the importance of education since they have been educating others (NCSL, 1991, p. 29).

Since many life-threatening behaviors, such as "drug and alcohol abuse and early sexual experi-

ences, begin during early adolescence, it seems logical that success in developmental tasks and positive interactions with adults may reduce the need that some adolescents feel to engage in those behaviors" (Irwin, 1996, p. 222). Even antisocial behaviors such as aggression and fighting can be affected by community service activities. A middle school student with a well-deserved reputation as a fighter and troublemaker, while doing service in a pre-school, found himself confronted with two small children about to come to blows on the playground. His developing self-awareness, combined with his service role as an authority figure, prompted him to reconsider his own behavior (NCSL, 1991).

For students at-risk of dropping out of school, the middle school can be the last place where they will receive formal education. Serna and Smith (1995) list several skills that can help these students be more successful in school and reduce the chances that they will leave without a diploma. These skills, all of which are integral to service learning projects, include the following: (1) asking for help and advice from trusted adults, (2) collaborating with others to achieve goals, (3) planning, (4) implementing, and (5) evaluating strategies, as well as (6) risk-taking, and (7) dealing with stress.

As students interact with others during service learning activities, they become engaged and develop a sense of what they can contribute to the world around them. These interactions contribute to motivation for school, for learning, and for participating in community life. Teachers who participated in a service learning program directed by the Social Science Education Consortium reported that one of the most positive aspects of the projects in which their students participated was the enthusiasm of the "troublemakers" who "did especially well in the service learning portion of the unit" (Schukar, 1997, p. 182).

At this point in the development of young people, community service can provide the concrete experiences through which they can examine values and beliefs from new perspectives, and develop habits of mind that will help them become thoughtful, compassionate, well-informed, and active members of their communities.

GUIDELINES FOR SUCCESSFUL SERVICE LEARNING ACTIVITIES

Because of the many individuals, agencies, even equipment involved, service learning requires an exceptional amount of organization, planning, and commitment. Ruggenberg (1993) suggests the following guidelines for planning successful service learning activities.

- Allow the students to do work of a significant nature;
- Connect the students directly with the people who benefit from their work;
- Present challenges that require students to test and expand their abilities;
- Require students to use decision-making skills; putting them in a position to "do" and not merely to observe;
- Reflect on and discuss the consequences of their work with staff and supervisors (p. 16).

Alan Haskvitz, a longtime practitioner of service learning in his own classroom, recommends using students' interests and behaviors to guide them into worthwhile service projects. "Go after what they're doing," he advises. "If you see a kid wad up a piece of paper and throw it in the corner, there's your recycling. Ask: 'Why did you do that?' 'How much are we really throwing away here?' 'What can we do about this?' " (Hayes, 1997, p. 12).

The ideal format for service learning is to encourage students to initiate them. They can create their own service projects by examining their communities and looking for needs and then thinking of ways to meet them. Schine (1997) describes one such activity. Following the shooting of a Dominican drug dealer by a police officer in their community, a group of sixth graders examined the relationships among the community members and the police. Deciding that one reason for the hostility stemmed from language differences, the students decided to participate in the cross-cultural training offered by the police department. They invented games to help officers learn Spanish, volunteered as language tutors at the police station, and produced skits to illustrate issues important to young people in the community.

Service learning, like all experiential learning, requires more of the teacher than traditional in-class instruction, even instruction based on active learning. One only has to visualize fifty or so thirteen-year-olds wandering an inner-city neighborhood unclear about what they are doing, unmotivated to accomplish it, and unsure about their reasons for participating, to appreciate the seriousness of careful planning for effective service learning activities. The meaning that students derive from the service learning activity has its roots in what happens in the classroom before, during, and after the project itself.

Classroom activities must give students an opportunity to expand their knowledge and skill base in ways that will help them better understand the reasons for the service learning project. Egan (1997) explains this essential link between concrete experience and abstract understanding. ". . . [T]he practical activity is certainly useful, but it can best support meaningful learning in a context of powerful abstractions, it is within the abstract context that the concrete content makes sense" (p. 52). A well-planned service experience can be an anchor to which the instructor can attach the material of the required curriculum.

Haskvitz explains, "Almost any factual knowledge that students acquire can be related to a service project either by research or an activity" (Hayes, 1997, p. 10). Haskvitz always requires research for service learning projects. "You can't just send students out to clean up a beach," he explains. "That's just free labor. If there's going to be a beach cleanup, my students must research how the beaches got dirty in the first place. . . . If students don't do research, beach cleanups will just go on forever" (p. 10).

The most significant component in student learning is the emphasis that is placed on reflecting on the experience. Conrad and Hedin (1981) explain, "Perhaps students can make personal meaning of their experiences on their own, but if this meaning is to affect their broader social attitudes and intellectual skills, systematic and directed reflection must be added" (p. 36).

The teacher's role in this process is significant because he or she structures the reflection experiences to focus on those aspects that are important for students: 1) to learn the factual, content material, 2) to think about values in terms of their own beliefs and what they have observed in the service experience, 3) to identify the communication and problem-solving skills they used, and 4) to place their own concrete experiences in broad, universal contexts. Because service learning experiences, if they work the way they should, are highly engaging and active, stopping to make personal and intellectual meaning of what is happening will probably not happen unless a teacher provides the opportunity.

CONCLUSION

Students at Mansfield Middle School in Tucson, Arizona, used their social studies knowledge to create a hunger awareness campaign within their own school. After a unit on world hunger, they produced a videotape about the local food bank, then traveled from homeroom to homeroom showing the video and soliciting food for the school food drive. As a result of their actions, Mansfield collected more food than any other middle school in their district (Schukar, 1997). This experience, one that they surely will not forget, allowed them to use knowledge about geography, demographics, and current events in a practical, authentic way. They also exercised their reading, writing, and speaking skills, while working with others in collaboration to accomplish real goals. Most important of all, they learned that they could *do* something about the events going on around them. Imagine the twenty-first century populated with people who learned this lesson early in life.

RESOURCES

Many organizations provide information about how teachers can connect community service with the curriculum: 1) The Citizenship Education Clearing House (CECH) located at the University of Missouri-St. Louis and 2) Learn and Serve America (http://www.whitehouse.gov/WH/EOP/cns/html/cns-index.html).

In addition, the following web sites have information related to service learning: 1) Prophets—www.kn.pacbell.com/wired/prophets/index.html; 2) the National Service Learning Clearinghouse—www.nicsl.coled.umn.edu/; and 3) Youth in Action Network—www.mightymedia.com/yia/mainmenu.cfm?StateTag=0).

Finally, several books offer ideas and resources for using service learning. *A Kid's Guide to Social Action* by Barbara Lewis has practical, specific advice for organizing service experiences and teaching students the skill they need to be successful. Also useful are *Combining Service and Learning: A Resource Book for Community and Public Service Vol. 1* edited by Jane C. Kendall; *Serving to Learn, Learning to Serve: Civics and Service from A to Z* by Cynthia Parsons; *The Kid's Guide to Service Projects* by Barbara A. Lewis and Pamela Espeland; *Social Issues and Service at the Middle Level* edited by Samuel Totten and Jon E. Pedersen; *A Student's Guide to Volunteering* by Theresa Foy Digeronimo; and *Enriching the Curriculum through Service Learning* edited by Carol Kinsley and Kate McPherson.

REFERENCES

Barber, B. (1992). *The aristocracy of everyone*. New York: Ballantine.

Conrad, D. & Hedin, D. (1981). *Experiential education evaluation project, executive summary of the final report*. St. Paul, MN: Minnesota University.

Eberly, D. J. (1989). National service and the high school. *NASSP Journal, 73* (516). 53–60.

Edgar, E. & Polloway, E. A. (1994). Education for adolescents with disabilities: Curriculum and placement issues. *The Journal of Special Education, 27*. 438–452.

Egan, K. (1997). *The educated mind.* Chicago: University of Chicago Press.

Hatcher, J. A. (1997). Reflection: Bridging the gap between service and learning. *College Teaching, 45.* Retrieved July 24, 1998 from the World Wide Web: http://www.elibrary.com.

Hayes, B. (1997). From the classroom to the community: An interview with Alan Haskvitz. *Social Studies Review, 36* (2). 10–12.

Irwin, J. L. (1996). Developmental tasks of early adolescence: How adult awareness can reduce at-risk behavior. *The Clearing House, 60.* 222–225.

Kohn, A. (1994). The truth about self-esteem. *Phi Delta Kappan, 76.* 272–283.

Marcia, J. (1987). The identity status approach to the study of ego identity development. In T. Honess & K. Yardley (Eds.). *Self and identity: Perspectives across the life span.* London: Routledge & Kagan Paul.

National Center for Service Learning in Early Adolescence. (1991). *Connections: Service learning in the middle grades.* New York: City University of New York.

National Council for the Social Studies. (1994). Expect excellence: Curriculum standards for social studies. Retrieved October 10, 1998, from the World Wide Web: http://www.ncss.org/standards.

National Council of Teachers of Mathematics. Curriculum and Evaluation Standards for School Mathematics. Reston, VA: National Council of Teachers of Mathematics, 1989. Retrieved October 10, 1998, from the World Wide Web: http://www.enc.org/reform.

National Education Goals Panel. National education goals: Building a nation of learners. Retrieved October 10, 1998, from the World Wide Web: http://www.negp.gov, last modified May 28, 1998.

Ruggenberg, J. (1993). Community service learning: A vital component of secondary school education. *Moral Education Forum, 18* (3). 11–19.

Schine, J. (1997). School-based service: Reconnecting schools, communities, and youth at the margin. *Theory into Practice, 36* (3). 170–176.

Schukar, R. (1997). Enhancing the Middle School Curriculum through Service Learning. *Theory into Practice, 36.* 176–183.

Serna, L. A. & Smith, J. L. (1995). Learning with purpose: Self-determination skills for students who are at risk for school and community failure. *Intervention in School and Clinic, 30.* 142–153.

Shymansky, J. A.; Jorgensen, M. A. & Marberry, C. A. (1997). Science and mathematics are spoken and written here: Promoting science and mathematics literacy in the classroom. In Reform in Math and Science Education: Issues for the Classroom. Columbus, OH: Eisenhower National Clearinghouse. Retrieved October 10, 1998, from the World Wide Web: http://www.enc.org/reform/.

Simon, K.; Parks, B. S.; & Beckerman, M. (1996). Effects of participatory learning programs in middle and high school civic education. *The Social Studies, 87* (3). 171–176.

Peggy A. Grant is Assistant Professor, School of Education, Purdue University Calumet, Hammond, Indiana.

QUESTIONS FOR REFLECTION

1. To what extent could service learning activities be incorporated into the curriculum across all levels of education (i.e., K–12 schools and higher education)? What "adjustments" would have to be made at the various levels?

2. How might you incorporate service learning into the curriculum with which you are most familiar?

3. How should teachers assess students' learning as a result of their participation in service learning activities?

Teach Middle School and All This Too? Teachers' Concerns about Standards-Based Curricula

TARIQ T. AKMAL

ABSTRACT: As part of the nationwide effort to improve student achievement by setting higher standards, Washington state has developed the Essential Academic Learning Requirements (EALRs), to be implemented in all K–12 public schools by 2001. Teachers at one middle school, however, wonder if mandated standards developed at the state level can be relevant to the lives of local middle school students. Four major components of the standards-based approach are described: state-level assessments, classroom-based assessments, professional staff development, and "context indicators." While teachers have numerous concerns about implementing the new standards, they welcome increased opportunities for collaborative curriculum development.

Educators who have seen many educational reforms come and go suspect that if they just wait long enough and say very little, the next reform will replace the previous one. The current national standards-based reform movement may seem to be just another trend-of-the-month, but it has slowly been gathering momentum over the last decade. Not only are states calling for K–12 public education to improve student achievement by setting higher standards, but groups such as the National Council for Accreditation of Teacher Education (NCATE) and the Interstate New Teacher Assessment and Support Consortium (INTASC) have also called for standards-based teacher preparation programs.

Basing K–12 education on a set of standards for all schools and districts in a state would seem to be a straightforward change. However, the impact of raising standards on curriculum development, assessment, student retention, meeting and planning times, teacher in-service, state funding for education, and teacher preparation programs is often not carefully considered (Lewis, 1997). In middle schools where limited time and resources have been set aside for program development, adjusting to higher standards can have significant consequences.

Middle school teachers have raised concerns about the implementation of new standards. Though effective middle schools have increased student achievement, large-scale evaluations of middle school programs indicate that they have not yet reached their potential, nor are they fully implementing the recommendations for transescent education described in the Carnegie Council on Adolescent Development's *Turning Points* (Felner, Jackson, Kasak, Mulhall, Brand, & Flowers, 1997). As the Council noted in 1995, middle schools must develop curricula that are built around concepts that are important to students (Muth & Alvermann, 1999). If curriculum standards are developed at the state or national level, will they be relevant to the lives of local middle school students?

A STANDARDS-BASED APPROACH TO EDUCATION

The state of Washington, like many states, has taken a standards-based approach to its school reform efforts. In 1993, Washington's Commission on Student Learning (http://csl.wednet.edu) was given the task of developing Essential Academic

Article written by Tariq T. Akmal for *Curriculum Planning: A Contemporary Approach*, Seventh Edition, 2000. Used by permission of the author.

Learning Requirements (EALRs) for all Washington students. For the first time, educators and students in the state would be accountable for reaching a common set of goals. The four overarching goals of the EALRs (pronounced "ē-lers") are as follows; (a complete set of EALRs may be found at http://www.ospi.wednet.edu).

1. READ with comprehension, WRITE with skill, and COMMUNICATE effectively and responsibly in a variety of ways and settings.
2. KNOW and APPLY the core concepts and principles of mathematics; social, physical and life sciences; civics, history and geography; arts; and health and fitness.
3. THINK analytically, logically, and creatively, and INTEGRATE experiences and knowledge to form reasoned judgments and solve problems.
4. UNDERSTAND the importance of work and how performance, effort and decisions directly affect future career and educational opportunities.

The EALRs are intended to improve student achievement and raise academic standards. Instruments for measuring student achievement were developed for the fourth-, seventh-, and tenth-grade levels. "Benchmarks"—points in time used to measure students' progress—were developed for the three grade levels, predicated on the assumption that students would have mastered certain skills and knowledge upon completion of those grades. Participation in the fourth-grade assessment became mandatory for all schools in Washington as of spring 1998. Assessments for seventh-grade and tenth-grade students are voluntary until spring 2001.

Washington's assessment system has four major components: state-level assessments, classroom-based assessments, professional staff development, and a "context indicator" system. The state-level assessments allow students to select and/or create responses to demonstrate their skills, knowledge, and understanding for each of the EALRs. Unlike traditional norm-referenced assessments, none of the state assessments are timed, so students feel little pressure to rush through their work.

The second component of the system is classroom-based assessment. These assessments address learning requirements not easily measured by the state assessment (e.g., oral presentations or group discussion); offer teachers opportunities to gather evidence of learning that best fit the needs of individual students; and assist teachers in gathering valid evidence of student learning (Ensign, 1998).

The third component of the new assessment system is professional development. Ongoing, comprehensive training and support for teachers and administrators improves their understanding of the EALRs, the elements of sound assessment, and effective instructional techniques that enable students to achieve the state standards. Learning and Assessment Centers have been established in several locations across the state to further facilitate use of the assessment system (Ensign, 1998).

The last component is the "context indicator" system. The context indicators will provide insight into why some students might not achieve to the desired level and identify factors that both inhibit and support students' learning. Context indicators might include such information as faculty experience and training, instructional strategies employed, condition of facilities and equipment, availability of appropriate instructional materials and technology, relevant characteristics of the students and the community, and school dropout and graduation rates (Ensign, 1998).

ONE SCHOOL'S RESPONSE TO THE EALRS

Lincoln Middle School* in Pullman, Washington, recognized locally and at the state level for academic excellence, is representative of the ease with which some elements of change can be effected as well as the difficulties encountered in redefining the middle school curriculum. The faculty at Lincoln Middle School decided to gradually phase in the new standards and their

---

*The author taught at Lincoln Middle School from 1988 to 1994.

corresponding assessments. Faculty spent the 1997–1998 school year realigning the curriculum at each grade level with the EALRs and organizing the benchmarks so that each grade would be responsible for a series of concepts and skills. The next year, 1998–1999, was devoted to developing classroom-based performance assessments to determine if students had achieved the required benchmarks. Each teacher was required to complete at least one performance assessment. During the next year, faculty members began to develop their ability to incorporate the new assessment tools into their lessons. This timeline would allow ample time to develop assessments and enable the school to meet the timeline for statewide compliance, the year 2000.

CONCERNS RELATED TO CURRICULUM REALIGNMENT AND IMPLEMENTATION

During the first phase of curriculum realignment, several questions surfaced among both veteran and novice teachers. For example, if the state expected teachers to make sweeping changes, would teachers be provided with appropriate training? If a teacher had not yet received training for using the new assessments, would he or she be held accountable for students' failure to achieve the standard? If, as rumor had it, Student Learning Improvement Grants that had been readily available to assist schools with curriculum redesign were withdrawn by the state in the year 2000, how would schools provide training to teachers? Were teacher education programs around the state prepared to provide necessary training?

The faculty also had concerns about student accountability. What would happen if students did not meet a standard? If classroom grades were based upon performance, what would happen if students did not "perform" according to the standards? Though teachers were reluctant to discuss student failure, they worried about students who show little interest in achieving the standards.

In addition, teachers were concerned about the time and resources needed to develop new curricula and assessments. While some state money was provided for "curriculum days" and in-service, many teachers believed it was not enough, and they wondered how they would find the time to make necessary changes in the curriculum. Furthermore, were these changes more important than the other demands of their jobs? In this regard, the school's principal pointed out to the author that "When Boeing builds a new plane, 60 percent of the project money is spent on research and development. They get to test the plane as much as they need to before it goes into operation. Teachers feel like they are building a new plane, but they have to reconfigure it in the air as they are testing it!"

TEACHER COLLABORATION

A major benefit of the effort to meet state standards was that teachers were spending more time on curriculum development. Teachers who rarely had the time or inclination to meet, now met regularly with their colleagues. Increased collaboration also created more opportunities for curriculum integration and team teaching.

Though not all teachers willingly embraced the required changes, they did embrace the spirit of collaboration. As Lincoln teachers worked on establishing performance-based assessments to meet state requirements, they were being more creative, cooperative, and diligent. Since the school's principal regularly reminded teachers that "there's no reason to reinvent the wheel," teachers made good use of materials already developed. In addition, many teachers took advantage of the state's Learning and Assessment Centers and attended workshops in nearby Spokane.

USING ASSESSMENTS TO TEACH CLASSROOM LESSONS

The assessments developed to measure student achievement vis-à-vis the EALRs were such that they could also be used for teaching. Performance-based tasks and activities often relegated to the position of tools for "testing" could now be used as teaching tools. For example, a performance assessment normally used at the completion of lessons on communication in mathematics and "number sense" could also be a learning activity for a lesson within the unit. Exposure to such assessments allows students to become familiar with critical thinking activities and different approaches to demonstrating their achievement. Students also become comfortable with scoring rubrics—they realize that high achievement comes when they are able to meet all the criteria within a rubric and that they, not the teacher, are responsible for their own learning.

THE INTERSECTION OF STANDARDS-BASED APPROACHES AND MIDDLE SCHOOL CURRICULUM

If middle schools are to meet the developmental needs of early adolescents and "foster academic success in all students" (Wiles and Bondi, 1993, p. 83), can they also meet standards such as Washington state's EALRs? Will the curriculum become too "content oriented"—in direct opposition to the effective middle-level curriculum as described by the Carnegie Council on Adolescent Development (1995)? While state-mandated standards do provide a way of expressing the high expectations that effective middle schools must maintain, and they promote the open-ended, student-centered approaches to critical thinking that should characterize middle schools, can teachers also be expected to meet the cognitive, social, emotional, and physical needs of transescent learners?

Washington state, like many other states, has chosen to invest its educational future in a standards-based, K–12 curriculum. As the case of Lincoln Middle School has shown, teachers do have valid concerns about a standards-based curriculum, and they need sufficient time to realign the curriculum and develop classroom assessments. However, these challenges are outweighed by the dual benefits of increasing communication and collaboration among teachers and providing middle-level students with thoughtfully developed curricula and assessments based on meaningful essential academic learning requirements.

REFERENCES

Beane, J. A. (1990). *A middle school curriculum: From rhetoric to reality*. Columbus, OH: National Middle School Association.

Carnegie Council on Adolescent Development. (1989). *Turning points: Preparing American youth for the 21st century*. Washington, DC: Carnegie Council on Adolescent Development.

Carnegie Council on Adolescent Development. (1995). *Great transitions: Preparing adolescents for a new century*. New York: Carnegie Corporation of New York.

Clabaugh, G. K. (1997). Body counts and standards-based reform. *Educational Horizons, 75*, 107–108.

Ensign, G. (1998). *The Washington assessment of student learning: An update—May 1998*. Washington Commission on Student Learning [online]. Available FTP: Hostname: ospi.wednet.edu Directory: csl.wednet.edu/Web%20page/3%20assessment%20system/subdocuments/1-

Felner, R. D., Jackson, A. W., Kasak, D., Mulhall, P., Brand, S., & Flowers, N. (1997, March). The impact of school reform for the middle years: Longitudinal study of a network engaged in Turning Points-based comprehensive school transformation. *Phi Delta Kappan, 78*, 528–550.

Lewis, A. C. (1997, March). Staying with the standards movement. *Phi Delta Kappan, 78*, 487–488.

Lipsitz, J., Jackson, A. W., and Austin, L. M. (1997, March). What works in middle-grades school reform. *Phi Delta Kappan, 78*, 517–519.

Muth, K. O. & Alvermann, D. E. (1999). *Teaching and learning in the middle grades* (2nd Ed.). Boston, Allyn and Bacon.

Wiles, J. & Bondi, J. (1993). *The Essential Middle School*. New York, NY: Macmillan Publishing Company.

Tariq T. Akmal is Assistant Professor, Department of Teaching and Learning, College of Education, Washington State University, and former teacher at Lincoln Middle School, Pullman, Washington.

QUESTIONS FOR REFLECTION

1.   What are the advantages and disadvantages of curriculum standards developed at the state level?
2.   Do standards developed at the state or national levels negatively affect the ability of teachers to provide relevant, appropriate curricular experiences to students at the local level?
3.   To what extent should teachers be held accountable if students do not achieve curriculum standards?

The Teacher as Counselor: Some Practical Considerations

JUDITH A. BROUGH

ABSTRACT: While their role is not the same as that of trained guidance counselors, middle-level teachers should possess practical counseling skills to help students make decisions and develop relationships. The activities that characterize effective "teacher–counselors" include developing a secure, comfortable classroom atmosphere; involving students in planning units of learning; encouraging students to solve their own problems; seeking professional assistance if a student has serious emotional problems; and recognizing that their role is not to "cure" mental illness but "in some small way to help prevent it."

Guidance has been widely recognized as a function of middle level education. But what is the role of the classroom teacher in this guidance function? It is certainly not to replace or even substitute for the trained guidance counselor. Instead, it is to assist transescents in their daily decision-making and in their relationships.

This function may be approached through a formal advisor-advisee program or even, to some extent, through values clarification type activities. But, there remains a general guidance-counseling perspective in classroom teaching which calls for some practical counseling skills. In addition, the effective teacher-counselor must possess knowledge about their needs and characteristics and have a genuine liking for transescents. With this attitude and knowledge of transescents in hand,

the following considerations and activities may be developed and used by the effective teacher-counselor.

Get to know each child as an individual.   Middle school teachers all talk with students as individuals; greet them at the door; show genuine concern; and become familiar with their various countenances. But we need to take it a few steps further. Get involved in informal groups of students; become a club advisor or chaperone. Home visitations can also be extremely enlightening, if you can somehow find the time. If you do not actually want to sit down in the home with parents and child, at least drive or walk by each of their homes. Literally go to see "where they're coming from."

From *Middle School Journal* 16, no. 4 (August 1985): 4, 8–9. Used by permission of the author and the publisher.

Frequent contacts with parents are invaluable. Call them with good news, not just the bad. Send home a memo about something special which the child has done or accomplished. This dissemination of good news helps to establish trust and a sense of fairness in the child—something of which middle school youngsters are acutely aware.

Observe the students and perhaps jot down some of your observations. Try to note who is not participating in class discussions; is that normal behavior for him/her? Who is monopolizing the conversation(s)? Who is sad? Who is moping? Who seems scared? Who needs some advice in cleanliness habits? Who just needs someone to care?

And finally, ask the kids. Ask them to put in writing anonymously what is troubling them, or what you should know about kids their age. The necessary role of the teacher as counselor becomes apparent when one considers a response I received on such an anonymous questionnaire: "Help us, because we want to grow up more faster than we should."

Develop a secure and comfortable classroom atmosphere.   Be certain that your students feel free to ask questions. Conrad Toepfer, that stalwart advocate of transescents, has frequently said, "the only dumb question is the question that isn't asked."

Try a little self-disclosure.   Let the students know that your life has not always been a bed of roses, and that you somehow managed to get through it. Emphasize that people can learn to deal with all sorts of problems. Try to come across as a real person. Let them come to know you as an individual with outside interests and a family.

Never downplay a student's problem or concern. Refrain from saying, "Don't worry, it'll get better." The student's problem may seem trivial to you, but it is monumental to them. Remember that they are in the throes of developing a sense of identity—trying to determine who they are and what is important to them. They are cogni-

tively unable to intellectualize emotional situations, but adults commonly expect them to do so. Try to envision crises which you encountered at that age: your diary falling into your brother's hands; not having a boyfriend/girlfriend when *everyone* else did (I made one up); pimples; the inability to do a cartwheel which excluded you from any cheerleading exploits; and the frayed carpet in your living room which precluded anyone from visiting your house in the daylight. You are talking basic traumas here!

Organize some units of learning with your students. These are not to be confused with units of instruction which center on the teacher doing the instruction. Rather, these are units which emphasize the students doing exploring wants and needs and learning the difference between the two. My co-teacher, students, and I developed one on respect for self, others, animals and the environment. The results were more than gratifying.

With caution, try some large group "What's Bugging Me" Sessions.   If it bugs one of the kids to be pushed in line, the students can discuss alternative ways of dealing with such a situation (besides pushing back). This is not intended to be a group counseling session to address deepseated emotional problems; it is meant to help kids learn to deal with various daily situations. Blount and Klausmeier (1968) listed the following emotional needs of emerging adolescents which could be used as guidelines for sessions:

1. Understanding socially approved methods for relieving emotional tensions and substituting those for childish or otherwise disapproved methods.
2. Analyzing emotional situations objectively.
3. Obtaining a broader understanding of situations in which disruptive emotions are produced.
4. Acquiring many social skills to meet new situations.
5. Eliminating fears and emotionalized patterns of response that are already firmly established.

Plan learning experiences appropriate to transescent developmental stages.   Community service projects work wonders. Students could tutor younger children, meet with and get to know senior citizens, organize food drives for the needy. There seems to be no substitute for community service as a means of building a sense of worth and accomplishment.

Let the children solve their own problems; do not attempt to solve problems for them.   Most often a shoulder to cry on or a listening post is all that is necessary. Isn't it easier to solve a problem once you have stated it out loud? The voicing of the problem seems to help put it into proper perspective. A few good questions asked at the right time might also be of value. "Why do you think so?" "What else could you have done?" But avoid didactic responses such as, "Why don't you try. . . ." Remember that your objective is to assist the children in solving their own problems.

The following guidelines are recommended:

1. Let the student release his/her emotions and try to tap into real feelings.
2. Encourage that the whole story be told.
3. Ask clarifying questions; try to get the student to identify specific instances and feelings.
4. Remember that silence is fine. It isn't necessary that someone is always talking. Silence gives time for choice making.
5. Look at alternatives to the problem's solution. Reframe it; look at the problem from a different perspective.
6. Remember that people are resilient.

Refrain from promising confidences which you may not be able to keep.   Be wary, if a student starts with "If I tell you something, do you promise not to tell my parents?" You cannot make such a promise, and should tell that to the student. Add that although you will do all in your power to help them with their problem, parental or administrative involvement may be necessary avenues to a solution.

Make and continually update a resource file. Know to whom or what to refer your students when it seems appropriate. Is there a book or pamphlet which may help them better than you are able? Is there another teacher about whom a child has expressed confidence?

Recognize serious problems as such and do not hesitate to seek assistance from counselors, psychologists, parents and administrators.   You are not trained to deal with deep-seated emotional problems; admit that and relinquish them to more qualified others in the particular realm. What you *can* do is help the student to become more willing to see a counselor. Ligon and McDaniel (1970, p. 78) commented:

> It takes counseling skill on the part of the teacher to help some students become willing to see a school counselor and be receptive to such counseling. Future counseling or therapy will be most effective if the teacher is able to prepare the student for help from the school counselor or other specialist. Merely asking the counselor to call in a student is asking him to counsel an unwilling student. Doing so without first asking the permission of the student is also breaking confidence with the student.

Note problems which seem to crop up often and alternative means of getting them out in the open. The most frequently encountered problems seem to fall into three categories:

1. a death in the family. The student develops a sense of vulnerability and loss. Then, to top it off, the other students do not know what to say to a grieving peer and consequently ignore him or her. Discussing suggestions on how to treat and talk to a grieving friend would help immensely—especially before any such tragic event occurs.
2. problems with parents. These may include separation, divorce, and subsequent parental dating and remarriage. Many transescents feel unaccepted (the myth that "It isn't happening

to anyone else"), abused, and/or overprotected. One of my students felt that her parents didn't trust her and weren't very proud of her. Her brothers had been very successful students and she felt that she wasn't up to par. All she needed was a little bit of my time and attention—reassurance and encouragement from an adult. Other students feel too pressured; their parents are overdemanding, or at least they appear that way to the transescent.

3. problems with peers. This one, of course, is a constant. It includes unpopularity, overpopularity. Who do you choose to sit next to at lunch when everyone wants to sit next to you and someone is bound to get mad? Then there is the age-old problem of being "different"—too smart, too dumb, too underdeveloped, too overdeveloped, just "too. . . ."

Recognize that as a teacher-counselor your job is not to cure mental illness, but in some small way to help prevent it. To help children to know themselves is of paramount concern. The following activities may help:

1. "Daily emotional release"—at the end of each day each student fills out a card answering the question, "How do you feel today and why?" The student has the option of then ripping it up.
2. Every day students name at least one thing which they did well and/or something nice which happened to them.
3. Make a list of courtesies each student did for someone else. Build the number slowly. One discourtesy necessitates doing two courtesies.
4. Brainstorm on items which make them feel well mentally and physically.

WHAT THE COUNSELING ROLE REQUIRES

The teacher who assumes the role of counselor inevitably gives unstintingly of time. Planning periods, lunch periods and alone time before and after school may fall by the wayside. Children cannot talk to you in confidence during class, so it is hard not to devote extra time to pressing situations.

You must be willing to work *with* your students in discovering problems, solutions, and alternatives. The teacher will not know all the problems, and certainly cannot know all of the answers. The counseling aspect, then, logically becomes a joint effort.

Learn to accept failure, as difficult as that may be. You cannot help all of the students all of the time. Some must be referred to others, some must be placed in different situations, and some, as harsh as it may sound, will just plod on as before. The students must recognize that they have a problem and seek help. You cannot hope to convince them that they need assistance. They might be perfectly content as they are.

Beane and Lipka (1984) differentiated between self-concept and self-esteem, which distinction has importance for the guidance oriented teacher. They defined self-concept as "the description of self in terms of roles and attitudes." Self-esteem, however, "refers to the evaluation one makes of the self-concept description and, more specifically, to the degree to which one is satisfied or dissatisfied with it, in whole or in part." (pp. 5–6). They illustrated:

Self-esteem judgments are based on values or value indicators such as attitudes, beliefs, or interests. For example, an adolescent might describe himself as a good student (self-concept), but may wish to change that (self-esteem) because he wants to be accepted by peers who devalue school success (value indicator) . . . a teacher working with the adolescent just described may have difficulty understanding why the student may begin to show a decline in school achievement. The teacher, not knowing the value-base of the student, may further complicate the situation by praising the students work in front of the peers who devalue school success, in an attempt to bolster self-esteem. The point of understanding the place of values in self-perception is that an individual may not have the same self-esteem judgments others would have under similar circumstances. (p. 6).

And finally, the teacher must be willing, sometimes, to subordinate subject matter to more pressing "guidance" concerns. Some subject matter may relate to transescent concerns, and therefore be "legitimately" covered. However, the middle level teacher must always keep in mind the social and emotional as well as academic objectives of the school. The students will not learn the academics if they are feeling insecure, so the counseling activities must take precedence when deemed a priority by the professional, the teacher-counselor. Both you and your students are able to distinguish among the teacher's various roles and responsibilities. Ligon and McDaniel (1970, p. 81) stated, "Teachers can learn to be counselors but they often have to make some changes. They can learn to shift from one role to another, from the one who must keep order in the classroom to the one who listens and understands. Students understand this dual role. One student approached a teacher who was supervising in the lunchroom. He started to ask her something, and then said, 'You have to be strict now, don't you? I'll see you after school.' "

CONCLUSION

The activities and suggestions given can be adapted to almost any teacher-counselor situa-tion. Their use will depend upon the characteristics and teaching methods of individual teachers. What is of paramount importance is not the particular activities used, but the spirit in which they are offered. A poem written by a student and quoted by Moss (1969, p. 189) has a message which should be heeded.

And Gladly Lerne

I trudge through endless halls
and sit in musty cubicles
(only they're labs, most of them)
and gaze through someones
(only they're no ones, most of them)
who look over my head to watch the clock
and scribble important nothings on blackboards
(only they're greenboards, most of them).
and sometimes
i meet a teacher

REFERENCES

Beane, J. and Lipka, R. *Self-Concept, Self-Esteem and the Curriculum.* Boston: Allyn and Bacon, Inc., 1984.

Blount, N. and Klausmeier, H. *Teaching in the Secondary School.* 3rd ed. New York: Harper & Row, 1968.

Ligon, M. and McDaniel, S. *The Teacher's Role in Counseling.* Englewood Cliffs, NJ: Prentice-Hall, Inc., 1970.

Moss, T. *Middle School.* Boston: Houghton Mifflin Co., 1969.

Judith A. Brough is Professor and Chair, Education Department, Gettysburg College, Gettysburg, Pennsylvania.

QUESTIONS FOR REFLECTION

1. What additional skills should "teacher-counselors" possess?
2. What professional experiences can help teachers of transescents and early adolescents develop the counseling skills described by Brough?
3. What is the difference between self-concept and self-esteem? Why is it important for middle-level teachers to understand the difference?

CASE STUDY IN CURRICULUM IMPLEMENTATION

Revitalizing the Middle School: The Guilford County Process

JERRY WEAST

LILLIE JONES

MIKE PRIDDY

LARRY ALLRED

PAUL GEORGE

ABSTRACT: The Guilford County Public Schools, formed by the merger of three North Carolina school districts in 1994, launched a revitalization effort for the seventeen middle schools in the new district. The following case study documents five strategies that have led to the partial, if not full, realization of seven goals for revitalization: (1) formation of a middle school task force, (2) development of a revitalization plan, (3) staff development, (4) leadership development for principals, and (5) regular, public evaluation of schools.

As in many other parts of the nation, the middle school concept came to the Piedmont area of North Carolina in the early '80's, for a combination of reasons (George & Alexander, 1993). Educators there discovered that racially desegregated middle schools could enhance the extent to which a district could be desegregated, while permitting elementary schools to remain as neighborhood schools. Opening middle schools also made it possible to avoid closing high schools where enrollment was down, by moving the ninth grade from former junior high schools into the high school building. Enrollment pressures of a different kind in the elementary schools could be eased by moving the sixth grades to newly organized middle schools. State legislation following the explosion of the *Nation at Risk* report (1983) may have also prompted the reorganization of middle level education there. By the end of the decade of the '80's, middle schools were widespread in this area of North Carolina.

REVITALIZATION PROMPTED BY THE MERGER OF THREE DISTRICTS

In 1994, three central North Carolina school districts (Greensboro, Guilford County, and High Point) merged to form the current Guilford County Public Schools, with approximately 60,000 students, one of the largest school districts in the nation. Guilford County includes urban, suburban, and rural housing, a wide range of socioeconomic levels, and a school population that is approximately 60% white and 40% minority. The new school board and district superintendent were dedicated to creating one comprehensive and unified district in place of three very different school systems. The highest

Reprinted with permission from National Middle School Association. The article originally appeared in the May 1999 issue of *Middle School Journal*.

priority was placed on the establishment of public confidence in the new school system. Schools in the new district would be safe, equitable, fiscally responsible, and places where academic achievement would reach new heights.

It quickly became clear, when the commotion connected to the merger began to pass, that among the many ways in which the three former districts had differed, the middle school concept had been implemented in each of the three former districts, but with widely varying degrees of success. Some middle schools had interdisciplinary teams; some did not, and where teams were in place, they often functioned minimally. Some schools had teacher-based advisory programs; some did not, and where they existed, most educators were dissatisfied with that aspect of the program. Some middle schools in the new Guilford County had successfully implemented heterogeneous grouping; many retained a system of strict ability grouping.

A number of the middle schools were giving large portions of the school day to exploratory curriculum; at the same time, academic achievement scores in the basic components of the curriculum were below state averages. This disparity led to confusion and dissatisfaction among parents, board members, and educators. Clearly, a common or unifying vision for seventeen middle schools was needed, one which was congruent with the drive to establish public confidence in the new system as a whole. This need led to the commitment for a comprehensive review and a plan for the revitalization of the middle school concept in Guilford County Schools.

REVITALIZATION STRATEGY ONE: A MIDDLE SCHOOL TASK FORCE IS FORMED

In the spring of 1995, the Board of Education of Guilford County Schools adopted a plan and approved a timeline for assessing and revitalizing its middle schools. To achieve this common vision, however, required lengthy discussions among members of the community and school system.

The Board of Education had called for the creation of a Middle School Task Force two years earlier which included teachers, administrators, and parents. Considerable time was spent in staff development for the members of the Task Force, focusing upon the middle school concept as well as emerging trends in areas of education that would affect middle level schools. Achievement patterns in each school, and across the district, were examined and probed for underlying factors. Numerous periodicals and books were reviewed, with subsequent discussions regarding equity and access for all students to a rigorous curriculum. A commitment to balancing equity and opportunities for excellence began to emerge. Various models of school organization, schedules, and components (e.g., advisory) were examined. In particular, considerable time and energy focused upon the pros and cons of curriculum tracking and ability grouping.

REVITALIZATION STRATEGY TWO: DEVELOPMENT OF A GUILFORD COUNTY MIDDLE SCHOOL REVITALIZATION PLAN—SEVEN CENTRAL ELEMENTS

After several months of intense dialogue and debate among the members of the Task Force, a common vision statement was adopted. That vision for all 17 Guilford County middle schools was, it turns out, an affirmation of the central components of the middle school concept (George & Alexander, 1993). The statement included these seven central elements:

- focus on academic achievement in the core curriculum,
- daily teacher advisory,
- team organization at every grade,
- flexible block scheduling,
- an expanded menu of electives and student activities (cultural arts, athletics, and intramurals), differentiated instruction, and
- heterogeneous grouping in science and social studies in all schools.

Academic Achievement

Increased student academic achievement was to be the primary objective of middle school revitalization efforts; it had already become the central focus of the superintendent and the Board. Test scores in the newly created district were lower than anyone wanted them to be, and the scores were distributed across the district in a way that correlated far too closely with the socioeconomic status of the students attending particular schools. The superintendent, the school board, and middle school educators in the district were committed to increasing student achievement and decreasing the variability of academic achievement on the basis of socioeconomic status within the district. Every component of the middle school concept in Guilford County was, therefore, expected to focus on, support, or at least not to detract from the emphasis on increasing academic achievement for all students.

The extent to which the other six components of the new plan were already in place, in 1995, was difficult to describe. The teacher advisory program was totally absent in some schools, in place only in name and time in others. Interdisciplinary teams were organized in most schools so that teachers on teams shared a common group of students, in the same area of the building, and had a common schedule allowing for team planning. But teams seemed to be accomplishing very little else. Few teams worked together to improve student behavior management; few attempted to create a sense of community on their teams; and fewer worked together to integrate the curriculum. Flexible, team-controlled schedules were in place in a number of the schools, but few teams made any attempts to modify or adapt the schedule to student-oriented uses.

The district did have a time-honored commitment to a rich and exciting unified arts, or exploratory curriculum, but there were real questions about the extent to which this aspect of the curriculum was actually contributing to increased academic achievement. Differentiated instruction may have been discussed, but traditional secondary large group, whole class, teacher-directed instruction was the norm. And, in a number of the middle schools, a rigid ability grouping plan was as dominant as it ever had been.

The establishment of these seven common components for all 17 schools was, given the immense diversity of the district, a bold and courageous move, both pedagogically and politically. As always, leadership was a crucial, and complicated, factor in determining the extent to which a new vision became reality. The new superintendent brought a fierce and uncompromising commitment to the creation of district unity, a non-negotiable demand for increased student achievement, and an unwavering insistence on new fiscal responsibility. In the district office and within the middle schools in each of the three former districts, however, there was a sizable group of professional educators who, as a result of years of experience within middle level education, were deeply committed to that concept.

Such situations have created volatile mismatches in other districts, where unresolved conflicts have led to the collapse of momentum for change. In Guilford County, fortuitously, the vision of the board and the superintendent coalesced with the deeply felt and knowledgeable commitment to middle school education and to the specific components of the Middle School Plan. This happened in a way that created an even sharper focus on needs at the middle level, brought a commitment of resources for revitalization, and heightened the sense of importance and accountability that gave force to the revitalization effort.

Tracking and Ability Grouping: An "Incident"

An incident connected to the early efforts at implementation of the new middle school plan, specifically the component of heterogeneous grouping, brought an increased sense of urgency to the revitalization effort. As a part of the development of the new vision by the school board, a review of instructional grouping practices had brought the members of the board, and the superintendent's staff, to an endorsement of increased heterogeneous grouping in all of the district's middle schools (Wheelock, 1992). A sense of the importance of equity accompanied the new board's realization of the immense diversity that the new district represented.

As a result of earlier attempts at implementation of the middle school concept, all but three of the new district's middle schools had attempted a considerable amount of heterogeneous grouping. Three schools representing historically high-achieving areas of the district had not yet been "detracked." Unfortunately, in a classically bimodal distribution of achievement, high achievement growth in these schools had been restricted to the upper range of the ability grouping classes, and students in low tracks maintained a level of comparatively low achievement. Furthermore, the three schools were caught up in a grouping plan that resulted in having the upper tracks composed predominantly of white, upper-middle class students and lower tracks comprised mainly of children from minority, lower socioeconomic groups. Thus, the schools were in a potentially combustible situation when asked to begin the detracking process.

When the district commitment to increased heterogeneous grouping in the middle school was announced, teachers, and parents of students in high track classes in these three traditional, racially diverse schools were less than enthusiastic about the change. One of the three school principals embraced the change to heterogeneous science and social studies classes; two others kept a "low profile" hoping, perhaps, that this might be one more dictate that they could eventually ignore.

Eventually, rumors mixed with district guidelines to the point that a group of parents of advanced students at one school, where the principal supported the changes, became alarmed at what they believed might be the elimination of gifted programs at that site. A relatively impromptu public meeting held at the school drew a group of nearly 500 concerned parents, teachers, students, and community members. During the meeting, angry, nearly physical, confrontations occurred between advocates for various positions as audience members literally wrestled for the microphone. The local media became involved, and alarming reports of the meeting spread quickly throughout the district. Board members immediately received dozens of phone calls from alarmed citizens and educators representing both sides of the grouping issue.

School board members, having earlier made a public commitment to equity in all its school programs, and having endorsed the middle school grouping strategies related to it, became openly concerned about the divisions within the community over ability grouping. Individual board members' clarity about what "the research" said seemed less certain in the midst of public furor. The members of the board were also concerned about whether teachers and school leaders had the "instructional prowess" to implement the new grouping policy effectively. Instructional grouping was clearly as political a component of the revitalization plan as it was a pedagogical one.

Nevertheless, the district leaders and the board maintained their commitment to detracking in science and social studies. That decision was not capricious or made too quickly, and it entailed extensive staff development for decision-makers. Effective implementation of more heterogeneous grouping would, it seemed clear, also require extensive staff development for those who would implement it in schools and classrooms. In addition to workshops, district leaders contracted with two universities to deliver additional services, including a course from High Point University leading to certification in teaching the academically gifted. Professors from the School of Education at UNC-Greensboro also observed in classrooms and offered assistance in the area of multiple intelligences. Other prominent national consultants also visited teachers in their classrooms, to offer specific strategies and increase confidence in this area.

Parental understanding was just as crucial. Several public forums were conducted. These forums focused upon the characteristics and needs of adolescent learners, elements of exemplary middle schools, and differentiated learning. A luncheon meeting with PTA presidents was typical of the opportunity for discussion and dialogue with parents.

Ultimately, public communication and staff development made it possible to keep the commitment to increased heterogeneous grouping. Staff development was supported by central office members' in-depth knowledge of the political maneuvers required to increase acceptance of heterogeneous grouping by members of the school and the community. School board members were pleased that heterogeneous grouping would focus primarily on science and social studies classes, not language arts or mathematics. They were also pleased to learn that grouping within classes could occur when appropriate, and that gifted programs would not be dismantled.

Teachers were relieved when staff development workshops centered on the skills for differentiating instruction that they would need to be successful in heterogeneous classrooms. Parents were pleased when they learned that their bright children would not be held back, or that their children would not be relegated to a school-based underclass. Eventually, test scores would affirm the effort.

Having experienced the positive resolution to the grouping incident produced by the combination of effective staff development and determined, skillful leadership, central office leaders moved ahead with the implementation of the other components of the new middle school revitalization plan. A common understanding and effective programmatic implementation of teacher advisory, interdisciplinary team organization, flexible scheduling, curriculum enrichment, and differentiated instruction became the next targets. Increased academic achievement would be the most important measure of the successful implementation of these program components. Staff development and a comprehensive model of program evaluation became center pieces in the strategy to implement the revitalization plan.

REVITALIZATION STRATEGY THREE: STAFF DEVELOPMENT

Comprehensive staff development was and continues to be necessary in middle level education, because middle schools are truly emergent,[1] developing and evolving as time passes. Staff development for middle school educators in Guilford County focused sharply on the seven components of the middle school revitalization effort, constantly keeping in mind the goal of restoring public confidence through increasing academic achievement. Professional development activity was characterized by variety and involvement, important elements for teachers and principals as well as students. Teachers and principals are adults; as adult learners, staff developers presumed, they must have variety as well as relevancy embedded within their staff development.

In the Guilford County School System, staff developers worked to make this premise an operational reality. Each middle school leader was required to submit a detailed staff development plan that included participation in system-wide initiatives as well as in building level staff development directly related to the seven components of the Middle School Revitalization Plan. In addition, through the efforts of the Associate Superintendent for Educational Program Services, Director of Staff Development, the Executive Directors, the Director of Middle Schools, as well as a partnership with the University of North Carolina at Greensboro, teams of teachers and principals formed a task force that has planned and delivered several summer institutes.

These institutes have focused upon strategies for strengthening and revitalizing Guilford County middle schools by the renewing of everyone's understanding of fundamental elements. In many cases, teachers and principals have led or presented at these sessions. In other cases, our university partnership afforded an expanded menu of consultants and services. Teams of local educators, formed at the institutes, have assumed leadership for subsequent training in their respective buildings. They had a common understanding and the necessary commitment, developed as a result of the district efforts. Their colleagues were receptive to training provided by colleagues from the classroom next door or down the hall.

Quadrant Meetings

Following the initial summer institutes, in 1995 and 1996, the district was divided into quadrants for further training in new middle school initiatives. Each quadrant was made up of at least two of the three former districts; in this way some degree of district-wide uniformity would emerge along with overall middle school revitalization. Informal meetings of middle school teachers and administrators from each quadrant continued to cement their knowledge of the pace of program implementation, and permitted them to share their knowledge, concerns, and best practices with each other. These quadrant meetings were well attended and afforded another opportunity for sharing, building a district-wide sense of momentum regarding the implementation of the components of the middle school plan.

REVITALIZATION STRATEGY FOUR: FOCUS ON THE PRINCIPALSHIP

"Sooner or later, every middle school takes on the characteristics of its leadership" (George & Anderson, 1989). Numerous sources cite the unparalleled importance of the principals' leadership on the establishment and maintenance of long-term high quality school programs. Because the middle school movement is uniquely based on the characteristics and needs of young adolescents, effective leadership in those schools is predicated upon a continuing understanding and commitment to the middle school concept and to young adolescents these schools serve.

In many school districts, however, quality middle school programs may fail to survive over the long term because dedicated school leaders who initially establish middle school programs are eventually replaced by principals who have no

training, little experience, or long-term career interest in middle school leadership. After a period as short as five to seven years after establishing middle schools, a school district may find itself with a whole new leadership team in place in its middle schools, a group of principals who may have come from the elementary principalship or high school assistant principalship. In either case, too many of these new middle school leaders have never had the opportunity to learn about the uniqueness of young adolescence or the special nature of the middle school. Succession planning in large school districts too rarely includes selection and training procedures that guarantee that new middle school leaders have what it takes to maintain high quality programs. School district leaders in Guilford County understood that middle school revitalization simply would not occur without the right kind of leadership in every school.

The Courage to Act

The initial and crucial step was for central office leaders to realize, themselves, the critical aspect of selection and training of new middle school principals and to commit to wrenching around the selection process in several important ways. First, central office leaders conducted a careful and confidential assessment of school principals in place at the beginning of the revitalization effort. As a result, more than a third of the middle schools received new leadership within the first year of the revitalization process. The message to those who remained was that the school district was, indeed, committed to the middle school concept and to retaining only those principals who fit the middle school well. New middle school principals would no longer be selected on the basis of time served in elementary or high school buildings.

Staff Development for Principals

To achieve a new level of principals' understanding and commitment to the revitalization effort required more than careful selection. Regular, frequent, and sharply focused principals' meetings became another important source of staff development. Beginning in 1995, and extending through each month of 1996 and 1997, a major portion of the district middle school principals' meetings focused upon components of exemplary middle schools, the accompanying research findings, and the implications for school leaders in Guilford County. Most importantly, these sessions were an opportunity for the district superintendent and other highly placed central office leaders to voice their firm commitment to the middle school concept and to endorse the direction in which the district was moving to implement the seven central components of the middle school plan. There was no doubt about where schools were expected to go and who was expected to lead them there.

Examples of topics from district principals' meetings during the 1995–96 school year include:

September—The Middle School Student: Implications for Curriculum, Organization, and Instruction
October—Team Organization: Effective Practices
November—Teacher Advisory: Building Relationships and Character Education
December—Differentiated Instruction
January—Explorations/Encore
February—Assessment and Evaluation

"Jawbone"

Large group meetings of middle school principals, of the sort described here, are necessary but not sufficient. In our experience, it is also almost always necessary for central office leaders to engage in a considerable amount of what Lyndon Johnson called "jawboning." To "jawbone," in this situation, is to meet one-on-one, face-to-face, with individual school leaders to reinforce the message and to make it eminently clear that one's current position and possible future in district leadership is related to the degree to which the principal can bring his or her school into compliance with the district commitments. Over a period of two years, several middle schools experienced additional changes in leadership when it became clear that the principal in place could not or would not exert the sort of leadership that was necessary to bring about the revitalization happening elsewhere in the district. Education is always and everywhere a complex dance between the pedagogical and the political, and middle school revitalization efforts clearly reveal this truism.

REVITALIZATION STRATEGY FIVE: REGULAR, PUBLIC EVALUATION OF MIDDLE SCHOOLS

As a part of the middle school revitalization plan, the Board of Education committed the district to an annual evaluation of its middle schools, in part because members were anxious to determine that effective implementation of the revitalization plan was occurring, and also because they believed that frequent feedback from such an evaluation would spur additional efforts to succeed. Considerable time and effort were required to develop what has become a comprehensive survey instrument for middle school teachers, parents, and students (Ward, 1998). A combined effort by the district Office of Assessment and Evaluation as well as the Office of Curriculum and Instruction enabled us to develop and implement a comprehensive evaluation system that provides feedback for annual school improvement plans. This assessment effort included a careful examination of academic achievement in each school, and a comprehensive survey of parents, students, and teachers.

Annual Publication of Achievement Scores from Each School

An important part of the evaluation process has included the annual publication of how each individual middle school has fared academically.

Not only were the data made available to school board members, and the local media, but colorful posters depicting the academic progress of each middle school, and of all the middle schools as a whole group, were displayed for weeks in the district office and in the chambers of the school board. Public attention and knowledge of progress, or the lack of it, has had a significant effect on the speed and energy devoted to curriculum alignment in Guilford County middle schools. Fortunately, the result has been steady upward growth, annually, of achievement in all areas measured by the state; Guilford County middle schools now exceed state averages in every area.

The Middle School Survey

The district's instrument for the annual middle school survey is quite comprehensive, focusing on all seven of the central elements of the new middle school plan (Ward, 1998). It includes these components:

- Questions about the middle school concept—advisory, flexible block scheduling, thematic/interdisciplinary curriculum and instruction, team organization, electives, and intramurals
- Questions about instruction and learning—expectations, effort, diversity and equity, student success, use of technology and media, and differentiated instruction
- Questions about school climate—safety, discipline, behavior, respect and caring, support programs, and building cleanliness
- Questions about parental involvement
- An opportunity for respondents to "grade" the school

Using Results of the Surveys. As with the achievement test scores, each year's survey results for each middle school, and for the middle schools as a group, are compiled and made public. The first two years of surveys have revealed that the basic components of the middle school concept are now in place in Guilford County middle schools, but that much remains to be done, particularly in the area of differentiation of instruction. The central office staff has used the survey data to plan annual summer middle school professional development institutes that aim to provide teachers with the skills they need to provide for a heterogeneous group of learners in virtually every class. High Point University, located in the district, has developed and delivered specially designed courses on the topic of differentiated instruction. The district has developed a *Handbook on Differentiated Instruction* and distributed copies to all middle school teachers, as well as a system-wide curriculum resource guide for the Teacher Advisory program.

Survey Data and Continuous School Improvement. Every one of the seventeen middle school principals studies the data from each annual survey and then comes to the central office for a school improvement planning conference. Prior to the conference, principals have identified, along with their school leadership teams, goals and objectives for school improvement, and a plan for addressing those aims. Plans differ from school to school, but there is often common focus.

Data from this survey process has enabled the school district to create a cycle of continuous improvement in almost every area of the middle school. For example, team effectiveness has been enhanced. The data revealed the need for a curriculum guide in the area of teacher advisory. The purposes of advisory needed to be clarified. Subsequent staff and curriculum development have led to improvements in this area. The data from the surveys has also revealed the need for closer working relationships between core and encore teachers. Consequently a district-wide goal has been developed to improve the collaboration that occurred between both of these areas.

A major thrust has been to provide teachers with the knowledge and skills that are essential in working with student diversity. As previously noted, numerous workshops have occurred in differentiated instruction. In addition teachers have been given the opportunity to pursue licensure in academically giftedness with little expense. We believe that all students should be challenged and all students should have access to such skills.

SUMMARY

The revitalization of middle schools in Guilford County is, as many say, a "work in progress." The seven goals of revitalization in Guilford County middle schools have been approached, if not fully achieved. The good news, to date, is that academic achievement is climbing higher each year, and the results of the most recent annual survey are very positive. In that survey, better than 88% of the middle school teachers continue to assert their belief that educators in their school are effectively implementing the middle school concept. Ninety percent of middle school teachers agreed that their schools deserve a grade of C or better; eighty percent awarded their school an A or B.

Even better, perhaps, is that 91% of parents agreed that their child's middle school deserved a grade of C or better, with approximately two-thirds saying that they would give the school an A or B! The students were not far behind, with 81% giving their school a C or better; 52% gave their school an A or B.

Generally, public confidence in the schools of Guilford County has risen, perhaps because of the open, candid nature of the district's revitalization effort. The district has received positive notice in other national journals, local media are much more generous in their praise, members of the school board are pleased. Local school leaders have begun to talk about a revitalization of the high schools in the district as a next step; what more positive evidence could there be.

NOTE

1. William Alexander, generally recognized as the "father" of the middle school concept, intentionally used the term "emergent" in the title of the first book on the subject, *The Emergent Middle School*, published in New York, in 1968, by Holt, Rinehart, and Winston. He believed that effective middle schools must always be undergoing revitalization or they would cease to be alive, growing, and meaningful places for learning.

REFERENCES

Felner, R., Jackson, A., Kasak, D., Mulhall, P., Brand, S., and Flowers, N. (March, 1997). The impact of school reform for the middle years. *Phi Delta Kappan, v78*, n7, pp. 528–532, 541–550.

George, P., & Anderson, W. (1989). Maintaining the middle school: A national survey. *NASSP Bulletin,* 73, 67–74.

George, P., & Alexander, W. (1993). *The exemplary middle school,* (2nd ed). New York: Holt, Rinehart.

George, P., & Shewey, K. (1994). *New evidence for the middle school.* Columbus, OH: National Middle School Association.

National Commission on Excellence in Education (1983, April 27). An open letter to the American people. A nation at risk: The imperative for educational reform. *Education Week.*

Tye, K. (1985). *The junior high: School in search of a mission.* Landom, MD: University Press of America.

National Center for Education Statistics (September, 1997). *Elementary and secondary school districts. Common core of data survey.* Washington, DC: US Department of Education.

Ward, M. (1998). *A systems approach to middle school evaluation: Guilford County Schools Formative Approach.* A paper presented at the Annual Conference of the American Educational Research Association, San Diego, CA, April 1998.

Wheelock, A. (1992). *Crossing the tracks.* New York: The New Press.

Jerry Weast is Superintendent; *Lillie Jones* is Associate Superintendent; *Mike Priddy* is Executive Director, Curriculum and Accountability; *Larry Allred* is Director, Secondary Achievement, all with the Guilford County Public Schools, North Carolina; and *Paul George* is Professor, College of Education, University of Florida.

QUESTIONS FOR REFLECTION

1. Review the seven elements of the plan to revitalize Guilford County middle schools. What might have led the authors to suggest that these elements represented a "politically bold" move within the district? Would each of these elements draw equal support in the school district with which you are most familiar?
2. Analyze the events surrounding the "detracking" effort at three middle schools that served historically high-achieving areas in the district. What factors contributed to the successful resolution of the detracking "incident"?
3. What are the characteristics and abilities of individuals who are able to provide effective leadership for large-scale curriculum reform such as the Guilford County revitalization effort?

TEACHERS' VOICES
Putting Theory into Practice

The Educational Benefits to Middle School Students Participating in a Student/Scientist Project

MARY FOUGERE

ABSTRACT: *A seventh- and eighth-grade teacher uses the Forest Watch Project and a research/inquiry approach to bring "authentic science" into her classroom. By collecting data, analyzing samples, conducting experiments, and writing lab reports, students "become" scientists and extend their problem-solving capabilities. In addition, the program helps teachers and students achieve state and national standards in science and mathematics. Through their participation in a long-term, environmentally oriented project, students become more optimistic about their ability to positively influence the future.*

INTRODUCTION

The Forest Watch Project developed by Barry Rock, a research scientist at the University of New Hampshire, and high school Biology teacher, Phil Brown, was generated in response to a real need in our communities to bring authentic science into the classrooms of our potential future researchers and expand the amount of data available to a worthwhile monitoring project. For the Middle School classroom teacher, Forest Watch has provided a vehicle with which to incorporate national

From *Journal of Science Education and Technology* 7, no. 1 (March 1998): 25–30. Used by permission of the author and publisher.

and state standards throughout the seventh and eighth grade curriculum. It has provided teachers with the academic and material support to accomplish this.

For students, the advantages are innumerable. Not only does the inquiry approach of the project give students the opportunity to solve problems, but they are also able to apply those skills to other situations. They are linked with other students throughout the New England region, comparing data and continuing in the program through high school. Students realize that research science is a long term process that requires patience and skill at all levels. Perhaps, for me, the most important advantage is the ability of the project to offer students the opportunity to affect their future. In doing this bit of real science, students feel as though they are being a proactive participant of their future.

A final advantage of programs like Forest Watch is that they provide valuable data to research scientists participating in the student scientist partnership (SSP). Student measurements and sample collections provide access to data from a wide area that would not otherwise be available.

"Wow!" "Neat!" "Can I see my house?" "Where's the road that the school is on?" "What do the colors mean?" "How far can I zoom in?" These are some of the enthusiastic questions seventh and eighth graders in Gilmanton raised when introduced to a Landsat satellite image of their community as part of the Forest Watch Program. This is the fifth year that Gilmanton has been actively involved in the program. Forest Watch has provided for us a long-term research/ inquiry based approach to teaching Science at the Middle School level.

THE FOREST WATCH PROGRAM AT GILMANTON MIDDLE SCHOOL

In 1992, I was introduced to Earth Day: Forest Watch by Gary Lauten and Phil Brown during the annual New Hampshire Science Teacher Conference. Our K–8 school is located thirty minutes from Lake Winnipesaukee in Central New Hampshire and services approximately 400 students. Forest Watch impacts anywhere from 100–120 students at both the seventh and eighth grade levels each year. This is the fifth consecutive year that Gilmanton School has participated in the Forest Watch Project. We have accumulated four years worth of data. Last year Gilmanton began construction of a new Middle School wing to the building and we lost our original five sampling trees to the construction. While this was disappointing, we discovered was that this offered to a new group of students the opportunity to set up a new Pixel Sized Sampling Plot and to choose the five new trees in this plot to study.

I have been teaching for fifteen years, coming out of college with an Elementary Education/ Secondary Social Studies degree in 1982. In the state of New Hampshire, there is no requirement for middle school teachers to be subject certified. Many of the smaller schools, such as Gilmanton, hire teachers who can be more flexible in what they can teach and how they can teach it. It is not unusual to find a middle school teacher teaching five science courses and one reading or math class depending on the school population and the budget of that particular year.

Once in the classroom, it was Science that interested me most. Courses such as ICE offered by the Institute of Chemical Education from Madison, WI, gave me a deeper background in chemistry. Project AIMS workshops offered the skills and techniques to integrate both Science and Math, and APAST helped to add the latest in activities and methodologies to my growing science portfolio. But, it was Forest Watch that offered the opportunity to integrate the sciences and social studies to make science relevant for my students.

When I took the Gilmanton position, there was no text available for classroom use. The position had been held by a deeply respected man whose entire curriculum, unlike many of his counterparts of the time, was hands on. Unfortunately, when he passed on, so did the curriculum he created. By '91, I had much in my bag of tricks to offer students.

However, it wasn't until partway through our second year of Forest Watch, that I realized that a metamorphosis had occurred: We were not only studying what science was about, but rather we became the scientists ourselves. The students knew that by collecting their data, sending their samples, doing their experiments, that this was the real thing! The six weeks in Spring that we spent learning the techniques for the protocols in seventh grade blossomed into a need to come back in eighth grade to analyze the data and a need to leave accurate records for the underclass students to follow. Today, Forest Watch is interwoven throughout both seventh and eighth grade throughout the year.

Forest Watch was developed in 1992 as a means of including K–12th grade students in hands-on science and math activities (Rock and Lauten, 1996). Business is actively involved in our high schools through such programs as "School to Work" and Business Partnerships under the assumption that by exposing and training youngsters early in certain work skills, students would then make a better transition into the work force. The Forest Watch Program offers that same opportunity for students in the area of environmental research science. It is an ongoing student/scientist partnership between professors, research scientists, and graduate students at the University of New Hampshire and K–12th grade students throughout the northeast. The difference between the business partnership and our Forest Watch partnership lies in the fact that our goal is to foster in children problem-solving capabilities that can be applied to any facet of life as well as providing opportunities for students to gain competency in Science and Math content area. Of course, we always welcome and encourage potential research scientists. . . .

In New Hampshire as well as other states across New England, it is becoming more and more important for a teacher to bring his/her curriculum in line with state and national standards. The paradigm of national standards and reform for Science, *Benchmarks for Science Literacy,* has the goal of reforming in science educa-

tion as a means of achieving scientific literacy for all Americans (AAAS, 1993; NRC, 1995).

In addition, New Hampshire recently instituted mandatory statewide proficiency standard testing in grades three, six and ten with the goal of gaining accountability and uniformity of the skills and content of its students' curriculum (NH Curriculum Frameworks, 1995). Forest Watch is a program that allows teachers to work within those Standards and Benchmarks. Hands-on activities, the linking of science and math, technology, and measurement and calculation are basic standards emphasized both at the state and the national level. Forest Watch addresses each of these as well as evaluating student measurement data for accuracy. Details on the measurement activities and data collection procedures can be found in Rock and Lauten (1996).

As part of the Gilmanton Middle Schools involvement in Forest Watch, we have permanently tagged five white pine trees and have been measuring both height and diameter at breast height (DBH-defined as 1.35m above the ground) of these five trees for the last four years. At all grade levels, accuracy of measurement is a major issue, especially when reporting data to an on-going research project. Because of the ramifications of incorrect data, students are required to be more responsible for their accuracy. The approach that we take begins with the overall question, "Why is accuracy important when you are collecting measurement data?" When presenting the concept to students, I hold up a simple bar graph that my seventh graders created in 1995 showing the cumulative DBH data from one of our five trees from 1992–1994. By examining the bar graph, students visualize the exaggerated shrinking and swelling of the trunk! Even at the seventh grade level, with limited math backgrounds, the mistakes are obvious.

Students logically come up with the next set of questions: What is being measured? What is DBH (diameter at breast height)? How can we be more accurate? What can we do to make sure we measure the correct DBH each year?

Students create the list of what they need to do to insure accuracy: making all measurements at the same height, using the same measuring device, making many measurements of the same tree, etc. There are activities embedded in the Forest Watch Program that allow students further investigation if students don't have the background for determining just how accurate a measure is.

The next phase allows students the opportunity to go out to our study site and measure the DBH based on their suggestions. Forest Watch provides a set of protocols that must be followed to control variables from one school to the next for the good of the overall program. I try to gently guide the students toward the correct approach without actually handing them a set of procedures.

This inquiry approach prevents students from forming many of the common misconceptions about how the DBH measurement is done. Rather, they are asked to be the scientist and to create an approach (with guidance from me) that is possible, accountable, repeatable, and accurate. It is by following this process that students 1) develop a better understanding of the inquiry approach of the scientific method, 2) insure accuracy in the measurements they make, and 3) develop the skills necessary to approach the problem of how to be sure they are accurate.

The evidence for this comes later in the year when students are asked to create an experiment using not the DBH of a white pine as practiced, but something entirely different: the hatching of brine shrimp eggs. I have yet to have a student want to do his/her experiment in isolation and with no repeat trials. More often than not, students ask each other to double check their numbers and to recount the numbers of eggs hatched. This, from a teacher's perspective, is the payoff for Forest Watch's inquiry approach: the ability to apply knowledge and skills learned in Forest Watch to other situations.

I attempt to integrate Forest Watch in almost every unit of Science at both the seventh and the eighth grade level. This allows students to appreciate the inclusiveness of the overall project. Students also are aware of opportunities to continue with this project when they go on to high school and that the project will be there when they reach college level. Knowing they have personal connections at UNH with Forest Watch researchers and the opportunity to bring useful knowledge with them to the Gilford High School, where Forest Watch is also a part of the curriculum, are great motivators for our children.

We use Forest Watch information on atmospheric and tropospheric ozone, as well as other air borne pollutants, when tracing pollutants as part of an introduction to the Forest Watch unit in seventh grade. The concepts are reintroduced in eighth grade chemistry when studying the chemical structure of molecules as we examine the shape of O_3. Students learn about the periodic table, but can only begin to appreciate the relationships and reactions that are possible between the elements once they understand the chemical formulas and molecular shape of some of these pollutants.

Another example of how we fit Forest Watch into an already crowded curriculum occurs just prior to our seventh grade Mt. Washington hike. Each spring, our seventh grade students hike to the summit of Mt. Washington, tour the observatory, stay overnight in the Hut in the Clouds, then hike back down. As part of our preparation, we examine slide pictures of and satellite images of spruce damage on Camel Hump Mountain in Vermont. We then use Landsat data with Multi-Spec to find the area of the trail that students will hike and to speculate as to which areas along this trail might have acid rain damage to the spruce trees. During the hike, students are asked to watch for areas of damage. Since our trees in Gilmanton are relatively healthy, this experience has quite an impact on our students.

THE ADVANTAGES OF PARTICIPATING IN AN SSP

Students develop an understanding that they are a significant part of a larger project. Our students learn to write lab reports, develop hypotheses, control variables, collect data and draw conclusions in an integrated series of activities rather than in isolated activities. With Forest Watch, our students realize for the first time that research science is a long term process: one experiment or protocol is performed, then another is done, and still a third is done, until all of the data are collected for that year. However, it takes looking at the data from *all of these* protocols in comparison to data collected from other students in other communities and in previous years in order to make appropriate conclusions.

We receive back from UNH the results of the portable spectrometer scan shortly after sending our white pine samples to UNH. These results come in the form of a line graph. (Later, we receive cumulative data from all the participating schools.) During training, we were provided with a graph entitled: *Landsat Thematic Mapper Bands Overlayed on a VIRUS Vegetation Spectrum* which indicates percent reflectance for healthy white pine. Various bands indicate leaf pigment, cell structure and water content. We particularly look at the NDVI which indicates the relationship of the biomass to chlorophyll, the REIP (Red Edge Inflection Point) which indicates cell structure, and 5/4 which is an indicator of water content. Students work in teams to examine the data. Danielle DiRosa and Kim Hyslop's assignment was to determine the condition of tree #41 in the south quadrant. They realized they needed to look at more than one year's worth of data. After examining data from '92–'94, their overall conclusions were:

> The results from our study from 1992 through 1994 T41S needles showed that the 5/4 and REIP stayed the same from year to year. The results showed that the NDVI was unhealthy each year also. The NDVI was the only unhealthy part of our test. The NDVI or the comparison and relationship of the biomass to the chlorophyll is continually unhealthy each year of our testing. The NDVI ranged from .768–.8223.
>
> The 5/4 test came out healthy for all three years, which means that the water level is healthy. The tree was not under any water stress. Also, the REIP was healthy. All three years the REIP was above 705. So, the results prove that the cell structure is healthy in tree 41south.

Clearly, these students came away with the realization that they next need to examine the results of other schools' data and with an appreciation of the technological tools available in helping to assess our forest. Not all students realized such positive news with their quadrant sample and this led students back to asking the question, "Why?" which in turn leads them to back to the wider data set.

There are many advantages to being part of the Forest Watch community of schools. University personnel have come to our rural school several times, bringing visitors from the Czech Republic, equipment like the portable spectrometer used to scan our samples that are sent to UNH, and offering the students both training and insights to the program. Several students have come with me to the university to gain a better understanding of the scope of the overall project.

This spring, we will be taking our entire eighth grade to UNH to meet with Forest Watch people from the university, tour the lab where our samples are sent and work directly with computers to analyze Forest Watch data. Building these relationships is an important aspect of this project. As a teacher, it makes me more accountable to other science teachers that I work with as well as to the professors at UNH. It keeps me in touch with current information and provides me with the added background, support, and confidence that I need to help make this a success.

From the students' perspective, Forest Watch offers an opportunity to feel as though they are interacting in a positive way with their future. Many young adolescents have developed a pessimistic attitude toward life and the world around them. Part of that attitude is an attempt to sort out his/her place in the world. Last fall while studying acid rain and other types of pollution, one of my brightest students asked the big question: "What's the use? We're just going to destroy this world in the end, and I can't do anything by myself anyway." After pulling my heart out of its pit, I didn't even have to think about the answer. It just flowed.

> This is the year, Sarah, that you will take charge of your future. Forest Watch is an opportunity for you to collectively make a difference. By monitoring this piece of the earth, by examining the health of our forests and comparing their health to other parts of the world, we gain a better understanding of the big picture. It is in understanding the whole picture that we can make legislation, raise awareness, and take proactive stances.

One of the biggest advantages that I see with Forest Watch is that it offers hands-on opportunities for my children to gain some control and hope over their future.

One of the important lessons learned from several years of Forest Watch student data is that improvement in air quality leads to healthier trees. The ozone levels along the seacoast of New Hampshire were unhealthful for several dates during the summer of 1991. Needles produced that year showed many symptoms of damage. Ozone levels were much lower in the summer of 1992 and needles produced in that year were much more healthy. If air quality can be improved, our forests will respond by becoming more healthy.

FITTING SSP ACTIVITIES INTO AN ALREADY CROWDED CURRICULUM

The Forest Watch program is designed in a manner that students must do several protocol-directed activities including: the methods used to set up the pixel sized sampling plot, the DBH, tree height, needle length, types and amounts of symptoms, etc. There are also other protocols that are not required but help to substantiate the information we receive back from UNH from the spectrometer scan of the branch samples sent. Chlorophyll extraction and microscopic study of

needle anatomy are two examples of optional protocols that can be accomplished in the lab. By comparing the data from the UNH spectral scan to the data students collect in the lab, students realize that there are many different ways to collect the same type of data and that it is important to cross-validate one technique with another.

The optional protocols and activities offer the teacher the flexibility of incorporating what fits best with his/her already crowded curriculum. Often, I make my judgments on what to include according to the time available and what needs to be covered under the standards. I attempt to relate whatever we are doing to the white pine or the overall Forest Watch project. Seventh graders, for instance, learn about life cycles, cell structure and disease. While we are studying life cycles and growing Wisconsin Fast plants, we examine the life cycle of the white pine. While studying cell structure, we learn how to make cross sections of the pine needles using carrots to hold the needles so that they can be cut with razor blades. We find stomates on the needles, look for areas of damage such as chlorosis and necrosis, and try to find evidence of other damage agents (insects, fungi, mechanical damage, etc.)

State curriculum standards include requiring students to "demonstrate an increasing ability to use technology to observe nature." (K–12 Science Curriculum Frameworks, 1995) What better example of applied technology than to take those same students who "Oohed and Aahed!" at the first sight of the Landsat image in seventh grade and allow them to take the data themselves and manipulate it. Our eighth graders spend a month each Fall in the computer lab doing just that. They use MultiSpec software and images of Beverly, Massachusetts, Pease International Tradeport and finally Gilmanton to conduct an unsupervised classification of the areas. Students are able to assign pixels with specific reflectivity a particular class. For example, knowing where the runway is at Pease, students can zoom in on the runway and choose a single pixel. Students assign that pixel the name 'asphalt'. During the unsupervised classification, all other pixels with that reflectivity automatically become 'asphalt'. Students choose a second pixel in what they know to be a stand of white pines and assign that pixel the term, 'white pine'. This continues until students have five or six classifications that they are confident of. Multispec will then classify the entire image and we are able to print out the image in color for the students. The image of Gilmanton is then 'ground truthed' for accuracy.

SUMMARY

As our community becomes larger and our student population becomes more and more mobile, there is ever increasing need to meet national and state standards within our classrooms. Forest Watch, an example of a student scientist partnership (SSP), offers many opportunities for participants ranging from direct participation with the professional scientific community, improvement in student attitudes and scientific growth, teacher enhancement, and offering teachers a sense of making a difference. The partnership developed between UNH and Forest Watch schools goes far beyond the classroom. It reaches across our communities, into our forests in many towns across New England, and indeed, across the globe.

REFERENCES

American Association for Advancement of Science (AAAS). 1993. *Benchmarks for Science Literacy.* New York, New York, Oxford Press.

National Research Council (NRC). 1995. *National Science Education Standards NRC.* Washington, D.C. Academy Press.

Rock, B. N. and Lauten, G. N. 1996. K–12th Grade Students as Active Contributors to Research Investigations. *Journal of Science and Technology,* vol. 5(4):255–266.

The New Hampshire K–12 Science Curriculum Framework. 1995. Regional Alliance for Mathematics and Science Education Reform. Plymouth, NH.

Mary Fougere is a middle school/Forest Watch teacher at Gilmanton School, Gilmanton Iron Works, New Heaven, New Hampshire.

QUESTIONS FOR REFLECTION

1. How might the research/inquiry approach be applied in the curricular area and at the level with which you are most familiar?
2. What approaches to assessing students' learning are appropriate for projects like the Forest Watch Program?
3. What criticisms might some parents make about curricular experiences such as the Forest Watch Program? How would you respond to those criticisms?

LEARNING ACTIVITIES

Critical Thinking

1. Which developmental changes discussed in Chapter 3 should guide curriculum planners in designing educational programs for transescents and early adolescents?

2. What are the essential elements of effective curricula for transescents and early adolescents?

3. William M. Alexander, generally acknowledged as the "father" of the middle school, once said, "Every student should be well known as a person by at least one adult in the school who accepts responsibility for the student's guidance." What does it mean to be "known as a person?" Why is such a relationship with an adult of critical importance to middle-level students? What steps can teachers and administrators take to ensure that each student has such a relationship?

4. What problems might a junior high/middle-level student have if he or she has not sufficiently resolved the first four psychosocial crises that are part of the human life cycle as described by Erik Erikson (see "Erik Erikson's Developmental Stages: A Healthy Personality for Every Child" in Chapter 3).

Application Activities

1. Pioneering work in developing curricula for transescents was done by Carleton W. Washburne at the Skokie Junior High School in Winnetka and is described in Chapter 7 of *Winnetka: The History and Significance of an Educational Experiment* by Washburne and Sidney P. Marland (Prentice-Hall, 1963). Would the activities described in that chapter be appropriate and challenging for today's transescents? Which of the four perspectives on curriculum that William H. Schubert discusses in Chapter 1 do those activities represent?

2. When you were a transescent and early adolescent, what school experiences helped you to grow and learn? What experiences hindered you? What implications do these experiences have for your current and future curriculum planning activities?

3. Drawing from the material in this chapter, develop a short questionnaire or set of interview questions that curriculum planners could use to learn more about transescents and early adolescents.

4. Invite a group of junior high/middle school teachers to your class and ask them to describe the steps they take in planning curricula for their students. What do they see as the most important curriculum criteria to use in planning?

Field Experiences

1. Talk with a group of transescents and early adolescents about the social forces of concern to them in their school, their community, their nation, and the world. Compare your findings with those of your fellow students.

2. Visit a junior high or middle school and ask to see the school's statement of philosophy (or mission statement) and/or set of schoolwide goals. To what extent do these materials reflect the points of view expressed in this chapter?

3. Visit an agency in your community that offers services to transescents and early adolescents and their families. Ask a staff member to describe the services that are offered. Report your findings to the rest of your class.

Internet Activities

1. Go to one or more of the following locations and gather information, research results, publications, and resources on effective educational programs for transescents and early adolescents.

   Center for Adolescent Studies (**http://education.indiana.edu/cas/**)
   National Middle School Association (**http://www.nmsa.org/**)
   Online Educational Resources (**http://quest.arc.nasa.gov/OER/**)
   Center of Education for the Young Adolescent
   (**http://vms.www.uwplatt.edu/~ceya/**)
   Middle Level Leadership Center (**http://www.mllc.org/home.htm**)
   The Middle School Information Center
   (**http://www.vmsa.org/VMCENT/default.html**)

2. Go to Kidlink (**http://www.org/english/index.html**), an organization dedicated to using the WWW to link children and youth through the age of fifteen from around the world. From this location, visit areas accessible to adults to determine the educational interests, needs, and concerns of transescents and early adolescents.

3. Go to Kidlink at **http://kidlink.org/english/general/curric.html**, an educator-oriented site where you will find instructional activities that integrate various areas of the curriculum. Compile a list of activities appropriate for transescents and early adolescents. From here you can "visit" school sites where students and teachers use Kidlink in the classroom.

BOOKS AND ARTICLES TO REVIEW

Research and Theory in Education for Transescents and Early Adolescents

Andrews. David W., et al. "The Adolescent Transitions Program for High-Risk Teens and their Parents: Toward a School-Based Intervention." *Education and Treatment of Children* 18, no. 4 (November 1995): 478–498.

Beane, James A. "Problems and Possibilities for an Integrative Curriculum." *Middle School Journal* 25, no. 1 (September 1993): 18–23.

Brady, Marion. "Beyond Interdisciplinary: Preparing Teachers for New Curriculum." *NASSP Bulletin* 80, no. 580 (May 1996): 1–8.

Brozo, William G., et al. "A Walk through Gracie's Garden: Literacy and Cultural Explorations in a Mexican American Junior High School." *Journal of Adolescent & Adult Literacy* 40, no. 3 (November 1996): 164–170.

Carnegie Council on Adolescent Development. *Turning Points: Preparing American Youth for the 21st Century.* Carnegie Corporation of New York, 1989.

Collins, Rhoda Powers. "Middle School Mathematics: Student Empowerment through Quality Innovations." *Clearing House* 67, no. 4 (March–April 1994): 180–181.

Corso, Marjorie, and Stewart, Ann B. "Middle School Successes." *Strategies* 9, no. 3 (November–December 1995): 26–29.

Dehart, Paula, and Cook, Perry A. "Transforming Middle Schools through Integrated Curriculum." *Voices from the Middle* 4, no. 2 (April 1997): 2–6.

Felner, Robert D., et al. "The Impact of School Reform for the Middle Years." *Phi Delta Kappan* 78, no. 7 (March 1997): 528–532, 541–550.

George, Paul S. *The Exemplary Middle School,* 2nd Ed. Fort Worth: Harcourt Brace Jovanovich College Publishers, 1993.

George, Paul S., Lawrence, Gordon, and Bushnell, Donna. *Handbook for Middle School Teaching,* 2nd Ed. New York: Longman, 1998.

George, Paul S., Stevenson, Chris, Thomason, Julia, and Beane, James. *The Middle School—and Beyond.*

Alexandria, VA: Association for Supervision and Curriculum Development, 1992.

Greenlaw, M. Jean, and Tipps, Steve. "A Literature Approach to Middle Grade Math." *Clearing House* 71, no. 9 (September–October 1997): 9–13.

Hawkins, Mary Louise, and Graham, M. Dolores. "Four Principles for Reforming Middle Schools." *Childhood Education* 73, no. 5 (1997): 278–281.

Holt, Dan G. "Positively Humorous: Teaching Gifted Middle School Students to Use Positive Humor to Cope with Stress." *Gifted Child Today Magazine* 19, no. 1 (January–February 1996): 18–21, 38–39.

Hope, Warren C. "Meeting the Needs of Middle Level Students through Service Learning." *NASSP Bulletin* 81, no. 587 (March 1997): 39–45.

Hough, David L. "The Elemiddle School: A Model for Middle Grades Reform." *Principal* 7, no. 3 (January 1995): 6–9.

Irvin, Judith L. *Transforming Middle Level Education: Perspectives and Possibilities.* Boston: Allyn and Bacon, 1992.

Kagan, Jerome, and Gall, Susan B., eds. *The Gale Encyclopedia of Childhood and Adolescence.* Detroit: Gale Research, 1998.

Kalafat, John, and Gagliano, Carla. "The Use of Simulations to Assess the Impact of an Adolescent Suicide Response Curriculum." *Suicide and Life-Threatening Behavior* 26, no. 4 (Winter 1996): 359–364.

Kennedy, Dora F., and De Lorenzo, William E. "Point: The Case for Exploratory Programs in Middle/Junior High School." *Foreign Language Annals* 27, no. 1 (Spring 1994): 69–73.

Lammers, Jane W. "The Effects of Curriculum on Student Health Behaviors: A Case Study of the Growing Healthy Curriculum on Health Behaviors of Eighth Grade Students." *Journal of Health Education* 27, no. 5 (September–October 1996): 278–282.

Lewis, Paul. "Why Humor?" *Voices from the Middle* 2, no. 3 (September 1995): 10–16.

Lipsitz, Joan, et al. "Speaking with One Voice: A Manifesto for Middle-Grades Reform." *Phi Delta Kappan* 78, no. 7 (March 1997): 533–540.

Lisman, David C. *Toward a Civil Society: Civic Literacy and Service Learning.* Westport, CT: Greenwood Publishing, 1998.

Long, John. "Survey of Montessori Adolescent Programs: Interpretive Commentary." *NAMTA Journal* (July 1994): 1–64.

Manning, M. Lee, et al. "What Works in Urban Middle Schools." *Childhood Education* 71, no. 4 (Summer 1995): 221–224.

Muth, Denise K., and Alverman, Donna E. *Teaching and Learning in the Middle Grades.* Boston: Allyn and Bacon, 1992.

Pollak, Judy P., and Mills, Rebecca A. "True Collaboration: Building and Maintaining Successful Teams." *Schools in the Middle* 6, no. 5 (May–June 1997): 28–32.

Powell, Richard, et al. "Sustaining a Nonlinear Integrative Learning Context: Middle Level Teachers' Perspectives." *Research in Middle Level Education Quarterly* 20, no. 2 (Winter 1997): 23–63.

Russell, Jill F. "Relationships between the Implementation of Middle-Level Program Concepts and Student Achievement." *Journal of Curriculum and Supervision* 12, no. 2 (Winter 1997): 169–185.

Schiddell, Betty L., and Ethington, Corinna A. "Teaching of Geometry in the Eighth Grade Mathematics Curriculum: Findings from the Second International Mathematics Study." *Focus on Learning Problems in Mathematics* 16, no. 2 (Spring 1994): 51–61.

Stevenson, Chris, and Carr, Judy F., eds. *Integrated Studies in the Middle Grades.* New York: Teachers College Press, 1993.

Tindal, Gerald, and Nolet, Victor. "Curriculum-Based Measurement in Middle and High Schools: Critical Thinking Skills in Content Areas." *Focus on Exceptional Children* 27, no. 7 (March 1995): 1–22.

Totten, Samuel, and Pederson, Jon E. *Social Issues and Service at the Middle Level.* Boston: Allyn and Bacon, 1997.

Wegner, Gregory. "What Lessons Are There from the Holocaust for My Generation Today? Perspectives on Civic Virtue from Middle School Youth." *Journal of Curriculum and Supervision* 13, no. 2 (Winter 1998): 167–183.

Theory into Practice: Strategies for Middle-Level/Junior High Programs

Doggett, Keri. "City Youth: A Middle School Core Curriculum Model." *Social Studies Review* 36, no. 2 (Spring–Summer 1997): 28–29.

Engelland, Holly. "Catapulting: Bringing the Middle Ages to the Middle Level Classroom." *Science Scope* 17, no. 5 (February 1994): 30–36.

Field, Sharon, et al. "Meeting Functional Curriculum Needs in Middle School General Education Classrooms." *Teaching Exceptional Children* 26, no. 2 (Winter 1994): 40–43.

Griffin, Kathy. "Writing in the Social Studies Classroom." *Voices from the Middle* 4, no. 2 (April 1997): 31–37.

Harrington, Randal. "New Standards for Teaching Middle School Science: Now that We Have Them, What Do We Do?" *Journal of Research in Rural Education* 13, no. 1 (Spring 1997): 37–46.

Holzman-Benshalom, Yona, and Cohen, Rimona. "Multimedia in Junior High." *Educational Leadership* 55, no. 3 (November 1997): 64–66.

Howe, Ann C., and Bell, Jerry. "Factors Associated with Successful Implementation of Interdisciplinary Curriculum Units." *Research in Middle Level Education Quarterly* 21, no. 2 (Winter 1998): 39–52.

Lockhart, James R. "Confessions of a High School Teacher." *English Journal* 86, no. 1 (January 1997): 105–108.

Morrow, Linda R. "Readers 'Fresh' from the Middle." *Voices from the Middle* 2, no. 2 (April 1995): 13–20.

Nidiffer, Linda G., and Moon, Sidney M. "Middle School Seminars: The Purdue Three-Stage Model Provides Exciting Opportunities for Pull-Out Programs." *Gifted Child Today Magazine* 17, no. 2 (March–April 1994): 24–27, 39, 40.

Peterson, Norman K., and Orde, Barbara J. "Implementing Multimedia in the Middle School Curriculum: Pros, Cons and Lessons Learned." *T.H.E. Journal* 22, no. 7 (February 1995): 70–75.

Taradash, Gloria. "Extending Educational Opportunities for Middle School Gifted Students." *Gifted Child Quarterly* 38, no. 2 (1994): 89–94.

Yeager, Elizabeth Anne, et al. "Now Is Your Time!: A Middle School History Unit." *Social Education* 61, no. 4 (April–May 1997): 207–209.

Videotapes

Interdisciplinary Team Organization is a two-part videotape on interdisciplinary planning and faculty teaming at the middle school/junior high school level. *Tracking and Ability Grouping: Which Way for American Schools?* Part One reviews the research and experience with ability grouping and tracking, and Part Two describes alternatives to current practices. *The Modern Middle School* is a four-part series that addresses topics such as the nature of the middle school learner, advisor–advisee programs, interdisciplinary team organization, exploratory programs, and student grouping options. (All available from Teacher Education Resources, P.O. Box 206, Gainesville, FL 32602, (800) 874-7777.)

CHAPTER 9

Education for Middle Adolescents

FOCUS QUESTIONS

1. What are the major developmental concerns of middle adolescents?
2. What are some of the "internal problems" that confront today's high schools?
3. What were the reasons behind the development of the comprehensive high school in America?
4. What recommendations have been made for restructuring high schools?
5. What are some appropriate curricular goals for middle adolescents?

The age range of adolescence in our society is approximately age ten to age twenty. Transescence and early adolescence were described in Chapter 8 as the period from approximately age ten to fifteen; middle adolescence, then, is the period approximately from ages fifteen to eighteen, the high school years.

DEVELOPMENTAL CHALLENGES OF MIDDLE ADOLESCENCE

Middle adolescents are beginning to seek some assurance of eventual economic independence from parents and other adults. They sense their new intellectual powers and their need to develop additional cognitive skills. Their dominant motivation most often is to achieve social status within the adolescent community and to meet the expectations of their peers. Often, they feel the tension between two orientations—engaging in behavior approved by adults versus engaging in behavior approved by peers.

Middle adolescents, according to Erik Erikson, seek a "sense of identity" and the development of values they can call their own. According to Bennett M. Berger, a well-known sociologist and author of *An Essay on Culture: Symbolic Structure and Social Structure* (1995), adolescence is one of the ways that culture violates nature by insisting that, for an increasing number of years, young persons postpone their claims to the privileges and responsibilities of common citizenship. At this point, you may wish to review the perspectives on human development that have been advanced by Erikson, Lawrence Kohlberg, Carol Gilligan, and others by turning to Chapter 3.

The world of today's middle adolescents is dramatically different from the one their parents experienced. Technological changes, a multiplicity of social options and values, the pervasiveness of crime and violence, the media's intrusion and influence, and the blurring of the lines separating adults and children have a tremendous impact on today's youth. Adults may have difficulty comprehending the realities that characterize the lives of many youth today—for example, results from the South Carolina Youth Risk Behavior Survey revealed that 47 percent of adolescent males and 13 percent of adolescent females carried weapons, and large numbers reported fighting; the strongest predictors of weapon carrying and fighting were alcohol and drug use and sexual intercourse (Valois and McKewon, 1998). In this chapter's Teachers' Voices article, "Making the Circle Bigger: A Journey in the South Bronx," Susan McCray describes how she provides her students with educational experiences to help them understand and transcend the harsh realities of their daily lives.

THE QUEST FOR SELF-IDENTITY

As young people move through the period of middle adolescence, they come to attach less importance to the reactions of their peers and more to their quest for a strong self-identity. They tend to move from relying on others to self-reliance; their own sense of what matters, rather than the reactions of peers, guides their actions. Eliot Wigginton, the originator of the Foxfire approach to the high school curriculum, says in *Sometimes a Shining Moment: The Foxfire Experience* that the needs of middle adolescents are best met by allowing them "to do things of importance—to do real work of real consequence in the real world"(1985, p. 236). To the extent that middle adolescents have these experiences they are less likely to see the school curriculum as meaningless and to turn to self-destructive activities such as drug abuse, dropping out, school absenteeism, suicide, teenage pregnancy, vandalism, criminal activity, and cultism.

Often, though, middle adolescents gain their independence and sense of identity only after going through a period of conflict with parents, teachers, and other adults. In far too many instances, middle adolescents express their defiance and rebellion by turning to the self-destructive activities mentioned above. The challenge for those who plan curricula for middle adolescents, then, is to provide them with appropriate ways to express their emerging sense of independence or, as Carolyn Mamchur (1990) suggests, opportunities to use their "power" to decide what and how they learn. To help middle adolescents traverse this challenging period of their lives and prepare for their eventual transition into adulthood, M. Lee Manning and Richard Saddlemire (see "Implementing Middle School Concepts into High Schools") suggest that high schools adopt four middle-level practices: advisor–advisee programs, exploratory programs, interdisciplinary teams, and school climate enhancement efforts.

CHALLENGES TO THE AMERICAN HIGH SCHOOL

In addition to being buffeted by frequent waves of criticism and calls for reform from external sources, high schools in the United States have been coping with a myriad of internal problems during the last few decades. Many high schools are plagued by hostility, violence, despair, alienation, and drug abuse. Their expansive campuses, large enrollments, and bureaucratic organizational structures make matters worse; and students often express underlying negativity toward teachers, administrators, and staff. Some students find their school experiences unenjoyable, if not painful. Minority group students may feel that they receive differential treatment. Typically, students ask for more openness and mutual respect. Neither students themselves nor teachers see students as influential in setting school policies. Many students believe they are not learning as much as they should. The high school typically does not use the rich resources of the community.

In addition, confirmation that high school curricula are not as rigorous as they ought to be comes from the students themselves. One survey of college students for their views on what should be included in the high school curriculum indicated that students wanted more reading, literature and vocabulary, speaking and writing skills, research papers, and computer courses (Sandel, 1991).

DEVELOPMENT OF THE "COMPREHENSIVE" HIGH SCHOOL

To meet the needs of middle adolescents and to catch up with the Soviet Union in the production of engineers and scientists, former Harvard University President James B. Conant and others called for the development of the "comprehensive" high school during the 1950s and 1960s. The comprehensive high school would "provide learning opportunities for all . . . adolescents within a range from barely educable to the gifted and talented. Its purpose [would be] to enable each pupil (a) to develop to his [sic] greatest potential for his [sic] own success and happiness and (b) to make a maximum contribution to the American society of which he [sic] is a part" (Gilchrist, 1962, p. 32).

Conant recommended that "every pupil who can do so effectively and rewardingly should take a minimum of eighteen academic subjects" (1962, p. 29). This course of study, which Conant estimated 15 to 20 percent of students could complete "with profit," would include four years of mathematics, four years of one foreign language, three years of science, four years of English, and three years of social studies.

Expectations for the comprehensive high school were high. As the superintendent of University City Public Schools in Missouri wrote in 1962: "America desperately needs the developed abilities of all its youth. Citizens and educators have, in the comprehensive high school, an exciting and valuable tool to fulfill America's needs for the future" (Gilchrist, 1962, p. 33).

The comprehensive high school, however, has proven inadequate for the program of education many middle adolescents need. Some observers (see, for example, Joseph Murphy's "Explaining 'Academic Drift' in High Schools: Strategies for Improvement" in this chapter) believe that attempts to develop comprehensive high school curricula that address the needs of all middle adolescents have resulted in curricula that lack coherence. Similarly, Fred M. Newman (see "Can Depth Replace Coverage in the High School Curriculum?" in this chapter) asserts that high schools tend to try to teach "too much" to students. As a result, high school curricula focus more on *covering content* than on *developing understanding*. Similarly, in "Rethinking the Benefits of the College-Bound Curriculum," Nel Noddings argues for a reconsideration of the benefits of breadth in the high school curriculum.

THE GREAT DEBATE ON HIGH SCHOOL REFORM

The 1980s saw a plethora of reform-oriented reports and books on American education, most of which focused on the high school and called for raising standards, promoting excellence, and rebuilding public confidence in the schools. The 1983 report by the National Commission on Excellence in Education, *A Nation at Risk: The Imperative for Educational Reform,* launched a great national debate on how to improve high schools in the United States. With alarm, the report claimed that the nation had "been committing an act of unthinking, unilateral educational disarmament" and cited the high rate of illiteracy among seventeen-year-olds and minority youth, a drop in SAT scores, and the need for college and business to offer remedial reading, writing, and computation. In response to the perceived ineffectiveness of America's schools, *A Nation at Risk* recommended raising standards (not clearly defined), requiring "Five New Basics" (four years of English, three years of mathematics, three years of science, three years of social studies, and one-half year of computer science) for graduation, assessing students' learning more frequently, and lengthening the school day and the school year.

Another widely discussed report was Ernest Boyer's (1983) *High School: A Report on Secondary Education in America* sponsored by the Carnegie Foundation for the Advancement of Teaching. *High School* recommends first and foremost a "core of common learnings" and service-oriented activities for all, more flexibility in scheduling, a program of electives to develop individual interests, the mastery of language, and a single track for academic and vocational students.

Broad, sweeping reform of America's high schools was also called for in *Horace's Compromise: The Dilemma of the American High School* by Theodore Sizer (1984). Through his analysis of the professional dilemmas encountered by Horace Smith, a hypothetical high school English teacher, Sizer built a case for "revamping the structure" of the high school. He asserted that higher-order thinking skills should form the core of the high school curriculum and they should be learned through students' confrontations with engaging, challenging problems. Sizer also believed that high schools should have fewer and clearer goals, and should require mastery of subject matter for graduation. Interdisciplinary nongraded curricula were essential, he believed, and instruction should be adapted to students' diverse learning styles. To put his ideas into practice, Sizer began the Coalition of Essential Schools at Brown University. From a modest beginning with five schools in 1984, the Coalition grew to more than one thousand schools and twenty-four regional support centers by the end of the century.

In *Horace's School: Redesigning the American High School* (1992), Sizer further described the Coalition's approach to restructuring high schools. A basic premise of the Coalition is that top-down, standardized solutions to school problems don't work and that teachers must play a key role in changing schools. Since no two Coalition schools are alike, each is encouraged to develop an approach to restructuring that meets the needs of faculty, students, and community. However, the restructuring efforts of Coalition schools are guided by ten common principles, two of which specifically address the content of the educational program:

1. The school should focus on helping young people develop the habit of using their minds well. Schools should not attempt to be comprehensive if such a claim is made at the expense of the school's central intellectual purpose. Schools should be learner centered, addressing students' social and emotional development, as well as their academic progress.
2. The school's academic goal should be simple: that each student master a limited number of essential skills and areas of knowledge. The aphorism "Less Is More" should dominate. Curricular decisions should be guided by student interest, developmentally appropriate practice, and the aim of thorough student mastery and achievement. Students of all ages should have many opportunities to discover and construct meaning from their own experiences (Coalition of Essential Schools, 1998).

In *Horace's Hope: What Works for the American High School* (1996), Sizer describes thirteen lessons he learned from a decade of efforts to reform America's high schools. In this chapter's "New Hope for High Schools: Lessons from Reform-Minded Educators," excerpted from *Horace's Hope,* Sizer describes four of those lessons.

GOALS FOR THE EDUCATION OF MIDDLE ADOLESCENTS

What goals should be included in programs of education for middle adolescents? As we have emphasized throughout this book, curriculum goals should be derived, in large measure, from the four curriculum bases—social forces, theories of human development, the nature of learning, and the nature of knowledge. With this perspective in mind, the goals would surely include the following:

1. Encouraging the development and practice of critical thinking, what the Coalition of Essential Schools has described as "the habit of using [one's] mind well"
2. Helping learners begin the process of career development, whether through vocational guidance, vocational education, or additional academic development
3. Providing learners with experiences that enhance their citizenship skills, sense of responsibility, and understanding of and concern for the world about them

4. Helping students to become self-directed, lifelong learners (In this chapter's "Case Study in Curriculum Implementation" article, "Horizonte—Where Students Come First," James P. Anderson and his coauthors describe a high school program that allows students to help direct their own learning.)

5. Assisting learners to become self-actualized and secure in their identities

6. Assisting learners in making the transition to the world of work, to participation in their communities, and to the world of the future (In "Technological Literacy: A Twenty-First-Century Imperative" in this chapter, Merrill M. Oaks, Richard Gantman, and Melvin Pedras explore the need to make technological literacy a national priority.)

At the start of the twenty-first century, virtually every state has responded to the recurring calls to reform high schools in America. Teachers are playing a greater role in restructuring and curriculum change. For example, many schools participate in collaborative school reform networks, and through these networks, teachers receive training and resources for facilitating change in their schools. As the articles in this chapter confirm, more and more educational programs for middle adolescents are being developed in light of the following recommendation from the Coalition of Essential Schools: " . . . decisions about the details of the course of study, the use of students' and teachers' time and the choice of teaching materials and specific pedagogies must be unreservedly placed in the hands of the principal and staff" (Coalition of Essential Schools, 1998).

REFERENCES

Berger, Bennett M. *An Essay on Culture: Symbolic Structure and Social Structure*. Berkeley: University of California Press, 1995.

Boyer, Ernest. *High School: A Report on Secondary Education in America*. New York: Harper and Row, 1983.

Coalition of Essential Schools. "Ten Common Principles." Oakland, CA: Coalition of Essential Schools, 1998.

Conant, James B. "The Comprehensive High School." *NEA Journal* LI, No. 5 (May 1962): 29–30.

Gilchrist, Robert S. "What Is a Comprehensive High School?" *NEA Journal* LI, No. 8 (November 1962): 32–33.

Mamchur, Carolyn. "But . . . the Curriculum." *Phi Delta Kappan* 71, no. 5 (April 1990): 634–637.

Sandel, Lenore. "What High School Students Need to Know in Preparation for Success in College." *The High School Journal* 74, no. 3 (February/March 1991): 160–163.

Sizer, Theodore R. *Horace's Hope: What Works for the American High School*. Boston: Houghton Mifflin, 1996.

———. *Horace's School: Redesigning the American High School*. Boston: Houghton Mifflin, 1992.

———. *Horace's Compromise: The Dilemma of the American High School*. Boston: Houghton Mifflin, 1984.

Valois, Robert F., and McKewon, Robert E. "Frequency and Correlates of Fighting and Carrying Weapons Among Public School Adolescents." *American Journal of Health Behavior* 22, no. 1 (January–February 1998): 8–17.

Wigginton, Eliot. *Sometimes a Shining Moment: The Foxfire Experience*. Garden City, NY: Anchor Press, Doubleday, 1985.

Explaining "Academic Drift" in High Schools: Strategies for Improvement

JOSEPH MURPHY

ABSTRACT: *The high school curriculum is described as nonacademic and fragmented—a "collection" of courses rather than a coherent educational program. Nine curriculum trends that have emerged in response to seemingly reasonable demands have contributed to this "curriculum sprawl." To restore coherence and rigor to the high school curriculum, educators must develop a deep understanding of curricular coherence, avoid the temptation to return to the past, and take greater responsibility for guiding students to make wise choices among various curricular options.*

A number of important studies over the last six years have painted a rather unfavorable picture of the coursework in America's high schools (Murphy, et al., 1986; Powell, et al., 1985; Sedlak, et al., 1986). The authors of these reports have concluded that a lack of attention to the structure of the curriculum, coupled with inadequate efforts on the part of adults to shape students' course selections, have created a situation where many students are more likely to leave school with a collection of courses than with an education. The purpose of this paper is to explain how this situation evolved and to offer a corrective agenda for enhancing the coherence of the high school curriculum.

The Trend Toward Drift: As we look back on what has unfolded over the last quarter of a century, we can identify nine broad trends that have contributed to the lack of coherence often found in patterns of student coursework (see Figure 9.1). While each individual trend is grounded in a rationale designed to improve educational opportunities for students, collectively they have exerted a powerful force to pull students away from integrated educational experiences.

One of these trends has been the introduction into the curriculum of courses in practical arts (e.g., jewelry making) and personal services (e.g., family living). A second related trend has been the addition of required courses (and curricular units) in response to pressures from special interest groups (e.g., consumer education) and pressing social needs in the larger society (e.g., AIDS education). Conjoined with these first two phenomena has been the transfer of historically cocurricular activities into the regular school curriculum (e.g., yearbook). By and large, courses in these first three areas have been added with little consideration for how well they fit into the overall curricular structure. Their addition has also meant the elimination of more important academic coursework. Thus, movement down each of these curricular paths has helped reduce the integrity of the basic curricular structure in high schools and the rigor of individual students' educational experiences.

A second set of erosive trends (items 4–9 in Figure 9.1) is concerned less with outside intrusions into the curriculum than with the consequences of internal reconfigurations of curricular structures. One of these trends has been the proliferation of introductory courses. Analysts are just awakening to the fact that it is possible for students to pass through high school without studying in depth any single concept or subject. Closely related to the growth of more and more introductory courses has been the expansion of mini courses. Both trends are based on the belief that students should be exposed, if only for a brief

Reprinted, with permission of the author and the publisher, from *The High School Journal* 74, no. 2 (December/January 1991). Gerald Unks, editor. © 1991 The University of North Carolina Press.

FIGURE 9.1
A Portrait of Academic Drift

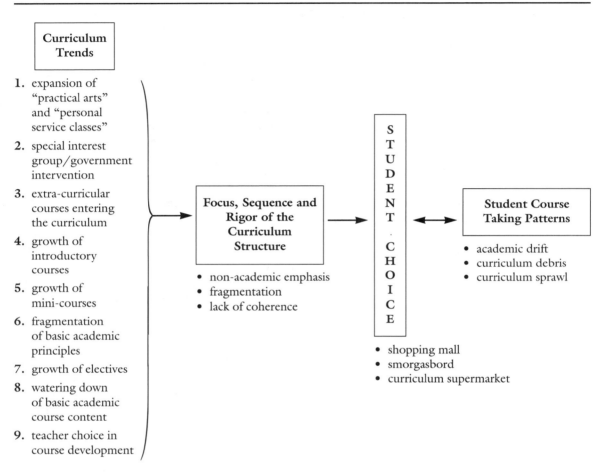

period of time, to as many areas as possible of our rapidly burgeoning knowledge base. However, two important problems arise when curricular programs are based upon this premise. First, such approaches require students to focus on content issues rather than on learning strategies. They also limit students to a surface knowledge of academic content. Second, this trend has provided the impetus for the creation of classes that often lack the rigor (extensive readings, writing assignments, examinations) of more traditionally organized ones. Transcript analysis reveals that introductory courses often (and these mini courses almost always) are taken during the senior year, when students craft schedules on the

basis more of convenience and ease of work than on intellectual demands.

Connected with, though slightly peripheral to, these two issues is the growth of electives—connected because electives were designed to increase student exposure to a variety of areas; peripheral because they also allow students to delve more fully into an area of study. However, because electives are often left unconnected to regular course sequences, in terms either of an overarching program design or of a sequential set of skills and knowledge, they have tended to contribute to the evolution of curriculum frameworks that lack cohesion. This condition can also be attributed to another of the nine curriculum trends (see Figure 9.1)—teacher choice in course development. The increasing professionalization of teaching, coupled with the opportunity created by the need for electives, has provided teachers with considerably more control over course development than they historically have enjoyed. Unfortunately, these new choices are often made on the basis of the teachers' areas of interest rather than with an eye toward ensuring integrity in the overall curricular structure. At the same time that the serious disadvantages of this professorial model of course construction are being recognized in universities, it continues to operate with insufficient scrutiny in high schools.

The high school curriculum is also being shaped by the proliferation of courses that mirror the increasing fragmentation of the academic disciplines. By patterning themselves on university disciplines, high school curricula have unwittingly adopted the lack of coherence that accompanies this fragmentation. Finally, as all these other dynamics have been gradually molding the high school curriculum, there has been a watering down of basic course content, thus reducing even further the likelihood that students will receive an integrated set of educational experiences.

The curricular structure that has emerged from all of these influences is not especially healthy (see Figure 9.1). It tends to be highly fragmented, non-academic, and incoherent. It has been variously labeled as a smorgasbord, a shopping mall, and a curricular supermarket. While it is quite possible to craft a coherent curriculum package from this type of structure—and many students, especially academic track students do—it is also possible not to craft coherence—and many students, especially general track and non-academic track students, do not. Since students are free to make selections from the smorgasbord, and do so often with minimal guidance from parents, teachers, and administrators, their transcripts frequently resemble a pattern of curriculum debris. Because learning in American public high schools is profoundly voluntary, as Powell and his colleagues (1985) have noted, students simply drift through school until they collect enough units to graduate.

An Agenda for Developing Curricular Coherence: Solutions to the problems of academic drift and curricular debris will not necessarily be easy to forge. The curricular trends discussed above were not set in motion by educators in order to destroy high schools. These forces have arisen in response to seemingly reasonable demands—more choice and better-balanced curricular experiences for students, greater professional discretion for teachers, and so forth. Yet it is known that collectively they have damaged the integrity of the system that they were designed to enhance. Worse, their effects have been most deleterious for those students who are most dependent on school for their learning and for the formation of their career aspirations; that is, for minorities, for students from low-income families, and for other students at risk.

Systematic and systemic efforts must be engaged in order to restore coherence and rigor to the high school curriculum. Listed below are three broad guidelines that can help create the agenda for that work.

First, the types of changes required will never occur until the educators leading our high schools develop a much deeper understanding of curricular cohesiveness as a critical component of the core technology of education. High school principals need to provide, and often act as, the glue that holds together the entire curriculum structure, and they need to ensure that each of its components reflects rigorous standards for content and demanding performance expectations. The list of reasons why principals have historically provided only minimal attention to curricular issues is quite lengthy—dysfunctional training in universities, district expectations that rivet their concern on other matters, a penchant for management issues, the professional nature of teaching, and so forth. However, the consequences of the failure to provide adequate leadership in this area are quite clear. When all of the explanations and excuses are cleared away, the bottom line is that principals are the chief executive officers of their organizations and are responsible for what happens in them. When a condition is as fundamentally unhealthy in an organization as is the picture of curricular sprawl in our high schools, the educators managing these institutions must take charge and begin to correct the situation. When the problem is as systemic as the above discussion indicates, principals must become much more personally involved in the healing process. In order to do this successfully, administrators must become considerably more proficient in their knowledge of important curricular issues.

Second, despite the temptation to do so, trying to solve the problem of academic drift by returning to the past must be avoided. While many valuable lessons can be gained from studying history, solution strategies that simply replicate what has been done in the past will fail because basic decisions made in the past were fundamentally flawed. At the outset of the movement to mass education in the early 1900s, education faced a key choice. They could differentiate curriculum, or they could differentiate instruction. They chose the wrong path, electing to provide different curricula for different groups of students. In retrospect, the more appropriate decision would have been to offer more unified curricular experiences while differentiating the strategies and procedures employed to help students master their content. Later, in response to the knowledge explosion that began to bombard schools in the middle of this century, a key choice was again confronted. Educators could elect to keep attempting to capture this mushrooming knowledge base in an ever-expanding array of courses, or they could shift their focus to helping students develop the skills and knowledge needed to learn. Again, the wrong path was chosen, with educators opting for more and more courses. Educators need to understand that by simply returning to yesterday's rules, they would institutionalize very serious problems, such as the two noted above, into tomorrow's educational system.

Third, educators need to take much greater responsibility for what happens academically to the young adults in their care than has been accepted in the past. While giving students choices is appropriate, abrogating the responsibility for helping students to choose wisely is not. Educators must also craft the array of options that are provided to students much more carefully. They must ensure that these options are integrated into a well thought-out curricular structure, and they must do a better job of helping students select those options that will open the maximum number of doors to them after they graduate. This is not a philosophical argument; it is an action agenda. Many high schools have begun the process of restoring credibility to the curriculum packages that students select. Some are tackling the issue of a meaningful senior year. Others are working out strategies to establish and shape long-range curriculum planning for individual students. Still others are creating rigorous learning experiences that require students to study one or more issues in depth. Much work lies ahead. Strong leadership is needed to get the job done. Educators need curricular leadership. And they need it from the men and women who lead our high schools.

REFERENCES

Murphy, J., et. al. (1987) "Academic Drift and Curriculum Debris: An Analysis of High School Course-Taking Patterns with Implications for Local Policy Makers." *Journal of Curriculum Studies, 19,* 4, p. 341–360.

Powell, A. G., Farrar, E., and Cohen, D. K. (1985) *The Shopping Mall High School: Winners and Losers in the Educational Marketplace.* Boston: Houghton Mifflin.

Sedlak, M. W., et. al. (1986) *Selling Students Short: Classroom Bargains and Academic Reform in the American High School.* New York, N.Y.: Teachers College Press.

Joseph Murphy is Professor and Chair, Department of Educational Leadership, Vanderbilt University, and Senior Research Fellow, National Center for Educational Leadership.

QUESTIONS FOR REFLECTION

1. Reflect on the high school curriculum you experienced. To what extent did it reflect the nine curriculum trends Murphy discusses?
2. Murphy states that "Educators need curricular leadership." Imagine that you are charged with providing curricular leadership at a high school—what would you do to ensure that your school's curriculum is cohesive and rigorous?
3. Is there evidence that the problem of "academic drift" characterizes the curriculum at the college and university level? If so, what examples can you cite?
4. At the educational level of greatest interest to you, what guidelines should educators follow when helping students choose from among curricular options?

Can Depth Replace Coverage in the High School Curriculum?

FRED M. NEWMANN

ABSTRACT: The emphasis on broad content coverage is a fundamental limitation of the high school curriculum. This "addiction to coverage" allows students to develop only superficial understanding of what they study. As an alternative, the curriculum should emphasize depth. If given time to differentiate, elaborate, qualify, and integrate, students will acquire a rich understanding of content. To overcome the obstacles to depth will require cutting content from the existing curriculum, developing new approaches to assessment, and changing instructional strategies.

Debates about the high school curriculum tend to focus on two general questions. First, are students studying the proper content? In other words, are they taking the right number of courses in each content area, and do these courses provide an appropriate blend of knowledge, skills, attitudes, and values? Second, what are the best ways to organize and teach a given body of content to certain groups of students? These important questions seem likely to persist, due to a lack of definitive research and to the political nature of education policy making. Meanwhile, a more fundamental problem continues to plague our efforts. Despite an abundance of sophisticated rationales, pedagogical approaches, and curriculum designs, we usually try to teach too much.

In our research on higher-order thinking in high school social studies classes, we asked students whether they ever had the opportunity to really dig into a given topic and study it in depth for at least two weeks. John responded to our question:

I got totally immersed in a project when the teacher forced us to do a paper on some guy. We couldn't pick him, but we had to read at least four books and write at least 100 note cards—big cards—and develop at least a 10-page paper. I got Montaigne. It ended up real interesting. As Mr. Foster pointed out, it was kind of cool that I got to

From *Phi Delta Kappan* 69, no. 5 (January 1988): 345–348. Used by permission of the author.

be a real expert and to know more than probably five million people in America about this guy. I'm not sure what made it so interesting—whether it was Montaigne's own works and life or just the fact that I got to know so much about him.

Asked whether he had such opportunities very often, John replied:

Most of the time, you don't get this in school. A lot of times it's a total skim; it's very bad. The course in European history is a classic example. We covered 2,000 years. Every week we were assigned to cover a 30-page chapter. The teacher is a stickler for dates and facts. We had 50 dates a week to memorize. The pity of it all is that now I don't remember any of them. I worked so hard, and now basically all I remember is Montaigne. There's like maybe five dates I remember, when I probably learned 300 or 400 dates all year. I can't even remember a lot of the important guys we studied.

I'd like to have worked where you dig in depth, but it's a double-sided sword, because if you're constantly going in-depth about each thing you come across, then you're not going to get very far. It's quantity versus quality. The only reasonable thing is you've got to find a balance. I guess there's more of a superficial quality to school now—teachers trying to cover as much as they can. They're not going into depth.

ADDICTION TO COVERAGE

We are addicted to coverage. This addiction seems endemic in high schools—where it runs rampant, especially in history—but it affects all levels of the curriculum, from kindergarten through college. We expose students to broad surveys of the disciplines and to endless sets of skills and competencies. The academic agenda includes a wide variety of topics; to cover them all, we give students time to develop only the most superficial understandings. The press for broad coverage causes many teachers to feel inadequate about leaving out so much content and apologetically mindful of the fact that much of what they teach is not fully understood by their students.

For several reasons, the addiction to coverage is destructive. First, it fosters the delusion that human beings are able to master everything worth knowing. We ought to realize that the knowledge explosion of this century has created a virtual galaxy of material worth knowing. Moreover, we ought to recognize that a crucial task of curriculum builders is to choose from this vast quantity of valuable knowledge a relatively infinitesimal portion to teach. The more we attempt to make this infinitesimal sample of knowledge representative or comprehensive, the more we delude ourselves, given the swift pace at which knowledge is accumulating. It is both arrogant and futile to assume that we can keep up with the knowledge explosion.

Furthermore, survey coverage is often a waste of time. Students learn most material in order to use it on one or two brief occasions (a quiz and a test), after which the material is quickly forgotten. When knowledge is used only rarely, it is seldom available for transfer to new situations.

Beyond simply wasting time or failing to impart knowledge of lasting value, superficial coverage has a more insidious consequence: it reinforces habits of mindlessness. Classrooms become places in which material must be learned—even though students find it nonsensical because their teachers have no time to explain. Students are denied opportunities to explore related areas that arouse their curiosity for fear of straying too far from the official list of topics to be covered. Teachers' talents for conveying subtle nuances and complexities are squelched. Not surprisingly, many students stop asking questions soon after they leave the early elementary grades. Instead, they passively allow teachers and textbooks to pour material into their heads, where they will try to store it for future use in educational exercises. However, the press to "cover" offers little opportunity to develop that material in ways that will help students meet more authentic intellectual challenges.

Most of us recognize the negative consequences of an addiction to coverage. We all want our curricula to foster fundamental understandings and complex, higher-order thinking. But despite our best intentions, we cannot break the habit.

THE ALTERNATIVE: DEPTH

The alternative to coverage, though difficult to achieve, is depth: the sustained study of a given topic that leads students beyond superficial exposure to rich, complex understanding. The topic might be "broad" (e.g., liberty, ecological balance) or "narrow" (e.g., John Winthrop's leadership in colonial America, the effect of acid rain on sugar maple trees). To gain rich understanding of a topic, students must master a great deal of information, use that information to answer a variety of questions about the topic, and generate new questions that lead to further inquiry. In demonstrating their knowledge of the topic, they should go beyond simple declarative statements to differentiation, elaboration, qualification, and integration.

Depth has been summarized as "less is more."* But *less* in this context does not mean less knowledge or information, for depth can be achieved only through the mastery of considerable information. Rather, *less* refers to less mastery of information that provides only a superficial acquaintance with a topic. In general, depth is preferable as a principle of curriculum development, because depth is more likely to facilitate lasting retention and transfer of knowledge, more likely to cultivate thoughtfulness than mindlessness, and more likely to enable us to cope in some reasonable fashion with the explosion of knowledge.

It is important to head off two possible misinterpretations of my advocacy of depth over coverage. First, I do not suggest that skills should replace knowledge as the focus of the curriculum. Instead, I maintain that knowledge in depth is

more valuable than superficial knowledge and that, in order to achieve knowledge in depth, we must radically reduce the number of isolated bits of information that are transmitted to children.

Second, some readers may worry that emphasis on depth will produce excessive specialization and thus undermine the quest for a common core of knowledge, which is necessary for communication and social cohesion. However, there is no logical contradiction between knowledge in depth and attempts to achieve a common core. A common core can consist either of in-depth knowledge of a few topics or of superficial knowledge of many topics. What to include in the common core and what proportion of the curriculum the common core should occupy are difficult questions, but they should remain separate from the issue of superficial familiarity versus complex understanding. I am arguing here only that we should be devoting a far greater proportion of formal education to the development of complex understanding of fewer topics, whether those topics are unique to certain classes and schools or common to all of them.

OBSTACLES TO DEPTH

Why is depth so difficult to achieve? What are some of the major obstacles?

First, we must recognize that the point of education *is*, in a sense, to cover material—that is, to expose students to and make them familiar with new information. Conversely, to be unaware of information considered "basic" for productive living within a society is to be uneducated. In our society, becoming educated involves learning the meanings of thousands of words and mastering hundreds of conventions for manipulating information and communicating effectively with others. Clearly, to master ideas and techniques, students must be exposed to information.

Unfortunately, this legitimate need for a certain degree of coverage has fostered the illusion (firmly held by professional educators and by the general public) that it is possible to teach a rea-

---

*Theodore R. Sizer, *Horace's Compromise: The Dilemma of the American High School* (Boston: Houghton Mifflin, 1984).

sonably comprehensive sample of all the worthwhile knowledge that is currently available. We are remarkably unwilling to accept the consequences of the knowledge explosion. Instead, we cling to a conception of education more appropriate to medieval times, when formal public knowledge was relatively well-defined, finite, and manageable. Although we know that times have changed and that we can't teach everything, we apparently retain our faith in the ideal of comprehensiveness, because we continue to try to cover as much as possible.

The mounting pressure for schools to be accountable and to prove their effectiveness through students' test scores gives added impetus to an emphasis on coverage over depth. It is more convenient to test for superficial coverage, because thousands of multiple-choice test items can be constructed to tap countless bits of knowledge.

We teachers have been socialized to construe knowledge as outlines of the content of introductory textbooks. Seldom in our own undergraduate or graduate education did our professors engage us in deep inquiry, except for such special experiences as participating in an honors program or writing a graduate thesis (rare instances that are reserved for individuals who have already endured many years of ritualistic coverage). Thus many of us would hardly know what to do with students if the pressure for coverage were suddenly lifted.

Even teachers who have a commitment to depth and a vision of how to achieve it in the classroom are frustrated by the lack of suitable textbooks and other instructional materials. Literary works, journal articles, and primary sources are useful with highly motivated and able readers, but such materials are too difficult for many students, and few alternatives are available.

Another obstacle to depth is the orientation that students bring to their schoolwork. They have been rewarded primarily for completing discrete tasks that require the recognition of countless bits of knowledge. Those knowledge bits are organized into many separate subjects, and students' learning schedules are divided into small chunks of time. A variety of topics must be studied each day. Therefore, continuous and sustained study of any one topic seems virtually impossible.

Television further undermines intense and sustained concentration on a single topic. Teachers report that young people of the television generation have no patience for study in depth; they want quick, simple, unambiguous answers. Moreover, college-bound students want some assurance that they have been exposed to the range of information covered by admissions tests.

OVERCOMING THE OBSTACLES

The obstacles are formidable indeed. But teachers, administrators, and state-level policy makers who seek to overcome them may find the following recommendations helpful.

First, schools and school districts must continue to develop a rationale for study in depth. At the same time, they must focus the public's attention on the problems of addiction to coverage. In other words, they must help policy makers, academics, business leaders, and the general public to see that well-intentioned efforts to cover a broad range of material have developed into an obsession that is undermining education.

Second, instead of focusing immediately on which courses to eliminate, schools and school districts would probably find it less divisive to work first on ways of achieving depth within existing courses. Later, criteria such as the following might be used to decide which content to cut from the curriculum:

- Does the topic occupy a critical position in a hierarchy of content, so that students must master it in order to understand the important ideas that follow? Does failure to understand this particular topic put students at risk?
- If the topic is of critical importance, could it be readily learned outside of school through reading, televiewing, or some other form of independent study? Or does mastery of this

topic require special guidance by a professional educator?

- Are teachers likely to spend a large amount of time developing this topic and assessing students' understanding of it, or will they simply give students a superficial exposure to the topic and then test for recognition or recall?

These criteria alone cannot resolve all the complicated issues related to the selection of curricular content. But they illustrate the kinds of educational principles (as opposed to teachers' personal preferences or faculty or school district politics) on which curriculum decisions might be based.

Third, in any individual school that tries to foster depth at the expense of coverage, the teachers will need special support as they wrestle with such issues as what content to cut from the curriculum, how to teach for depth, and how to assess new and more complex forms of mastery. Such support ought to include resources that would enable teachers to participate more fully in the development of curriculum materials and new approaches to testing and that would enable them to help one another more frequently in planning, teaching, and evaluating lessons.

At the state level, policy makers affect the coverage of content in at least five areas: assessment, textbook selection, curriculum requirements, school improvement programs, and teacher education. Let us consider the nature of state influence in each area and how the states might encourage a greater emphasis on depth.

Assessment. To the extent that state testing programs rely primarily on short-answer, multiple-choice tests that cover a broad range of subjects, the states contribute to the disease of coverage. There are two basic strategies for improving assessment. First, test developers can reduce the number of isolated bits of information covered by the tests, using instead items that allow students to demonstrate in-depth mastery of a smaller number of topics. Second, test developers can replace multiple-choice, short-answer

questions with writing exercises—perhaps even speaking exercises—that require students to synthesize their ideas and to show the development of their thinking on selected topics.

Textbook selection. States spread the disease of coverage when they adopt textbooks written primarily for survey courses aimed at comprehensive exposure. Publishers must be persuaded to prepare textbooks that take a more selective, in-depth approach; meanwhile, the states should adopt and publicize existing textbooks and other instructional materials that reflect this approach. One of the students I interviewed remarked that he had enjoyed a course in European history. "What made the course so interesting?" I asked. "Was it the teacher?" "No, the teacher was not particularly exciting," he said. "But the textbook was really terrific." He recalled neither the title of the book nor the name of its author. What he remembered was that the book did not inundate readers with dates and facts, headings, review questions, and test questions. "It was like a book you'd find in the library—a real book," he added.

State curriculum requirements. State legislators are pressured by every conceivable organization to insert subjects into the curriculum, and a reasonable case can be made for almost every proposed course or unit of instruction. Individually, each requirement seems legitimate; collectively, however, they often resemble a disorganized smorgasbord. Current efforts to reduce the number of electives and to return to a common core of required courses may seem to address the problem. But elective courses often enable students to inquire more deeply into specific topics than do core courses, which often become superficial surveys. We should avoid sanctifying either approach and instead support having students study fewer topics in greater depth.

School improvement programs. Moving away from an emphasis on coverage will be difficult.

Many teachers regard coverage as a primary educational goal. Others recognize that the pace of instruction makes thoughtful inquiry impossible, but they worry that they will do a disservice to students if they fail to cover all the territory required by state mandates and standardized tests. To resolve this complex professional dilemma, teachers need time to think, to argue, to select, and to develop new instructional materials. States should appropriate funds to help the schools pay for programs of staff development and for the production by staff members of curricula and tests that emphasize in-depth study.

Teacher education.   Colleges and universities perpetuate the addiction to coverage through survey courses and broad distribution requirements. These offerings permit many students to complete their degrees without ever having to engage in a sustained struggle to master the complexity of a field or topic. Thus higher education encourages teachers to conceive of knowledge as that which is contained on the table of contents of an introductory text. The states should counter this tendency by requiring that prospective teachers devote a greater proportion of their training to the in-depth study of an academic area.

Regardless of what we teach or how we teach it, we try to teach too much. The addiction to coverage is a futile attempt to offer students a comprehensive education; it wastes time and it undermines intellectual integrity. Instead of superficial exposure, curricula should emphasize sustained study aimed at developing complex understanding. But powerful obstacles—illusions about the nature of knowledge, pressures for accountability, patterns of socializing teachers and students, the organization of schooling, and the quality of instructional materials—stand in the way of a shift to study in depth. Moving in that direction will require action at the school, district, and state levels to cut content from the curriculum, develop new approaches to assessment, and change instructional materials and pedagogy. Most important, schools, districts, and states will have to carefully reexamine the goals of education.

Fred M. Newmann is Director, National Center on Effective Secondary Schools, School of Education, University of Wisconsin, Madison.

QUESTIONS FOR REFLECTION

1.   To what extent does an "addiction to coverage" characterize curricula at the elementary, junior/middle, and postsecondary levels of education? What examples can you cite?
2.   In what ways does an emphasis on coverage "reinforce habits of mindlessness?"
3.   What steps can curriculum planners take to help policy makers, other educators, business leaders, and the general public understand how the "addiction to coverage" undermines the educative process?

Technological Literacy: A Twenty-First-Century Imperative

MERRILL M. OAKS
RICHARD GANTMAN
MELVIN PEDRAS

ABSTRACT: Technological literacy, the ability to understand and use technology, is an imperative for the future. Technology education, which has its roots in manual training and industrial arts programs of the past, provides students with the skills and knowledge to "solve problems and extend human capabilities." Initiatives by several professional organizations have shaped today's secondary-level technology education curricula. Among the innovative approaches that help students in technology education programs connect theory and practice are applied learning, thematic curricula, and project-based learning.

The meaning of the term *literacy* depends upon an individual's personal and professional context. For example, the level of literacy expected of a 10th grade student is different from that expected of a research scientist. Similarly, the literacy that Benjamin Franklin spoke of when he stated that it requires a "literate electorate" to make a democracy work is not the same literacy required to make our advanced technological society prosper. In today's society, there is a strong rationale for making technological literacy a national priority. It is imperative that we be able to make informed decisions about what technologies should be developed, when and how they will be used, and what the benefits and consequences of their use should be.

This article explores the concept of *technological literacy* and its relationship to technology education at the secondary level. Technology education is an emerging curriculum trend that provides new and exciting connections and opportunities for secondary teachers and students within the current framework of school restructuring, reform, and revitalization.

TECHNOLOGY AND TECHNOLOGICAL LITERACY

Technology may be viewed as the sum of man-made means to satisfy human needs and desires and to solve specific problems in a given situation. Similarly, "Technology for All Americans" defines *technology* as "human innovation in action that involves the generation of knowledge and processes to develop systems that solve problems and extend human capabilities" (International Technology Education Association, 1996, 16).

Technology has three major components: processes, knowledge, and contexts (International Technology Education Association, 1996). The *processes* of technology are the actions people take in designing, producing, and controlling things. Technological *knowledge* addresses the nature and history of technology and its impact on society. The *contexts* of technology involve understanding and developing technical systems that are made up of specific technologies.

"Technology for All Americans" defines *technological literacy* as the ability to use, manage, and

Article written by Merrill M. Oaks, Richard Gantman, and Melvin Pedras for *Curriculum Planning: A Contemporary Approach*, Seventh Edition, 2000. Used by permission of the authors.

understand technology. The ability to use technology requires knowledge of the components of existing macrosystems, or human adaptive systems, and how those systems behave. The ability to manage technology requires that all technological activities are efficient and appropriate. Understanding technology involves more than the acquisition of information; it involves the ability to synthesize that information into new insights.

EVOLUTION OF TECHNOLOGY EDUCATION

The study of technology and its subsequent integration into the school curriculum as technology education had its roots in early movements such as *manual training* of the late 1870s. One of the most influential educational figures of the time was John Dewey who saw manual training as an essential part of the curriculum. Manual training was one of the "methods of life" to be integrated into the curriculum, with broad and rich content (Hamilton and Pedras, 1975). Manual training was expanded to include the study of industry to provide an understanding of the production, distribution, and consumption of the things that constitute material wealth. Individuals such as Frederick Bonser and James Russell also maintained that the study of industry would provide an understanding of humankind's relation to industry and enable people to appreciate the dignity of work.

This thinking continued well into the early 1900s, at which time other educational leaders began to suggest further broadening the study of industry. This led to a social-industrial philosophy, which culminated in a program of study called *industrial arts* that lasted well into the early 1960s.

Industrial arts was integrated into the school curriculum as a program of study that, when properly organized, would revitalize other subject areas of the school curriculum. The 1960s saw numerous innovative industrial arts programs such as American Industries, the Maryland

Plan, Industriology, and career education which broadened the study of industry to include an understanding of how our present technological society emerged.

As our society became more complex and dependent upon advanced technology, it became apparent that the need for education that focused on technological principles and concepts had become stronger. During the 1970s and 1980s, this need led to a shift in curricular emphasis from industrial arts to technology education and, eventually, to the goal of achieving a technologically literate citizenry.

Technology today is about meeting human needs through the creative processes of designing, making, and servicing products that satisfy human requirements. Technology education, then, represents a concerted national effort to provide today's students with the skills and knowledge needed to solve problems and extend human capabilities. Currently, appropriate national standards, curricula, and leadership are being developed to integrate technology education into all school grade levels. Major initiatives such as Technology for All Americans are providing guidance and standards for the development of quality technology education programs that are in concert with the needs of society.

A critical dimension of technology education is the preparation of secondary-level students who understand how technology will influence their future personal and professional lives. Whether students move from the secondary to postsecondary level or enter the world of work directly, the message is the same; a strong secondary-level technology education curriculum is becoming a national educational imperative.

THE SECONDARY TECHNOLOGY EDUCATION CURRICULUM

Three initiatives have had a major impact on the design of the secondary technology education curriculum: (1) Technology for All Americans and Standards for Technology Education, both developed by the International Technology Education Association; (2) the National Curriculum for Design and Technology developed in England; and (3) Science for All Americans and Benchmarks for Science Literacy, both supported the American Association for the Advancement of Science.

The International Technology Education Association, in collaboration with the National Science Foundation, has developed a conceptual framework for technology education and technological literacy and established a set of national standards. "Technology for All Americans" redefines technology education and offers a clear rationale for technological literacy as a requirement for all students. "Standards for Technology Education" lays out a clear scope and sequence for students in kindergarten through twelfth grade. The secondary-level technology education curriculum builds on learners' prior experiences using technology to construct products and to apply principles and concepts of production systems. At the secondary level, the technology education curriculum is expanded to include links to other fields of study that are critically important to technology, such as mathematics and science. Technology programs at this level, which require teachers who are certified in technology education, typically focus on specific technologies and career paths and are conducted in specially equipped technology laboratories. "Standards for Technology Education" (International Technology Education Association, n.d.) calls for the following curricular experiences: designing, developing, and producing products and systems, and using and managing technology. Students master the concepts of "systems thinking" and assess the impacts and consequences of technology; they also study the nature and history of technology, and they identify connections between technology and other fields of study.

The British Department for Education and Employment has, over the last decade, been actively developing and implementing a national curriculum and standards for technology education. The "National Curriculum for Design and Technology" (Department for Education and Employment, 1995) is part of the "National Curriculum" of required subjects. The British technology education curriculum is organized around the study of designing and making products. Program goals are designed to help students draw from a wide range of areas, including the study of familiar products, the characteristics of materials, and the form and function of production processes, as they develop their understanding of the design process. Additionally, students are required to communicate their design solutions and rationale. At the secondary level, the curriculum is organized around the following concepts: designing skills, making skills, materials and components, systems and controls, products and applications, quality, and health and safety.

The American Association for the Advancement of Science (AAAS) has, for the past several years, been actively involved in establishing benchmark standards for science. These efforts, *Science for All Americans* (Rutherford, 1990) and *Benchmarks for Science Literacy* (American Association for the Advancement of Science, 1993), make a strong argument for the study of technology:

> In a sense, then, many parts of our world are designed—shaped and controlled, largely through the use of technology—in light of what we take our interests to be. We have brought the earth to a point of where our future well being will depend heavily on how we develop and use and restrict technology. In turn, that will depend heavily on how well we understand the workings of technology and the social, cultural, economic, and ecological systems within which we live. (American Association for the Advancement of Science, 1993, p. 107)

Mathematics, science, and technology are so closely related that it is often difficult to separate them and impossible to study one without understanding the others. This interrelationship becomes evident if we define *technology* as the application of science and mathematics to meet human needs and wants. Therefore, it is not surprising to find that technology is intricately woven throughout the national standards for science education in *Benchmarks for Science Literacy*. The nature of technology, the design world, historical perspectives, common themes, and habits of mind are all benchmarks in the science literacy initiative, and they speak directly to the interwoven nature of science and technology.

CURRICULAR APPROACHES IN TECHNOLOGY EDUCATION

Throughout the 1980s and 1990s, technology education evolved from a materials processing based curriculum to one that emphasizes technological literacy (International Technology Education Association, 1996). During the same time, secondary level programs moved toward a more pragmatic, "real world" based curriculum emphasizing authentic, practical connectedness between subject matter and its application. This movement away from the separation of "theoretical" and "practical" courses has been both revolutionary and highly encouraging. The transition—prompted by increased student apathy toward the "traditional," century-old secondary school curriculum and a growing dissatisfaction by both teachers and parents with the traditional curriculum—was made possible by national initiatives such as "Transition to Work," "Tech Prep," and "Work-Based Learning." As a result, cooperation and exploration between technology education and other academic and vocational areas are increasing. For example, many secondary schools are currently using commercially marketed technology laboratories as a catalyst for merging technology education and the general secondary curriculum. A more meaningful and relevant secondary curriculum is made possible by combining the unique features of technology education with emerging curricular initiatives in other areas.

One such curricular innovation is "applied learning," a simple but highly effective means of establishing initial collaboration between a technology education teacher and other general or vocational subject matter specialists. Applied learning activities can be as simple as having mathematics students work in a technology laboratory to construct mathematical models or as complex as having them design and develop a community mass transit or water purification system. Applied learning does not require teams of teachers working together in a fully integrated plan; rather, it can involve any subject matter specialist such as a science, mathematics, or social studies teacher who wishes to make the curriculum more meaningful and motivating by infusing technological literacy concepts and activities in his or her teaching. Conducting applied learning activities such as material processing, construction, assembly, and testing typically creates high student interest and motivation; moreover, it greatly enhances, for both teacher and students, the perceived relevance of and appreciation for courses such as mathematics, science, social studies, and English.

Another curricular innovation within technology education is the "thematic curriculum." The thematic curriculum is a series of experiences, programs, courses, or units that focus on a common subject or theme. Secondary schools are increasingly setting up thematic schools, clusters, academies, and programs as subunits within the traditional school. Examples of thematic organizers include art, fashion design, health, music, manufacturing and technology, agriculture, military science, engineering, medical science, business, communications, and construction.

Other thematic approaches are based on technological "content organizers" such as manufacturing, communication, transportation, bio-related and medical technology, design technology, physical systems, and information systems. These clusters or thematic content areas integrate technology education with one other course or an entire curriculum. A technology-centered thematic approach can provide students with extensive experiences in research, problem solving, analysis, and evaluation. Lastly, technology-based thematic instruction provides secondary students with an impressive inventory of work and career related skills to help them make the transition from secondary schools to the workplace or to postsecondary education.

"Project based learning" (PBL) is yet another strategy for integrating technology education with subject matter areas across the curriculum. Since technology education has a rich tradition of project-centered curricula, there are many opportunities to merge technology education and the general and vocational curriculum areas. PBL can be defined as a curricular approach or structure that transforms teaching from *teachers telling* to *students doing*. Five key elements of PBL include:

1. Engaging learning experiences that involve students in complex, real world projects through which they develop and apply skills and knowledge
2. Recognizing that significant learning taps students' inherent drive to learn, their capability to do important work, and need to be taken seriously
3. Learning for which general curricular outcomes can be identified up front, while specific outcomes of the students' learning are neither predetermined nor fully predictable
4. Learning that requires students to draw from many information sources and disciplines in order to solve problems
5. Experiences through which students learn to manage and allocate resources such as time and materials

Successful interdisciplinary project based learning requires a format and structure that encourages student freedom while it focuses on long-term outcomes and strategies for completion. The *design brief* is an excellent tool for this purpose. Much like a traditional lesson plan format, there is no single "right" way to develop a design brief. Nevertheless, design briefs have certain commonalties, including:

- Identification of the project or issue
- Research questions, hypotheses, or ideas on how to solve the problem
- Established criteria and a plan for completion
- Setting the scope and sequence of the project
- Final selection of the chosen project materials and resources needed
- Design solution(s)
- Assessment of project results

The design brief method of planning is used in technology education to provide structure and organization for project based learning. When used with other disciplines, the design brief has the added advantage of providing a means of consistent communication among students and teachers from participating curriculum areas. Ideas for innovative, challenging design briefs are available for teacher and student use in publications such as *TIES Magazine*. Some examples include:

1. Identify a large island in the south Pacific and design a way to reduce it to table-top size, but maintain its scale.
2. Design and make a system for collecting and counting macroinvertebrates that can assure the integrity of the sample.
3. Aerodynamics plays a major role in the handling of today's motorcycles. Design and build a motorcycle model from wood. Build a wind tunnel and test the motorcycle. Describe what happens to the motorcycle when there is a missing or damaged fairing.

Whether researching the implications of a proposed freeway through an urban residential area, designing and building a prototype of a new harvesting method for fruit growers, or solving a virus problem with apples prior to importation, the project based learning method captivates students with highly motivating, real life situations. PBL is a highly effective means of teaching students how to go far beyond school resources to access knowledge and information needed to solve real world problems and make significant contributions to the community and society. Technology education is well positioned to serve as a catalyst for merging the traditional academic subject areas while it promotes the quest to ensure technological literacy for every American secondary school graduate.

TECHNOLOGY EDUCATION AND THE TOTAL SCHOOL CURRICULUM

This discussion of technology education would be incomplete without a short explanation of how it fits into the total school curriculum. While our emphasis has been on the secondary level, elementary and junior high/middle school programs cannot be ignored.

Technology education should be integrated into all levels of study, from kindergarten through high school, and should be made especially appealing to those students who traditionally have not been served by technology programs (Oaks and Pedras, 1992). To do so will ensure a well-educated student population that understands and is able to adjust to and provide leadership for a rapidly changing technological society.

At the elementary school level, the study of technology should help students learn broad concepts about our society and environment. Teachers should take advantage of children's needs for psychomotor activity and cooperative learning environments to enhance their learning about technology. At this level, the study of technology can help students develop critical-thinking skills and give them opportunities to engage in creative problem solving, thereby helping them make connections between subjects learned and the needs of society.

Junior high/middle school technology education strategies should help students learn broad concepts of technology and how they apply to society. At this level, students should begin to develop the ability of assessing the impact of technology and technological systems on individuals, society, and the environment. Technology education at the junior high/middle level and beyond requires qualified technology education teachers who understand and can teach the interrelationships of technology to other areas of study. Furthermore, such teachers are able to make liberal use of problems and processes as they apply to the design, development, and use of technological products. Junior high/middle school students should also receive instruction in how technology relates to other fields of study such as mathematics, science, computers, social studies, and language arts.

Similarly, technology at the high school level should be taught by qualified technology education teachers who understand how technology is related to other subjects across the curriculum. Methods such as inquiry, cooperative problem solving, research, and discussion should be used extensively, and every effort should be made to ensure that technology is studied within a broad context.

"Technology for All Americans" suggests that, as a result of studying technology at the high school level, students should be able to:

- Evaluate technology's capabilities, uses, and consequences on individuals, society, and the environment;
- Employ the resources of technology to analyze the behavior of technological systems;
- Apply design concepts to solve problems and extend human capability;
- Apply scientific principles, engineering concepts, and technological systems in the solution of everyday problems; and
- Develop personal interests and abilities related to careers in technology (International Technology Education Association, 1996).

Upon graduation from high school, all students should be technologically literate. Anything less will reduce our ability to develop technological advancements that enhance the quality of life for our citizens and for the world.

REFERENCES

American Association for the Advancement of Science. (1993). *Benchmarks for Science Literacy.* New York: Oxford University Press.

Department for Education and Employment. (1995). "The National Curriculum for Design and Technology. London: Author.

Hamilton, B., and Pedras, M. (1975). "An Historical Perspective on Industrial Arts with Implications for Career Education." *Man/Society/Technology,* 34(4), 112–113.

International Technology Education Association. (1996). "Technology for All Americans: A Rationale and Structure for the Study of Technology." Reston, VA: International Technology Education Association.

International Technology Education Association. (n.d.) "Standards for Technology Education." Unpublished. Reston, VA: International Technology Education Association.

Oaks, M., and Pedras, M. (1992). "Technology Education: A Catalyst for Curriculum Integration." *The Technology Teacher,* 51(5), 11–13.

Rutherford, J. (1990). *Science for All Americans.* New York: Oxford University Press.

Merrill M. Oaks is Professor, Department of Teaching and Learning, and former Director of Technology Education at Washington State University; *Richard Gantman* is Curriculum Director, Stephenson School District, Stephenson, Washington; and *Melvin Pedras* is Professor, College of Education, University of Idaho.

QUESTIONS FOR REFLECTION

1. How might technology and technological literacy be integrated into the curriculum with which you are most familiar?
2. Similarly, how might the five elements of project based learning be incorporated into the curriculum with which you are most familiar?
3. In what ways is students' learning enhanced when instruction is transformed from *teachers telling* to *students doing*?

Implementing Middle School Concepts into High Schools

M. LEE MANNING
RICHARD SADDLEMIRE

ABSTRACT: Four middle school concepts shown to increase students' achievement; promote positive, humane behaviors; and improve attitudes toward school hold promise for the high school level: advisor–advisee programs, exploratory programs, interdisciplinary teams, and efforts to promote a positive school climate. Discussions of each concept include implementation tasks, characteristics of effective high school efforts, and recommended readings.

During the last ten years, research and scholarly writing on effective middle school concepts and practices have resulted in clear directions for middle level educators. A wealth of information on effective middle school practices has come from several sources: *Turning Points: Preparing American Youth for the 21st Century* (Carnegie Council on Adolescent Development 1989), the National Middle School Association's position paper *This We Believe* (National Middle School Association 1992), middle school textbooks (Allen, Splittgerber, and Manning 1993; Irvin 1992; Manning 1993), recommendations of professional associations (National Association of Secondary School Principals 1993), and reports from several state departments of education (California State Department of Education 1987; Maryland Department of Education 1989).

Responding to this information, middle schools increasingly have implemented concepts that have the potential to increase students' academic achievement, promote positive and humane behaviors, and improve attitudes toward school. In this article, we propose that there are four middle school concepts that hold promise for being effective in high schools. For each concept, we list implementation tasks, the character-

istics of effective high school efforts, and recommended readings.

Before choosing to implement one or more of the concepts, high school educators should ask themselves the following question: Considering the characteristics of our high school, which concepts hold the most promise for (1) improving academic achievement, (2) improving student behavior, (3) fostering positive interpersonal relationships between students and between educators and students, and (4) enhancing the school's ability to address adolescents' cognitive and psychosocial needs?

CONCEPT 1: ADVISOR-ADVISEE PROGRAMS

The advisor-advisee program, sometimes called a teacher advisory, ensures that each student has at least one adult who knows him or her well and also that each student belongs to a small interactive group. Advisory groups promote students' social, emotional, and moral growth, while providing personal and academic guidance. To reduce the student-teacher ratio, all professional staff members serve as advisors. Advisories

From *Clearing House* 69, no. 6, 339–342, July/August 1996. Reprinted with permission of the Helen Dwight Reid Educational Foundation. Published by Heldref Publications, 1319 Eighteenth St., N. W., Washington, DC 20036–1802. Copyright © 1996.

should be held daily and can be twenty-five to forty minutes long, depending on the school schedule (Allen, Splittgerber, and Manning 1993). Advisories can focus on students' concerns and suggestions or can be based on "advisory plans" prepared by professional writers.

Most high schools have guidance counselors and guidance programs that operate in accordance with district policy and/or accrediting associations. It should be noted that adding advisor-advisee programs to the high school guidance program neither negates nor undercuts the work of counseling professionals.

Implementation Tasks

To implement an advisor-advisee program, members of the school staff will need to

- write a rationale for implementing the program based on an examination of actual student behaviors and school conditions;
- list ways that the program and the guidance and counseling services can work collaboratively toward agreed-upon goals;
- design an advisory guide that shows daily or monthly topics; and
- write a letter to parents describing the newly implemented advisor-advisee program.

Characteristics of Successful Programs

Successful advisor-advisee programs share several characteristics: (1) all students feel known by at least one caring adult; (2) students participate in advisor-advisee sessions on concerns and issues that they consider personally relevant (e.g., developmental matters, school rules and policies, higher education opportunities, and dealing with parents and other adults); (3) students and educators get to know one another on a personal teenager-adult basis; and (4) educators have sufficient professional development to know how to

select appropriate topics and plan effective advisor-advisee sessions.

Recommended Reading

High school educators will find two publications especially useful in the area of advisor-advisee programs: *Advisor-Advisee Programs: Why, What, and How* (James 1986) and Neila Connors's "Teacher Advisory: The Fourth R" in *Transforming Middle Level Education: Perspectives and Possibilities* (Irvin 1992). Also, an article in the May 1994 issue of the *Middle School Journal* addresses teacher attitudes and advisor-advisee programs.

CONCEPT 2: EXPLORATORY PROGRAMS

An exploratory program gives students the opportunity to explore areas of interest and concern. Recognizing adolescents' developing interests and capacities to learn, such a program introduces a variety of topics, skills, and content fields, without requiring mastery. The program may consist of short courses or elective units, each of which should give students a sense of control over the kind of learning they are pursuing. Various numbers and types of exploratory programs may be established, depending on school schedules, student interest, and teacher expertise. An exploratory usually lasts a month or six or nine weeks; a semester-long exploratory may be too long, considering adolescents' changing interests (Manning 1993).

Exploratory programs provide an interesting "retreat" from the prescribed curriculum and the rigid routine of the school. Also, for students who have few opportunities to explore areas of interest outside the prescribed curriculum, exploratory courses can spark new interests, lead them to take previously unconsidered academic courses, or even motivate them to investigate new career fields.

Implementation Tasks

To undertake an exploratory program, administrators and teachers will need to perform the following tasks:

- write a rationale for having exploratory programs on the high school level;
- identify what the teachers' roles will be in the program;
- identify appropriate time frames (minutes per day, days per week, six or nine weeks, and so forth) for the exploratory program;
- select topics for the program;
- write a syllabus that outlines an exploratory program; and
- write a letter to parents that describes the program, its rationale, and possible topics.

Characteristics of Successful Programs

Several characteristics of effective exploratory programs can be identified: (1) The high school considers students' interests when choosing exploratory topics. (Possible topics include dramatic, home, and industrial arts; technology; developmental and health concerns; foreign languages; extensions of specific academic areas; theatrical performances; independent study opportunities; historical, cultural, and studio art; various elements of visual art, drawing, and pottery; and consumer education.) (2) The exploratory program has a time frame shorter than a semester (e.g., six or nine weeks), so that students can explore a number of topics rather than only one or two during the school year. (3) The program does not assign grades to students' work, so students do not feel pressured to achieve in areas that they are only exploring.

Recommended Reading

An extensive discussion of exploratory programs, *Teaching and Learning in the Middle Level School* (Allen, Splittgerber, and Manning 1993) suggests time frames, topics, and procedures. Also, *Exploration: The Total Curriculum* (Compton and Hawn 1993) provides readers with a comprehensive treatment of this key middle school concept.

CONCEPT 3: INTERDISCIPLINARY TEAMS

Interdisciplinary teaming has proved to be a workable concept that is highly valued and enjoyed by both middle school teachers and students. It can be equally successful in the high school, especially when teachers see its advantages and are allowed to maintain allegiances to their subject area departments.

Interdisciplinary teams are made up of three or more teachers representing different subject areas. The team shares the same students, schedules, and classroom areas and thereby has increased autonomy and responsibility for significant decision making. It is important to note that while teachers from various subject areas plan together, they do not teach together in the same classroom.

Most high schools are organized by subject area departments. Teachers are experts in their respective subject areas; however, they are often unfamiliar with the skills and abilities of other subject area teachers. As a result, little curricular integration occurs, and students are left with knowledge of individual courses but without a clear perspective of the many relationships between subject areas.

Suggestions that teachers break away from their subject area teams and reorganize into interdisciplinary teams may be met with opposition. Teachers' concerns might be assuaged by allowing them to continue with their respective departmental organizations (thus having both subject area departments and interdisciplinary teams) either permanently or during the transition periods. Such a decision could be made by administrators and teachers.

Implementation Tasks

Tasks that need to be undertaken in order to put interdisciplinary teams into effect include the following:

- write a rationale for adopting the interdisciplinary approach;
- list several characteristics of effective interdisciplinary teams;
- list the roles and responsibilities of team leaders;
- list several means of evaluating interdisciplinary projects; and
- identify any conflicts that might arise and possible ways of handling them.

Characteristics of Successful Programs

The characteristics of effective interdisciplinary teams are (1) teams that are balanced among content, instruction, and skills; (2) teams that emphasize the fruits of positive teamwork, such as caring, respect, success, and a sense of interdependence; (3) teachers sharing time, materials, and resources; (4) the participation of team members in conflict resolution training; and (5) for team leaders, training in effective leadership skills.

Recommended Reading

Helpful publications on interdisciplinary teaming include *The Team Process: A Handbook for Teachers* (Merenbloom 1991), *Interdisciplinary Teaching in the Middle Grades: Why and How* (Vars 1993), and the March 1994 issue of the *Middle School Journal*, which includes articles that focus on integrating subject areas and selecting interdisciplinary themes.

CONCEPT 4: EFFORTS TO PROMOTE A POSITIVE SCHOOL CLIMATE

The middle school philosophy holds that the overall climate of the school is itself a "teacher."

This We Believe compares a good middle school to a good family—all people in the building are respected and all have particular roles and responsibilities (National Middle School Association 1992). A true middle school provides evidence of warmth, caring, and respect; those conditions should be apparent in all aspects of the school and should be firmly rooted in a sense of harmony and togetherness (California State Department of Education 1987).

Undoubtedly, high school students will benefit from a positive school climate. Such a climate promotes better interpersonal relationships, more humane environments, improved student behavior, and more helpful behavior-management methods. Some high schools subscribe to aggressive (and, in fact, sometimes abrasive and offensive) discipline policies. Educators often place rules and punishments upon students, sometimes in a harsh manner. Although educators have a responsibility to maintain safe and orderly environments, programs designed simply to suppress aggressive or negative behaviors often fail. Teachers and administrators who, on the other hand, implement humane behavior-management programs and model positive behaviors will influence students to treat educators and other students in the same positive manner.

Implementation Tasks

To promote a positive school climate, adults in the school community will need to do the following:

- identify school "hot spots"—either times of the day or locations of the school where aggressive behaviors might begin;
- extend "invitations" for positive school environments (such as listening to students; speaking courteously; using students' interests as a basis for conversations; and refraining from making hurtful remarks) (Kostelnik, Stein, and Whiren 1988);
- identify ways that students can become involved in the governance of the school; and

- name specific alternative (and positive and humane) practices that promote positive behavior and reflect middle school concepts.

Characteristics of Successful Programs

Several characteristics are shared by schools with positive climates. (1) Educators understand the importance of positive interpersonal relationships and their effect on daily school routines. (2) A positive verbal environment sets a tone for students to emulate. (3) Educators plan behavior management systems that enforce school rules and policies yet allow students to retain self-respect. (4) Educators encourage behavior that demonstrates respect for all cultures and both sexes.

Recommended Reading

Irvin's (1992) *Transforming Middle Level Education: Perspectives and Possibilities* includes an article (Johnston 1992) that addresses school climate and collaborative behavior. Also, Thomas and Bass (1993) examine the relationship between school climate and the implementation of middle school practices. Last, the *Middle School Journal* and *The Clearing House* periodically include articles on promoting positive school behaviors.

TIME FRAME

High school educators should be commended for their visions of more positive and humane high schools. They will find, however, that the implementation of middle school concepts into the high school requires both dedicated effort and considerable time. For example, staff development sessions that give educators only an introduction to middle school concepts likely will result in "business as usual." A sustained yet patient effort will prevent educators from feeling overwhelmed by change, will provide time for a genuine change of attitudes and improvement of skills, and will allow educators to feel that they are a part of the change process rather than that change is being imposed on them. Determining a time frame will require a consideration of the individual school, its current practices and policies, the extent to which the middle schools that feed into the high school adhere to the concepts, and the enthusiasm of administrators and faculty. An excellent resource for educators wanting to implement middle school concepts is *Planning for Success: Successful Implementation of Middle School Organization* (Williamson and Johnston 1991).

SUMMARY

Implementing middle school concepts into the high school years can have a positive impact on both adolescents and their educators. Adolescent learners will benefit from advisor-advisee and exploratory programs. They and their teachers will benefit from interdisciplinary teams and from a positive and humane school climate. The challenge lies in determining which middle school concepts to adopt and in reaching agreement on a realistic time frame for implementation. Although implementing the concepts into a high school requires considerable time and effort, educators should not feel overwhelmed in their efforts, especially because students might already have a working knowledge of essential middle school concepts. Similarly, many valuable journal articles and books provide clear directions for implementing those concepts.

REFERENCES

Allen, H. A., F. L. Splittgerber, and M. L. Manning. 1993. *Teaching and learning in the middle level school.* Columbus, Ohio: Merrill.

California State Department of Education. 1987. *Caught in the middle.* Sacramento, Calif.: California Department of Education.

Carnegie Council on Adolescent Development. 1989. *Turning points: Preparing American youth for the 21st century.* Washington, D.C.: Carnegie Council on Adolescent Development.

Compton, M. F., and H. C. Hawn. 1993. *Exploration: The total curriculum.* Columbus, Ohio: National Middle School Association.

Connors, N. A. 1992. Teacher advisory: The fourth r. In *Transforming middle level education: Perspectives and possibilities,* edited by J. L. Irvin, 162–92. Boston: Allyn and Bacon.

Irvin, J. L. 1992. *Transforming middle level education: Perspectives and possibilities.* Boston: Allyn and Bacon.

James, M. 1986. *Advisor-advisee programs: Why, what, and how.* Columbus, Ohio: National Middle School Association.

Johnston, J. H. 1992. Climate and culture as mediators of school values and collaborative behavior. In *Transforming middle level education: Perspectives and possibilities,* edited by J. L. Irvin, 77–92. Boston: Allyn and Bacon.

Kostelnik, M. J., L. C. Stein, and A. P. Whiten. 1988. Children's self-esteem: The verbal environment. *Childhood Education* 65:29–32.

Manning. M. L. 1993. *Developmentally appropriate middle level schools.* Wheaton, Md.: Association for Childhood Education International.

Maryland Department of Education. 1989. *What matters in the middle grades.* Baltimore, Md.: Maryland Department of Education.

Merenbloom, E. 1991. *The team process: A handbook for teachers.* Columbus, Ohio: National Middle School Association.

National Association of Secondary School Principals. 1993. *Achieving excellence through the middle level curriculum.* Reston, Va.: National Association of Secondary School Principals.

National Middle School Association. 1992. *This we believe.* Columbus, Ohio: National Middle School Association.

Thomas, D. D., and G. R. Bass. 1993. An analysis of the relationship between school climate and the implementation of middle school practices. *Research in Middle Level Education* 16:1–12.

Vats, G. F. 1993. *Interdisciplinary teaching in the middle grades: Why and how.* Columbus, Ohio: National Middle School Association.

Williamson, R., and J. H. Johnston. 1991. *Planning for success: Successful implementation of middle school organization.* Reston, Va.: National Association of Secondary School Principals.

M. Lee Manning is an associate professor in the Department of Educational Curriculum and Instruction, Darden College of Education, Old Dominion University, Norfolk, Virginia; *Richard Saddlemire* is superintendent of the Antilles Consolidated School System, Fort Buchanan, Puerto Rico.

QUESTIONS FOR REFLECTION

1. Select one of the four middle school concepts discussed in this article and critique the recommendations for implementing that concept. What additional implementation strategies would you suggest?

2. Review the articles in Chapter 8 on educational programs for transescents and early adolescents. What additional middle school concepts would you suggest for the high school level?

3. The authors identify four general characteristics shared by schools with positive climates. If you were evaluating the climate of a school, what specific "evidence" would you look for to indicate the presence, or absence, of each characteristic?

New Hope for High Schools: Lessons from Reform-Minded Educators

THEODORE R. SIZER

ABSTRACT: This excerpt from Horace's Hope: What Works for the American High School *examines four factors that account for the "extraordinary gap between common sense and common school practice": the symbolic, rather than substantive, purposes of high schools; the highly complex and interconnected high school "mechanism"; similar high school routines across the country; and decisions about policy and practice made by those who do not have to live with those decisions. The author then discusses four of the thirteen lessons he has learned from working with reform-minded schools—these schools have stable leadership; perceive each child as an individual; continually readjust goals based on children, staff, and community; and have a climate based on respect and genuine communication.*

The leap from traditional school practice to commonsense reform is for most Americans a heroic one. Contrast familiar life outside school with that commonly found inside school. Few parents want to spend, or can even rationally contemplate spending, a full day all alone penned up in one room with 27 12-year-olds, day after day.... Nonetheless, most parents assume that a middle-school teacher can cope well every day of the week with five groups of 27 12-year-olds drawn from every sort of community, following a regimen over which that teacher has almost no control.

Most college English department faculty members would mightily object—and do strenuously object—if those of them who teach writing classes are forced to carry more than 60 students at once, in four classes of 15 students each. Nonetheless, most school boards assume that high school English instructors can teach 120 to 180 students, in groups of 20 to 40, to write clearly and well.

Few businesses hire people on the basis of test scores alone, or even principally so. Most businesses hire people on the basis of evidence about their previous work, its substance, and how faithfully and imaginatively they dealt with that substance. Yet most policy makers assume that for

serious purposes of judgment, one can pinpoint the present effectiveness and future chances of a child, or even an entire school, on the basis of some congeries of numerical data.

Few successful businesses change the content of each employee's work every hour and regularly and insistently interrupt the workers' efforts with announcements on a public address system. Nonetheless, a seven- or eight-period day and an incessant blare of administrative matters over PA systems characterize most high schools.

Few serious enterprises let all their employees take long vacations at the same time every year. Few such enterprises assume that all work can be reduced to a predictable schedule, which implies that every worker will produce at the same speed. Few serious businesses believe that those who are immediately swifter are always better. Nonetheless, most high schools accept these practices without challenge.

And more. The typical routines of high school . . . often defy elementary logic and the experience of the typical citizen. Yet, curiously, they seem exceedingly difficult to change.

I believe that there are at least four reasons for this extraordinary gap between common sense and common school practice.

Excerpted from *Horace's Hope*, by Theodore R. Sizer. Copyright © 1996 by Theodore R. Sizer. Reprinted by permission of Houghton Mifflin Company. All rights reserved.

First, high schools in America serve more symbolic than substantive purposes. The routines of adolescence carry great weight—taking the expected courses, coping with Mom and Dad over a report card festooned with challenging letter or numerical grades, meeting girls or boys, dating (made possible by the rituals of the high school hallways), attending homecoming, the prom, and above all graduation, that choreographed rite of passage expected of every American around the age of 18. One messes with these very familiar icons of practice at one's peril. . . .

Second, the high school mechanism is highly complex and interconnected. The curriculum, for example, is divided into familiar subjects. To teach a particular subject in a public school, one has to be formally certified in that academic area by the state. One gains certification by attending a college where specified courses leading to that credential are given. The college is divided into departments that correspond with the certification needs of those at the high school. College faculty get their tenure by providing the expected courses and writing their books in the expected areas. The collective bargaining agreements reflect these subject categories. State and federal assessments and regulations depend on them. . . . Seemingly everything important within and outside a high school affects everything else. To change anything means changing everything. The prospect is daunting, usually paralyzing.

Third, and not surprisingly, school routines tend to be remarkably similar in high schools across the country, even those in the private sector, where one might expect significantly different approaches. There are few examples, especially state-endorsed examples, of a school organized in ways and on assumptions that diverge sharply from the conventional. Thus we have a chicken-and-egg problem; there is no critical mass of different schools across the country to bear witness to a better kind of schooling, and this makes the argument in their favor a difficult one, based on promises rather than evidence.

Finally, the people who make many crucial decisions about educational policy and practice—those at the top—do not have to live with those decisions. After giving the order to charge, they do not have to lead the troops—that is, to serve directly in the schools. Accordingly, there is little incentive for many of them to study the realities. . . . They can require and recommend and finance with little immediate accountability. If kids do not improve, someone else is always there to blame. . . .

Change comes hard, even when the need for the change is blatantly obvious. The system carries on, even when the carrying on is irrational. In Essential schools as well as in schools in kindred projects, there is usually a battle over even the most obviously needed reforms. Realistically, we must expect that a majority of the schools attempting significant change will flounder, smothered by the forces of mindless tradition, fear, and obstruction, which, because of the complexity of high school work, are so easy to rally. As a result, we have learned to be very straight with the schools and with the authorities directing them about the rigors and costs of serious change. . . .

Human-scale places are critical. "I cannot teach well a student whom I do not know." How many students at once can one high school teacher know well? At the start, the Coalition, somewhat arbitrarily, asserted that no teacher should have responsibility for more than 80 students. Even though the leap to this number from the more usual 100 to 180 students is heroic, the record of demonstrably successful Essential schools shows that this number is still too large.

However, we have learned that there is much more to the whole matter of scale. It is not only that each teacher must have a sensible load of students. It is that the school itself has to be of human scale—a place where everyone can know everyone else. Of course, smallness is just the beginning, but it is a necessary precondition.

More than one teacher must know each child (and her family) well, and there must be time for those teachers, and, as necessary, her parents, to discuss that child. It is fine for me to know Jessica, a ninth-grader; but my knowledge of her is necessarily limited to her participation in my classes and our personal relationship. She may well be known quite differently by another teacher, who is a different person and who teaches her a different subject. Together that teacher and I and her parents can construct a fuller, fairer portrait of Jessica than any of us can alone.

Such sharing of knowledge about kids requires trusting colleagueship among teachers. If we are hired merely on the basis of our certification areas ("secondary school U.S. and European history teacher") and seniority in the school system ("First hired, last fired"), we join a school as independent operators, are given our classrooms, and consult and collaborate only when the spirit moves us. But when we are chosen to work in a school on the basis of a commitment to the philosophy of that school and because our arrival will strengthen the corps of staff members already there, the relationship of each of us to the others is always crucial, particularly so if the school is taking on tough reforms.

How many colleagues can work effectively together? No more, our hunch is, than can attend a crowded potluck supper. So much of importance in schools depends on trust, and trust arises from familiarity and from time spent together getting divisive issues out on the table and addressing them. A team of 25 to 30 teachers, a number large enough for variety and small enough for trust, might be ideal. This implies, given average secondary school pupil-teacher ratios, a school of 325 to 420 pupils, itself a human-scale number. Adolescent anonymity is unlikely in such a place.

How, some protest, does one create such small units when school buildings are very large? The answer is to divide the students into small, fully autonomous units, each in effect its own school within a large "educational apartment building."

What does it take to work together effectively? A mix of inspired leadership, candor, and restraint. Schools are difficult places, filled with issues over which reasonable people will disagree. A process to work the inevitable kinks out is necessary, as is the time for that process to proceed.

A kid has just been caught with a pinch of marijuana; he is a first-time offender. Should we suspend him? "We need to set an example." Or do we just slap his wrist hard? "He's really scared—he needs support now."

Those English prize essays; which is best and why? Who gets the prize? Should there be a prize? What signals, good and bad, do prizes send?

An unmarried teacher is pregnant. As she comes to term, should she continue to teach? "She models the very behavior that we must not condone." "She's a stellar teacher; the kids love her." "Her private life is her own business." "Each case deserves to be decided on its merits." . . .

The very existence of such confrontations, of course, makes teaching an endlessly stimulating occupation. These are real issues that affect real people every day, and they are issues as influential in people's lives as they are controversial. They can be dealt with well only in schools small enough to allow for trusting relationships among the staff and with the students.

Human scale is only the beginning. The culture of the place is also critical. Essential schools with high morale reflect the dignity deserved by teachers as well as students. The little things symbolize it well. Teachers are given not only the time to struggle with the substance and standards of the students' daily work but also the civilities of access to telephones and trust in their use. A copying machine is available for all, not just the administrative staff. There are no time clocks or check-ins. Teachers are expected to consult with one another, and easy relationships among colleagues—formal or informal, as the individuals like—are the norm. These matters are the important minutiae of school keeping, the little things that send institutional signals.

Work in an Essential school (as in most others) is hard. The pressure is bearable if the work is respected, not only in word but in the way the adult community functions. Essential schools that have worked out their relationships clearly serve their students better than those in which the adults go their own ways civilly or are full of tension and disrespect. . . .

The evidence in favor of human-scale environments and a teacher-student ratio of one to 80 or fewer comes largely from negative findings. Some schools, however devoted to redesign, have not been able to reduce teacher loads dramatically. They thereby remain wracked with faculty dissension, which paralyzes all reform beyond generalized rhetoric. Big schools remain the prisoners of procedures rather than relationships to get through a day, and many of their students thus remain aloof and difficult to engage. The poor performance of such students reflects this.

The limited but growing number of small Essential schools (or small autonomous units within a larger institution) that have been able to build coherent relationships demonstrably outperform their large and bureaucratically ensnared brethren. . . .

Clusters of schools proceed more effectively than schools alone. The Coalition in its early years was a group of individual schools, each making its own way in its own setting. As the numbers of schools grew, for administrative convenience we organized regional centers to provide the kind of support usually delivered from the Coalition's central office at Brown University. We have since realized that clustering has important substantive virtues.

The schools play off against one another, comparing work, consulting on new directions, promoting honest talk by faculty members across schools, serving each other as sustained "critical friends." A cluster of schools can help others in their midst get started, both through the small staffs they hire and by lending veteran teachers as consultants.

The schools protect one another politically. In one extraordinary instance, a new district superintendent threatened to fire a principal because she had raised substantial moneys on her own for her school's library, which made it far richer than comparable libraries in nearby schools. The superintendent found this inequitable; no school should have a much bigger library than others. The principal had to cease this fund-raising, he ordered. Principals at the other schools in the cluster and the cluster's staff had contacts with the local newspaper, and the story quickly reached page one. The superintendent backed off. Entrepreneurial energy was applauded, and the poverty of school library budgets was exposed.

In some places, such as New York City, clusters in fact operate in some respects as formal school districts. They collectively prepare standards and expectations for exhibitions, and they make the work of their students public. They monitor and support one another. When it is efficient, they make collective purchases. They have negotiated with the state for collective waivers of regulations. They are professional and governmental units in all but name. They profoundly redefine what is meant by the top and the bottom.

The relationship between the top and the bottom of the educational hierarchy must be fundamentally rethought. Our experience with the governance of schools has led to four principal conclusions. First, stability of leadership within the system is crucial. Schools endlessly affected by changes—new superintendents, each with a new plan; new governors, also with "new initiatives"; new legislative leadership—are pulled in frustratingly different directions. We have seen school principals and teachers figuring out practically, and often cynically, how to fend off the worst of any new order, knowing that this year's innovation may well not be operative next year. . . .

Second, the way the policy community and the bureaucracy view schooling is crucial. If the metaphor of the bloodless assembly line persists, little change happens. Dealing with children in the aggregate ("all the eighth-graders in this state," "all children from families below the poverty line") and perceiving each child as an individual ("just like each of my own very different children") lead policy in very different directions. The latter, obviously—as it reflects reality—is preferable.

Policy makers, of course, have to view the large scene, but they do not have to reduce the scene to crude generalities. Accepting both the diversities implicit in schooling—the differences among children, neighborhoods, and professionals—and the need to attend carefully to the wishes, commitments, and proper rights of parents make system policy and practice complex, and thus a nuisance. We have found that when the subtleties are honored and when there has been bipartisan commitment to a reform direction, the results are promising.

In 1988, the Coalition of Essential Schools formally allied with the Education Commission of the States (an association of state governments for collective study of educational policy and practice) in a project dubbed Re:Learning to pursue what we called a strategy of reform "from the schoolhouse to the statehouse." The assumption here was that the governmental "top" and the school-level "bottom" would work as close allies, with the demands and particular needs of the bottom—the individual schools—profoundly shaping the top's specific policies.

Over the past years some 15 states have been involved, directly or indirectly, in this project, which has led to efforts to bring together the teaching and policy communities for greater understanding of each other's roles (gatherings rarely held in previous times), state assignment of staff to support Essential schools and kindred reforming schools, state funds to support the reform, and waivers of regulations to give the schools room to redesign their work. In several states this activity has led to reform legislation—specific support to risk-taking schools. Most important, Re:Learning has given legitimacy to the work of those schools trying to break with unwise practices. The informed blessing of the top has provided substantial support for the bottom, as the rapid growth of Essential schools after 1988 evidences.

Third, leaders at both the top and the bottom have to understand that managing a school is rather like sailing a boat. There is a chart, there is a planned course, and there are plotted shoals and sandbars, but those on board have to adjust all the time to changing winds and attitudes, even redrawing the course to the destination from time to time. There are goals for a school and a framework of expectations for how those goals may be reached, but the means, and even the framework itself, are subject to constant adjustment on the basis of what is going on with the children, the staff, and the community. The hand of government has to be a light one, and a trusting one. Directing the sailboat from an office ashore is as imprudent as directing the activities of an individual school from a school system's central headquarters.

Finally, respect and sustained, genuine communication between top and bottom are essential. Where there are differences, they should be addressed. Too often they are swept under a rug while the state or district tries to ram its views home and the locals sit on their hands, griping.

Of course, the conventional wisdom implies that higher government has the right to overrule lower government. The fact that these "levels" of government arise more from the realities of scale (towns are smaller than states) and from political arrangements than from citizens' rights obscures the fact that the compulsory nature of public education puts an enormous responsibility for restraint on governmental leaders. Some give that responsibility too little respect, with predictable resentment and opposition at the bottom.

The shape and obligations of all the pieces of the public school system as we know it are under fresh scrutiny. State and city leaders' willingness to contemplate radical changes in that system is strikingly more prevalent today than when the Coalition's work started. The system is under criticism unprecedented in this century. We hope that the new forms it takes adhere carefully to the convictions represented by Re:Learning's slogan, "*from* the schoolhouse *to* the statehouse."

Theodore R. Sizer is university Professor Emeritus, Brown University, and Chairman of the Coalition of Essential Schools, Oakland, California.

QUESTIONS FOR REFLECTION

1. After his brief discussion of the symbolic purposes of high school, Sizer says "One messes with these very familiar icons of practice at one's peril. . . ." What does he mean by this statement?

2. After discussing the complexity and interconnectedness of the "high school mechanism," Sizer concludes that the prospect of change is "daunting, usually paralyzing." Do you agree? Can you cite evidence to suggest that Sizer's view is too pessimistic?

3. Reflecting on the educational setting with which you are most familiar (K–12 through higher education; school or nonschool program), to what extent does the climate of this setting reflect concern for the "human scale"? How does this concern (or lack of concern) affect students' learning?

Rethinking the Benefits of the College-Bound Curriculum

NEL NODDINGS

ABSTRACT: Pointing out that "elite" colleges exert too much control over the curriculum for noncollege-bound students, the author recommends rethinking two beliefs that support the current top-down model of education. First, the belief that all children should have an opportunity to qualify for the best colleges may lead to students being "forced" to follow a desired curriculum. Second, the belief that breadth, rather than specialization, is desirable in the precollege curriculum leads many to look for evidence that students have taken a subject rather than know *that subject.*

Deborah Meier and Susan Ohanian invite us to think about how secondary schools and colleges might approach education if they were modeled on the early elementary grades and the needs of students instead of on the images and demands of the elite colleges and universities. They claim that such education might be characterized by greater freedom, sustained activity, playfulness, sense of purpose, and a healthy skepticism born of genuine curiosity. The elite colleges and universities do in fact exercise more control than they should over a vast number of students who will never enter their doors. Can anything be done to change this?

I will argue that we should rethink two sets of beliefs that support the current topdown model:

one, a set of faulty notions about equal opportunity, sameness, and the inherent worth of the college-bound curriculum; the other, an equally faulty set of beliefs about the dangers of specialization and the benefits of breadth. Rethinking these matters may weaken the rationale for our current mode of operation.

FAULTY NOTIONS ABOUT EQUALITY AND SAMENESS

Advocates of the standard precollege curriculum usually offer one or both of two arguments for requiring students to take college-preparatory

From *Phi Delta Kappan* 78, no. 4 (December 1996): 285–289. © 1996, Phi Delta Kappa. Used by permission of the author and publisher.

mathematics, science, English, history, and foreign language. One argument seeks to persuade us that all children should have the opportunity to qualify for an elite education. The second maintains that a curriculum designed as preparation for Harvard or Stanford is, inherently, the best education for everyone. It seems to me that both of these arguments are wrong and, in some forms, actually harmful.

Let's consider the first argument—that all children should be given an opportunity to qualify for the best colleges. The first thing to notice is that opportunities might be provided without coercion. Too often those who insist on equal opportunity want to force students into the curriculum that will "give" them the desired opportunity. They argue that high school students are simply not mature enough to make important curriculum choices; for their own good, then, the school must make these choices for them.

Mortimer Adler, for example, has insisted that, left to their own choices, some students will "downgrade" their own education; therefore, adults should control these crucial choices so that such downgrading does not occur.[1] But there are two powerful responses to Adler's concerns. First, it should not be possible for students to downgrade their education no matter what choices they make. Why should responsible educators allow schools to offer a set of "good" courses and a set of "bad" courses? As John Dewey pointed out years ago, a course in cooking, well planned and well executed, can induce critical thinking, increase cultural literacy, and provide valuable skills—it can be a "good" course. In contrast, a course in algebra may discourage critical thinking, add nothing to cultural literacy, and lead students to despair of acquiring useful skills—it can be a "bad" course. Thus, before we abandon the variety of courses typical of the "shopping mall" high school, we should ask genuine and penetrating questions about the value of these courses. I've already offered three criteria for judging courses good or bad. I'd also ask, Are they interesting? Are they challenging? Do the teachers treat the students with respect?

Are the students likely to grow as whole persons—in other words, is it reasonable to predict that the students will grow socially, morally, and intellectually? When I say that these questions should be asked genuinely, I mean that we should not decide a priori that the conventional academic subjects are superior to others. We should investigate. We should ask teachers to justify what they do in light of the criteria we establish, and we should continually ask penetrating questions about the criteria themselves.

The second response to Adler's worry is equally important. When some of us object strongly to the coercion inherent in a standardized curriculum, defenders often suppose that we are recommending a permissive, "hands-off" freedom for students. In fact, what we are recommending is something much more demanding and realistic. We are recommending a system of teacher counseling and guidance that approximates parental interest in students. We reject the simple (and highly deceptive) notion that students can be given equal opportunity by force. The very notion is antithetical to democratic education. We need to live with our children, assess their gifts and interests both realistically and generously, talk with them, listen to them, and help them to make well-informed decisions.

But, sincere advocates of standardization protest, despite commendable guidance (and it won't always be available), some students will land in the wrong slots. They will not be prepared if they change their minds and want college after all. This complaint underscores the criticisms raised by Meier and Ohanian. Why *should* the colleges be allowed to continue their stranglehold on the school curriculum? Why should rigorous alternative courses not be acceptable for college admission? And why shouldn't our education system be flexible enough to accommodate the changes of mind that increasingly characterize a postmodern society? The crucial educational point here is that students may learn better how to learn and may have greater confidence in their capacity to learn if they are encouraged to make well-informed decisions about their own education. Changing their minds should lead to new challenges, not to helpless despair.

Before leaving the discussion of the "equal opportunity" argument, I want to say something about political aspects of the argument. Politicians often affirm that education is, or should be, the way out of poverty. Teachers are urged to have the same expectations for poor children as for rich children: all should meet the rigorous standards that are now being recommended. This advice may be well intentioned, but its logic is muddled. We know that, by and large, children from stable, economically secure homes do fairly well with standard schooling (I am *not* arguing that they are, therefore, well educated—just that they do well on standard measures). In contrast, children from poor homes often have a difficult time with the usual pattern of schooling. How will this be changed by simply declaring that poor children now *will* do as well as richer ones? It would be more logical to launch a massive social program against poverty on the assumption that the formerly poor would now do better in schools.

Many of us worry that the current emphasis on high achievement for all is a monumental distraction from the social problems that should command our attention. Consider what would happen if we succeeded in bringing all students to whatever standards we establish. Our society would still need people to grow and harvest our food, to pack and deliver it, to sell it in supermarkets; we would still need waiters, cooks, and people to clean up; we would still need people to drive our trucks, buses, and taxis; we would still need hotel maids, street cleaners, repair persons, retail clerks, and servers of fast food. What excuse would we then have for letting many of these people live in poverty? Would we argue that, although they met the standard, they did less well than others? What excuse do we have now? It is clear that poverty is a social problem—a moral problem—not an educational one. No person who works at a legitimate job should live in poverty.

As we wake up and acknowledge our interdependence and the obvious worth of so many jobs that are now devalued, we should begin to look at our students with greater appreciation. What a wonderful range of talents and interests they bring to their first years in school! Howard Gardner has identified seven intelligences, only two of which are recognized and developed in schools.[2] Whether or not further research confirms seven (or 49!) intelligences, anyone who has taught knows that children have different gifts. To expect all children to do well in a course of study designed for a few seems very unfair. Moreover, such a system is wasteful; it demands higher degrees and harsher methods of coercion, loses more students through discouragement, and wears teachers out. Ultimately, it is disrespectful, denying the very talents and interests on which the society depends.

When we face the fact that the schoolchildren of today will do all kinds of work as adults, we have to ask why they should all have the same education. I have already argued that the equal opportunity rationale is faulty; to suppose that a child who is interested and talented in a subject has the same opportunity as one whose interests and talents lie elsewhere is heartless. But there remains the possibility that the standard curriculum is inherently valuable, that it is important for all children no matter what occupations they enter.

This is an argument made popular early in this century by Robert Maynard Hutchins. Hutchins reasoned that "education implies teaching. Teaching implies knowledge. Knowledge is truth. The truth is everywhere the same. Hence, education should be everywhere the same."[3] In today's atmosphere of recognized pluralism, Hutchins' syllogism sounds both arrogant and ludicrous, but the standard curriculum reflects an underlying acceptance of similar notions. Many believe that the truth is somehow discoverable (or has already been discovered) and that it should somehow be made into a standard curriculum. I am not suggesting, of course, that our curricula should be liberally sprinkled with falsehoods. I am simply pointing out that notions of universal truth are, in reality, too parochial and too limited to serve as the foundation of education. Further, much education is properly aimed at skills, attitudes, and forms of thinking that cannot be characterized as "truths," although they may serve in the continuing inquiry that leads in the direction of a form of truth.

However, there is an important point to consider in Hutchins' argument. To the degree that people are alike and share a common human condition, they need some common education. Deborah Meier emphasizes citizenship, and surely each new generation of citizens needs some knowledge and skills associated with that status. But it is unlikely that students need the chronological history demanded by some policy makers or that they need a great deal of specific information about the holders of various offices, the number of congressional representatives, or the dates on which various laws were enacted. Much that is regarded as necessary for citizenship is probably not essential, and what is essential is usually overlooked. Too often we concentrate on cramming students' heads with easily testable facts and ignore the discourse of responsibility, interdependent sociality, community, and commitment. Further, we often fail to provide our students with the practice they need to participate effectively in democratic citizenship.

Moreover, as human beings, we have more in common than citizenship. The emphasis on citizenship as contrasted with private life is, at least in part, a product of masculine domination of the curriculum. Where are all the matters traditionally assigned to women? Our children need to know something about the commitment required for intimate relationships, what it means to be a parent, what it means to make a home. They should become good neighbors, responsible pet owners, concerned guardians of the natural world, and honest colleagues in whatever activities they pursue. They should know something about the stages of life, the various approaches to spirituality, suffering and compassion, violence and peace. These are the common learnings teachers should include in their courses; these are the topics that arise in common human experience.

It is perhaps understandable that successful people educated in the traditional way might mourn the demise of the curriculum they studied. To some it is deplorable that English teachers no longer find Shakespeare essential. But many English teachers are working with young people who carry weapons to school, who may be assaulted or killed, or who will produce babies while they are themselves still children. To insist on the traditional curriculum in such circumstances is irresponsible.

Advocates of the traditional curriculum might grant my point but insist that something must be done to prepare students for the standard curriculum. They might argue that resources should be made available so that young people will be ready for a "real" education. In a sense, these advocates want the curriculum to be made safe for Shakespeare. In opposition, I would argue that *all* children need a new sort of common studies, as outlined above, and that Shakespeare, like so many other staples of the traditional curriculum, should become a treasured option, not a requirement.

Today, we cannot think in terms of one ideal model of the educated person. There are obviously many such models living and working all around us. Some well-educated and successful people cannot recognize the music of Beethoven, some cannot tell a Monet from a Manet, many have no concept of mathematical functions, most cannot name the parts of an insect or any of the great geologic ages. Unavoidably, as knowledge continues to expand, we will become more ignorant as well as more knowledgeable. What is truly deplorable, however, and what must be avoided is raising generations of violent, irresponsible, uncaring, and unhealthy adults.

FAULTY NOTIONS ABOUT SPECIALIZATION

This part of my argument is tied very closely to the first part. On the one hand, many Americans fear early specialization and argue for a breadth in precollege (and sometimes even college) education that will "keep the doors open" and not commit their children to any specific form of work or field of study. On the other hand, many of the same people have accepted an array of narrow specializations as an adequate representation of breadth. This is the kind of anomaly that arises when we fail to think deeply enough about an issue.

One wonders whether the parents and educators who argue against early specialization really want something called "breadth" or whether what we are hearing is just another variant of the "change of mind" argument. If it is the latter, we can reiterate and deepen our earlier response. The *system* must be transformed to make such changes of mind easier and to keep the pursuit of learning vital and meaningful.

But suppose people really want breadth; suppose, that is, that the argument is for broad cultural knowledge—knowledge that spans the array of human disciplines. I have already argued that advocates of the standard curriculum cannot have in mind the full range of human *concerns,* or they would not leave out of the curriculum most of the matters traditionally assigned to women and associated with private life. Hence our focus must be on the recognized disciplines—history, literature, philosophy, mathematics, and so on. Is the aim of breadth accomplished by requiring students to take a wide variety of courses in these disciplines?

Here I will argue that the present system accomplishes nothing of the kind. Consider one powerful piece of evidence. In high school, students aiming for college must take such a variety of courses. They study four, five, or six disciplines, but their teachers know only one. Their teachers have, for the most part, been subjected to the same required breadth and over several more years, and yet the end result is an "educated" adult who knows only one discipline and rarely has any breadth even in that. How often can a student get help on an algebra problem from her English teacher? And try asking the math teacher for help in interpreting *Heart of Darkness* or *Moby Dick.*

As the disciplines are taught now, the breadth argument is a sham. The true objective has little to do with knowledge; its focus is credentialing. We are not so concerned that students *know* some mathematics, for example; we are far more instrumentally concerned that their records should show that they have *taken* mathematics. Then, if they decide to apply to college, they are "prepared." I am not condemning this argument. Indeed, it is the most powerful and convincing one that can be given for going along with the required curriculum. But we ought not to deceive ourselves and suppose that there is a sound educational rationale for the present structure.

If we really wanted breadth in the disciplines, we would begin to broaden each discipline from within. We would reconsider our views on specialization. As it is now, we reject specialization when it means that a child will be allowed to concentrate on an area of his own special interest. But we accept presentations of the disciplines that are overly narrow and often specialized to the point where few generalists can find anything to whet their interest.

The development of narrower and narrower specialties is, of course, one of the manifestations of the Weberian bureaucratic system in which we now live. Its signs are all around us. We regularly ask exactly who should do what, scarcely questioning the supposition that every agency and role should have well-stated functions and that these functions should not overlap. Thus we ask, "Who should provide moral guidance for our children?" and argue over whether it should be the parents or the school. It rarely occurs to us that in some matters—surely in education—the organization should be more holistic. In holistic enterprises, the answer to questions about who should perform certain tasks is "everyone concerned." In such domains we refuse to chop everything into small pieces, each one handled by a particular expert, technician, or assembly-line worker.

"Prescriptive technologies" have their place, of course. They are enormously powerful in fields of material production. The physicist Ursula Franklin remarks, "Today, the temptation to design more or less everything according to prescriptive and broken-up technologies is so strong that it is even applied to those tasks that should be conducted in a holistic way. Any tasks that require caring, whether for people or nature, any tasks that require immediate feedback and adjustment, are best done holistically."[4] Franklin explicitly names education as a quintessential holistic enterprise. By dividing the disciplines in a narrow and exclusive way, we have in fact fragmented the mental life of schooling. Perhaps even worse, we have made it impossible for students to catch a glimpse of their teachers as whole persons—as models of educated persons.[5]

It is possible to teach the individual disciplines in a way that does not sacrifice the special quality that attracts a few to each and yet connects each discipline to the wider intellectual and social world. Wayne Booth has described the influence on his own life of a high school chemistry teacher who taught the liberal arts in his chemistry classes.[6] Booth does not mean by this that his chemistry teacher literally taught bits of disjointed mathematics, literature, or history. Rather, he means that the teacher shared with his students great ideas and how they arose, something of the aesthetics and epistemology of his subject, pieces of biographical and historical information when those were relevant or potentially interesting—that he could move about freely in the various domains we declare to be important and draw out stories and concepts that enriched both his chemistry instruction and the cultural literacy of his students.

I have myself argued in several places that mathematics teachers should be prepared to teach in this way.[7] Of course, mathematics as a school subject—just as art, music, and all other subjects—should retain the special identity and encourage the special talent that draws students to it, but it should also broaden students' moral and aesthetic sensibilities, increase their cultural literacy, and reveal the teacher as an educated person. Mathematics teachers should have a wide repertoire of stories connecting mathematics (or mathematicians) to theology, logic, and science but

also to classism, sexism, mysticism, militarism, and a host of other topics of general interest. They should be prepared to discuss what it means to live in a mathematicized world and how to cope with that world. The mathematics teacher, like every other teacher, should feel an obligation to discuss the great existential questions: What is the meaning of life? What are its origins? Its destination? How should I live? Why is there suffering and what is my obligation in relieving it? Have mathematicians thought about these questions? Of course! But one would never guess it from what occurs in most high school classes.

We would not have to worry seriously about early specialization if everything taught in schools were approached in this way. Students could pursue their own interests with the enthusiasm of children and experts and still expand their horizons. They would gain specialized skills and, at the same time, get a sense of how their subject, talent, or special interest fits within the larger culture.

CAN HIGHER EDUCATION CHANGE?

By way of concluding remarks, I want to explore the feasibility of changes in higher education. Susan Ohanian says that she has "no quarrel with the entrance requirements of Harvard," but that she refuses to accept a system of precollege education designed to prepare all students for Harvard. The problem here, of course, is that some parents want their children prepared for Harvard. They are quite right in assuming that, even if their children are not accepted at Harvard, some other "good enough" school will be impressed by the preparation. It will take courage and imagination for other colleges to break away and establish their own criteria. A very few have done so already.

Many people in higher education admit that the traditional admissions criteria are faulty. But the criteria are well established and widely accepted by a huge public. Even though several features of the system have been attacked as unfair, it is thought to be more fair than a system that might be more responsive to individual talents and more specialized preparation. Any change in a system so widespread and so deeply entrenched would have to be gradual. Two separate standards of preparation—for scientific and nonscientific fields—might be a start.

I think it is more feasible to work toward broadening the disciplines from within and toward the establishment of a solid variety of pre-college courses of study. The latter must grow out of a genuine commitment on the part of parents and educators to provide an excellent education for the work-bound as well as the college-bound. It is a project in which industry could be a valuable partner.

However, higher education could take the lead in broadening the disciplines from within, in restoring the liberality to liberal education. The most obviously pressing need in this project is to educate teachers adequately. To do what I suggest, however, requires the courage to insist that teachers need a highly specialized form of education—that is, one designed especially for teachers. When they are undergraduates preparing to teach, their majors should reflect the breadth described earlier. Excellent teachers possess more than narrow subject-matter knowledge plus some tricks of the trade. They have both broad general knowledge and an impressive range of knowledge in their own discipline.

The course of study I've outlined for teachers could in no way be considered "watered down." Indeed, its richness and rigor might well be the envy of those majoring in the nonteaching versions of the same subjects. Oddly enough, even here we encounter the "change of mind" argument. People have actually said to me, "But what if a student majors in math-for-teaching and then decides to do something else?" My first answer is that he or she will probably have a better mathematics education than most other mathematics majors—one characterized by deeper understand-ing of basic concepts and a fuller appreciation of mathematics in the wider culture. But my second answer is "Would you ask a question like this of preparation for, say, engineering?" If people decide to be social workers or ministers after preparing for engineering, then they must acquire the requisite preparation for their newly chosen field. Why should we suppose that preparation for nothing-in-particular is sound preparation for teaching?

Ohanian and Meier are basically right. Education modeled from the bottom up would be characterized by greater freedom, a more energetic pursuit of continuing interests, and a greater sense of purpose. But to bring off such a change will require that greater trust be placed in both students and teachers. Will students make wise choices? Will teachers guide them well? And will teachers prepare themselves so well that every course they offer is rich with the details of a wide range of human concerns?

NOTES

1. Mortimer Adler, *The Paideia Proposal* (New York: Macmillan, 1982).
2. See Howard Gardner, *Frames of Mind* (New York: Basic Books, 1983).
3. Robert Maynard Hutchins, *The Higher Learning in America* (New Haven, Conn.: Yale University Press, 1936), p. 66.
4. Ursula Franklin, *The Real World of Technology* (Concord, Ont.: Anansi Press, 1992), p. 24.
5. See Bruce Wilshire, *The Moral Collapse of the University* (Albany, N.Y.: SUNY Press, 1990).
6. See Wayne C. Booth, *The Vocation of a Teacher* (Chicago: University of Chicago Press, 1988).
7. See Nel Noddings, *The Challenge to Care in Schools* (New York: Teachers College Press, 1992); idem, *Educating for Intelligent Belief or Unbelief* (New York: Teachers College Press, 1993); and idem, "Does Everybody Count?," *Journal of Mathematical Behavior,* vol. 13, 1994, pp. 89–104.

Nel Noddings is Lee Jacks Professor of Education at Stanford University, Stanford, California.

QUESTIONS FOR REFLECTION

1. Are high school students mature enough to make important curriculum decisions for themselves, or should the schools make these decisions?
2. At the level of education and in the curricular area with which you are most familiar, do students (and their teachers) have the perception that there are "good" and "bad" courses? On what bases are these judgments made?
3. According to Noddings, why is the "equal opportunity rationale" faulty? Do you agree?

CASE STUDY IN CURRICULUM IMPLEMENTATION

Horizonte—Where Students Come First

JAMES P. ANDERSON
BARBARA FLOISAND
DAVID MARTINEZ
DALMAR P. ROBINSON

ABSTRACT: Horizonte is an alternative Utah high school that enables students to help direct their own learning. The school's educational program is organized around five guiding principles or fundamental beliefs, rather than specific strategies: (1) students' needs and learning styles shape the curriculum, (2) students and staff have universal access to technology, (3) the curriculum is inclusive and multicultural, (4) students are assisted to reach their full potential, and (5) teachers are enthusiastic, adaptable, lifelong learners.

To a scientist, a horizon is the line between the earth and the sky. To anthropologists, it can refer to artifacts from varied origins that display cultural similarities. But for an educator, *horizon* means the potential that each student strives to develop. Two years ago, when our alternative public school, the Salt Lake Community High School, moved into a newer facility, we renamed it the Horizonte Instruction and Training Center, deliberately selecting the non-English term.

At the outset, many people wondered whether students would feel alienated and uncomfortable attending an institution with a Spanish name, unless, of course, they themselves happened to be

From *Educational Leadership* 54, no. 7 (April 1997): 50–52. © 1997, Association for Supervision and Curriculum Development. Used by permission of the authors and publisher.

Hispanic. But Horizonte's largest single minority is indeed Latino (45 percent). So Horizonte prevailed. The other minority groups are Pacific Islanders, African Americans, Asians, Eastern Europeans, and Native Americans. Total enrollment is 1,800 students. Along with high school students, Horizonte serves adults whose education has been interrupted for a variety of reasons.

In our logo, the word *horizon* is printed in English, Tongan, Russian, Vietnamese, Piute, and Arabic. Many Utah place names have Native American origins. We wanted our school to become an intentional symbol of multiculturalism. Everyone is welcome here—Navajos, Bosnians, Somalis, Caucasians, Hispanics. Students may wear the apparel of their homeland without being considered abnormal. Horizonte encourages student success despite the many challenges in their lives—poverty, discrimination, teenage pregnancy, and disrupted childhoods.

Even though other educators in the city may find it bewildering and maybe even threatening, Horizonte is proving that a public school in an area with rapidly growing urban, minority, and low socioeconomic student populations can improve students' learning. That is our mission.

HORIZONTE'S MISSION

It took more than a year for Horizonte staff to agree on a mission statement:

> Valuing the diversity and individual worth of students, Horizonte Instruction and Training Center, a multicultural learning center, will provide the education and skills necessary for students to achieve self-sufficiency and become contributing participants within their communities.

As a result of their work on the mission statement, Horizonte staff members insist that the school provide a nontraditional environment driven by student needs. Students perceive—and appreciate—the differences (see Figure 9.2). For example, in traditional instruction, class and teacher assignments are largely arbitrary; but at Horizonte, the staff provides as many choices as possible, even in such traditionally school-controlled areas as schedules, locations of classrooms, and endpoints of courses.

We believe that schools should be democratic institutions. We are a service organization and live in the neighborhood as fellow citizens. Our priorities are as follows: students first, teachers second, classified staff third, and administrators fourth. Above all, every student must be treated fairly and with dignity. We tell students: "You can't pick your parents or where or when you are born. It is perfectly natural to want to belong, to be acknowledged, to succeed, regardless of your circumstances."

Most high school students who find themselves at Horizonte have not been successful in the regular school setting. Their self-esteem may be low. They may feel alienated from their peers. Some may believe that society has set them up for failure. Horizonte's task is to provide a supportive environment that motivates and allows students to recognize windows of opportunity and to reach their educational and career goals.

FIVE GUIDING PRINCIPLES

The five principles that propel Horizonte's vision resemble fundamental beliefs more than specific strategies.

1. *Curriculum is shaped to meet student needs and learning styles.* We address all state standards, but our methods are as diverse as the teachers themselves. Humanities and language arts teacher Tim Lineback recently grouped good readers, poor readers, and artistic students together to create a modern version of the Edgar Allan Poe story "The Fall of the House of Usher" and to build a scale model of the house. The outcomes revealed talents no standardized test could have assessed.

FIGURE 9.2
Traditional versus Horizonte Schooling—As Students See It

Perceptions of Traditional School	*Perceptions of Horizonte*
1. The school arbitrarily assigns students to teachers and classes.	1. Students select courses and teachers whenever choices exist.
2. The faculty and administration determine student schedules.	2. Students set their own schedules, and student-parent-advisor teams set goals at conferences.
3. Teachers pay attention to students only while the student attends their class.	3. Teachers support students and act as their advocates in all school-related activities.
4. Teachers are accountable only for teaching curriculum content.	4. Teachers respond to their students, not only as learners, but as people.
5. Students have access to teachers only during formal class periods.	5. Teachers are accessible in classrooms and halls and share a common lunchroom and restrooms with students.
6. Participation in activities is limited to the elite, ignoring the full spectrum of school ethnicity.	6. All activities are open to everyone and reflect the school's total ethnic, cultural, and economic make-up.
7. The school measures student success only by SAT scores, college placement status, and athletics.	7. The school measures student success by a mix of academic, service, cooperative, and behavioral factors.
8. Classrooms are passive places where teachers tend to do the talking and teaching and students do most of the listening and learning.	8. Classrooms are dynamic, interactive places where students and teachers both teach and learn.
9. Student interaction with teachers is superficial and cold rather than self-affirming and warm.	9. School staff treat students as individuals, and students often work one-on-one with teachers.
10. Learning is restricted to classrooms in the school building.	10. Students and teachers use the community at large as a learning resource.

2. *Access to all technology is a total need for everyone.* Every student has an e-mail address and learns to use the Internet, CD-ROMS, fax machines, voice mail, and other electronic equipment in the school technology lab. Teachers require students to conduct intensive research and to analyze, evaluate, and interpret data as information *users*, not just efficient information *gatherers*.

3. *Horizonte is an inclusive, multicultural learning community.* Forty-five percent of the participants in any Horizonte activity (in school or out of the building) must proportionally represent each minority group. In addition,

we celebrate ethnic holidays with food, dance, music, and costumes. The curriculum reflects a wealth of cultural perspectives. A Russian-born pianist performed at a recent graduation ceremony. An in-depth study of the ancient Anasazi Indians preceded a field trip to the Valley of Fire historical site in Nevada.

4. *All students should be assisted to reach their full potential.* For example, one Horizonte student was a pregnant, unmarried 16-year-old whose parents had rejected her. She attended classes with adults in the school's prenatal-postnatal care program and found a room at the local YWCA. She graduated from high

school. After struggling for several years, she was able to develop a realistic goal, qualify for some benefits, and organize her time. Last year, she graduated with a degree in nursing from the University of Utah.

5. *Horizonte teachers are enthusiastic, adaptable, lifelong learners.* Building construction instructor James Yates came to Horizonte from a career as a contractor in industry. He and his student crew, including girls and students with special needs, do cement, drywall, and other construction jobs to restore older inner-city homes, under an agreement with the Salt Lake Housing Authority. Yates has the ability to share his firsthand knowledge and to motivate students to take pride in the quality of their craftsmanship.

CURRICULUM INNOVATIONS

These principles have led to innovations in curriculum, such as service learning and minicourses in intriguing topics.

Service learning. Every Horizonte teacher involves students in service projects. Last winter, students collected commodities for the Utah Food Bank. They also helped build a haunted house for Halloween that benefited the March of Dimes, restored plant life along the banks of the nearby Jordan River, and volunteered as tutors for a local Head Start program.

Curriculum integration. Two annual intersessions, or minicourses, supplement core studies. Students choose topics such as writing stories for children, culture of ancient societies, sewing for fun, endangered species, and film study and analysis. A project at Horizonte's Garfield site has used archaeological digs and grids to teach math, social studies, science, English, and humanities. The study of communicable diseases is improving the skills of young parents in communications, social studies, and science.

PERFORMANCE GAINS

Is Horizonte's all-for-one–one-for-all approach to education effective? The evidence is impressive:

- Ninety percent of Horizonte students passed the Salt Lake City School District writing competency test in 1995–96, although many of them had failed to pass it the previous year.
- Also last year, youth with ethnic-minority and low socioeconomic backgrounds who had been at Horizonte for one or more years achieved the greatest Scholastic Assessment Test (SAT) performance gain among secondary schools in the district.
- Horizonte students enrolled in the federal Job Training Partnership Act program in the summer of 1996 demonstrated an average of two years' growth in mathematics and reading.

Horizonte is an empowering place, not just because of what it teaches but how—with acceptance of all students for who they are. Perhaps the letter from a grateful parent says it best:

I have seen my daughter go from *F*s to *A*s in less than a year. She actually looks forward to school again as a place where there is kindness and respect. You have given her back the confidence every teenager needs to get through life. She has learned that if you believe in others, they will believe in you.

James P. Anderson is Principal at Horizonte Instruction and Training Center, Salt Lake City, Utah; *Barbara Floisand* is an Applied Technology Specialist, and *David Martinez* is Assistant Principal at Horizonte; *Dalmar P. Robinson* is Public Information Officer at the Utah State Office of Education, Salt Lake City.

QUESTIONS FOR REFLECTION

1. The authors state that Horizonte's priorities are: "students first, teachers second, classified staff third, and administrators fourth." How are these priorities arranged at the school, college, or university with which you are most familiar? What are the consequences of these priorities for students' learning?

2. Horizonte students are given many choices throughout their educational program. What "lessons" do students learn as a result of making such choices?

3. At any level, what arguments are often made against empowering students to play a role in designing their own curricular experiences?

TEACHERS' VOICES
Putting Theory into Practice

Making the Circle Bigger: A Journey in the South Bronx

SUSAN McCRAY

ABSTRACT: The author, an Outward Bound instructor at a South Bronx high school in New York City, describes some of her experiences while coteaching a course within an integrated curriculum. In mid-December, she realizes that her recent efforts at "creating a rich, dynamic curriculum . . . always seemed to fall flat." The author hopes that a previously arranged "urban exploration" trip to the Lower East Side of Manhattan will enliven the curriculum and enable students to see course content as relevant and real. The trip enables students to learn one of life's more important lessons: "Never give up on life. Always keep trying to be the best."

The following article describes some of my experiences while working as an Outward Bound instructor at the South Bronx High School in the school year 1991–92. For 4 years I co-taught a course that integrated the philosophy and methodology of experiential learning with a social studies and English curriculum. The course met daily for a double period, and the alumni of the class formed a club that gathered regularly after school. The school is located in Mott Haven, a section of the Bronx in New York City, and serves the local community, whose population is primarily Puerto Rican and Dominican, with a growing number of residents from other Latin American countries and a small percentage of African Americans. I myself, a white woman, grew up three subway stops and 15 minutes away on the Upper East Side of Manhattan. Ironically, the closer I became

Excerpted from McCray, S. (1996). "Making the Circle Bigger: A Journey in the South Bronx." In D. Udall and A. Mednick (Eds.), *Journeys through Our Classrooms,* (pp. 149–161). Dubuque, IA: Kendall/Hunt Publishing Company. Used by permission of the author.

to these young people, the more profoundly aware I became of just how far those three subway stops and that 15 minutes are. So, while trying to capture the reality of our work together, I realize that even this description is from my own perspective.

Also, I am telling this story from journals and memory, and I know that recollection is inevitably a process of re-creation. In many instances, moments and individuals have wandered through my mind and landed on the page in slightly new forms and sequences. The details may not be exact, but it is the essence of the story that remains most powerful. . . .

Each day I heard another story, because each young person has a story to tell. These stories were often of their personal struggles, but because of my students it seemed impossible for me to lose myself to despair. In response to the violence in their lives, the students of both the class and club decided to organize a series of events dedicated to peace and unity. They planned to build a park next to the school, Unity Park, and to prepare a week of workshops, assemblies, and speak-outs for the rest of the school. Their indefatigable spirit and our closeness as a community were the foundation of the park.

One morning I pushed through the school's heavy, metal front door and walked into Ramon's jubilant smile. He came gliding up and wrapped his arms around me. "Oh, Susan," he whispered in that gorgeous Dominican accent. He began to escort me to my office, "Susan, you look tired. You work too much. How are you? Did I tell you . . . ?" Ramon always had news that he dispatched with hushed intensity. His warmth was contagious. He led me up the stairs and right into "the desk mob." After 2 years of bureaucratic battles, I had procured a space for the program big enough to house an intimate miniclub. I said my hellos, letting the group of students know how sincerely good it was to see them. And before I could ask them where they were supposed to be, they assured me that Veronica had finished her test and Louis had been kicked out of science. After a long pause, Alex quickly added that he was on his way back to class. It was always tempt-

ing to let them stay; I sensed that they flocked here because they could find connection and caring. But I knew, and they knew, that they also had to hold each other accountable for all their academic responsibilities.

At this time of the year, in the middle of December, it was always hard to hold their attention in class. No matter how much I focused on creating a rich, dynamic curriculum, it always seemed to fall flat. The club attendance had dwindled, and the class was bored. I was bored and boring. We had completed our introductions, in which they interviewed each other and wrote biographies; we had been on our first backpacking trip; we had written a group contract; we had begun our cultural studies, and they had completed interviews of their own families. Now, in desperation (and lethargy), I tried having them write about themselves; I tried discussion; I even tried my old standby—debates. In reality, there was little solid content, nor was there an engaging project.

Fortunately, we put an urban exploration trip on the calendar. In many ways it became a pivotal juncture of the curriculum—an opportunity for them to see the lessons of the course as relevant and real. I hoped that studying other communities would help us develop ideas for our project. We would go to another neighborhood in the city, the Lower East Side of Manhattan, searching for examples of parks and murals and meeting people who could be role models and inspire our work.

But it took a lot of convincing. Students wondered why we should bother wandering the streets of Manhattan, a place they knew and sometimes feared. On a school trip they assumed there was always the chance of danger or, worse, ridicule from strangers. The Lower East Side is demographically and physically similar to the South Bronx, but once we were there it was far enough away from home that we could enter with an explorer's perspective, both anxious and open.

I helped them find their way to a collection of murals known on the Lower East Side as the "protest murals," but when we arrived and found the gate locked, we just stood on the corner aimlessly. We had spent hours in class practicing approaching and interviewing people in the street, but still the students were hesitant and resistant about moving beyond our group. Garfield took the initiative. He walked toward a man sitting on a nearby stoop, while the rest of the group stood riveted, watching and waiting in awe. This is not something a young Black Jamaican man wearing baggy jeans and a baseball cap does outside of his own neighborhood in New York City. The time passed; Garfield continued talking with this man, while the rest of us stared at Garfield. Eventually he took his journal out and began writing. Then he and the man began walking back toward us. "This is David." Garfield introduced each of us, and then he told us that David knew all about the neighborhood. He had been homeless for years, but he had spent that time in the area and even had a key to the park. He had helped build it, had organized a rally when the city officials threatened to destroy it, and was continuing to watch over it. So we followed David into his garden and spent the next hour of this bitter cold December day standing beneath the huge murals hearing about his life and his views of the homeless situation and of the social and political history of the community.

Later Hugo, who had recently come to this country from El Salvador, captured the moment in writing. He was usually so quiet and shy. He rarely spoke or wrote in class; but now he responded to a phrase in the mural painted beneath a crystal ball: "La Lucha Continua means that the struggle never ends. You always have to keep fighting for a better future. Never give up on life. Always keep trying to be the best." This is why I leave the classroom with my students; I could never have planned this experience.

As we walked away and left David sitting on his bench, Garfield pulled on the "hoody" of his full-length Fat Goose jacket and wrapped his arm around Carmen's shoulders. For that hour none of us had noticed the cold.

Susan McCray is a teacher at Graham and Parks School, Cambridge, Massachusetts.

QUESTIONS FOR REFLECTION

1. What should teachers do if they observe that their efforts at "creating a rich, dynamic curriculum . . . always seem to fall flat"? What curricular changes might they consider?
2. What are the educational benefits to students (and teachers) of occasional "field trips" into their surrounding communities?
3. In addition to realizing the importance of never giving up and striving to do one's best, what other "lessons" might McCray's students have learned as a result of the urban exploration trip?

LEARNING ACTIVITIES

Critical Thinking

1. Are a common high school curriculum and uniform standards appropriate in a pluralistic society? Can a common curriculum and uniform standards be implemented with diverse groups of students? Can individual differences be accom-

modated? Should they be? Review the comments Joseph Murphy makes about curricular coherence ("Explaining 'Academic Drift' in High Schools: Strategies for Improvement") before responding to these questions.

2. Reflect on this chapter's recommendations for changing the curriculum for middle adolescents in light of curricular goals for middle adolescents, the four bases of the curriculum, and curriculum criteria. Which recommendations from the articles in this chapter would you like to see implemented?

3. Which developmental changes discussed in Chapter 3 should guide curriculum planners in designing educational programs for middle adolescents?

4. What are the essential elements of effective curricula for middle adolescents?

5. What are some of the challenges that today's middle adolescents face that were unknown or little known to their parents or grandparents? To what extent can (or should) these challenges be addressed in educational programs for middle adolescents?

Application Activities

1. When you were a middle adolescent, what school experiences helped you to grow and learn? What experiences hindered you? What implications do these experiences have for your current and future curriculum planning activities?

2. Drawing from the material in this chapter, develop a short questionnaire or set of interview questions that curriculum planners could use to learn more about middle adolescents. Compare your questions with those of your classmates.

3. Invite a group of high school teachers to your class and ask them to describe the steps they take in planning curricula for their students. What do they see as the most important curriculum criteria to use in planning?

4. Obtain a statement of philosophy (or mission statement) from a nearby high school. Analyze the statement in regard to this chapter's six recommended goals for educational programs for middle adolescents. How many of the goals are reflected in the statement?

Field Experiences

1. Visit a nearby high school and obtain permission to interview a few students about their curricular experiences. Take field notes based on these interviews. The following questions might serve as a guide for beginning your interviews: Do the students like school? What about it do they like and dislike? What are their favorite subjects? What about those subjects do they like? What are their plans for the future? Then, analyze your field notes; what themes or concerns emerge that would be useful for curriculum planners at this level?

2. Visit an agency in your community that offers services to middle adolescents and their families. Ask a staff member to describe the services that are offered. Report your findings to the rest of your class.

3. Talk with a group of middle adolescents about the social forces of concern to them in their school, their community, their nation, and the world. What implications do their concerns have for curriculum planners at this level?

Internet Activities

1. At the Center for Research on the Education of Students Placed at Risk (CRES-PAR) (**http://scov.csos.jhu.edu/crespar/CreSPaR.html**), gather research results and curriculum-related resources useful to those who plan educational programs for middle adolescents placed at risk.
2. Go to the State Curriculum Frameworks and Contents Standards page maintained by the U.S. Department of Education's Office of Educational Research and Improvement (OERI) (**http://www.ed.gov/offices/OERI/statecur/**) and obtain your state's secondary-level curriculum frameworks. Critique these frameworks in light of the recommendations in Chapter 9.
3. Go to OERI's Blue Ribbon Schools Program (**http://www.ed.gov/offices/OERA/BlueRibbonSchools/**) which recognizes outstanding public and private schools. From that site, "visit" a few exemplary high schools. To what extent do they reflect the recommendations made throughout Chapter 9?

BOOKS AND ARTICLES TO REVIEW

Research and Theory in Education for Middle Adolescents

Bartnick, William M., and Parkay, Forrest W. "A Comparative Analysis of the 'Holding Power' of General and Exceptional Education Programs." *Remedial and Special Education* 12, no. 5 (September/October 1991): 17–22.

Bechtel, Dave, and Reed, Cynthia. "Students as Documenters: Benefits, Reflections, and Suggestions." *NASSP Bulletin* 82, no. 594 (January 1998): 89–95.

Boccia, Judith A., ed. *Students Taking the Lead: The Challenges and Rewards of Empowering Youth in Schools.* San Francisco: Jossey-Bass, 1997.

Boyer, Ernest. *High School: A Report on Secondary Education in America.* New York: Harper and Row, 1984.

Bracy, Gerald E. "An Optimal Size for High Schools?" *Phi Delta Kappan* 79, no. 5 (January 1998): 406.

Brown, Cynthia Stokes. *Connecting with the Past: History Workshop in Middle and High Schools.* Portsmouth, NH: Heinemann, 1994.

Bugaj, Stephen J. "Intensive Scheduling and Special Education in Secondary Schools: Research and Recommendations." *NASSP Bulletin* 82, no. 594 (January 1998): 33–39.

Carey, Nancy. *Curricular Differentiation in Public High Schools.* Washington, DC: U.S. Department of Education, 1994.

Cawelti, Gordon. *High School Restructuring: A National Study.* Arlington, VA: Educational Research Service, 1994.

Davidson, Ann Locke. *Making and Molding Identity in Schools: Student Narratives on Race, Gender, and Academic Engagement.* Albany: State University of New York Press, 1996.

Dryfoos, Joy G. "Adolescents at Risk: Shaping Programs to Fit the Need." *Journal of Negro Education* 65, no. 1 (Winter 1996): 5–18.

Edison, Carrie Baylard. *The Accelerated High School: A Step-by-Step Guide for Administrators and Teachers.* Thousand Oaks, CA: Corwin Press, 1998.

Fenske, Neil R. *A History of American Public High Schools, 1890–1990: Through the Eyes of Principals.* Lewiston, NY: E. Mellen Press, 1997.

Fine, Michelle, ed. *Chartering Urban School Reform: Reflections on Public High Schools in the Midst of Change.* New York: Teachers College Press, 1994.

Gilbert, Robert N. *Welcome To Our World: Realities of High School Students.* Thousand Oaks, CA: Corwin Press, 1998.

Jenkins, John M. *Transforming High Schools: A Constructivist Agenda.* Lancaster, PA: Technomic Publishing Co., 1996.

Jorgensen, Cheryl. *Restructuring High Schools for All Students: Taking Inclusion to the Next Level.* Baltimore, MD: P. H. Brookes Pub., 1998.

Lester, Julie H., and Cheek, Earl H., Jr. "The 'Real' Experts Address Textbook Issues." *Journal of Adolescent & Adult Literacy* 41, no. 4 (December–January 1997–98): 282–291.

Lightfoot, Sarah. *Good High Schools: Portraits of Character and Culture.* New York: Basic Books, 1983.

Maurer, Richard E. *Designing Interdisciplinary Curriculum in Middle, Junior High, and High Schools.* Boston: Allyn and Bacon, 1994.

Maxwell, Rhoda J. *Writing Across the Curriculum in Middle and High Schools.* Boston: Allyn and Bacon, 1996.

Muncey, Donna E., and McQuillan, Patrick J. *Reform and Resistance in Schools and Classrooms: An Ethnographic View of the Coalition of Essential Schools.* New Haven: Yale University Press, 1996.

Newmann, Fred M., et al. *Authentic Achievement: Restructuring Schools for Intellectual Quality.* San Francisco: Jossey-Bass, 1996.

Olszewski-Kubilius, Paula. "Developing the Talents of Academically Gifted High School Students: Issues for Secondary School Administrators." *NASSP Bulletin* 82, no. 595 (February 1998): 85–92.

O'Shea, David. *Implementing the American History Curriculum in Public Senior High Schools: A Comparison of the Perceptions, Characteristics, and Activities of Teachers of General Enrollment and Advanced Placement Courses.* Los Angeles: National Center for History in the Schools, 1994.

Parkay, Forrest W. "The Success-Oriented Curriculum: Its Effect on Student Achievement and Attitudes." *Clearing House* 61, no. 2 (October 1987): 66–68.

———. "The Authoritarian Assault Upon the Public School Curriculum: An Additional 'Indicator of Risk.' " *The High School Journal* 68, no. 3 (February–March 1985): 120–128.

Parkay, Forrest W., and Damico, Sandra B. "Negotiating the Implementation of Educational Policy in an Urban American High School." In S. J. Crump, ed. *School-Centered Leadership: Putting Educational Policy Into Practice.* Melbourne, Australia: Thomas Nelson, 1993, 237–246.

Parkay, Forrest W., Shindler, J., and Oaks, M. "Creating a Climate for Collaborative, Emergent Leadership at an Urban High School." *International Journal of Educational Reform* 6, no. 1 (January 1997): 64–74.

Powell, Arthur G. *Lessons From Privilege: The American Prep School Tradition.* Cambridge, MA: Harvard University Press, 1996.

———, Farrar, Eleanor, and Cohen, David K. *The Shopping Mall High School.* Boston: Houghton Mifflin, 1985.

Reinstein, David. "Crossing the Economic Divide." *Educational Leadership* 55, no. 4 (December–January 1997–98): 28–29.

Rettig, Michael D., and Canady, Robert Lynn. "All Around the Block: The Benefits and Challenges of a Non-traditional School Schedule." *School Administrator* 53, no. 8 (September 1996): 8–14.

Roellke, Christopher. *Curriculum Adequacy and Quality in High Schools Enrolling Fewer Than 400 Pupils (9–12).* Charleston, WV: Clearinghouse on Rural Education and Small Schools, 1996.

Scheuerer, Daniel T., and Parkay, Forrest W. "The New Christian Right and the Public School Curriculum: A Florida Report." In Jane B. Smith and J. Gordon Coleman, Jr., *School Library Media Annual: 1992, Volume Ten.* Englewood, CO: Libraries Unlimited, 1992, 112–118.

Shmurak, Carole B. *Voices of Hope: Adolescent Girls at Single Sex and Coeducational Schools.* New York: P. Lang, 1998.

Sizer, Theodore R. *Horace's Hope: What Works for the American High School.* Boston: Houghton Mifflin, 1996.

———. *Horace's School: Redesigning the American High School.* Boston: Houghton Mifflin, 1992.

———. *Horace's Compromise: The Dilemma of the American High School.* Boston: Houghton Mifflin, 1984.

Spies, Paul. *Interdisciplinary Teams for High Schools.* Bloomington, IN: Phi Delta Kappa Educational Foundation, 1997.

Stern, David, et al. *School-Based Enterprise: Productive Learning in American High Schools.* San Francisco: Jossey-Bass, 1994.

Wood, George H. *A Time to Learn: Creating Community in America's High Schools.* New York: Dutton, 1998.

Wooster, Martin Morse. *Angry Classrooms, Vacant Minds: What's Happened to Our High Schools?* San Francisco: Pacific Research Institute for Public Policy, 1994.

Wraga, William G. *Democracy's High School: The Comprehensive High School and Educational Reform in the United States.* Lanham, MD: University Press of America, 1994.

Theory into Practice: Strategies for High School Programs

Barker, Joel A. "Preparing for the 21st Century: The EFG Experiment." *Educational Horizons* 73, no. 1 (Fall 1994): 12–17.

Carline, Marianne B., et al. "Improving High School Students' Performance via Discovery Learning,

Collaboration and Technology." *T. H. E. Journal* 24, no. 10 (May 1997): 62–65.

Cawelti, Gordon. *Effects of High School Restructuring: Ten Schools at Work.* Arlington, VA: Educational Research Service, 1997.

Gerson, Mark. *In the Classroom: Dispatches from an Inner-City School That Works.* New York: Free Press, 1997.

Goetz, Jill. " 'City Bugs' Website Turns Teens into Taxonomists." *California Agriculture* 52, no. 1 (January–February 1998): 4–5.

Inger, Sharon S. "The Barnstable High School P. M. Program: One Approach to the Education of High-risk High School Students." *Journal of Education for Students Placed at Risk* 2, no. 1 (1997): 11–28.

Lozada, Marlene. "The Making of a High-Tech High School." *Techniques: Making Education and Career Connections* 72, no. 5 (May 1997): 18–21, 32.

———. "Getting off the Track to Nowhere." *Techniques: Making Education and Career Connections* 72, no. 8 (November–December 1997): 38–41.

Nehring, James. *The School Within Us: The Creation of an Innovative Public School.* Albany: State University of New York Press, 1998.

Pasi, Raymond J. "Success in High School—And Beyond." *Educational Leadership* 54, no. 8 (May 1997): 40–42.

Penn, Alexandra. *Integrating Academic and Vocational Education: A Model for Secondary Schools.* Alexandria, VA: Association for Supervision and Curriculum Development, 1996.

Queen, J. Allen, et al. "The Road We Traveled: Scheduling in the 4 × 4 Block." *NASSP Bulletin* 81, no. 588 (April 1997): 88–89.

Rop, Charles. "Breaking the Gender Barrier in the Physical Sciences." *Educational Leadership* 55, no. 4 (December–January 1997–98): 58–60.

Rossman, Gretchan, and Wilson, Bruce L. "Context, Courses, and the Curriculum: Local Responses to State Policy Reform." *Educational Policy* 10, no. 3 (September 1996): 399–421.

Rossuck, Jennifer. "Banned Books: A Study of Censorship." *English Journal* 86, no. 2 (February 1997): 67–70.

Sabo, Sandra. "A Blueprint for Change: A Learner-Focused Curriculum Drove the Design of Minnesota's Chaska High School." *Techniques: Making Education and Career Connections* 73, no. 2 (February 1998): 16–19.

Schaller, Sue, and Wenk, John. "A Humanities Class for the Twenty-first Century." *English Journal* 86, no. 7 (November 1997): 75–78.

U.S. Department of Education. *New American High Schools: Profiles of the Nation's Leading Edge Schools.* Washington, DC: U.S. Department of Education, 1998.

Vail, Kathleen. "Keeping Fernando in School." *American School Board Journal* 185, no. 2 (February 1998): 30–33.

Visher, Mary G., et al. *School-to-Work in the 1990s: A Look at Programs and Practices in American High Schools.* Berkeley, CA: MPR Associates, Inc., 1998.

Von Villas, Barbara A. "High Schools Can Visibly Improve: The District That Became a Model." *NASSP Bulletin* 80, no. 578 (March 1996): 68–74.

Zeeman, Kenneth L. "Grappling with Grendel or What We Did When the Censors Came." *English Journal* 86, no. 2 (February 1997): 46–50.

Videotapes

Character 101: Reading, Writing, and Respect focuses on the issue of character education and shows what some schools are doing to combat violence, vandalism, and cheating and to teach good citizenship and moral behavior. *Heroin: The New High School High* examines the increasing prevalence of heroin among today's middle adolescents (both available from Films for the Humanities and Sciences, P.O. Box 2053, Princeton, NJ 08543-2053 <http://www.films.com>).

Integrating Teaching Models for Secondary Teachers features highly effective teachers demonstrating models of teaching such as concept attainment, inductive thinking, mind mapping, cooperative learning, and academic controversy. *Cooperative Learning & Multiple Intelligences for High School Teachers* features teachers demonstrating how to teach content through cooperative learning and multiple intelligences strategies. *The Technology-Infused High School Classroom* shows how to design problem-based activities utilizing technology. (All available from The Video Journal of Education, 8686 South 1300 East, Sandy, UT 84094 (888) 566-6888, <http://www.videojournal.com>).

CHAPTER 10

Education for Late Adolescents and Adults

FOCUS QUESTIONS

1. What are the major developmental challenges of late adolescence and adulthood?
2. What are several types of community college programs?
3. What challenges confront today's colleges and universities?
4. How has adult education evolved to meet the needs of adult learners?
5. What educational opportunities are available to senior learners?

Late adolescence, the period from approximately age fifteen or sixteen through nineteen, is a critical period in the development of self-concept. This period is important for the individual's psycho-social identity, work or work-related success in terms of what is valued by society, and integration into the life of the local, national, and global communities. Late adolescence and early adulthood can be a tumultuous period in our society. At this time, the quest for identity shifts from relying on others to self-reliance. The individual critically examines values, begins to form intimate relationships with others, and develops an identity as worker, parent, and citizen. No longer children, late adolescents want to use newly acquired knowledge, skills, and strengths to achieve their own purposes whether through employment, marriage, parenthood, postsecondary education or training, a career, or military service.

DEVELOPMENTAL CHALLENGES OF LATE ADOLESCENCE AND ADULTHOOD

Erik Erikson's eight-stage model for the human life cycle identifies three salient psychosocial crises that characterize late adolescence through adulthood. During young adulthood (intimacy versus isolation), the individual must develop intimate relationships or experience feelings of isolation. Then, during middle adulthood (generativity versus stagnation), the individual must develop a way to satisfy and support the next generation or experience stagnation; this care for the next generation can be expressed through parenting or a career in teaching, for example. Finally, during late adulthood (integrity versus despair), the individual must accept oneself as one is and thereby experience a sense of fulfillment; without this self-acceptance, the individual experiences feelings of despair.

Robert J. Havighurst (1900–1991), a University of Chicago professor who made outstanding contributions to life span developmental psychology, found that some individuals, during late adolescence and early adulthood, lead highly individualistic lives and grow into alienation, loneliness, or ruthlessness with little feeling for the values of community life. While Havighurst (1972, p. 5) believed that early adulthood is the period most full of "teachable moments," he found that period of life "emptiest of efforts to teach." One of the challenges to community college and university programs, then, is to capitalize on these "teachable moments."

HIGHER EDUCATION ENROLLMENTS

Higher education enrollments have steadily increased during the last few decades. Enrollments in public and private, two-year and four-year institutions totaled more than 9 million in 1972. By 1996, this figure had risen to more than 14 million; and by 2008, the figure is expected to rise to more than 16 million (National Center for Education Statistics, 1998a). Since the early 1980s, women have played a major role in the increased higher education enrollments. Between 1983 and 1996, the enrollment of women increased from 6.4 million to 8.0 million, and this figure is expected to increase to 9.2 million by 2008 (National Center for Education Statistics, 1998a). The enrollment of students over age thirty-five increased from 2.2 million in 1988 to 3.0 million in 1996; and this figure is expected to remain unchanged by 2008 (National Center for Education Statistics, 1998a).

Total enrollments in public and private two-year colleges were 5.6 million during fall 1996; by 2008, this figure is expected to increase to 6.1 million (National Center for Education Statistics, 1998a). Among the students enrolled at this level in 1996, almost 50 percent were under 25; about 25 percent were in the 25–34 age group, and 25 percent were in the over-35 age group (National Center for Education Statistics, 1996).

TWO-YEAR COLLEGES

Two-year colleges offer education and training programs that are two years in length or less. These programs usually lead to a license, a certificate, an associate of arts (A.A.) degree, an associate of science (A.S.) degree, or an associate of applied science (A.A.S.) degree. Colleges with programs less than four years in length are usually called *community colleges, technical colleges,* or *junior colleges.*

The community college, a relatively new educational institution developed in the United States, has become a major element of the American system of postsecondary education. Although it evolved from the junior college, the community college is designed to serve many more social purposes. Community colleges provide their communities with adult education programs in a variety of fields. They provide a college-parallel program for those who wish to transfer to four-year colleges or universities after two years. They offer terminal education in many vocational, technical, and commercial subjects for those who desire a two-year course of study. Several states have developed master plans to provide community colleges within commuting distance of all high school graduates.

The community college has grown from one that served a limited number of students to one that provides education for many youth not in four-year colleges and for many adult learners. Community colleges also offer many programs to help meet the needs of their communities and society. Typically, community colleges offer five types of programs:

1. **Junior college transfer programs.** High school graduates can pursue the equivalent of the first two years of undergraduate work at a four-year college or university. This program of study leads to the associate of arts (A.A.) degree. For many students, a nearby community college may be preferable to a larger, often more impersonal, college or university.

2. **Technical and/or vocational programs.** Our technological society provides excellent opportunities to young people who wish to prepare for jobs that require completion of a two-year, or less, preparation program. For example, the *Occupational Outlook Handbook,* published annually by the U.S. Department of Labor, Bureau of Labor Statistics, includes many careers that require two years of training or less.

3. **Adult education programs.** These programs serve an entire community. Classes, usually formed according to interest and demand, might offer instruction in photography, acting, playing a musical instrument, self-defense, meditation, retirement planning, cooking, or horseback riding, to name only a few. Adult education programs are particularly appealing to individuals who are retired or semi-retired.

4. **Developmental programs.** These programs serve students whose educational backgrounds may prevent them from enrolling in and successfully completing academic or technical courses of study. Most community colleges offer GED programs for students who have not graduated from high school and need a high school diploma to enroll in a postsecondary program.

5. **Community service programs.** Some community colleges provide their communities with education and training when and where they are needed. Multiservice outreach programs, extension centers, in-plant training, and programs for traditionally underrepresented groups are examples of community service programs.

Since the 1970s, the number of community colleges and their enrollments have increased dramatically, and the functions and importance of the five types of programs have changed considerably. At first, community colleges emphasized transfer programs because of the expanded opportunities they gave high school graduates to attend college. Later, the emphasis shifted to "nontraditional" students—women "reentering" education after their childbearing years, middle-aged adults seeking new educational experiences and career opportunities, the unemployed, new immigrants, and members of groups traditionally underrepresented in postsecondary educational programs.

A major concern for community colleges today is the large number of students who drop out before completing their programs. Because many students seem unable to succeed, attention to individual learning needs and problems is an important part of curriculum planning and teaching at this level.

The community college serves many young people who mature late (often called "late bloomers") and would not be permitted to enter a four-year college or university on the basis of their high school grades. Many students who need remedial work in basic skills can make up these deficiencies in noncredit "guided studies" programs. Completion of such a program enables them to enroll in other areas of study.

FOUR-YEAR COLLEGES AND UNIVERSITIES

Total undergraduate enrollments in public and private four-year colleges and universities for fall 1996 were about 12.3 million; by 2008, this figure was expected to increase to about 14.0 million (National Center for Education Statistics, 1998a). Among the students enrolled at this level in 1996, about 71 percent were under 25; about 17 percent in the 25–34 age group; and 12 percent in the over-35 age group (National Center for Education Statistics, 1996).

Total graduate enrollments in public and private universities for fall 1996 were about 1.7 million in 1996; by 2008, this figure was expected to be about the same (National Center for Education Statistics, 1998a). Total first-time enrollments in professional schools (medical, law, etc.) for fall 1996 were about 285,000; by 2008, this figure was expected to be about the same (National Center for Education Statistics, 1998a). Among the students enrolled at this level in 1996, about 19 percent were under 25; about 45 percent in the 25–34 age group; and 36 percent in the over-35 age group (National Center for Education Statistics, 1996).

Since the start of the last decade of the twentieth century, the university has been challenged and its benefits questioned in ways that were unheard of previously in that century. Clearly, universities cannot continue to do for the next twenty years, only better, what they have done for the last twenty. The demand for alternatives and alternative programs is as strong at this level as at the other levels of education addressed in this book. Many students have gone to college after high school by default because they didn't know what else to do, and their parents had been conditioned to believe that higher education was something they owed their children. Over 50 percent of high school graduates in the United States now go on to college (in some communities, 70 or 80 percent) expecting to get better jobs as a result of getting a college degree—in spite of the fact that 80 percent of jobs in the country do not require a college degree. The broad general goals of education at this level are the same as those at the other levels we have studied—*citizenship, equal educational opportunity, vocation, self-realization,* and *critical thinking.* However, alternatives should continually be developed to serve the needs of late adolescents and adults in attaining these goals. And, the curriculum should reflect a "balance" between liberal and professional study, between education for life and education for work.

At one time, the word *college* may have meant four uninterrupted years of full-time enrollment at one institution. During the 1970s, however, alternatives for undergraduate education for late adolescents and adults were increased considerably in many parts of the United States by the development of "colleges without walls" and their "external" (or "extended") degrees. Today, thousands of students earn their bachelor's degrees through such programs. The academic community's acceptance of the best of these programs is indicated by the number of recipients of external degrees who are able to gain admission to graduate studies.

Similar to the "great debate" on high school reform discussed in the previous chapter, several national reports addressing the goals and practices in higher education were released in the mid-1980s. For example, the Carnegie Foundation for the Advancement of Teaching's 1985 report, *Higher Education and the American Resurgence,* called for the restoration to higher education of its original purpose of preparing graduates for lives of involved and committed citizenship. The report also called for increased efforts to recruit minority students into higher education and renewed efforts to develop creativity and independence of mind. In response to the increased focus on academic disciplines and the "gradual retreat from values," the report proposed "active learning" and the "ideal of service."

The National Institute of Education's 1984 report, *Involvement in Learning: Realizing the Potential of American Higher Education,* called for more active modes of learning. The report claimed that college curricula had become excessively vocational in orientation and that curriculum content should address not only subject matter but also the development of students' abilities to analyze, to solve complex problems, and to synthesize. Furthermore, students and faculty should integrate knowledge from various disciplines. Similarly, in "Connectedness through Liberal Education" in this chapter, the late Ernest Boyer draws from the 1987 Carnegie Foundation report titled *College: The Undergraduate Experience in America* and identifies five essential priorities for undergraduate education.

There has also been a widespread recognition that higher education curricula should prepare students to live in a society that continues to become increasingly culturally diverse. For example, in "Curriculum Planning and Development for Native Americans and Alaska Natives in Higher Education" in this chapter, Ella Inglebret and D. Michael Pavel point out that "Native peoples are once again playing a key role in defining their own educational landscapes and the directions for their journeys; however, this time the journey constantly intersects with that of many other peoples from widely varying backgrounds." In "Multiculturalism Yes, Particularism No," Diane Ravitch presents a thought-provoking discussion of the distinction between pluralism and particularism in the university curriculum. And finally, in this chapter's Case Study in Curriculum Implementation section ("Faculty Collaboration for a New Curriculum"), Peter Gold describes some of the key decisions and critical policies surrounding the collaborative development and teaching of a course titled "American Pluralism" at the State University of New York-Buffalo.

ADULT EDUCATION

Adult education is changing dramatically. Before 1945, it was generally believed that adults, once past adolescence, had little learning capacity. When thousands of World War II veterans returned to college campuses, supported by the Servicemen's Readjustment Act (popularly known as the G. I. Bill of Rights), there was great fear that they would be unable to learn and would lower academic standards. Just the reverse happened; they did better academically than their younger classmates—because they were older, more mature, and often highly motivated. Today, we know that adults, regardless of age, can learn almost anything they are motivated to learn. The fact that almost one-third of all undergraduate students now are over twenty-five and that this percentage will continue to increase for the foreseeable future is compelling evidence of adults' ability to learn.

A major educational issue well into the twenty-first century will undoubtedly be to establish an equilibrium between what might be termed *youth-terminal* and *adult-continuing* education. Two traditionally held assumptions about postsecondary education are being questioned: 1) that the need for organized educational opportunities can be met during the first one-fourth of the life span; and 2) that the need for education during the remaining three-fourths of a lifetime can be met adequately by incidental learning through the daily experiences of living and working. Today's students must develop the ability and desire to continue learning throughout their lifetimes, and they must be provided with appropriate, recurring learning opportunities to achieve that goal. In a world characterized by rapid social, technological, economic, and political changes, continuing education will be essential—a person's education now becomes obsolescent with a rapidity never before known. We must remember that one of the primary purposes of schooling is for students to learn how to learn.

A major emphasis in adult education is to continue to expand learning opportunities for people previously underrepresented in higher education: African Americans, Latino and Hispanic Americans, Asian Americans and Pacific Islanders, Native Americans and Alaskan Natives, and the poor. In this chapter's Teachers' Voices—Putting Theory into Practice section ("How Critical Are Our Pedagogies? Privileging the Discourse of Lived Experience in the Community College Classroom"), Leonor Xóchitl Pérez and Anna Marie Christiansen describe how the first author created a mechanism through which students' psychological, social, and cultural characteristics were acknowledged, discussed, and integrated into a course for students aged seventeen to fifty-five at a community college in a low-income Latino community in Los Angeles.

MEETING THE NEEDS OF NONTRADITIONAL STUDENTS

Colleges and universities are beginning to take seriously the challenge posed by the reentry of adult, "nontraditional" students, who, as Naomi Jacobs (1989, p. 329) points out, may be "unsure of their abilities, rusty in their study habits, and encumbered by family and work responsibilities." Colleges and universities are meeting the educational needs of many nontraditional students whose employment, family obligations, and geographic location make on-campus attendance difficult through distance education—"education or training courses delivered to remote (off-campus) locations via audio, video, or computer technologies" (National Center for Education Statistics, 1998b, p. 1). In addition to creating greater access to higher education, especially for students in rural areas, distance education is seen as a way of reducing costs. For example, in the state of Washington, the Washington Higher Education Telecommunication System (WHETS) is a two-way audio-video microwave system that links ten cities and fourteen educational institutions. As a member of WHETS, Washington State University delivers about seventy courses per semester to several sites around the state, including three branch campuses and two community colleges. More than thirty classrooms on campus are capable of sending and receiving over the system.

Examples of other university and state networks for distance education include the Colorado Electronic Community College, EdNet in Oregon, the Iowa Communications Network, the TeleLinking Network in Kentucky, and BadgerNet in Wisconsin. Other systems involve cooperatives and consortia that cross state lines, such as the Western Governors University, a "virtual university" sponsored by the governors of fifteen states and one U.S. territory); and the Committee on Institutional Cooperation, a network of twelve large universities, including Pennsylvania State University, University of Iowa, Ohio State University, University of Minnesota, University of Wisconsin, and University of Illinois (National Center for Education Statistics, 1998b).

Distance education is becoming an increasingly important element of higher education. In 1994–95, an estimated 25,730 distance education courses with different catalog numbers were offered by colleges and universities. That year only 4 percent of institutions offered no distance education courses, while 25 percent offered 11 to 25 courses, and 26 percent offered more than 25 courses (National Center for Education Statistics, 1998b). Out of about 14.3 million students enrolled in higher education in 1994, almost 800,000 enrolled in distance education courses. Among the target audiences for distance education courses, 49 percent of institutions targeted workers seeking skill updating or retraining; 39 percent targeted professionals seeking recertification; 16 percent targeted individuals with disabilities; 12 percent targeted military personnel; 7 percent targeted Native Americans/Alaskan Natives on tribal lands; and 3 percent targeted non-English-speaking individuals (National Center for Education Statistics, 1998b).

SENIOR LEARNERS

Another group of learners that is increasing rapidly is senior learners. With computer-age advances in health care—from artificial heart implantation, to diagnoses using magnetic resonance imaging, to the possibility of individuals cloning vital organs for later replacement—the life span of Americans is steadily being extended. The population over the age of 65 is increasing twice as fast as the population as a whole. For example, a *U.S. News & World Report* article titled "If You Live to Be 100—It Won't Be Unusual" estimated that the number of Americans 65 or older will nearly double between 1983 and 2033; more than one out of five Americans in 2033 will be 65 or older. Also, in 1998, approximately 61,000 persons were 100 or older; by 2040, this number is expected to increase to 1.4 million. As John Glenn's return to space in 1998 at the age of 77 dramatically portrayed, older Americans will increasingly be better educated and more physically, intellectually, and politically active than their predecessors. Thus, it seems highly possible that new opportunities for curriculum planners will become available as educational gerontologists, individuals who specialize in developing educational programs for an aging population.

Many colleges and universities are now opening their doors widely to senior citizens; roughly one-fifth of the 3,000 institutions for higher learning offer courses for retirement age students (many offer free or reduced tuition). Courses vary from cultural enrichment, retirement services, and crafts to liberal arts programs and vocational reeducation.

The greatest group participation of older adults in regular college-level courses has been through Elderhostel, which began as a nonprofit organization in 1975 and offered people sixty and over the chance to take courses, staying in residence while paying only for living expenses. The Elderhostel program, originally based on a few college and university campuses in the New England states, now operates in all states and in many countries. In 1998, more than 270,000 individuals participated in Elderhostel educational programs, and 3,000 courses were offered. Increasingly, curriculum planners are realizing that more attention should be given to teaching senior learners and that the fight against ageism should begin in the minds of the elderly. Elderhostel is based on the idea that retirement does not mean withdrawal and that "learning is a lifelong process; sharing new ideas, challenges and experiences is rewarding in every season of life" (Elderhostel, 1998).

HIGHER EDUCATION AND THE FUTURE

What will be the shape of higher education in the future? In "The Decline of the Knowledge Factory" in this chapter, John Tagg maintains that colleges will need to become "learning-driven institutions" if they are to provide society with its best hope for the future—the educated person. In "The University in the Twenty-First Century," Richard L. Rubenstein suggests that "The marketplace will play an ever-increasing role in the structure, curriculum, curriculum delivery, research, and nature of the student body in the information age university." Similarly, Clark Kerr (1997, p. 355), former president of the University of California, believes "The dominant fact is that higher education serves the labor market; and enrollments will follow labor market needs, not intellectual, cultural, and social needs." Clearly, linkages with other institutions will be all-important to the survival and significance of the university of the future. Since more and more jobs depend upon contacts with people throughout the world, what is taught in our colleges and universities must reflect the interrelatedness of global and national events. Colleges and universities should provide young people and adults in our society with the skills and knowledge needed to function in a world community.

In addition to continued calls to provide students with a rigorous liberal education and to prepare them to meet the challenges of a rapidly changing society and world, today's universities are experiencing strong pressure to make their curricula more student centered. For example, in "The Student-Centered Research University" in this chapter, Gershon Vincow maintains that student learning is the principal goal of the research university and that the principal rationale for research should be the extent to which it promotes learning among undergraduate and graduate students. As universities continue to become more student centered, many different approaches to curriculum planning and teaching will be utilized, and much faculty time will be devoted to diagnosing students' needs and prescribing individual courses of study.

What goals of education should be established for late adolescents and adults? As mentioned earlier in this chapter, the broad general goals of education at the postsecondary level are the same as those at the other levels we have studied—*citizenship, equal educational opportunity, vocation, self-realization,* and *critical thinking.* In addition, a major goal of postsecondary education should be to provide a wide array of educational opportunities for learners. Curriculum planners must recognize that the life span for everyone includes critical transitional events that require new adjustments to meet life's challenges.

REFERENCES

Boyer, Ernest L. *College: The Undergraduate Experience in America.* New York: Harper & Row, 1987.

Carnegie Foundation for the Advancement of Teaching. *Higher Education and the American Resurgence.* Lawrenceville, NJ: Princeton University Press, 1985.

Elderhostel. "Elderhostel Mission Statement." Boston: Elderhostel, Inc., 1998.

Havighurst, Robert J. *Developmental Tasks and Education,* 3rd Ed. New York: Longman, 1972.

Jacobs, Naomi. "Nontraditional Students: The New Ecology of the Classroom." *The Educational Forum* 53, no. 4 (Summer 1989): 329–326.

Kerr, Clark. "Speculations about the Increasingly Indeterminate Future of Higher Education in the United States." *Review of Higher Education* 20, no. 4 (Summer 1997): 345–356.

National Center for Education Statistics. *Projection of Education Statistics to 2008.* Washington, DC: National Center for Education Statistics, 1998a.

———. "Distance Education in Higher Education Institutions: Incidence, Audiences, and Plans to Expand." Washington, DC: National Center for Education Statistics, 1998b.

———. *The Condition of Education 1996.* Washington, DC: National Center for Education Statistics, 1996.

National Institute of Education. *Involvement in Learning: Realizing the Potential of American Higher Education.* Washington, DC: U.S. Government Printing Office, 1984.

Connectedness through Liberal Education

ERNEST L. BOYER (1928–1995)

ABSTRACT: Drawing from the 1987 Carnegie Foundation report, College: The Undergraduate Experience in America, *Boyer identifies five essential priorities for undergraduate education. Students should (1) become proficient in the written and spoken word, (2) be liberally educated, (3) acquire moral and ethical principles, (4) be taught by teachers who emphasize active rather than passive learning, and (5) be helped to establish connections between theories presented in the classroom and the realities of life.*

In the past 3 years, the Carnegie Foundation has been looking at undergraduate education in the United States. In our report, "College," we recommended many changes to strengthen the undergraduate experience. I would like to highlight what I consider to be five essentials of quality undergraduate education.

Let me begin with a personal illustration. In 1972, I was sitting in my office in Albany, New York, on a dreary Monday morning. To avoid the obligations of the day, I turned instinctively to the stack of third-class mail that I kept perched precariously on the corner of my desk to create the illusion of being very busy. On top of the pile was the student newspaper from Stanford University. The headline read that the faculty at Stanford had reintroduced a required course in Western civilization after having abolished all requirements just 3 years before. The students, in a front-page editorial, opposed the brash act of the faculty. They declared that "a required course is an illiberal act," and concluded that editorial with this blockbuster question. "How dare they impose uniform standards on nonuniform people?"

At first I was amused, and then deeply troubled, by that query—and it has nagged me to this day. I wondered how it was that some of the nation's most gifted students could not understand that while we are not uniform, we still have many things in common. Is it conceivable that we are educating our students to see themselves in isola-

tion while failing to help them discover their connections? Is it possible that, through formal education in the United States, we are stressing our independence but not affirming the interdependent nature of our existence?

This anecdote brings me to the central theme of my remarks. I believe that all worthy goals we pursue in undergraduate education might be captured by the simple word, "connections." Let me give four or five examples to illustrate my point.

First, we are connected through the exquisite use of symbols. Language is our most essential human function. Our capacity to capture feelings and ideas sets us apart from all other forms of life, the porpoise and the bumble bee notwithstanding. And the top priority of those in undergraduate education must be to help all students become proficient in the written and spoken word. I find it quite amazing that children learn very early that words are both magical and powerful. When I was a young boy in Dayton, Ohio, they used to say "Sticks and stones may break my bones, but names would never hurt me." "What nonsense," I'd usually say, with tears running down my checks, thinking all the time, "For goodness sakes, hit me with a stick but stop those words that penetrate so deeply and last so long."

Language begins before birth as the unborn infant monitors the mother's voice in utero. We know that the three middle ear bones—the hammer, the anvil, and the stirrup—are the only

Excerpted from *Journal of Professional Nursing* 5, no. 2 (March–April 1989): 102–107. Based on a keynote presentation at the semiannual meeting of the American Association of Colleges of Nursing, Washington, DC, March 14, 1988. Used by permission of the author.

bones fully formed at birth. So, we start language development before we're born. We learn language from our parents and our grandparents and all those people around us. It is through this process that we are connected to each other. And now that I am a grandfather and see this process of language acquisition and development unencumbered by dirty diapers and burpings late at night, I stand in awe that this magical, God-given, gene-driven capacity of symbols emerges so majestically. Yet we take language development so carelessly for granted. We accept it unthinkingly, just as we do breath itself. Consider the miracle of this very moment: I stand here vibrating my vocal cords, molecules are bombarded in your direction, they touch your tympanic membrane, signals go scurrying up your eighth cranial nerve, and there is a response in your cerebrum which I trust approximates the images in mine. It is this process through which we are personally and socially empowered and connected.

We say in our report that every college freshman should take a basic course in language. We say that writing should be taught in every class, since it's through clear writing that clear thinking can be taught. We conclude that every student should, before he or she graduates from college, be able to write carefully, think critically, listen with discernment, and speak with power and precision.

In the teaching of language, we should also teach the value of silence, listening to each other and to ourselves. We live in a culture where noise too often is the norm. In fact, we feel uncomfortable in the presence of silence. And yet listening is often a crucial condition for those in the healing arts. I wish that in the classroom students would begin to have periods of silence, not just to keep order but to reflect on what they have heard.

There is, in too many professional arrangements, the protection of our labels that conceal us from each other. Some years ago, when we were having dinner at our home, the children were playing a record at a decibel level that was calculated to destroy the tympanic membrane. I asked them to please tell me what I was hearing. They gave me the lyrics of the song "Eleanor Rigby," the story of a woman who wore a mask she kept in a jar. I think that song quite rightly is a parable of many of our institutions. We protect ourselves as deans, professors, scientists, scholars, and one wonders where's the humanity of it all. We scurry about, caught up in the thick of things, unwilling and often unable to take the time to listen carefully to each other. I'm talking about teaching language, not as the parts of speech, not just as a process that's technically correct, but as the means by which humans are connected to each other.

When I was chancellor of the State University of New York, I was about to speak to a group of faculty from across the state, when 350 students came barging in through the door, as they often did in those days. They were chanting slogans and waving placards and they demanded that I help free a group of students who had been arrested on another campus. For almost an hour we shouted back and forth. Finally, I concluded we weren't listening to each other. The meeting was in a shambles and, even worse, I realized that I was talking not to people but to a faceless mob. So more out of desperation than inspiration, I left the platform, walked into the crowd, and began to talk to a single student. I asked her name; I asked her about her family; I asked her why she was so angry. Soon several others joined us and I described what I could and couldn't do. Well, to make this story short, the session ended, we reached a compromise, and in the process I learned to know some most attractive students.

What I'm suggesting is that our shared use of symbols connects us to each other, and it is through liberal education that students should be asked to consider the quality of the messages they send. Recently, I happened across a fascinating little anecdote about an 18th century Quaker named John Olmen. He tells of a meeting he had with Indians in Pennsylvania. Olmen said he struggled to communicate with them through an interpreter who was having an extremely bad time with his messages. So Olmen shifted to silence and occasionally to prayer. At the end of the exchange, he was intrigued by what one of the Indian chiefs said of his message. "I love to feel where the words come from." In the end, the quality of the message is not in its correctness alone, but in the integrity of the meaning. Those around us know whether we are just sending messages or are listening as well.

I want to make one final point on the issue of connectedness through language. Connectedness is achieved not just through cleverness or even clarity of expression, but through integrity as well. To borrow again from the Quakers, in the 18th and early 19th centuries, Quakers were unwilling to swear "to tell the truth, the whole truth, and nothing but the truth" in a court of law. It wasn't just that they were against swearing, although they were. The problem was that they were unwilling to swear to tell the truth in a court with their hand positioned on a Bible because to do so meant raising the question of whether or not, outside the courtroom, truth might be an option. So they would say, "Your Honor, I speak truth." "No, No, you have to swear you'll speak it now." "But your Honor, I speak truth." Now, I'm not sure I would be willing to hang for a delicate point like that, but the larger principle cannot be denied. I am suggesting that students should be taught that truth is the obligation they assume when they are empowered with the use of symbols. And that in the end, the quality of a college can be measured by the quality of communication on the campus.

This brings me to priority number two. I believe that students not only need empowerment and connectedness through language, they need to be liberally educated so they can put their work in larger context. As I look at the nature of our world, I'm deeply disturbed that many of our students are becoming increasingly parochial at the very moment the human agenda is more global. And I do not believe that they can act as wise professionals in an interdependent world unless they are able to put their work in an international context.

About 3 years ago, 40 per cent of the community college students we surveyed could not locate either Iran or El Salvador on the map. During our study of the American high school, we discovered that only two states require students to complete a course in non-Western studies. And 2 years ago, when we surveyed 5,000 undergraduates, we learned that over 30 per cent of them said that they had nothing in common with people in underdeveloped countries. The simple truth is that our graduates will live in a world that is economically, politically, and environmentally connected and they increasingly will work with a population in the United States that is more and more diverse. Yet somehow we are not providing a general education that offers the larger perspective that is urgently required, one that affirms our connectedness, not just socially but ecologically as well.

When I was US Commissioner of Education, Joan Ganz Cooney, the creator of Sesame Street, came to see me one day with an idea she had for a new program on science for junior high school students. We found funding for the show, which was called "3-2-1 Contact." Cooney and her staff conducted research to prepare for the show. They asked some junior high school students in New York City such questions as where water came from. A disturbing percentage said, "the faucet." They asked where light came from and the students said, "the switch." And they asked where garbage went and students said, "down the chute." Their answers indicate a frightening almost "anti-connectedness" to much of their world.

We are, as Lewis Thomas put it, embedded in the natural world as working parts. It is no longer possible for us to consume and produce without asking about discarding, too. We must become increasingly sensitive to the interdependent nature of our physical world and our responsibility to live according to the laws of nature, both as a global community and in our personal lives as well. This kind of interdependence, in my judgment, is at the heart of professional education. Lewis Thomas once wrote that "if this century does not slip forever through our fingers it will be because education will have directed us away from our splintered dumbness and helped us focus on our common goal."

This brings me then to priority number three, how we live and how we work—the challenge to bring moral and ethical perspective to our profession. Many of us have been worried about such issues as gene splicing research that might introduce mutations on the planet earth. We have also questioned whether human subjects should be used during experimentation. These, in my judgment, are questions in which there are no experts. There are only human beings trying to solve new and complicated problems.

Again, the challenge is to put our professions in social and ethical perspective. If we do not, we run the risk of creating what I call the "Boesky syndrome," people who know how to succeed but who do not make their decisions within the context of moral judgment; people whose confidence is not guided by conscience. In the Carnegie report on college, we suggest something called the enriched major. We suggest that every professional field should be asked to place its own work in historical, social, and ethical perspective. We drew some of our inspiration from Norman Cousins, who observed some years ago that the doctor who knows only disease is at a disadvantage alongside the doctor who knows as much about people as he or she does about pathological organisms.

Cousins goes on to say that the lawyer who argues in court from a narrow legal base is no match for the lawyer who can connect legal precedence to historical experience. So we suggest in our report that the values professionals bring to their work are every bit as crucial as the work itself. And we argue that general and specialized education should be blended during college; just as inevitably, they should be blended during life.

This discussion leads me to say a word about teachers. We can have a good curriculum in professional training and we can have all the priorities spelled out in a syllabus or in a national report. However, in the end, connectedness is established in the classroom by teachers who serve as models and as mentors.

Several years ago during a sleepless night, I counted all the teachers I've had, instead of counting sheep. I remembered 15 or more rather vividly. There were, I must admit, a few nightmares in the bunch. But I tried to think of all the great teachers, the outstanding individuals in colleges and schools who genuinely changed my life.

First I thought about Miss Rice, my first grade teacher. My mother walked with me my first day of school. On the way, I asked her if I would learn to read that day. I badly wanted to learn to read. My mother said, "No, you won't learn to read today but you will before the year is out." Well, she didn't know Miss Rice. I walked into the room and there she stood half human, half divine. After a meaningful pause, Miss Rice looked at 28 frightened, awestruck children and said, "Good morning class, today we learn to read." Those were the first words I ever heard in school.

I probably learned to memorize that day, not decode, but Miss Rice taught me something much more fundamental. She taught me that language is the centerpiece of learning. And I find it really quite miraculous that 50 years later in our book on high school, there was a chapter on the centrality of language, and again in our book on college there was a chapter on language. If we do a book on graduate education, I'm sure there will be a chapter on language. And I mention that to credit the influence of an unheralded first grade teacher at Fairview Avenue Elementary School, Dayton, Ohio, 1934.

I also recall Mr. Wittlinger, a high school history teacher, who one day said quietly as I passed his desk, "Ernest, you're doing very well in history. If you keep this up you just might be a student." It sounds like a put-down but it was the highest academic accolade I'd received. I went home that night thinking to myself, "I'm not a baseball player, I'm not a cowboy, I'm not a fire chief, I just might be a student." The redefinition of who I might be at a time when I wasn't very sure was immeasurably powerful.

Great teachers live forever. What made them truly great? First, these teachers were knowledgeable and well-informed. They had something to teach; thus, their knowledge base was firm. Of course, we've all had teachers who were very knowledgeable but also were dreary and ineffectual, so there had to be something else. Second, these teachers could communicate at a level the student understood. They knew their students and they made connections between their knowledge and their students' readiness to receive it.

The third and final characteristic that brought all together was the fact that the truly outstanding teachers in my life were open, authentic, and believable human beings. They laughed, they cried, they said "I don't know," and above all, they made connections. Mentoring by great teachers makes the difference. I suggest that as we look for ways to strengthen the undergraduate experience we need new models of teaching in the classroom. We need, among other things, active learning rather than passive relationships. We need teachers who inspire not conformity, but creativity in the classroom.

During our study of high school and college, we were enormously impressed by the passivity of students. John Goodlad, who has done an excellent job of studying schools, reports that in many classrooms, 6 per cent of the time is devoted to student speech in the classroom and almost all of that has to do with logistics such as "Will we have this on this test?" and comments about procedural arrangements, not the substance of their work. Now I wish I could tell you that that's not true in colleges, but passivity dominates the classroom in higher education as well. We are teaching lethargy, not engagement.

During our study of undergraduate colleges, we were on the campus of a well-known university. Just before we got there, one of the ranking professors had observed the graduating senior class. He asked how many of them went through 4 years at this institution, got a baccalaureate degree, and said not one word in class. What would you guess? Seventy-five per cent of the students said they could go through that university, never say one word in class, just take notes, and slip in and out. They admitted that they would perhaps have to avoid a few teachers, but that by and large they could do it.

We need to create a climate not only in which there are teachers who mentor, but in which students are teachers, too. Students, as they continue to learn, must accept an obligation to be increasingly engaged. We also need cooperative learning as a part of this process. I'm impressed that through all of school, students are in competition with each other, yet in the end, our serious problems will be resolved through collaborative efforts in the sciences, the professions, and in the workplace, too.

It is not insignificant that increasingly we are talking about the health care "team." That language demonstrates clearly that we are going to have to share information and pursue collaborative problem solving. The teaching model in all fields should be built around the collaborative approach where students are pursuing problems together, and even being graded on their group effort rather than in competition with each other. In the end we are going to survive on planet Earth through an understanding that our problems are collective and our solutions must be found through collaboration.

This leads me to one final observation. I believe we must establish connections between the theories of the classroom and the realities of life.

John Gardner said on one occasion that the deepest threat to the integrity of any community is an incapacity on the part of its citizens to lend themselves to any worthy, common purpose. Gardner goes on to reflect on the bareness of a life that encompasses nothing beyond the self. I believe we are creating a culture in which the sense of engagement is increasingly diminished.

When we did our study on high school, for example, I became quite convinced that we have not just a school problem but a youth problem in this nation. Many of our young people during their teenage years are not socially engaged. This is worrisome, because it's particularly during this time that young people need to find out who they are and how they will fit into the larger world. Many college campuses are youth ghettos, too, places where students talk only to themselves. Today in our society we're organizing ourselves horizontally; putting children in day-care centers, young people in high schools, and then finally our seniors into retirement villages. Instead of connections, we're having intergenerational fragmentation. There is something unhealthy about a culture in which the different generations are separated from each other.

My parents will be celebrating their 89th birthdays in a retirement village soon. There's something particularly redeeming about that village. They have a day-care center there, so every morning 50 or more 4- and 5-year-olds come trucking up. It may not be your idea of retirement, but there's something authentic about a community in which the young and the older mingle with each. My father has a little boy whom he calls "his little friend." All of the day-care children have adopted grandparents and they spend time together throughout the day. When I call my father, he talks about the child's drawings on the wall and the conversations they've had. A community in which young children are able to see the agonies and the dignities of aging and in which 80-year-olds can spend time with children who are on the threshold of a hopeful life offers a deep, joyous opportunity for connections.

Increasingly, I believe that an authentic part of education is building connections between the theory of the classroom and the reality of life outside. The school is not simply a monastic retreat; it is a base of operation. And it is my opinion that every professional field has to build in this component of connectiveness so that students can see the relationship between theory and it application.

For that reason, in our report called high school and then later in college, we propose a service term, not just in the professions but in other fields as well; a time when students can teach others, serve as tutors or spend time in retirement villages or work with young children in day-care centers. All of this is to demonstrate a validity between who they are and the realities of life. Vachel Lindsay wrote on one occasion that "It is the world's one crime its babes grow dull. . . . Not that they sow, but that they seldom reap, not that they serve, but have no gods to serve. Not that they die, but that they die like sheep." Students should understand that the tragedy of life is not death. The tragedy is to die with commitments undefined, convictions undeclared, and service unfulfilled.

Ernest L. Boyer was president of the Carnegie Foundation for the Advancement of Teaching from 1979 to 1995; prior to that he was U.S. Commissioner of Education under President Carter and chancellor of the State University of New York.

QUESTIONS FOR REFLECTION

1. Do you agree with Boyer that all worthy goals for undergraduate education might be captured by the word *connections*? What other word captures what the goals for undergraduate education ought to be?

2. In terms of importance, how would you rank order the five priorities Boyer has identified? What is the rationale for your ranking?

3. To what extent do you agree with the following observation by Boyer: ". . . passivity dominates the classroom in higher education as well. We are teaching lethargy, not engagement"? What factors limit the amount of *engagement* found in the college curriculum? What steps can curriculum planners and teachers take to change this?

Multiculturalism Yes, Particularism No

DIANE RAVITCH

ABSTRACT: The author asserts that the study of American culture is vulnerable to "reconstruction, deconstruction, and revision" and that two versions of multiculturalism are vying for dominance in how American culture is taught. The pluralist approach sees American culture as the creation of many groups and emphasizes commonality and unity; the particularist approach, based on the notion of racial and ethnic purity, denies that a common American culture exists and promotes separatism and a narrow view of the world.

The controversy at Stanford in 1988 over changes in a required course in Western culture has grown into a national debate about the issue of multiculturalism. College campuses, school districts, and even state boards of education are presently examining what is taught and asking whether the history and literature that are offered reflect accurately, the different cultural strands in our society and our world.

Unfortunately, the Stanford battle cast the argument in the wrong terms. Defenders of the existing Western-culture course opposed those who advocated adding works by women and members of minority groups and thus created the impression that Western culture excludes the voices of people who are female, black, Hispanic, and Asian. That image is, of course, ridiculous; we need only look around to see that all of these groups are very much part of Western culture and that their members have made important contributions to its literary and historical traditions.

The debate over multiculturalism follows a generation of scholarship that has enriched our knowledge about the historical experiences of women, blacks, and members of other minority, groups in various societies. As a result of the new scholarship, our schools and our institutions of learning have in recent years begun to embrace what Catharine R. Stimpson of Rutgers University has called "cultural democracy," a recognition that we must listen to "a diversity of voices" to understand our culture, past and present.

Teachers of history and literature have discovered that it is not very difficult, in fact that it is rewarding, to broaden their perspective beyond the one that they learned when they were in school.

Of course, students should still study Western culture, and they should learn about the emergence of the democratic ideology and the concept of individualized freedom that have been so crucial in the history of the world. But they must also learn about the cultures of Asia, Africa, and Latin America. These all represent complex civilizations, containing many cultural groups and different languages.

But today, when educators argue about multiculturalism, they are usually not talking about disciplined study of other major civilizations. They refer instead to American culture, which, because it is ours and because it is relatively new, is vulnerable to reconstruction, deconstruction, and revision. From which perspective should it be taught? Who should be included?

The real issue on campus and in the classroom is not whether there will be multiculturalism, but what kind of multiculturalism there will be. Two versions presently compete for dominance in the teaching of American culture. One approach reflects cultural pluralism and accepts diversity as a fact; the other represents particularism and demands loyalty to a particular group. The two coexist uncomfortably, because they are not different by degree. In fact, they are opposite in spirit and in purpose.

From *The Chronicle of Higher Education* 37, no. 8 (October 24, 1990): A44. Used by permission of the author.

The pluralist approach to American culture recognizes that the common culture has been shaped by the interaction of the nation's many diverse cultural elements. It sees American culture as the creation of many groups of immigrants, American Indians, Africans, and their descendants. American music, art, literature, language, food, clothing, sports, holidays, and customs all demonstrate the commingling of diverse cultures in one nation. Paradoxical though it may seem, the United States has a common culture that is multicultural.

The particularist approach to American culture can be seen most vividly in ethnic-studies programs whose goal is to "raise the self-esteem" of students by providing role models. Such courses are animated by a spirit of filiopietism and by fundamentalist notions of racial and ethnic purity. Students are encouraged to believe that something in their blood or their race memory or their cultural D.N.A. defines who they are and what they may achieve. Particularists seek to attach their students to their ancestral homelands as the source of their personal identity and authentic culture.

The pluralists promote a broader interpretation of common American culture by recognizing first that there *is* a common culture, and second that it has been created by many different groups. At its most basic, our common culture is a civic culture, shaped by our Constitution, our commitment to democratic values, and our historical experience as a nation. In addition, our very heterogeneity sets us apart from most other nations and creates styles of expression that the rest of the world perceives as distinctively American. The pluralists seek due recognition for the ways in which the nation's many racial, ethnic, and cultural groups have transformed the national culture. They say, in effect, "American culture belongs to all of us, and we remake it in every generation." The cohesive element in the pluralistic approach is the clear acknowledgement that, whatever our differences, we are all human. The thread that binds us is our common humanity, transcending race, color, ethnicity, language, and religion.

Particularists have no interest in extending American culture; indeed, they deny that a common culture exists. They do not appeal to the common good, because their idea of community is defined along racial or ethnic lines. They reject any accommodation among groups, any interactions that blur the distinct lines among them. They espouse a version of history in which everyone is either the descendant of victims or of oppressors. By doing so, ancient hatreds are fanned and recreated in each generation.

There is not a fine line that divides pluralism from particularism; they are as different as secularism and sectarianism. The pluralist approach to teaching culture accords with traditional academic ethics, in that students learn to approach their subject with a critical eye. They learn *about* the subject, and they know that they may criticize its strengths and weaknesses without offending the professor. For example, in a traditional academic setting, the object of learning about Confucianism or Islam or Judaism is to study its history and philosophy, not to become an adherent of the faith. Similarly, there is a valid place for special courses and programs in black studies, women's studies, gay studies, or any other kind of cultural studies, so long as they are taught critically and not as doctrinal faiths.

By contrast, particularism has spurred a separatist ethic in higher education. In the particularist classroom, students are taught to believe in the subject, to immerse themselves in its truths, and to champion them against skeptics. They are taught to believe, not to doubt or criticize. In this sense, particularism resembles a religious approach to teaching. Students are taught a faith, and the professor expects them to believe what he or she believes. In this sense, particularism resembles a sectarian approach to teaching.

On our campuses today, courses in black studies, Asian studies, and all other special cultural studies should welcome all students, not just in theory but in fact. The severing of such courses from established disciplines probably encourages separatism and ideological extremism. All too often, even though the catalogue implies that such courses are for everyone, the particularism of the professor or the department may discourage students who are not members of the in-group from signing up. The tendency to turn such courses into separatist enclaves violates a major purpose of higher education, which is to broaden one's understanding of the world. No special status should be accorded to students who are of the group being studied, nor should scholars be expected to specialize only in the culture of their ancestors.

The essential difference between pluralism and particularism is that the former actively combats ethnocentrism and the latter purposefully teaches it. Ethnocentrism is the specter that has been haunting the world for centuries—causing war, injustice, and civil conflict. Ethnocentrism tells people that they must trust and accept only members of their own group. It tells them that they must immerse themselves in their own culture and close their mind to others. It says to members of the group that they have nothing in common with people of a different race, a different religion, a different culture. It breeds hatred and distrust.

Ethnocentrism has no place in our schools and institutions of higher learning. Academic institutions have an obligation to introduce students to a larger culture than the one they learned at home.

The purpose of education is not to reproduce and reinforce the prejudices of our inherited culture. Education must prepare people to live in a world of competing ideas and values, to be able to work with people from different backgrounds, to be able to question their own beliefs.

The novelist Salmon Rushdie's recent comments are germane to the ongoing debate about multiculturalism. This past summer, he published an essay called "In Good Faith," his reflections on the events that forced him into isolation. Mr. Rushdie wrote that those who oppose his novel "are of the opinion that intermingling with a different culture will inevitably weaken and ruin their own." He goes on to say:

"*The Satanic Verses* celebrates hybridity, impurity, intermingling, the transformation that comes of new and unexpected combinations of human beings, cultures, ideas, politics, movies, songs. It rejoices in mongrelization and fears the absolutism of the Pure. Mélange, hotchpotch, a bit of this and a bit of that is *how newness enters the world*."

True believers in all societies have never been comfortable with the kinds of ideas and activities found in the university. They have seen the university as a citadel of doubt, skepticism, nonconformity, unorthodoxy, and dissent; a place where young people learn to question the faith of the elders; a safe haven for those who criticize the conventional wisdom.

And so it should remain.

Diane Ravitch is Professor of History and Education, Teachers College, Columbia University.

QUESTIONS FOR REFLECTION

1. How does Ravitch distinguish between cultural pluralism and cultural particularism?
2. Do you agree with Ravitch's assertion that cultural pluralism "actively combats" racism, while cultural particularism "purposefully teaches" it?
3. Does a multicultural emphasis in the curriculum "exalt racial and ethnic pride at the expense of social cohesion"?

Curriculum Planning and Development for Native Americans and Alaska Natives in Higher Education

ELLA INGLEBRET
D. MICHAEL PAVEL

ABSTRACT: An historical overview of curriculum development practices provides insights for meeting the educational needs of Native Americans and Alaska Natives who will enroll in higher education institutions in the twenty-first century. Three orientations to curriculum planning for Native peoples are discussed: (1) changing the student to fit the curriculum, (2) creating culturally congruent curricula, and (3) empowering students and communities. The authors see evidence that Native peoples are "once again playing a key role in defining their own educational landscapes and the directions for their [educational] journeys."

For Native Peoples in America, this is a great time to be alive. We are the children of cultural magnificence; the parents of the visions and dreams of our ancestors. We are the modern evidence of our ancient continuums (Harjo, 1994, p. 5).

There is a renewed sense of optimism in Indian country. After decades of being silenced, Indian and Native voices are being heard and their views considered within the postsecondary arena (see, for example, Indian Nations At Risk Task Force, 1990; Native Education Initiative of the Regional Educational Labs, 1995; White House Conference on Indian Education, 1992). Native concerns regarding the educational achievement of their peoples are strengthened as they join with national agendas focused on better preparation of students for citizenship in a culturally diverse society (see, for example, Adams, 1992; Bennett, 1995; Justiz, 1994). While this recent trend represents a significant social force for change, underrepresentation of Native Americans and Alaska Natives in higher education remains a critical issue (U.S. Department of Education, 1998). Only when we address the needs of all peoples in this land will our country be positioned to continu-

ally meet the complex challenges of a highly interdependent world.

The curricula of higher educational institutions might serve as powerful catalysts for social change or might perpetuate social inequalities that impede the forward movement of a culturally diverse nation. This article advocates that curriculum planning issues be examined to increase Native American and Alaska Native achievement in higher education. The first section provides a historical review of Native American educational curricula dating back to its roots, bringing it forward through the assimilationist period imposed by the federal government and up to more recent efforts toward self-determination. Following this historical overview, various approaches associated with curriculum development specific to Native Americans and Alaska Natives are discussed.

Information presented is derived from various sources. Due to limitations in available literature specific to Native Americanns and Alaska Natives in higher education, this article draws upon literature addressing elementary, secondary, and postsecondary curriculum development. The review of literature is integrated with research

Article written by Ella Inglebret and D. Michael Pavel for *Curriculum Planning: A Contemporary Approach*, Seventh Edition, 2000. Used by permission of the authors.

completed by the authors as well as personal experiences in designing, implementing, and evaluating educational programs for Native Americans and Alaska Natives in higher education. The goal is to provide the reader with insights into curriculum planning that will be pertinent to the education of college students in the new century.

HISTORICAL REVIEW

Prior to fifteenth-century European contact, higher education was, as it still is, a fundamental part of Native American societies. Contrary to the popular image of Native Americans as uneducated savages, "many of the American Indian peoples devoted their lives and talents to the search and development of knowledge—a practice that arose from the cultural group needs and in part focused on learning how to better provide for the practical well-being of the people" (D-Q University, 1996–97, p. 2). Traditional educational processes were associated with formal higher education institutions (Crum, 1991) and with a "total way of life" (McKay & McKay, 1987, p. 64). Educational curricula focused on facilitating awareness of an individual's relationship to the universe and of one's place in history, as well as on the development of "inner strengths and depth of character" (D-Q University, 1996–97, p. 3). However, with the advent of widespread European colonialism, traditional education systems were severely challenged by multiple forces including: (a) foreign diseases spread by explorers, missionaries, and profiteers which left many of the Native teachers dead; (b) competing philosophies fueled by Eurocentric positioning which disregarded the Native people's ancestral means of educating their citizens; and (c) benign and feigned efforts to morally save the Indian savage more ruthless than altruistic.

Foreign disease brought profound devastation. Snipp (1989) has paralleled the magnitude of Native American depopulation after 1500 to the medieval plagues of Europe. Possessing neither the resistance to European diseases introduced by early explorers nor the cures that were developed to combat the diseases, Native American populations were quickly decimated. Large-scale depopulation created upheaval in existing social and cultural systems, including education, and caused redistribution of entire population centers. As a consequence, what White settlers encountered were often only the remnants of once complex Native civilizations.

White European contact quickly revealed incompatibilities with Native American philosophies and lifestyles. The Native people were viewed as impediments to the country's settlement and westward expansion. Their very existence was further challenged through warfare, genocide, and assimilationist policies. Where the "Indian problem" was not eliminated on the battlefield, it was to be eradicated using education as a tool. It was believed that as Natives learned the ways of the White people, they would willingly give up their own ways to become part of the dominant society (Utley, 1984).

Some of the very first higher education institutions established by the English in this country had chartered missions to educate Native Americans. The charters of Harvard College (1636), the College of William and Mary (1693), and Dartmouth College (1769) all incorporated curricula that were designed to educate and "civilize" Native Americans (Wright & Tierney, 1991). However, this intent was not readily accepted by the Natives themselves. The following reaction of the Six Nations of the Iroquois Confederacy to an offer by the Government of Virginia to enroll their sons at the College of William and Mary exemplifies the Native attitude toward Western education.

. . . you, who are wise, must know that different Nations have different Conceptions of things and you will therefore not take it amiss, if our Ideas of this kind of Education happen not to be the same as yours. We have had some Experience of it; Several of our young People were formerly brought up at the Colleges of the Northern Provinces; they were instructed in all your Sciences; but, when they came back to us, they were bad Runners, ignorant of every means of living in the Woods, unable to bear either Cold or Hunger, know neither how to build a Cabin, take a Deer, or kill an enemy, spoke our Language imperfectly, were neither fit for Hunters, Warriors, nor Counsellors; they were totally good for nothing. We are however not the less oblig'd by your kind Offer, tho' we decline accepting it; and, to show our grateful Sense of it, if the Gentleman of Virginia will send us a dozen of their Sons, we will take Care of their Education, instruct them in all we know, and make Men of them. (Franklin, 1794, p. 28–29)

While colonial colleges largely failed in their attempts at assimilating Native Americans, the assimilationist philosophy was carried forward to the federally funded, boarding school era beginning in the late 1800s. The target became young children who were considered "ideal agents for uplifting an older generation still stranded in the backwaters of barbarism" (Adams, 1995, p. 335). In contrast to the focus of the colonial college on higher academic study, boarding school curricula emphasized vocational training and domestic arts. To facilitate adoption of White cultural values and knowledge, Native children were removed great distances from their families and tribal surroundings. Use of Native languages was strictly forbidden and subject to corporal punishment (Szasz, 1977). Due to the high transportation costs involved and the objections of families to having their children forcibly removed, on-reservation day schools were eventually established. During this period few Native Americans received formal education beyond the high school level.

The quality of education provided at federal boarding schools of this era was highly criticized in the U.S. government–sponsored study now commonly referred to as the Meriam Report (Meriam, 1928), which served as an indictment of the federal government's assimilationist policies (Bill, 1987). The Meriam Report exposed the shocking and substandard conditions that existed within boarding schools and suggested that pre-adolescent Native children should no longer be sent to these schools. Vocational training provided for older students was also criticized for its irrelevance to the workplace and to the skills necessary for life on the reservations. It was recommended that education for Native children be provided within their home communities and that they incorporate elements of both White culture and the local Native language and culture.

Some educational reforms followed the release of the Meriam Report. Native enrollment in boarding schools did become less prevalent. However, the federal policy shift toward incorporation of Native languages and culture into the curriculum of Native schools was only short-lived. Curriculum planning would remain outside of the control of Native Americans themselves because entrenched negative attitudes of non-Native teachers and school administrators presented significant barriers to the enactment of the new policies.

Reflecting the limited impact of education reform efforts, the Meriam Report's criticisms were mirrored forty years later in what is commonly referred to as the Kennedy Report, *Indian Education Tragedy—A National Challenge* (U.S. Senate, 1969). High dropout rates, low academic achievement, and low self-esteem characterized Native American and Alaska Native students. The report indicated that "most schools serving American Indian and Alaska Native students had consistently belittled the students' cultural identity and integrity while systematically ignoring parental voices of concern and pleas for justice" (Pavel, Swisher, & Ward, 1995, p. 34). The limited accomplishments of Native American and Alaska Native students across elementary, secondary, and postsecondary education indicated that an externally imposed system and curricula developed by members of the dominant society did not address the educational needs of Native people (Lomawaima, 1995). It was time for Native people to determine the course of their own educational futures and take the lead in developing the mission, scope, and influence of their own curricula.

The civil rights movement of the 1950s and 1960s set the stage for Native American and Alaska Native voices to be heard. No longer would the assimilationist policies designed to eliminate indigenous cultures and beliefs be tolerated. No longer would low levels of educational attainment be accepted. Curricula emphasizing vocational training would not suffice for higher academic study. Native American and Alaska Native people had a long and proud history of self-education that would no longer be squelched. For the first time since the advent of White Europeans, Native American and Alaska Native people would have the opportunity to build an educational system that incorporated their values, needs, and visions of the future (The Carnegie Foundation for the Advancement of Teaching, 1989).

Over time, increased control has been assumed over Native education policies, administration, and curriculum. Efforts of higher education institutions as well as tribal, state, and federal governments have resulted in increased enrollments of Native students. Passage of the Indian Self-Determination and Educational Assistance Act of 1975 led to the first large-scale participation of Native people in contemporary education. Perhaps the most significant step forward in higher education involved the passage of the Navajo Community College Act of 1970 and the Tribally Controlled Community College Assistance Act of 1978, which paved the way for the tribally controlled college movement.

Today there are thirty tribally controlled colleges that enroll nearly a quarter of all full-time equivalent Native American and Alaska Native students attending the 3,000 plus higher education institutions in America (U.S. Department of Education, 1998). While serving different tribes, the tribally controlled colleges have similar institutional missions that influence curriculum development. These include: (a) preserve, enhance, and promote tribal language and culture; (b) serve the economic development, human resource development, and community organization; and (c) provide academic programs for students seeking two-year and/or four-year degrees in addition to transfer courses.

CONTEMPORARY CURRICULUM PLANNING

The learning experience for Native American and Alaska Native students extends far beyond the formal curriculum of the classroom. Therefore, the following discussion will present curriculum planning as it exists within the broader context of higher education. Various approaches that have been advocated for increasing Native American and Alaska Native representation in higher education will be presented within the framework of three orientations: (a) changing the student to fit the curriculum, (b) creating culturally congruent curricula, and (c) empowering students and communities. These orientations are not mutually exclusive, but rather are based on different theoretical foundations that have significant and varying implications for curriculum planning for Native American and Alaska Native students.

Changing the Student to Fit the Curriculum

Early attempts at fostering Native American and Alaska Native success in higher education have focused on students adapting to the existing curriculum and to overall institutional expectations. Various authors have drawn attention to the mismatch that frequently exists between the culture of mainstream education institutions and Native communities (Deyhle, 1995; Henry & Pepper, 1990; Lipka & Ilutsik, 1995; Pipes, Westby, & Inglebret, 1993; Swisher, 1990). Native American and Alaska Native students are often confronted with institutional policies and curricular content and practices that are unfamiliar or even contradictory to what they have experienced in their home communities. To increase academic achievement, students have to learn the rules and dominant practices associated with a particular institutional culture as well as in receiving supplemental educational instruction and psychosocial support.

With this approach the student is expected to make the primary adjustments while standard curriculum planning is maintained. This framework can ease the demands put on faculty; however, it brings disadvantages. It relies on Native student assimilation to the dominant culture of the institution, giving little regard to the cultural background the student brings to the academic setting. In fact, Deyhle and Swisher (1997) point out that, consistent with cultural deficit theory, the cultural characteristics of the student are likely to be viewed as deficiencies that lead to failure in the educational process. They contrast this assimilationist perspective that omits the student's home culture from the curriculum with their review of related research indicating that "Native languages and cultures correlate positively with school success" (p. 136). Consequently, it behooves the educator to explore means for considering a Native student's cultural background during the curriculum planning process.

Content and Process of Creating Culturally Congruent Curricula

Content. Modification and extension of content provides one means for increasing the cultural congruence of curricula for Native American and Alaska Native students. Cummins (1994) and Lomawaima (1995) emphasize the importance of incorporating the cultural and linguistic background of Native students into the curriculum. Native American students attending universities have indicated that inclusion of cultural content in the core curriculum is "very important" to their academic success (Inglebret, 1991). When students do not see the concepts and contributions of their cultural groups reflected in coursework, a message is sent—educators do not value these concepts and contributions. This subtle, yet powerful, message can undermine attempts to increase participation of Native Americans and Alaska Natives in higher education.

In attempting to extend curricular content, it is typical for college and university faculty to first look to written documents for information. However, when striving to learn about Native culture, faculty are likely to encounter a paucity of accurate written resources (Mankiller, 1991). Native Americans and Alaska Natives have traditionally passed down information orally and only recently have used the written medium to record cultural information. Consequently, much of the literature available has been written by non-Natives who tend to portray Natives through the perspective of Western philosophies and values. This has resulted in significant discrepancies between the Native view of themselves as compared to their portrayal in books (fiction and nonfiction). Furthermore, much of the popular literature depicts Native American and Alaska Native people as a sort of monolithic, generic population (Geiogamah & Pavel, 1993). In reality, there are over 500 federally recognized tribal and Native groups in the United States that vary widely in worldviews, history, values, traditions, governance, and language (Bureau of Indian Affairs, 1991). Therefore, care must be taken in selecting written materials to ensure their accuracy, as well as relevance to a particular group of students.

In the spirit of sharing control over curricular content, it seems more appropriate to initially bypass this inclination toward the written word and to first listen to the concerns of Native people. Members of Native and tribal communities are in the best position to determine what content is most relevant for inclusion in the curriculum. Culturally congruent strategies can be used to learn about culture, such as observing and participating in tribal events and activities of the communities. According to Badwound (1991), "the most effective way to learn about tribal culture is to live among and interact with the tribal community" (p. 19). In this way an instructor can gain valuable insights into tribal views of what constitutes knowledge, dominant values and beliefs, and issues of particular relevance to the community. Crazy Bull (1997) further specifies that "oral histories about individuals, families, communities, events, and time periods are a remarkable source of information about tribal life. There are many solutions to our everyday problems in the stories of our elders" (p. 19). Further conceptual knowledge and understanding of underlying beliefs can be gained through becoming familiar with oral history dealing with the origin of a particular Native people (Srivastava, 1997).

As curricular content is determined, faculty also need to decide how the content will be included. This poses the challenge of where to center the curriculum. If separate courses are designed to cover cultural areas, this content can remain marginalized from the core of the curriculum. If Native cultural content is integrated in a comparative manner, there is a risk of perpetuating an "us" versus "them" mentality that views "we" as natural and "they" as exotic and strange (Schmitz, 1992). Butler and Schmitz (cited in Schmitz, 1992) recommend that we respond to these dilemmas by teaching from "multiple centers (traditions, perspectives, bodies of knowledge), rather than a single center. . . . Reflecting reality, these centers overlap: they represent the multiplicity of individuals and groups, shared heritages and traditions, influences, borrowings, and legacies" (p. 65). Thus, different cultural groups become the central focus at specific times for specific topics.

Process.   Just as curricular content contributes to cultural congruence for Native students, the process used to teach this content plays an important role in bridging the gap between institutional and home cultures. Deyhle and Swisher (1997) explain that early, culturally specific socialization patterns influence "the ways in which children learn to learn or approach learning" (p. 139). Native American students carry early-established learning patterns along with their underlying cultural ethics and values into the higher education realm. Awareness of the ethics and values in which the learning process is grounded can positively impact the postsecondary experience for these students.

Caring is central to education in Native communities and important in the process of planning and implementing curriculum. In her theory of moral development, Gilligan (1982) focuses on care as an essential element in relationships among people, and the ethic of care as developing along a continuum that reaches its highest level with the integration of responsibility for self with responsibility for others. Arvizu (1995) observed this ethic in the perspectives of both Native American educators and students. Pavel (1997) found caring to be essential in making higher education accessible to tribal college students. The importance of care within education for Native students cannot be overstated. There is a preponderance of evidence that indicates uncaring teachers and educational administrators were primary factors related to student dropout (Bowker, 1993; Deyhle, 1992; Swisher, Hoisch, & Pavel, 1991).

Caring behavior can take on a variety of forms within education. Deyhle and Swisher (1997) suggest that teachers who watch and listen to their Native students, as well as have high expectations for their achievement, are demonstrating caring behavior. Within tribal colleges, Pavel (1997) identifies sincerity and honesty as primary attributes of caring interactions with further recognition given to the encouraging, comforting, reassuring, and helpful nature of caring relationships. In recognizing the collective nature of tribal communities, care extends beyond the individual student to his/her family, as well as to the larger community. Care is also synonymous with a firm belief in the capacity of Native students to learn. As a result, caring faculty involve themselves, first, in taking the time to learn about cultural values and concepts and, second, in taking action to integrate these values and concepts into the educational process.

Moreover, through the ethic of care, faculty recognize Native students' cultural backgrounds as presenting strengths that can be used to enrich the learning experience for other students in the classroom. Two cultural concepts are highlighted here to demonstrate this assertion. First, Native communities often emphasize cooperation and sharing in both knowledge acquisition and in the demonstration of learning (Pease-Windy Boy, 1995; Swisher, 1990). Cooperative learning strategies have become increasingly popular in university classrooms with positive effects observed in relation to "critical thinking, self-esteem, racial and ethnic relations, and prosocial behavior" across groups of students (Cooper, Robinson, & McKinney, 1994, p. 78). Schmitz (1992) also contends that a collaborative mode of learning has served to decrease the distance inherent in faculty–student relationships and has given more responsibility to students for their own learning. As a second example, members of Native communities view life as a whole emphasizing the interconnections that exist among all things (Crazy Bull, 1997). This cultural concept has been translated into an interdisciplinary curricular emphasis (Pease-Windy Boy, 1995; Schmitz, 1992) that is now viewed as an asset for students grappling with the highly complex problems of today's rapidly changing world.

Cultural discontinuity theory can serve as the foundation for the curriculum development approach described in this section because it assumes that culturally based differences in the values of the Native American and Alaska Native students' home and the mainstream American culture of the school lead to "conflicts, misunderstandings, and ultimately, failure for those students" (Dehyle & Swisher, 1997, p. 162). Conversely, it is assumed that a better match between the home culture and the school culture will lead to increased academic success. While the creation of culturally congruent curricula can contribute to positive academic experiences for Native American and Alaska Native students, cultural matches or mismatches do not provide a sole explanation for either student persistence or for student dropout. Therefore, we must address additional dimensions of the educational process that intersect with cultural continuity in order to facilitate Native American and Alaska Native student achievement. One such dimension involves the power relationships existing within the contexts of classroom and community.

Empowering Students and Communities

Lomawaima (1995) portrays Native American education as "a 500-year-old battle for power" (p. 331). During the past half century the power to define education, to develop educational pro-

grams and policies, and to decide what constitutes research has predominantly resided outside of Native communities. This historic imbalance in power has perpetuated racism and discriminatory practices that have kept the voices of Native Americans and Alaska Natives out of the forefront in academic dialogue. Higher education curricula built on an ethic of care can play a key role in creating a more balanced power structure in our society. Underlying this focus on modification of power relationships is the theory of sociostructural conflict, which locates the cause of school dropout within the broader social structure of society (Ogbu, 1993). Oppressive practices are viewed as systematically embedded in everyday practices and, as such, must be unearthed and held up for scrutiny from the various participants. At the same time, new systems for daily functioning must be collaboratively built. This can be accomplished, at least in part, within the context of the classroom, as well as through the formation of linkages with tribal communities.

As a microcosm of society, the classroom can serve as a forum for challenging social inequalities that impact the lives of all who live in an interdependent world (Bell, 1997). Power relations that exist within teacher–student interactions can be made explicit as they interweave with those of other societal institutions. The power structure of the classroom can be transformed to recognize the capacity of students to assume both learning and teaching roles, while a parallel teacher/student role is assumed by the faculty member. Attention can be given to the role that various values and assumptions play in legitimizing certain types of knowledge, while delegitimizing others. The impact of membership in specific social identity groups can be made visible. Taken collectively, these strategies can serve to empower both Native and non-Native students in a manner that impacts the immediate educational process, as well as long-term participation in a democracy.

Community lies at the heart of traditional Native education. Therefore, as educators look to make strategic moves both addressing power imbalances and consistent with an ethic of care, their focus will move to the formation of linkages with tribal communities. These linkages will involve reciprocal relationships whereby universities become partners with tribal communities in building continuous progress curricula (Stiggins, 1997). These curricula will grow out of dialogue among the various stakeholders—students, families, tribal educators, tribal leaders, business people, and postsecondary educators—and will bring Native voices to the forefront in defining educational needs, in developing educational models for meeting these needs, and in evaluating the eventual outcomes of these efforts. Continuity will undergird these educational frameworks to ensure both a smooth transition between educational institutions and coordination of content and process across academic levels.

CONCLUSION

Curriculum development specific to Native Americans and Alaska Natives in higher education can be likened to a journey. The journey begins with Native peoples deciding the paths to be taken, the rivers to be crossed, and the mountains to be challenged as they strive to develop knowledge that promotes the well-being of their peoples. The course of the journey becomes radically altered with the advent of European Americans. Control over the route to education is removed from the hands of Native peoples with disastrous results.

Now we see another radical change in direction. Native peoples are once again playing a key role in defining their own educational landscapes and the directions for their journeys; however, this time the journey constantly intersects with that of many other peoples from widely varying backgrounds. The educational journey can no longer take place in isolation. As the paths of these peoples join, part, and join once again, there is a need for an ethic of care. As a nation, we must strive to build caring relationships among peoples that promote understanding and respect for each other's perspectives, in recognition that

the quality of our lives and of our educational journeys have become highly interdependent. Only when we attend to the needs of all who journey with us will we be able to build a country that exemplifies the principles of democracy and meets the demands of the complex social, economic, and political issues we now confront on a daily basis. The curricula we develop in higher education can play a crucial role in directing us toward these ideals.

REFERENCES

Adams, D. W. (1995). *Education for extinction.* Lawrence, KS: University Press of Kansas.

Adams, M. (1992). *Promoting diversity in college classrooms: Innovative responses for the curriculum, faculty, and institutions. New Directions for Teaching and Learning, No. 52.* San Francisco: Jossey-Bass.

Arvizu, D. R. (1995). The care voice and American Indian college students: An alternative perspective for student development professionals. *Journal of American Indian Education, 34*(3), 1–17.

Badwound, E. (1991). Teaching to empower: Tribal colleges must promote leadership and self determination in their reservations. *Tribal College, Journal of American Indian Higher Education, 3*(1), 15–19.

Bell, L. A. (1997). Theoretical foundations for social justice education. In M. Adams, L. A. Bell, & P. Griffin (Eds.), *Teaching for diversity and social justice: A sourcebook* (pp. 3–15). NY: Routledge.

Bennett, C. I. (1995). *Research on racial issues in American higher education.* (ERIC Reproduction Services No. ED 382 733).

Bill, W. (1987). *From boarding schools to self-determination.* Olympia, WA: Superintendent of Public Instruction.

Bowker, A. (1993). *Sisters in the blood: The education of women in Native America.* Newton, MA: WEEA Publishing Center.

Bureau of Indian Affairs. (1991). *American Indians today: Answers to your questions.* Washington, DC: Department of the Interior.

Carnegie Foundation for the Advancement of Teaching. (1989). *Tribal colleges: Shaping the future of Native America.* Lawrenceville, NJ: Princeton University Press.

Cooper, J. L., Robinson, P., & McKinney, M. (1994). Cooperative learning in the classroom. In D. F. Halpern & Associates (Eds.), *Changing college classrooms: New teaching and learning strategies for an increasingly complex world* (pp. 74–92). San Francisco: Jossey-Bass.

Crazy Bull, C. (1997). A Native conversation about research and scholarship. *Tribal College Journal, 9*(1), 17–23.

Crum, S. (1991). Colleges before Columbus. *Tribal College, Journal of American Indian Higher Education, 3*(2), 14–17.

Cummins, J. (1994). The empowerment of Indian students. In J. Reyhner (Ed.), *Teaching American Indian students* (pp. 3–12). Norman, OK: University of Oklahoma Press.

Deyhle, D. (1992). Constructing failure and maintaining cultural identity: Navajo and Ute school leavers. *Journal of American Indian Education, 31,* 24–47.

Deyhle, D. (1995). Navajo youth and Anglo racism: Cultural integrity and resistance. *Harvard Educational Review, 65,* 403–444.

Deyhle, D., & Swisher, K. (1997). Research in American Indian and Alaska Native Education: From assimilation to self-determination. In M. W. Apple (Ed.), *Review of research in education, 22* (pp. 113–194), Washington, DC: American Educational Research Association.

D-Q University. (1996–97). *D-Q University general catalog 1996–97.* Davis, CA: D-Q University.

Franklin, B. (1794). *Two tracts: Information to those who would remove to America, and remarks concerning the savages of North America, 2nd ed.* London: Printed for John Stockdale.

Geiogamah, H., & Pavel, D. M. (1993). Developing television for American Indian and Alaska Native children in the late 20th century. In G. Berry & J. Asamen (Eds.), *The effects of television on the psychosocial development of children* (pp. 191–204). San Francisco: Jossey-Bass.

Gilligan, C. (1982). *In a different voice: Psychological theory and women's development.* Cambridge: Harvard University.

Harjo, S. S. (1994). Guest essay. *Native Peoples, 7*(2), 5.

Henry, S. L., & Pepper, F. C. (1990). Cognitive, social, and cultural effects on Indian learning style: Classroom implications. *Educational Issues of Language Minority Students, 7,* 95–97.

Indian Nations At Risk Task Force. (1990). *Indian nations at risk, summary of issues and recommendations from regional hearings.* Washington, DC: U.S. Government Printing Office.

Inglebret, E. (1991). *Retention of Native Americans in a communication disorders training program.* Paper presented at the Annual Convention of the American Speech-Language-Hearing Association, Atlanta.

Justiz, M. J. (1994). *Minorities in higher education.* Phoenix: Oryx.

Lipka, J., & Ilutsik, E. (1995). Negotiated change: Yup'ik perspectives on indigenous schooling. *Bilingual Research Journal, 19,* 195–207.

Lomawaima, K. T. (1995). Educating Native Americans. In J. A. Banks & C. A. McGee Banks (Eds.), *Handbook of research on multicultural education* (pp. 331–347). NY: Macmillan.

Mankiller, W. (1991). Entering the twenty-first century on our own terms. *National Forum: The Phi Kappa Phi Journal, 71*(2), 5–6.

McKay, A., & McKay, B. (1987). Education as a total way of life: The Nisga'a experience. In J. Barman, Y. Hebert, & D. McCaskill (Eds.), *Indian education in Canada volume 2: The challenge* (pp. 64–85). Vancouver: University of British Columbia Press.

Meriam, L. (1928). *The problem of Indian administration.* Baltimore, MD: Johns Hopkins University Press.

Native Education Initiative of the Regional Educational Labs. (1995). *Promising programs in Native education.* (ERIC Reproduction Service No. ED 385 420).

Ogbu, J. U. (1993). Variability in minority school performance: A problem in search of an explanation. In E. Jacob & C. Jordan (Eds.), *Minority education: Anthropological perspective* (pp. 83–111). Norwood, NJ: Ablex.

Pavel, D. M. (1997). *Postsecondary access via the tribal colleges: A gateway to the center of being.* Washington, DC: American Association of Community Colleges and The Ford Foundation.

Pavel, D. M., Swisher, K., & Ward, M. (1995). Special focus: American Indian and Alaska Native demographic and educational trends. In D. J. Carter & R. Wilson (Eds.), *Thirteenth annual status report: Minorities in higher education* (pp. 33–60). Washington, DC: American Council on Education.

Pease-Windy Boy, J. (1995). Cultural diversity in higher education: An American Indian perspective.

In C. E. Sleeter & P. L. McLaren (Eds.), *Multicultural education, critical pedagogy, and the politics of difference* (pp. 399–413). Albany, NY: State University of New York Press.

Pipes, M. A., Westby, C. E., & Inglebret, E. (1993). Profile of Native American students. In L. W. Clark & D. E. Waltzman (Eds.), *Faculty and student challenges in facing cultural and linguistic diversity* (pp. 137–172). Springfield, IL: Charles C. Thomas.

Schmitz, B. (1992). Cultural pluralism and core curricula. In M. Adams (Ed.), *Promoting diversity in college classrooms: Innovative responses for the curriculum, faculty, and institutions. New Directions for Teaching and Learning, No. 52*. San Francisco: Jossey-Bass.

Snipp, C. M. (1989). *American Indians: The first of this land*. NY: Russell Sage Foundation.

Srivastava, R. (1997). A report from the trenches: Cultural integration in science and math. *Tribal College, Journal of American Indian Higher Education. 9*(2), 16–18.

Stiggins, R. J. (1997). *Leadership for excellence in assessment*. Portland, OR: The Assessment Training Institute.

Swisher, K. (1990). Cooperative learning and the education of American Indian/Alaska Native students: A review of the literature and suggestions for implementation. *Journal of American Indian Education 29*(2),36–43.

Swisher, K., Hoisch, M., & Pavel, D. M. (1991). *American Indian/Alaska Natives dropout study 1991*. Washington, DC: National Education Association.

Szasz, M. C. (1977). *Education and the American Indian: The road to self-determination since 1928*. Albuquerque: University of New Mexico Press.

U.S. Department of Education, National Center for Education Statistics. (1998). *American Indians and Alaska Natives in Postsecondary Education*. NCES 98-291, by D. Michael Pavel, Rebecca Skinner, Elizabeth Farris, Margaret Cahalan, John Tippeconnic, and Wayne Stein. Project Officers, Bernard Greene and Martha Hollins. Washington, DC.

U.S. Senate. (1969). *Indian education: A national tragedy—a national challenge*. Washington, DC: U.S. Government Printing Office.

Utley, R. M. (1984). *The Indian frontier of the American West, 1846–1890*. Albuquerque, NM: University of New Mexico Press.

White House Conference on Indian Education. (1992). *The final report of the White House Conference on Indian education (executive summary)*. Washington, DC: Author.

Wright, B. & Tierney, W. G. (1991). American Indians in higher education: A history of cultural conflict. *Change, 23*(2), 11–18.

Ella Inglebret is a doctoral student in higher education and Program Coordinator, Department of Speech and Hearing Sciences, Washington State University; *D. Michael Pavel* is Assistant Professor of higher education, Washington State University and an enrolled member of the Skokomish Indian Nation in western Washington.

QUESTIONS FOR REFLECTION

1. How can concepts from Native students' cultural backgrounds be used to enrich higher education curricula for *all* students?

2. What do the authors mean when they state that "community lies at the heart of traditional Native education"? What would be the distinguishing elements of a higher education curriculum based on this view of community?

3. In what ways can education (at any level) be likened to a journey?

The Student-Centered Research University

GERSHON VINCOW

ABSTRACT: *A model for the goals, priorities, and desired outcomes of the student-centered research university is presented. Ten key actions are essential for an institution to make the transformation to a student-centered research university, a central feature of which is the student-centered course, which focuses more on students' learning and less on faculty interests. Common faculty objections include lowering of standards, an abandonment of research, lack of training in pedagogy, and lack of time.*

THE NEED FOR CHANGE

Research universities—independent and state-supported alike—have been the object of society's severe criticism in recent years. Some of it is justified; much of it is uninformed and unfounded. I'm tired of this criticism, but I'm also dismayed by our weak and ineffective response. We need a new approach, the student-centered research university.

Yes, I'm tired of "Profscam," of the charge that the research I did in my day, with such dedication and creativity, published in the leading journals, was arcane, irrelevant and unnecessary. How do you feel about your research and its significance? Is it a "scam"?

I'm annoyed that people claim we cost too much. Is $35,000 a year for an assistant professor in the Humanities too much compared to the starting salaries of engineers and lawyers who have less education and less proven creativity? Beyond that comparison, do you think you are overpaid?

I'm tired of the mindless carping about teaching assistants, most of whom are inspired, involved, and helpful to students. I'm dismayed by the lack of understanding that supervised teaching assistants are like medical residents. They are society's way of regenerating an important profession. Why can't we make that clear?

I'm upset by the imagery of the professor as fat-cat consultant, always on the airplane, hardly ever at the university, and certainly not dedicated

to students. How many of us in this room does that picture portray?

I must admit, however, that our responses to these attacks have often been weak and typically ineffective. We acknowledge that we need to put some more effort into undergraduate education, but we assert that overall our house is in order. After all, aren't American research universities the envy of the world—sought by students from around the globe? Don't we still receive the lion's share of Nobel awards?

"Irrelevant," reply our critics, "what we want is better results for our children, improved learning outcomes as they join a globally competitive work force. The solution is simple. Just teach more hours per week, and all will be well." We know that this oversimplified solution will not produce the desired results, but we will not win their hearts and minds so long as the playing field of our discussion is society's conventional exaggeration of the research university model.

Our best course of action is to pursue a new model. I propose that we create a student-centered research university. This student-centered model will produce the learning outcomes our students need, will therefore be valued by society, and will again bring us society's strong support.

My goal in this presentation is to describe one view of the student-centered research university and to persuade you of its value. The theme of this symposium, "Toward a Student-Centered Research University," suggests that you may be

From *Innovative Higher Education* 21, no. 3 (Spring 1997): 165–178. © 1997, Human Sciences Press, Inc.
Used by permission of the author and publisher.

disposed to develop your own version of such a model, one best suited to the strengths and traditions of an outstanding university.

THE STUDENT-CENTERED MODEL: GOALS, PRIORITIES, AND DESIRED OUTCOMES

To provide an overview I will first sketch a conceptual framework for the student-centered research university. I start by reformulating the mission statement of the research university. In my view, it ought not be the conventional "teaching, research and service," however elegantly we might phrase it, but rather the following:

> The mission of the research university is to promote learning through teaching, research, scholarship, creative accomplishment, and service.

Our goal is to promote learning. Teaching, research, and service are simply the means to achieve this goal, not the ends in themselves. We will judge the value of each program and each activity by how much and how well it contributes to promoting learning. This statement is important because it helps us prioritize our actions, but even more important because it serves as the clear and ultimate performance measure of our success.

How much and how well has our teaching promoted learning by our undergraduate and graduate students? How much and how well has our research contributed to promoting learning among our students as well as among our colleagues in the discipline? How much and how well has our public service contributed to promoting learning among the citizens of our state and society in general?

Another advantage of this revised mission statement is that it leads us naturally to a student-centered model. Whom do we first think of as the learners at a university? Certainly, our undergraduate and graduate students.

So the mission statement to promote learning refocuses our attention away from a university centered mostly on the faculty and what it does—

teaching, research and service—toward a university in which faculty and students share center stage, both as learners. We see the student as learner in our educational programs, the faculty member as learner in his or her research program.

Now we proceed to defining the student-centered research university. Simply put, it is a special kind of research university—in which the principal focus is on students, both undergraduate and graduate.

Since our institutional mission is "to promote learning" and our principal focus is on students, our number one priority becomes promoting learning by our students. We take a fresh look at all our activities from this viewpoint, centered on students. What are some immediate consequences?

- We—the faculty—will judge our success as educators not simply by how well we teach, or transmit knowledge and skills, but rather by how well we promote learning by students. This change in emphasis—that is, the faculty thinking about education not simply as "teaching" but as "teaching and learning"—is the single most important transformation to be achieved by the vision of a student-centered research university.

- A second consequence is that successful research and creative performance will have a significant impact on our students. Our principal rationale for research will be how it promotes learning by our students, both undergraduate and graduate students, including doctoral students. Our secondary rationale for research will be how it promotes learning as it advances our discipline. Among faculty, this flip-flop of rationales for research is the most controversial aspect of the new model. But think of its positive impact on society. Our legislatures, our critics can be led anew to appreciate and value research. They will come to understand that research is essential because it promotes learning by our students.

Another aspect of becoming student-centered follows from recognizing that enormous learning and personal growth occur outside the classroom during the college years. We in Academic Affairs must work together in new ways with Student Affairs so that academic learning and personal development become two mutually supporting, reinforcing, enhancing parts of one whole—the collegiate experience of the student. An improved "campus culture" becomes an important goal.

Having outlined what I mean by student-centered, let me make a few remarks about the research university aspect of the new model. Our basic character will remain that of a research university, with greater emphasis put on the role of research in promoting learning. As a research university, we will continue to feature graduate education, especially doctoral education. The student-centered model will apply both to undergraduate and graduate students. In fact, undergraduate and graduate education should be mutually reinforcing in such a research university and their synergy an important component of the student-centered approach.

How can the research university provide added educational value to students? I believe that a faculty engaged in research and creative professional activity can bring to the classroom not only the cutting edge of new knowledge but also a creative spirit that adds a special quality to education. I believe that we can model in our teaching a curiosity about the world and an excitement in learning and discovery, both of which are essential to inspire students with our passion for the life of the mind. Further, we can better motivate students to be engaged in learning since we are seen by them as fellow active learners and not simply as transmitters of knowledge and skills. Outside the formal classroom, we can and should involve undergraduates, insofar as possible, in research or in a research type of experience. Many science and engineering faculty have long led the way in providing such opportunities for undergraduate students in their laboratories.

I'll conclude this general portrait of the student-centered research university by summarizing it in another way. The following ten key actions are required for becoming a student-centered research university:

- We view each aspect of the university from the perspective of its impact on students.
- We affirm student learning as our principal goal, and our principal rationale for research is the extent to which research promotes learning among undergraduate and graduate students.
- We judge our success in education by how well students learn and not simply by how well we transmit knowledge.
- We revise our courses and our majors to become more centered on students' learning.
- We continually improve courses and academic programs through assessment of learning outcomes.
- We emphasize the value added by a research university experience in promoting students' learning.
- We develop a holistic approach to the experience of students and the culture of the institution—scholarly learning and personal development become mutually supporting goals.
- We support students' success leading to graduation so that student-faculty relationships, including improved advising and mentoring, are central to our efforts.
- We modify faculty roles, evaluations, and rewards to increase the emphasis on teaching and advising; and we redirect institutional incentives and reallocate resources to support these actions.

THE STUDENT-CENTERED COURSE: A MAJOR FEATURE OF THE STUDENT-CENTERED RESEARCH UNIVERSITY

To create the student-centered research university we must proceed from the conceptual to the concrete. We must implement each of these ten key actions. For example, we must revise our courses and our majors to become more centered on students' learning. I will illustrate this point by describing in detail a student-centered course, focusing on how it promotes leaning.

We conceptualize and develop the student-centered course from the point of view of its impact on students and their learning. We abandon the old refrain—I teach Physics, not students. We modify the traditional faculty-centered focus on the subject matter content we wish to convey and the skills we wish to impart. To begin the student-centered approach to teaching, we try to understand the starting point from which students enter our classroom. We ask such questions as the following.

- What is our students' background knowledge in our subject and their prerequisite preparation in allied disciplines such as mathematics?
- What are their goals in taking the course? How can we relate their goals to ours?

Answering these leads us to the most important questions:

- What are our goals for the course as they relate to student learning outcomes?
- What do we wish students to come away with in their knowledge of subject matter, critical-thinking skills, communication skills, awareness of values issues, and so on?
- And how will we accomplish these goals in our student-centered course?

There are many additional questions to answer as we focus on the teaching and learning process.

- How can we acknowledge and support our students' learning within their diverse learning styles? (Some are concrete thinkers, others abstract; some are verbal, others visual.)
- How can we communicate high expectations of all our students, motivate their involvement in learning, and provide the support they need to produce optimal learning outcomes?
- How can we get them actively involved in their studies?

- How can we approach each student as an individual, personalizing the experience?
- How can we stimulate students' intellectual curiosity and introduce them to the meaning of scholarship and discovery?
- How can we help students achieve the same pleasure and satisfaction we experience in the process of learning?

These are all important questions we need to answer in order to design a student-centered course. But for most of us, who have developed our careers as subject-matter experts in research universities, they are difficult and indeed uncomfortable questions. I do not pretend to be an expert on pedagogy but will simply report a few illustrations of what some master teachers and experts in the literature of effective teaching have suggested.

Many instructors make special efforts to get to know their students personally, even in large courses. Classroom anonymity—often a contributor to students' lack of involvement and absence from class—can be broken down. Faculty gather information from students, such as their year of attendance, major, reasons for taking the course, background in the subject, and so on. This information helps the instructor shape the course; asking for it indicates a personal interest in students and provides "icebreakers" when students visit during office hours. In some cases, the instructor in large classes can learn the name of each student. One colleague, who teaches a large-enrollment "Introduction to Political Science" course, requires that each student visit him once during office hours, just to get acquainted and give their impressions of the course. Such increased student-faculty contact is essential to promoting students' involvement in learning.

Students frequently tell me that they want to know more about us as people. They want to know where we hail from, our educational background, family, hobbies, and so on. That small degree of personalization adds to a constructive relationship and stimulates their engagement in the course.

Among our first communications with students is the course syllabus that we pass out and review during the first class period. Think about it. Aren't our syllabi typically bureaucratic in tone and course-centered rather than student-centered? What should we add to syllabi from the student's point of view? An interesting statement of the goals, objectives and outcomes of the course is essential.

- These are the main ideas and areas of knowledge that you will learn.
- These are the academic skills that you will acquire, and this is how.
- These are the ways we will support your learning.

Reviewing such a syllabus in class communicates our teaching and learning goals and can set an inspirational tone at the outset. Students will sense our love of the subject, our genuine enthusiasm for teaching it, and will understand our expectations for what they will learn. Such an introduction can go a long way toward promoting student interest in the course.

And what should the syllabus say about classroom attendance? At Syracuse we have a new policy: "Attendance in classes is expected in all courses at Syracuse University. Class attendance requirements and policies concerning nonattendance are established by the instructors of each course and are detailed in the course syllabus." This policy conveys our belief that classroom attendance is essential to promoting learning. (My freshman seminar class last semester was amazed at the back-of-the-envelope calculation that each class costs them the same as a good rock concert, about $30; they won't easily forget that comparison.)

As we teach our course we should look at each aspect to consider how it is student-centered, that is, how it promotes learning by students. For example, are we giving enough assignments early in the semester with prompt feedback? This is particularly important in lower division courses, to help first-year students understand college-level expectations and to guide them in developing skills of independent learning.

In all levels of courses we should ask if we are working our students hard enough. "Reading, writing, thinking, and a lot of it," that's how one master teacher describes his approach. The conventional format—lectures, assigned readings, a midterm, a paper, and a final are far from adequate in a student-centered course.

And what about papers? Are they designed to promote learning? Traditionally many faculty have assigned a topic for a paper, read the paper, assigned a grade and made some comments in the margins. This approach focuses on the faculty evaluating the student. It does not optimally promote the learning of analytic and communication skills. Perhaps a shorter paper should be assigned, with a requirement first to submit an outline, then a draft of the paper and then a revised final version, each of these receiving constructive feedback. That process models our professional approach to research and writing and is much more student-centered and learning centered.

Two other examples to improve learning in the area of writing involve student collaboration:

- In the basic writing course at Syracuse students often work together as a writers workshop, reading and critiquing each other's papers.
- A colleague at Rochester tells me that his students' papers are read by two other students in the class, critiqued by them, and then rewritten and resubmitted for a grade. All three students are graded, the two student readers based on the quality of their critiques.

These are examples of active learning, a variety of approaches stressing the active participation of students with other students in learning. Research shows that students involved in academically-focused groups are more engaged in their learning and learn more. There is a whole variety of active learning strategies to complement the more traditional lectures, seminars, and laboratories. These strategies include study groups, project teams, group work in class, informal discussion groups, learning communities, cooperative learning, and collaborative learning. Active learning is an important feature of the student-centered course.

Despite our best efforts to provide feedback first-year students frequently are not clear about how well they are doing. At Syracuse we have recently introduced mid-semester progress reports. First-year students receive S or U, satisfactory or unsatisfactory, in four categories: attendance, participation, submitted work (assignments, papers, projects), and exams and quizzes. This feedback signals some students that they need to party less and study more or ask for help in a particular course. These reports also signal advisers and deans' offices about students "at risk" who may need special attention.

It is important that the student-centered course reflect our claim that the faculty's involvement in research and graduate education is a great advantage for undergraduates. We should incorporate into our lectures and course material references to our scholarly activities as well as those of faculty and students at our university. These references may be quite natural in graduate courses or advanced upper-division courses. In lower-division courses it may be necessary to digress intentionally to connect the course material with our scholarship or that of others. In this way, we illustrate the value and importance of a spirit of inquiry, discovery, and creativity and make students aware and proud of their research-university environment.

At the end of each course, I encourage a return to the syllabus, and a review of our goals—now as achieved results. What were the highlights of the course? What have students learned? What have they accomplished? Students need assistance in performing such reflective integration of their educational experience. It's very satisfying for both faculty and students to preview and review teaching and learning accomplishments.

And how can we promote learning at the very end of the course—the final exam? In my opinion, the notion of a cumulative final examination that requires students to review and integrate the entire course is an important capstone experience. At Syracuse, we have a new Academic Calendar starting next year. I pressed for six reading days in fall and four reading days in spring—a significant increase. I will call on the faculty to provide students, whenever possible, a cumulative final exam as yet another aspect of promoting their learning experience.

OBJECTIONS TO THE MODEL CHANGE

Having proposed the new model of the student-centered research university, having summarized it with ten key actions, and illustrated it with the student-centered course, I will now respond to some of the concerns about it that have been raised by my colleagues.

Some faculty object to a student-centered approach, fearing that it might lead to a lowering of standards. That is a possibility, but it can be avoided. Although we will try to promote learning by each student, we ought not achieve or claim success by artificially lowering standards so that all students have "successful" learning outcomes. It is essential that we continue to articulate our standards clearly, teach to standards, and in the long run, strengthen these standards. This is a fundamental part of our value system and must be preserved.

Some faculty fear that the new model will destroy the research university. How far will we go along this path, they ask? What will the university look like when we get there? Will we be spending so much of our time on undergraduate teaching and advising that we are forced to abandon research?

Although that is not our intention, the truthful answer is that we can't know in detail what the student-centered research university will look like in the future. This model cannot yet be understood as a "product"—a defined end point but is rather a "process"—a direction of development. We are just beginning to describe its path and to create the "vehicles" that will propel us along it.

How fast will we change? We should not assume that a dramatic transformation will occur in the short term. Just as the current research university model took several decades to develop, this new model will evolve over time, with more than one generation of faculty involved. The pace of change will depend on the faculty's commitment and on society's positive reinforcement of our efforts.

Faculty must be motivated to proceed along this new and challenging path. To speed this culture change at the university we must revise faculty evaluation and reward systems and align institutional incentives to our new criteria for successful performance.

How much will we change? One fundamental limitation to the degree of student-centeredness that we can achieve is our student-to-faculty ratio, currently in the range 10–15 to one. But who knows how the use of advanced information technology may radically transform teaching and learning, the nature of the student-faculty relationship, and therefore the significance of this limiting ratio?

Another faculty objection to pursuing this model is that it emphasizes improvements in pedagogy that go far beyond what we were trained for. We are basically subject matter experts who have a lot of on-the-job teaching experience. Although this is a legitimate concern, I have great confidence in our flexibility and creativity. We are smart, energetic, and dedicated problem solvers who can take major steps toward creating the student-centered research university.

En route, we must also transform the Ph.D. degree so that it better educates not only in research but also in teaching. At Syracuse we have such a "Professoriate of the Future" project underway, involving more than 150 faculty mentors who are training advanced doctoral students in teaching.

One final and major objection is that faculty members are already working 50–60 hours per week and can't take on additional activities. I fully agree. Developing the student-centered research university can't be viewed as an "add on"; it must be a substitution, achieved through eliminating some low-priority activities and reallocating our time commitments. Some more time will have to be spent on improving teaching and advising and less on research.

What are some specific suggestions for improving faculty productivity—here defined not as numbers of students taught or as classroom hours spent teaching per week but rather as effectiveness in supporting students' learning?

- We can improve overall productivity by increasingly measuring it at the department level, with each faculty member contributing optimally, through an individualized mix of teaching, research and service, which may change with time and stage of career.
- Since research remains an essential component of our mission, faculty can improve productivity by focusing on the quality of their research, scholarship, and creative activity. We should prioritize our scholarly efforts more carefully. With somewhat less time available during the academic year, the quality of research accomplished rather than its quantity should become the leading criterion of performance. Some universities have already reflected this idea by limiting the number of articles that faculty can submit for their tenure evaluation.
- Keeping in mind that the end product is student learning, we can also enhance productivity by requiring students to work harder, longer hours, and more effectively in our courses. This will call for better motivation and engagement by students and better support by faculty.
- To promote instructional efficiency in student learning, we can increase our use of advanced undergraduate students as preceptors, particularly in large-enrollment courses. Some universities involve such undergraduates on a volunteer basis; others give course credit, and still others pay small stipends.
- Faculty can increasingly explore the use of information technology to improve the efficiency and effectiveness of student learning.
- Faculty can reduce the total number of undergraduate courses offered—eliminating many

low-enrollment elective courses—so that they can focus more time and effort on improving the quality of teaching and learning in the remaining courses. The result can be a rich but simplified curriculum, coherent and internally reinforcing.

- Finally, faculty can trim the number and sizes of committees at all levels—department, college, and university while exercising caution not to relinquish faculty governance responsibilities and prerogatives.

CONCLUSION

The obvious difficulty of implementing some of these suggestions to improve our productivity in promoting learning exemplifies the general challenge that faces us in moving toward a student-centered research university. Not all research universities are yet ready to meet that challenge, but some have begun to ask themselves critical questions. Answers can lead to most of the 10 key actions required for becoming a student-centered research university. A few examples of such questions, leading to a change in the campus culture, are as follows:

- Are we too alcohol- and sport-centered?
- Should teachers be more involved in extra-curricular activities?
- Should teachers be concerned with teaching character, tolerance, and an ethic across the curriculum?

Positive answers to these and related questions invite us to "develop a holistic approach to the experience of students and the culture of the institution—scholarly learning and personal developments become mutually supporting goals."

To strike at the heart of the matter is to focus on promoting learning as the best way of further-ing the interests of students. We might ask ourselves the following:

- What is good teaching?
- Are we really teachers, or do we "facilitate learning"?
- What are the advantages of being a research university?
- How does student involvement in research promote learning?

Answers to such questions will "affirm student learning as our principal goal," will acknowledge that "we judge our success in education by how well students learn and not simply by how well we transmit knowledge," and will "emphasize the value added of a research-university experience to promoting students' learning."

The topic of creating student-centered courses and programs raises issues of building a curriculum in a culturally pluralistic academic community. We ask ourselves such questions as the following:

- Are courses taught to meet the needs of students and to promote learning, or are they taught to accommodate the interests of faculty?
- Does the university's curriculum promote learning and meet the needs of students today?
- Should the core curriculum include required courses on other cultures or languages?

Answers lead us to the key action to "revise our courses and our majors to become more centered on students learning."

This symposium at the University of Georgia and other similar efforts beginning at research universities across the country manifest a courageous and visionary response to society's messages. Within the academy we can decide to break the logjam of criticism and denial, to take a positive stance, to move toward the new model of the student-centered research university.

Gershon Vincow is Vice Chancellor for Academic Affairs, Syracuse University.

QUESTIONS FOR REFLECTION

1. What additional key actions should research universities take to become more student-centered?
2. Should teachers at the higher education level be concerned with teaching character, tolerance, and ethical behavior across the curriculum?
3. Why is the development of a student-centered research university a *process* rather than a *product*?

The Decline of the Knowledge Factory

JOHN TAGG

ABSTRACT: Knowledge—rather than capital, labor, or raw materials—will be the "organizing and animating principle" of the twenty-first century. Thus, the educated person will be the hope for America's future, and colleges, the "engine" of the knowledge society, should be our best hope for producing such persons. However, if one considers the criteria against which colleges should be judged—what students learn—it is evident that colleges are failing. Evidence indicates that the quality of undergraduate education on many campuses has been declining, and college selectivity, prestige, and resources have little influence on students' learning. Standardization and bureaucratization in "knowledge factories" has resulted in an undergraduate education characterized by mediocrity and incoherence. An "atomized" curriculum results in students' inability to think globally and to transfer methods of analysis from one subject or problem to another. To reverse their current decline, colleges must become "learning-driven institutions."

The organizing and animating principle in the world of the next century will be neither capital nor labor nor raw materials but knowledge. As management theoretician Peter Drucker observes, "The shift to the knowledge society . . . puts the person in the center. In so doing it raises new challenges, new issues, new and quite unprecedented questions about the knowledge society's representative, the educated person." If knowledge is the key to our future, the educated person will embody the hope for the future.

When we speak of the "educated person" today, we often assume as a framework for the discussion the institution that defines and certifies education: the college. At a time when high schools cannot persuasively claim to produce even literate graduates, we focus our hopes for the educated person on colleges and universities.

The United States leads the world in the proportion of its people who attend college. We see college as the bridge to social mobility; discussions about the prospects of disadvantaged groups or individuals often become disputes about access, or the lack thereof, to college. In many ways college has become the engine of the knowledge society; if it breaks down, we will be stranded in a strange new place.

Unfortunately, this engine of progress is failing. It makes more noise than ever, but it is no longer turning the wheels. Yet this will not be instantly evident to the casual observer. Behemoth University carries on public and private research in

This article appeared in the June 1998 issue and is reprinted with permission from *The World & I,* a publication of *The Washington Times Corporation,* copyright © 1998.

a dizzying array of fields, provides graduate and professional schooling and community service, and offers a stage for the political and cultural dramas of a variety of social causes and groups; with so many shells in constant motion, most observers would be hard pressed to find the pea of undergraduate learning. Most of what we read in the newspapers about colleges and universities concerns the inputs to those institutions—entering students, faculty hired, revenue from taxes or tuition—or the research outputs, such as discoveries in the physical or social sciences. We encounter little news about the central product of colleges—the product that justifies most public investment in higher education. Even the well-informed citizen will find little information in the public press on the issue on which colleges should be judged: what the students learn.

DO COLLEGES WORK?

That question has been asked, and with increasing persistence, over the past two decades—and the answers have been discouraging. In 1985 the Association of American Colleges (now the Association of American Colleges and Universities) assembled a select committee under the leadership of Mark Curtis, then president of the AAC, to address "the loss of integrity in the bachelors degree." Their report, Integrity in the College Curriculum, asserted that "evidence of decline and devaluation is everywhere." An examination of what students study in college revealed that "what is now going on is almost anything, and it goes on in the name of the bachelor's degree." Assessing the qualities of those who teach undergraduates, they concluded that "if the professional preparation of doctors were as minimal as that of college teachers, the United States would have more funeral directors than lawyers."

Eight years later, in 1993, the Wingspread Group on Higher Education, chaired by former Labor Secretary William Brock and including several prominent college presidents, surveyed the same prospect. They noted that the Depart-

ment of Education's National Adult Literacy Survey (NALS) found that "surprisingly large numbers of two- and four-year graduates are unable, in everyday situations, to use basic skills involving reading, writing, computation, and elementary problem-solving." They concluded that

> a disturbing and dangerous mismatch exists between what American society needs of higher education and what it is receiving. Nowhere is the mismatch more dangerous than in the quality of undergraduate preparation provided on many campuses. The American imperative for the 21st century is that society must hold higher education to much higher expectations or risk national decline.

A growing body of research over the last two decades has helped to fill in the sketchy picture of what colleges do. A relatively few scholars at our major universities have turned their attention to the central questions that define the value of the institutions where they work. And what they have found is disturbing. In 1991, Ernest Pascarella of the University of Illinois, Chicago, and Patrick Terenzini of the Center for the Study of Higher Education at Pennsylvania State University published a massive volume, *How College Affects Students: Findings and Insights from Twenty Years of Research*. Their assessments are carefully weighted and qualified, and they find, not surprisingly, that college students learn a good deal while in college and change in many ways. College does make a difference. But perhaps their most striking conclusion is that while attending college makes a difference, the particular college one attends makes hardly any predictable difference at all.

One of the foundational assumptions that guides parents, students, alumni, and taxpayers in thinking about colleges is that a greater investment in human and economic resources produces a better product in terms of educational outcome. Conventional thinking holds that those who run these institutions have some coherent conception of *quality,* and that this conception of quality is embodied in the best colleges, which others seek to emulate. Parents pay the breathtaking tuition charged by Ivy

League institutions, and legislators invest public money in enormous state universities, because they believe quality is worth paying for—and because they believe that while they may not be able to define just what that quality consists of, those professionals who govern higher education can define it and, given adequate resources, create it.

But Pascarella and Terenzini found that

> there is little consistent evidence to indicate that college selectivity, prestige, or educational resources have any important net impact on students in such areas as learning, cognitive and intellectual development, other psychosocial changes, the development of principled moral reasoning, or shifts in other attitudes and values. Nearly all of the variance in learning and cognitive outcomes is attributable to individual aptitude differences among students attending different colleges. Only a small and perhaps trivial part is uniquely due to the quality of the college attended.

In other words, if colleges know what quality is in undergraduate education, they apparently do not know how to produce it.

In 1993 Alexander Astin, director of the Higher Education Research Institute at UCLA, published a new study: *What Matters in College: Four Critical Years Revisited*. Astin attempted to assess the effects of college using longitudinal studies of students at many varied institutions and finding correlations between the institutions' characteristics and selected student outcomes. His research, like Pascarella and Terenzini's, leaves us with a disappointing picture, a picture of colleges that attend least to what matters most and often act in ways that seem almost designed to assure they fail at their avowed mission.

Astin's research reveals that what colleges actually do bears little resemblance to what we would be likely to extract from college catalogs or commencement speeches. This probably should not surprise us. Harvard organizational theorist Chris Argyris has demonstrated that the way people say they act in business organizations—their "espoused theory," Argyris calls it—has little relationship with their "theory-in use," which governs how they actually behave. Astin has discovered essentially the same thing in American colleges:

> Institutions espouse high-sounding values, of course, in their mission statements, college catalogues, and public pronouncements by institutional leaders. The problem is that the explicitly stated values—which always include a strong commitment to undergraduate education—are often at variance with the actual values that drive our decisions and policies.

For an outsider—and for not a few insiders—the first barrier to realistically assessing baccalaureate education is simply finding it in the morass of muddled missions that make up the contemporary multiversity. Astin quotes "one of our leading higher education scholars" as dismissing research about undergraduate learning with the remark, "The modern American university is not a residential liberal arts college." Indeed, Astin responds that

> all types of institutions claim to to be engaged in the same enterprise: the liberal education of the undergraduate student. While it is true that certain kinds of institutions also do other things—research, vocational education, and graduate education, to name just a few—does having multiple functions "give permission" to an institution to offer baccalaureate education programs that are second-rate?

Does engaging in research and graduate education justify shortchanging undergraduate education? Does engaging in vocational education justify offering mediocre transfer education? The answer to that question today is, for all practical purposes, "yes." A multiplicity of functions does justify mediocrity and incoherence in undergraduate education, at least to the not very exacting standards of most of our colleges.

WHAT HAPPENED?

Why are our colleges failing? Because they have substituted standardized processes for educational substance. They have become bureaucratized assembly lines for academic credit and have largely ceased, at the institutional level, to know or care what their students learn.

If we look at higher education as it exists today, what we see is counterintuitive. In a nation with over thirty-five hundred colleges serving more than fourteen million students, we find an amazing homogeneity. Despite the vast number of colleges, they display more sameness than difference. Why?

Today's system of higher education is a product of the postwar world. With the impetus of the GI Bill of Rights, rapid economic growth, and the baby boom, the college population surged after World War II. Between 1950 and 1970 college enrollment more than tripled. The percentage of Americans over twenty-five who completed a bachelor's degree doubled between the end of the war and 1970 and nearly doubled again by 1993. And the most dramatic growth has taken place in public colleges. In 1947 less than half of the nation's college students attended public institutions. By 1993 nearly 80 percent did.

Today's colleges have developed as part of a nationwide system of higher education, and hence they have become nearly interchangeable. In such a system, colleges, especially public colleges, have been able to thrive only by growing. Thus their operations have become standardized and focused on providing more of their product to more students. The mission of colleges in this system is to offer classes. My colleague Robert Barr has labeled the governing set of assumptions, attitudes, and rules that define colleges in this system—the theory-in-use of most colleges—the Instruction Paradigm. In the Instruction Paradigm, the product of colleges is classes; colleges exist for the purpose of offering more instruction to more students in more classes.

In this system, the "atom" of the educational universe is the one-hour block of lecture and the "molecule" is the three-unit course. The parts of the educational experience have transferrable value only in the form of completed credit hours. For almost any student at nearly any college

today, the essential meaning of "being a student" is accumulating credit hours.

A credit hour is a measurement of time spent in class. I do not mean to suggest that credit is automatic for students who merely show up. They must, of course, pass the course. But the amount of credit, the weight of the course in the transcript, is based on the length of time the student sits in a room. What the student does in the room, what the teacher does in the room, what they think after they leave the room—these things are irrelevant to academic credit. The qualifications and experience and attitudes of the teacher are irrelevant to academic credit—three units from a creative scholar passionately interested in her subject and her students are equal to three units from a bored grad student who finds teaching a largely avoidable irritation. The attitude and involvement of the student are irrelevant to academic credit—three units earned by a committed and involved student who finds a whole new way of thinking and a lifechanging body of ideas in a course are equal to three units earned by a student who thinks about the course only long enough to fake temporary knowledge with borrowed notes.

Public funding mechanisms in most states reward colleges for offering courses, credit hours. Not for grades, not for course completion, and certainly not for learning. States pay colleges for students sitting in classrooms. You get what you pay for.

THE KNOWLEDGE FACTORY

The Instruction Paradigm college of the postwar period is a knowledge factory: The student passes through an assembly line of courses. As the students pass by, each faculty member affixes a specialized part of knowledge. Then the students move on down the assembly line to the next instructor, who bolts on another fragment of knowledge. The assembly line moves at a steady pace. Each instructor has exactly one semester or quarter to do the same job for every student, who is assumed to be as like every other as the chassis of a given model of car. The workers on this line tend to view their jobs narrowly, as defined by the part of knowledge that it is their business to affix. No one has the job of quality control for the finished product.

In the college as knowledge factory, students learn that the only value recognized by the system, the only fungible good that counts toward success, is the grade on the transcript. It is a fractured system dedicated to the production of parts, of three-unit classes. The reason colleges fail is that the parts don't fit together. They don't add up to a coherent whole. They add up to a transcript but not an education.

Most of the lower division, the first two years of college, is dominated by general education requirements. These requirements at most colleges consist of lists of classes—in a variety of categories such as the humanities, social science, and physical science—from which the student may choose. William Schaefer, emeritus professor of English and former executive vice chancellor at UCLA, describes general education as "a conglomeration of unrelated courses dedicated to the proposition that one's reach should never exceed one's grasp."

The incoherence of the curriculum flows from the internal organizational dynamic of the knowledge factory. Required classes are shaped by the dominant organizational unit of college facilities: academic departments. At nearly all colleges, the fundamental duty and allegiance of the faculty is to their home departments. Most academic departments hire their own faculty. Most faculty members literally owe their jobs not to the college as an institution but to their departments. Most of the crucial decisions about a faculty member's workload and duties are primarily departmental decisions. As Schaefer notes, "Departments have a life of their own—insular, defensive, self-governing, compelled to protect their interests because the faculty positions as well as the courses that justify funding those positions are located therein."

Departments become large by bolting more of their distinctive parts onto more student chassis

in the educational assembly line, by offering those bread-and-butter required general education courses that garner large guaranteed enrollments. But these are often just the kinds of innocuous survey courses that faculty prefer not to teach. And the highest rewards in most universities are reserved not for those who teach undergraduates but for those who are recognized for their research contributions to their academic disciplines. Academic departments have achieved the "best" of both worlds by hiring large numbers of graduate students or part-time instructors, at low salaries and often with no benefits, to teach undergraduate courses, while freeing up senior faculty for research activities.

Our great research universities have for many years subsidized their research programs and graduate schools at the expense of undergraduate programs. They have, in effect, pawned their undergraduate colleges to buy faculty the jewel of research time. There is no penalty to pay for this transaction, because undergraduate programs are funded based on seat time; learning doesn't count; the failure of students to learn exacts no cost to the department or the institution.

Academic departments are ostensibly organized in the service of "disciplines"—coherent and discrete bodies of knowledge or methods of study. While many of the academic disciplines that make up the sciences and humanities are of ancient and proud lineage, their configuration in the modern university is largely a product of academic politics. And their trajectory in the development and deployment of general education courses is almost entirely a product of competition between departments for campus resources. On the academic assembly line of the knowledge factory, each part must be different, so the incentive is to emphasize what makes a discipline unlike others and to shape all knowledge into these highly differentiated disciplines.

Even skills of universal relevance to virtually everything we do in life have become the property of one department or another. Thus, writing in the student's native language becomes the concern of the Department of English; speaking the student's native language is relegated to the Department of Communication. Quantitative reasoning belongs to the Department of Mathematics. The atomized curriculum has taken an increasingly conspicuous toll: the inability of students to think globally or to transfer methods of analysis from one subject or problem to another. The evidence mounts that what students learn in one course they do not retain and transfer to their experience in other courses or to their lives and their work. The fragments never fit together. This has led to a growing demand for the teaching of "critical thinking." But even the subject of thought itself becomes in the knowledge factory an object of competitive bidding among academic departments. Adam Sweeting, director of the Writing Program at the Massachusetts School of Law at Andover, warns that "if we are not careful, the teaching of critical thinking skills will become the responsibility of one university department, a prospect that is at odds with the very idea of a university."

But then much about the modern university is at odds with the very idea of a university. The competition between "academic disciplines" for institutional turf generates a bundle of fragments, a mass of shards, and no coherent whole at all. It lacks precisely that quality of *discipline* that provided the rationale for the enterprise from the beginning. It creates a metacurriculum in which students learn that college is a sequence of disconnected parts, valuable only as credits earned. And what comes off the assembly line of the knowledge factory in the end is an "education" that might have been designed by Rube Goldberg, with marketing advice from the Edsel team.

The result is an institution that satisfies nobody. College faculties complain bitterly, often about the administration, but most often about the students. History and philosophy professors complain that students can't write. English professors complain that students know little about history and culture. Science professors complain that students have only a rudimentary grasp of mathematics. And everyone complains that students can't think. Yet grades have never been

higher. The mean grade point average of all college graduates in 1994 was 3.0 on a scale of 4. It seems unfair to penalize students with poor grades for deficiencies that really fall outside the scope of the course, deficiencies that could not possibly be addressed in a three-unit, one-semester class. So the professors blame the students or the administration and fight pitched battles in the faculty senate. Yet nothing seems to work, because the deficiencies that plague students are almost by definition problems that cannot be addressed in any three-unit class. But three-unit classes are all there are; they are what the college is made of.

Perhaps least satisfied with the knowledge factory are the students. Those students who come to college from high school today come hoping for something better, but with no framework of educational value to bring to the experience themselves. For many of them, the defining experience of college becomes drunkenness. While some colleges have begun belatedly to recognize the costs of the culture of irresponsibility that has grown up on many campuses, it remains the case that substance abuse is one of the few measurable outcomes of a college education. A commission chaired by former Health, Education, and Welfare Secretary Joseph Califano Jr. reported in 1994 that a third of college students are binge drinkers and that the number of college women who reported that they drink in order to get drunk had tripled since 1973, now matching the rate for men.

William Willimon, dean of the chapel at Duke University, and Thomas Naylor, emeritus professor of economics at Duke, have characterized the chaos and aimlessness that college is for many students in their book *The Abandoned Generation: Rethinking Higher Education*. They offer an especially telling statement of the experience of the knowledge factory from a University of Michigan senior:

> So you get here and they start asking you, "What do you think you want to major in?" "Have you thought about what courses you want to take?" And you get the impression that that's what it's all about—courses, majors. So you take the courses.

You get your card punched. You try a little this and a little that. Then comes GRADUATION. And you wake up and you look at this bunch of courses and then it hits you: They don't add up to anything. It's just a bunch of courses. It doesn't mean a thing.

DO COLLEGES HAVE A FUTURE?

The knowledge factory is breaking down as we approach the twenty-first century. The transformation to the knowledge society means that the demand for higher education will increase both in quantity and quality: More students will require more sophisticated knowledge and skills. But this transformation has also brought into existence something new on the higher education landscape: competition.

Competition has emerged for two reasons. First, private employers who need skilled employees have found that the graduates of conventional colleges are poorly prepared to do the work they need to do. Many corporations have either established their own "universities" or sought the support of outside vendors to provide educational services. The second reason competition has burgeoned is that contemporary information technology has made possible immediate access to educational services from anywhere. Education is no longer bound to the campus. Hence many providers can compete to serve students who were formerly too distant. The competition is real. Stan Davis and Jim Botkin—in *The Monster Under the Bed*, their book about the growing imperative for corporate education—offer little hope to the conventional college: "Employee education is not growing 100 percent faster than academe, but 100 times—or 10,000 percent—faster.

In the face of such competition, if conventional colleges hold fast to the Instruction Paradigm and continue to grant degrees on seat time, many of those colleges will wither and die—going down, we can hardly doubt, in a blaze of acrimony as the nation's great minds culminate in faculty senates across the land. If colleges are to thrive, and in some cases if they are even to survive, they must change.

Colleges need to make a paradigm shift, to set aside a whole body of assumptions and implicit rules and adopt a fundamentally different perspective, a new theory-in-use. They must recognize that the Instruction Paradigm mistakes a means for an end, confuses offering classes with producing learning. To put that end in its proper place would be to embrace what Barr calls "the Learning Paradigm." From the perspective of the Learning Paradigm, the central defining functions of the knowledge factory are trivial. What counts is what students learn. That the mission of colleges is to produce learning should be fairly noncontroversial, since it is consistent with what nearly all college faculty and administrators already say in public.

The problem is that most colleges do not assess in any meaningful way what students have learned. They can tell you what classes their students have taken but not what their graduates know or what they can do. The shift to the Learning Paradigm would require that colleges begin to take learning seriously, to assess and measure it, and to take responsibility for producing it.

A large and growing number of faculty and administrators have seen that major changes in the way colleges do business are both desirable and inevitable. The prestigious California Higher Education Policy Center, in a 1996 report, urged that "colleges and Universities . . . begin a transition toward making student learning, not the time spent on courses taken, the principal basis on which degrees and certificates are rewarded."

Excellent models of such colleges exist. Alverno College in Milwaukee has for decades been developing "assessment-as-learning," an approach that seeks to both monitor and guide students' development toward the mastery of a set of core competencies that define a liberal education. The new Western Governors' University will reward students with credit only when they have established through rigorous assessment that they have mastered the required skills. According to Alan Guskin, chancellor of Antioch University, more than two hundred colleges across the country are seriously discussing major restructuring.

Nonetheless, if we contrast the glacial rate at which colleges and universities seem inclined to change with the lightning speed with which the society they serve is transforming itself, we must be disturbed by the contrast. Many believe that undergraduate colleges cannot meet the challenge of the knowledge society. Davis and Botkin, for example, foresee that "corporations will continue to need traditional universities to carry out basic education and research. Nevertheless they will increasingly take on teaching themselves." Drucker predicts: "Thirty years from now the big university campuses will be relics. Universities won't survive. . . . Such totally uncontrollable expenditures, without any visible improvement in either the content or the quality of education, means that the system is rapidly becoming untenable. Higher education is in deep crisis."

Should we, after all, care? What matter if many of our colleges pass away or diminish into support institutions for market-driven forces that can adapt more flexibly to the needs of a changing world? What would be lost? Perhaps not much. Perhaps a great deal. For colleges hold a place in American society that no other institution is likely to fill. They hold the place of liberal education, of education for liberty, of the kind of experience through which children grow into citizens, through which men and women learn the exercise of the freedom that is tempered by choosing responsibility. I say that colleges "hold the place" of liberal education today because I cannot say that they serve the function. But they remain the institutional focus of the ideal, which survives as an ideal.

While private industry and the Internet may supplant many of the existing functions of colleges in our society, these media do not seem likely venues for a rebirth of liberal education. Part of the vulnerability of our existing undergraduate colleges lies in the fact that they have become institutions whose chief activities could be done better by others. If what we want is a knowledge factory, let us at least apply the insights of American efficiency engineer Frederick Taylor and organize the work in the most effi-

cient way. If we want an academic assembly line, let us at least give the workers real responsibility for a real product and reward those who do good work more than those who do poor work. If what we want is an efficient knowledge factory, it will not look anything like a modern college.

The real claim that existing colleges have on our loyalty and our resources is not based upon what they are now or what they do now; it is based on what they could be and what they could do, on the ideal of which they remain the emblems. A college, a real college, is a human community, not a civil service bureaucracy or an industrial factory. A college that can become a learning community, can become more than the sum of its parts. John Henry Cardinal Newman wrote over a century ago in *The Idea of a University:* "A University is, according to the usual designation, an Alma Mater, knowing her children one by one, not a foundry, or a mint, or a treadmill."

Changing the governing paradigm, becoming learning-driven institutions, may seem a daunting task for today's knowledge factories. It seems a little like asking the post office to become a church. Yet the reason that the ideal of liberal education survives in our cultural imagination is that it addresses an ongoing need, the need to nurture in the young the development of both heart and mind, the need to set young people on a course that offers not just facility but maturity, not just cleverness but wisdom.

I am not ready to give up on the ideal of liberal education. Our society is a poorer place because we so often fail to achieve that ideal, and it would be a far richer place if we could revive that ideal in a manner fitting for our time. It is not likely to be revived in any place other than our colleges. The question we face is really what we want the "educated person" of the new millennium to be. Is it worth the trouble to prepare people for life in the knowledge society with a foundation experience that genuinely opens to them the rewards of learning and the satisfactions of discovery, that empowers them with the independence and the discretion to seek not just information but understanding? I think it is worth the trouble. It is, at least, worth a try.

John Tagg is associate professor of English at Palomar College, San Marcos, California.

QUESTIONS FOR REFLECTION

1. Is the "knowledge factory" an appropriate metaphor for colleges? What other metaphor(s) can you suggest?
2. Reflect on your undergraduate education; to what extent does (did) it "fit" Tagg's portrayal of undergraduate education in America? Do you possess a "transcript" or an "education"? Were the general education requirements you satisfied "a conglomeration of unrelated courses dedicated to the proposition that one's reach should never exceed one's grasp"?
3. What are the salient differences between an "efficient knowledge factory" and a "learning-driven institution"? In which direction do you think colleges will evolve during the twenty-first century?

The University in the Twenty-First Century

RICHARD L. RUBENSTEIN

ABSTRACT: For centuries, American colleges and universities have responded to the needs of a changing marketplace, and there is no reason to expect that this function will cease in the information age. The role of the university in the twenty-first century is examined. Among the problems and issues universities will face are technologically fostered economic demands, limited resources, and diminished government support. The changing relationships among universities, the corporate world, and the state are explored.

In his essay on contemporary higher education [see previous article], John Tagg argues that colleges and universities, the engines of progress of the contemporary knowledge society, are failing badly and are not meeting the need for their radical transformation. This author is in agreement with Tagg that much reform is needed. However, I am far less skeptical concerning the ability of American colleges and universities to transform themselves. Although they have often been characterized as "ivory tower" institutions and remote from the "real world," over the centuries they have in fact responded to the needs of a changing marketplace. There is no reason to believe that they will cease to do so in the information age.

One of the most important functions of the university has always been to train personnel for knowledge—intensive professions in the labor market. In eleventh-century Bologna, that market consisted of the two most important institutions of the time, church and state. Not surprisingly, the only courses of study initially offered by the University of Bologna were canon and civil law. In eighteenth-century Prussia, the state came to regard inherited feudal status as a woefully inadequate basis for the appointment of public officials. It required a professionally trained corps to hold public office. In addition to the administrative and judicial bureaucracy, these included teachers and professors in state-controlled schools and

This article appeared in the June 1998 issue and is reprinted with permission from *The World & I*, a publication of *The Washington Times Corporation*, copyright © 1998.

universities and the ecclesiastical hierarchy of the established Lutheran Church. The academic offerings of Prussian universities expanded to meet this demand.

Apart from law, medicine, and theology, professional and scientific training did not become an important part of the university's mission until late in the nineteenth century. Germany was the first country to respond to the rapid industrialization that was taking place in western Europe and North America. It created the university as a complex of graduate schools performing advanced research and experimentation that became the worldwide model.

GROWTH OF THE MODERN UNIVERSITY

The rationalization of agriculture and the growth of industry in the second half of the nineteenth century were principal factors in the expansion of the modern American university system. In 1862 Lincoln signed the Morrill Act granting thirty thousand acres of land for each representative and senator "for the endowment, support and maintenance of at least one college . . . to teach branches of learning as are related to agriculture and mechanical arts." The act provided the basis for the extraordinarily successful American land grant system of agricultural education and research without excluding "scientific and classical studies." Many of the land grant colleges have become great universities. These include Ohio State University, Michigan State University, Cornell, and the Universities of Maryland, Georgia, Florida, Wisconsin, Illinois, and West Virginia.

With its insatiable demand for ever more effective weapons systems, war has contributed enormously to the growth of the modern university system. In World War I, chemists and physicists worked on weapons development in government laboratories. In World War II, the government contracted its weapons research projects to the universities themselves. Physicists first produced plutonium at the University of Califor-

nia at Berkeley. On December 2, 1942, the first man-made, self-sustaining nuclear reaction was achieved in a squash court beneath the unused football field of the University of Chicago. The war also created a heightened demand—largely met by American colleges and universities—for economists, sociologists, demographers, political scientists, psychologists, managerial experts, historians, cryptographers, professionals skilled in foreign languages, and, in general, those who possessed knowledge concerning both Allied and enemy countries.

After the war, returning veterans and the Cold War provided the basis for the further expansion of the university system. Sophisticated weapons of all sorts, both nuclear and nonnuclear, the hardware and software necessary for their delivery systems; and the system of defense developed in the postwar period all rested upon a university-created knowledge base. Inevitably, there were civilian spin-offs, including the invention of the transistor, the semiconductor, the microprocessor, and other types of computer chips. Both the imperatives of the Cold War and the expansion of global conununications, commerce, finance, and transportation required a concurrent expansion of personnel in the history, culture, languages, religion, and economics of distant lands. The sheer size of the enterprises necessary to maintain civilian and military activities created an unprecedented demand for skilled managers. This led in turn to the proliferation of business schools and schools of public administration. Almost all the advances of the postwar period have been knowledge-based to a far greater extent than ever before. To meet the demands of the new situation, the U.S. government was willing to render an unprecedented measure of support to institutions of higher learning and their students.

Undoubtedly, one of the most important Cold War enterprises involving government-university cooperation was the development of the Internet. The network system originated in 1969 in a U.S. Department of Defense program called ARPANET (Advanced Research Projects Agency Network). Its purpose was to provide a communications network for organizations engaged in defense-related research that was secure and survivable in a military catastrophe. During the 1990s there was a quantum leap in the growth of the Internet as a result of the development in 1989 of the World Wide Web, the Internet's most important information retrieval system. Never before has so powerful an instrument of information gathering and exchange been available to human beings. More than any other device, the Web created the practical basis for the intellectual, academic, commercial, and financial development of the information age.

CHALLENGE OF THE INFORMATION AGE

As Tagg indicates, today's students seek an education that differs markedly from that sought as little as a decade ago. He is not alone in suggesting that an emerging learning franchise is in the process of joining the teaching franchise, or in his language, the instructional paradigm. The teaching franchise is defined as "the current system by which teaching and the awarding of course credits and degrees are bundled together in accredited institutions of higher education." By contrast, the learning franchise "provides access to powerful learning systems, information and knowledge bases, scholarly exchange networks, or other mechanisms for the delivery of learning." Authors Michael Dolence and Donald Norris observe that "learning modules are open to anyone who wishes to access them and has the power to compensate the provider." The latter system is more suitable to the needs of a huge number of information age workers who must constantly enhance their knowledge as their fields of endeavor are transformed and in many cases their vocational roles became redundant. The traditional curriculum will not disappear, but the majority of the learners will seek and pay primarily for only that content which they deem relevant to the jobs they either have or aspire to have.

In all likelihood, in the twenty-first century the most important test for traditionally constituted universities will be to meet the challenge of the information age. As Tagg argues, if the universities fall, other institutions will undertake the task of post-secondary-school learning.

Tagg argues that colleges and universities must abandon granting degrees on the basis of "seat time." Few educators would disagree, nor is there much disagreement among responsible educators that the "learning paradigm" must replace the "instructional paradigm." The job market alone will guarantee that the transformation takes place. I would, however, caution against an overemphasis on training for competence within a single discipline. Many of today's students may require the flexibility to seek further training and make a vocational change in midcareer.

Nor are educators unaware of the need for new approaches to the delivery of educational content: In the developed world, technologically induced vocational redundancy compels an ever-increasing number of adults to seek training for vocational slots other than those for which they originally prepared. This is as true of those with university degrees as those who have little or no advanced schooling. In the developing world, a large number of men and women seek advanced education in either domestic institutions or overseas to qualify for current and future vocational slots. At the University of Bridgeport, for example, students from Japan, Korea, Mongolia, India, Russia, Bulgaria, Taiwan, Malaysia, and other countries are enrolled in our graduate and undergraduate programs. Moreover, the university is currently working with academic institutions in Pakistan and the United Arab Emirates to make our curriculum available to students in those countries.

Recently, the University of Connecticut opened a $70 million branch campus in Stanford, one of America's leading corporate centers. Financed by the taxing power of the state, the branch campus offers the same business and education degrees as the University of Bridgeport's

Stanford campus for considerably less money. Nevertheless, our enrollment in Stanford continues to grow because we offer weekend programs such as a two-year M.B.A. course with classes on both Saturday and Sunday. No other institution in the Stanford area offers such a schedule, nor are they likely to. For many corporate employees seeking advancement, the University of Bridgeport offers the only feasible course schedule that promises a degree in a reasonable time frame.

RATIONALIZING THE UNIVERSITY

A major difference between American and European universities relates to the nature of university administration. As universities evolved and huge resources were necessary to maintain them, they became bureaucratically managed. In Europe, university administration has tended to take state bureaucracy as its model; in the United States, the modern corporation has been the model, in which the president is seen as the chief executive officer of a not-for-profit corporation. The tendency to bureaucratize has been an inevitable consequence of the need to rationalize medium- and large-scale enterprises. Nevertheless, it has not been possible to completely rationalize the universities. Traditions such as tenure, faculty autonomy in curricular matters, and the generally guildlike structure of the academic profession have served as a break in a time of growing technologically fostered economic demands, limited resources, and diminished government support.

Some of the restraints on rationalization have considerable academic merit. Nevertheless, enhanced rationalization is likely to be forced on all but the elite universities if they are to survive. In the larger society, the economic gap between the very affluent and the rest of the population is growing ever wider. The same tendency is visible in the gap between elite academic institutions and those institutions that train the information age workforce. Elite private institutions do not need to meet the pedestrian demands of the marketplace. They will continue to flourish through the largesse of wealthy alumni and corporations. The act of significant giving to such institutions confers status. In addition, elite institutions can expect some measure of generous federal funding to continue. When a research project is deemed a matter of urgent public interest, the government is likely to invest in those institutions that promise the least risk. Similarly, the great American state institutions are likely to continue to offer a degree of resistance to thoroughgoing rationalization, because they are in the business of training regional elites. Nevertheless, most nonelite public and private institutions will, in all probability, have no choice but to commit to increasing rationalization if they are to survive. Since market conditions prevail at the majority of such institutions, that process is well under way.

THE UNIVERSITY, THE CORPORATE WORLD, AND THE STATE

Finally, universities will continue to face problems in their relations with both the corporate world and the state. In a knowledge-based society, universities are wealth-creating institutions. This trend is likely to accelerate in the information age. Among the issues to be resolved, if possible, are the following: Universities will have to either agree to train corporate personnel and enter into agreements for profit-making endeavors in fields such as biotechnology, computer science, computer engineering, nuclear physics or else other institutions, including the corporations, will do it in their stead. How shall universities deal with such contractual arrangements when foreign corporations are involved? This is already an issue with some Japanese corporations and American universities, as well as American multinational corporations overseas. When such arrangements are entered into, is it proper for universities to permit the foreign corporations to bar access to their campus facilities and to the work done there? Are there fields such as weapons production, counterintelligence, and police training for foreign governments that ought to be avoided? To what extent, if any, ought faculty members' involvement in corporate life be limited?

With regard to the state, no university can exist wholly independent of the state. All private universities in the United States are highly regulated by state departments of education or boards of regents. They are also regulated by the federal Department of Education and its designated regional accreditation institutions, such as the New England Association of Schools and Colleges. The university's fundamental power to grant legally recognized degrees rests upon state and federal licensing. Without federally guaranteed loans, it would be impossible for a large proportion of America's students to attend college or university. Thus, the state exercises considerable control over all universities, both public and private. Bureaucratically mandated regulations govern hiring and enrollment practices, some budget priorities, and procedural safeguards.

One of the most controversial examples of such control has been "affirmative action," a program designed to overcome the effects of past discrimination by giving some form of preferential treatment in admission and faculty and staff appointment primarily to some minorities and women. The term is usually applied to those programs that set forth goals and timetables required of schools receiving public funds. According to affirmative action statutes, the school must demonstrate a "good faith" effort to recruit minority students and to employ minority faculty. Critics of the system claim that the system has led to the es-

tablishment of state-enforced racial quotas. The system is highly controversial and has recently met with considerable opposition. State mandates also cover elements of the curriculum. In some cases, colleges and universities are required to offer courses on religious and ethnic diversity.

To the extent that more schools follow the University of Phoenix model, insistence on "affirmative action" is likely to diminish. Such schools are concerned with successful outcomes. They are interested in hiring the instructor most qualified to give the instruction required by their workingforce student population. Were they to permit any extraneous consideration to determine their choice of either faculty or curriculum, they would be subject to the harsh judgment of the most impersonal of all arbiters, the marketplace.

These are but some of the issues that will confront the colleges and universities in the twentyfirst century. Of necessity, this discussion is not comprehensive. Nevertheless, it offers an indication of the transformations I believe are taking place in the information age. If I could summarize my views in a single sentence, it would be as follows: The marketplace will play an everincreasing role in the structure, curriculum, curriculum delivery, research, and nature of the student body in the information age university.

REFERENCE

Tagg, John. (1998). "The Decline of the Knowledge Factory." *The World & I* (June 1998): 292–305.

Richard L. Rubenstein is president of the University of Bridgeport.

QUESTIONS FOR REFLECTION

1. What are the salient differences between the university-level education sought by students today and the education sought by students one or two decades ago?
2. What are the distinctions between a "teaching franchise" and a "learning franchise"? Between the "instructional paradigm" and the "learning paradigm"?
3. What should be the relationship between the marketplace and the information-age university?

CASE STUDY IN CURRICULUM IMPLEMENTATION

Faculty Collaboration for a New Curriculum

PETER GOLD

ABSTRACT: *Describes how faculty at the State University of New York–Buffalo collaborated on the development of an interdisciplinary course titled "American Pluralism and the Search for Equality." The course has become the "centerpiece" of a new curriculum for all arts and sciences students. Several key decisions and critical policies that ensured continuation of the course are examined, including responses to vocal critics of the new course and a strategy for involving both supporters and critics in the curriculum development process.*

Eight years ago, the State University of New York–Buffalo first offered a pilot section of the course "American Pluralism and the Search for Equality." The course considers issues in contemporary American experience—race, gender, ethnicity, religion—through the disciplinary lens of faculty instructors using a variety of contemporary and historical sources and teaching styles. Five years ago, the course became the centerpiece for the general education core in a new curriculum required of all arts and sciences students. A recently completed fifth-year evaluation of the course strongly supports its continuation because the course meets its goals and is taught according to the principles agreed upon when it was founded. How has "American Pluralism and the Search for Equality" managed to reach this milestone and maintain faculty, administrative, and student support—especially when so many attempts at curriculum reform are short-lived?

THE MAKING OF A COURSE

Hindsight identifies key decisions and critical policies that ensured the continuation of the course. Certainly, they include the successful manage-ment of campus debate, commitment to faculty development, and deliberate use of criticism to focus development of the course and ensure its longevity. Readers familiar with AAC&U's *Strong Foundations*, a report on successful general education programs, will recognize many of its principles in this course. And participants in the American Commitments project and other earlier AAC&U initiatives will recognize those influences. Discussed at national meetings and in print, what follows is an overview of "American Pluralism," its success problems, and some reasons for its survival.

During the past five years, forty-five faculty members from twenty-two departments—in the arts, humanities, social sciences, law, education, and student-support programs—have taught 122 sections of "American Pluralism." Approximately eleven hundred students annually enrolled in a mix of large and small sections. A course committee of teaching faculty members supervised "American Pluralism" and reports were made to the deans of arts and sciences via an arts and sciences curriculum committee. Course review was conducted by that curriculum committee, and only some on the committee had direct experience with the course. Students who completed

From *Liberal Education* 83, no. 1 (Winter 1997): 46–49. Used by permission of the publisher. Copyright 1997, Association of American Colleges and Universities.

the course were asked to participate in focus groups and identify strengths and weaknesses of the course as well as its impact on campus life.

At the time "American Pluralism" was being planned, reports of similar initiatives and how they had torn apart other campuses were being publicized. "Political correctness" stories were rampant in the popular press. But faculty and administrative leaders here were determined not to have divisiveness characterize our debates. For a while, debate about the course was nasty, personal, and stereotyped. However, the leadership exerted by the planning faculty members was successful in keeping the volume low. Instead, attention was directed to the problems with the existing curriculum and the national—and nonpartisan—calls for courses shaped around issues of diversity. The survey of freshmen, administered on campus for many years but never used in curriculum planning, contained data on shifting student attitudes and demographics; these data were introduced to support the curricular need for addressing pluralism, such as was already present on our campus. Still, a few critics resorted to name-calling in widely circulated position papers and in the campus newspaper. But as provocation mounted, so did deliberate efforts by supporters of the course to keep the focus on the course syllabus and to keep the teaching process public. Over time the tone of the criticism became more reasoned; the course committee continued planning and developing the means for evaluating pilot sections.

The course has lasted for eight years because of the controls on the contentiousness surrounding its planning and approval process. Respecting faculty criticism of the course helped ensure its curricular integrity. For example, critics who objected to requiring "American Pluralism" of all students charged that the course indoctrinated students and celebrated victims. From the first offering, course reviews examined these allegations by critically studying syllabi and assigned readings. In addition, student focus groups, course evaluations, and the fifth-year review focus groups all explicitly asked for evidence to support the charges. There was no evidence. On the contrary, focus groups showed that students are even less tolerant of indoctrination than are faculty members. Furthermore, students were concerned that indoctrination was possible in other sections—but reported none in their section. They said they wouldn't hesitate to complain or to switch from sections that they found unpalatable. In fact, two sections had a larger than usual percentage of students drop the course after one or two class meetings. Students were offended by what they considered inappropriate—and insensitive—teaching.

Challenges from supporters and critics alike often called for adding topics such as freedom or for alternative courses such as civics or American history. The response of the planning group was for supporters and critics alike to contribute to the development of such courses and to identify teaching faculty for the proposed substitute curriculum. In reality, the pluralism course is not a replacement for any existing course and is only tangentially related, to an existing requirement. The usual concerns for departmental enrollments and departmental resources did not emerge. "American Pluralism" survived these challenges. It is now a viable core course with a widely supported curriculum and sufficient faculty to meet student demand, in other words, a good idea for a course matched to realistic campus resources and needs.

CRITICS AND RESPONSES

Early in the development process, critics complained about the motives of the faculty members promoting a course in pluralism and—even more seriously—challenged their qualifications. Paradoxically, these charges spurred successful recruitment of faculty members from many departments and with diverse political persuasions. The consequence is that course ownership is now more widely shared than was at first envisioned. The course committee continues to respond to critics by circulating the course syllabi of all sections. This quiets complaints while also reminding course faculty members that their sections are under scrutiny. Later, some early supporters of the course criticized what they perceived as "loss of direction" in the many sections; however, they took responsibility, wrote a text, and assembled readings to present what they deemed "missing" material.

Some other critical junctures occurred. A critic of the course pedagogy began to teach his own section to prove the prevailing pedagogy wrong. When department chairs critical of the course argued that they were not willing to provide faculty members to teach the core course, they nevertheless claimed ownership of the subject matter. The solution was that with certain conditions, departmental collaboration was approved, and they have provided needed capacity and faculty participation.

FACULTY COLLABORATION

Faculty peer responsibility has been critical to the longevity of "American Pluralism." Faculty members assume responsibility for the review of syllabi, student evaluations, and the introduction of new faculty to the course. Once faculty members learned how to discuss a syllabus and course evaluation in a collegial fashion, they found it refreshing, especially since collegial examination of curriculum and pedagogy rarely occurs in their home departments. Participating faculty members agreed to teach several common topics enumerated in the course principles; flexibility is in the means, which may include histories, narratives, novels, reports, films, exercises, and research reports. Faculty members teaching the materials to other faculty members became the basic resource of many of the development programs. These development programs are regularly offered, while information sessions, such as those needed for recruiting volunteer instructors for future semesters, are offered as necessary.

From the outset there were "windows" into every "American Pluralism" classroom—windows through which every curious critic and supporter was welcome to look. While there is little or no peer review for most campus teaching, nor are syllabi circulated nor student evaluations made public, the course committee wanted to open those windows on "American Pluralism." They distributed regular reports on the curriculum, syllabi, student evaluations, and faculty development programs. Moreover, a book of readings was prepared and its table of contents distributed for discussion. Even more surprising, faculty members visited each other's classrooms and discussed their observations with the committee.

This extraordinary openness came to seem ordinary. At first, several of the strongest proponents of the course were uncomfortable with a peer-reviewed syllabus and, even more, with a window into their classroom. "In my twenty-five years on this campus," one person said, "no one has ever talked to me in this way about my course—and I don't like it!" A few early participating instructors even chose not to continue teaching the course after their first-semester report was discussed in the course committee.

The introduction of a new required course outside any particular discipline is a rare occurrence. Unaccustomed to teaching courses to nonmajors outside their disciplines, some of the faculty members interested in teaching the curriculum were not prepared for the substantial emphasis on pedagogy. On the other hand, an unexpected benefit of talking about the course and circulating course information was the creation of a campus conversation about the issues and ideas being taught. The more typical description of "my" course, "my" discipline, "my" expertise became muted. In a way, requiring this course of students furnished a vehicle for the "general education" of the faculty.

SUPPORT FOR THE COURSE

Administrative support for the course included financial compensation for participation in the development programs, a modest budget for teaching materials, support for national presentations, and, more centrally, the shifting of teaching responsibilities to allow "American Pluralism" as part of the teaching load. In hindsight and without minimizing its necessity, however, the financial contribution was probably less important than other forms of public support: teaching sections, public backing for the core courses in general education, and support from all administrative levels of the institution. Professional and graduate program faculty members were recruited to take part in undergraduate general education—a rare event on campus.

Initially, and as a sign of the administration's commitment to the course, participants in the summer faculty development programs were compensated. Recently, sessions have become routinized: shorter, uncompensated, and distributed throughout the year. Moreover, the then-provost—now president—himself cotaught a pilot section of the course. And the arts and sciences deans insured a steady supply of teaching faculty members; further, by requesting a faculty vote a few years ago, they reasserted faculty support for the course. These "mandates" reduced administrative ambivalence and were forceful in persuading faculty members that the course had permanence.

With so many faculty members teaching "American Pluralism," all with ties to their home departments, the descriptions of its successes and failures are multiple and varied. Besides the disciplinary lens, campus opinions are colored by the legacy of public controversy, the public mandate of requiring a thousand students to take a course outside the major, and asking faculty members to be prepared to discuss a curriculum publicly. Perhaps, too, this diversity of opinion developed because it is unusual to give sustained attention to campus curricula for an initiative generated like this. An unanticipated result of this attention is participating faculty's somewhat unrealistic expectations of speedy and responsive changes. Also unanticipated is the pronouncement/rumor by both supporters and critics of "the death of general education [land this core course]"—despite evidence to the contrary. For some otherwise supportive faculty members, the failure of "American Pluralism" is their announcement that the requirements to teach the course will keep them from volunteering. On the other hand, those who volunteer to teach agree to adhere to common principles, not common sections, and discussion of curricular issues within the course committee.

In the focus groups, students commended the course for allowing consideration of issues they had little experience discussing in a public setting. In the midst of a heated campus debate in which race figured prominently, we noted that it was students enrolled in the course who were informed about the issues. The reviewers were unprepared for the finding of the fifth-year evaluation focus groups: students are advocates of the course. They support it as a required course.

"American Pluralism" has found its place on campus and won the support of faculty, staff, and students. Its longevity comes from maintaining faculty oversight for curricular integrity and the enrichment of faculty bringing a pedagogy and curricular components from their disciplines to this core course.

Peter Gold is associate dean of the undergraduate college at the State University of New York–Buffalo.

QUESTIONS FOR REFLECTION

1. How should curriculum planners respond to those who openly oppose a particular curriculum development effort (at any level)?
2. Why is it that "so many attempts at curriculum reform are short-lived"?
3. What accounts for the success and the continued survival of the "American Pluralism" course at SUNY-Buffalo? What are the implications of this case study for curriculum development efforts in the educational setting with which you are most familiar?

TEACHERS' VOICES
Putting Theory into Practice

How Critical Are Our Pedagogies? Privileging the Discourse of Lived Experience in the Community College Classroom

LEONOR XÓCHITL PÉREZ
ANNA MARIE CHRISTIANSEN

ABSTRACT: *The first author describes her experiences teaching a "Success in College" course at a community college in a low-income Latino community in Los Angeles. The development of a learning community, the author realizes, requires more than an appropriate textbook and teaching strategies. The curriculum should include strategies for addressing the psychological, social, and cultural issues minority students bring to the classroom. By providing students with opportunities for collaborative learning and sharing personal opinions, the author acknowledged, discussed, and integrated students' backgrounds into the course objectives.*

The need for socialization within the academic culture is a common theme in research and recommendations for practitioners that teach or work with minority college students (Bower, 1996). Among factors that place minority students in need of this socialization are: (a) minority students' beliefs about valued adult roles and about the part played by education in structuring access to those roles; (b) minority students' preparation, which involves both developing expectations about higher education and participating in experiences that approximate going to college; and (c) minority students' style of attending college, which distinguishes students who follow traditional full-time patterns of college attendance and those who enter college with adult roles and responsibilities (Richardson & Skinner, 1992). Given this need for socialization about academic culture, many community colleges now offer courses that teach "success in college." The content of these courses most often includes three general topics—the college experience, academic skill development, and life management.

What becomes problematic at the community college level, however, is how minority students must negotiate everyday experience with formal academic learning. Such negotiations complicate the academic socialization process for these students. While the acquisition of knowledge is expected to impact students' abilities to think critically about the world outside of the academic institution, many educators believe that the elemental experiences of everyday living should not impact what happens in the classroom. For students balancing school with their various nonacademic identities and responsibilities, such negotiation of their experiences can lead to what

Article written by Leonor Xóchitl Pérez and Anna Marie Christiansen for *Curriculum Planning: A Contemporary Approach*, Seventh Edition, 2000. Used by permission of the authors.

Signithia Fordham (1988) terms academic "race-lessness," in which students "unlearn or modify their own culturally sanctioned interactional and behavioral styles and adopt those styles rewarded in the school context if they wish to achieve academic success." Often, the mere act of attending an institution of higher learning suggests either a conscious or semiconscious rejection of their home culture(s) (Fordham, 1988).

As a novice instructor preparing to teach a class in "success in college" at a community college in a low-income Latino community in Los Angeles, I* invested many hours in developing the curriculum. I thought much about the appropriate textbook and about ways to develop learning communities. I anticipated using Supplemental Instruction (SI), which increases academic achievement and promotes the development of learning communities through collaborative learning. In SI, regularly scheduled, out-of-class, peer-facilitated sessions are held in which students have the opportunity to discuss, process, and interact by reading, studying, and preparing for examinations (Martin, Blanc, & Arendale, 1996). These learning communities have been noted to increase coherence in what is being learned, promote intellectual interaction, and help promote academic and social connections with faculty and students (Tinto, Russo, & Kadel-Tara, 1996).

It wasn't long, however, before I learned that a curriculum should include more than the appropriate textbook and strategies to develop a learning community. A curriculum should include the complete environment for learning that instructors provide. Giroux and McLaren (1994) point out that a curriculum embracing students' cultural politics, or the myriad of everyday negotiations they face as raced, gendered, and social subjects, addresses the nexus of social and curricular theory. Such curricular change can, they argue, provide a "commitment to hope and emancipation [as well as] the desire to link educational practice to the public good" (Giroux &

McLaren, 1994). Therefore, the depth and complexity of the educational process must be considered, and thus a curriculum should also account for how an instructor will address the psychological, social, and cultural issues that minority students bring to the classroom, which will in turn affect learning.

The first day of the "success in college" course was important to me personally. Not only was it my first day teaching at the college level, I was also returning as an instructor to the same college where I started my own higher education, inhabiting the role of Gramsci's (1987) organic intellectual who furthers the interests of her community in scholarly activity. I was making a full circle and anxiously awaiting the opportunity to give back to the Chicano community in which I was raised by teaching at the local community college. As I walked to class, I looked around the campus and noticed that not much had changed. Half of the classrooms were still housed in beige World War II surplus bungalows. Concrete and asphalt, more than grass and trees, covered the campus grounds. I also looked in the women's bathroom and saw that graffiti still covered the walls and doors, the towel dispensers were still empty, and water leaked from under one of the stalls.

My first impression of the students who sat in my class led me to consider what others have said about classrooms at the community college. The classroom was at one time a community of students with shared experiences. The classroom at the community college today, however, is composed of individuals who have nothing more in common than if they were all waiting at a bus stop (Ritschel, 1995). Before me sat students who ranged in age from seventeen to fifty-five. Among them were housewives and grandmothers, while others were recent high school graduates or full-time workers who supported an entire family.

During the first week of instruction I learned that the demands in the lives of most of these students interfered with my plans to use out-of-class Supplemental Instruction (SI) to build learning

---

*Throughout this article, "I" refers to the first author.

communities. Olivia, a Latina in her late forties with brown curly hair, large brown eyes, and a noticeable Spanish accent, shared something with the class that demonstrated the personal and cultural conditions that would keep her from participating in SI activities. "My husband, he gets angry when I come to the college," she said in a heavy Spanish accent. "At first I came to school behind his back. He went to work and I went to the college." Eventually he found out that she was attending community college and became enraged. In his view, a woman should never surpass the educational or career status of her husband. His attitude reflected the patriarchal ideology of traditional macho culture as well as Fordham's (1988) notion of how, for some students, further learning functions as cultural two-timing. Olivia's husband started threatening to hurt her physically if she continued attending classes. Eventually he made good on his threat and physically abused her. She chose to report her situation to the police and as a result received a restraining order so that she could continue attending classes. The class was silent as they listened to her story. They also seemed to be moved. This is only one of a variety of stories I heard about what keeps many of these students from participating in traditional college activities that would incorporate them into academic culture.

It then became apparent that learning communities in this class, at this community college, could not be developed through interactions with the institution as a whole or with peers in out-of-class SI sessions but would be developed only in interactions between the students and myself in each individual class session. I had to make adjustments to my planned curriculum to meet the needs of this class. I quickly developed activities and exercises that provided in-class opportunities for collaborative learning that facilitated the development of learning communities.

Even after I developed the opportunity for collaborative learning and thus for the development of learning communities, I often found that many students could not make the connection between what they learned in class and their life experiences. This was the case with Angela. She was one of two African American students in this predominately Latino class. I noticed that something was happening in her life when, during a class session, I heard tapping on the glass window behind the chair in which I sat. It was Angela. By motioning with her index finger she indicated that she wanted me to attract the attention of a fellow student. I obtained the attention of that student. She pulled out a book from her bag and went outside and took it to Angela. When Angela returned to class, I asked her if all was well. She stated that her mother-in-law was hospitalized. She was dying of cirrhosis of the liver, and Angela was spending a great amount of time caring for her mother-in-law's nine children, aged one through twenty-four. Angela is twenty-seven years old. Later that month, she said in a calm and nonchalant manner, "I thought I almost went into labor last night. I have been having contractions and I went to the doctor. My doctor he said I am three centimeters dilated." "And how many do you need to be, six?" I asked. "I need to be at least five, so I have two more to go. I'll be glad when it comes. I'm tired," she said. "You have been working hard too," I responded. She said, "This year just started off bad. Maybe it will get better, God willing." I then asked her what was happening with the nine children, and she said, "A lot, ooh, well, remember I told you that we were helping with the children? Well, now starting last weekend they are coming out here. The children are staying with me." "With you at your house?" I asked. "Yeah. Just every weekend they've been coming down here and I love them so much but I can't take care of them much longer." "All nine of them are coming to your house?" I asked in disbelief. "Well, actually, only eight are, plus my own baby and then I'm having another baby now. It's hard because those kids can eat! And we don't have that much food in the house. So it's just hard and they, they, I have to have a lot of energy and patience in dealing with them. It's just dreadful, but I can't just say 'no' because they don't have anybody else to turn to," she said. I asked her how her personal situation had been affecting her school work. She said she had not been studying like she was supposed to. She had been too busy at home to give school her all. Angela was in class the day that we discussed the theory of challenge and support, which states that every challenge that is adequately supported dissipates in intensity. Thus I asked her if anything that she had learned in class so far had helped her with this situation. She said, "not this situation, not this situation," as she shook her head. For Angela, challenges in her personal life interfered with her ability to fully benefit from the class. However, had Angela not had external pressures, she still might have not benefited any more from the class. She learned through the Meyers-Briggs inventory that she was an introvert. However, she was unable to translate this knowledge into insights on how her introversion could be affecting her help-seeking behavior in dealing with the challenges in her life. Walsh (1996) points out that educators should collaboratively study with students their real-life problems and find "active, creative ways to make these realities the knowledge base from which other learning emanates and evolves."

I soon learned, however, that for students to consider their real-life problems and beliefs to be a valid springboard from which to learn, they must be encouraged to voice them. Alex, a male Latino who is about twenty years old, appeared to be what we call "the loner type." He always wore polyester pants, T-shirts with slogans on them, and a baseball cap. He also carried a Walkman around that he listened to, shutting himself out further from the world that surrounds him. He carried around a binder with a picture of the revolutionary Che Guevara. This student never participated in class discussions. One day, however, as I asked students how they felt about certain issues, he started to speak about the evils of American corporations. The class laughed. I firmly stated, "Do not laugh at him! He has a right to voice his opinion whether it agrees with yours or not." The class was silent. Embedded within liberatory theories of education is the corollary of student voice. To give students voice is to let them reinvent the world according to

what they already know, even if their paradigm questions that of the dominant structures. Through voice, the context of the learning situation is made familiar to the student. I continually encouraged students to share their personal opinions with the class as well as to make connections between these opinions and what was learned in class by keeping an in-class journal.

My experiences in listening to and observing Olivia, Angela, Alex, and many other students in this class taught me that the curriculum I had planned did not provide a mechanism in which the different psychological, social, and cultural factors brought in by the students could be acknowledged, discussed, and integrated into the course objectives. My ability to adapt to the needs of the class and to apply critical pedagogical practices, however, increased the possibility that students would make meaningful connections between what they learned in class and what goes on in their lives. The Freire (1997) model of education posits a problem-solving methodology in which students practice the power to "perceive critically *the way they exist* [author's emphasis] and in which they find themselves." In this way, their reality is not fixed, but in process and capable of being transformed.

Although I found pedagogical practices that worked for this class, pedagogical practices must constantly be reconceptualized to address each new teaching assignment. Through continual interrogation of how we teach, it then becomes, as Freire (1988) points out, "the form that knowing takes as the teacher searches for particular ways of teaching that will challenge and call forth in students their own act of knowing," thus privileging lived experience alongside formal academic endeavor.

REFERENCES

Bower, B. L. (1996). Promoting new student success in community college. In J. N. Hankin (Ed.), *The community college: Opportunity and access for America's first-year students.* Columbia, SC: National Research Center for the Freshman Year Experience and Students in Transition, University of South Carolina. (ERIC Document Reproduction Service No. ED 393 486).

Fordham, Signithia. (1988). Racelessness as a Factor in Black Students' School Success. *Harvard Educational Review*, 58, 54–84.

Freire, Paulo. (1988). Letter to North American Teachers. In Ira Shor (Ed.). *Freire for the Classroom: A Sourcebook for Liberatory Teaching*. Portsmouth, NH: Boyton/Cook Publishers.

Freire, Paulo. (1997). *Pedagogy of the Oppressed*. New Revised Ed. Trans. Myra Bergman Ramos. New York: The Continuum Publishing Company.

Giroux, Henry A., & McLaren, Peter. (1991). Radical Pedagogy as Cultural Politics: Beyond the Discourse of Critique and Anti-Utopianism. In Donald Morton & Mas'ud Zavarzadeh (Eds.). *Theory/Pedagogy/Politics: Texts for Change*. Urbana, IL: University of Illinois Press, 152–186.

Giroux, Henry A., & McLaren, Peter. (1994). *Between Borders: Pedagogy and the Politics of Cultural Studies*. New York: Routledge.

Gramsci, Antonio. (1987). *The Modern Prince & Other Writings*. Trans. Louis Marks. New York: International Publishers.

Martin, D. C., Blanc, R., & Arendale, D. R. (1996). Supplemental instruction: Supporting the classroom experience. In J. N. Hankin (Ed.), *The community college: Opportunity and access for America's first-year students*. Columbia, SC: National Research Center for the Freshman Year Experience and Students in Transition, University of South Carolina. (ERIC Document Reproduction Service No. ED 393 486).

Richardson, R. C., Jr, & Skinner, E. F. (1992). Helping first-generation minority students achieve degrees (pp. 29–43). In S. L. Zwerling & H. B. London, (Eds.), *First generation students: Confronting cultural issues. New Directions for Community Colleges*, No. 80. San Francisco: Jossey Bass.

Ritschel, R. E. (1995, Feb./March). The classroom as community. *Community College Journal*, 65(4), 16–19.

Tinto, V., Russo, P. E., & Kadel-Tara, S. (1996). Learning communities and student involvement in the community college: Creating environments of inclusion and success. In J. N. Hankin (Ed.), *The community college: Opportunity and access for America's first-year students*. Columbia, SC: National Research Center for the Freshman Year Experience and Students in Transition, University of South Carolina. (ERIC Document Reproduction Service No. ED 393 486).

Walsh, Catherine E. (1996). Making a Difference: Social Vision, Pedagogy, and Real Life. In Catherine E. Walsh (Ed.). *Education Reform and Social Change: Multicultural Voices, Struggles, and Visions*. Mahwah, NJ: Lawrence Erlbaum Associates, Publishers. 223–240.

Leonor Xóchitl Pérez is a doctoral student in higher education and organizational change and Graduate Research Associate, Community College Outreach Programs, University of California-Los Angeles; *Anna Marie Christiansen* is a doctoral student in English at Idaho State University, Pocatello.

QUESTIONS FOR REFLECTION

1. How can the curriculum contribute to minority and nonminority students' "academic socialization" in institutions of higher education?

2. What characterizes a genuine learning community at the higher education level? Is this description different from that of a learning community at other levels of education?

3. How can students' "real-life problems and beliefs" be a catalyst for learning?

LEARNING ACTIVITIES

Critical Thinking

1. The introduction for this chapter states that the general goals for educational programs at the higher education level—citizenship, equal educational opportunity, vocation, self-realization, and critical thinking—are the same as at other levels. Should the relative emphasis on these goals remain the same for learners at the different stages of life covered in this chapter—late adolescence through all phases of adulthood? What changes in emphasis would you recommend?

2. What is the role of higher education in regard to today's trend toward lifelong learning? How has this role changed during the last two decades?

3. Reflect upon the college curricula you have experienced thus far in your education. Was most emphasis placed on liberal or professional studies? To what extent were the two integrated? How might this integration have been more extensive and effective?

4. Carl Eisdorfer, noted gerontological psychiatrist, once said that older Americans are less like one another than any other segment of the population. What do you think might be the basis for this statement? If true, what implications does it have for programs of lifelong education?

Application Activities

1. In "Nontraditional Students: The New Ecology of the Classroom" (*The Educational Forum*, Summer 1989, pp. 329–336), Naomi Jacobs suggests that " . . . it will become more and more crucial to develop methods of instruction acknowledging and creatively unifying the varieties of experience to be found in such diverse groups, and even harnessing the potential energy in conflict." Identify and describe three methods of instruction that would be effective for such groups of students. In addition, how would you describe the curricular materials that would be most effective for this group?

2. What curriculum criteria do you consider most important for curriculum planning at the community college level? At the university level? At each level, how should these criteria be applied?

3. The introduction to this chapter states that a major emphasis in adult education is to expand learning opportunities for people previously underrepresented in higher education: African Americans, Latino and Hispanic Americans, Asian Americans and Pacific Islanders, Native Americans and Alaskan Natives, and the poor. How can adult and continuing education curricula meet the needs of students from these groups? Does Diane Ravitch's article, "Multiculturalism Yes, Particularism No," suggest any guidelines for developing these curricula?

Field Experiences

1. Visit a nearby community college and interview a few students about their curricular experiences. Take field notes based on these interviews. The following questions might serve as a guide for beginning your interviews: What are the students' long-range goals? How will their community college experiences enable them to reach those goals? What emphasis do the students place on the following goals: citizenship, equal educational opportunity, vocation, self-realization, and critical thinking?

2. Obtain materials that describe the undergraduate general education requirements at your college or university. To what extent do they reflect the following curricular goals: citizenship, equal educational opportunity, vocation, self-realization, and critical thinking?

3. Interview an instructor in an adult and/or continuing education program to determine the curricular strategies he/she uses to meet students' needs. To what extent do these strategies reflect the points of view presented in this chapter?

Internet Activities

1. Visit the ERIC Clearinghouse on Higher Education (**http://gwu.edu/~eriche/**) and gather curriculum-related research results and resources related to the issues and trends discussed in this chapter.

2. Go to the home page of the Association for the Study of Higher Education (ASHE) at **http://www.coe.missouri.edu/~ashe/**. From there go to the "Abstracts to the Research Papers" presented at the annual national conference. What issues and trends are reflected in the abstracts? How do they relate to the material presented in this chapter?

3. Go to the Office of Adult Learning Services (OALS) (**http://www.collegeboard.org/offals/html/indx001a.html**) maintained by College Board Online (**http://www.collegeboard.org/**). Gather information related to the recruitment, instruction, and assessment of adult students. Compare this information to the material presented in this chapter.

4. At the National Institute on Postsecondary Education, Libraries and Lifelong Learning sponsored by the Office of Educational Research and Improvement (OERI) (**http://ed.gov/offices/OERI/**), gather information of interest on the education and training of adults in postsecondary institutions, community-based education programs, and the workplace.

BOOKS AND ARTICLES TO REVIEW

Research and Theory in Education for Late Adolescents and Adults

Altback, Phillip G., and Finkelstein, Martin J., eds. *The Academic Profession: The Professorate in Crisis.* New York: Garland Publishing, 1997.

Arthur, John, and Shapiro, Amy, eds. *Campus Wars: Multiculturalism and the Politics of Difference.* Boulder, CO: Westview Press, 1995.

Ball, Howard, Berkowitz, S. D., and Mzamane, Mbulelo, eds. *Multicultural Education in Colleges and Universities: A Transdisciplinary Approach.* Mahwah, NJ: Lawrence Erlbaum Associates, 1998.

Benjamin, Michael. *Cultural Diversity, Educational Equity, and the Transformation of Higher Education: Group Profiles as a Guide to Policy and Programming.* Westport, Conn: Praeger, 1996.

Bok, Derek. *Universities and the Future of America.* Duke University Press, 1990.

Cross, Patricia K. "New Lenses on Learning." *About Campus* 1, no. 1 (March–April 1996): 4–9.

———. *Educating for the 21st Century.* ERIC Document No. ED 386 232, 1995.

Diamond, Robert M., and Adam, Bronwyn E. *Changing Priorities at Research Universities: 1991–1996.* Syracuse, NY: Syracuse University, 1997.

Ehrenberg, Ronald G. *The American University: National Treasure or Endangered Species?* Ithaca, NY: Cornell University Press, 1997.

Feagin, Joe R., Vera, Hernan, and Imani, Nikitah. *The Agony of Education: Black Students at White Colleges and Universities.* New York: Routledge, 1996.

Hackney, Sheldon. "The University Is Not the U.S. Army: A Conversation with Lawrence W. Levine." *Humanities* 18, no. 1 (January–February 1997): 4–9, 50–54.

Handy, Charles. "A Proper Education." *Change: The Magazine of Higher Learning* 30, no. 5 (September/October 1998): 12–19.

Johnson, David W., Johnson, Roger T., and Smith, Karl A. *Academic Controversy: Enriching College Instruction through Intellectual Conflict.* ERIC Clearinghouse on Higher Education, 1996.

Kumar, Amitava, ed. *Class Issues: Pedagogy, Cultural Studies, and the Public Sphere.* New York: New York University Press, 1997.

Lattuca, Lisa R., and Stark, Joan S. "Will Disciplinary Perspectives Impede Curricular Reform?" *Journal of Higher Education* 65, no. 4 (July–August 1994): 401–426.

Lucas, Christopher J. *Crisis in the Academy: Rethinking American Higher Education in America.* New York: St. Martin's Press, 1996.

Matthews, Anne. *Bright College Years: Inside the American Campus Today.* New York: Simon & Schuster, 1997.

Meister, Jeanne C. *Corporate Universities: Lessons in Building a World-Class Work Force.* New York: McGraw-Hill, 1998.

Merisotis, Jamie P., and O'Brien, Colleen T., eds. *Minority-Serving Institutions: Distinct Purposes, Common Goals.* San Francisco: Jossey-Bass, 1998.

Nightingale, Peggy, et al. *Assessing Learning in Universities.* Sydney: University of New South Wales Press, 1996.

Noll, Roger C., ed. *Challenge to Research Universities.* Washington, DC: Brookings Institution Press, 1998.

Nussbaum, Martha C. *Cultivating Humanity: A Classical Defense of Reform in Liberal Education.* Cambridge, MA: Harvard University Press, 1997.

O'Brien, George Dennis. *All the Essential Half-Truths about Higher Education.* Chicago: University of Chicago Press, 1998.

Rhoads, Robert A., and Howard, Jeffrey P. F., eds. *Academic Service Learning: A Pedagogy of Action and Reflection.* San Francisco: Jossey-Bass, 1998.

Rosenzweig, Robert M. *The Political University: Policy, Politics, and Presidential Leadership in the American Research University.* Baltimore, MD: Johns Hopkins University Press, 1998.

Shils, Edward. *The Calling of Education: The Academic Ethic and other Essays on Higher Education.* Chicago: University of Chicago Press, 1997.

Swenson, Craig. "Customers & Markets: The Cuss Words of Academe." *Change: The Magazine of Higher Learning* 30, no. 5 (September/October 1998): 34–39.

Tierney, William G., ed. *The Responsive University: Restructuring for High Performance.* Baltimore: Johns Hopkins University Press, 1998.

Trosset, Carol. "Obstacles to Open Discussion and Critical Thinking: The Grinnell College Study." *Change: The Magazine of Higher Learning* 30, no. 5 (September/October 1998): 44–49.

Williams, William H., and Naylor, Thomas H. *The Abandoned Generation: Rethinking Higher Education.* Grand Rapids, MI: W. B. Eerdmans Publishing Co., 1995.

Theory into Practice: Strategies for Higher Education Programs

Burrell, Karen Irene, et al. "How Do We Know What We Are Preparing Our Students For? A Reality Check of One University's Academic Literacy Demands." *Research and Teaching in Developmental Education* 13, no. 2 (Spring 1997): 55–70.

Eldred, Marilou, and Fogarty, Brian E. "Five Lessons for Curriculum Reform." *Liberal Education* 82, no. 1 (Winter 1996): 32–37.

Fritz, Janie M. Harden. "Curricular Fidelity, Diversity with Connection: The Duquesne Experiment." *Journal of the Association for Communication*

Administration (JACA) no. 1 (January 1997): 24–31.

Grob, Leonard, and Kuehl, James R. "Coherence & Assessment in a General Education Program." *Liberal Education* 83, no. 1 (Winter 1997): 34–39.

Haecker, Dorothy A. "Windows and Mirrors, Stages and Masks: Strategies for the Borderlands." *Metropolitan Universities: An International Forum* 7, no. 2 (Fall 1996): 51–59.

Sedlak, Robert A., and Cartwright, G. Phillip. "Two Approaches to Distance Education: Lessons Learned." *Change* 29, no. 1 (January–February 1997): 54–56.

Videotapes

Moyers/Sports for Sale is based on the Knight Foundation Commission Report on Intercollegiate Athletics; Bill Moyers explores the role of athletics at colleges and universities and includes visits to top-ranking schools where the debate on the commercialization of sports and academics is most heated. (Available from PBS Video, 1320 Braddock Place, Alexandria, VA 22314-1698 (800) 344-3337).

Campus under Siege: Rights, Responsibilities, & Academic Freedom, 1994, examines three cases of academic freedom involving controversial, sometimes unproven and often offensive ideas in the classroom. *Diversity in Higher Education,* 1994, focuses on the development of diversity programs in higher education. *Higher Education: Paying the Price,* 1996, examines how universities are changing in an era of increased costs and shrinking revenues. *Retention Strategies for Campus Diversity: Constructing Effective Learning Environments,* 1995, emphasizes the development of learning communities where minority students feel comfortable. (All available from PBS Adult Learning Satellite Service (800) 257-2578.)

Index